Second Edition

987654321

Copyright ©1975, 1982 by Random House, Inc.

Library of Congress Cataloging in Publication Data
Goleman, Daniel
    Introductory psychology.
    First ed. / by Anthony Davids and Trygg Engen.
    Bibliography: p.
    Includes index.
    1. Psychology. I. Engen, Trygg, 1926-
II. Davids, Anthony. III. Title; Davids, Anthony.
Introductory psychology. IV. Title.
BF121.G63 1981   150   81-8632
ISBN 0-394-32090-5   AACR2

Cover photograph: ©Erich Hartmann/Magnum

INTRODUCTORY PSYCHOLOGY

SECOND EDITION

RANDOM HOUSE
NEW YORK

DANIEL GOLEMAN
Senior Editor
Psychology Today magazine

TRYGG ENGEN
Brown University

ANTHONY DAVIDS
Brown University

INTRODUCTORY PSYCHOLOGY

CONTENTS

■ v

PART FIVE HUMAN DEVELOPMENT   301

PART SIX   NORMAL AND ABNORMAL BEHAVIOR   368

PART SEVEN SOCIAL BEHAVIOR 475

PREFACE

In accepting an invitation to collaborate with Anthony Davids and Trygg Engen in their revision of *Introductory Psychology*, I set out to maintain the excellence of content coverage while making the second edition as clear and engaging as possible.

I remember my own first introduction to psychology in college. The book we used was exhaustive in its coverage, but it was not lively and interesting. The text covered in depth a plethora of facts, details, and studies that bewildered many of us. Its authors made little effort to engage our interest, or to make clear how the concepts described might help us understand our own lives. That textbook's implicit goal for us was technical mastery of the field of psychology, and its immediate objective was to turn us into instant psychologists by the time we finished the course.

In writing the second edition of our own textbook, my coauthors and I have held to more modest goals, which we feel are also more realistic ones. We seek to increase students' awareness of how psychology applies to their lives, to show them how it can help them understand their own and others' behavior, and to suggest some ways in which psychology may be useful to society. We

have sought to offer better students the detailed information they can integrate, while not intimidating others who are not so verbally sophisticated by overloading them with information. We have tried to describe sophisticated research and complex concepts selectively and with directness and clarity.

UNIQUE FEATURES

In reshaping *Introductory Psychology* from its first edition into its present form, we have produced an almost entirely new book. Throughout, we have sought ways to increase reader involvement. Several of these devices are, we believe, unique among psychology textbooks.

☐ **Applying psychology.** These minichapters deal with ways in which a pertinent aspect of each major text topic touches people's lives. Applying psychology chapters discuss either an issue (such as shifting sex roles) or an applied technique (such as how to study more effectively).

□ **Imagine that.** These easily imagined vignettes of familiar situations illustrate psychological concepts in the students' everyday lives.

□ **Common myths.** At the start of each chapter, a half dozen or so erroneous, but widespread, beliefs are presented—and corrected.

While other textbooks may have one or two of these features, only this textbook has them all—in addition to standard boxes that feature intriguing current research and biographies of key figures who have contributed to psychology's development. These attention-boosting devices have not been added at the sacrifice of substance; they are designed to draw the reader more directly into a cognitive involvement with the basics of psychology presented throughout the text.

Following is a more detailed description of each of the major special features.

Applying psychology

Each major section of the book ends with an "applying psychology" minichapter that elaborates in detail a relevant topic that bears on the life of students. These are practical; they present specific skills or further insight into issues and needs of special importance to students. They include:

□ **Understanding methods and statistics.** Over and above presenting basic research methods and statistical concepts, this minichapter shows students how these methods and statistics would be brought to bear in answering a specific research question. A hypothetical study used as a running example provides a cohesive thread in linking the explanations of each stage of research.

□ **How to learn.** The principles of learning and memory suggest a range of strategies that can help the student be more effective. This minichapter offers practical tips for approaching learning, studying, remembering, and taking exams.

□ **Nature and nurture.** The issue of the degree to which human behavior is innate or learned crops up in many areas of life. This perennial question in psychology is discussed in terms of the basics of heredity and illustrated by some provocative postulates of sociobiology.

□ **Understanding power, the blues, and intimacy.** Findings on motivation, emotion, and sexuality are applied to situations with which every student is familiar: displays of personal power, feelings of loneliness and depression, and the dynamics of coupling and breaking up.

□ **Caregivers: mothers, fathers, and others.** An increasing proportion of students are themselves divorced or the children of divorce, or working mothers, or the parents of children in day care. This minichapter surveys research on how these widespread phenomena affect children.

□ **Adjustment to stress and transition.** The one constant in life is change, and change is the essence of stress. This minichapter reviews findings on the nature of stress, offers strategies for coping with it and examines ways to deal with the transitions of leaving home, living alone, and finding a job.

□ **The sexes.** Issues raised by the women's and men's movements over the last decade are addressed in a review of research on sex differences and sex roles.

These short applying psychology chapters are separated from the main body of the text in order to give the instructor greater flexibility in assigning them. Each is designed to evoke a great deal of student interest; all of them should be excellent springboards for class discussion.

Common myths

Many people believe that . . .	*Actually . . .*
Every symbol in a dream has a specific, universal meaning.	The meaning of symbols in dreams depends on how the dreamer interprets them.
Anxiety harms performance.	Moderate anxiety can help performance; only when anxiety is too high does it hamper performance.
"Psychoanalyst" and "psychologist" are interchangeable terms.	Each term refers to a person with a different professional role, training, and expertise.

Students come to an introductory psychology course with a number of common misconceptions. Many students, for example, will believe that 'psychoanalyst' and 'psychologist' are interchangeable terms, or that there is a specific meaning to every symbol in people's dreams, or that anxiety invariably harms performance.

My coauthors and I have collected dozens of common myths from research others have done (e.g. Vaughn, 1977) and from our own teaching experience. At the start of every chapter a few of these myths are presented, just as they are above, both in the untrue form that many people mistakenly believe, and in a corrected version that explains what actually is the case. To the degree that these myths represent the misconceptions of a given student, they should serve as a challenge to learn why the facts are as they are. Besides intriguing students, the myths and their corrections should meet head-on the task of clearing up many common misconceptions about psychology.

Imagine that . . .

Imagine that you're preparing a lecture on language acquisition in children. You invent a running example of conversations between a small girl and an aunt or uncle whom she visits periodically over a period of months and years. At each visit she has passed a different landmark in language mastery, as displayed in her conversational abilities.

Or, suppose you're going to talk about altruism and bystander apathy. You might tell a story about a gentleman who suffers what might be a heart attack in a busy subway station, posing to the class the question of when they would help out–and when not–and why.

Or, let's say you want to discuss brain disorders. You tell a vignette about an elderly sufferer of senile dementia who has a visit from an old friend but doesn't make the connection between the grown adult who visits and the small child he used to know.

We've used vignettes like these in the running feature called **Imagine That.** These scenes appear regularly to keep the reader involved as the chapters unfold. The purpose of these vignettes is identical with the aim of the instructor who wants to deliver an interesting lecture: to keep students attentive, to illustrate key points with understandable examples, and to show how the concepts of psychology can explain familiar facets of life.

CONTENT CHANGES IN THIS REVISION

Additional chapters

The face of psychology changes constantly. While a textbook must cover classic studies and basic principles, the demand of currency requires that the contents of a new book reflect the shifting focus of research and thought in the field. This revision reflects those changes in a number of ways. For example, two new chapters cover fields that have risen to recent prominence, both in student awareness and in professional research: *Human Sexuality* and *States of Consciousness.*

The chapter on human sexuality is a thorough review of the topic, covering its biological roots, the nature of

sexual arousal, developmental factors, the influence of culture, and the range of sexual behavior. Topics of special interest to students include psychological factors–such as fantasy–that affect sexual arousal, the role of sexual intimacy in love and marriage, and what surveys reveal about the range and frequency of people's sexual behavior–including that of college students. The chapter also addresses key social issues, such as the relationship between pornography and sex crimes, and homosexuality.

The new chapter on states of consciousness surveys areas that have been the focus of recent research. The coverage is first put in the context of the spectrum of arousal, from waking awareness, to the stages of sleep, through altered states. Major sections are devoted to sleep and dreams, hypnosis, and drug-induced states. Of particular interest to students are the sections on dreams, meditation and biofeedback, and explanations of the effects on consciousness of marijuana and alcohol.

Two notable changes in this revision are in the chapters *Abnormal Psychology* and *Therapies.* In keeping with the recent publication of the new Diagnostic and Statistical Manual (DSM-III), our abnormal psychology chapter has been completely redone to reflect the way psychopathology will be taught in the 1980s. Without abandoning well used concepts such as neurosis, we have made our descriptions of mental disorder compatible with the new criteria set down in the DSM-III.

The therapy chapter is innovative in a different way. At the outset the reader is presented with the detailed case history of an obsessive-compulsive housewife, Mrs. C. As each major type of therapy is covered, there is a description of how a therapist of that orientation (e.g., analytic, behaviorist, family) would treat her. This provides the reader with a vivid means to compare and contrast the major therapies.

An entirely new introductory chapter sets the stage by showing the student how psychology evolves, taking behaviorism as a case in point. The legendary case of Little Albert is described, including its influence–and misuse–as behaviorism took hold in American psychology. Depicting the contributions of Watson and B. F. Skinner in formulating behaviorist theory, and the interplay of these key theorists with a large body of behaviorist research, gives the student a more realistic sense of how psychology actually grows.

Current topics

While a textbook must cover classic studies and basic principles, its contents must also reflect the shifting focus of research. Thus, many sections have been expanded to cover important issues and new areas of research. For example, new findings on how children can acquire speech have been given their due in a rewritten updated major section. The current dispute over whether primates can master language has also been given significant coverage. The chapter on the brain and biological substrata of behavior has been reorganized to focus on recent findings, such as discoveries of new neurotransmitters, revised theories of the localization of brain function, and a serious look at laterality. The surge of interest in cognitive psychology has led us to increase the coverage of topics such as attention, perception and language, and how perception is organized.

We have made other additions in response to current interest in issues of social concern. The social psychology chapters, for example, now include added sections on environmental psychology, on the ethics of research, and on confronting the "tragedy of the commons," the need for personal sacrifice in response to dwindling resources. The debate over how much of intelligence is due to nature, how much to nurture, is updated in detail. The applying psychology chapter on caregivers highlights research findings on the impact of single-parent families, working mothers, and day care on child development.

Biographies

Psychology has been developed through the theories and research of vast numbers of people. But the impact of certain key figures looms large in its history. The psychologists whose biographies we have chosen to present are Ivan Pavlov, Herman Ebbinghaus, William James, Jean Piaget, Sigmund Freud, and Stanley Milgram. These biographical sketches not only describe the significance of these people's work, but emphasize the interplay between their personal outlooks and the nature of their contributions.

The biography of Herman Ebbinghaus, for example, emphasizes his role in bringing the scientific method to bear on questions in psychology. The sketch of William James depicts the intellectual climate of turn-of-the-century psychology and shows that the issues he addressed in his classic works are still of primary importance to the field. Sigmund Freud's personality is shown to be a shaper of both his outlook and the way in which he handled the initial negative reaction his theories received.

Each biography tries to depict, then, the human story and the style behind the contributions each of these thinkers has made to the body of knowledge modern psychology reflects.

IN CONCLUSION

The most effective lecturer is the one who holds the audience's attention while covering the topic in detail. The art of writing an effective textbook is the same: it must keep the reader engaged and the presentation of content solid. Thorough, understandable, engaging—these are the hallmarks of an ideal textbook, and these are the qualities we've strived for in writing of this edition.

We have used a combination of format devices, such as **Common Myths, Imagine That...** and topical **Applying Psychology** minichapters to keep the text engaging. At the same time we have included in our updating of this edition a range of new topics that should intrigue the student while reflecting the most important current concerns in the field, including human sexuality, states of consciousness, current findings on neurotransmitters, and living with diminishing common resources. The point that psychology can be useful in the student's life will, we hope, be driven home to the student in such applying psychology chapters as those on how to study, how to cope with stress and depression, finding a job, and similar "brasstacks" applications.

The result is, we trust, a textbook that instructors will find thorough and up to date and students will find readable and engaging. We've enjoyed preparing this revision, and we hope you'll enjoy using it.

D.G.

IN APPRECIATION

We wish to thank the many people who have assisted us in revising *Introductory Psychology*. Of particular help have been: Susan Anderson, of the University of California at Santa Barbara, who provided blueprints for the new chapter on human sexuality as well as for the revisions of the social psychology chapters; Richard Davidson of the State University of New York at Purchase, who advised us on the revision of our chapter on the brain and behavior and the new chapter on states of consciousness; Kathleen Speeth, who consulted in revising the chapter on learning and Elizabeth Engen for her assistance in revising the chapter on language. Valuable assistance in gathering and preparing boxes, summaries, and glossaries was provided by Patricia Hodgins, Leslea Newman, Daniela Kupar, and Alan Spragen.

Paul Shensa, our editor at Random House, deserves special thanks for having gathered us to join forces on the second edition, and for steering us safely through the hazards of the project from beginning to end. Patsy Matthai was of great help in orchestrating our efforts, and Deborah Connor has done an excellent job of polishing them into final shape. Special thanks go to Ann Underwood, who meticulously typed the manuscript.

The final shape and tone of this revision owes much to the consultants who reviewed chapters in progress:

Andrew Baum	Uniformed Services University
Murray Benimoff	Glassboro State College
Norma Benimoff	Camden County College
Steven L. Cohen	Bloomsburg State College
Donald Cook	Northeastern University
Patricia Crane	San Antonio College
Richard J. Davidson	SUNY College at Purchase
Stephen F. Davis	Emporia State University
Carl L. Denti	Dutchess Community College
Gary Greenberg	Wichita State University
Lilian Gershman	Erie Community College
Barry R. Haimson	Southeastern Massachusetts University
John H. Harvey	Vanderbilt University
Gladys Hiner	Oscar Rose Junior College
Sidney Hochman	Nassau Community College
Ralph W. Hood	University of Tennessee at Chattanooga
Susan Locke	Baruch College of CUNY
Roslyn Mass	Middlesex County College
Kenneth B. Melvin	University of Alabama
Steven P. Mewaldt	Marshall University
George Mount	Mountain View College
Raymond F. Paloutzian	University of Idaho
Dan G. Perkins	Richland College
J. Randall Price	Richland College
Albert E. Roberts	Catawba College
Barbara Robinson	Portland Community College
George Rogers	Northern Kentucky University
Connie Schick	Bloomsburg State College
Dru Sherrod	Pitzer College
Charlotte Simon	Montgomery College
Joel D. West	Northern Michigan University

D.G., T.E., A.D.

INTRODUCTORY PSYCHOLOGY

PART ONE

THE SCIENCE
OF PSYCHOLOGY

1

THE STUDY OF MIND AND BEHAVIOR

THE SCOPE OF PSYCHOLOGY

Psychology: that's life ■ Common myths

HOW PSYCHOLOGY EVOLVES

The case of Little Albert ■ The influence of research ■ The saga of behaviorism ■ Key contributions ■ Schools of thought

THE STUFF OF PSYCHOLOGY

Fundamental issues ■ Applying psychology ■ What psychologists do

The object of all psychology is to give
us a totally different idea of the things
we know best.

PAUL VALÉRY

THE SCOPE OF
PSYCHOLOGY

Imagine that you've arrived at a bus
station half an hour early, and you sit down for a
few minutes to watch the passing scene. The people walking by catch your attention, and you notice what a varied lot they are: tall and short; fat
and thin; blond, dark-haired, and bald; their skin
color ranges from pale white to dark brown; you
see faces that strike you as homely, or handsome,
or somewhere in-between. There's a teenager
with a rucksack, an old man leaning on a cane, a
young mother carrying a wailing baby.

Everyone listens as a loudspeaker booms out
an announcement of another bus leaving, and
many turn to the wall clock to check the time. In
the babble of voices, you hear unfamiliar
sounds—is that Japanese?

In the distance a radio blares a pop tune. Your
nose catches the mingled smells of pizza and frying hamburgers from a nearby food stand, and
you realize that you're hungry.

You notice a couple behind you laughing up-
roariously, while a young girl sitting nearby looks
anxious and fearful, and a man on your right argues heatedly with the ticket agent.

As you watch and listen, your mind not only registers the things that are going on around you, but
also wanders. You think of your trip home and
wonder if you'll get along better with your brother
now than you did before you went away to school.
You daydream about the evening you hope to
spend with a friend you haven't seen for several
weeks. You worry about whether you passed that
chemistry test. You plan how to organize the English paper you have to write, and you remind yourself to fill out the application for a job.

Psychology is the study of mind and behavior.
It deals with the things we know best, such as this
hypothetical scene in the bus station. Psychology
studies life, but in doing so it gives us a new understanding of familiar moments.

Psychology: that's life

The scope of psychology includes what you have
been observing in the bus station: the range of differences in how people look and act, how they

sense and perceive, what they need and feel. Psychology is concerned, too, with many areas that cannot be observed directly—the innermost thoughts and dreams of someone like yourself; how you have been influenced by your family; the kinds of fantasies you have; how you have learned to solve your problems; your plans for the future.

Because psychology informs us about what we know best, you will find imaginary but perhaps familiar scenes from daily life throughout this book. Each of them illustrates a principle or concept of psychology in terms of moments that many of us have experienced ourselves. These vignettes will be introduced by "Imagine that...." When you read one, try to imagine yourself in the same situation, or try to remember a similar experience you've had yourself. It should make the explanations that follow more pertinent to your own life.

Common myths

Psychology teaches you secret ways to control and manipulate other people.

Do you agree with the statement above? Many people do—but they're wrong. Psychology can help you to understand yourself and others better, but it doesn't give you any magical means to manipulate people.

There are many such false beliefs that people hold about psychology and their own behavior. Reading this book will correct many of the mistaken notions you may hold. Each chapter will begin with a list of common myths about its topic; within the chapter will be facts that set each myth straight.

Many myths about psychology become established because they represent a commonsense or intuitive understanding of life. But common sense and intuition are not the same as objective knowledge, the goal of psychological research. The results of psychological research often run counter to intuition.

For example, it is often believed that it is best to face the truth and that denying reality is unhealthy. But this is not always the case—in many stressful situations in which there is no direct action a person can take to lessen the stress, denial is psychologically useful (Lazarus, 1979). For instance, hospital patients who deny the dangers of an impending operation recover more quickly and have fewer postoperative complications than those who face the truth and seek out all the details they can about their surgery.

Take another example. It seems obvious that severely disturbed children very likely grew up in disturbed families—where a parent is psychotic. Actually, autistic children, who are extremely disturbed, typically come from families whose members are quite normal, or even superior in intelligence and adjustment.

Like all scientific disciplines, psychology seeks to observe, describe, and explain the facts it studies. In the case of psychology, the facts are about our lives. Psychology often reveals a different understanding of the familiar from the one that either common sense or intuition would suggest. Only objective study can allow psychologists to formulate the theories and laws that might enable them to understand and even predict our actions, thoughts, and feelings.

HOW PSYCHOLOGY EVOLVES

The case of Little Albert

The year was 1919, the place a hospital in Baltimore. John B. Watson was conducting a series of experiments with a nine-month-old baby whom he called Albert. A healthy and stolid infant, Albert was to become one of the most famous experimental subjects in psychology (Harris, 1979).

Watson had seen a child frightened by a dog; he reasoned that if a child was frightened by an animal once, similar animals would make it afraid thereafter. To test his supposition, Watson needed a child young enough not to have already been exposed to an animal that might have frightened it. Nine-month-old Albert was a likely candidate.

Watson, the father of the school of thought in American psychology called "behaviorism," sought to answer three questions: (1) Could a baby be made to fear an animal if a loud, startling noise accompanied the animal's presentation? (2) Would the fear transfer to similar animals or objects? and (3) How long would the fear last?

First Albert was tested for preexisting fears by

John B. Watson (1878–1958), a founder of the behaviorist school of psychology. (The Granger Collection)

struck the steel. After seven pairings of touch and sound, Albert cried when the rat was presented to him without the noise. Watson's first question was answered. Albert had become afraid of the rat.

Five days later, Watson presented Albert various animals and objects; the infant showed no fear of some familiar wooden blocks, but was afraid of the rat, a dog, and a sealskin coat. Watson's second question was answered—Albert's fear of the rat had transferred to similar objects.

After an interval of more than a month, Watson tested whether Albert was still afraid. Albert, with some fear, touched the sealskin coat and the rabbit, but avoided a Santa Claus mask and a dog. He let the rat crawl over him, but covered his eyes with both hands. The third question was answered—the fear had persisted.

From this study, Watson verified to his satisfaction several parts of the behaviorist theory he proposed. Watson's research test of his theory illustrates the studies on which psychology is based. Each experiment establishes, confirms, or clarifies a concept in psychology—or refutes one. Because the principles of psychology are founded on research, you will find several experiments described in every chapter of this book. They should give you a sense of how psychologists in each field have established the facts and theories you will learn in this book.

having a series of animals and objects presented, including a white rat, a rabbit, a dog, cotton, and masks. He showed no fear of any of them. But when a steel bar was hit with a hammer behind his back, Albert was afraid.

Two months after this first test, the experiment began in earnest. A white rat was put near Albert; whenever Albert reached to touch it, the hammer

Figure 1.1 Little Albert

Before conditioning, Albert was unafraid of the rat. After the rat was paired with a jarring noise, he became afraid of it. His fear generalized to a rabbit, among other things.

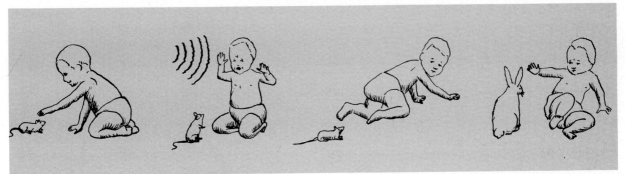

The influence of research

The story of Little Albert became widely known, even though other researchers over the following two decades were unable to duplicate Watson's results in studies of their own, suggesting his results were flawed. One reason for Albert's popularity was that Watson wrote about the study often during the next decade, both for his fellow psychologists in journals and for the general public in such articles as "What About Your Child?" in 1928 for *Cosmopolitan* magazine. Largely through Watson's writings, behaviorism captured the imagination of both psychologists and the public at large. In psychology, behaviorism held center stage for several decades after Little Albert's encounter with the white rat.

The story of the study was retold time and again in textbooks as an illustration of the fundamental tenets of behaviorism. As often happens, the more often it was retold, the less accurate the telling (Harris, 1979). Some textbook versions had Albert fearing spurious objects, such as his mother's fur neckpiece. Some gave the story a happy ending by claiming that Watson removed Albert's fear.

Still other psychologists have revived the story of Albert because it seems to support their own theory. In 1960 Joseph Wolpe, who developed a therapy based on the principles of behaviorism, cited the case of Albert as evidence that a single experience can give a person a phobia—although Albert was never seen by Watson after the study, and there is no clear evidence the child did develop a lasting fear of rats throughout life.* According to Harris (1979), in 1971—more than half a century after Albert's trials—another psychologist, M. E. P. Seligman, pointed to the study as evidence that people are prone to fear furry things like rats more than they fear other kinds of objects.

Watson's test of Albert is actually of uncertain

scientific value. There were several flaws in the way Watson conducted it. For example, on one occasion, a dog that Albert was to be presented with began to bark so loudly that it frightened both Albert *and* Watson. The flaws are severe enough that the study seems to belong to the category of "interesting but uninterpretable results" (Harris, 1979).

The lasting significance of the case of Little Albert—and Watson's writings—stems from the fact that it prompted others to do their own research on the same problems. The result has been more than half a century of growing knowledge about how people learn and the role of learning in behavior.

The saga of behaviorism

Watson created a new wave in American psychology, one that rerouted the course of inquiry from its earlier direction. Before Watson, American psychology was dominated by "introspectionists," who tried to observe their own mental processes. For example, an introspectionist might look at a rose, then try to analyze all the thoughts about elements of that experience. The endeavor proved elusive—in part because introspection itself is a mental process that may change the very thing it tries to observe. The telling flaw in the introspective method was its subjectivity. Behaviorism's objective methods were more appealing to other psychologists trying to make a science of their discipline.

Watson expanded on the work of the Russian physiologist Ivan Pavlov, who just after the turn of the century had shown that stimuli in the environment can change an animal's—or a person's—behavior. Watson agreed. He felt that introspectionists were heading toward a dead end. Psychologists, said Watson (1914), should be objective: they should observe behavior, not try to watch their own minds operate.

Watson and other behaviorists did not deny the existence of such subjective processes as thinking, feeling, or dreaming. They simply considered these aspects unimportant sidelights to the real concerns of psychology. Watson emphasized conditioning and the scientific method of observation as it is applied in the natural sciences.

*If you're wondering what happened to Little Albert, the answer is that nobody knows. Albert and his mother lost touch with Watson when the experiment ended, and despite efforts to track him down later, there is no trace of him—nor any evidence that he continued to fear rats. Watson's experiment with Albert would never be allowed today; ethical standards for experiments with humans have changed radically since then. Psychologists would not condone conditioning fears in children for experimental purposes.

The behaviorist approach focused on the study of how people acquire various physical responses. But could such an approach deal with the obviously psychological problems of thinking and feeling? According to Watson, thinking and feeling are "implicit" behavior. For example, he believed that thinking is nothing more than subvocal speech—that is, talking to oneself inaudibly. By studying observable actions, Watson contended, the principles that also control thought and feeling could be discovered.

Watson was a revolutionary in psychology and, especially during the latter part of his career, expressed his views on human nature in strong language that sometimes shocked his contemporaries. In 1924 he confidently declared the potential power of the conditioning method:

> Give me a dozen healthy infants, well-formed, and my own specified world to bring them up in and I'll guarantee to take any one at random and train him to become any type of specialist I might select—doctor, lawyer, artist, merchant-chief, and, yes, even beggarman and thief, regardless of his talents, penchants, tendencies, abilities, vocations, and race of his ancestors. I am going beyond my facts and I admit it, but so have the advocates of the contrary been doing it for many thousands of years. (Watson, 1924)

Such denial of free will was unpopular and led to the charge that Watson's approach dehumanized people. It implied determinism: that people's behavior was not freely chosen, but rather fixed by their past. But Watson was able to produce data such as his study of Little Albert to support some of his contentions, and he gained many followers among psychologists.

Key contributions

Psychology evolves through the contributions of great thinkers like Watson, whose work guides and inspires large numbers of researchers. The thinkers propose theories or insights that the researchers who follow test and refine. Relatively few of Watson's original principles have survived to this day unchanged or unchallenged, but his insights provided an intellectual foundation in which behaviorism could flourish.

Watson's view of learning guided several generations of psychological research on the topic, and

his emphasis on objective methods established the groundwork for research in the entire field. Not all Watson's theories and hypotheses held up under later tests, but the stage was set for a new theory of learning. That theory was proposed by B. F. Skinner.

Skinner had come upon the works of Watson, and they excited him enough to set him out on a career in psychology. Skinner formulated and tested his own theories on learning and conditioning, using animals instead of people to test his hypotheses. The control he achieved over the behavior of his laboratory animals was so precise that during World War II Skinner proposed a top-secret project: to train pigeons to guide missiles to enemy targets. The project was never actually approved by the government, let alone put to the test in battle.

After the war, Skinner went on to apply his techniques to people. He built an "air crib" to allow his baby daughter to spend time in a clean and

An "air crib" like the one B. F. Skinner used to raise his own daughter when she was an infant. Skinner contended that air cribs were a better, cleaner environment for an infant than the conventional crib, but the idea did not become popular. (Courtesy of B. F. Skinner, photo by Robert Epstein)

B. F. Skinner (1904–   ), an influential behaviorist.
(Photo by Hans-Peter Biemann. Courtesy, B. F. Skinner)

controlled environment, which he felt would make her a healthier child. He also developed the "Skinner box," a chamber in which an animal's environment can be precisely controlled and its behavior recorded. (Many people mistakenly call the air crib a "Skinner box.") The Skinner box immediately became popular in psychological laboratories, in part because it allowed elegant tests of Skinner's theory of learning.

Skinner looked beyond his laboratory to life. One application was in the classroom: Skinner and his followers devised teaching machines that led students through a topic in small steps. In keeping with Skinnerian principles, each correct response to a question on the topic earned a rewarding confirmation. Others applied these principles to relieve mental patients of their symptoms. While Watson had launched behaviorism in America, Skinner's theories and research methods consolidated its hold.

Schools of thought

Behaviorism is but one of many schools of thought in psychology. Most psychologists these days no longer consider themselves to be mem-

bers of any particular school. Even so, in their approach or technique they may be working in the tradition of one or another school.

Behaviorism attempts to explain much or all of people's behavior in terms of a person's learning history. But psychobiology, another school of thought, looks to biology, especially to the workings of the brain, as the key to understanding behavior. Still another school of thought holds that psychodynamics—a person's internal mental conflicts and needs—can reveal what behaviorism and biology cannot.

The developmental psychologist argues that to understand a person, you must study the course of infancy, childhood, and life's later stages and assess the impact of each. Humanistic psychologists contend that a person's hopes and potentials matter most. Still other psychologists look to the study of cognitive processes—including memory, perception, and thought—as a source of insights. Social psychologists, on the other hand, try to understand how interaction with others shapes a person's behavior.

We will survey each of these schools of thought. Each perspective offers a rich pool of findings and insights on the complexities of human behavior; the proper study of psychology includes them all. Throughout this text, the focus will vary from one approach to another. But as you read about each, you will see that no single method, perspective, or school dominates psychology.

THE STUFF OF PSYCHOLOGY

Imagine that you're talking to a friend who is a chain smoker.

"I don't understand it," she says. "I know I shouldn't smoke, I know how it increases my chances of getting cancer or a heart attack. But I can't seem to stop, no matter what I do. I tried chewing gum instead. I was hypnotized. I spent a hundred dollars on a weekend course. Nothing helps. Smoking makes me feel better. I go crazy without cigarettes.

"I think I'm just fated to be a chain smoker." ◼

Fundamental issues

Your friend's fatalistic attitude about smoking reflects part of a fundamental issue in psychology: are people free to choose how they behave, or is their behavior determined by forces beyond their control? Such concerns and questions cut across all schools of thought. While many schools address these issues directly, none has come up with any decisive answers. For example, take the question of whether a person is master or victim of her fate. A behaviorist might say that your friend's actions are dictated by her past conditioning, while a humanistic psychologist would counter that through an act of will she could break free of her past.

The perennial issues in psychology crop up in various forms at different times (Wertheimer, 1972). Another debate concerns the ancient question of whether human nature is good or evil. In psychology this question is framed in terms of whether a person is rational and able to make realistic decisions, or whether decisions are based on emotions or conditioning; here the opponents might be a cognitive psychologist and a behaviorist.

Then there is the issue of which factors matter most in people's behavior: past or present, nature or nurture. A psychodynamic view holds that a person's past holds the key to understanding present behavior, while a humanist would say that the past is not nearly as important as the present. The question of nature versus nurture opposes a biological perspective against a social one: the former contends that heredity largely fixes behavior, while the latter maintains that the influence of society shapes behavior.

Finally there is the question of simplicity versus complexity. How should people's behavior be explained? Is the simplest explanation the best? For example, would you be satisfied with the explanation that your friend has a biological deficit that compels her to smoke? Or that she unconsciously wants to die? Or that she has learned a habit that gives her short-term benefits that are more powerful than the long-term risks?

Probably no single explanation will hold the answer to why, despite its dangers, people smoke. Human behavior is complex; many factors are involved in even the simplest act like smoking.

While in science it is desirable to find the most simple explanation, psychology deals with intricately interwoven factors. There is frequently no single, simple answer to the whys of behavior.

Imagine that you work in a building where the thermostats are set at 65° in winter to save fuel. On your lunch break you go to a small cafe for a bite to eat. The place feels boiling hot to you.

"What's the thermostat set at?" you ask the proprietor.

"Seventy-two degrees. We like to keep our customers nice and warm. Good for business."

"What about the fuel shortage? If everyone did that, we'd be even worse off than we are."

"It's not my problem. I've got my own business to think about. Let other people save fuel—I want to save my customers." ■

Applying psychology

"It's not my problem"—a frustrating attitude to encounter if you're concerned about energy shortages, ecology, or any of the other social issues that affect us all. How can you get people to care—or at least to cooperate?

This is the sort of question that psychologists grapple with when they try to apply what they've learned. The situation of the fuel-hogging restaurant, for example, has been dealt with by social psychologists who study the factors that lead people to cooperate and conserve scarce resources or to compete for them. In these situations, each person can get a short-term gain (for instance, keeping customers warm) but will in the end suffer a long-term loss (for instance, the fuel shortage that such self-interest will aggravate).

Research has shown, though, that certain measures will make people more likely to conserve voluntarily: increased information about the severity of the problem, a set of penalties for those who don't cooperate and incentives for those who do, and information about alternatives. These are by and large tactics the government is using in its effort to increase energy conservation.

Some research in psychology is "pure," in the sense that it contributes to an area of knowledge in the field but has no immediate application to life. Other research is directly applied to specific problems. But all research increases the sum of our knowledge about human behavior—and that itself is useful.

As you progress through this book, you will find short "applying psychology" chapters that deal with the ways that psychology can be applied to your own life or to understanding current social trends. Applying psychology chapters on understanding methods, on how to learn, and on coping and adjustment are all designed to be of practical use to you. Applying psychology chapters on the controversy over nature and nurture, on caregivers, and on sex differences and sex roles are meant to give you insight into trends and issues such as the debate over race and IQ, new patterns in the family and child care, and the relations between the sexes.

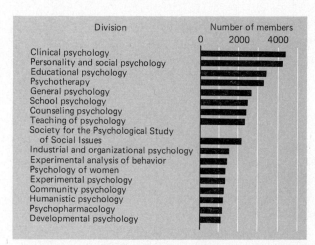

Figure 1.2 Fields of specialization in psychology
Most psychologists are members of the American Psychological Association (APA) and belong to divisions of the organization related to their work and professional interests. A psychologist can belong to more than one division—e.g., a therapist might belong to the divisions of Psychotherapy and Clinical Psychology. This chart shows membership in the seventeen most populous divisions of the APA in 1977.

Imagine that you've been working in a large insurance company for a few months. Lately one of your officemates has been seeming more and more preoccupied and looking rather glum.

"Is something bothering you?" you ask.

"Sure is," he replies. "I've been feeling really depressed these days. Don't know why. There's a psychologist in personnel. I think I'll go see if she can help me."

What psychologists do

Your friend might be making a mistake if he consulted the psychologist in personnel about his depression. A personnel psychologist is trained to select the right person for a given job, and to consult on interpersonal problems in business and industry. But there is little in the training of a personnel psychologist that would allow her to help with someone's depression.

The kind of psychologist your friend should seek out for help is a *clinical* psychologist. Clinical psychologists specialize in treating psychological problems. Clinical training focuses on

diagnosing and helping people with problems. Clinical psychologists work with troubled children or adults in guidance clinics, residential treatment centers, and institutions for delinquents, criminals, or mental patients; they may also work in private practice. Many clinical psychologists staff community mental health centers, where they deal with entire families in conjunction with physicians, police officers, teachers, ministers, and other community figures who encounter troubled people. The largest number of psychologists specialize in clinical psychology, but there are many other types of psychologists (see Figure 1.2).

The psychologists you probably have most contact with are teaching or doing research; that is, they work in colleges and universities. Like medical specialists, psychologists who do research tend to concentrate their interest on one particular field. *Physiological* psychologists emphasize the biological processes involved in behavior. *Experimental* psychologists are concerned mostly with cognitive and learning processes in perception, thinking, problem solving, and language. *Social* psychologists focus on people-to-people and people-to-environment interactions. *Developmental* psychologists study how people grow and change from infancy through old age.

School and *counseling* psychologists are concerned primarily with assessing intelligence and scholastic abilities, diagnosing personality and motivational problems, and providing counseling for students with personal, social, or academic difficulties.

Some psychologists work in business and industry. *Industrial* psychologists study factors such as worker motivation, efficiency of performance, and productivity. *Personnel* psychologists, subspecialists in the industrial field, use scientific methods to select workers best suited for various jobs, such as sales, accounting—or an airport traffic controller. Another subspecialty is the *consumer* psychologist, who studies the effects of advertising, packaging, labeling, and other aspects of goods and services produced by industry.

Human factors psychologists are concerned with relations between people and machines. These scientists use their knowledge of sensory processes, learning, motivation, and motor skills to design equipment that will maximize human performance. Human factors psychologists apply their expertise, for example, to design air traffic control rooms to minimize the risk of error.

There are many other sorts of work settings for psychologists. Psychology is a rapidly changing field, and, increasingly, young professionals find themselves in jobs for which their training was not specifically directed, for example, police work, publishing, or business management. Many of the general skills that psychology teaches transfer easily to other occupations.

The range of psychology itself blends into other professions: a specialist in psychobiology can hardly be distinguished from one in neurophysiology, since both study the brain with much the same methods; at the other extreme, a humanistic or existential psychologist is close to a philosopher or theologian in outlook.

People sometimes confuse psychologists with psychiatrists and psychoanalysts. They are not the same. A psychiatrist is a physician with special training in treating mental disorders. A psychiatrist has an M.D.; a clinical psychologist—who also treats mental disorders—has a Ph.D. The psychiatrist and clinical psychologist differ in training, outlook, and some of the treatment each is likely to offer. A psychoanalyst is someone who follows the theory and practices first set forth by Sigmund Freud for treating mental disorder. A psychoanalyst can be either a psychologist or a psychiatrist, but relatively few members of either profession are psychoanalysts.

In sum, the business of psychology is to understand human behavior and to apply that understanding to solving human problems. There are a multitude of outlooks and methods within psychology for achieving these objectives, and each has its appropriate arena in the study of human affairs. No specialty or school within psychology has all the answers, but each offers a particular expertise that is useful in the total endeavor to understand mind and behavior. Psychology, as Paul Valéry put it, can sometimes "give us a totally different idea of the things we know best"—an idea that is both more objective and more helpful than our everyday understanding of life.

GLOSSARY

Behaviorism A school of thought based on the principles of learning theory.

Clinical psychologist A Ph.D. trained to diagnose and treat people with mental problems.

Developmental psychologist One who studies how people grow and change throughout the lifespan.

Experimental psychologist One who studies processes of cognition and learning.

Personnel psychologist One who assesses a person's suitability for a given job and consults with employees on interpersonal problems.

Physiological psychologist One who studies the role of biological processes in behavior.

Psychiatrist A physician with special training in treating mental disorders.

Psychoanalyst A therapist who follows Sigmund Freud's theories and applies his techniques for treating mental disorder.

Psychobiology The study of the brain's influence on behavior.

Social psychologist One who studies how interactions between people affect behavior.

UNDERSTANDING METHODS AND STATISTICS

APPLYING PSYCHOLOGY / ONE

BASIC METHODS

Forming hypotheses ■ Testing hypotheses ■ Experimental
treatment ■ Evaluation ■ Confounding factors ■ Drawing a conclusion

ORGANIZING DATA

Dependent and independent variables ■ Graphs

STATISTICS

Descriptive and inferential statistics ■ Sampling ■ Averages ■ Variability ■ Correlations

UNDERSTANDING STATISTICS

Statistical hypothesis testing ■ Error ■ Significance level ■ Correlation coefficients

MISUSING STATISTICS

Common research pitfalls

Much of psychology may seem to you like common sense, but it is common sense with a difference. The difference is that while psychology grows from everyday impressions of people's behavior and experiences, it is refined through scientific methods that can verify, clarify, or disprove ordinary observations.

Take cigarette smoking. Its harmful effects on health have been well-documented. But what about its effects on the quality of a person's life? For example, have you heard that after a person smokes a cigarette, food doesn't taste as good? There are several reasons why you might share this common impression. Perhaps you are yourself an ex-smoker, and it seems that now that you've stopped, food tastes much better than it did while you were a smoker.

The question is why this might be so. You might suppose that cigarette smoke deadens a person's taste buds. Or you might theorize that the nicotine in tobacco has some chemical reaction in the body that interferes with the sharpness of a person's senses, including taste. Or you may have read that researchers have found that nicotine alters the level of certain chemicals and influences brain waves (Westfall *et al.*, 1967); perhaps changes in the brain function of a smoker diminish the sense of taste.

But there is another possibility entirely: You may be wrong about smoking deadening taste. A measurement of smokers' ability to taste might reveal that there is no actual difference—smokers only *seem* to be less acute tasters. Once we believe something, we tend to see and remember events that confirm it. You might have somehow convinced yourself that smoking deadens taste, selectively remembering the times that smokers observed that they couldn't taste very well and failing to notice or remember the times that their sense of taste was as sharp as nonsmokers'.

BASIC METHODS

Because our everyday observations are prey to such distortions, psychologists put their impressions of how people think and act to a systematic test. As in any other science, the basic method in psychology is to observe, to form a hunch, and to test it and verify its truth. A psychologist begins by observing the event: the effect of smoking on taste. The observation is restated in the form of a *hypothesis*, a proposition that can be proven right or wrong. A hypothesis needs to be stated precisely, in order to be testable; for example: "people who smoke cigarettes are less sensitive to taste than nonsmokers." The test in this case would be to rate people on their sensitivity to taste after they have smoked. What we call "taste," though, is mostly the perception of odors; the flavor of a food is largely the result of how it smells. Thus testing a person's sensitivity to taste in foods requires testing the ability to discriminate odors.

Forming hypotheses

Hypotheses in psychology are rarely as simple as the idea that nonsmokers taste food better than smokers. Hypotheses generally attempt to explain a relationship, not simply establish that the relationship exists. Thus, if and when you establish that smokers have poorer sensitivity to taste, you can entertain hypotheses about why that might be so. Three have been mentioned: smoke deadens the sense of taste or smell; nicotine interferes with the sharpness of the senses; and nicotine alters brain function.

There are two kinds of hypotheses: *inductive*, propositions about empirical (observable) facts, and *deductive*, propositions that follow logically from a theory that springs from your own experience. The hypothesis that smoking deadens the sense of smell is inductive—it is based on a simple observation of what seems to be the case. The hypothesis that nicotine alters brain function and interferes with odor sensitivity is deductive—it does not follow from a simple observation, but rather from a theory about how the nervous system works.

A *theory* is a statement about the relationship between many different factors, a kind of working model of how they interact and a tool for dealing with them. A theory is far more comprehensive than a hypothesis; a hypothesis is a proposition that follows from a theory. Where there is no theory, a hypothesis is like a "minitheory" proposed

to explain a specific relationship. A general theory that applies to your question about smoking and taste might be that the senses vary in their sharpness according to shifts in the body's condition; smoking could produce a physiological change that affects taste.

For many researchers, perhaps most, the real fun is in forming hypotheses and putting them into testable form. This is the creative part of research, where a person can see beyond the facts and propose as yet unproven, but testable, ideas. The actual experimental test, such as measuring people's sensitivities to odors, can be boring drudgery compared to the pleasure of thinking through the hypothesis and a way to test it.

To form a testable hypothesis, you need more than insight; you need to do your homework. Other people who have worked in the area will have their own findings and theories. You'll need to review these, find out which fit your line of thinking, and whether what others have found might modify your insights. For example, a review of the literature on smoking would show that some studies have found it does affect odor sensitivity, and some have found no effect. However, since all these studies used different procedures, it is impossible to reach a consensus. You could try to resolve the differences by conducting a more decisive experiment.

You might note that nicotine has been found to be particularly harmful in its biological effects, and that it has at least one psychological effect: it makes smokers less irritated by an obnoxious noise (Schachter, 1980). Nicotine may be the culprit in dulling taste. A specific hypothesis you might then propose for your experiment is: the nicotine in cigarette smoke dulls odor sensitivity.

Testing hypotheses

To test your hypothesis, you could follow some standard steps. In the present case, you would first recruit a group of "subjects," or people to study. Say you find twenty-four students of nearly the same age, background, and other relevant considerations, such as whether they are smokers or not, how much they smoke, and so on. You then

"Oh, nothing much. Just experimenting with some rabbits."

Drawing by Levin, © 1980, The New Yorker Magazine, Inc.

divide them at random into two groups of twelve, telling them as little as possible about the purpose and nature of your test and theory.

It is important that there be no initial difference between the groups that might bias your own results, for example, one group with many heavy smokers, the other with few. Also you must be careful to not treat the groups differently so as to inadvertently produce differences unrelated to smoking. If you tell them what kind of tobacco you want them to smoke and how you expect it to affect them, the results might reflect their expectations or their own contrary ideas about the influence of the factors tested. If possible you would want someone else to run the test who does not know the specifics of the differences between how the groups will be treated. Then this will be a *double-blind* experiment, that is, one in which neither the experimenter nor the subject knows the particular conditions of the test (such as exactly what hypothesis is being tested, or which subject is getting which treatment).

Experimental treatment

The second stage is to treat the two groups differently. The difference should be calculated to test your hypothesis—for example, to have one group smoke a high-nicotine cigarette. This is the *experimental group.* The selection of the cigarette you use must be made according to its amount of nicotine. Let's say you select a brand that is fairly high: Kool filter cigarettes, containing 1.6 milligrams of nicotine.

The other group, the *control group*, should not receive nicotine, the factor to be tested. Thus your control group could smoke a nicotine-free cabbage cigarette (Triumph menthol) that looks like the Kool.

Smoking itself might for some reason make a difference; for example, aspects of smoking other than nicotine might interfere with odor sensitivity. You should observe the subjects' reactions to the cigarettes carefully to be sure subjects in both groups believe they are smoking a regular men-

TABLE A.1 **ODOR DETECTION ABILITIES:** Number of hits out of 100 tries after smoking a tobacco cigarette (experimental group) or a cabbage cigarette (control group)

Experimental Group		Control Group	
Subject	Score	Subject	Score
1	26	1	46
2	48	2	71
3	71	3	67
4	77	4	66
5	70	5	76
6	66	6	64
7	58	7	57
8	60	8	65
9	69	9	66
10	66	10	62
11	91	11	81
12	71	12	72
MEAN	64.4	MEAN	66.2
STANDARD DEVIATION	16.0	STANDARD DEVIATION	9.1

tholated cigarette. To aid in this deception, both cigarettes should have the brand name covered by tape.

You would instruct each subject to smoke "naturally" up to the tape. Waiting just long enough for the nicotine to take effect—about five minutes after smoking the cigarettes—you would give the subjects an odor sensitivity test in an otherwise odor-free chamber. Their task is to sniff a test tube containing either a hard-to-detect amount of food odor (e.g., banana flavor or meat extract) or a substance which looks the same but has no odor. Table A.1 shows a percentage of "hits," that is, correct responses to test tubes actually containing an odor, for this hypothetical experiment.

Evaluation

You can now observe the effect of the nicotine by comparing the results for the two groups. The measure observed should be appropriate to the hypothesis; a hit would fulfill this criterion because it shows how sensitive a person is to an odor. Your conclusion would be stated as a comparison of hits for the two groups. Looking at the results in Ta-

ble A.1, it is clear that the subjects were not equally sensitive. The average (mean) shows that the experimental group, which had the nicotine, was less sensitive to odor than the control group, but there were differences within the group; not all experimental group members did poorly. You need to take these differences into account before drawing a conclusion.

Confounding factors

The assumption that underlies the interpretation of results in this sort of experiment is simple: if the people in the study were the same at the start, but different later, then it must have been the treatment that made the difference. If you had found that the group that smoked high-nicotine cigarettes had poorer odor sensitivity than the nonnicotine group, you could conclude that nicotine lessened their sensitivity. This interpretation does not hold, though, if some unintended factor apart from the treatment actually caused the difference. Say, for example, light smokers are more affected by nicotine than heavy smokers, and that the high-nicotine group happened to have more light smokers in it.

Such extraneous factors are *confounding*—inadvertent factors that cause the effect attributed to the treatment. Experimenters have to be cautious in designing a control condition that will duplicate the treatment in every way but the specific variable being tested. If light smokers are more likely to be affected by nicotine than heavy smokers, you'd have to be sure that there were equal numbers of light smokers in both the experimental and control groups. Another confounding factor might have been that the nonnicotine brand of cigarettes used in the control condition tasted strange to smokers; their reaction to a strange-tasting cigarette may have somehow distorted their responses on the odor sensitivity test afterward. It is hard to anticipate all the possible confounding factors in any experiment. Often one experiment will reveal problems in the method that will then mean another experiment must be run that will eliminate the confounding factor. Only after the second experiment can there be a true test of the hypothesis.

Drawing a conclusion

Your conclusion would be stated as a comparison of the two groups. For example, you might find that "People who smoked cigarettes high in nicotine did about as well on odor sensitivity as people who smoked cigarettes with no nicotine. Nicotine does not seem to lessen odor sensitivity." These (imaginary) results would indicate that your hypothesis was wrong, in which case you would have to discard it and propose a new one that fit your results. It might be something like "Smoking cigarettes of any kind will lessen odor sensitivity."

Your next step would be to test whether simply smoking—regardless of nicotine content—lessens odor sensitivity. To do that you'd have to test a group of smokers and a group of nonsmokers.

Using experimental findings to refine, discard, or validate the original hypothesis means that the resulting theory is grounded in facts. In this way theory and findings strengthen each other; the theory guides research, while the findings reshape the theory. The result is a body of theory that is scientifically sound—the goal of research in psychology.

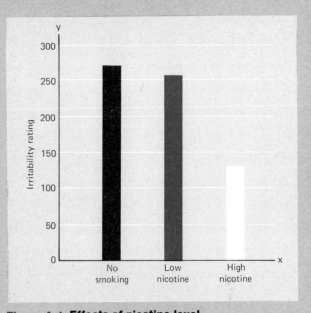

Figure A.1 Effects of nicotine level
Heavy smokers had the least tolerance for obnoxious noises when they were not allowed to smoke. A low-nicotine cigarette made them less irritable, but smoking their favorite brand made them least irritated by the noise. Irritability, the dependent variable, is plotted along the vertical axis, while the type of cigarette smoked, the independent variable, is displayed along the horizontal axis.

ORGANIZING DATA

Dependent and independent variables

Your research design was one of the most common: you tried out the effect of one variable (nicotine) and observed its effect on another variable (odor sensitivity). The factor that is varied systematically is called the *independent variable;* the factor it affects is called the *dependent variable.* The value of the dependent variable depends on that of the independent variable.

Graphs

A helpful way to grasp the patterns that your results show is to graph them. The most common graph is a pair of coordinates—two lines at right angles to each other (see Figure A.1). Typically,

the horizontal line, commonly called the x axis, or abscissa, is used for the values of the independent variable. It is divided into whatever units are appropriate for the particular measure, in this case, how much nicotine was smoked. The vertical line, the y axis, or ordinate, is used for values of the dependent variable—in this case, irritability.

Another common graph displays the *frequency distribution,* in which the scores on a measure are plotted on the x axis, with the number of people in the group who got each of those scores plotted on the y axis. The best-known frequency distribution is the *normal distribution, or bell-shaped curve.* A bell-shaped curve is highest at the middle range and drops gradually toward the lowest and highest ranges of scores.

A famous bell-shaped curve was obtained when an IQ test was given in 1937 to a sample of 3,184 children presumed to be representative of the average American child. About one-quarter of the children got the average score of 100, while about one-tenth scored 80 and another tenth scored 120. The results for the whole group were balanced on both sides of the middle peak, producing a bell-shaped curve (Figure A.2—1937 Stanford-Binet distribution).

But distributions do not always produce such a neatly symmetrical bell curve. Distributions are *skewed* when there is a preponderance of scores toward the lower or higher end. *Negative skewing* has more scores toward the high end—what you might expect to see, for example, in IQ scores if a large number of college students were included in the sample. *Positive skewing* has more scores

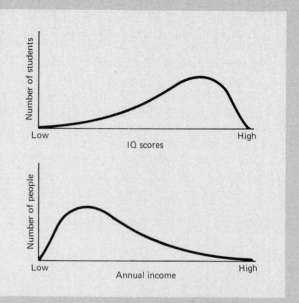

Figure A.3 Negative skewing

Negative skewing occurs when a relatively high number of scores fall at the high end of the scale, positive skewing when a high number fall at the low end. An easy exam, for example, would result in a negative skew, while a hard one would produce scores in a positive skew.

toward the low end—what you might see if you plotted annual incomes in a country where many people were poor and a few quite wealthy (see Figure A.3).

Figure A.2 Distribution of IQ scores plotted at 10-point intervals

The table shows the percentage of children receiving scores in each 10-point range.

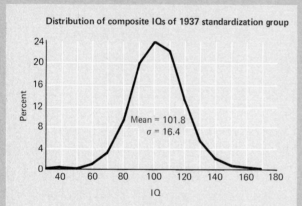

Distribution of composite IQs of 1937 standardization group

Mean = 101.8
σ = 16.4

Distribution of the 1937 standardization group

IQ	Percent	Classification
160–169	0.03	
150–159	0.2	Very superior
140–149	1.1	
130–139	3.1	
120–129	8.2	Superior
110–119	18.1	High average
100–109	23.5	
90–99	23.0	Normal or average
80–89	14.5	Low average
70–79	5.6	Borderline defective
60–69	2.0	
50–59	0.4	
40–49	0.2	Mentally defective
30–39	0.03	

STATISTICS

One of the most general principles in psychology is that people vary. No two people are exactly alike, nor are any two groups. If in your experiment you do find a difference between two groups of people on a measure (e.g., odor sensitivity), how do you know if it is due to the treatment (i.e., nicotine) or to chance? It could be that the groups just happened to differ, and that your results had nothing to do with your treatment.

Because of the possibility that a chance variation has occurred rather than a real treatment effect, psychologists use statistics to analyze their results. *Statistics* is a branch of mathematics that deals with the collection, analysis, and interpretation of numerical data. You find statistics used everywhere: to report on changes in the cost-of-living and employment rates, to compare baseball players' batting records, to report public opinion on issues in the news, to predict the outcome of elections. Using statistics to analyze any numerical outcome allows us to say with confidence that the effect reported is real and consequential, rather than just a chance variation. An effect is *significant* when statistics tell us it is not the product of chance alone.

Descriptive and inferential statistics

Statistics can summarize facts or help us infer what the facts may imply. *Descriptive* statistics simply summarize the characteristics of a set of numbers. Averaging the odor hits of two groups of people is an example of descriptive statistics; it summarizes the results of the experiment. Baseball players' batting averages and IQ scores are descriptive statistics. *Inferential statistics,* on the other hand, are procedures for estimating the characteristics of a whole population from data on a part of the population. That is, do the results for one small group hold for everybody, or do they only reflect the performance of the people you happened to use in your experiment?

Sampling

A *sample* in statistics is a subset of a larger population. The population can be any group you choose to study: fat people, women, redheads, or whales. You could never gather and study all the members of such populations. You can, however, gather a sample from the population. Inferential statistics allow you to look at the sample, study it, and draw conclusions about the population as a whole. Political polls use inferential statistics: a sample of people who represent the national population are polled, and the results are taken to represent the opinions of the whole country. The Nielsen index rates the popularity of television shows by sampling only about 1,500 TV sets out of the several million in the country. If there is some meaningful factor that sets the people in the Niel-

sen group apart from other TV watchers (e.g., if all of them were well-to-do or lived in large cities), then this sample would be "biased"—it would not truly represent the whole population.

To pick a sample that can be generalized to the whole population it represents, the sampling must be random. A *random sample* is one in which every person in the population stands an equal chance of being selected. If a pollster were to choose a sample from a list of registered Republicans, then the sample could be random only for people with two characteristics: Republicans who were registered to vote. The results could not be generalized to all Republicans, nor to the entire voting public.

There are several methods of picking a random sample. One is to flip a coin. You can randomly assign people to two groups in that way: heads they go to the experimental group, tails, to the control group.

Averages

If a person is a member of a sample you've tested, the most likely prediction you can make about his or her value on any measure you've taken is that it will be average. You can find that value by computing the *central tendency*, or average of scores, for the group. But in general, the average represents the effect of the independent variable (e.g., nicotine) on the group (see Table A.1, p. 18).

There are many kinds of averages in statistics, each useful in its way. Each kind of measure for central tendency yields different information. The *mode* is simply the most popular number. But when numbers are distributed more haphazardly than a bell curve, the mode is not a trustworthy gauge of the central tendency. A better indicator would be the *mean,* or simple average. The mean in Table A.1 was obtained for the experimental and control group separately by adding all the scores in a group and dividing the total by the number of scores in the group.

Another measure of central tendency is the *median,* the one score in a series that is the midpoint—an equal number of scores fall above and below the median. For example, given the scores 5, 7, 9, 10, and 13, 9 is the median. When the number of scores is even, like 3, 6, 8, and 11, then the median falls midway between the two middle scores, 6 and 8; the median is 7 in this case. The median corresponds to the 50th percentile; you may be familiar with percentiles from scores on aptitude or achievement tests. A percentile divides a set of scores into 100 parts; if you are at the 50th percentile, then 50 percent of scores are below yours, and 50 above. Percentiles provide a finer way of breaking up distributions of scores than the median, but the principle is the same.

In general, the mean is most often used as a measure of central tendency, since it is more useful than the other measures in statistical tests.

Variability

Since people differ, the group average may not be a good description of any specific person in the group. The spread, or *variability*, of individual differences in scores tells you how well or poorly the average describes any given person in the group. If the individual values within a group cluster together, the variability is small and the average is a fairly good estimate for anyone in the group. If they cover a wide spread, variability is large and the average value is a poor way to describe any given person in the group. The difference between the two groups in Table A.1 seems small relative to the individual differences in each group. Therefore, the difference between groups is not likely to be significant. There is also variability in the scores of a single person measured at different times. One measure of the variability is the *range* of scores, from highest to lowest. The greater the range of the difference between highest and lowest score, the less representative are measures of central tendency such as the mean. But the range can be misleading if, for example, there are unusually high or low scores, as in the control group in Table A.1.

The most common way of expressing the variability within a group of values is the *standard deviation*, defined as "the square root of the average of the squares of the deviations from the mean." This is not as forbidding as it sounds. In effect, the standard deviation weights the degree

each score differs from the mean by a value corresponding to the frequency of each score. It is a mathematical method for more truly representing a distribution. Note that the control group in Table A.1 shows less variation than the experimental group.

Correlations

A *correlation* is a relationship between variables. For example, if the value of one rises, the other does too. Or, when the value of one lowers, the other rises. Or, within a certain range of values for the first variable, the second rises; past a certain value for the first, the other lowers, or stays constant. There are innumerable patterns of correlation possible.

The relationship between variables can be shown by making a *scatter plot*, a diagram in which the scores for two variables are placed on a graph. A scatter plot gives you a visual impression of the relationship between the two (see Figure A.4).

When scores for two variables are obtained for a sample, there is a correlation between the two if knowing the value for one improves your ability to predict the value for the other. Let's say you found that by and large, the more a person smoked, the lower that person's odor sensitivity. If a person smoked just a few cigarettes each day, you'd predict a higher sensitivity score; if she smoked two packs, you'd predict a lower sensitivity score.

But correlations are not causes. If two variables are related, one does not necessarily *cause* the other. For example, there is a high positive correlation between a city's crime rate and the number of churches. The more churches, the more crime. Does this mean churches cause crime, or that crime leads people to church? Not at all. The relationship may be related to a third factor: density of population. The more people in a city, the more churches—and the more crime.

Nothing is simple, especially when it comes to interpreting the causes of human behavior. Most behavior has many underlying causes, and, what's more, these causes interact. *Interaction* occurs

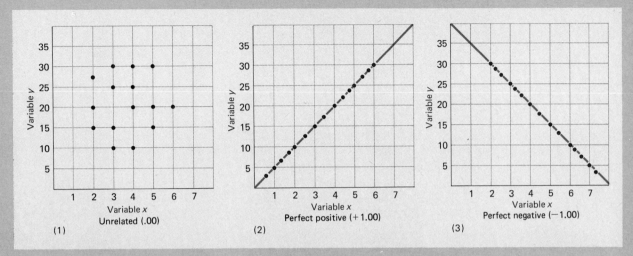

Figure A.4 A scatter plot showing the relationship between two scores

Zero correlation between them is at the left (1), a perfect positive (+ 1.00) correlation in the middle (2), and a perfect negative correlation (− 1.00) at the right (3).

when the effects of one independent variable change the effects of another independent variable. For example, nicotine may influence a nonsmoker's odor sensitivity more than that of a smoker. In this case, then, the effects of odor sensitivity and nicotine interact.

UNDERSTANDING STATISTICS

Statistical hypothesis testing

A hypothesis, remember, is a hunch that can be tested. A *statistical hypothesis* predicts the values that should be found in a sample under certain conditions. The research question is, basically, whether a difference between an experimental group and a control group is the result of chance or the result of experimental treatment. The hypothesis that the difference is an effect of the treatment (e.g., nicotine), is tested by establishing that the difference discovered is *not* the product of chance.

Statistics tests the proposition that the difference found *is* attributable to chance. If this proposition is disproved, then the treatment must account for the difference. A *null hypothesis* states that there is no systematic difference be-

tween experimental and control groups. If the null hypothesis holds, then the treatment had no important effect. The alternative, or *research hypothesis*, is that the difference between experimental and control groups is more than the product of chance. In other words, the treatment made a real difference. For example, the null hypothesis in the smoking study might be that the sensitivity scores of the nicotine group and the control group are the same, or differ only by chance. The research hypothesis, on the other hand, would be that the difference between these scores is greater than chance and is related to the experimental factor—nicotine.

The research hypothesis is more likely to be true (1) if the difference between the group scores is great; (2) if the differences in scores between the people within each group are small; and (3) if the number of people in each group is large. A difference in sensitivity scores between the experimental and control groups would confirm a research hypothesis, then, if (1) it was a large difference; (2) the scores clustered around the average values for each group; and (3) there were many people in the groups. In all three respects, the results of the smoking experiment in Table A.1 fail to confirm the research hypothesis and so support the null hypothesis. In short, nicotine had no significant effect on odor sensitivity.

Error

There are two kinds of error that can occur when testing null and research hypotheses. In a *Type I error*, the null hypothesis is rejected when it is actually true. In this sort of error, you conclude that the difference found between the groups is greater than chance alone would produce, when in fact it is not. In a *Type II error*, the research hypothesis is rejected when it is actually true. You conclude that the difference between the groups is the result of chance alone, when in fact it is greater than chance alone would produce.

Significance level

How do you know whether a difference is due to chance or not? In statistics you can never know for sure, but you can be highly certain when a difference is probably not due to chance. The convention in psychological research is to establish a level of significance, an arbitrary value of probability that provides an acceptable level of certainty. This value is typically one chance in twenty, or 5 percent, usually stated .05. Let's say you flipped a penny eight times, and it came up heads seven times and tails just once. If the level of probability of getting this outcome is only .05 or less, then your result would be expected to happen by chance only one time out of twenty. Thus, this result would be considered significant, and if it had been the outcome of an experiment or treatment—say trying to influence the flip of a coin by picturing in your mind the side you want to come up—then we would assume the outcome was not the result of chance, but of the treatment.

Correlation coefficients

The *correlation coefficient* is a measure of the extent of a correlation. If two variables don't correlate at all, their correlation coefficient is zero. If two variables correlate perfectly—a change in one producing a comparable change in the other—their correlation coefficient is 1.00; such variables show a perfect *positive* correlation. Most correlations are imperfect. A correlation coefficient of .60

describes a less strong, but positive, correlation. If an increase in variable x produces a steady decrease in variable y, then there is a perfect *negative correlation* between them, with a value of -1.00. A correlation coefficient of -0.15 describes a weak, negative correlation. The correlation between students' IQ scores and their grades should be positive, while the correlation between IQ and errors on college exams should be negative.

Scatter diagrams like those in Figure A.4 show these patterns of correlation. When the values of variables plotted in a scatter diagram are unrelated, the dots are scattered randomly, and the correlation coefficient is zero. A positive correlation slopes upward; a negative correlation slopes downward. You'll frequently find correlation coefficients expressed in terms of r in journal articles or psychology textbooks.

MISUSING STATISTICS

Mark Twain wrote, "There are three kinds of lies—lies, damned lies, and statistics." In the same vein, a research director of one of the national communications networks distinguished between "objective research" and "research with an objective." Statistics can make sense of otherwise confusing data, but the results of statistics can all too easily be misinterpreted or misrepresented, either purposely or unknowingly.

A frequent misuse of statistics is to jump to broader, more generalized conclusions than are warranted. For example, say you conclude that nicotine influences odor sensitivity after observing only the first two subjects in each group. When you see the results for all the subjects, your conclusion turns out to be premature. Generalization of statistical results can be made only from *representative* samples of the whole population, with adequate control of extraneous variables that might account for or distort the results.

Another common way to misuse statistics is to present or cite them out of context. Graphs and tables are an important part of statistics and can easily be manipulated to give a self-serving impression. An example of using results out of context would be emphasizing the one type of crime that may have diminished over an interval in a city, such as bank robberies, giving only passing attention to all other types of crime, such as muggings, rapes, and homicides, which may have increased. This abuse of statistics can create a comfortable illusion that the efforts of law enforcement officers are successful. Such manipulation distorts research to gain an objective, rather than using research to arrive at a sound understanding of what the evidence actually shows.

It is tempting to make inferences that exaggerate the strength of a statistic. Say you have a correlation coefficient that is quite low, around .30. You can say that you found a positive correlation between the two variables, or you can be more accurate and say you found a weak but positive correlation. The first statement makes the correlation sound much stronger than it is. In fact any inferences drawn from such a weak correlation should be seen as hypotheses needing further research before they can be accepted.

Another common misuse of statistics is in graphs that visually distort a difference, making it look important when in fact it is not statistically significant. To sensationalize a set of values on a graph there are some standard tricks: (1) select the data that make your point, and leave out any that weaken it; (2) expand the units on one axis to visually exaggerate the effect you're trying to emphasize; (3) exaggerate by eliminating the numbers on one axis, so that the reader will have no real sense of what the seeming change actually represents numerically; and (4) eliminate zero, starting the graph in the lower left, thus making it seem that the effect represents more than it actually does. To see the total effect of these simple rules for distortion, see Figure A.5.

Beware of the commonly misused phrase "the average." As we have seen, there are several kinds of average—mean, median, and mode (plus two other statistical averages we haven't discussed). Each can serve a good purpose, and each can represent a different value for the same group. Any average chosen can be to the advantage of the chooser, probably supporting some claim rather than best representing the data. Remember also that the concept of average is true of scores, not people. There is so much variability

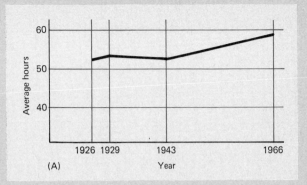

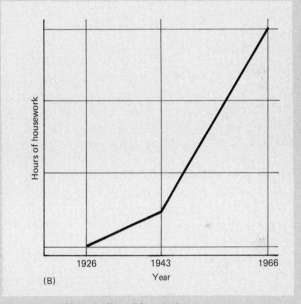

Figure A.5 How to lie with graphs

Part A is an accurate graph of the average hours per week devoted to housework in selected years between 1926 and 1966. There was no great change, as the graph shows.

Part B distorts the data by eliminating numbers, expanding the y axis to exaggerate the change, and omitting the point for 1929. The result gives the impression that the amount of time spent on housework increased dramatically during the forty years.(From G. A. Kimble, *How to Use (and Misuse) Statistics*, © 1978, p. 30. Reprinted by permission of Prentice-Hall, Inc., Englewood Cliffs, New Jersey.)

among people on so many different dimensions that there is no "average person."

Common research pitfalls

One set of distortions in research is due to the presence of the researcher—it has been called the "onstage effect." This simply means that people who are aware that they are being observed for a psychological study become self-conscious and act unnaturally. For example, people sometimes tell a researcher what they think they "should" say, rather than what they truly feel. If a person feels the researcher is evaluating his adequacy or mental health, he may become apprehensive and try to behave in ways he feels people should. Or a subject can try to please a researcher by acting in a way she guesses will fulfill the goals of the study. Such effects are research *artifacts*, effects created by the research itself, rather than the behavior it attempts to study.

An antidote to onstage effects is *unobtrusive measures*, research that assesses behavior unbeknownst to the person assessed (Webb, Campbell, Schwartz, and Sechrest, 1966). For example, one study measured which exhibits in a museum were most popular by observing where the tiles were most worn. There are other ways that researchers can protect their experiments against artifacts. If the researcher doesn't know what's being measured, then he or she won't inadvertently influence subjects to respond in a certain way; this can be done in a research team if the person who briefs the subjects doesn't know what's being measured, while another researcher who has no contact with subjects does the scoring.

This same strategy is used in double-blind experiments, where both the researcher and the subject don't know which treatment the subject is getting. For example, in testing a new drug, half the subjects will get the experimental pill, the other half a *placebo*, an inert pill that resembles the experimental one in shape, appearance, and taste,

but has no physical effects. This procedure guards against the possibility that a subject or researcher might influence the drug effect by expecting some particular reaction.

Many studies claim that one treatment or another changed the experimental groups for the better. This may or may not be true, though. In a famous study, factory workers were found to produce more when just about *any* change was introduced: dimming the lights or brightening them, having breaks at different times, and so on. This kind of change, called the *Hawthorne effect*, is a change that *any* novelty seems to produce, and so no special claims can be made for a treatment that works in this way. The safeguard here would be a control group that is treated the same as the experimental group, save for the treatment.

Finally, watch for *sample bias*, when an experimental group is supposed to represent a larger population, but actually does not. In general, the larger the sample, the more likely it is to represent the whole population. Nevertheless, there can be a systematic bias in sampling—even in large populations. For example, if a survey on nuclear power is made with a disproportionate number of nuclear physicists in the sample, then the results will not be likely to reflect accurately the national population's views. The best sample is, of course, a random sample—but almost no sample is truly random.

Even if you never have the opportunity to do any research, a grasp of these basic concepts can make you a critical consumer when you read reports of research.

GLOSSARY

Artifacts Effects created by the research itself, rather than by the behavior it studies.

Central tendency The average value for a group of scores.

Confounding factors Inadvertent factors that cause an effect which is then wrongly attributed to the treatment.

Control group Subjects comparable to those in the

treatment group in every way except that they do not receive the experimental treatment.

Correlation coefficient A measurement of the degree to which two variables are related.

Dependent variable A factor affected by an independent variable; its value changes as the independent variable changes.

Double-blind An experimental condition in which neither the experimenter nor the subject knows the specific objectives of the test nor other details that might influence its outcome.

Experimental group Subjects that receive the treatment to be tested.

Hawthorne effect The tendency for *any* novel treatment to produce a change in behavior.

Hypothesis A proposition that can be proven or disproven.

Independent variable A factor that is varied systematically in an experiment to test its effects.

Interaction A situation in which the effects of one independent variable alter the effects of another.

Mean The simple average, obtained by dividing the total number of scores by the number of members in the group.

Median The score at the midpoint in a series of values.

Mode The most common value in a group of scores.

Normal distribution (or bell-shaped curve) A distribution that is highest at the middle range and drops off toward the low and high ends of the range.

Null hypothesis The proposition that the difference between experimental and control groups is due to chance.

Random sample A subset of a population in which every person stands an equal chance of being selected.

Range The spread from lowest to highest in a group of scores.

Research hypothesis The proposition that the difference between experimental and control groups is not the product of chance, but due to the independent variable.

Sample A representative subset of a larger population.

Sample bias A situation in which the experimental group does not actually represent the total population being assessed.

Significant effect An experimental effect that is not the product of chance alone.

Skew A distribution with more scores toward the lower or higher end.

Statistical hypothesis A specific prediction of the values that should hold for a sample under certain conditions.

Statistics A branch of mathematics dealing with the collection, analysis, and interpretation of numerical data.

Theory A statement about the relationship between many different factors.

Type I error The null hypothesis is rejected when it is actually true.

Type II error The research hypothesis is rejected when it is actually true.

Unobtrusive measures Research that assesses behavior unbeknownst to the subject assessed.

Variability The spread of differences in scores.

PART TWO

COGNITIVE PROCESSES

2

LEARNING

COMMON MYTHS

MANY PEOPLE BELIEVE...	ACTUALLY...
Practice makes perfect.	Practice by itself will not always do the job; it is more effective when associated with reward for correct performance.
The best way to ensure that a desired behavior will persist after training is completed is to reward the behavior every single time it occurs.	Once reward is withdrawn, behavior trained under intermittent reward (i.e., rewards for some trials, but not all) will persist longer than behavior trained under 100 percent reward.
A person can never learn to control physiological functions like heart rate and blood pressure.	Biofeedback training can teach a person to regulate functions such as these.
Humane considerations aside, punishment is more effective than reward.	Reward is more consistently effective; punishment produces variable results and can sometimes backfire.
People will work much harder for a salary than if they are paid "by the piece."	People work harder if paid by the piece than if they get a salary.

Well maybe it's the time of year
or maybe it's the time of man
I don't know who I am
But life is for learning . . .

JONI MITCHELL, "WOODSTOCK"

Life is for learning. Perhaps life *is* learning. A baby learns to crawl, walk, put a verb with a noun in a sentence. A child learns to add, subtract, multiply, divide, and to talk and move in ways that are acceptable to friends and family. A married couple learns the little signs and signals each gives for wanting to be closer or wanting to withdraw. Americans learn "The Star-Spangled Banner," and the French learn the "Marseillaise."

The amount we learn is vast, and much of it is imperceptible. Each time we learn something, no matter how seemingly trivial, we are changed by it. We are not precisely the people we were before—and what we have learned makes us the people we are.

Imagine that

it's been years since you've driven a car with a standard gearshift; your own car is an automatic. One day your car is in the shop for repairs. A friend is kind enough to loan you hers for the day. There's only one catch: it's a standard shift. As she drives you to where you're letting her off, you watch closely as she smoothly changes gears. It's as though you're learning it for the first time.

Your friend gets out, leaving you there alone with the gearshift. You study the diagram on the gearshift knob. First gear: to the left and forward. Cautiously, you slide the gearshift to the left and ease it forward—then freeze as a horrible grinding growls from the car's innards.

You sit and gather your thoughts. Then, you remember: of course—the clutch! You push the pedal in, and the gears shift into first. You let your foot off the clutch, an action followed by the car lurching forward with a stomach-wrenching growl, and stopping dead.

After half a dozen tries, you get better and better until finally the placing of your foot on the clutch meshes with the placing of your hand on the gearshift. All in one swift motion.

You head off down the road. As you drive, you remember how smoothly your friend shifted. You find yourself making the same smooth motions you saw her make. From then on it's easy.

When you return her car, your friend asks, "Have any trouble?"

"None at all." ■

KINDS OF LEARNING

In technical terms, *learning* is a relatively permanent change in behavior resulting from rewarded practice. Real learning involves a change that is both sustained—for not every new change in behavior lasts—and rewarded. If in fumbling to use a clutch you happen to do it right once, you have not necessarily learned to use the clutch. You have learned it only after you can do it again and again. Reward and practice cement learning. The satisfaction you feel at mastering a new skill and the exhilaration you feel in using it can both be rewards for learning to clutch properly.

When we learn, a new or changed response becomes part of our repertory of responses, to be called upon as needed. Once you know how to use a clutch, you can do it automatically. Or when you learn Spanish, "¿Como está Ud?" elicits an automatic "Bien, gracias." Psychologists recognize four main kinds of learning:

1. In *classical conditioning,* a previously neutral stimulus comes to elicit a response similar to that of an original stimulus after the two have been paired a number of times. While fumbling with the clutch, you became anxious (the elicited response) when you heard the gears grind (the stimulus). If just using the gearshift itself (a previously neutral stimulus) were to make you anxious, it would be an instance of classical conditioning.

2. In *operant conditioning,* actions that are followed by rewards are more likely to be repeated. With experimentation and practice, you refined your control of the clutch pedal until it meshed with your shifting gears; your reward was a smooth ride. When a form of behavior is more likely to occur because it is followed by a satisfying event in this way, we say it has been *reinforced.*

3. *Imitation,* or observational learning, is the means by which you follow the example of someone else in learning something new. By imitating your friend at the wheel, you learned how to shift smoothly. Learning by imitation plays a large role in increasing our repertory of abilities. Children, for example, acquire much of their socialization through imitation.

4. *Cognitive insight* is learning that occurs as a result of a sudden breakthrough in understanding. When you realized that the clutch was the answer to your agony with the gearshift, that might well have been learning by insight. Cognitive insight is at work when you solve a problem or have a creative thought. The feelings of pleasure, closure, and capability that the insight brings are its reward.

Some changes in behavior that resemble learning are not in fact learned changes. Change often occurs without either reward or practice, but such change is not learned. A canary need not learn to sing, nor does a puppy learn to worry a bone. Newly hatched turtles head directly toward water from the dry land of their birth. This is not a learned response. Such behaviors are innate, or inborn.

It is not always useful to respond to each stimulus that presents itself. An animal in the wild, for example, may stop eating, freeze, and become alert to see if rustling leaves signal a predator; if the rustling proves to be just the wind, then the animal stops its defensive response and goes back to eating, even though the leaves keep rustling. This waning of a response to a repeated stimulus is *habituation.* When a stimulus is repeated over and over, the response it produces will gradually decrease in intensity or magnitude, typically until it stops altogether. Habituation, sometimes described as "learning what not to do," is very useful: it keeps an animal or a human from endlessly repeating wasteful responses. The first response is useful—for example, the rustling might have signaled a predator—but repeating it wastes valuable time and energy (Fantino and Logan, 1979).

Other changes, such as those due to biological maturation, have nothing to do with learning—a girl does not "learn" to menstruate, though she will learn what to do about her menstrual periods as well as a set of attitudes about her experience. Nor does an adolescent boy grow taller because he is rewarded for it, though he may have rewarding experiences as a result of his new height.

Imagine that it is a warm day and you are eating a carry-out hamburger with a group of your friends. Suddenly a large wasp buzzes loudly into the middle of the group and lands right on your French fries. At the sight of it, one of your friends cries "A WASP!" and leaps into the air and charges off across the lawn, leaving a trail of shredded lettuce and catsup.

When he returns, your friend explains that his fear began when he was a baby. As he crawled around the backyard one day, he discovered a fuzzy, yellow-and-black bug that buzzed around him. After a few misses he managed to grab it. The nice bug was a bee, and he got a painful sting.

Afterward, he began crying whenever he saw a bee or any other insect. Later he learned that not all bugs would sting him, and he no longer cried at the mere sight of a bee. However, he is still afraid when a stinging insect comes near him, and sometimes he panics completely. ■

CLASSICAL CONDITIONING

Reflex, stimulus, and response

Your friend's story illustrates the kind of learning known as classical conditioning. Classical conditioning was made famous by Ivan Pavlov, a celebrated Russian physiologist, at the turn of the century. (Actually, an American psychologist, A. B. Twitmeyer, reported on classical conditioning before Pavlov, but the significance of his discovery was ignored.) Classical conditioning was

accidentally discovered by Pavlov during research on the digestive system. In a study of the digestion of dogs, Pavlov was measuring the amount of saliva produced when they tasted food. The rate of the dogs' saliva flow was being timed by a metronome. At one point Pavlov noticed that the dogs began salivating when they heard the metronome, before the food was placed in their mouths.

Classical conditioning begins with an unconditioned reflex, which is a relationship between a stimulus and a response. A *stimulus* is any event that makes a person or animal behave in a certain way, for example, the dogs' food. The behavior the stimulus elicits is a *response*, such as salivation. The automatic—or unconditioned—responses used in classical conditioning are typically natural processes, such as blinking in response to a puff of air on the eye or salivating at the smell of food.

The stimulus and response that form an automatic reflex are known as the *unconditioned stimulus* (UCS) and *unconditioned response* (UCR). Unconditioned responses are not learned. A baby needs no training to respond to the unconditioned stimulus of a bee sting with the unconditioned responses of releasing the grip and crying. Nor does a dog need to learn to salivate in response to food. When Pavlov's dogs associated the unconditioned stimulus of the food with the sound of the metronome, the sound then became a conditioned stimulus (CS) causing the conditioned response (CR)—salivating—by itself.

Classical conditioning, then, creates a new pair-

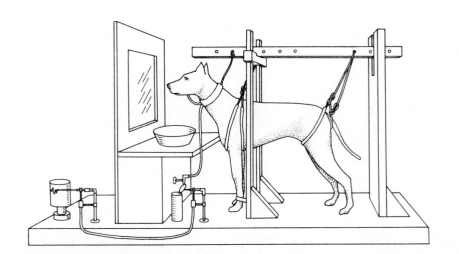

Figure 2.1 Pavlov's experiment
In Pavlov's experiments, the dogs' saliva was collected as a measure of the conditioned response.

ing between a given stimulus and response, for example, a metronome and salivation, or a bee and fright. Before conditioning, they are not related; afterward, the conditioned stimulus evokes the conditioned response—the metronome evokes salivation, the bee evokes fright. In Pavlov's terms, the new pairing of the stimulus and response marks "acquisition": a CS evokes a CR.

Extinction and recovery

A conditioned response will die out if it is not occasionally paired with an unconditioned stimulus. When the CS no longer evokes a CR, we say that the conditioned response has *extinguished*. For example, if the metronome no longer made Pavlov's dogs salivate, then the CR would be extinguished. If the baby was not stung every time he saw a bee, he would stop crying at the mere sight of one. You might think he had forgotten about the sting, but extinction is not the same as forgetting. Forgetting would mean that the baby could not recall the fact that a bee had stung him. In this case, however, his conditioned response was extinguished because he no longer associated the sight of the bee with the sting.

Extinction is not always the end of a response. Sometimes it will recur in a *spontaneous recovery*, the reappearance of a conditioned response that has been extinguished; the CS once again evokes the CR. For example, a successful businesswoman, long past the pain of a childhood auto accident, might occasionally find herself afraid of downtown traffic. In the long run, however, it is necessary for a conditioned response to be paired with the unconditioned stimulus from time to time for the conditioning to remain strong; otherwise it will die out. Your friend's periodic encounters with stinging insects most likely kept his conditioned response—fright—alive.

The strength of a conditioned response can be measured by its intensity, for example, the amount of saliva the dog produces. Its strength can also be measured by the *latency*, or time elapsed, between the stimulus and response, that is, the time it takes the dog to begin to salivate. The more stimulus-response pairings, the more intense and rapid will be the response.

■ It was a strange scene—an adult coyote retreating from a lamb. The coyote was hungry, the lamb was healthy, and in that inescapable enclosure all that was missing for an instant meal of lamb was a parsley garnish. What went wrong?

The coyote had learned through aversive conditioning to hate lamb.

Operating on the principle that if an animal ate a meal that made it sick, it would avoid that meal in the future, Carl Gustavson and John Garcia (1974) conducted an experiment in aversive conditioning using seven adult coyotes. Lithium chloride, which causes nausea and vomiting, was slipped into their hamburger. All became ill. Two days later the coyotes were offered untainted hamburger. They sniffed it, retched, then either rolled on the food, urinated on it, or buried it.

Live lambs and rabbits were the next course on this experimental menu, and these creatures were gobbled up without hesitation. But on the fifth day, our coyotes were given minced lamb meat seasoned with lithium and wrapped in fresh lamb hide. A week later, live lamb was back as the entree. This time only two coyotes were biting, and they ate with great reservation.

After another serving of lamb à la lithium two days

Generalization and discrimination

After a conditioned response (e.g., salivation) has been acquired to one stimulus (e.g., a metronome's ticking), another similar stimulus (e.g., the tick of a clock) may elicit the response. This is *generalization:* a stimulus similar to an already conditioned stimulus elicits the conditioned response. As a baby, your friend generalized from bees to any flying insect—they all made him cry.

Discrimination, in contrast to generalization, is the ability to detect differences among stimuli. Stimulus discrimination is adaptive in helping us

PULLING A GAG ON THE WILY COYOTE

later, not one coyote would attack a lamb, though they still devoured rabbits with relish. The coyotes had learned not to attack their normal prey. Instead, they nibbled grass the way a sick dog will, sometimes snapping at their greens as if frustrated by their inability to bite into the lambs.

The coyotes had become classically conditioned. The lithium, an unconditioned stimulus, led to nausea and vomiting, an unconditioned response. When lithium was paired with the taste of lamb, then the lamb became a conditioned stimulus: it, too, then caused the coyotes to get sick.

The coyotes' fickle taste buds could mean a solution to the problem of controlling sheep-killing coyotes without slaughtering them into extinction. Researchers now want to apply this method of control on the open range as an alternative to the guns, poisons, and traps now being used to control coyotes. There remains the problem of moving this method of control from the lab to the land. With success, the predator coyotes will develop such a strong aversion to lamb that they will abandon the sheep range entirely.

A coyote running away from a lamb? A strange sight, but it may lead to a peaceful method of protecting our sheep *and* our coyotes. ■

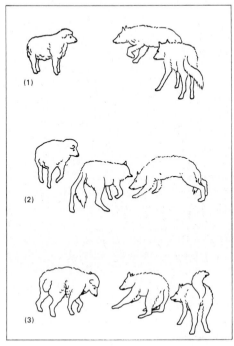

Figure 2.2 Aversive conditioning of wolves
Like the coyotes, wolves who have eaten lamb laced with lithium are wary of sheep afterward—1) wolves encounter a live sheep; 2) they back away, and 3) retreat when it charges at them.

to ignore irrelevant stimulus differences and to react one way to one stimulus and a different way to another. Through discrimination, your friend learned not to cry when he saw a butterfly.

OPERANT CONDITIONING

Imagine that you have an old Shetland wool sweater that you hardly ever wear. One day you decide to wear it, because your favorite sweater is at the cleaners.

You're surprised to find your friends complimenting you on this sweater. By the end of the day you've decided the Shetland sweater is your new favorite. ■

Your change of mind about the old sweater is an instance of operant conditioning. While in classical conditioning a response is controlled by the stimulus that goes *before* it, in operant conditioning, behavior is controlled by the stimuli that *follow* it. *Operant behavior* is simply spontaneous activity that can be conditioned. In *operant conditioning* the positive or negative consequences of an act determine whether it will be performed

more or less often in the future. The effects of operant behavior determine whether it is repeated. You spontaneously wear the old sweater and get many compliments, so you're more likely to wear it.

B. F. Skinner (1974) has been a pioneer of operant conditioning and has developed many methods and tools for its study. His best-known creation is the experimental chamber that bears his name, in which animals are put for operant conditioning.

For example, a pigeon is put in a Skinner box like the one in Figure 2.3. The pigeon is hungry and moves around pecking here and there. Sooner or later it accidentally pushes down a disc by pecking or just bumping it. Pushing the disc releases a food pellet into the box. So the pigeon's own behavior has made food appear. The pigeon eats the pellet, and then pecks and bumps around again, this time nearer the disc. The disc is pushed down again, and another pellet appears. Soon the pigeon begins to peck the disc repeatedly, until it is no longer hungry.

Reinforcers

The events that follow an action are called *reinforcers* if they increase the chance of that action occurring again. There are primary, secondary, and generalized reinforcers.

A *primary reinforcer* is any event that increases the frequency of the behavior it follows. Feeding a hungry dog when it does something that pleases you is a primary reinforcer. Food is a primary reinforcer if you're hungry, as is water if you're thirsty. Receiving a pellet is a primary reinforcer for a hungry pigeon.

A *secondary reinforcer* is an event that has been paired with a primary reinforcer and that be-

Figure 2.3 Pigeon in a Skinner box

Since pecking is the pigeon's most easily elicited operant behavior, the Skinner box pictured here was designed to dispense food pellets when the pigeon pecks a disc. (Photo by Will Rapport/Courtesy, B. F. Skinner)

Through systematic application of principals of reinforcement, animals such as this porpoise can be trained to perform complicated tricks. (Copyright © Gordon Smith/National Geographic Society/Photo Researchers, Inc.)

comes rewarding in a similar way. Although secondary reinforcers are not innately satisfying, when they become paired with a primary reinforcer they take on the same value. Saying "Good boy" to your dog can have a reinforcing effect similar to feeding it, if you've paired "Good boy" and food in the past.

Shaping

When reinforcement is used in a step-by-step manner to develop a particular response, it is called *shaping*. In shaping, any behavior that comes close to what you want the subject to learn is reinforced at first. Later, the subject is reinforced only for behavior that is closer to what you want. Finally, the subject actually performs the desired behavior and is reinforced only for that. Shaping is akin to blindman's bluff, where a blindfolded player is guided to the goal by calls of "warmer" and "colder." Shaping is at work when a child learns to write or an animal learns a trick.

An interested "Uh-huh" is a common shaper in conversations: it keeps a person talking. If you want to shape someone's conversation systematically, you can reinforce them with an "Uh-huh" response when they talk about the subject you choose, and not about others. Therapists often do this with their clients—not always knowingly—thereby getting the client to talk about those topics that interest the therapist most. There are stories of college classes conspiring to shape their professor's behavior during lectures. For example, a class could be very attentive whenever the professor performed a target behavior—like coughing, walking to the left or gesturing in a certain way—and could act very bored at other times. What should be the result of such shaping on the professor's lecturing performance?

When reinforcement follows operant behavior without delay, it is called *immediate reinforcement.* This is the case when you feed your dog as soon as she does what you want her to. A *delayed reinforcement* is one that is presented after a period of time has passed, sometimes a very long period, as, for example, getting a grade of A for a paper turned in several days before or being told about a merit bonus for good work in the past. Experiments have shown that immediate reinforcement is more successful in strengthening operant behavior than delayed reinforcement because it is more easily associated with the behavior that precedes it.

Events can be positive or negative reinforcers. *Positive reinforcers* (like food or praise) increase the likelihood of the operant behaviors they follow. *Negative reinforcers* (like disapproval or an electric shock) increase the likelihood of operant behaviors that *remove* the negative reinforcers. For example, a rat learns very quickly to press a lever that turns off an electric shock.

Aversive conditioning

In *aversive conditioning*, negative reinforcers are used. The conditioned response is an attempt to avoid or escape an unpleasant stimulus. In the laboratory, a rat will learn to press a bar to postpone shock or avoid it completely. This is *conditioned avoidance.* Rats can also learn to press a bar to escape a cage with an electrified floor grid. This form of aversive conditioning is called *escape learning.* Aversive conditioning is used in parole programs in which visits to the parole officers can cease only if the former convict behaves acceptably in the community.

A *punishment* is different from a negative reinforcer because it is an event used to *decrease* the likelihood of the operant behavior it follows— for example, a crowd boos a football player after he clips an opponent. A punishment *decreases* the likelihood of undesirable behavior by producing an aversive situation after that behavior occurs, while a negative reinforcer *increases* desired behavior by ending when the behavior is displayed.

Punishment in therapy was avoided for many years because it was seen as ineffective and unethical; in recent years it has become used, with the patient's consent, to help suppress behavior people want to be cured of, such as alcoholism, or self-destructive behavior, as with autistic children (Fantino and Logan, 1979). "Aversion therapy" makes use of punishment to eliminate undesirable behavior. For example, a disturbed child who for several years had severe temper tantrums was cured of them by the punishment of isolation in a "time-out" room (Wolf, Risley, and Mees, 1961).

To be effective in shaping behavior, punishment must be given skillfully. If the punishment is too severe and inescapable, then it may produce *learned helplessness*, a condition in which the subject stops giving responses altogether (Seligman, 1974). In the prototype study of learned helplessness, dogs were given electric shocks that were inescapable: no matter what the dog did, it was shocked (Seligman and Maier, 1967). After this training, the dog was put in a treadmill box where it could jump over a barrier to escape more shock. The dogs generally were unable to learn this simple escape response. Dogs who were not first put through the learned helplessness situation easily learned to escape.

Measuring operant conditioning

In studying operant behavior, the measure of greatest importance is the rate at which the response is taking place. The effect of reinforcement is usually to increase that rate, but satiation can slow it down even if reinforcement continues. In laboratory investigations, these variations in response rate, from minute to minute, hour to hour, and one experimental condition to another, are totaled and graphed against time to make a cumulative response curve. In real life, it may seem not so easy to keep track of the frequency of responses as you practice the piano, play the stock market, or do a disco dance, but serious students of a skill often do just that (see Fig. 2.4).

Figure 2.4 A cumulative record kept by B. F. Skinner of his own operant behavior— writing

Skinner measured his output in terms of the number of words he wrote between 1930 and 1958. In 1930 his output was just over 10,000 words; by 1958, it was 150,000 words and accelerating. (B. F. Skinner, *Cumulative Record,* © 1961, p. vii. Reprinted by permission of Prentice-Hall, Inc., Englewood Cliffs, New Jersey.)

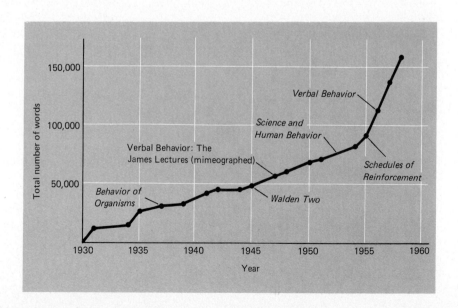

Operantly conditioned behavior persists as long as it is reinforced. When it is no longer followed by a reinforcer, it begins to diminish gradually until it occurs no more often than it would have without training. Firmly established operant behavior will take longer to extinguish than new or casually learned responses.

Behavior modification

While operant conditioning methods were developed in experiments with animals, they have proven their efficacy with people as well. Operant conditioning with people, usually called "behavior modification" (see also Chapter 17), has proven to be a powerful method of reducing problem behaviors and psychological symptoms (Birk, 1978). For example, one of the most practical uses of behavior modification has been in the area of one of life's thornier lessons: toilet training. Many parents agonize over how to toilet train their children. Early toilet training—before about twenty months—can lead to serious emotional problems in children, since their bladder and bowel muscles haven't matured enough for the voluntary control that their parents are demanding of them.

An efficient method for toilet training children applies the principles of operant conditioning. Its worth was demonstrated with a group of children whose resistance to toilet training had led their parents to seek professional help (Foxx and Azrin, 1973).

Thirty-four children between the ages of twenty and thirty-six months were given training sessions at home. Their training was aimed at the following skills: approach potty, grasp and pull down pants, sit on potty, rise after urination, pull up pants, remove and empty bowl, flush toilet, return bowl to potty.

The children were given plenty to drink to ensure frequent urination. All toys and distractions were removed during the session, as trainers carefully led them through each skill, offering food as the positive primary reinforcer. Secondary reinforcers included smiles, hugs, kisses, applause, and praise. Reinforcers were given immediately after any skill was performed correctly.

As punishment for wetting their pants, children were reprimanded and made to go immediately to the potty. The trainer would show them snacks, but withhold them. Eventually children associated these annoyances with wet pants.

The experiment was a success. After an average of $3\frac{1}{2}$ hours of such toilet training, accidents decreased from about six per day to only one a week, and remained at this level for a four-month follow-up period, to the delight of the parents.

Imagine that your cousin, Helen, is married, has two small, highly energetic children, and gets a splitting headache every afternoon. Aspirin doesn't agree with her stomach, and doesn't seem to help much anyway. Tranquilizers make her too drowsy to handle the kids. Doctor after doctor has seen her, and none has been able to help.

Her latest doctor, though, has tried something new, and it seems to be working: biofeedback. He diagnosed her headaches as caused by muscle tension. His remedy was to monitor the muscle tension levels in her forehead, so that as her muscle tensed, a tone got higher in pitch and louder in volume. By listening to the tone, she could tell when her forehead tensed or relaxed.

After several sessions of practice Helen learned, through trial and error, to keep the tone low and quiet. Once she knew how to lower her muscle tension in the calm of her doctor's office, she brought the skill home. Now no matter how frustrating, irritating, or overwhelming the kids get, her forehead stays relaxed. Most important: no headaches. ■

Biofeedback

Helen is the beneficiary of the application of operant conditioning to human biology. "Biofeedback" (see also Chapter 17) allows a person to control internal bodily processes by giving immediate information about bodily changes. An electronic sensor monitors the changes and sends a signal through an amplifier that varies in tone or intensity with the bodily changes. Once Helen could hear the tone that told her how her muscle tension levels were changing, she could experiment with herself and learn through shaping how to keep tension low. The tone was the reinforcer for the operant conditioning of her muscle tension.

Biofeedback represents a new way of thinking about people's ability to control their bodies. The traditional view in human physiology was that functions such as heartbeat, sweating, and muscle tension were beyond a person's conscious control. In the 1960s there were reports of yogis who could control their heart rate, but these were viewed with skepticism. Psychologist Neal Miller, however, hit upon a finding which—though debatable in itself—opened the way for biofeedback.

Miller had been studying the behavior of rats that had an electrode implanted in a part of the forebrain called the "pleasure center," because electrical stimulation there seemed to send rats into ecstasy. A rat trained to press a bar for the reward of stimulation of its pleasure center will press more than 2,000 times per hour for twenty-four consecutive hours. Miller (1969) injected his rats with curare, a South American arrow poison that paralyzes the skeletal system. He then rewarded the rats with a shot of pleasure when they increased their heart rate. Through shaping, the paralyzed rats learned to increase their heart rates. Although no one (including Miller himself) has subsequently been able to replicate this study (Miller and Dworkin, 1974), these results inspired other researchers to try the same procedures with humans—without the curare.

Miller and others went on to teach humans to use biofeedback to control their heart rate, blood pressure, stomach acid secretions—in fact, almost any human bodily process that can be monitored can also be brought under some degree of control. Biofeedback has become a widely accepted clinical tool, especially for the control of symptoms in psychosomatic disorders where people's psychological problems lead to physical symptoms. The most common clinical uses of biofeedback are for tension and migraine headaches, muscle control disorders, high blood pressure, poor blood flow, irregular heartbeat, and the control of anxiety (Birk, 1978).

Biofeedback allows people to regulate physiological processes like brain waves and blood pressure that are normally beyond their voluntary control. (Nick Passmore/Stock, Boston)

Figure 2.5 Curarized rat learning to control its heart rate

The rat's breathing is maintained by a respirator; the wire electrodes are for administering a pleasant stimulation and for recording the rat's heart rate.

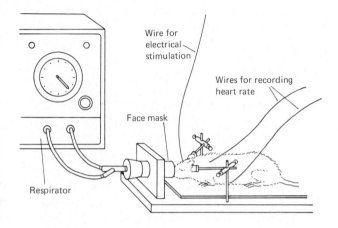

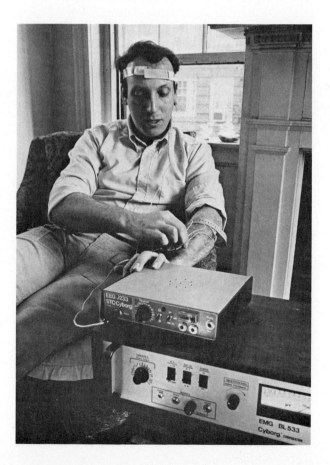

SCHEDULES OF REINFORCEMENT

Imagine that your sister's four-year-old hates vegetables but loves desserts. Your sister doesn't serve dessert every night, but when she does, your nephew must finish his vegetables in order to get any. At first he only ate his vegetables on nights when there was dessert. After a while, though, he ate all his vegetables even though he only occasionally got dessert as a reward. ■

Timing

The timing of reinforcers makes a great difference in conditioning. Reinforcement can be *continuous*, with each response reinforced, or *intermittent*, with some but not all responses reinforced. Continuous reinforcement is the quickest way to condition operant behavior, but it is not the most economic way to maintain it. Once behavior has been conditioned, it is more easily maintained with intermittent reinforcement. If your sister had served ice cream every night, and given your nephew some each time he ate—continuous reinforcement—he probably would have learned more quickly to eat his vegetables. But once he

"Oh boy! A whole dollar. I hope it doesn't spoil me."

had learned to eat his vegetables, an intermittent reward was enough to maintain the habit.

Extinction is quicker when continuous reinforcement ceases than when intermittent reinforcement stops. It is as if the intermittently reinforced person thinks an unreinforced response is just one of those that didn't bring a reward, while the continuously reinforced person thinks all reinforcement is over if a response brings no reward. If your sister had produced a dessert after each time your nephew ate his vegetables, it would have been continuous reinforcement; if she had then stopped giving him any desserts at all, he'd be more likely to stop eating his vegetables.

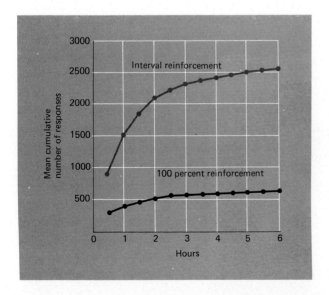

Figure 2.6 Effects of continuous and intermittent reinforcement on extinction

The effects on extinction of continuous and intermittent reinforcement differ. Two groups of animals were trained with operant conditioning to give a specific response. Their training took 200 reinforced trials. Then extinction began. The animals trained with continuous reinforcement quickly extinguished the conditioned response: they made an average of a little over 500 cumulative responses during the first 6 hour period of no reinforcement. But the animals trained on an intermittent schedule took much longer to extinguish the behavior. During the 6-hour period they gave an average of over 2,500 cumulative responses.

Interval schedules

Reinforcement of an operant activity at regular intervals is a *schedule*. For example, if a pigeon in a Skinner box gets a pellet of food every few minutes, it would be on a reinforcement schedule. There are different types of schedules. *Interval schedules* are based on the passage of time. If the pigeon got a pellet for its first proper response after every thirty seconds, it would be on what is called a *fixed-interval schedule*. Reinforcement that varies around an average time is a *variable-interval schedule*. If the pellets come after a correct response at irregular intervals, say ranging from sixty seconds to ten seconds with an average of thirty seconds, then it is on a variable-interval schedule.

A pigeon on a fixed-interval schedule of thirty seconds will peck little after receiving its last pellet, but will begin to peck faster as the end of the thirty-second interval draws near. When the thirty seconds are up, there will be a burst of pecking. Pigeons, monkeys, and other animals (including humans) can learn to estimate such intervals accurately.

Life holds many instances of interval schedules. You may know the time your mail usually comes; odds are you check your mailbox much more frequently around that time. You do the same sort of increased checking when a kettle is about to boil. When you're waiting for a bus you don't look down the road an hour before it is due; as its scheduled time nears, you look for it more and more frequently.

Ratio schedules

While interval schedules are determined by time, *ratio schedules* depend on the number of operant responses. The ratio is the number of operant responses that precede a reward. For example, if a pigeon gets a pellet after every twenty pecks, then it is on a ratio schedule. A *fixed-ratio schedule* requires a specific number of responses between each reinforcement. The pigeon, for example, would be on an FR-20 (for "fixed-ratio of twenty") schedule, where there is a reward after each twenty responses. In a *variable-ratio schedule*, however, the reinforcement comes after a varying number of responses; the ratio is given in terms of the average number of responses before reinforcement. A VR-20 schedule, for example, means there are, on the average, twenty responses before each reward. The exact number of responses before any given reward, though, might vary from two to fifty, with an average of twenty.

A pigeon on a fixed-ratio schedule will peck at a steady, high rate to get food pellets, but if the rewards stop, the pecking will cease rather quickly. On a variable-ratio schedule, a pigeon will also peck very rapidly. But if reinforcement stops, the pigeon will continue to peck rapidly, since it is unclear just how many pecks are required for reward. Behavior learned under a variable-ratio schedule becomes solidly established, and extinction can take a long time.

"Piecework," where a worker gets paid for each piece or finished product, is a form of ratio schedule. A weekly or monthly salary is a form of inter-

Gambling is based on a variable-ratio schedule; the pattern of random winning keeps people betting despite their cumulative losses. (Tony Korody/Sygma)

HAVE MONEY, WILL GAMBLE

■ Tonight, at a casino, all eyes are on the roulette wheel. A man bets $5,000 on 33 black. The wheel spins. The man sweats as he watches the little ball tease around the wheel. He's a dedicated gambler who knows what it's like to win—and to lose.

All gambling is organized on a variable-ratio schedule, and this random pattern of winning may be what hooks a gambler in the first place. Using an encounter between man and slot machine, psychologists studied how someone can become a serious gambler (Lewis and Duncan, 1958). Each person was given a supply of quarter-sized discs and told to play the machine as long as he wished. If he won, each disc could be cashed in for a nickel—the reinforcer.

There was no chance involved in this betting since the odds were rigged. Some subjects won 100 percent of the time. Others, on a variable-ratio schedule, won only one-third or two-thirds of the time, and so were intermittently reinforced. After a practice session, no one was reinforced. Every player lost every time.

The people who had been intermittently reinforced during practice continued to plug away at the machine, hoping for a change in luck, and knowing that the machine would not pay off every time. But the group that had won all of the practice tries quit much sooner. This hard-luck period may have been more than they could handle after sweet success.

B. F. Skinner (1971) sums up the role of the variable-ratio schedule in gambling: ''it pays on a kind of schedule which sustains betting even though, in the long run, the amount paid is less than the amount wagered.'' The gambler may have a streak of good luck, followed by intermittent losses. Skinner notes that ''an early run of good luck which grows steadily worse may create a dedicated gambler.''

Like the man who bet on 33 black. He waits. The wheel is slowing down, the ball is dropping in and out of numbers. His chances of winning are slim at best. He closes his eyes and hears the ball click from slot to slot. It stops. Silence. He's afraid to open his eyes. He opens them. The ball rests on 33 black.

The crowd explodes. He's ecstatic. He has won.

But has he? ''In the long run,'' says Skinner, ''the 'utility' is negative: the gambler loses all.''

The call comes for new bets. His winnings never reach his hands; the gambler places all his chips on 23 red . . . ■

val schedule. Like the pigeon on a fixed-ratio schedule, piecework leads a worker to turn out pieces more rapidly and continuously than she would if she were on an interval schedule, that is, if she got the same paycheck every week regardless of productivity. Many salespeople work for commissions, so that their salary depends on how many sales they make—a common form of the fixed-ratio schedule.

A high rate of productivity for relatively little reward can be maintained on a fixed-ratio schedule, which makes it appealing to employers. Also, raising the ratio of reinforcement, so that a worker has to produce more pieces for the same pay, does not carry too great a risk of extinction. But from the workers' point of view, this would simply mean they must work harder for the same pay. Can you see why labor unions have opposed pay scales based on a fixed-ratio, preferring instead a fixed-interval schedule for salaries?

IMITATION

Imagine that you're taking tennis lessons. Your teacher watches while you serve. Do what you will, none of your serves lands in the magic square on the other side of the net.

"Not bad," he says, "but you're hitting the ball too soon. Try to wait longer before you swing—like this." He serves three or four, each one a perfect drive into the far corner of the serving square.

"Now you try."

Your first serve is a hit, your second a near-miss, your third as bad as ever.

"You're getting it—watch me again." Three perfect serves. You watch more closely now, imagining your body going through the motions of each serve.

"Go ahead—try again."

You feel your body serve just as you saw your coach do it—and hit three smashes in a row, bull's-eye. ■

When you copy your coach's stroke so that your serve lands on the mark, you've learned by imitating him. Imitation, or observational learning, is the duplication of another's actions through observation. Imitation is at work while a baby learns to speak, to get along with others, to play games. The first time a child goes to a concert, she mimics others to learn the right way to follow an usher or the right moment and manner for applause. A student in a chemistry class watches his instructor titrate chemicals, then duplicates the feat with his own test tubes.

Learning through imitation is an efficient way to master a new body of behavior. Unlike classical or operant conditioning, which take several repetitions, a person can sometimes learn in a single try through imitation how to do a thing properly. While learning through imitation is quick and easy, its reward is not always obvious. The most likely reinforcer for this kind of learning is the satisfaction that mastery brings.

Imitation seems to be a powerful force in shaping a child's social behavior (although other kinds of learning certainly operate too). In a well-known study of how children imitate adult aggression (Bandura, Ross, and Ross, 1962), boys and girls watched a movie of rather savage adults with a large knock-em-down balloon doll—punching, throwing, kicking, shouting "Hit it down, punch it!" and hitting it with a hammer. Children who had seen the movie and then had a go at the same balloon doll treated it much more aggressively than a group of children who played with the doll

Many skills are acquired through imitation.
(© Guy Le Querrec/Magnum)

but hadn't seen the movie. The imitation of aggression was strongest for boys who saw a movie of an adult male attacking the doll, presumably because the urge to imitate was buttressed by identification with the male model.

The implications of this study for real life are many; for example, the study has been marshalled as an argument to cut down on television violence (Comstock, et al., 1978). Children are heavy viewers of television, with viewing time increasing through the elementary school years. Since Bandura's study of aggression, there have been many more designed to see whether television violence increases aggression in children. A review of the findings shows that television may indeed increase aggression by teaching children hostile acts that were previously unfamiliar, encouraging aggression in various situations, and triggering imitative aggression. On the other hand, because television is a major influence on children growing up in America, it could also serve to promote socially desirable behavior. In either case, imitative learning is the mechanism by which television seems to teach children to be "good" or "bad."

A six-year study of 1,565 teenage boys in London assessed the degree to which long-term exposure to television violence increases serious

PAVLOV

(Culver Pictures)

■ During the Russian Revolution there was shooting in the streets. It was a time when people hid in their rooms in order to survive. Ivan Pavlov, who was then studying conditioned responses, arrived at the lab with customary punctuality—his own conditioned response perhaps. The lab was deserted, but after about ten minutes one of his assistants arrived. Pavlov criticized his lateness; the man reminded him of the bloody revolution just outside their doors. "What difference does a revolution make when you have work to do in the laboratory?" Pavlov replied.

Although Pavlov's laboratory was a model of efficiency, he was notoriously careless about mundane details in his private life. Once, after a promotion that brought with it a sorely needed cash bonus, Pavlov lent an untrustworthy friend most of the money before he got home. The money was never repaid; Pavlov's wife handled all the finances after that. Although he was living at the time just above the poverty level, Pavlov often forgot to pick up his paycheck.

Pavlov's impractical bent in his personal affairs is perhaps best illustrated by a gift he gave his wife when they were just engaged. Typically he would get her luxuries, like candy or theater tickets. Once, though, when she was about to leave on a trip, he bought her a pair of shoes. When she opened her trunk she found only one shoe. In response to her query, Pavlov wrote her, "Don't look for your shoe. I took it as a remembrance of you and have put it on my desk."

Pavlov's early work on the circulatory system led him to discover the laws governing the regulation of blood pressure and cardiac activity. For his data he performed surgery on live dogs, an operation which typically terrified the animals. But when Pavlov was the surgeon, the dogs were not bothered. They jumped willingly onto the operating table and often did not require tying down. Pavlov's biographer attributes this to the meticulous care he took in making incisions, the lightning speed with which he operated, and his compassion toward the animals. He would often take them home after an operation and nurse them back to health. Another reason for Pavlov's delicate precision during the operations: blood made him queasy.

In 1904 Pavlov won the Nobel Prize for his research on the digestive glands—not for the conditioning experiments for which he is remembered. While studying the digestive glands, he realized that they operated not only when food was in the dog's mouth, but when it saw, smelled, and even heard someone approaching with food. To distinguish these reactions from innate reflexes, he called them "conditioned reflexes." These discoveries led Pavlov to the insight that the nervous system can learn new connections between stimuli.

From the start Pavlov felt his discoveries on conditioning held vast implications. Despite the fact that his work received constant criticism, he had the strong conviction that it would bring happiness to the human race, lead mankind to freedom of the will, and even allow an understanding of the religious impulse, which he referred to as "the highest of all conditioned responses." ■

violence as well as the less serious sorts, such as swearing, aggression in sports, or threats to other children (Belson, 1978). This study found that specific sorts of violence on television led to more real-life violence. The particularly potent kinds of violence included verbal or physical abuse between people in a close personal relationship (e.g., husband and wife, father and son), extremely realistic violence, violence by good guys pursuing good causes, and violence that has nothing to do with the plot. Unrealistic violence, such as in slapstick comedies, cartoons, and science fiction, did not inspire real-life violence. The reason suggested by the researcher: unrealistic violence is hard to imitate.

INSIGHT

Connect all the dots with four continuous straight lines without retracing your path:

```
.    .    .

.    .    .

.    .    .
```

(See page 51 for answer.)

When you puzzle over the solution to a problem, then get the answer in a flash, you learn in a manner that may involve not only imitation and conditioning. An *insight* is a sudden discovery of new relations among things or events. Unlike the other kinds of learning discussed in this chapter, insights apparently occur as a result of a restructuring or reinterpretation of our perceptions or thoughts, and not so much as a result of the influence of events around us. Insight seems to be one-trial learning, while many trials or repetitions are usually required for classical and operant conditioning.

Like imitation, insight—when it occurs—is an efficient way to learn, since it requires only one correct experience. A classically conditioned response requires many pairings of stimulus and response. In operant conditioning a spontaneous

activity that happens to be followed by a reinforcer slowly increases in frequency. Shaping may take many attempts before the desired behavior is achieved. But learning through insight takes a single correct try.

Single-trial learning

While he was detained by the British on the Canary Islands off the coast of Africa during World War I, German psychologist Wolfgang Köhler spent his time testing the capacities of caged chimpanzees. While he expected to find his chimps learning according to Pavlov's theories of classical conditioning, Köhler was amazed to find that they seemed to invent new behaviors on the spot to solve problems. This was *single-trial learning,* acquisition of a response on a single try.

One chimp, for example, was placed in a cage with a long stick and with a banana outside out of reach. The chimp vainly reached for the banana, then turned to play with the objects inside the cage. From time to time he would reach for the banana through the bars of the cage, to no avail. Then suddenly the chimp saw the banana and the stick in the same line of sight, and immediately reached for the banana with the stick. The insight was not only sudden, but lasting. The chimp had learned.

Köhler challenged Pavlov's simple stimulus-response theories of learning with these cases of insight in chimps. When Pavlov heard about Köhler's chimps, he replied with his own theory, claiming that the chimps were probably experienced and had learned through prior conditioning to use sticks as tools. What Köhler considered to be insight, Pavlov saw as a conditioned stimulus eliciting an effective conditioned response.

Don Dougherty, © Saturday Review 1978

IMPRINTING: BIRDS TO BEINGS

■ If you mention "imprinting" to anyone familiar with psychology, the picture below leaps to mind: ethologist Konrad Lorenz, trudging along in baggy overalls, imprinted mama to a brood of goslings who cheerily follow him, single file, across a field.

Lorenz (1935) coined the term "imprinting" to describe an animal's encounter with a moving object (usually its mother) during specific critical or sensitive periods. Imprinting occurs as the image of that object is irreversibly stamped on its nervous system. Imprinting seems to be a kind of single-trial learning; in ducklings it can happen in as little as one minute's worth of following.

Each species seems to have its own critical period for imprinting. For mallard ducks, it peaks at thirteen to sixteen hours after hatching. After that, the duckling reacts to strange objects with fear. For dogs the imprinting age is around thirteen weeks;

"Oh, go away!"

Goslings imprinted on Konrad Lorenz. (Konrad Lorenz/LIFE Magazine, © 1955 Time Inc.)

after that they are harder to make someone's pet. Kittens not handled in the first few weeks later shy away from people.

Some researchers believe that there may be imprinting in humans (Hoffman and De Parelo, 1977). The new mother who sees her baby for the first time may be convinced her baby recognizes her from the start by the feel of her body or sound of her voice—but the baby knows better. Not until she has fed, nursed, comforted, and cuddled the infant will it notice those features unique to its mama. This is called "filial imprinting"—a process by which a newborn becomes familiar with a person to whom it will respond as that person's child.

Klaus Immelman (1973) conjectured that an imprinting experience in infancy can stamp a person's sexual preference for life. There are two types of sexual imprinting: intraspecific and interspecific. In *intra*specific imprinting, for example, birds of one color, reared by foster parents of another color, prefer to mate with birds the color of the foster parent. Here, birds of a feather do *not* flock together. In *inter*specific sexual imprinting, sexual attachments may be directed toward another species or a human as the result of an early imprinting experience with that species.

In other words, Lorenz's ducklings—if they underwent interspecific sexual imprinting—may have spent the rest of their lives in a vain search for a duck in baggy overalls. ■

Learning set

The debate was settled by later studies that took a closer look at how chimps learned the stick-and-banana trick. Harry F. Harlow used a similar task requiring insight: He presented a chimp—or a small child—with three objects on a board, two similar and one different. Under the odd one was a reward. The problem was to choose the object that was odd in color, shape, or size. What needed to be learned was not the characteristics of the odd object, but its relation to the others. The odd object changed from trial to trial. At first mon-

The test apparatus used by Harlow to study learning sets. The monkey must choose the odd object in a set of three in order to get a reward. (The Wisconsin Regional Primate Center)

keys fumbled with the problem, doing no better than chance would predict. But after perhaps a hundred different problems, they eventually caught on and grasped the oddity principle. From that point they solved each problem every time.

The way chimpanzees learn to solve problems has since been studied in more detail than in Köhler's original experiments. In one such study, young chimps given sticks showed no signs of using them as tools at first (Harlow and Kuenne, 1949). Then, gradually, by trial and error, the chimps learned to use the sticks to pull in objects beyond their reach. The younger and less experienced the animals, the longer they took to solve Köhler-type problems, and none of them came to the solution suddenly with a flash of insight. Young children, it seemed, went through a similar gradual process as did the chimps in learning to use the sticks as tools.

What was learned was not an association, but an idea, or *learning set,* the readiness to respond in a given way to a specific kind of situation. Once a learning set is acquired, it immediately comes into play when the situation is right. The Harlows concluded that learning sets—the ability to solve a certain kind of problem—are acquired slowly on the basis of experience, often in an operantly conditioned manner. When a learning set is applied to a new problem, the answer comes at once, and so seems to be an insight (Harlow and Kuenne, 1949). Both Pavlov and Köhler were right, to a degree.

Concept learning

Learning through insight does not seem to be totally explainable in terms of stimulus-response principles like learning set. The mathematician Henri Poincaré, for example, has described how a solution to a difficult problem came to him "in a flash"; Einstein tells of first "seeing" the laws he described in his equations as a visual image in the mind's eye.

Such sudden, spontaneous insights seem to be instances of *concept learning,* a learning task that requires the reorganization of stimuli according to some rule or set of rules. In the case of Poincaré and Einstein, the reorganization of rules

was a creative act of the first order, yielding original insights into the nature of the physical universe. A creative artist uses the same sort of
reorganization of familiar stimuli—paints, words,
or clay—to form an original pattern. And when
you solve the puzzle of the dots at the start of this
section, you are also involved in concept-learning,
which includes problem solving. Learning of this
sort may be more readily approached through cognitive psychology—the study of how knowledge is
acquired, organized, and used—than through the
principles of learning.

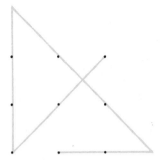

Figure 2.7
Correct answer to puzzle on page 48.

SUMMARY

Learning is a relatively permanent behavior
change brought about by classical conditioning,
operant conditioning, imitation, or insight.

Classical conditioning. Classical conditioning
is based on an innate stimulus-response reflex.
Conditioning pairs a neutral stimulus with the
stimulus that elicits the spontaneous response, so
that over time this new conditioning stimulus generates the response. In responding, subjects can
learn to generalize across stimuli and to discriminate among them.

If a conditioned reflex is not occasionally reas-
sociated with the original unconditioned reflex, it
will eventually be extinguished, although spontaneous recovery is sometimes experienced after extinction.

Operant conditioning. Operant conditioning
reinforces spontaneous behavior with a subsequent rewarding event. Primary reinforcement
provides direct rewards; secondary and generalized reinforcement, rewards associated in some
way with primary ones. Shaping reinforces behavioral change in small steps, until a new complex of
activity has been learned. Immediate reinforcement is generally more effective than delayed reinforcement.

Aversive conditioning uses negative rather than
positive reinforcement to produce desired behavior. In punishment, an aversive stimulus elimi-
nates an undesired response. If administered
indiscriminately, punishment may result in a general state of learned helplessness.

Schedules of reinforcement. The timing of reinforcement is important in the conditioning process. Continuous reinforcement is the fastest, but
most easily extinguished, training method. A response may be rewarded once in a time period
(fixed interval), or at variable intervals, or a response may be rewarded in a fixed or variable ratio of reinforcements. Intermittent reinforcement
schedules usually result in more stable mainte-
nance of the learned behavior.

Imitation. The learning that takes place
through imitation is often relatively quick and
easy, and can be a powerful shaper of behavior,
especially children's social behavior.

Insight. Insight—unlike the other main types
of learning—generally occurs "in a flash," and
seems to consist of a sudden restructuring of perceptions. Repetition is generally not involved in
this kind of learning, but the application of a previously acquired learning set may be a component
of insight.

GLOSSARY

Aversive conditioning The use of negative reinforcement to produce a desired behavior or of punishment to reduce unwanted behavior.

Classical conditioning The repeated pairing of a neutral stimulus with an unconditioned stimulus that produces a certain response, until the neutral stimulus alone produces that response.

Concept learning Sudden, spontaneous insight based on the reorganization of stimuli according to some rule or set of rules.

Conditioned avoidance Behavior learned to postpone or avoid aversive stimuli.

Conditioned response (CR) The response evoked by the conditioned stimulus after conditioning.

Conditioned stimulus (CS) The stimulus to which a new response is related through conditioning.

Continuous reinforcement An operant conditioning method in which each correct response is reinforced.

Delayed reinforcement A time lag occurs between operant behavior and reward.

Discrimination The ability to detect differences in stimuli that are somewhat similar to a conditioned stimulus, so that not all similar stimuli will evoke the conditioned response.

Escape learning Behavior that is learned to escape aversive stimuli.

Extinction The dying out of a conditioned response due to lack of pairing with an unconditioned stimulus.

Fixed-interval schedule Reinforcement that is given for the first response only after a set amount of time passes between correct responses.

Fixed-ratio schedule Reinforcement that is given every time there is a fixed number of responses.

Generalization An event similar to a conditioned stimulus produces a conditioned response.

Habituation The waning of a response to a repeated stimulus.

Imitation Learning by observing and duplicating another's actions.

Immediate reinforcement A reward directly follows operant behavior.

Insight Learning that occurs as a result of a sudden breakthrough in understanding.

Intermittent reinforcement The rewarding of some, but not all, correct responses.

Interval schedule The reinforcement of correct responses on the basis of the length of time passed between responses.

Latency The time between a stimulus and its response.

Learned helplessness A condition produced by inescapable aversive stimuli; the subject stops responding altogether.

Learning Relatively permanent change in behavior that results from reward or practice.

Learning set A readiness to respond in a given way to a specific kind of problem.

Negative reinforcer An aversive stimulus that increases the frequency of a response by ceasing when the response occurs.

Operant behavior An activity by a subject that produces a change in its environment.

Operant conditioning Situation in which behavior is influenced by rewards or punishments that follow the behavior.

Positive reinforcer A reward that, when presented, increases the likelihood of a behavior.

Primary reinforcer An innately satisfying event that increases the frequency of the behavior it follows.

Punishment An unpleasant event that decreases operant behavior.

Ratio schedule The reinforcement of correct responses based on the number of correct responses given.

Reflex An automatic response to a stimulus.

Reinforcers Events that increase the chance that an action will occur again.

Response A behavior elicited by a stimulus.

Schedule of reinforcement The timing of rewards for operant behavior. Schedules are either continuous or intermittent.

Secondary reinforcer An event that is paired with a primary reinforcer and that becomes rewarding in a similar way.

Shaping The use of reinforcers in a step-by-step manner to develop a behavior.

Single-trial learning The immediate acquisition of behavior, for example, through imitation or insight.

Spontaneous recovery The reappearance of a conditioned behavior after its extinction, in response to the conditioned stimulus.

Stimulus Any event that elicits a response.

Unconditioned response An innate, unlearned reaction to a stimulus.

Unconditioned stimulus A stimulus that innately elicits an unconditioned response.

Variable-interval schedule Reinforcement that is given after an average interval of time.

Variable-ratio schedule Reinforcement that is given after an average number of responses.

3

MEMORY

COMMON MYTHS

MANY PEOPLE BELIEVE ...	ACTUALLY ...
The rate at which we forget is constant.	After we learn something, we forget more of it in the first few hours than we do in the next several days.
Difficult material is more easily forgotten than is easy material.	Difficult and easy material, if equally well learned, are both forgotten at the same rate.
An experienced bridge player is no better at remembering card hands than anyone else.	An expert has better recall than a novice in his or her area of expertise; a bridge expert will have better recall than a beginner.
Faster learners remember better than slow learners.	The speed of learning does not determine how much a person will remember.
The main cause of forgetting is the decay of memory traces in the brain.	There is no evidence that there are "memory traces" in the brain.

Zen students are with their masters at least ten years before they presume to teach others. Nan-in was visited by Tenno, who, having passed his apprenticeship, had become a teacher. The day happened to be rainy, so Tenno wore wooden clogs and carried an umbrella.

After greeting him, Nan-in remarked: ''I suppose you left your wooden clogs in the vestibule. I want to know if your umbrella is on the right or the left side of the clogs.''

Tenno, confused, had no instant answer. He realized that he was unable to carry his Zen every minute. He became Nan-in's pupil, and he studied six more years to accomplish his every-minute Zen.

PAUL REPS, *ZEN FLESH, ZEN BONES,* P. 354

Do you remember the name of your third grade teacher? What you had for breakfast yesterday? Who you were with on your first date? What you wore last Tuesday? How much you paid for the last record you bought? The color of your mother's eyes?

Without memory, we would have no personal identity, no sense of who we are. Our personal history is etched in the tender thread of our memories; the mosaic of our identity is built of bits of moments remembered. Yet memory is tied to forgetting; if we did not forget a vast amount of our experience, we would be overwhelmed with trivia, as was the young boy Ireneo Funes in a story by Jorge Borges. Because of a fall from a horse, Funes could no longer forget. Borges writes of this strange state of unforgetfulness:

> The present was almost intolerable, it was so rich and bright; the same was true of the most ancient and most trivial memories.... He remembered the shapes of the clouds in the south at dawn on the 30th of April of 1880, and he could compare them in his recollection with the marbled grain in the design of a leatherbound book which he had seen only once, and with the lines in the spray which an oar raised in the Rio Negro on the eve of the battle of Quebracho ...

Memory is an intricate balance of things remembered and things forgotten. We are bombarded every minute through our senses with more information than we can possibly handle. While you read this page, for example, these thoughts register in your mind while your span of vision also takes in the shape of the page itself, details of the room near the book, and any other visual detail your eye may meet should it momentarily glance about the room. Meanwhile your other senses are busy too: if you pay attention, you'll notice a variety of sounds, smells, and pressures on your body. From this vast array of sensations, your mind selects details to notice, think about, and, finally, remember.

Imagine that it's 7:00 A.M. You just have time to take a shower and get over to campus for your history midterm.

Standing under the hot water, you begin to feel almost human. You run through a list of dates—the years the various kings of England ascended the throne. Then you begin to link the names of the kings to their dates. 1382. Whose year was

55

that? Wait a minute. Was that year in your list? Did anybody take the throne that year at all?

Time to hit the road. Pencils and pens, your notebook has plenty of paper, out the door and down the stairs. You leap on your bicycle and head off down the street. You begin to cross reference your lists of dates and kings with another list. Groups of kings: the Saxons, the Normans. William the Conqueror in 1066—that's one you won't forget; you've known it since the sixth grade. ■

KINDS OF MEMORY

Memory is simply the ability to bring to mind past experience. But our memories do not link together our whole past; remembering goes hand-in-hand with forgetting. The ways in which we remember—or forget—the events of our lives are complex. The varieties of the ways we remember include:

☐ short-term sensory storage, the brief recording of whatever is in awareness in a given moment. Short-term sensory storage is the split-second registering of immediate unnamed sensory experience. As you watch the road pass by underneath your car or bike, a multitude of details—rocks, potholes, textures—pass through your awareness, but you forget them almost as soon as you see them.

☐ short-term memory, the immediate lodging of information in the memory. A short-term memory lasts as long as you focus on it, then either disappears or becomes a more permanent memory. When you try to memorize the dates that British kings ascended the throne, the process of memorizing each date begins with short-term memory.

☐ long-term memory, relatively permanent storage of information. A long-term memory is any information that can be retrieved after the event itself is past. When a short-term memory—such as the date of a British king's ascension—is rehearsed, it becomes a long-term memory. The date 1066 was lodged in long-term memory years ago.

Imagine that it's a humid afternoon and you're sitting in the shade of a tree doing your best to study your geology assignment. You notice that a girl sitting nearby is poring over the same book. Seizing the chance to not study, you strike up a conversation. Her name's Jan, she's from Ohio, she's a sophomore . . .

As you talk you half-notice a young man walking by. Your eyes meet for a split-second, but you think nothing of it. But there's something about that blond cowlick that seems familiar. Then suddenly it hits you: that's Binky McGovern! He lived next door to you until you were seven! You haven't seen him in all these years, but you'd recognize him anywhere.

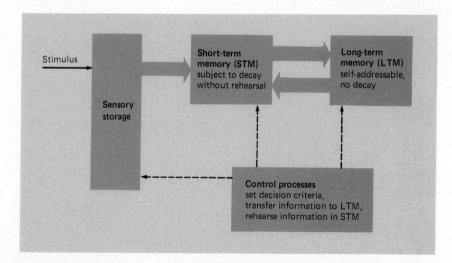

Figure 3.1 How information flows between the three kinds of memory

Information registers for a split second in short-term sensory storage. Most of the impressions that reach sensory storage are forgotten. Information that is attended to reaches short-term memory; short-term memories last only as long as they are the focus of awareness. If information is noticed and rehearsed, it becomes lodged in long-term memory, and can be recalled later. Control processes determine what sorts of information are rehearsed in short-term memory, and which should pass into long-term memory.

As you leap to your feet to catch up with Binky you turn to excuse yourself to . . . how could you have forgotten her name already? ■

Memory passes through several stages, from a brief sensory impression to short-term, and then, sometimes, to long-term storage (Simon, 1979). The flow of remembering is part of *information processing*, the way the brain registers, codes, and stores our experience. In the first step, we notice a raw sensory impression—a barely familiar face. If we focus on it for a moment and keep it fresh in mind, the impression is briefly stored in memory—a familiar cowlick. When the impression is coded, it is given a name and entered in long-term memory—the name Binky McGovern was there all these years waiting for the moment it would be called up, but Jan's name never entered long-term memory. *Memory retrieval* is the calling up of a long-term memory.

Short-term sensory storage

There are several kinds of short-term sensory storage, each of them involving a different sense. In art, an icon is a picture of something. *Iconic storage* is the brief registration of visual sensations in awareness. Iconic storage occurs constantly while we are awake and aware. Each of the other senses has a similar process of brief registration; *echoic storage*, for example, is a briefly held auditory memory. All the forms of sensory storage are split-second processes, momentary stages between immediate perception and memory proper.

Short-term sensory storage goes on constantly, though we rarely note it. If you slap your knee, the sensation continues for a moment; if you look at a light while it is turned off, the image outlasts the light for a fraction of a second. To get an idea of how brief this kind of storage is, try the following (Lindsay and Norman, 1977): Make a fist and raise your forefinger. Wave your finger back and forth slowly about a foot in front of your eyes. You can see your finger moving against the background behind it. Now move your finger faster and faster. The image begins to blur: you seem to see it in several places at once. When you wave

your finger fast enough, it becomes a kind of fan-shaped set of images. The shadowy images of your finger are your iconic storage of it.

Experiments have shown that iconic storage lasts only about one-quarter of a second before it fades. It is simply an image storage, and does not involve any naming or meaning. By the time an image is recognized and named, such as Binky McGovern's cowlick, it has already passed to the stage of short-term memory. If someone tells us "There's a great movie playing tonight," we do not so much hear the sounds that make up the sentence as remember the meaning of the words. Once an impression has been named, it has outlasted the instant life span of iconic storage.

Imagine that your upstairs neighbor has talked you into going to a movie tonight. While she is getting ready, you look up the phone number of the theater so you can find out when the movie starts. 443-6298. You put away the phone book and move toward the phone. 443-6298. You repeat the number to yourself. You dial 4 . . . 4 . . . BANG! Your back door flies open and your neighbor bounces in. "When's it start?" You stare at her, receiver in one hand, the other hand tangled in the dial, your mind a complete blank. "I don't know," you answer. "I was just calling, but I forgot the number." You look up the number again; your friend takes the phone. "What's the number?" she asks. "It's 443 exchange, right?" "That's right. 6298." She dials. Busy. She tries again. "443 what?" "6298." This time you don't even need to look in the book. ■

Short-term memory

Short-term memories persist only while you keep your mind on them. When you looked up the phone number in the directory, you had to keep repeating it until you got to the phone. When your friend distracted you, you had to look it up again.

In *short-term memory*, information is easily retrieved and stored for a short time only. As long as you focus on the phone number you have registered in short-term memory, you can use it to dial. But you must either keep a visual image of the number directly in your mind or you must rehearse the number, silently or aloud, as you did by repeating it over and over to yourself. After using the number several times, you were able to remember it without having to look it up. This indicates that the number had passed from short-term to long-term memory.

In addition to being temporary, short-term memory also seems to have a limited capacity. It has been observed that only about seven items, plus or minus two, can be stored in it (Miller, 1956). A series of seven digits, such as a typical phone number, is just about the limit. Other researchers have proposed that the "magic number" for the basic number of units held short-term is five, not seven (Simon, 1979). The significance lies not in the exact number, though, but rather in the principle that the capacity of short-term memory is a fixed number of units, independent of what exactly is being remembered.

However, we can greatly increase the meager capacity of short-term memory by "chunking," a process of recoding information. *Chunking* involves combining several different items which can then be remembered as a single item. If you could chunk three digits of a number into one item to remember, you could retain twenty-one digits. In fact, your friend may have done just this in the case of the phone number by remembering the three-digit exchange as if it were a single item. Or a social security number is much easier to memorize as 347-82-1445 than it would be if you tried to remember it as 347821445.

Hermann Ebbinghaus did the first important research on memory using himself as his experimental subject. In his classic book on memory, published in 1885, he reports how he invented nonsense syllables, such as KOF or CEH, which arouse few if any prior associations. He then set himself the task of memorizing long lists of them, and recorded the rate at which he forgot them.

More recent experiments have shown that without aids such as chunking and rehearsing, the items in short-term memory are quickly forgotten. In a study of the duration of short-term memory, college students could remember very few nonsense syllables longer than eighteen seconds (Peterson and Peterson, 1959). They were prevented from rehearsing or maintaining a visual image of the syllables by means of an intervening task, much like the neighbor's arrival interfered with memorizing the phone number. Immediately after being shown the syllables, the subjects were shown a three-digit number and asked to count backwards from it in threes or fours. Recall of the nonsense syllables dropped sharply a few seconds after the intervening arithmetic task and was less than 10 percent after eighteen seconds.

When the subjects were given three meaningful

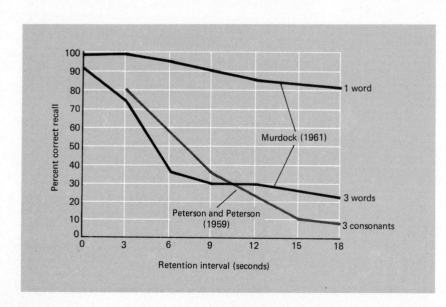

Figure 3.2 The percentage of words and consonants correctly recalled after delays ranging from zero to eighteen seconds

Even meaningful words such as "table," "plant," and "bear" will be forgotten after just a few seconds if instructions to count backward prevent a person from rehearsing them. Note that the rate of recall for a single word with no interruptions is much higher.

words, like "table," "plant," and "bear," they recalled them only slightly better, probably because three unrelated words are not much more meaningful than three unrelated letters. But in another experiment, recall from short-term memory improved when the students were allowed up to three rehearsals of the nonsense words before the arithmetic task began. And when material could be organized logically in chunks, recall was even better (Murdock, 1961).

If an item in short-term memory does not enter long-term memory, it is soon forgotten. Short-term memory is the door to long-term memory for many sorts of information. Some items—especially those of personal significance—are held while we rehearse, organize, and code the information. After this the information enters our long-term memory, from which we may retrieve it later, sometimes years later.

Long-term memory

Some information from the senses, such as visual scenes or auditory events, is coded directly into long-term memory. Before most other information enters long-term memory, it must first be registered by the senses, then organized and coded in the short-term memory, then rehearsed often enough to "sink in" or "make a lasting impression." In studying for a history exam, you have to hold the information in your short-term memory, then organize it in some meaningful way, then rehearse it enough that you retain it and have access to it during the test.

Retrieval from long-term memory seems to depend to a large degree on the coding or organization given the information when it was stored. Thus, we are not always able to retrieve information unless we think of it in the right way. As in a library, a large amount of information is stored in long-term memory. In a library, you must find the right catalog card before you can get the book you want; similarly, your memory can produce full-fledged images or representations of past events if it is given the proper questions or instructions.

Sensory information is similarly organized. When you saw the familiar cowlick, that visual image immediately triggered the name of Binky McGovern. But if a short-term memory is not held long enough for coding and rehearsing, it will not enter long-term memory—as was the case with the name of the girl under the tree in the story on page 56 . . . What *was* her name, anyway?

Semantic versus episodic memory

Our long-term memory stores a vast quantity of information from the long string of episodes that forms our lives. Long-term memory holds data such as what we had for breakfast this morning, who came to our last birthday party, and what it was like to learn to ride a bike. The record of personal life experiences is called *episodic memory* (Tulving, 1972). Episodic memories are generally retrieved through an association with a particular time and place.

Figure 3.3 Semantic vs. episodic memory
Semantic memories deal with general concepts, relationships, and rules; episodic memories deal with specific life experiences. The semantic memory of "father" evokes a general concept, while the episodic memory of "father" refers to a person's own father.

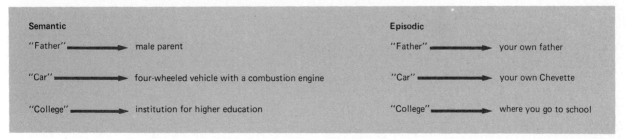

Semantic		Episodic	
"Father" →	male parent	"Father" →	your own father
"Car" →	four-wheeled vehicle with a combustion engine	"Car" →	your own Chevette
"College" →	institution for higher education	"College" →	where you go to school

REAL LIFE MEMORY

■ How long will you remember a passionate kiss, a hilarious joke, the pain of childbirth, or the first snowfall of 1981? You may not have an answer to this, but Marigold Linton does. Using herself as the subject in a six-year study of long-term memory, Linton (1978) painstakingly recorded on cards two real events per day (about 5,500 items altogether) and assigned each a number with a date. Once a month, she took a random sample of all the cards she had written before. She tested herself on her recall of the date the event described had occurred, and on whether she remembered the event at all.

From this detailed experiment she learned that people forget at a much slower rate than the Ebbinghaus curve of forgetting would predict. Linton forgot a total 32 percent of the material at a relatively even rate over the six years she tested. Rehearsals (the number of times she thought about an item and retested herself on it) helped to slow down the rate of forgetting. In the real world re-

hearsals are either formal, like studying for a test, or informal, as when we think about an event spontaneously from time to time so it lingers in memory. Formal rehearsals can themselves be more accurately pinpointed or remembered later; informal ones are harder to recall.

To test yourself as Marigold Linton did, answer this question:

Which came first, the Egypt-Israel peace treaty, or the visit of Pope John Paul II to America?

Now try this question:

What were you doing the day the American hostages were released from Iran?

Chances are the second question will be much clearer and sharper in your memory—for at least two reasons: it requires less inferential problem solving, and it connects a world event with your life, so the chance of rehearsing and remembering it is greater. ■

Our memory is also the repository for a vast amount of information that is not tied to a particular time or place, such as the fact that mountains have slopes or that presidents are elected for a fixed term. *Semantic memory* is the term for our knowledge of words, concepts, and the relations among them (Tulving, 1972). Semantic memories deal with the relationships and rules that organize our knowledge. They do not depend on our recalling a particular episode in the past in order to bring them to mind. Thus, in order to remember what eight times seven is, we don't have to recall the time when we learned that part of the multiplication table. Some, however, question the distinction between semantic and episodic memory (Anderson and Ross, 1980).

Semantic memory, our knowledge of how events or concepts are related, can distort episodic memory, recall of what actually happened

(Loftus and Loftus, 1976). Take the following example involving a traffic accident—a complex and sudden event. College students watched films of a traffic accident and then answered a series of questions (Loftus and Zanni, 1975). Some were asked questions with an indefinite article, like "Did you see a broken headlight?" Others were asked the same question with a definite article: "Did you see *the* broken headlight?" There was no broken headlight in the film, but even so the questions with a definite article got many more "yes" answers. This false recognition was, presumably, an effect of the workings of semantic memory. The rules governing use of definite articles like "the" imply a particular object or event, while an indefinite article does not. The semantic memory for the rules of using articles, then, overrode the episodic memory of what was actually seen in the film.

MEMORY AND THE BRAIN

The exact mechanisms that allow our brains to remember are unknown. Most researchers believe that memory must involve some physical change in the brain, but they have yet to discover the nature of such a change. One model for such a change is the general concept of an *engram*, a lasting mark caused by a stimulus of any sort on a living organism. Learning, as we have seen, is a behavioral change that endures. Since the turn of the century the engram has been proposed as a lasting physical residue in the brain formed during learning that remains dormant in the brain until the moment it is retrieved.

One version of this theory, proposed by Donald Hebb in 1949, holds that a "trace," a physiological change in brain cells, is the basis for short- and long-term memory. According to Hebb's theory, stimuli cause *activity traces* in nerve cells that hold a short-term memory until a *structural trace* can form that will hold a long-term memory. *Consolidation*, when the activity traces are transformed into stable structural traces, marks the change from short-term to long-term memory. Activity traces, then, hold short-term memory, and structural traces are the brain changes that house long-term memory—or so the theory goes. Since the theory is based on the existence of things and events that are hard to observe—activity traces, structural traces, and consolidation—it is difficult to prove or disprove. There is, however, some indirect evidence consistent with the theory.

A blow to the head, for example, can cause *retrograde amnesia*, in which a person doesn't recall events that immediately preceded the blow, but remembers events that occurred earlier. Electroshock therapy also produces retrograde amnesia. Presumably, the trauma of the blow or of electroshock somehow interferes with the process whereby activity traces are consolidated into structural traces. This interference means that what would have been short-term memories never become long-term memories.

The theory that memory traces are structural was given a boost by the discoveries of neurosurgeon Wilder Penfield, who performed brain surgery on epileptics who could not be helped by any other means. The operations were done using only local anesthesia; his patients were aware, though they felt no pain. Penfield took advantage of this unusual situation to perform a brief experiment that did not interfere with the safety of the operation: he stimulated the patients' temporal lobe with weak electrical currents. As he touched the electrode to their exposed brains, the patients reported vivid memories of long-past experiences, some of which they thought they had long since forgotten. Penfield (1958) reported:

> A patient may hear music, for example. But, if so, he hears a single playing of the music, orchestra, or piano, or voices; and he may be aware of himself as present in the room or hall. He may hear voices, the voices of friends or of strangers.... He may, on the other hand, see things that he saw in an earlier period without being aware of sound. If he felt a pleasurable admiration then, he feels it now.

Penfield's electrodes, however, were not touching an engram; when in the course of surgery he removed the parts of the temporal lobe from which the memory was evoked, his patients were still able to recall these events. Yet not all memories

The exposed right brain hemisphere of one of Penfield's patients. When Penfield's electrode stimulated the numbered sections the patient gave a response, such as recalling a vivid memory. (Courtesy, W. Penfield, Montreal Neurological Institute, McGill University)

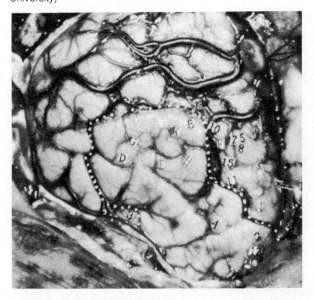

are permanent; some can be destroyed (Loftus and Loftus, 1980).

Researchers generally agree that several areas of the brain are essential for memory, particularly the hippocampus, the temporal lobes, and the association areas in the cortex. A study of sixteen patients with organic dementia, a disease that destroys brain tissue, found that all of them suffered impaired memory. An analysis of blood flow patterns in their brains showed that they had damage to these brain zones (Hagberg, 1978). Patients with Korsakoff's psychosis, a disease caused by alcohol abuse that results in deterioration of the brain, revealed the same pattern of damage to the hippocampus and severe memory loss, especially short-term memory (Vinocur and Olds, 1978; Mair *et al.*, 1980).

A tragic living experiment on memory and the brain began during a brain operation for epilepsy (a brain disorder that causes episodes of blackouts and seizures) when a patient's hippocampus was removed entirely (Blakemore, 1977). While parts of the hippocampus had been removed in previous operations on severe epileptics with no adverse effects on memory, with this patient—called H.M.—total removal resulted in extreme memory loss: he cannot form new memories. While all his memories from before the operation are intact, he seems incapable of retrieving new ones. For example, H.M. works in a state rehabilitation center assembling parts of cigarette lighters, but cannot say what he does, where he works, or how he gets there. While H.M. can still learn simple routines, he cannot bring them to conscious awareness in his memory. His world of experience is just a few minutes long.

Most recent research does not seek to find a part of the brain that houses anything like "memory banks." The most likely candidates for the repository of memory within the brain are large molecules that are a part of every cell: *RNA*, the ribonucleic acid that translates the genetic message from the genetic code of DNA, and follows its blueprints to assemble protein molecules in keeping with the DNA code. *DNA*—complex genetic molecules—are found in the nucleus of every cell in the body, and pass on each cell's contribution to the blueprint for the species. RNA molecules are the messengers for DNA, stimulating

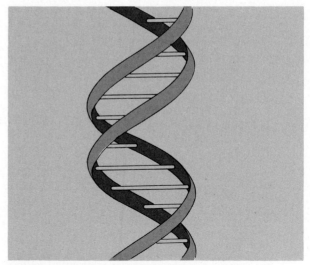

Figure 3.4 The molecular basis for the genetic code
The DNA molecule contains the genetic code in its ladderlike spiral structure.

the production of the complex substances that the blueprints for each cell demand. Each RNA molecule is a storehouse of information, a sort of microscopic library.

The brains of animals that have learned a new task—and so have had to enter it in memory—synthesize more RNA than usual; drugs that block RNA also block the ability to learn. Also, inhibiting RNA immediately after an animal has learned produces retrograde amnesia for the task, suggesting that RNA plays a role in consolidation (Schneider and Tarshis, 1980). Some researchers dispute these results on several grounds—e.g., one points out that they could just as well be due to an impurity in the RNA used in these tests; protein is an alternative candidate (Ungar *et al.*, 1972). In fact no single theory of memory and the brain has yet been proven conclusively.

The biochemistry of memory is extremely complex; the pieces of this scientific puzzle have yet to be entirely assembled. For example, lithium chloride, a drug used as an antidepressant, seems to impair short-term memory (Kusumo and Vaughn, 1977). Similarly, GABA, a chemical that governs transmission of nerve impulses in the brain, also decreases memory consolidation (Katz and Liebler, 1978). The search is on for chemicals that might enhance memory, and thus lead to a "memory pill." Several chemical compounds have seemed to be promising memory aids in research studies but none has proven itself a surefire memory pill (Kovac, 1977).

WHY WE FORGET

Why do we forget? No single theory has general acceptance among psychologists; of the three theories that are most widely accepted, one says we forget because a memory trace fades, another says we forget because other memories interfere, and the third says forgetting is shaped by our motives. All seem to have some grain of truth.

The decaying memory trace

One theory holds that a *memory trace*—a yet-to-be-identified physical structure of memory—is created for every event we remember. The theory posits that a memory trace will decay as time goes on, with the details of memory gradually becoming lost, unless the memory is brought to mind from time to time (Norman, 1969). Rehearsal of the memory strengthens the trace; without rehearsal it decays.

If you learned Spanish in high school but haven't practiced it much since, your memory for it will be much poorer than if you had kept it up over the years. Common sense would seem to support the memory trace theory, except for one thing: it fails to explain how we can suddenly remember skills or events from our distant past that we have not thought of or rehearsed in the meantime. If you haven't ridden a bike since grade school, you'll still be able to hop on one and pedal away.

The best test of the memory trace theory calls for a person to do nothing with a memory, in which case it gradually should be forgotten. While we are awake, we are constantly thinking of things; we are much closer to doing nothing when we are asleep. When people are asked to memorize new material just before going to sleep, they remember it better than material they memorized before staying awake for several hours (Jenkins

and Dallenbach, 1924). Here again the memory trace theory does not seem to hold up: the people who went directly to sleep probably did less with their new memories, and the memories therefore should have faded more, not less.

Imagine that you've played guitar for three years, and you're pretty good. One day you find yourself moving into a house with four other guitar players. Unfortunately, jamming with five guitars doesn't work too well. You take up the banjo.

You can learn the chording all right, but when you really get into a song you seem to forget what you're playing. You start playing guitar chords on your banjo, which ruins a song fast.

You keep practicing and, after a while, become a decent banjo picker. Then banjo picking gets you interested in bluegrass music. You begin picking the guitar again to learn some bluegrass licks on it. But now you find yourself trying to play banjo chords on the guitar. ■

The interfering association

Another view of forgetting attributes it to interference by new memories that inhibit old ones. In forgetting that is caused by *interference*, one set of memories inhibits the recall of another. As B. J. Underwood (1964), a proponent of this theory, puts it, "all forgetting results basically from interference between the associations" that each person carries in memory. Playing the banjo creates a whole new set of habits and associations that can interfere, for a time, with the ability to play the guitar. Or if you memorize a list of vocabulary words for your French class, and then learn another list, you won't recall the second list as well as the first; associations from the first list will crop up when you attempt to recall the second. If you learn twenty lists, you will forget still more.

There are two kinds of memory interference: proactive and retroactive. In *proactive* interference, material learned earlier interferes with recall of material learned later. Your old telephone number proactively interferes with your attempts

"Don't ask questions. Just see if my umbrella's under the sink."

Imagine that two old friends from high school are having drinks together and reminiscing.

"You remember that blond girl? You dated her. What was her name?"

"Ellen? Elaine?"

"You remember, she was rich—a cheerleader—you used to follow her around."

"Oh, Eleanor Clark. I didn't follow her around. And I didn't date her. Except once—that big bash at Richard's house in Creekwood. We had a good time. Danced all night."

At that remark, the first old friend snorts in his beer and chokes. He stamps his feet while he coughs. Finally, he manages to talk again. "Yeah you had a good time. You got drunk, and she went off with another guy—the quarterback, whatsizname." ■

Motivation

Our drives and goals, or motivations, influence memory by making things that we find important easier to remember than uninteresting things. Motivation can aid memory by making a person more attentive to certain information, such as whether someone you're interested in dating is already seeing somebody else regularly. In the same way, motivation can make some things easier to forget. *Repression* is the exclusion of painful experiences from memory; repression is a form of selective forgetting. Recall of such experiences may bring up associated anxiety or guilt; repressing them guards against these negative feelings. Sigmund Freud proposed repression as a major defense mechanism that is the cause of motivated forgetting (Clemes, 1964), such as the convenient inability to remember Eleanor Clark.

Repression seems to cause many cases of *psychogenic amnesia*, the loss of memory or personal identity for psychological, rather than physical, reasons. A person who develops psychogenic amnesia may feel that she has violated her moral or religious beliefs and, because her guilt is so unbearable, may forget everything, including her identity. Since brain damage does not cause this condition, such a person's memory usually returns

to learn a new one; this theory predicts that interference might be still greater if both numbers share some digits, so that old associations interfere with the new ones you're trying to learn. Or if you begin to learn the banjo after years as a guitarist, you may find your hands playing familiar guitar chords instead of the banjo riffs you're trying to master.

In *retroactive* interference, newly learned material interferes with the memory of material learned earlier. If you memorized the dates of ascension to the throne of the kings of France last semester, and learning a similar set for the kings of England this term made you forget the French ones, that would be retroactive interference. When you tried to play guitar chords on your banjo, that was proactive interference, but when your banjo chords interfered with remembering the guitar chords you had learned earlier, you were experiencing the effects of retroactive interference.

if her emotional and motivational situation changes (Stengel, 1964). Such cases bring home the point that forgetting may simply be difficulty with recall, not loss of a given memory altogether.

A person's motivation can also influence how he reconstructs memories, as in the case of confabulations. *Confabulations* are falsifications that a person makes up to fill in gaps in memory and that the person accepts as true. Confabulations are likely to be agreeable to the person making them up, possibly more agreeable than the actual events that occurred during the gap in memory. The high school friend who mentioned Eleanor Clark brought up an unhappy memory. His friend's confabulation of dancing all night had replaced the repressed memory of the actual event.

The curve of forgetting

Forgetting follows a pattern. At first forgetting occurs rapidly, but as time passes, the rate of forgetting slows—an effect first studied by Hermann Ebbinghaus in experiments he did on

Figure 3.5 The curve of forgetting
Most forgetting occurs soon after material has been learned. The percentage of what a person remembers decreases rapidly at first, and so the curve of forgetting drops steeply at the beginning, then becomes more horizontal.

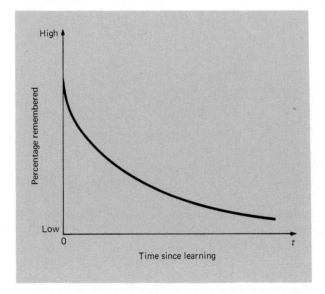

himself. If you make a graph plotting how much you will forget on the y axis and the passage of time on the x axis, you will draw a curve that is steep at first but levels off as time goes by. This is the *curve of forgetting*, the rate at which learning is lost from memory. The shapes of all the curves of forgetting are roughly the same, e.g., for nonsense syllables and familiar words, for complex ideas, the names and faces of old friends, or phone numbers. The drop is more rapid at first (meaning forgetting is faster), and slows down as time passes. The specific shape depends on the material learned, as does the final level the curve eventually reaches.

One experiment compared the forgetting curve for a series of fifteen nonsense syllables with that for the simple motor skill of keeping a pointer on a dime-sized target as it revolves on a turntable (Leavitt and Schlosberg, 1944). True to the curve, forgetting of both skills took place rapidly for the first week or two, then continued at a gradually reducing rate for the next eight weeks. However, the subjects retained the motor skill much better than they did the verbal skill.

This experiment shows that we forget motor skills less rapidly than verbal ones. Moreover, we seem to remember complex motor skills, such as riding a bicycle, typing, skating, or swimming, even better than simple ones such as the tracking skill in the experiment. The curve of forgetting for more complex skills becomes nearly flat after a time, although performance excellence may fall off a little. Riding off on your roommate's bicycle, for example, was easy; because you forgot so little of how to do it during your year without one, it felt perfectly natural and didn't even register in your preoccupied mind. If you tried to take a history exam on material you learned a year ago, however, the going would be tougher.

It is likely that motor skills are easier to remember because each one tends to be unique—swimming requires much different movements than typing—so there is less chance that the memory of one motor skill would interfere with another. These sorts of complex motor skills may also be easier to remember than simple ones because they must be learned much more thoroughly to be learned at all.

THE TIP OF YOUR TONGUE

■ How many times has this happened to you?

You're doing a sparkling monologue about, say, a Woody Allen movie. You sketch Allen's career, discuss the morality of ghostwriting, and recount in detail Allen's own debut as a serious actor. You're at the peak of your brilliance, when somebody asks, ". . . but what was the movie called?"

Nothing. Your mind is blank. Frantically, you free-associate: it has something to do with ghostwriting . . . with deception and misrepresentation . . . *The Liar* . . . no . . . *The Fraud* . . . closer . . . *The Rotten People* . . . no, no. You are losing credibility by the minute.

Desperately you try another route: mental charades. Sounds like runt? *The Runt* . . . can't be . . . stung, bunt, so close and yet . . . you just can't quite get . . . "*The Front*!" yells someone. You've been beaten. It's not fair. The answer was right on the tip of your tongue.

If it's any consolation, you are certainly not alone.

In a systematic study of the "tip of the tongue" (TOT) state (Brown and McNeill, 1966), volunteers were given definitions and asked for the correct word. The TOT state was tough to catch. Some people guessed the answer immediately, others claimed they didn't know the word at all.

When the TOT state did occur, it had a number of characteristics. The person would "feel" he knew the word; he sometimes remembered the initial sound, correct number of syllables, or the first letter. Often he knew which words were incorrect. This recollection of the general characteristics of a word is called "generic recall."

Brown and McNeill surmised that a TOT word is stored in our long-term memory and can be retrieved either by sound, meaning, or association.

For example, I give you the meaning: "a strong vessel in which material is pounded or crushed with a pestle" and you, of course, respond with . . . Tarter? Barter? Martyr? Mortal? It's right on the tip of your tongue . . . *

* Mortar.

Anxiety

Just as anxiety can interfere with learning, it can also make it harder for us to remember. Forty-eight college freshmen were selected for an experiment on recall; half had been identified on a previous test as low in anxiety, half as high (Radin and Wittmaier, 1979). They were all given the same learning task: to memorize a list of sixty words, each presented for four seconds. Some were told they had done well; others were made to feel they had done poorly—an anxiety-producing condition. Those made to feel anxious did less well four weeks later on a test of recall than those told they had done well. The worst recall performance was among those freshmen who were high in anxiety to begin with, and who were also made to feel anxious. One implication is that people who are generally anxious would do well to learn memory aids to help them compensate for the negative effects of anxiety on recall.

MEMORY AIDS

Coding

Even though factors such as anxiety or the simple passage of time make us forget some of what we have learned, there are several steps we can take to aid our memory. For example, how much you remember depends on how well you *code*, or organize, it. We can recall materials organized in related categories two or three times better than items learned randomly (Bower, 1970).

For instance, in an investigation of conceptual learning (Tulving and Pearlstone, 1966), two groups of subjects learned lists of from twelve to forty-eight words. The lists one group learned were broken down into categories, such as four-footed animals like "cow" and "rat" or weapons like "bomb" and "cannon." The other group was given the same lists, but the words were not categorized. The subjects whose retrieval was cued by seeing the categories did much better in recalling the words. Although we may remember certain uncategorized items, our recall is better when retrieval is assisted by a system of organization.

Even greater retrieval was found in subjects who built narrative stories around the lists of words than in control subjects who simply learned the words serially (Bower and Clark, 1969). The subjects aided by their stories recalled six or seven times as much as the control group and also made very few errors. So chunking, or relating the items on a list to each other in a meaningful way, improves memory and diminishes forgetfulness. If you're studying for a quiz on the kings of England, for example, you might place the kings in groups, and better still, within the framework of the social and political climate in which they reigned. Such methods improve both the efficiency with which you code facts into memory and your ability to retrieve them during a test.

Imagine that your best friend is in both your French class and your tennis class. You are presently studying a list of French verbs to prepare for a ten-minute quiz tomorrow. You whip through it. It's easy for you. So you call your friend on the telephone and suggest she meet you at the tennis court to practice together. "Sorry," she replies, "I've got to study these verbs for French. I'll be out on the court after I have this list down."

For two hours you practice your tennis serve alone. By the time your friend gets there you have lost a can of balls and your shin is hamburger. But you're serving hard and fast, just inside the line. And you destroy your friend in the first set.

By the fourth set, however, her serve is better than yours, and she's destroying you. "Well," you say, "you're taking these sets. But I'll beat you on the French test; you had to study that list twice as long as I did."

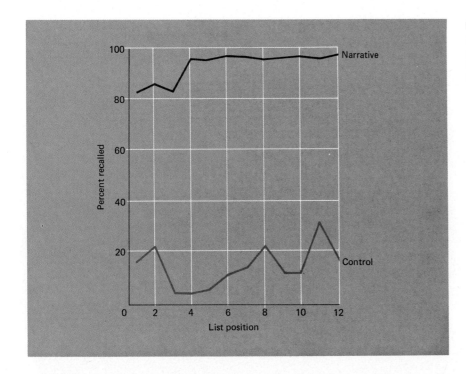

Figure 3.6 Memory aids improve recall

Average recall for subjects using mnemonic ("narrative") versus normal ("control") methods of study.

The next day, however, you both do equally well on the quiz in French. And, to your surprise, after a week of practicing you are keeping up with her tennis game. ■

Learning speed

How fast you learn does not determine how much you will remember. If a slow learner has enough time to learn or code materials into her memory, her retention score will be the same as that of a fast learner (Underwood, 1964). Slow learners may not be able to code, chunk, and organize material as quickly as fast learners but, having mastered the material to the same degree, they can remember it as well. In other words, with more time devoted to studying, students of average ability can do as well as students of greater ability who study less. For this reason, your friend has to spend a lot more time on her French lessons to keep up with you, but she could do as well in the end. And, of course, that gave you time to keep up with her tennis game.

Imagine a beaker that is wide at the bottom and narrows toward the top. If you fill such a beaker with water, the higher it is filled, the less quickly it will evaporate, since it will have less surface area. The water level can be considered to represent how well material is learned, and evaporation can symbolize forgetting. Thus the better the material is learned (higher water level), the slower it will be forgotten (less surface area). A fast learner would be like a beaker that is filled quickly. It will take the slow learner longer to get material entered into memory to the same level as the fast learner, but after reaching that level, both will forget at the same rate.

Easily learned material is not any easier to remember than more difficult subject matter. When easy and difficult material are equally well learned, as if to the same level in a beaker, they are forgotten at about the same rate (Underwood, 1964). If you struggle to learn the dates that British kings were crowned, but breeze through the rules for conjugating French verbs, in the long run it won't matter which was easier to master. You'll forget both stacks of information at about equal rates.

Imagine that you can talk football with your dad. He's an armchair quarterback, actually played in college, and you have to admit that he does know the game.

You're watching a game together on television. The Cowboys score on an astounding seventy-one-yard run. "That reminds me of Johnson last season," you comment. "Ninety-one yards on a turnover."

"I don't remember that," says your father.

"Yeah, against Baltimore. He intercepted on his own nine-yard line and ran it all the way back."

"Oh, yeah. No, that wasn't a turnover," your father explains. "That was a lateral pass. Johnson's an offensive back. He wouldn't have intercepted. Defensive men intercept." ■

Schemata

We seem to reconstruct the past according to a personal frame of reference called a *schema* (plural: schemata). Schemata are rules for memory governed by one's attitudes, needs, and interests (Bartlett, 1932). What you remember about last night's party is guided by the schema of your interests and attitudes. If you dislike dancing but enjoy talking to members of the opposite sex, you'll remember little of the music but much about the conversations you had. And you'll probably remember most about who you left the party with and what you did afterwards. Your particular schema determines, at least in part, how you reconstruct the party.

In *reconstruction*, a past experience is pieced together according to a person's schema. The role of schemata in reconstruction can be seen in gamesmanship. Expert players of bridge or chess—or football fans—seem to remember specific and complex plays and moves better than nonexperts. Experts may use reconstruction to recall the plays already made—the key moves of the black queen, or the strategy that destroyed the defense in a football game ten years ago. Experts understand the probable and important plays by means of well-learned schemata, so they can concentrate on these in reconstructing the events. They may not have better memories, but they are more aware of the significance of events and, because of their knowledge, they can reconstruct more efficiently (Norman, 1969).

MEMORY RETRIEVAL

There are many tests of remembering and forgetting. Your history test, for example, is meant to measure how much you remember—or have forgotten—about a certain period of English history. Your grade point average reflects in part how well you do on such memory tests. How much you can show you remember will depend to some extent on both the type of memory test you take and the method of measurement used. There are two types of remembering: recognition and recall. Although a person may not be able to remember every word of a poem she has learned, she may be able to recall some of it. Or, although she may recognize the poem as one that she has read before, she may not be able to recite any of it. Generally, recognition is much easier than recall. You might be able to recognize dates on your history exam if you saw them in a multiple-choice format. To make the test more of a challenge your professor would probably increase the level of difficulty of the details you must remember.

"I never forget a face." (© Joel Gordon, 1976)

Recall

When you *recall* an event, you retrieve it from memory. Recall is a search of memory to find particular information. You search your memory for answers when you take a test, when you try to remember a phone number, or when you try to think back to the last place you saw something that you've lost. As you scan your memory for details of last night's dream, you are engaged in recall.

Recall may be either free or aided. In a free-recall situation, the order of the items recalled is unimportant. We may reconstruct or create our own order to aid the recall; for example, if you are asked to name the fifty states in any order, you might recall them *aided* by geographic area or alphabetical order. But free recall would be simply searching your memory until you *freely* ran across the name of a state.

In aided recall, the order or organization of the items is important. *Serial learning* is aided recall of data that was learned in a particular sequence—in other words, a *memorized* list. If you want to remember the names of the presidents from George Washington on, you would probably learn them in order, because the recall of Truman may aid the recall of Eisenhower, and Eisenhower may make you think of Kennedy.

The *probe technique* is a test of recall in which a specific item from the list, or a subset of items, is requested. A question such as "Who was the fifth king of England after the Norman conquest?" requiring you to select a particular name from your memory list of English kings is an example of the probe technique.

If you have studied a foreign language, you already know the *paired-associate* method of recall, where the item to be learned is linked with one you know well. First, you learn the equivalents of English words in the foreign language. Then, given the English, you try to recall the foreign words. They are paired associates, with the former serving as cues for recalling the latter; for example, the word "number" brings to mind the Spanish word "numero." Likewise, you could pair the dates of kings ascending the throne with their names, so that the name would bring to mind the associated date—William the Conqueror is linked with 1066, George III with 1760.

HIGH? FORGET IT

◼ It's a Saturday night party, and you've had plenty to drink. You run into an old friend, have a great time with her, and promise to call her the next day. She tells you her phone number, and you repeat it several times to be sure you'll remember. Sunday morning, despite a mild hangover, you decide to give her a call. But when you try to remember her number, your mind's a blank.

This scenario fits what has been learned about the effects of intoxication on memory, whether from alcohol or marijuana. According to a review of findings by Elizabeth Loftus (1980), whether you're high from drinking alcohol or smoking pot, your ability to retrieve information from long-term memory will not suffer—but your capacity for storing new information in memory will be impaired while you stay high.

In general, a person's recall for words on a list fits what is termed the ''serial position curve'' (see Figure 3.7). When a person tries to recall the list in whatever order comes to mind, she typically remembers the last few words on the list first, then words from the beginning, and finally words in the middle. For this reason, words at the end of the list have the best chance of being recalled, those at the start a good chance, and those in the middle a poor chance.

In one study, volunteers were given either the equivalent of four to six mixed drinks, or the same amount to drink with no alcohol (both mixtures were disguised to taste the same). They were shown a list of words, and then immediately asked to recall them. The effects: those who had the non-alcoholic drinks had the usual serial position pattern of recall. However, the drunk volunteers could remember the last words on the list, but had trouble with those from the beginning and middle (Jones, 1973).

Short-term memory is thought to last up to fifteen or twenty minutes; after that the information must pass into long-term memory or be forgotten. That seems to be what happened: the last words on the list were still in short-term memory during the recall test, while those in the beginning and middle should have passed into long-term memory. This pattern of recall suggests that alcohol interferes with long-term memory, but not short-term.

Alcohol may interfere with the formation of new long-term memories, but it does not seem to interfere with long-term recall of information learned while sober. In another study, volunteers memorized word lists while sober, then tried to recall them while drunk (Birnbaum and Parker, 1977). The intoxicated group could recall the list as well as the sober group. The factor that made the difference in memorizing had nothing to do with sobriety: the more adept at using schemata, the better the person's recall (Birnbaum *et al.,* 1980).

Marijuana has similar effects on memory. In a study parallel to that done with alcohol, volunteers ate ordinary brownies or brownies laced with THC (the active chemical in marijuana) and then memorized word lists. As with alcohol, the marijuana high did not affect memory of the last words on the list, although it did hamper recall of those at the start and middle (Darley and Tinklenberg, 1974).

In a later study, though, volunteers smoked their marijuana instead of eating it in brownies (Miller, 1974). Because smoking the drug works more quickly and intensely than eating it, this group was more ''stoned'' than those in the earlier study. This more-intoxicated group did poorly in recalling all parts of the list, including the last part. Being mildly stoned, then, hampers long-term memory but not short-term memory; being very stoned interferes with even short-term recall. Presumably, the same would be true for being very drunk, although there has been no test of this as yet (Loftus, 1980).

''Drink to forget'' is an old saying. But if you drink—or smoke—you'll forget mostly the new, not the old. ◼

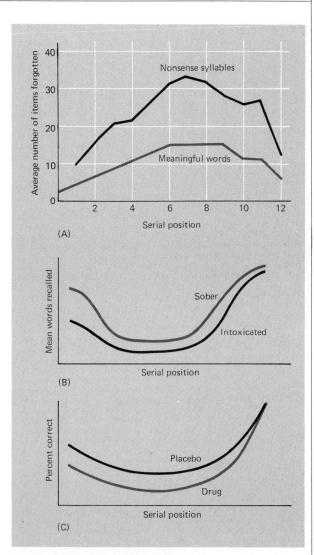

(A)

(B)

(C)

Figure 3.7 Serial position effect

(A) When a person memorizes a list of words or nonsense syllables and then has to recall them, the words memorized last are usually recalled best, the words at the start of the list next best, and the words in the middle are least well recalled.

(B) When sober subjects were asked to recall a list, their recall followed the usual serial position curve. But when subjects who had consumed alcohol recalled the lists, their recall was uniformly poorer.

(C) When subjects were tested for memory of words learned while high on marijuana, they did very poorly.

Imagine that you're observing a police lineup. You sit in the darkened spectators' area. Your swollen jaw reminds you that you're a mugging victim. Some guy just walked right up to you last night and knocked you down and took your wallet. And then, unbelievably, you couldn't even describe him to the police.

But when the suspects walk out like performers onto a stage, you suddenly spot him: the one on the right in the brown jacket. You're sure of it; you would know him anywhere. ■

Recognition

In *recognition,* a particular memory is triggered as you perceive again all or part of familiar information. Recognition requires a strong, definite cue, whereas recall involves either minimal cues or no cue at all. Recall depends on the ability to associate the information to be remembered with something in the conscious mind. For example, the question "Who are your cousins?" requires a

Which face did you see before on page 69? (© Joel Gordon, 1976)

search of your memory to retrieve the names associated with "cousins." On the other hand, the question "Is Gail your cousin?" gives you a definite, clear cue—you simply compare the name "Gail" with your memories of "cousin" to see if it fits. Multiple-choice questions test recognition: "Who was the first king of England—Alfred the Great, William the Conqueror, or George I?" A police lineup also tests recognition.

Recognition is generally easier than recall. A recognition task may, however, become as difficult as a recall task, if not more so, when the incorrect alternatives or distractions are similar to the correct item, as on a tricky multiple-choice question.

Imagine that you're in a strange city for the first time, walking through the door of a large museum, when suddenly you have the strongest sensation that *this has all happened be-*

fore. Yet you know this is the first time in your life you've gone through that museum door. ■

Memory quirks: déjà vu

You've just experienced a *déjà vu* ("already seen" in French), the seeming memory of an experience that is actually happening for the first time. The *déjà vu* experience, the strong feeling of having been here before but knowing you haven't, is an anomaly of recognition. One theory says that a *déjà vu* is caused by subtle features of the event that, perhaps subconsciously, are similar to something previously experienced. Another theory proposes that the present event somehow registers in memory before we are consciously aware of it, and so presents itself as something remembered.

At any rate, let's say you're in a strange city for the first time, walking through the door of a large museum, when suddenly you have the strongest sensation that this has all happened before . . .

SUMMARY

Memory is an intricate balance of things remembered and things forgotten. It involves the ability to bring past experience to mind, but also to reject information that is unnecessary or undesirable.

Kinds of memory. Basically, there are three kinds of memory: short-term sensory storage, short-term memory, and long-term memory.

Short-term sensory storage is the temporary, split-second registering of sensory experience.

Short-term memory is the immediate lodging of a limited amount of information in the memory, information which will be quickly forgotten unless deliberately converted into long-term memory. Short-term information storage can be increased by chunking and rehearsing.

The establishment of a relatively permanent long-term memory involves sensory registration of information, organization and coding in the short-term memory and, finally, adequate rehearsal. Long-term memories include episodic ones,

such as personal life experiences, and semantic ones, such as knowledge of words, concepts, and the relationships among them.

Memory and the brain. Although the exact mechanics that allow our brains to remember are unknown, and no single memory theory has been proven, most researchers believe that some physical change must be involved. The general concept of the engram, a lasting physical residue in the brain formed during learning, has been proposed as one model of such change. Hebb's version of the concept holds that an activity trace holds a short-term memory until the formation of a structural trace that will hold a long-term memory. Consolidation marks the change.

The trace theory seems to be supported by the phenomenon of retrograde amnesia, in which a trauma causes loss of memory of events that immediately preceded the trauma, but leaves earlier memories intact.

Recent research suggests that the repositories of memory in the brain are the large ribonucleic acid (RNA) molecules that are part of every cell in the body. RNA translates the genetic message from the code of DNA, a complex molecule also found in every cell.

Why we forget. One theory of forgetting holds that the memory trace, a yet-to-be-identified physical structure, decays over time if the memory is not rehearsed. According to another view, forgetting is caused by the interference of one set of memories with another: in proactive interference, the memory of old material interferes with the recall of material learned later; in retroactive interference, new material makes the recall of old material more difficult.

Various kinds of motivation can also influence forgetting. Painful experiences may be repressed, a form of selective forgetting. Psychogenic amnesia, an extreme form of repression whereby one loses the memory of one's personal identity, is caused by feelings of guilt in people who have violated their own basic beliefs. Gaps in memory are sometimes filled with confabulations, which are likely to be improvements on the actual forgotten events.

Learning fades in a pattern that can be plotted on a graph, forming a "curve of forgetting." The shape of the curve remains the same no matter what the material being forgotten, although motor skills seem to be retained longer than verbal ones. Anxiety can accelerate forgetting.

Memory aids. Recall of material organized, or coded, into related categories is two to three times more effective than recall of uncoded material. The speed at which material is learned has no effect on how well it will be remembered. Schemata, or personal frameworks for memory governed by one's attitudes, needs, and interests, can provide the basis for reconstruction of past experience.

Memory retrieval. There are two different types of remembering, recall and recognition. Recall involves a search of one's memory to find information. Serial learning is a type of aided recall in which data is learned in a particular sequence. The paired-associate type of recall links an item to be learned with one that is already familiar.

In recognition, generally an easier task than recall, a memory is triggered by a strong, definite cue.

The sensation of *déjà vu*, the feeling that one remembers an event that is actually happening for the first time, is a memory anomaly.

GLOSSARY

Activity trace Short-lived electrical activity in brain cells that is thought to hold a short-term memory.

Chunking Recoding information to aid short-term memory by combining several items so they can be remembered as a single item.

Coding Organizing material in related categories to aid memory.

Confabulation Falsification—usually unwitting—to fill a gap in memory.

Consolidation The transformation of an activity trace into a stable structural trace, marking the change from short- to long-term memory.

Curve of forgetting The rate at which learning is lost from memory.

Déjà vu The seeming memory of an experience that is actually happening for the first time.

DNA Complex molecule found in the nucleus of every cell in the body and containing the genetic code.

Echoic storage A briefly held auditory memory.

Engram According to one theory, a lasting physical residue in the brain that stores a memory.

Episodic memory The record of personal life experiences, generally retrieved through an association with a particular time and place.

Iconic storage The short-term sensory storage of visual impressions.

Information processing The way the brain registers, codes, and stores experience.

Interference A cause of forgetting in which one set of memories inhibits the recall of another.

Long-term memory The relatively permanent storage of information.

Memory The ability to bring past experience to mind.

Memory retrieval The calling up of long-term memory.

Paired-associate recall The linking of an item to be learned with one that is already familiar.

Proactive interference What occurs when material learned earlier interferes with recall of new material.

Probe technique The test of recall in which a specific item or subset of items is requested.

Psychogenic amnesia A form of repression whereby people who feel they have violated their basic beliefs forget their own identity.

Recall The search of memory to retrieve specific information.

Recognition The process whereby memory is triggered by a strong cue that elicits stored information.

Reconstruction The piecing together of a past experience according to a schema.

Repression The exclusion of painful experience from memory.

Retroactive interference What occurs when newly learned material inhibits the recall of material learned earlier.

Retrograde amnesia The inability to recall events that immediately precede a trauma, while memory of earlier events is retained.

RNA Ribonucleic acid, or large molecules that are part of every cell. RNA follows the blueprint of the genetic code in DNA, and it may be the repository of memory.

Schemata The frame of reference that guides our choice of what to remember.

Semantic memory The long-term memory of words, concepts, and the relationships among them.

Sensory storage The constant, split-second registering of sensory experience, forgotten in seconds.

Serial learning A kind of aided recall whereby data is learned in a particular sequence.

Short-term memory The temporary lodging of information in the memory.

Structural trace A memory trace in the nerve cells of the brain that may hold a long-term memory.

Trace A physiological change in brain cells; the basis for memory, according to one version of the engram theory.

4

LANGUAGE AND THOUGHT

LANGUAGE

The "purity" of languages ■ Language and the brain ■ Animal language ■ What's human about language? ■ Can other primates learn human language?

LANGUAGE ACQUISITION

The child's capacity for learning ■ How children learn to speak ■ Babble ■ First words ■ Shades of meaning ■ Grammar ■ Surface and deep structures ■ Meaning

LANGUAGE AND THOUGHT

Culture, language, and reality ■ Are thought and language the same? ■ Language and problem solving

COMMON MYTHS

MANY PEOPLE BELIEVE . . .	ACTUALLY . . .
Black American English is a substandard dialect of English.	No variation of a language can be considered to be inferior to any other.
Human language is basically no different from the "language" of animals.	Unlike animals, whose "languages" consist of a ready-made stock of forms and meanings, humans constantly create novel utterances.
Children learn to speak properly by being corrected by their elders when they make mistakes.	Children learn language almost entirely without direct instruction.
Thought is silent speech.	Words and thoughts are related but not identical.

"When *I* use a word," Humpty Dumpty said, in rather a scornful tone, "it means just what I choose it to mean—neither more nor less."

"The question is," said Alice, "whether you *can* make words mean so many different things."

LEWIS CARROLL, *THROUGH THE LOOKING-GLASS*

LANGUAGE

How do you know what a word means—what a string of words, like this sentence, means? Is language just a collection of words? What does it mean to "know" a language? To know a language, you must be able to make certain sounds that signify certain meanings, and to understand the meanings of such sounds when others make them. Language, then, relates meanings to sounds. To know a spoken language is to master its sounds, and know how to combine them into words and arrange the words into meaningful utterances. Whether spoken or heard, written or read, *language* is a system of symbols that relates sound or sign to meaning.

The relationship between sounds and meaning in a language is arbitrary. The range of sounds utilized differs from language to language; the particular sounds available will limit the combinations that are possible. You probably pronounce "Bach" as though it ends in *k;* a person speaking German would pronounce it with a guttural sound that has no English equivalent. The rules governing how sounds are combined also differ from language to language. What may be a proper combination in one language may violate rules in another. When Hermann Ebbinghaus created his list of 2,300 nonsense syllables in his native German tongue, he undoubtedly included many combinations of sounds that make perfect sense as words in other languages. Some international companies, wanting to ensure the ready marketability of their product around the world, have hired linguists to concoct names that can be pronounced in any language. One such word is "Kodak."

All normal children learn to use sound to express meaning, but sound is not a necessary aspect of language. Many children who are born deaf learn sign language instead of spoken language. Sign language, like spoken language, has a *syntax*, a set of rules that govern how words are combined into meaningful utterances. Syntax is

TABLE 4.1 **"TREE" IN THREE LANGUAGES**

English	tree
Portuguese	arvore
Korean	namu

77

TABLE 4.2 **SOME UNIVERSALS OF HUMAN LANGUAGE**

---

1. All languages use nominal phrases and verbal phrases, corresponding to the two major classes of noun and verb, and in all of them the number of nouns far exceeds the number of verbs. One can be fairly sure that a noun in one language translates a noun in another.

2. All languages have modifiers of these two classes, corresponding to adjectives and adverbs.

3. All languages have ways of turning verbal phrases into nounal phrases (*He went*—I know *that he went*).

4. All languages have ways of making adjectivelike phrases out of other kinds of phrases (*The man went*—The man *who went*).

5. All languages have ways of turning sentences into interrogatives, negatives, and commands.

6. All languages show at least two forms of interaction between verbal and nominal, typically "intransitive" (the verbal is involved with only one nominal, as in *Boys play*) and "transitive" (the verbal is involved with two nominals, as in *Boys like girls*).

---

an essential part of human language, but sound is not.

Language could be based on a medium other than sound or sign. Animals, for example, communicate with each other through visual displays, touch, and even smell. But there are certain advantages to sound-based communication, which perhaps brought about the evolution of oral languages. Sound travels quite rapidly, at 1,100 feet per second in air, and works as well in the dark as in the light. Unlike visual messages, sounds can be heard no matter where one is looking, and whether or not people are touching. And odor, besides being difficult to turn on and off at will, depends on an intimate closeness and the direction of the wind.

Imagine that it's a late night rap

session at International House, a campus dorm for foreign students. You're visiting an engineering grad student from New Delhi.

Somehow talk has drifted to languages. A French student is bemoaning the decline in the use of French as the international language. "No language is as precise or sophisticated as French," he claims. "Why there's even an official academy that guards its purity. But now wherever

you go, you need to speak English—a messy tongue if ever there was one."

"I beg to differ," pipes up an Englishman. "English as we British speak it is as pure as ever. It's these Americans who have ruined it. I was in Texas last summer and I couldn't understand a soul."

Your hackles raised, you're searching for an articulate putdown when your host from New Delhi says, in his Indian-English accent:

"It is absolute rubbish you are speaking. If you know your history, it tells us that Sanskrit—as spoken by my Indian ancestors—is the parent to European languages. French and English are only descendants of pure Sanskrit."

The Frenchman and the Englishman retreat into a fuming silence. ■

The "purity" of languages

Language is a particularly universal human attribute; every culture has its language. Language may be among the most ancient skills of the human species, predating even stone tools and making fire. And although the arts and technologies of different peoples can be seen as primitive or sophisticated, language defies such a judgment. New Guinea tribesmen speak as rich a tongue as the most snobbish Parisian—or resident of New Delhi.

Languages continually change as new words and phrases are coined, borrowed, and adopted, and others become obsolete. While languages change, they do not degenerate. While some versions of a language may be considered more grammatically correct than others, every new variation serves its speakers well. The same holds true for dialects, the regional variations of a language. The English spoken in Harlem, Maine, or Texas is perfectly adequate. No local variation can be considered a "corrupted" version of any other.

Language and the brain

Language has been called the distinctive human trait. While other species have their own systems of communication, none seems to come near the complexity of human speech. Differences between the brains of humans and our closest animal relatives, subhuman primates like the gorilla, may explain the human capacity for language. The single major difference between human and nonhuman brains is the highly developed human cerebral cortex, the top layer of the brain which controls speech and thought.

Even our close cousins the apes lack well-developed links between visual and auditory senses, an interconnection highly developed in the human cortex. This tie between sight and sound is vital for speech; it enables humans to make the leap between seeing an object and using the word for that object. An ape can see a peanut and reach for it, but a human can call it by name. To call it a "peanut," a person must have learned to associate this specific sight with the sound combination "peanut" (Geschwind, 1964).

Neurologists have known for years that damage to the left half of the brain—but only rarely to the right—can cause *aphasia*, a language disorder whereby the intelligence is intact but a person is unable to speak properly. There are many kinds of aphasia: some aphasics substitute words that mean the same thing (e.g., "spouse" for "wife"), others substitute words that sound somewhat alike (e.g., "sparse" for "spouse"), some simply "can't find the right word" although they can write it or point it out, and still others invent words that sound like language but that no one else understands.

A more recent confirmation that the left half of the brain controls speech comes from operations performed in the 1960s on severe epileptics (Gazzaniga, 1977). When no other treatment would help, certain epileptics underwent an operation whereby most of the connections between the two halves of the brain were severed. Each half of the brain controls the opposite half of the body; if you scratch yourself with your right hand, your left hemisphere is responsible. The split-brain patients now had "two brains," one for each half of the body. These "split-brain" patients could still do most things they did before the operation, even though the two halves of the brain became separate control centers, operating in parallel. (See Figure 4.1.)

One limitation in these patients was that they were hampered in understanding words spoken into the left ear, which were heard by the right brain. They had no trouble understanding words

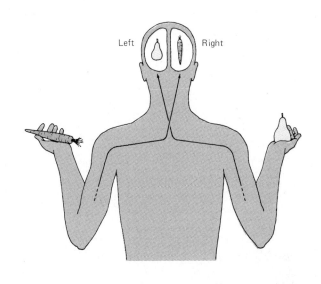

Figure 4.1 The split brain
Information from the right half of the body is registered in the left hemisphere, while the right hemisphere registers information from the left half.

spoken in the right ear and heard by the left brain. They also could talk only about things the left brain knew; if only the right brain knew it, they could not put it into words. There was no crossover; if their left hand felt an object, they could not say its name, although they could point to the correct word with their left hand (Gazzaniga, 1977).

Evidence from split-brain patients and aphasics, along with studies of normal people, has confirmed that the center for speech in most people is in the left half of the brain's cortex. One exception to this rule of brain organization is among some—but not all—left-handers, and certain right-handers (Levy, 1976).

Imagine that you and your cat understand each other. When you get her can of food from the cupboard, she rubs against your legs in appreciation and runs to her bowl. When she wants to go out, she comes over to you and meows, then walks to the door. When you want to pet her, you call her name and she comes to you, purring loudly.

But today you're furious with her. While you

were at class she knocked over a glass of water on your freshly typed term paper, turning it into something resembling a crumpled paper towel. Five hours of typing down the drain.

You call her name. She comes to you purring.

"You idiot!" you shout. She purrs more loudly.

"You utter imbecile!" The purr is almost a roar. Fuming, you stalk around the house. As you pass the cupboard she rubs against your legs, then runs to her bowl.

Frustrated, you stalk out the door. She quickly follows you out, thanking you with a loud "Meow." ■

Animal language

Many kinds of animals make sounds to each other that seem to mean something to others of their species. Crows caw, geese honk, hens cluck, cats meow, and dogs bark. But are they talking to each other? Do they have languages like humans? What kind of information can they communicate?

The Austrian Konrad Lorenz is a well-known ethologist, a student of animal behavior, who has observed the calls of many animals and birds. According to Lorenz, jackdaws say "zick, zick" in courtship, "kia" to tell others they are flying away, and "kiaw" to announce when they are flying back. They warn of a threatening cat with a rattling "krackrackrack."

The "language" of bees, on the other hand, is dance. When a bee has found a likely source of food, such as a patch of flowers, it returns to its hive and does a dance that directs other hive members to the food. Depending on the distance from the hive, the bee's dance will be in a round, sickle-shaped, or wriggly tail-wagging pattern. The vivacity with which the bee dances tells the quality of the food. The direction of the dance reveals the angle the food is from the sun, pinpointing the exact location.

Fiddler crabs wave their claws to signal to others of their species. There are forty different varieties of fiddler crab, each with its unique timing, movement, and posture, all exactly alike for all fiddler crabs of any given clan. Whatever the signal means, it never varies in form or meaning. While other animal species, like jackdaws or bees, have very different kinds of signals, like the fiddler crabs their communication system is confined to a frozen, inflexible form and meaning.

What's human about language?

If language is seen simply as a means to communicate, then many species besides man—in fact, probably all species—can be said to have a language. The question is, then, are animal and human language alike?

Unlike animals, whose languages consist of a ready-made stock of forms and meanings for messages, humans constantly create novel utterances. Human language is an open-ended system; there is no limit to possible variations. Once we know the rules of a language, we can generate any number of sentences. We can say things we never heard before, things that are unrehearsed but conform to language rules, and that will be understood by our listener (Chomsky, 1967). Human language is creative.

When an animal like a parrot learns to imitate human words, this does not mean the animal "speaks the language." The bird's utterances carry no meaning—it is as likely to say "hello" as "goodbye" when people are leaving. A parrot says what it hears, and no more. Simply producing the sounds of human language is not the same as speaking it.

While animal languages such as the jackdaws' and the bees' are highly effective for their immediate purpose, they are limited in ways that human speech is not. Animal languages are fixed-action patterns, behavior automatically released by the appropriate event. Your cat's language repertoire was too limited to make a fitting reply to your fit of anger. The jackdaw makes the same cry whether the threat is a cat or a dog; the bee has no way to add any thoughts of its own to its food dance.

Animals have a limited and unchanging set of calls or signals. They do not add new names, they cannot describe a novel situation, nor can they invent new expressions. Animal calls are very predictable. For all of these reasons, the answer to the question of whether animal and human languages are alike seems to be no (Brown, 1973).

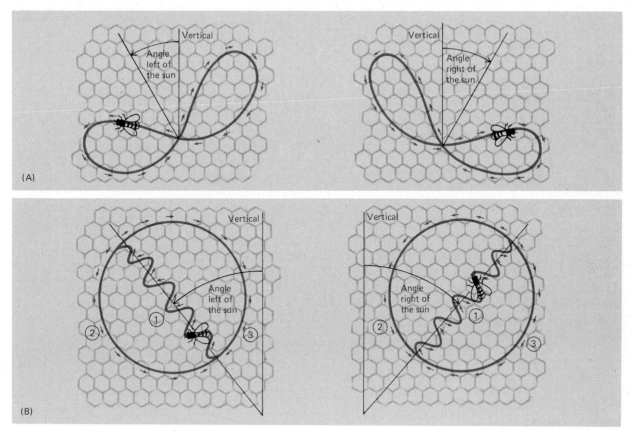

Figure 4.2 The language of bees

(A) The bee's sickle-shaped dance. The path traced in the dance signifies that there is a food source 20 to 60 feet from the hive. (B) The bee's tail-wagging dance. In this dance, the number of patterns completed each minute indicates the distance to the food source.

Can other primates learn human language?

In the late 1960s linguists like Noam Chomsky were of the opinion that "all normal humans acquire language, whereas acquisition of even its barest rudiments is quite beyond the capacities of an otherwise intelligent ape" (1968, p. 59). Soon after, however, a group of research teams working with chimpanzees began to report success in teaching the chimps human language. Since it is difficult for chimps to vocalize as humans do, the trainers taught the chimps various kinds of sign language.

A chimp named Washoe was raised by people using American Sign Language, also called Ameslan, a language system used by deaf people (Gardner and Gardner, 1969). In Ameslan, a specific hand position and movement is the same as a word of spoken English. By age three, Washoe could use thirty-four signs and would carry on dialogues with her trainers at the level of the simplest two-word sentences of a two-year-old child. But there were some problems. Washoe paid little attention to word order, so that she would sign "tickle you" as likely as "you tickle," when she asked to be tickled. Roger Brown (1973) has concluded that Washoe mastered the rudiments of language, but did not show any sense of the rules of syntax, which are vital to full mastery of language.

By now a handful of chimps have learned to "speak" using nonvocal systems. There is still controversy regarding the question of whether their communication is comparable to a child's learning to speak. For one, no chimp seems to be

THE NIM CHIMPSKY CONTROVERSY

■ Is language still the exclusive domain of humans? For several years psychologists have been presenting evidence that shows chimps and apes can learn an extensive vocabulary and, in some cases, produce sentences in special sign languages. But after a five-year research project, Herbert Terrace (1979), a psychologist at Columbia University, came to doubt such claims.

He set out to prove that chimps do more than imitate their human teachers—that they learn and use grammatical rules just as do humans. He worked with Nim Chimpsky (named for Noam Chomsky, the linguist who argued that language is unique to humans), a chimp who from the age of two weeks was surrounded by human "parents" and teachers.

Nim was raised like a child: he slept in a bed, dressed himself and was toilet trained by age 2½. These activities provided natural opportunities for him to learn a sign language. More than sixty volunteer teachers worked with Nim during the four years he lived in New York.

Nim learned 125 signs in forty-four months—for example, the signs for "angry" and "bite." He would sign these to people he was about to attack, along with an aggressive warning: his teeth bared and his hair standing up on end. After signing the

Nim Chimpsky and a trainer during one of Nim's exercises. The trainer points to different parts of the body and Nim imitates. (© Susan Kuklin 1977/Photo Researchers, Inc.)

words, Nim's angry expressions would disappear. It seemed Nim expressed this emotion through the symbol rather than the act.

Nim used the word "dirty" to express his need to go to the toilet; his teachers would interrupt whatever they were doing and take him to the bathroom. At times Nim signed "dirty" when he didn't want to cooperate with his teacher. Terrace feels that Nim learned to manipulate his teachers' behavior by using the word "dirty" to get out of situations he didn't like.

Over 20,000 of Nim's utterances that contained two or more words were recorded. There were several differences between Nim's speech and that of a child. As children grow older, the length of the phrases they create increases. After a child learns the phrase "eats breakfast" he expands that to "Daddy eats breakfast" and "When will Daddy eat breakfast?" Despite Nim's vocabulary increase, the average length of his utterances remained between 1.1 and 1.6 words.

Nim's "conversations" with his teachers bore only a superficial resemblance to a child's conversations with his or her parents. Only 12 percent of Nim's utterances were spontaneous; 88 percent were prompted by his teachers. Not only are children more spontaneous in their speech, they are also more creative. At three years of age, 42 percent of a child's utterances are expansions of things they've heard their parents say. Less than 10 percent of what Nim said followed this pattern.

Terrace finally gave up trying to teach Nim human language skills. He concluded that while the sequences of Nim's words looked like sentences, they actually were subtle imitations of his teachers' sentences. He could find no conclusive evidence of a primate's grammatical competence in his own, or any other researcher's, work.

When children learn to speak, they learn a grammar. Most sentences are not learned by rote. Rather, if a child learns the sentence "John hit Bill," the subject-verb-object order is comprehended and the

Washoe learns the sign for brush. (© Paul Fusco/ Magnum)

TABLE 4.3 **Some of Washoe's Utterances** (Washoe combined words to form what seem like primitive sentences)

Washoe sorry	Out open please hurry	Clothes yours
Baby down	You me in	You hat
Go in	Gimme flower	Roger tickle
Hug hurry	More fruit	You more drink
Open blanket	Baby mine	Comb black

child can then make new sentences such as "Bill hit John" or "Bill ate the apple."

Apes, for example, can tap out messages like "please machine give Lana apple" on a special keyboard. But it is difficult to say whether such utterances depend on knowledge of grammar. They could simply be imitations of what teachers had shown them, not genuine syntactic creations. Even pigeons, Terrace points out, can be taught to peck an array of keys in a particular sequence.

Washoe, a female chimp, combined many words without being trained to do so—or so her trainer, Roger Fouts, claimed. For example, when she saw a picture of a swan, she made the signs for "water bird." Fouts concluded she had made an elemen-

Koko signs "mad," referring to the mother cat in the story.

tary sentence, but Terrace feels this conclusion cannot be drawn unless one knows if Washoe frequently combined other adjectives and nouns, such as "blue crayon." Such combinations, if infrequent, Terrace contends, may be pure chance.

Other psychologists who have taught chimpanzees have been quick to respond to Terrace's critique of their efforts (Bazar, 1980). Fouts notes two major flaws in Terrace's approach. Nim had sixty teachers, while Fouts' own chimp, Washoe, had only six major people in her life—a much more stable learning environment. And Terrace used a carefully structured program to teach Nim language; Fouts pointed out that this is antithetical to the normal freewheeling social situations in which people— and other chimps—have learned to speak. Nim's failures could be due to Terrace's methods, rather than a lack of chimp language talent.

What's more, when the utterances of Koko, a gorilla, were analyzed using Terrace's criteria, only 11 percent was imitation, 36 percent expansion on what was said to her, and up to 45 percent spontaneous, as in the give-and-take of human talk (Bazar, 1980). Koko has also come up with some original, cogent terms of her own: for example, calling a mask an "eye hat."

But some of Terrace's criticisms have yet to be conclusively disproven. The most telling is the inability to show that these primates understand grammar or syntax, the key to true language learning. And until then, the controversy remains unresolved. ■

able to duplicate the human child's feat of creating and understanding sentences that conform to syntactic rules but which they have not been specifically taught. Other important questions remain unresolved. Do the chimps perform only if rewarded or only for those who taught them? Can they use their language skills in new situations or with new people? Will they teach it to their young? A convincing demonstration of the equivalence of chimp language skills to that of humans would be for one to put together the words it knew in a new way to comment on a novel event—if, one cloudy day, Washoe signed to a stranger, "I think it's going to rain, don't you?"

LANGUAGE ACQUISITION

The child's capacity for learning

The newborn infant seems to come into the world equipped with surprising sensory and cognitive talents. At one month, an infant can discriminate between subtly different sounds like *b* and *p* (Eimas *et al.*, 1970). Newborns have also been found to discriminate among odors, showing aversion to some and preference for others (Engen and Lipsitt, 1965). And infants only a few months old are interested enough in looking at pictures of human faces, geometric patterns, and cartoon figures that these can be used as reinforcement for the operant conditioning of the infant's sucking response (Siqueland and Delucia, 1969). All these studies suggest a genetic blueprint of capacities in the biological makeup of infants that will later help them with tasks such as learning language. The infant comes into the world already knowing how to learn.

Starting with these innate perceptual and cognitive skills, the child gradually develops her abilities. Her practice arena is her life: interacting with people and things in the world sharpens her senses, thought, and speech. Jean Piaget (1976) described four critical stages of development through which a child moves in developing cognitive abilities, beginning with dealing with the world physically and ending with dealing with it abstractly through language and symbols, such as

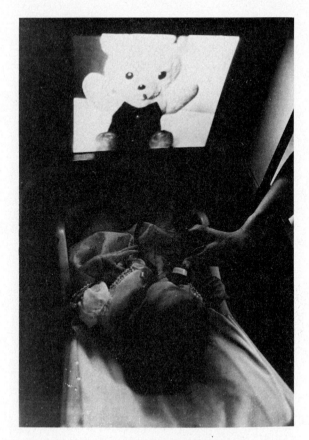

When the infant increases the rate of sucking on the nipple, a sensor is activated, causing a picture to be shown. The picture is the infant's reward for the operant response, increased sucking. (Courtesy, Dr. Lewis P. Lipsitt)

mathematics. Jerome Bruner calls Piaget's stages the "trouble theory": a child uses a simple approach in dealing with the demands of the environment until it no longer works and instead gets her into trouble. Then she moves on to the next stage of cognitive interpretation.

Imagine that your niece is fifteen months old. Every time she's come to visit for the last four months, she's carried on the same conversation with you. Madly hopping around your room, she points and squeals with wild enthusiasm. "Wassat? Wassat?" Your skis, your typewriter, your stereo, your wastebasket. Always the same "Wassat?" And you always give the same response, telling her the right names.

Today, though, she puts on a demonstration that amazes you. She hops through her same frantic routine, but this time she recites a different litany: "Your 'ki . . . your 'writer . . . your 'tereo . . . your ba'ket . . ."

Then she stops, turns to you with a broad, beaming smile, waiting for your praise. She's broken the code. ■

How children learn to speak

A child's mastery of language is one of the most impressive feats of human learning. For one thing, children learn language at an astounding rate; for another, they do so on the basis of often faulty information—the sometimes halting and ungrammatical speech of those around them (Chomsky, 1965). By age four, a child will master most of the rules that guide proper speech. Yet almost none of this learning will come as a direct lesson, such as being told to form a sentence by putting a verb together with a noun, or to form a plural by adding an *s* sound. The child learns language almost entirely on his own, in deliberate stages that reach the level of adult grammar bit by bit. Children in all parts of the world learn language in very similar stages, leading some linguists to think that the blueprint for language learning is built into the infant's brain.

Noam Chomsky (1957) has convincingly argued that in learning language a child does not simply memorize a large repertoire of sentences, but slowly masters a set of rules that show him how to speak and understand an immense variety of possible sentences. The young child seems to extract the rules for speaking his language from hearing what those around him say. No one teaches him these rules. In fact, many of the basic rules of a language are usually unknown even to its adult speakers, who nevertheless follow them to the letter despite their inability to say exactly what they are.

One theory of how children learn to speak suggests that they simply imitate what they hear adults say. But a careful observation of what children actually say as they learn to speak shows

TABLE 4.4 **UTTERANCES BY TWO-YEAR-OLDS, NOT LIKELY TO BE IMITATIONS**

My Cromer suitcase	You naughty are
Two foot	Why it can't turn off?
A bags	Put on it
A scissor	Cowboy did fighting me
A this truck	Put a gas in

that this can't be the case: where would a child hear a sentence like "Byebye boat"? While it is obvious that imitation is involved to some extent, it can't be the whole story. The major argument against the imitation theory is that children say things they've never heard before.

Another notion of how children learn to speak emphasizes the importance of expansions and corrections, where a grownup corrects a child's mistake or supplies the missing parts of the sentence (Snow and Ferguson, 1977). The child says "Me want milk," and you answer "*I* want milk." The problem here is that children have a way of ignoring or missing the point of the expansion (Bellugi, 1970). Their own sense of language rules seems to prevail over the corrections; for example, the child responds to your correcting reply "*I* want milk" with the question, "You want milk too?"

A third theory, the reinforcement theory, holds that parents reward a child for speaking correctly by saying things like "that's right" or "very good" when a child gets it right. In actuality, however, parents hardly ever say this sort of thing in response to correct grammar. When they do supply such reinforcement, it is typically in response to the truth of what the child has said, not the accuracy of the syntax (Brown and Hanlon, 1969). Parents do, however, alter the way they speak with children learning language, which may possibly make language rules easier to acquire. Most often, parents use a "nondirective" way to verify the accuracy of a child's language (Nelson, 1973). For example, if a toddler makes a correct identification, her mother might verify, "Yes, it *is* a doggie."

The prevailing notion of how children acquire language relies on none of these theories. Rather, the rate and sequence of language learning is seen to be a product of the child's stage of maturation, her mental readiness, and the complexity of what is to be learned (DeVilliers and DeVilliers, 1978). The critical gauge of language learning is the acquisition of meaning, as demonstrated by how the child actually uses language (Bates, 1976).

If a child masters a large vocabulary, but does not understand how to use these words in a meaningful way, then they do little good. For this reason, researchers have turned to studying *pragmatics,* the child's use of language in context (Bates, 1976). Using words meaningfully depends on matching their use to context, both in fitting the word to an appropriate syntax, and fitting the entire utterance to the social situation. The context of language learning, then, involves both the speaker and the listener, the social aspects of what's said and its specifics. Saying the word "banana" may not produce a banana for a two-year-old; but saying "banana" in the right context— with some in sight, and a grownup around—is more likely to.

One theory of language acquisition that is undergoing revision is that there is a "critical period" for a child to learn language (Lennenberg, 1967). The theory proposed that a child's maximum sensitivity to learning to talk is from the age of two until puberty. The basis for this proposal was that the speech areas in the brain were thought to take shape during this period. Later brain research, however, seems to show that the language area is fixed from birth, rather than emerging at around age two (Kinsbourne, 1975).

There seems to be a universal course to the earliest stages of language acquisition. Children begin to coo around three or four months. Their babbling peaks around nine months and then tapers off as they speak their first word—somewhere between twelve and eighteen months. Furthermore, puberty seems to mark the point at which learning a second language becomes more difficult; preadolescent children are much more able to learn to sound like a native speaker. The newer view of the theory of "critical periods" is that it may be true for the sounds of a language, but it does not seem to be true for other aspects, such as meaning (Devilliers and Devilliers, 1978).

Imagine that you're at your older sister's house, and your 15-month-old niece is hanging on to your sleeve, tugging insistently.

"Babababa goog ooz," she says. You stare back mystified.

"Babababa goog *ooz,*" she says. She repeats more emphatically, "Ooz, ooz." She must mean *something,* you think.

"OK dear, Mommy get you ooz," your sister says, as she pours a cup of juice. ■

Babble

An infant at about three or four months begins the first, essential step in learning to speak: she babbles. Most infants increase the rate of their babble to a peak between nine and twelve months, then slowly babble less and less between ten and fifteen months of age as they start to say their first clear words. The goos and bababas of the infant seem to serve several purposes. For one, babbling lets the infant play with her vocal apparatus, and so slowly begin to gain control of its movement. Although some infants will babble more when by themselves than when others are near, at a later stage babbling may serve to attract attention and even to communicate the infant's feelings (Nakazima, 1968). Babbling infants can give an uncannily "correct" intonation to their nonsense sounds; to many parents it seems to be an infant language that would make complete sense if only they had a guidebook.

While linguists are still uncertain about the main function of babble, it seems to mark the infant's earliest mastery of *phonemes,* the distinct speech sounds that make differences in meaning. Before babble can give way to recognizable words, the infant must learn to hear and say the same speech sounds that adults do, a difficult task. For one, she must learn to disregard the various clicks and coos mixed in with the English that adults speak to her; some evidence shows that infants can discriminate speech from nonspeech sounds very early, and that this ability may even be innate (DeVilliers and DeVilliers, 1978).

Many parents think that when their child speaks these first words she means much more than she

TABLE 4.5 **HOLOPHRASTIC SENTENCES**

allgone sock	beepbeep bang
hi Mommy	it ball
byebye boat	Katherine sock
allgone sticky	dirty sock
more wet	here pretty

is saying. Parents will often say, for instance, "Oh, 'ooz' is just her word for 'give me some juice.'" An old theory held that in using these single words the child actually meant a whole complex thought; a single word was thought to mean as much as an adult's whole sentence. For this reason the young child's single-word utterance came to be called a "holophrase," or one-word sentence. Later linguists have criticized this view on the grounds that at the stage where a child uses a holophrase, she does not yet comprehend language constructions as involved as a whole sentence. Others generally agree with the original theory, and argue that at this stage a child does mean to say more than the single word she utters, and is rapidly acquiring the mastery of language that will allow her to fit words together in a meaningful string. At the very least we can say that the child can use her single word together with gesture and tone to communicate her full meaning; a tug on the sleeve plus "ooz" tells you "Get me some juice."

First words

Late in the babbling period the infant starts to use certain sounds consistently to mean a given act, object, or situation. These consistent sounds are the infant's version of adult words. Your niece's word "ooz" was her word for "juice." These approximations of real words provide a link between babbling and the child's first adult words. They seem to show that the child understands that there is a correspondence between sound, meaning, and use.

A child most often speaks her first clear word between ten and thirteen months of age—around her first birthday, give or take a month or so. The child's first word is usually a combination of a con-

sonant and a vowel, sometimes in a repeated chain such as *pa* or *papa*. The most common consonant sounds in first words are stops (sounds made by interrupting the flow of air through the mouth) like *baba*, *up*, or *dada*, or nasals (sounds made through the nose) like *mama*.

The meaningful sounds of a language, its phonemes, are not identical with the letters of a language's alphabet; for example, although there are twenty-six letters in the alphabet, there are more than forty basic speech sounds in English. Every language has its own unique set of phonemes from which words are constructed. The infant learns to ignore variations in phonemes that don't matter in its native language, and to pay attention to those that do. The need to ignore phonemes that don't belong to one's native tongue can make it difficult in later life to learn languages where these once-ignored phonemes are important. Although there is large overlap in phonemes from language to language, the "non-English" clicks that an English-speaking adult makes to an infant, for example, may be a phoneme in certain African languages.

There are many subtle differences in the phonemes of various languages. In Japanese, for instance, there is a sound that approximates both the English *l* and *r*. Because the child raised in Japan learns no distinction between these sounds, when a Japanese-speaker learns English, he has great difficulty with a sentence like "Larry runs lyrically along." Conversely, English-speakers have great difficulty with phonemes strange to their native tongue, such as *chha* in Hindi, the guttural *cha* in Hebrew, and the Spanish *ñ*.

Imagine that its your niece again: It's a rainy day and you're enjoying coffee when she comes bounding in the door with her mother.

"Amuudy!" she announces.

"Amuudy?" you ask. "You mean it's all muddy outside?"

"Me amuudy." You blanch slightly as she points to her mud-covered shoes.

"You mean 'I'm all muddy,' dear," her mother corrects. ■

BABY TALK SPOKEN HERE

■ "Does Timmy like the iddy biddy kitty?" a mother asks her two-year-old in a singsong.

You recognize it at once: it's Baby Talk (BT), the distinctive way that adults talk to small children. Baby Talk has been studied in detail by linguists trying to understand its role in children's language acquisition (Snow and Ferguson, 1977). Its hallmarks are fairly obvious: a lyrical, high pitch of the voice, a rising tone of voice at the end of a sentence, using proper nouns in place of pronouns, exaggerated intonation, and—above all—simplicity.

But BT is not spoken only with babies: many of these same speech patterns are sometimes used with other special sorts of conversational partners, such as lovers, or with speakers who are felt to be unable to understand normal adult speech: foreigners, retarded people, pets, and even plants.

Baby Talk serves different purposes with each of these categories of conversational partners, according to Roger Brown (1977). In some cases it serves to communicate clearly and simply, for example, with foreigners, the retarded, or the deaf. But people would not use cute words ("iddy biddy") or a singsong with a foreigner, while they might with a pet or plant. With lovers, BT serves to express affection and capture attention. With babies, too, both functions come together; they are the object of affection, and respond best to simple speech. The two main characteristics of BT, then, are clarity and affectionateness.

Baby Talk has a special role in the world of language acquisition. Grownups use it frequently with two-year-olds, but by the time a child is about three or four, they talk normally with her or him. Indeed, one of the features of language that children master is Baby Talk; children as young as three will use it when talking to babies.

Adults adjust the way they speak to fit the level of comprehension of a child. Consider the names given common objects. For example, a dime is also a coin and money. "Dime" is its most specific name; "coin" can also mean a nickel or penny, while "money" can refer to a dollar bill as well. Anglin (1976) asked mothers to identify a series of pictures as they would for a young child and for an adult. What was "money" for a child was "dime" for an adult. The reasons for the difference seem to lie in interest and understanding: a two-year-old doesn't care if it's a dime, a quarter, or a dollar; they all taste terrible.

Shades of meaning

A child's first attempts at connected language are telegraphic; minor words and word endings are left out, but the message still gets across. The words the child includes are mainly the essential nouns and verbs necessary for bare meaning. Your niece's "Me amuudy," while ungrammatical, was an effective communication. The words included in telegraphic speech are those that have clear meanings and receive heavy emphasis in normal speech; they may be easier for the young child to hear, remember, and produce readily (Brown, 1973). The child's pattern of speech seems to be a consequence of both the nature of language and her own mental powers.

Once a child learns to say words that carry meaning, she is ready to learn that the differences in the ways things are said also make differences in meaning. The smallest unit of language that carries meaning is called a *morpheme;* the shades of meaning that are carried in words and phrases vary by differences in combinations of morphemes. A word can contain many morphemes, or may in itself be a morpheme. *Mud* is a morpheme, since it cannot be divided into smaller units that

In the same way, adults carefully cue their Baby Talk to fit what the child can understand; as he learns more about language, the BT spoken to him will change accordingly. Although at first glance BT might seem intended to teach children to learn to speak, that does not seem to be its purpose. The chief aim of BT is simply to communicate effectively with children too young to grasp many basics of speech. Its characteristics are tailored to that purpose: the singsong rhythm, for example, captures attention and the simple grammar ensures understanding.

But while BT is not meant to teach language skills, it may serve to help a child consolidate what she has learned. The order in which a child masters grammar, words, and inflections is determined by their complexity, not by the frequency with which the child hears them (Brown, 1973). She learns simple things first, and goes on to master others in the order of their complexity. As she masters new language skills, grownups will adjust their BT to her new level of mastery (Snow, 1977). In a sense, then, the youngster guides the grownup in how to talk Baby Talk—not the other way around. ■

still retain meaning. *Mud-dy* is two morphemes, mud + dy; the additional morpheme *dy* gives a new shade of meaning to *mud*.

As the child masters morphemes, the subtlety of meaning she can express expands enormously.

TABLE 4.6 **TELEGRAPHIC SPEECH**

Cat stand up table	Andrew want that
What that?	Cathy build house
He play little tune	No sit there

But before a child can use morphemes properly, she must be able to distinguish them in the speech she hears. Your niece could not tell that *all* and *muddy* were different morphemes, so she couldn't say exactly what she meant. Her telegraphic message "amuudy" was too abbreviated to make sense. But by adding the word "me" she got across the full meaning of her message.

Children begin to master morphemes around two years of age. They do not learn these fine details of language in random bits and pieces, but seem to master them in a relatively fixed order. Roger Brown (1973) and a group of researchers

Children master language in gradual stages. By two years old they can construct very simple sentences. (© Michael Weisbrot)

studied the way two- and three-year-olds learned a group of fourteen common morphemes, including *in* and *on*, the possessive *s* (as in "Mommy's brush"), the past tense and common verb forms such as the gerund ending *-ing*. In learning a morpheme, they found, a child uses it at first rather indiscriminately. But as she hears its proper use, the number of times she uses it correctly slowly increases. Finally the child will always use it correctly; once mastered, a morpheme is rarely used improperly.

Grammar

Just as the arrangement of morphemes within a word determines its meaning, the way words are combined within a sentence determines its meaning too. The rules whereby words are arranged into meaningful sentences are the *syntax* of a language. Syntax, along with the rules governing the combining of phonemes and morphemes, is part of the language's grammar. One part of learning a language is mastering its syntactical rules.

While a two-year-old uses simple sentences, as she grows more competent in speaking, simple noun-and-verb messages give way to more complex syntactical constructions with richer meanings. The two-year-old may ask for milk; her four-year-old brother will have expanded this to "a big glass of milk" or "some of that milk in the carton." With this added complexity of syntax, the child is able to express a richer variety of ideas. It also takes the burden of interpretation off the listener. The progression by which children master more complex rules of syntax is a gradual one. At two or three years of age, a child tells a story by strings of simple unjoined sentences, like "I lost my cat. It was named Tigger." Later a child joins two ideas together with a simple construction like "and": "I lost my cat and it was named Tigger." By five or six, a child is able to embed a clause within a sentence: "I lost Tigger, my cat" (Ingram, 1975).

Surface and deep structures

The rules that the child must master to achieve an adult competence, however, involve features more complex than those described thus far. To have a full adult mastery, he must develop a different kind of knowledge of grammar. The meaning of a sentence is not always apparent from the order of words alone. Chomsky (1965) described this aspect of language in terms of *surface structure*, which governs what is actually said, and *deep structure*, which defines the basic grammatical relations of

TABLE 4.7 **TWO-YEAR-OLDS LEARNING TO MASTER THE MEANING OF SENTENCES**

Peter (male, 2 years, 8 months)

Interviewer: Can you tell me what a dog is?
Peter: It goes woof, barks.
Interviewer: They bark. What else is a dog like?
Peter: Food.
Interviewer: Food?
Peter: And a dog likes water.
Interviewer: And a dog likes food, too.
Peter: Yeah.
Interviewer: What do they look like?
Peter: Big dogs.
Interviewer: Big? What else do they look like?
Peter: I saw a dog out in the schoolyard.
Interviewer: You saw a dog out in your schoolyard, right?
Peter: Yes. I did. It was big like Martha's dog. It was big like I and Martha.

the utterance, and therefore determines its meaning. The surface and deep structures of a given sentence are distinct; what is actually said can be very different from the deep structure of the sentence. *Grammatical transformations* are the rules that change the form of the sentence from what the speaker means to what is actually said; in other words, transformations relate deep structure to surface structure.

For example, take the sentences:

1. John is easy to please.
2. John is eager to please.

Although these sentences seem to have the same structure a child has to learn that in sentence (1), John is the *object* of "please," as in the paraphrase, "It is easy to please John." In sentence (2), John is the *subject* of "please," as in "John is eager to please someone." The understanding of sentences such as these is necessary for full competence in a language.

Imagine that a bachelor uncle has agreed to babysit for his four-year-old nephew for the weekend. Engrossed in a TV thriller, he has sent his nephew off to get ready for bed by him-

self. He hears a shrill call from the bathroom: "The sink's stopped up!"

"So what?" he calls back. The hero and his beautiful accomplice are running for their helicopter. A Land Rover with a machine gun and about fifty fascist troopers appears at the top of the hill.

"I can't brush my teeth!"

Machine gun bullets begin marching toward the frail aircraft. "Bail out the water with a glass."

"There's no glass in here."

The helicopter takes off. "Yes there is," yells the uncle. "I put your glass in there."

"There's no glass, Uncle Henry!" Absolute panic in the bathroom. "Uncle Henree-e-e . . .!"

In the living room bullets rake the fuselage. The helicopter finally soars into the blue, out of reach of bullets and bad guys. Ah.

Uncle Henry strolls into the bathroom where his nephew is in tears. "What's this, honey?" he inquires in a conciliatory voice, holding up a pink Tommee Tippee cup.

"That's plastic," sobs the nephew. ■

Meaning

Along with grammar, the child must master the meanings of words, relations between words, and sentences. All children seem to learn the same relational meanings at about the same age, no matter which language they are learning to speak. Some 70 percent of utterances by children around age two are accounted for by word relationships with eight basic meanings. These include possessor-possessed (e.g., "Daddy car" for "Daddy's car"), agent-action ("girl run"), and entity-attribute ("car blue"). At this stage a child has begun to express the relationships he has just begun to grasp between people and objects (Brown, 1973).

When adults name an object for a one- or two-year-old, they give it the name that makes sense at the child's level of behavior and understanding. The babysitting uncle didn't tell his young nephew that he had put a "receptacle for liquids" in the bathroom, though an adult would understand that this phrase could refer to the Tommee Tippee cup. One common error of young children is the overextension of just-learned words to inappropriate objects; another error is too limited an application, such as "That's plastic."

The rate at which young children acquire words is astounding; by the age of six, a child can use between 8,000 and 14,000 words (Carey, 1977). To know that many words he will have had to learn between five and eight words every day from age one. It seems that when a child first uses a new word, he most often doesn't know its full meaning. The more he uses and hears it, the better his grasp of its meaning: the nephew most likely acquired a better sense of the range of meanings for "glass" from his trauma in the bathroom.

LANGUAGE AND THOUGHT

Culture, language, and reality

Each language "slices" reality differently, according to the linguist Benjamin Whorf (1950). Whorf proposed a hypothesis of *linguistic relativity*, that language determines the differing views of reality held by people in various cultures. In English, for example, we divide words into nouns and verbs, distinguishing between things and events. But in the language of the Hopi Indians, events of short duration (e.g., spark, wave) are referred to by verbs, while those of long duration (e.g., storm, night) are designated by nouns. Still another Indian language, Nootka, has a single category of words that includes all things and events. An Eskimo has fourteen different words for kinds of snow, a yogi as many for kinds of meditation. The Whorfian theory proposes that people who speak different languages are led to think differently by virtue of their language's unique way of parceling and describing reality.

The anthropologist Edward Sapir also noted how various languages make very different subtle distinctions:

> When we observe an object of the type that we call a "stone" moving through space towards the earth, we involuntarily analyse the phenomenon into two concrete notions, that of a stone and that of an act of falling, and ... we declare that "the stone falls." We assume, naively enough, that this is about the only analysis that can be properly made. [However] ... the Russians may wonder why we consider it necessary to specify in every case whether a stone, or any

WHAT'S YOUR SIGN?

■ Do you know what are the four most common languages in America? After English, Spanish, and Italian, more than a half million people use American Sign Language (Ameslan, or ASL), making it the fourth most used language in America. Yet few people who are not ASL speakers realize how widespread it is, or know much about it.

Unlike finger spelling, where different hand shapes stand for the letters of the alphabet, sign language is not based on spoken language. Most signs are "iconic," meaning that their forms resemble in some way what they denote. In ASL, for example, the sign for "eggs" looks somewhat like a person breaking an egg (see Figure 4.3A).

Although ASL is composed of gestures, it is not the same as pantomime. Bellugi and Klima (1978) asked twelve people to convey in pantomime the word "egg." Most of them did something like the sequence depicted in Figure 4.3A(1)—picking up a small object, cracking it, opening it, throwing away two parts. The ASL sign for "egg," though, is the single hand shape shown in Figure 4.3A(2), which is similar to the hand's motion in breaking an egg into two parts.

Every community of deaf people seems to invent a sign language, and deaf parents teach a sign language to their children, whether or not the children can also speak (Schlesinger and Namir, 1978). While there have been attempts to systematize sign languages, by and large they spring up spontaneously and evolve over time, as does every other language.

Sign language is not international, although sign languages from different countries sometimes resemble one another far more than spoken languages. For example, when the Israeli and Arab sections of Jerusalem were reunited after twenty years in 1967, a group of deaf Arabs came to visit the Israeli center for the deaf. The two groups at

(A)

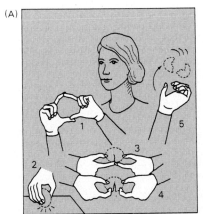

(1) Pantomime sequence for "egg"

(2) The ASL sign "egg"

(B)

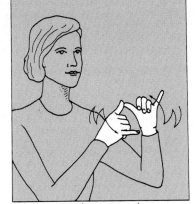

(1) "Measure"

(2) "Measuring" (derived form)

Figure 4.3 American Sign Language
(A) The ASL sign for "egg" (1) is different from the motions people make when trying to pantomime "egg" (2).
(B) The word "measure" (1) and a concept derived from it, "measuring" (2).

once found themselves able to sign with each other. Even so, American Sign Language is incomprehensible to a user of British Sign.

Although an interpreter can translate easily from spoken English to ASL, the two are not at all the same (Bellugi and Klima, 1978). For one, the principles of grammar that govern ASL are different from those that govern spoken English. For another, new words are added to ASL by compounding old ones in a fashion unrelated to the spoken

English forms: the sign for "thrill" combined with "inform" means "news" or "entertainment"; "wrong" and "happen" means "accidentally"; "hot" and "swirl" means "whirlpool."

Abstract meanings that derive from a concrete process (e.g., "to measure" and "the general activity of measuring") are indicated by movements that build from the sign for the basic meaning [see Figure 4.3B(1) and 4.3B(2)]. There is simply no equivalent principle in spoken English. ■

other object for that matter, is conceived in a definite or an indefinite manner, why the difference between "the stone" and "a stone" matters. "Stone falls" is good enough for Lenin, as it was good enough for Cicero. And if we find barbarous the neglect of the distinction as to definiteness, the Kwakiutl Indian of British Columbia may sympathize with us but wonder why we do not go a step further and indicate in some way whether the stone is visible or invisible to the speaker at the moment of speaking, and whether it is nearest to the speaker, the person addressed, or some third party. (1949, p. 157)

These differences between languages often make it difficult for translators to duplicate the sense of a concept from one language in the words of another. For example, the single word *hinke* in Norwegian requires a verb, an adverb, a prepositional phrase, and a noun to render its English equivalent: "to hop around on one foot."

Are thought and language the same?

Because language is central to thinking, an understanding of the nature of language and the way it works can explain much about our mental lives. Words stand for things, events, or relationships, for example, "dog," "hurricane," "upside down." They are part of *cognition,* the acquisition, organization, and use of knowledge. But language may not be essential to all cognition; words and thoughts are related, but not identical.

The distinction Chomsky makes between surface and deep structures seems to parallel the difference between thought and language. Thoughts organize ideas, language expresses them. In order to become clear about the precise distinction between thought and language, it is necessary to decide what each is, and then discover the relationship between them. However, oddly enough, there is no unanimous agreement among psychologists regarding what thinking is. An extreme, early behaviorist position held that thinking is simply a form of speech. On the other hand, the cognitive viewpoint is that there are qualities of thought that do not come from language.

The first spokesman for the behaviorist position was John Watson, who viewed thinking simply as subvocal speech. Thoughts, said Watson, are simply tiny movements of the larynx in the throat. This fits in with the classical conditioning view of language, which holds that after a spoken word is paired frequently enough with the object for which it stands, the word becomes a conditioned stimulus for our response to that object. When a person thinks about an object, said Watson, what he actually does is say the word silently to himself, making tiny, subvocal movements of the larynx. When you hear a person speak, you understand what he is saying by mimicking his words with your own vocal cords.

This theory has not stood up to tests. For example, one of its implications is that a person unable to control his larynx could not think. In an ingenious experiment, a volunteer was injected with curare, the South American Indian arrow poison that paralyzes all of a person's muscles. As the drug took effect, the volunteer gave answers to simple questions, signaling with his thumb until even that was impossible. The volunteer was so paralyzed that he could not even breathe without artificial respiration, let alone speak. But after the curare wore off, he reported that his mind had been "clear as a bell" all the while; he remembered everything said and done to him while paralyzed (Slobin, 1971). This demonstration is hard for behaviorists to explain, because it shows that thinking can go on in the absence of any sort of speech.

The major alternative to the behaviorist view is the cognitive position typified by Jerome Bruner's (1961) proposal that people know more than they are taught. A person has habitual ways of thinking that organize what he hears so that certain ideas are easier to grasp and remember than others. This suggests, for example, that a child is active in learning skills like language and in understanding how to make sense of the world. While the behaviorist stimulus-response-reinforcement sequences play a role in the child's development, including language acquisition, they matter less and less as the child grows older. What happens inside—the person's thoughts, plans, and schemata—determines more and more of what she or he does. This means that speaking, like other behavior, arises from thought, rather than the other way around.

Other psychologists who hold the cognitive view include the Swiss developmental psychologist Jean Piaget and L. S. Vygotsky, a Russian psychologist. Vygotsky (1962) sees speech and thought as quite separate: "The flow of thought," he writes, "is not accompanied by a simultaneous unfolding of speech. The two processes are not identical, and there is no rigid correspondence between the units of thought and speech." Vygotsky points out that this is obvious at those moments when we know what we are trying to say, yet can't put our thoughts into words. When you see yourself driving your friend's car, you conceive the thought as a whole, not broken into separate items. It is only when you say in words "I'd like to borrow your car" that you have to go from thought to the string of words that stand for the thought. "Thought," says Vygotsky, "has its own structure," which goes through transitions on its way to becoming spoken words.

Evidence that the influence of language on thought is limited to specific instances comes from tests done on deaf children. A group of seven- to ten-year-old deaf children and a comparable group of children with normal hearing were both given simple cognitive tests (Furth, 1961). The deaf children did as well as those with normal hearing when both groups had had the same experience with the skills tested, for example, picking out shapes that were the same from those that were different. But when a problem depended on language for its solution, the deaf children did not do as well, for example, in picking opposites, such as shortest and longest, from a set of shapes. Such tasks involve the concept of opposites, which is easily conceived in words. The results of the study suggest that language helps with problems such as those, but does not matter for others. More generally, the influence of language on thinking is limited, and language is certainly not essential to every kind of thought.

Thought does not have to be put into words at all; thinking can also be purely visual (Arnheim, 1969). When you picture a familiar scene in your mind—a favorite beach, or your route to school—you bring to mind an image that needs no words to make sense. This is a visual thought. The eighteenth-century philosopher George Berkeley went so far as to claim that thought cannot exist without an image of some kind. For Berkeley it was images, not words, that are essential to thought. If you were to think of yourself driving your father's car, Berkeley would say that this thought in your mind would consist of a single visual image, or several strung together. He believed, for example, that abstract ideas, such as beauty, are in our thoughts simply concrete images, such as of beautiful things (Heidbreder, 1961). Modern cognitive psychologists generally agree that thoughts can be images without words, or even sounds or physical feelings, but that images can mix with words in our thoughts, and that thinking can also consist of words without images.

Imagine that a small private airplane crashed, killing the pilot and injuring his son. The young man was rushed to a hospital where he was taken immediately to the emergency room and prepared for surgery. When everything was ready for the operation, the patient was wheeled in. But the surgeon, on seeing the patient, was too upset to operate, saying, "That's my son!"

How could this be?* ■

Language and problem solving

One of the most convincing justifications for the cognitive position that thought and spoken language can differ is the way in which people solve problems. It is the nature of a problem to present one with a novel situation never before encountered for which one has not yet learned a response. A problem demands creative thought, a novel response. Strangely, there is evidence that language can sometimes interfere with problem solving.

The solution to problems often comes about through new *cognitive organizations*, or perception of the patterns of things and events, and through new *response sets*, readiness to give a particular response in a given situation. Since language is itself a set of rules, the possibility arises that these rules may sometimes act as habitual

* The surgeon was the patient's mother.

sets on our thoughts, giving us a readiness to respond to certain problems in a helpful way, but hampering us in solving others.

When a person who is trying to solve a problem is anxious—as is often the case on difficult and important exams—she can fall prey to *functional fixedness,* the inability to break out of a fixed set. Take the example of a problem that requires seeing a familiar object in a new way, such as using a hammer as a bob for a pendulum. Functional fixedness would prevent a person from coming up with a resourceful solution. The name and idea

"hammer" stops a person from thinking of the object as a possible plumb bob, just as your set on the word "surgeon" can lead to the stereotyped idea that the person in question is a man.

Language can help or hinder learning. If information is to be useful, it must be couched in language that fits one's way of understanding. If it isn't, then the information is useless. A person just learning to ski will not be helped much by being told "shift to your uphill edges," but "lean into the hill" may be information that can be used (Bruner, 1966).

SUMMARY

Language. To know a language is to master its sounds, to know how to combine them into words, and to arrange the words into meaningful utterances. The range of sounds utilized and the combinations possible differ from language to language. Sound is not essential for language, but its advantages are many and compelling. The languages of even "primitive" peoples are rich and complex, and all languages are constantly changing. No language is "purer" than any other.

Human speech. Other species have systems of communication, but none seems to rival human speech. The highly developed human cerebral cortex enables us to make the ties between sight and sounds—to make the leap between seeing an object and using the word for it. The speech center is usually in the left half of the cortex.

Animals and language. Animals have "languages" of various kinds, but their communication systems, unlike human language, are confined to a frozen, inflexible form and meaning. They cannot create novel utterances. Experiments in teaching human sign language to chimps have resulted in some mastery of simple two-word sentences. But some researchers have concluded that chimps are unable to create or understand sentences that follow syntactical rules that have not been specifically taught to them.

Language acquisition. Children are born with surprising sensory and cognitive abilities. In building on these talents, they go through four critical stages of development, from dealing with the world physically to dealing with it abstractly through language and symbols, such as mathematics.

Children learn language quickly and for the most part without direct lessons or precise models. They usually master all the rules for proper speech by age four. Some linguists think that the blueprint for language learning is built into the infant's brain.

Current theories attribute the rate and sequence of language learning to the child's stage of maturation and mental readiness, and the complexity of what is to be learned. The acquisition of contextual meaning—as opposed to the accumulation of vocabulary—is a critical gauge for learning. The notion that there is a "critical period" for language learning has been narrowed to a critical period for mastering the sounds of a language.

The steps in learning language. The first, essential step in learning to speak is babbling, which seems to mark the infant's initial mastery of phonemes, the distinct speech sounds that make differences in meaning. Babbling begins at the age of three or four months.

Late in the babbling period, the child begins to

use sounds that approximate real words consistently and with meaning. These sounds, when combined with gesture and tone, communicate a meaning wider than the single word itself. They are the infant's version of adult words.

The child then gradually begins to acquire the rules of syntax that allow him to put his words together in meaningful combinations, and eventually in sentences.

The next step in language learning is the mastery of morphemes, the smallest units of language that carry differences in meaning. Around the age of two, children begin to learn these fine details, not randomly but in a relatively fixed order.

Finally, sometime between the ages of five and ten the child fully masters the capacity to understand the distinction between the surface structure and the deep structure of a sentence, and hence the sentence's meaning.

Language and thought. Linguists and anthropologists have pointed out that, since language is central to thinking, the nature of one's language may influence one's view of reality.

But behaviorists and cognitive psychologists disagree on the relationship between language and thought. Behaviorists have argued that thinking involves tiny movements of the larynx, that is, subvocal speech—a theory that has been largely discounted. Cognitive psychologists hold that the habitual ways that a person thinks help to organize information, and that thought and speech are quite separate.

Language is not essential to every kind of thought, and the influence of language on thinking is limited. In certain kinds of problem solving, in fact, there is evidence that language sets can have a negative impact on the ability to supply novel, creative solutions.

GLOSSARY

Aphasia A language disorder in which the intelligence is intact but a person is unable to speak properly.

Cognition The acquisition, organization, and use of knowledge.

Cognitive organization The perception of the patterns of things and events.

Deep structure The structure of an utterance that determines its basic grammatical relations, and hence its meaning.

Functional fixedness The inability to break out of a fixed set, hindering problem solving.

Grammatical transformations Rules that change the form of the sentence from what the speaker means to what is actually said.

Language A system of symbols that relates sounds or signs to meaning.

Linguistic relativity The hypothesis that language determines the differing views of reality held by people in different cultures.

Morpheme The smallest unit of language that carries meaning.

Phoneme Any distinct speech sound that makes a difference in meaning.

Pragmatics The study of the child's use of language in context.

Response set The readiness to give a particular response in a certain situation.

Surface structure The structure of a sentence that governs what is actually said.

Syntax The rules that govern the arrangement of words into a meaningful sentence.

HOW TO LEARN

APPLYING PSYCHOLOGY/TWO

GENERAL STRATEGY

Tip #1: Tailor your tactics ■ Tip #2: Get feedback ■ Tip #3: Turn failure into feedback ■ Tip #4: Stuck? come back later ■ Tip #5: Build your vocabulary

STUDYING: TACTICS

Tip #6: Find a place to study—and do nothing else there ■ Tip #7: Reward yourself ■ Tip #8: Stay alert, but not tense ■ Tip #9: SQ3R: survey, question, read, recite, review ■ Tip #10: Talk to yourself ■ Tip #11: Understand rather than memorize ■ Tip #12: Spread out your studying

MEMORY AIDS

Tip #13: Memorize in chunks ■ Tip #14: Overlearn ■ Tip #15: Mnemonics ■ Tip #16: Meaningful mnemonics make material more memorable

EXAMS

Tip #17: Be prepared ■ Tip #18: Effective cramming

All through school, teachers most likely have exhorted you to study, but probably no one has ever taught you how. Yet, given equal mental ability, those students who study most efficiently do the best. Psychological research on learning, memory, and thinking has yielded a range of techniques that can make any student a better learner—if he or she wants to be. The drive to do well is a critical factor in success, but such motivations are hard to teach. If you have the motivation to learn more efficiently, this application chapter offers you some practical tips on how you can do so.

The methods you use to study can matter far more than the number of hours you put in. Research indicates that the methods of learning and memory to be detailed here can greatly increase your basic academic skills (e.g., Bower, 1970; Furukawa and Cohen, 1979). The principles of learning and memory can be applied to any course.

GENERAL STRATEGY

Tip # 1: Tailor your tactics

Courses vary in content and the way they are taught; tailor your tactics accordingly. Chemistry courses require that you master laboratory skills as well as basic concepts, while history courses require remembering many detailed facts; English composition demands a very different set of skills than a math course. Apart from differences that stem from the nature of each topic, every professor will have a distinct style of teaching. Your tactics must fit the course and its teacher. If the instructor follows a textbook closely, concentrate on the text and tie your lecture notes and other reading to it. If the course uses many different books or if the instructor ranges far from the text, you'll need to take notes more thoroughly in lectures and to outline the reading carefully.

Tip # 2: Get feedback

Feedback is information about how you are doing. When you answer a question in class and the teacher says "That's right," you've gotten feedback. If she says "That's wrong," it's still feedback. Feedback about how well you've learned lets you know whether you've mastered a topic or still need to work on it. A quiz or test is feedback too, if you receive information about your performance—say in the form of a graded quiz.

Feedback works best when it follows soon after learning. Since a test is feedback on how well you've learned, testing yourself is an excellent source of feedback. When you study, give yourself a quick quiz on what you've just learned, or ask a friend to quiz you. Many textbooks—including this one—have sample questions in a study manual for students to use in self-quizzing. If you get an answer wrong, you need to study it again until you get it right. You should be able to understand *why* you got it wrong, so that you grasp the general principle behind it. Remember, you'll probably never be asked that exact question again, but you will be tested on questions like it.

A good drill for an exam is to get advance feedback by taking parts of the material you find difficult and testing yourself on them. Or get a friend or group of friends taking the same exam to fire questions back and forth.

Tip # 3: Turn failure into feedback

If you get a poor grade, how you react to it can hurt you or help you. If you take it as a punishment and react resentfully, or take it as a judgment and feel badly about yourself, you could end up in a state of helpless inactivity that will keep you from doing better.

One way to turn failure to your advantage is to use it as feedback. If you did poorly on a paper, see your instructor and find out what you might have done to make it better. If you failed a test, see your failure as a message that you need to study again whatever it was you failed to understand.

Tip # 4: Stuck? come back later

If you're at an impasse—say in writing a paper or solving a physics problem—put it aside for awhile and come back to it later. Take a walk, work on something else, have a cup of coffee. Sleeping on it may change your mental set so that you can tackle it again differently. While you let something sit, its solution seems to incubate. When you return to it, you're much more likely to have a new insight that will help solve your problem.

Tip # 5: Build your vocabulary

Each course has its own vocabulary, the keys to its basic concepts and rules. Behaviorists, for example, use an entirely different set of concepts than psychoanalysts. You'll need to learn both vocabularies—and more—to know psychology fully.

Learning can be frustrating.
(© Spencer Carter 1980/Woodfin Camp & Assoc.)

Develop the dictionary habit. Use glossaries, if your textbooks have them. Learn the exact, technical meaning of the key words for each field. A vague idea of what a word means is not good enough on an exam question that requires you to know the precise meaning. The better your specialized vocabulary on a topic, the better your understanding will be.

STUDYING: TACTICS

Tip #6: Find a place to study— and do nothing else there

Have you ever tried to read an assignment in a textbook, and found that you were constantly stopping to get a snack, read a magazine, talk to a friend, or watch a bit of television? The problem is a common one, and the solution is straightforward: control yourself. Teach yourself the habit of sticking with your work until it's done, letting nothing distract or interrupt you.

Condition your own study habits. It can be done easily if you're willing. For example, in one experiment a young woman was taught to use her desk as a signal to control her studying (Goldiamond, 1965). She was instructed to do schoolwork and only schoolwork while sitting at the desk; even letter writing was to be done in another place, as was daydreaming. During the first week, she spent only ten minutes at her desk, but by the end of the semester she was spending three hours a day there, all of it studying. In effect, what she had

done was to condition herself to study whenever she sat at her desk.

You can do the same. Pick a place where you will study—a desk in your room, a certain table in the library, or any place that is quiet and always available to you. Do as much of your studying as you can there—but nothing else. Whenever you find yourself daydreaming or doing anything but studying, get up and go somewhere else. When you're ready to study, come back to your place and do it there. Be firm with yourself about doing nothing else there but studying. It will help if you keep track of the amount of time you spend studying there; you can make a graph that charts the time you spend studying each day.

Tip #7: Reward yourself

If you sometimes find it just impossible to concentrate any longer on what you're studying, you may be trying to do too much all at once. Let your capacity for studying increase in stages.

Here's how this was done in a pilot study: On the first day, a student whose worst subject was physics was instructed to go to a particular room in the library in the free period immediately after his physics lecture and to study physics (Fox, 1962). He was told that as soon as he felt uncomfortable or began to daydream, he was to leave the room; before he left the room, however, he was to read one page of the text or to solve one easy problem. From the second day on, the counselor gradually increased the amount of work the student was to do after he decided to leave the

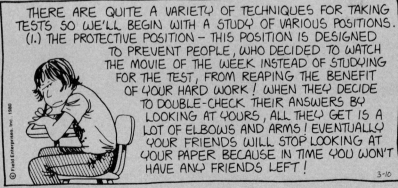

room. Once he reached a certain level, perhaps five pages of reading or three problems, the student was told that he could stay if he wanted to and do another unit of work of exactly the same size—five pages or three problems—and that he could repeat that unit again and again, provided he made an independent decision to continue working after completing each unit. Soon, he was spending all of his free period studying, and the counselor was ready to move on and use the same method with another subject. At the end of the pilot study, all the students trained in this way had improved their grades and many were so efficient that they completed their studying in free periods during the day and had evenings and weekends free.

To use the same method, notice every time you feel an impulse to stop studying and do something else you'd enjoy more, like talking to a friend. At that moment, decide to do a certain small amount more before you stop. Likewise, if you can't stand to study for another minute, then stop. But before you stop, do just a bit more. Slowly increase the amount of studying you do after deciding to stop, and before getting up to do something more enjoyable. In this way you reward yourself for studying more.

By breaking your work up into equal units—such as five pages of reading or three problems—and then deciding after each is finished if you want to try another, you increase and spread out the number of times you reinforce yourself for studying. Each time you finish a study unit, you're free to decide if studying is still enjoyable; if not, you're free to take a break then for something you enjoy more.

Tip #8: Stay alert, but not tense

As you know if you've ever dozed off during a lecture, a certain amount of arousal is needed for learning. But as you also know if you've ever been so worried about an exam that you couldn't even study, too much arousal interferes with learning. And if you've ever been so relaxed about a subject that you didn't even pay attention in class, you know that too little arousal can mean you don't learn or remember anything at all.

The connection between remembering and tension was demonstrated in a simple study in which students were assigned a memory task and then asked to grip a dynamometer, using different degrees of pressure (Courts, 1939). As a subject's grip tightened, memorization improved up to a certain optimal point; after that, it deteriorated. Similar results have been obtained when subjects learned motor skills under stress. The stress load was gradually increased, for example, by requiring subjects to pay attention to an increasing number of factors, and once again the learning of the motor skills improved up to a point and then diminished (Ellis, 1972). A graph of the results, with stress marked along the horizontal axis and learning along the vertical one, would produce an inverted U-shaped curve; learning ability rises, levels off, and then drops.

The trick is to be alert enough that you can pay close attention but relaxed enough that you're not worried or distracted. One way to help stay alert while you study is to deliberately set up conditions that are not too comfortable. Don't study curled up in an easy chair, or lying on a couch or bed; sit in a hard chair. From time to time take breaks that

TEST POSITION #2 (THE PRAYER POSITION) — DESPITE THE RULING BY THE SUPREME COURT BARRING PRAYER IN PUBLIC SCHOOLS, A LOT OF IT STILL GOES ON AROUND MID-TERMS AND FINALS! THIS POSITION CAN OFTEN BE PASSED OFF AS A CONTEMPLATIVE POSE WITH LITTLE RISK UNLESS YOU'RE THE TYPE WHO MOVES YOUR LIPS A LOT WHEN YOU PRAY. THE PRAYERS CAN RANGE FROM OUTRIGHT PLEAS FOR MERCY TO A RELIGIOUS VERSION OF 'LET'S MAKE A DEAL' IN WHICH ETERNAL GOOD BEHAVIOR IS BARTERED FOR THE IDENTITY OF THE TWENTY-THIRD PRESIDENT OF THE UNITED STATES!

© Field Enterprises, Inc., 1980   3-11

stir your metabolism: stretch, move around, take a walk.

Watch out for boredom. If one subject is beginning to bore you, switch to another, and come back to the first later. If a textbook is dull or too difficult, boredom is a particular danger. You can ward off boredom by finding ways to spice up the subject. For example, if a book is simply too abstract and overly general, try to discover some details on your own; the more you know about a topic, the more interesting it becomes. If a topic is presented in a boring way, find an alternate source that interests you more. For example, if *Les Misérables* does not inspire you as an introduction to advanced French, some sexy French magazines or cartoon books might appeal to you more.

If you are anxious much of the time, short-term therapy or counseling may be a help. Meditation has also been found to lower anxiety and strengthen alertness and concentration at the same time.

Tip #9: SQ3R: survey, question, read, recite, review

The SQ3R method can improve your comprehension when you study (Fox, 1962):

1. *Survey*—first skim the headings in a chapter to get a loose outline of what it covers.

2. *Question*—skim it again, posing questions to yourself as suggested by the headings.

3. *Read*—keeping those questions in mind, read the chapter without underlining or taking notes.

4. *Recite*—close the book and recite to yourself an outline of what you've just read.

5. *Review*—check your mental outline by re-reading the chapter, watching for errors or parts you've left out.

Tip #10: Talk to yourself

In normal studying, you learn more efficiently if you say the words to yourself, at least silently. This seems to code the words by their sound as well as visually. Such acoustic coding seems to hold the meaning of the words longer in short-term memory, making it more likely that they will be lodged in long-term memory (Conrad, 1972).

If you say the words to yourself as you read, you're also less likely to skip parts of sentences you might miss if you only scan visually. Speed-reading courses will advise you to read silently and stop saying words. But speed is not always best; comprehension is more important with textbooks. If you speed-read, save it for novels and pleasure reading.

Tip #11: Understand rather than memorize

In studying, it is far better to understand the material than to learn it by rote. By forming many associations on the subject you can build a network of related material. Then you can examine new information against the familiar context of the old.

Facts are not as important as principles, the rules by which you organize the facts. Sometimes facts are not even needed, once you know rules and principles. If you can conjugate one regular verb in French, for example, you can conjugate all similar regular verbs just by knowing the rules. Whenever possible, concentrate on learning not only facts, but also rules and principles, since they relate facts and add new connections to your network of meaningful associations. In assembling associations, you are mastering the basics of the subject.

When you study, think about what you read and tie it in to your own ideas. Ask questions or make up examples to illustrate points to yourself. Actively reading will place the ideas in a web of associations.

Tip #12: Spread out your studying

If you have to choose between cramming for four hours the night before a test to learn a new chapter, or spending one hour each night on it for four nights, you'd do better to take the four nights. Studying that is spread out is more efficient. A

TEST POSITION #3 (THE SEMI-PRONE POSITION) — THIS POSITION IS OFTEN FAVORED BY THOSE WHO FEEL A RELAXED APPROACH TO TEST TAKING IS THE BEST BET. IT ALSO HAS THE ADVANTAGE DURING A MATH TEST OF ALLOWING YOU TO COUNT ON YOUR FINGERS BY PRESSING THEM ONE AT A TIME ON THE BACK OF YOUR NECK, THUS KEEPING PEOPLE FROM REALIZING WHAT A DUMMY YOU ARE. HOWEVER, COUNTING ON YOUR FINGERS IN THIS MANNER SHOULD BE RESERVED FOR SIMPLE MATH PROBLEMS, SINCE ATTEMPTING SQUARE ROOTS CAN RESULT IN SEVERE WHIPLASH!

© Field Enterprises, Inc. 1980

3-/2

spread-out schedule of study allows more time for mental rehearsal of what you've learned, which improves your retention (Underwood and Schulz, 1961). It also reduces the negative effects of fatigue during long study sessions.

MEMORY AIDS

Tip #13: Memorize in chunks

Whether studying or memorizing, if the material is difficult you should chunk it. When you chunk, divide the material into roughly even lengths. To do this, look over the whole task and spot the parts that will need more time because they are important or harder. Make your chunks meaningful, short enough to manage with ease, and divided so that each ends with a good transition to the next.

If you want to be able to recall material for an exam, the best way to organize it is in chunks. About seven plus or minus two items can be held in immediate memory (Miller, 1956). If you are trying to memorize a list of the kings of England, organize the list into chunks of about seven names.

You can subjectively change what is treated as an item for learning by chunking—grouping several items into a batch and then remembering each batch as an item. For example, a telephone number can be learned as 6179683547, but it is easier if you chunk the number by breaking it into three items in the usual way: 617-968-3547. You could use the same principle with the list of the

kings of England, chunking them according to historical period, then remembering each list of kings in a period as a single item.

Tip #14: Overlearn

When you can recite something without an error, you have learned it. When you keep practicing after you have learned it, then you are overlearning. The more you overlearn, the better you will remember (Dolinsky, 1973).

If you have a part in a play, for example, overlearning is the best way to ensure you'll know your lines without a flaw. Overlearning is not a waste of time; in general, the amount you retain roughly parallels the amount you practice. If you practice far beyond the point of a single perfect recitation, you increase your chances of remembering perfectly.

Tip #15: Mnemonics

Suppose you had to learn a list of the names of the cranial nerves, or key dates in French history. This kind of list is hard to organize by groupings—it does not lend itself to being grouped by natural patterns (at least until you master the topic). Your best bet is memorization and drill.

Mnemonic devices are memory aids that peg material to be memorized with a coding rule. Mnemonic devices are a great help to memory. In one experiment, students asked to study several lists of forty items used forty campus locations as memory aids (Ross and Lawrence, 1968). Their immediate recall averaged thirty-eight of the forty items, and thirty-four of the forty were recalled one day later. Such results are staggeringly good.

The mnemonic they used was the "method of loci," where you first memorize a series of familiar locations, such as the rooms in your house or the houses along your street. Then you pair the items to be memorized with vivid images of the locations. The same set of locations can be used for any number of lists to be remembered.

A related technique is to embed the information to be remembered in a rhyme. A classical example is "In fourteen hundred ninety-two, Columbus sailed the ocean blue." Medical students know "On Old Olympus' Towering Top, A Fat Ancient German Vaults And Hops"—a reminder of the first letters of the cranial nerves (Olfactory, Optic, Oculomotor, Trochlear, Trigeminal, Abducent, Facial, Auditory, Glossopharyngeal, Vagus, Accessory, and Hypoglossal).

Another well-known mnemonic sentence translates into the value of the mathematical symbol pi: "How I wish I could recollect of circle round, the exact relation Archimedes unwound." The number of letters in each word corresponds to a number in the sequence of pi: 3.1415926535897.

In another mnemonic device, numbers are combined with rhyming words. In a study of mnemonics, subjects learned a series of words that rhymed with the numbers from one to ten: one-bun, two-shoe, three-tree, four-door, and so on (Bugelski, Kidd, and Segman, 1968). Then they learned a list of new words by associating vivid images of these words with images of the objects in the rhymes. "Pencil" might be imagined as a pencil stuck through a bun, "battleship" as a ship in a tree. A shopping list could be memorized this way, too.

Finally, the acronym is a tried and true mnemonic. It condenses the first letters of a series of words into a single word. For example, ROY G. BIV is an acronym for the colors of the visible spectrum: Red, Orange, Yellow, Green, Blue, Indigo, and Violet.

Tip # 16: Meaningful mnemonics make material more memorable

The drawback of mnemonics like acronyms or rhyming jingles is that they don't always register

the actual items in long-term memory. The medical student may remember the rhyme about the old German on Mt. Olympus long after she's forgotten the list of cranial nerves. A more effective mnemonic includes hints for remembering the items themselves (Bower, 1973). The cranial nerves would be better remembered by using key words that sound like their names: "At the oil factory (olfactory nerve), the optician (optic) looked for the occupant (oculomotor) of the truck (trochlear). . . . "

Associations strengthen memory. Mnemonics that connect words with a meaningful tie are more powerful. One way is to form a connection by imagining the two words interacting in some way. To remember the meaning of the Spanish word *calle*, for example, you might picture someone calling down a *road*. The word's meaning—road— would be recalled by the image suggested by its sound.

Another way to remember a list of words is by concocting a story around them. In one study, this method was found to improve recall about seven times more than simply trying to remember the word list (Bowers, 1973). This sort of method is useful, for example, when you have to remember the main exports of a given country, a list of vocabulary words in a foreign language, or definitions of basic concepts.

Finally, if you have to remember a series of numbers, such as your social security number, the populations of countries, or historical dates, a number-to-letter association works well. First you assign consonants to the numbers zero through nine. Zero might be B; one, C; two, D; three, F; and so on. Then the date 1066 would be CBJJ, which you could convert to the sound "cabbage," using the image of cabbage to recall it.

EXAMS

Tip # 17: Be prepared

On the day of a test, the extent to which you have prepared can make all the difference in how well you perform. When anxiety develops during a test, it tends to worsen performance by interfering with thinking (McKeachie, Pollie, and Speisman, 1953; Ellis, 1972). One common source of anxiety during tests is a feeling of helplessness and uncertainty. Able students with high anxiety are much more likely to fail than students of the same ability with low anxiety (Speilberger, 1966).

The best way to ward off this kind of anxiety is to prevent it by being prepared. To the extent that you have studied well for the exam, you can control the anxiety that stems from helplessness and uncertainty. Be thoroughly prepared—but don't stay up all night cramming for the exam. Lack of sleep also increases nervousness. Be sure to give yourself enough time the night before an exam to both study and sleep.

Tip # 18: Effective cramming

Suppose you have an exam tomorrow. These "night before" tactics may help you:

1. Study only the subject of the exam. If you study other subjects, you may have "negative transfer," as learning one subject interferes with learning others. Concentrate only on the subject you'll need to know the next day.

2. Review just before you go to sleep. Sleeping after learning results in better recall. Studying just before sleep seems to help especially with remembering details.

3. If you can, study in the room where the course lectures were given, or where the exam will be. Students often report that they can recall what a teacher said in the familiar lecture room better than anywhere else.

4. Read slowly and carefully—don't skim. Skimming during a review may keep the material in your short-term memory only for a few seconds. To maximize retention in long-term memory, focus on each key idea or basic definition, and talk to yourself about it. The more you focus on an item of information and the more associations you have for it, the more likely you'll be to recall it.

5. Read three times. The first time, read through a chapter to get a general idea of what it says. The second time, underline or highlight with a magic marker the points you consider to be important. The third time, go through and concentrate on the parts you've marked.

6. Look for exam questions. As you review a chapter, try to find ideas, concepts, definitions, and conclusions that look like they'd be the basis for good questions. Be sure to highlight all such points. (This tactic works best for objective questions; an essay exam requires that you understand the major ideas so that you can give them a critical analysis or review.)

PART THREE

PHYSIOLOGICAL AND PERCEPTUAL PROCESSES

5

BRAIN, BODY, AND BEHAVIOR

NEURONS

The action potential ■ Synaptic transmission ■ Neurotransmitters ■
Types of neurons ■ The endocrine system

BRAIN STRUCTURE

The cortex ■ The hemispheres ■ The limbic system ■ The brain stem

BRAIN FUNCTION

The visual system: how cells work together ■ Localization: tying brain location to
behavior ■ Functional units

THE CENTRAL AND PERIPHERAL NERVOUS SYSTEM

COMMON MYTHS

MANY PEOPLE BELIEVE THAT . . .	ACTUALLY . . .
Specific parts of the brain control complex mental tasks like memory and attention.	Such complex tasks are not performed by one single location in the brain, but depend on the coordination of many regions.
Damage to the brain is irreparable.	While brain cells, once damaged, cannot be replaced, other brain cells can sometimes take over their function. Undamaged brain cells sometimes can also grow new circuitry cells.
A headache is inside the brain.	The pain of a headache originates in the walls of blood vessels in the scalp or head, not in the brain itself.
The human brain loses vast amounts of cells as it ages.	There is no evidence that the brain of a healthy person loses damaging amounts of cells with aging.

Not only our pleasure, our joy and our
laughter, but also our sorrow, pain,
grief and tears arise from the brain,
and the brain alone. With it we think
and understand, see and hear, and we
discriminate between the ugly and the
beautiful, between what is pleasant
and what is unpleasant and between
good and evil.

HIPPOCRATES, FOURTH CENTURY B.C.

The whole of human psychology is based on the working of the nervous system and its extensions into the body—particularly the *brain,* the part of the nervous system enclosed in the skull. Yet for most of the last century, as psychology has been taking shape, there have been few if any research tools adequate to the task of tracing the links between the brain and behavior. Sigmund Freud, for example, held that we are captives of our physiology and that our inborn tendencies exert a profound effect on how we think and act—yet he himself abandoned the search for the specific ways our brain rules our mental life (Pribram and Gill, 1976).

For the first part of the century most psychologists, unable to specify how the brain affects behavior, treated the brain and nervous system as if they were in a "black box." The last decade or two has seen psychologists begin to fill in the details of the box by studying how the complexities of behavior stem from our physiological makeup and the workings of the brain (Russell, 1980). We are able to understand more about both the brain's anatomy (its structure and parts) and its physiology (how these parts function).

Although we can identify the main parts of the brain and their principal roles in awareness, psychologists and biologists who study the nervous system still don't know exactly how the parts of the brain work together to create consciousness. Researchers have barely begun to map the intricate workings of the brain and its role in behavior and consciousness; the possible interactions among the brain's cells and zones is so complex that most details of brain function remain a mystery.

Imagine that you're in bed enjoying the vague images and dreamy thoughts that float through your mind as you drift off to sleep. Suddenly your whole body goes into a spasm.

You wake up in a startled panic, confused. You're still in bed, yet you have the strong sense of having fallen. You settle back to sleep, puzzling over what could have happened.

■

NEURONS

The brain is a huge mass of cells that controls every aspect of your awareness and activity. An elaborate coordination of these cells allows them to act in an orderly fashion. This orderly working of brain cells in turn allows us to perform all the activities we take for granted: moving, thinking, sensing, sleeping—every act of living. When the cells don't coordinate their efforts, we notice things going awry: a fall, mental confusion, misperception, insomnia.

That feeling of falling that most people occasionally experience as they drift off to sleep is one such sign of miscoordination among cells. Called a "myoclonic jerk," it is a spasm of muscles throughout the body, one of many sorts of involuntary twitches due to mistiming of the cells that regulate muscle movement (Goleman and Engel, 1976). Although it indicates miscoordination of brain cells, it is perfectly normal; though people

rarely mention it, most can recall having had the sensations of a myoclonic jerk.

The human body contains trillions of cells. If each of them acted independently, we would be nothing more than a massive jumble of microorganisms. The body coordinates this mass of cells through a special type of cell, the *neuron*, the building block of the brain and nervous system (Stevens, 1979). Everything the nervous system does depends on the coordinated activity of neurons.

Although it is occasionally said that a person's brain loses tens of thousands of neurons each day, there is no evidence that this is the case. Poor circulation to the brain can kill vast numbers of neurons, but ordinary aging need not (Diamond, 1978).

Just like other cells in the body, each neuron has a cell membrane, a nucleus, and internal structures, but the size and shape of these features are distinctive in the neuron. What particularly sets a neuron apart from other cells is its unique projections, long protrusions that extend toward other neurons. One single, long projection, the *axon*, transmits messages to other neurons. Short, branched projections—the *dendrites*—receive messages from adjacent neurons (see Figure 5.1).

The action potential

By placing microscopic electrodes on each side of a neuron's cell membrane, researchers are able to get a closeup view of a neuron in action. They have discovered that the inside of the neuron is electrically negative relative to the outside. This electrical difference, called the *resting potential*, is minuscule—on the order of -60 to -90 millivolts. Other cells have similar electrical variation from inside to out, but the neuron is unusual because its membrane is electrically excitable. That is, if an electric current touches one point on its axon, the neuron's resting potential decreases. If the decrease is large enough, a sudden voltage change occurs in the membrane in what is called the *action potential*. This change in electrical charge travels along the neuron in a wave, or *impulse*, and it is the "language" in which a neuron passes information along its entire length—sometimes over several feet, as is the case for the neu-

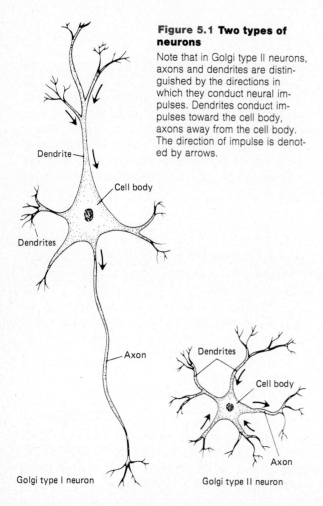

Figure 5.1 Two types of neurons

Note that in Golgi type II neurons, axons and dendrites are distinguished by the directions in which they conduct neural impulses. Dendrites conduct impulses toward the cell body, axons away from the cell body. The direction of impulse is denoted by arrows.

Dendrite

Cell body

Dendrites

Axon

Dendrites

Cell body

Axon

Golgi type I neuron

Golgi type II neuron

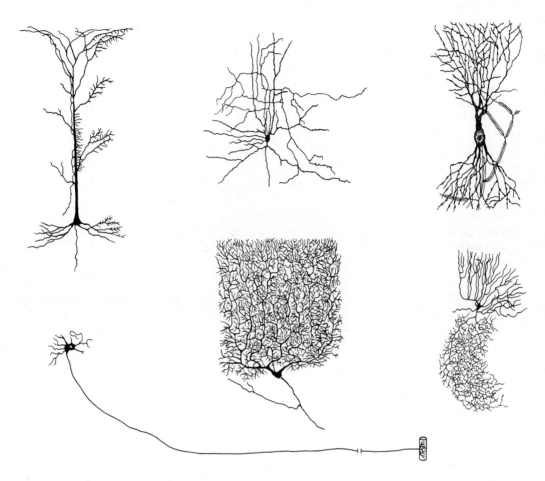

Figure 5.2 Types of neurons
There are many types of neurons. They differ in the lengths and branching of their dendrites.

rons that stretch from the fingertips all the way to the spinal cord (Thompson, 1967). (See Figure 5.2.)

The electric current of an impulse in one area of the membrane sets off a chain reaction through all other parts of the membrane. This shift in potential takes the form of a flow of ions, electrically charged atoms formed by the loss or gain of an electron (see Figure 5.3, p. 114). The impulse travels at speeds of about 200 miles an hour to the far ends of the cell. The impulse stays the same throughout this journey. When a cell changes from resting to action potential in this way, it is said to have "fired."

Having fired, the cell quickly returns its electri-

cal charge to its original level. Having reached this resting level, it is ready to fire again, always in the same pattern. A neuron's firing is all-or-none: only when the shift in electrical charge reaches a critical *threshold* level will there be an impulse.

Synaptic transmission

Neurons are continually in action, firing again and again. Each time a neuron fires, it passes a "message" to an adjacent neuron. Although the impulse travels only the length of the neuron itself, each firing triggers a flow of chemicals across a

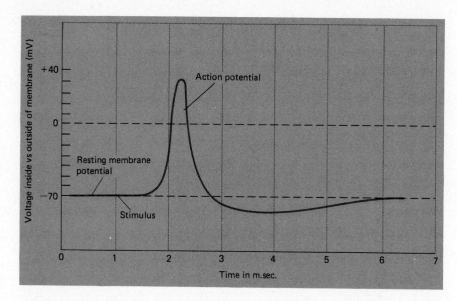

Figure 5.3 The action potential

A sudden voltage change in the membrane of a neuron causes a flow of ions throughout the cell that shifts the balance of electrons throughout the neuron.

synapse, the gap located at the junction of two neurons. Under the magnification of an electron microscope, a synapse is seen to be the gap between the membranes of two cells, with a synaptic cleft of about one fifty-thousandth of a millimeter between them. It is across this cleft that messages—in the form of spurts of brain chemicals—pass between cells when one of them fires.

Neurotransmitters

The membrane at the terminal of an axon contains tiny vesicles that release a chemical substance when an impulse reaches them. This substance, called a *neurotransmitter,* is the neuron's chemical messenger (Snyder, 1980*a*). When the neuron fires, it releases a neurotransmitter that spreads across the synaptic cleft to reach receptor sites on the adjacent neuron, usually on the dendrite (see Figure 5.4). The response of the dendrite is graded: the more neurotransmitter it receives, the greater the frequency at which it will fire.

Neurotransmitters can either *excite* the adjacent neuron, making it fire, or *inhibit* it, making it less likely to fire. When a neurotransmitter inhibits the adjacent neuron, it shifts that neuron's electric charge away from its firing threshold, making it need greater excitation in order to fire. A neurotransmitter causes firing when it creates

a shift in electric potential toward the firing threshold in the receiving neuron. It takes many packets of neurotransmitters to create a shift in potential great enough to reach the firing threshold.

When one cell excites another to fire, that cell in turn releases a neurotransmitter to a new adjacent cell, and that releases another, and so on, from neuron to neuron (Mandel, 1980). In this way neurons send a string of messages throughout the brain and the nerves in the body.

There are about 5 billion neurons, each with hundreds of excitatory and inhibitory synapses (Nauta and Feirtag, 1979). The complexity of possible transmission patterns between neurons is almost limitless. The sum total of all neurons firing at any given moment is what we mean by "brain activity." It controls every aspect of our mental life and behavior.

Types of Neurotransmitters. Neurotransmitters are the chemical messengers that regulate brain activity (Iversen, 1979). Each type of neurotransmitter fits with only certain neurons—those having receptors for that particular chemical substance—just as a key fits only a certain lock. Although researchers know that neurotransmitters control cell firing, they do not know with certainty how many different types of neurotransmitters there are in the nervous system. There may be as many as 200, each with a different chemical struc-

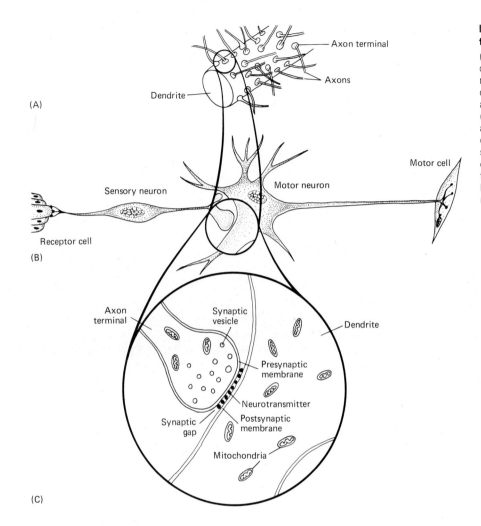

(A)

Dendrite

Axon terminal

Axons

Sensory neuron

Receptor cell

(B)

Motor neuron

Motor cell

Axon terminal

Synaptic vesicle

Dendrite

Presynaptic membrane

Neurotransmitter

Postsynaptic membrane

Synaptic gap

Mitochondria

(C)

Figure 5.4 Transmission at the synapse

(A) A distant view of a single dendrite encrusted with axon terminals. (B) A view of a single dendrite connecting, at the synapse, with a single axon terminal. (C) A magnified view of the synapse. Information is passed from one neuron to the next across the synaptic gap in the form of chemical neurotransmitters. The transmitter is produced in the cell body, stored in the vesicles, and released by the neural impulse.

ture and network of cells that will receive it (Snyder, 1980b). Even of the two dozen or so that have been positively identified, the exact nature and impact on neuronal activity remain largely unknown (Barchas *et al.*, 1978).

There are two kinds of neurotransmitters: excitatory and inhibitory. Acetylcholine, the first neurotransmitter identified, excites neurons to fire; gamma amino butyric acid (GABA), one of the more recently discovered neurotransmitters, inhibits their firing. Until the 1960s, neurotransmitters were thought to be confined to the brain and central nervous system. More recently, though, body chemicals such as certain amino acids (the building blocks of protein) were discovered to be neurotransmitters. For example, certain peptides

abundant in the intestines have been identified as regulating the neurons that relieve pain (Snyder, 1980a). The major neurotransmitters are listed and described in Table 5.1.

While most of the listed neurotransmitters are excitatory, just as important for balanced brain function are those chemicals that inhibit neurons. The inhibitory neurotransmitters serve as a brake on the system, countering the cell activity of the excitatory chemicals. Brain function is a delicate balance of excitation and inhibition of neurons, all regulated by the neurotransmitters.

Researchers hope to find in neurotransmitters clues to a wide range of behavior, from memory to schizophrenia. For example, amphetamine, a stimulant, triggers the release of dopamine. Excessive

TABLE 5.1 **THE MAJOR NEUROTRANSMITTERS**

Acetylcholine	Acts on neurons that control the voluntary muscles, as well as some nerves in involuntary muscles.
Norepinephrine	Regulates emergency responses, such as increased heart rate and blood pressure; may play a role in dreaming and moods.
Dopamine	Regulates movement; its destruction causes the rigidity and tremor of Parkinson's disease.
Serotonin	Found in very large neurons called the raphe nuclei; seems to regulate sleep and body temperature, and is related to the effects of psychedelic drugs.
Enkephalin	Acts on the same neurons that are the receptors for opiates, such as heroin and morphine; regulates pain, euphoria, breathing rate, dilation of pupils.
Substance P	Transmits pain messages from the skin to the brain.
GABA	Inhibits the firing of between 25 to 40 percent of the brain's neurons; may be the main inhibitory neurotransmitter.
Glutamic acid	May be the main excitatory neurotransmitter, causing neurons to fire. Connects major portions of the brain, and may regulate vision.
Histamine	Regulates emotions; outside the brain, plays a role in allergic reactions and secretion of stomach acid.

use of amphetamine can produce hallucinations and other symptoms of schizophrenia, leading researchers to suggest that an overactivity in the brain's dopamine system may underlie schizophrenia (Snyder, 1980a). In fact, many drugs that have been found to allay the symptoms of schizophrenia (e.g., chlorpromazine, the active ingredient in brand-name drugs like Thorazine) act by binding chemically with dopamine receptors, thus preventing the dopamine from activating those neurons.

Certain antidepressants (such as iproniazid, in Morsilid) inhibit the enzyme MAO, which ordinarily controls norepinephrine, dopamine, and serotonin. When this enzyme is blocked, the effects of these neurotransmitters become stronger. The result: depression lifts. The stimulant cocaine works in the same way as two commonly prescribed antidepressants (imprimine, known as Tofranil, and amitriptyline, or Elavil) in blocking the synapse

from collecting norepinephrine and serotonin. The effect seems to be a mild euphoria. Such findings suggest that depression may be the product of low levels of amines reaching the synapses that usually receive them, while mania—an excited, inappropriately happy "high" —may be due to too high levels of these same neurotransmitters.

Imagine that you're heating some water for coffee when the phone rings. It's a call you've been expecting, and you talk for several minutes. When you hang up, you go back to making coffee.

You've forgotten whether you turned the heat on under the water, and you automatically reach out to touch the pot to test if it's hot. Your finger jerks back, blistered, as you yell, "Ouch!" The water is boiling.

Which happens faster: your finger pulling away from the coffee, or your yell of pain? ■

Types of neurons

Your finger pulls away before you yell "Ouch." In this case, the reason your finger is faster than your tongue is that different types of neurons are involved in each of these acts. Your finger jerks through a reflex, which involves only two neurons that meet in the spinal cord, while your pained yell involves many more neurons that have to follow a complex path from your finger (along slower pain nerves) through a maze in your brain to the muscles that control your speech.

There are many kinds of neurons within the nervous system, each specialized for specific tasks (Schneider and Tarshis, 1980). *Afferent* neurons transmit sensory information to the brain. Some afferent neurons receive information directly from the environment, such as nerve endings in the skin. Others transmit the nerve impulse in a chain to the appropriate centers in the sensory cortex. *Efferent* neurons transmit information from the central nervous system to the periphery, such as the muscles.

Afferent and efferent neurons comprise only a small portion of the neurons in the body. All the

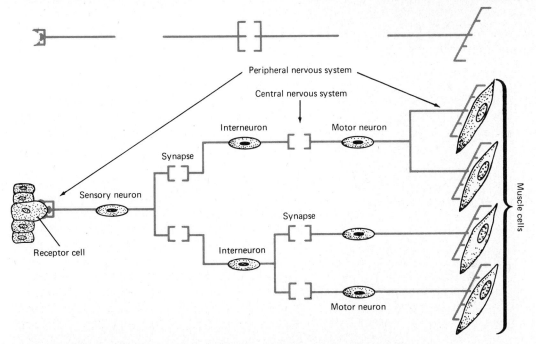

Figure 5.5 The relationship between afferent neurons, interneurons, and efferent neurons
Afferent neurons send information from the senses to the brain through interneurons. The brain in turn sends nervous impulses to muscles through interneurons and, finally, efferent neurons.

others are called interneurons; their task is simply to receive information from one neuron and pass it to another (see Figure 5.5). The simplest kind of behavior does not even involve interneurons: a simple reflex like the knee jerk requires only one afferent and one efferent neuron that meet in the spinal cord, without ever reaching the brain.

Even some of the higher-level reflexes that involve interneurons are automatic and involuntary. In fact we are usually not aware of a reflexive action until after it happens. When you touch a hot pot, you reflexively pull your hand away before the pain message has reached your cortex and elicited an "Ouch." The withdrawal reflex happens at the spinal cord level, so it occurs before your yell of pain.

The nonreflexive "Ouch" depends on interneurons that connect the spinal cord to many brain centers, and still others that connect those brain areas in turn. Interneurons then transmit your reaction to effectors in the muscles required for speech. It takes a fraction of a second for your finger to pull away, and a slightly longer fraction for the "Ouch!"

Imagine that you're in a hurry and traffic is very slow. As you approach a light, it turns yellow; you speed up and race through the intersection as the light turns red. Just made it.

But you notice a flashing red light in your rearview mirror: a police car right behind you. Your heart pounds and your body feels shaky and tense, ready for anything. You can hardly control your trembling as you go through the ritual of presenting your driver's license and registration. This time you're lucky—the officer lets you off with a warning.

As you drive away it seems to take forever for your body to calm down. ■

The endocrine system

Apart from the nervous system there is another coordinating system in the body. The circulatory system, best-known for transporting energy-rich nutrients and oxygen throughout the body, also carries *hormones,* chemicals that bring signals to

HOW DRUGS FOOL THE BRAIN

You're tired, but you've got to study. You drink some coffee and perk up.

You're feeling tense at the end of a hard day. You have a drink and start to relax.

You've had a wisdom tooth pulled and are in agony. A teaspoonful of codeine numbs your pain.

In each of these instances, the substance you took produced the effects you wanted by acting on your brain (Iversen, 1979). Caffeine, alcohol, codeine—and a host of other drugs—have chemical make-ups that resemble in some way the brain's own chemicals. This resemblance allows them to activate or inhibit specific aspects of brain function, such as getting the brain to perk you up, relax you, or numb your pain.

The 5 billion neurons in your brain are regulated by the neurotransmitters that pass between them. There are several dozen—perhaps hundreds—of different neurotransmitters. Each neurotransmitter has a unique molecular makeup that allows it to fit the receptors possessed by only one type of neuron. Some drugs mimic the makeup of a given neurotransmitter (Snyder, 1980*a*).

Alcohol, for example, shares its activity with mep-

robamate (marketed as Miltown) barbiturates, and benzodiazepines (such as the tranquilizer Valium). All these chemicals produce relaxation and sedation. Researchers reason that they also must share certain sites of action in the brain, since "cross-tolerance" exists among them. This means that the withdrawal symptoms of a barbiturate addict can be relieved by alcohol, Miltown, or Valium, and indicates that all these chemicals act on the same neurons.

While the molecules in each of these chemicals differ in many respects, they all share at least one factor that allows them to fit the same receptors. Presumably those receptors ordinarily receive a neurotransmitter—the brain's own tranquilizer. These chemicals mimic the action of that neurotransmitter, "fooling" the receptors into absorbing them instead of the natural substance.

Hallucinogenic drugs resemble neurotransmitters in structure. Mescaline, for example, is similar to norepinephrine and dopamine; both psylocibin and LSD resemble serotonin. Even caffeine and theophylline (a compound found in tea) seem to produce their mildly stimulating effect by interfering with an inhibitory neurotransmitter.

---

regulate the body's organs. The *endocrine glands* secrete hormones which the blood carries throughout the body to regulate activities such as sleep, emotion, and sex. While the brain and nervous system also regulate these activities, the two systems work differently.

Neurotransmitters act quickly and concisely in the brain. Hormones, by contrast, act in a slow and diffuse fashion on organs throughout the body. Hormones and neurotransmitters control different aspects of the same activity. While the neurotransmitters influence brain activity (where speed is essential), such as deciding to race through a yellow light, hormones influence slower

processes, such as your body's overall arousal under stress or fear. Thus hormones and neurotransmitters are both classified as "neuroregulators," chemicals that transmit messages between cells in every part of the body, including the brain (Barchas *et al.*, 1978). Hormones operate through the bloodstream, and neurotransmitters in the nerves and brain.

The shakiness you feel when the police stop you is regulated by two chemicals, adrenaline and noradrenaline (also called epinephrine and norepinephrine, respectively), which act as neurotransmitters in the brain cells and as hormones in the bloodstream. Noradrenaline's role in the circula-

The most detailed knowledge of how drugs fool the brain has been learned by studying opiates such as morphine and heroin. These drugs have been found to bind with neurons in the brain centers that regulate pain and euphoria, slow the breath, and dilate the eyes. These neurons have receptors that fit in a lock-and-key fashion with enkephalin, a neurotransmitter sometimes called "the brain's own morphine" (Snyder, 1980b). Drugs like morphine act as *agonists,* a term meaning "something that acts like." *Antagonist* is the term for a chemical that blocks the effects of another. Drugs like morphine and heroin mimic enkephalin, and so are agonists. Another drug, naloxone, blocks the activity of enkephalins at the receptors, and so is an antagonist.

Since one of the effects of enkephalin agonists like heroin is to slow breathing, a great danger of heroin overdoses is respiratory failure, resulting in a coma or death. Someone on the verge of death from a heroin overdose can be restored almost immediately by a small dose of naloxone. In the case of heroin, the opiate receptors absorb it as though it were enkephalin; naloxone, on the other hand, "plugs up" the opiate receptors, making them unavailable to either heroin or enkephalin. In either case, the drugs fool the brain. ■

pecially if you can't act by fighting or fleeing). Or, the same response can mobilize your body's abilities to act forcefully to cope with the emergency.

These hormones are secreted by two endocrine glands, the *adrenals,* located one above each kidney. The outer layer of the adrenals, the adrenal cortex, secretes chemicals called steroids that interact with ACTH, a hormone secreted by the pituitary gland, to regulate metabolism, that is, the rate at which the body converts food to energy. Under stress of any kind, the amount of these hormones in the body increases; the increase in the body's energy level that results is so important that without it even minor injuries could be fatal.

BRAIN STRUCTURE

Imagine that you've been up most of the night studying for your economics final. It's 2 A.M. and you're on your tenth cup of coffee when you notice a dull throb in your skull. It steadily intensifies to what feels like a pounding roar in your brain. It's the middle of the night and you've got a headache.

You rush to the bathroom and open the medicine cabinet. Somebody has used your last aspirin, thoughtfully leaving you the empty bottle. It feels as though your brain is about to explode.

In a panic, you search for anything that might help. Then, in the back of your closet, with odds and ends in the bottom of an overnight bag, you find another bottle of aspirin. You take two.

Fifteen minutes later you're on your eleventh cup of coffee, with only ten pages left to study. ■

tory system, for example, is to increase blood pressure. Adrenaline is formed from noradrenaline through a simple chemical reaction and is also carried in the bloodstream where, as a hormone, it regulates bodily responses such as fear and anger, and acts on many organs throughout the body.

Both of these neuroregulators produce what has been called the "fight-or-flight" response, where the body mobilizes itself to cope with an emergency. Any stress can trigger this response; the familiar signs include an increase in the force of the heart's pumping, and an increase in the body's energy, which can make you feel shaky (es-

While all of our experience is the product of the working of the brain, we do not directly experience the brain itself. The feeling that a headache is a "pain in the brain" is illusory; the pain of a headache comes from nerves in the walls of the blood vessels that lead into the head and brain, or the muscles of the forehead and neck. The brain has no nerve endings inside it, although all nerves send messages to the brain. For this reason, patients undergoing brain surgery need not receive a general anesthetic, for the surgeon's knife causes no pain as it slices through the brain.

To the anatomist the brain readily separates into large regions, each of which controls various aspects of behavior, such as moving and sensing. These large anatomical areas are built of an immense number of brain cells that work together to control all aspects of behavior.

The cortex

To the eye, the human brain resembles a massive, pinkish gray, three-pound walnut. The topmost layers of the brain, called the *cortex*, appear as a wrinkled wrapping around its surface. Like a walnut, the cortex is divided into two twin structures, the cerebral hemispheres, roughly identical halves to the left and right of a midline depression. It is the size and complexity of the cortex that separates the human brain from those of other mammals; the distinctly human intellectual abilities depend on it. An animal whose cortex is surgically removed can survive, but exhibits only stereo-typed, automatic responses (Rose, 1973); the richness of our memory as well as thought and creativity are attributable to cortical activity.

The brain evolved by adding new areas on top of older ones. The brain structures toward the bottom are shared by most species; those at the top are found only in higher animals. The cerebral cortex is unique to higher animals, like monkeys, chimpanzees, dolphins, and humans. There is no cortical tissue in fish and amphibians; mammals like rats and cats have a small, smooth cerebral cortex. Compared to that of other mammals, the human cortex is huge; if it were stretched out flat if would cover an area twenty feet square. The cortex can fit in the skull because it is compressed into folds, or fissures, which mark off the cortical lobes.

The wrinkles of the cortex are landmarks that appear in almost the same place in every human brain. Neuroanatomists use them to demarcate the cortex's major regions or lobes. The main regions of the cortex are the occipital lobe located at

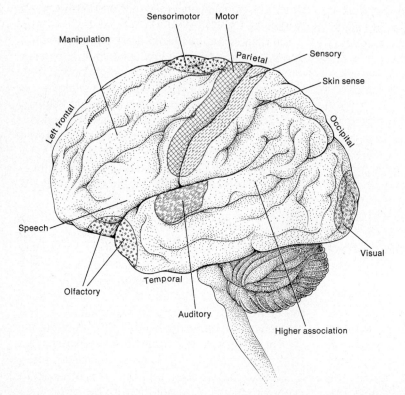

Figure 5.6 Motor and sensory areas
The motor and sensory functions are localized in adjacent areas of the human cortex.

the rear of the brain, the temporal lobe above the ear, the frontal lobe behind the forehead, and the parietal region at the top of the head (see Figure 5.6).

Motor cortex. In the 1860s Hughlings Jackson, a London neurologist, noticed that some of his epileptic patients had seizures that always began with fits in the same part of the body, such as a thumb, a toe, or a corner of the mouth. Since epileptic seizures are the result of irritation in the brain, Jackson was able to tie the region of injury that caused the seizures to the place in the body where the fits began. In doing so he discovered the *motor cortex*, a strip that runs across the top of the cortex down each side. The motor cortex on each hemisphere controls the muscles on the opposite side of the body. Many movements of the body's muscles begin with the activation of cells in the motor cortex (Evarts, 1979).

Sensory Cortex. Scattered toward the rear of the cortex are zones that receive messages from the senses. Directly behind the motor cortex is a second strip, the *sensory cortex*, that represents a map of the entire body, etched in the particular skin areas whose receptors end there. It is as if

the body were drawn out on the surface of the brain, but in a distorted fashion: the skin is mapped proportionately to the amount of receptors in each part. This "map" traces how messages from the skin reach the brain. The more sensitive the area, the larger its proportion on this body map. The "homunculus" in Figure 5.7 is a human figure drawn to these proportions. It has a huge face and hands—especially the lips and thumbs—and a tiny trunk, legs, and arms.

At the rear of the cortex is the visual area; it is here that cells will react if you look at something. On the sides of the hemispheres are the auditory zones, where cells respond when you hear sounds. At the bottom of the cortex on either side are the olfactory zones, where smells and tastes register.

Association areas. Although a great deal is known about the sensory and motor zones of the cortex, they represent only about one quarter of its area. The rest of the cortex neither registers sensory messages nor directs muscle movements. Called the *association areas*, these brain zones integrate the information gathered by the senses and coordinate the muscles. While the neurons in the sensory area are highly specialized and respond to certain types of stimuli only, cells in the

Figure 5.7 The sensory motor homunculus

(A) The human body reconstructed by the proportion of brain cells that monitor its parts. On the right side of the brain is a slice through the motor cortex; arranged around it are the parts of the body drawn in proportion to the amount of cortical space devoted to each. On the left side of the brain is a slice through the sensory cortex, with a similar representation of body features. (B) A "homunculus"—a human body drawn to represent the degree different parts of the skin's surface send their signals to the brain.

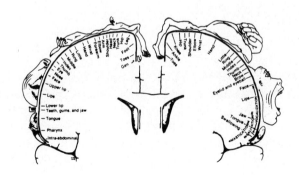

(A)

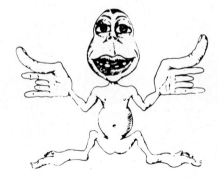

(B)

association areas may respond to many kinds of stimuli, such as light, sound, and touch. The association areas seem to bring together inputs from all the senses. Interestingly, the more advanced the animal on the evolutionary scale, the larger the percentage of brain that is association cortex; a monkey has more than a cat, and a human vastly more than a monkey. Quite possibly those mental abilities considered uniquely human reflect this quantitative increase in the association cortex (Kolb and Whishal, 1980).

Imagine that you're trying to remember how a song goes. You remember some of the lyrics, and start repeating them to yourself. As you do that, a snatch of melody floats through your mind. You hum it, until lyrics and melody click.Then you can sing the song.

Speaking, humming, and singing involve different sides of your brain. Can you guess which? ∎

The hemispheres

Assuming you're like most right-handers (lefties can vary), speaking the lyrics was controlled by the left side of your brain, humming the melody by your right, and singing by both together (Davidson and Schwartz, 1977). Some mental activities rely more on one half of the cortex than the other. When a person talks, for example, there is relatively more underlying cell activity in the left half than in the right. When this is the case, researchers categorize the task—in this case speech—as a left-hemisphere task. By the same token, humming would be a right-hemisphere task.

The cortex of the human brain is divided down the middle into two halves, or *hemispheres*. They are connected across the fissure between them by a bundle of nerve fibers called the *corpus callosum*, which transmits impulses between the hemispheres. Each hemisphere controls and monitors the opposite side of the body; the right half of the brain is tied to the body's left side, the left half to the right side (see Figure 5.8).

The two halves of the brain are specialized for different abilities. For example, neurologists have

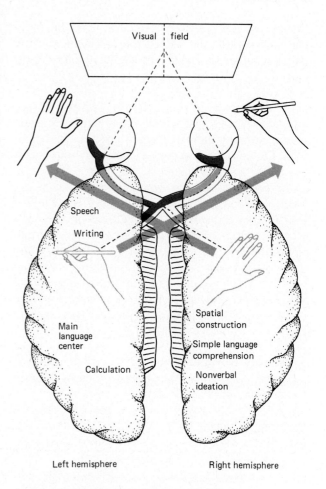

Figure 5.8 Hemispheric localization
The hemispheres each control different mental functions; severing the corpus callosum makes direct communication between them impossible: each hemisphere will not know about the tasks that the other hemisphere controls.

long known that in most right-handers, a zone on the left side of the brain, known as Broca's area, controls speech (in left-handers, brain organization can vary). To study what mental skills might be governed by one or the other hemisphere, researchers ask a person to perform various tasks while an electroencephalogram (EEG) measures the relative degree of activity in each hemisphere. If, for example, during a given task the left hemisphere becomes more active while the right becomes less, then that task is said to be a left hemisphere dominant task. This line of research suggests that many abilities are regulated by one or the other hemisphere (Andreassi, 1980).

The pattern of specialization of abilities in each hemisphere may vary with a number of factors, such as handedness. For most right-handers, the left hemisphere is more adept at analyzing things into their parts, while the right is better at integrating patterns and relations. The left brain is dominant during verbal tasks such as writing a letter or speaking the lyrics of a song. But the right brain dominates in tasks that entail pattern recognition, such as humming a tune. Other left-brain tasks include fine motor movements, such as fixing a watch, and mathematical and logical reasoning. The right hemisphere is more important in tasks like drawing a picture, recalling a familiar scene, and recognizing faces.

Each of these modes complements the other; the left hemisphere, for example, can logically analyze a problem, while the right might intuit the pattern that could solve it. Some educators, however, argue that our educational system puts too much emphasis on left-hemisphere skills, too little on the those of the right (Sperry, 1975).

Imagine that

you have six library books that will become overdue if you don't return them today. You've already been in trouble with the library twice this term for overdue books; you dread another run-in. Two minutes until it closes. Your heart is pounding madly as you race up the library steps.

You gasp as you reach the last step. The guard has just closed the door—you can see him locking it from inside through the glass. They can't do this to me! you think. But they have.

As you turn away in rage, you have the strange sensation that a tiny person is jumping up and down inside you, throwing a tantrum. ■

The limbic system

The anger you feel as the door is locked in your face is triggered by the *limbic system,* a series of brain structures that rise up from the brain's base toward the cortex at the top. The limbic system is "subcortical": it lies below the cortex. The limbic system not only plays a key role in negative feelings like fear and anger; it is also the source in the brain of feelings of pleasure, sexual desire, and satiation (MacLean, 1969). The limbic system regulates more basic processes as well, such as feelings of hunger, thirst, nausea, suffocation, choking, and the need to defecate or urinate.

The chain of structures that compose the limbic system include the hypothalamus, the septal area, amygdala, and hippocampus (see Figure 5.9). Since these structures are also found in the brains of reptiles and other primitive animals, they are sometimes termed the "old brain." Experiments with animals show that stimulation of one part of the limbic system can put an animal into a rage, while stimulating another part provokes play.

Because parts of the limbic system regulate anger and rage, some surgeons have advocated surgically severing these parts from the rest of the

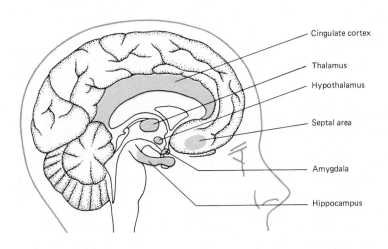

Cingulate cortex

Thalamus

Hypothalamus

Septal area

Amygdala

Hippocampus

Figure 5.9 The main structures of the limbic system

This series of interconnected areas of the brain regulate a broad range of behavior, particularly emotions.

ON HAVING TWO BRAINS

■ In the 1940s neurosurgeons began to treat some cases of severe epilepsy by cutting the corpus callosum, thus splitting the brain. While this procedure minimized or stopped seizures in many cases, it had another remarkable effect: it seemed to change little of the patient's behavior or personality otherwise.

Puzzled by the seeming lack of importance of the corpus callosum, Roger Sperry (1975) began to study the effects of severing it in cats and monkeys. He learned that when animals had the two halves of the brain severed surgically, each half had a life of its own—private sensations, learning, and memory—outside the awareness of the other.

In humans the effects of severing the connections between the halves of the cortex are not readily apparent; patients who have undergone the operation seem unchanged in casual encounters. Under closer testing, though, Sperry (1975) and Gazzaniga (1972) discovered that, as in the experimental animals, the halves of the brains were semi-independent.

One man, for example, exhibited the following symptoms of impaired communication between the halves. When he saw an object like a spoon in the left half of his visual field, he could not name it, though he could identify it by touch with his left hand from among several objects he could not see. In other words, his right brain could identify but not label the spoon. If his skin was tapped on the left side of his body, he could locate the point with his left hand, but not with his right; if touched on the right side, his right hand could locate the spot, but not his left hand. In short, his right and left hemispheres were not speaking to each other.

A woman who underwent the operation showed the same phenomenon when tested with a tachistoscope, a device that very briefly presents one picture to one side of the visual field and a different picture to the other side (Sperry, 1975). In effect, in a split-brain patient, the tachistoscope displays different pictures to each half of the brain. When the right side of the brain saw a picture of a naked woman, she began to giggle in embarrassment—but she could not tell the experimenter what it was she found so funny!

What seems to occur in split-brain patients is that the two halves of the brain operate in tandem,

brain in patients who are prone to violent fits of rage that are otherwise uncontrollable (Mark and Ervin, 1970). Critics of this procedure have attacked it as too severe and risky; because of the controversy surrounding it, psychosurgery is rare.

The brain stem

At the base of the brain is the *brain stem*, a thick cordlike structure from which the spinal column projects downward. The brain stem is the source of the *reticular formation*, a series of structures that connects upward, spreading like a net to all parts of the cortex, and downward to the spinal cord. Through its connections downward to the spinal cord, the reticular formation regulates tension in the muscles. Through its diffuse links upward to the cortex, it controls levels of arousal, or wakefulness.

While the reticular formation doesn't relay specific messages, it puts the cortex into a general state of arousal, preparing cortical areas to react to the sensory signals they receive. This general cortical alertness and preparedness was called by Pavlov the *orienting reflex*. When the reticular formation arouses the cortex, pupils dilate, muscle tone increases, and blood rushes to the brain. In this aroused state, the cortex is better able to re-each doing what it does best, but neither fully aware of the other. The remarkable fact is that in most cases their behavior does not give any hint that they are "two-brained."

What does this tell us about brain function in normal people? The split-brain work, suggests Galin (1976), may provide a model for such psychological conditions as repression. With the corpus callosum intact, the two hemispheres are, of course, in close contact. But the two halves of the brain may not always be well integrated, even in normal people. If that is so, then one half could harbor desires, memories, and feelings of which the other was unaware.

This possibility fits well with Freud's descriptions of the role of the "unconscious." He described the unconscious as a separate realm inaccessible to conscious recall. This realm of awareness had its own goals, logic, and ability to influence behavior outside the person's full awareness. The polarity he posited between the unconscious and the conscious parallels the split between the hemispheres, where the nonverbal, nondominant half of the brain operates semi-independently of the verbal, dominant hemisphere. ■

ceive sensory messages and act on them (Sokolov, 1963). In short, then, the reticular formation plays a pivotal role in alerting the cortex.

Imagine that you're renewing your driver's license, and you have to take an eye test. It's not easy. The bottom line looks blurry.

Is it a *D* or an *O*? Maybe a *U*? You can't tell at all, so you make a guess. "It's an *O*," you say.

You breathe a sigh of relief as the examiner says, "Fine, that's all now. You can pay the cashier." ■

BRAIN FUNCTION

The visual system: how cells work together

The brain is orchestrated by groups, nets, and chains of cells that work together for specific tasks. One of the most exacting studies of how brain cells coordinate their efforts examined how vision is transformed in the brain, tracing the process from the time light strikes the eye to the perception of a recognized image. In the early 1960s David Hubel and Thorsten Wiesel at Harvard Medical School studied the activation of cells in the visual system during this process.

In their experiments, Hubel and Wiesel placed tiny microelectrodes inside cells in the visual cortex of anesthetized cats. They then faced the cats toward a screen on which they beamed various patterns of light with a projector (Hubel, 1963). In this way, they recorded the responses of individual cells to the light patterns: whether a cell went "on" or "off" when the pattern was flashed. Any given cell they happened to measure, they knew, was only part of a huge number of visual cells; a stimulus that might excite it would undoubtedly inhibit others.

When they recorded how the cells responded to various light shapes, they found several distinct types of cells, including two they called "simple" and "complex." The simple cells responded to lines, such as slits, bars, or edges, when the lines were oriented in specific positions. Thus a simple cell might respond to a vertical bar, but not one slanted forty-five degrees to the left. The complex cells were not so discriminating, firing in response to lines in a greater range of positions, and—unlike the simple cells—also responding with sustained firing to moving lines.

From these results, Hubel and Wiesel (1979) concluded that the visual cortex contains many types of cell, each specialized to respond to a specific visual pattern. Any given pattern will make a specific set of cells active or turn them "on," while it makes another set inhibited, turns them "off." Each cell seems to have its specific duties, responding to a particular shape of stimulus in a particular orientation.

HOW THE BRAIN EVOLVED

■ The ancestry of the human brain can be traced back some 300 million years to the earliest stirrings of life on this planet, simple one-celled creatures (Rose, 1973). The evolutionary ascent of the nervous system is impressive; its most primitive forebear was a single cell, while in humans the brain and nervous system contain 5 billion cells that control several trillion cells throughout the body.

The most primitive forms of life, single-celled organisms such as the paramecium, exhibit only the most rudimentary forms of behavior. Whipping around in a drop of water, they sometimes bump into something, at which point they back up and seek a new path. They also seek out areas where there is food. And that's about it. A single-celled animal has nothing akin to a nervous system, although it "behaves."

The next rung on the evolutionary ladder—and the first step toward a nervous system—is seen in multicellular organisms. A typical one is the hydra, a tiny sea creature that attaches itself to a rock, waving its poisonous tentacles to catch small animals that wander by. This sort of complex behavior demands both that groups of cells be specialized for specific functions (grasping, poisoning, eating), and that they be able to communicate so as to coordinate their efforts. Here nerves—cells specialized to communicate and coordinate—are first found.

A semblance of a brain, though, doesn't appear until more sophisticated species evolve, for example, the flatworm. These little creatures have a fundamental improvement in the way their neurons are arranged: they are clustered in groups, with nerves leading out from the clusters. This marks the link in evolution between simple nets of nerves and their centralization into a brain.

Flatworms can learn, the key property of a full-fledged brain. For example, if touched with a rod, a flatworm will curl up to protect itself and cautiously uncurl after a while. But if it is touched repeatedly each time it uncurls, it will eventually stop curling up at the touch of the rod. The flatworm has habituated itself to the rod; it has learned that it is safe.

But the ability of a brain to learn seems to be roughly related to the proportion of brain cells to body cells. That proportion is quite low in simple species like flatworms. Larger brains, for structural reasons, required protective sheaths such as the skull and spinal cord, and vertebrates had such essential equipment. The most primitive vertebrate brains have three swellings; each connects with a major sense. The forebrain registers smell, the midbrain, vision, and the hindbrain, movement and balance. This is the basic design, for example, of a fish or bird brain (see Figure 5.10).

The human brain contains these structures and more. As species move up the evolutionary ladder, they don't discard brain structures, but add new ones and elaborate on old ones. For example, in the first land-based animals, reptiles and amphibians, the forebrain expanded much more than in fish, perhaps because the sense of smell is more important out of water than in.

Thus, for example, when you look at a black square on a white background, your eye is likely to fix on a certain point. At that moment, Hubel and Wiesel would predict, the image of the edge of the square nearest to that point would "turn on" a particular group of simple cells, for example, cells that respond to edges with light to the right and dark to the left, and oriented horizontally. Different cell types will be activated in a similar manner by the other three edges. Should your eye stray to another point, all these cell types would turn off, and yet other groups would turn

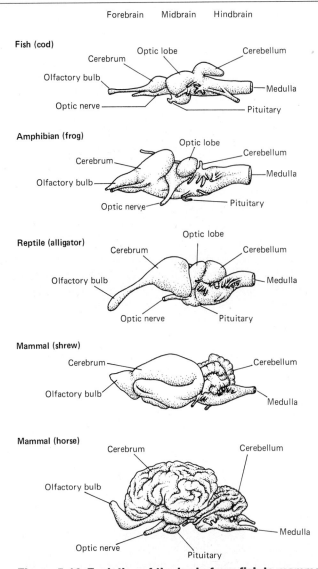

Forebrain   Midbrain   Hindbrain

Fish (cod)
Cerebrum
Optic lobe
Cerebellum
Olfactory bulb
Medulla
Optic nerve
Pituitary

Amphibian (frog)
Optic lobe
Cerebellum
Cerebrum
Medulla
Olfactory bulb
Optic nerve
Pituitary

Reptile (alligator)
Optic lobe
Cerebrum
Cerebellum
Olfactory bulb
Medulla
Optic nerve
Pituitary

Mammal (shrew)
Cerebrum
Cerebellum
Olfactory bulb
Medulla

Mammal (horse)
Cerebrum
Cerebellum
Olfactory bulb
Medulla
Optic nerve
Pituitary

Figure 5.10 Evolution of the brain from fish to mammal
Note the change in size of the mid- and forebrain.

Mammals alone developed a neocortex, primarily a zone where information about movement and senses is analyzed. The next leap in brain development is in the expansion of the association areas of the neocortex, the region where sensory information is coordinated with responses to it. Here complex learning can occur.

Primates—our branch of the mammal family—lived in trees, where they needed keen eyesight to survive. For this reason vision became the most relied-upon sense, and the visual cortex outpaced other senses in development.

But the outstanding feature of the human brain is its large cortex, the topmost layers of the brain. The tightly packed cerebral cortex allows the human brain to perform those functions we think of as distinctly human. The great number of cells in the cerebral cortex is made possible by its special twisted and convoluted surface. This way of packing cells allows a vast increase in the number the skull can hold. While there is no direct relationship between the size of the cortex of a species and its intellectual capacities, humans have among the highest ratios of cortical cells to body weight of any species.

Where do we go from here? Nowhere very soon: today's humans have the same skull capacity—and presumably the same sort of brain—found in the earliest *Homo sapiens* fossils, which date back several hundred thousand years. But that is a tiny span of time given the millions of years it has taken the brain to evolve. The brain is probably still evolving, but at too slow a pace for us to detect. ■

on, depending on exactly where your gaze rested at a given moment, whether it was moving or stationary, and so on. The total effect of the pattern of cells turned on and off would yield the information that you were looking at a square—or, in the case of the eye test, an *O*.

Localization: tying brain location to behavior

Since different kinds of specialized brain cells work together on a single task, neuroanatomists have tried to map the main groupings of such cell units to determine where in the brain various mental activities occur. *Localization theory* holds that specific parts of the brain control particular mental activities, such as sensing or movement. The strongest evidence for localization theory has come from people who have suffered brain damage, and from studies in which laboratory animals have had parts of their brains surgically removed. From such data, neuroanatomists have been able to map the links between the brain's major zones and the aspects of behavior these zones control.

Localization theory would seem to be the best explanation for why stroke victims or others with brain damage lose specific functions associated with the site of their brain problem. But there are exceptions to the rule; some people with severe brain damage sometimes surprise neurologists by completely recovering functions thought lost forever. Since a brain cell, once destroyed, does not regenerate, such cases have long puzzled neurologists.

One theory of brain function proposed by E. Roy John (1976) reconciles these facts. Called *statistical configuration theory*, it posits that brain functions are distributed throughout several regions of the brain, but some regions contribute more than others to any given function. John's theory is based on research whereby tiny microelectrodes were placed in single cells of a cat's brain. The microelectrode could record activity from a single cell, then move on through the cat's brain to record activity from another cell. In this way, a record was made of the firing rate of neurons in many regions of the cat's brain.

Readings from various cells were made while the cat performed the same tasks—pressing a lever to get milk when it saw lights flashing at one flash per second, or jumping a hurdle to avoid a shock if the light flashed five times per second. The microelectrodes revealed that cells in different parts of the brain responded to the same light flashes with identical firing rhythms. For example, when the cat saw lights flashing once per second, the cells fired at the same rate—once per second.

John concluded that it is the rhythm of the cells firing, not where in the brain the cells are located, that indicates that they are involved in a particular mental operation. Any given cell can contribute to the work of other cells spread throughout the brain by firing at the identical rhythm. In this way, cells cooperate to perform mental processes; it is the *rhythm* of their average firing rate that controls the mental function.

Since cells also fire spontaneously, seemingly at random, it is the *average* firing rate of innumerable cells that indicates that they are involved in a unified task. The statistical average does not predict the firing rate of a particular cell, only of the general trend for a group of cells. Thus when we move a muscle, the motor system has the most cells firing at the specific rhythm connected with the movement and the least firing at random. But at the same time the visual system will also have many cells firing at the same rate, although proportionately more will fire at random.

John's research shows that brain regions do not make an all-or-nothing contribution to mental operations. In fact, each brain region makes some contribution to almost every mental operation, such as movement or vision, but some are more involved than others. That is, more brain cells in some areas participate in a given operation than do cells in the other regions. Those regions that have the highest concentration of cells involved in a given activity are the ones that localization theorists point to when they say that a given activity is governed by a specific brain area, for example, that the visual cortex regulates vision (John, 1980).

Imagine that you hear it faintly at first, then persistently louder. An annoying buzz, like a wasp. You look around puzzled. You're lying in a strange, dimly lit room. You have no idea where you are. And there's that bothersome buzz.

Then it comes back in a flash. The noise is a travel alarm you set. You're at your sister's place for a visit, felt jet-lagged from your flight, took a nap. The strange room is her bedroom; you recognize it now. You reach for the alarm, turn it off. Oh yes, you think to yourself. Now I remember. ■

Functional units

There is no single part of the brain that controls actions as seemingly simple as waking from a nap, identifying the buzz of an alarm, reaching out to turn it off, or recognizing where you are. Such behavior depends on the orchestration of activity throughout the brain.

The most detailed understanding of the links between the zones of the brain and complex behavior has come from the work of a Russian neuropsychologist, A. R. Luria (1966). Luria treated hundreds of Russian soldiers who had suffered injuries to the brain during World War II, and so was able to map the relationship between the location of brain damage and the loss of mental faculties. Luria saw that the then-prevailing notions of how the brain works were too naive when they related a given locale in the brain to a complex faculty of mind, such as perceiving an object or logical reasoning. Instead, said Luria, the higher mental faculties were based on the complex interplay of cells from many parts of the brain.

Luria, on the basis of his research with brain injuries, was able to map *functional units* in the brain, each of which integrates a mosaic of cell activity into a single working whole. Thus a complex mental activity like object perception does not occur at one circumscribed point on the brain. Instead, it depends on the coordinated excitation and inhibition of cells throughout the visual system and association areas.

Luria (1970) proposed that the human brain has three major units, each of which includes scattered brain structures that work together to perform a specific function. The first unit regulates the energy level of the cortex. The main parts of this unit are at the base of the brain, in the upper and lower parts of the brain stem, connecting to the cortex via the reticular formation. This unit regulates alertness, from keen wakefulness to deep sleep. An injury to some part of it can, for example, put a person in a coma, a prolonged sleep.

The second unit, in the rear of the cortex, analyzes, codes, and stores information. The structures within this unit each have highly specific assignments. Some, for example, specialize in visual stimuli, others in auditory, others in bodily sensations. Data from different senses also overlap; here, for example, what a person sees and hears is brought together into a coherent whole. Injury to this unit can lead to such specific problems as visual disorientation in space, or the inability to tell where a sound is coming from.

The third unit, based primarily in the frontal lobes, programs, regulates, and verifies all conscious activity. It is here that plans for behavior—such as a body movement—are made. This unit participates in every complex behavior, and it is the seat of intentions; yet an injury to the frontal lobes will not interfere with processes such as sensation, movement, perception, or speech.

While the major function of each of these units can be described separately, Luria (1973) points out that any given psychological process relies on the combined working of all three. Seeing an object, for example, requires first that there be the necessary cortical alertness, a function of the first unit. The second unit analyzes the light patterns the eye hits upon, while the third controls the slight searching movements of the eyeball needed to pick out the essential cues about the object.

When the alarm awakened you, it was the first functional unit—particularly the reticular formation—that aroused your brain to the level of alertness at which it could make sense of what it was hearing and respond accordingly. It was the second functional unit that recognized the buzz as an alarm, and the room as your sister's. And the third unit organized and directed your reaching out to turn the alarm off.

Imagine that you're at an interview for a job, one you want very badly. It's almost over, and you think you've made a good impression. But as you've talked, you've grown aware of your pounding heartbeat and—what's worse—beads of sweat forming on your forehead.

The interviewer doesn't seem to notice the sweat on your brow. But when she turns away to get a brochure for you, you discreetly wipe your forehead with your sleeve.

Relieved, you continue the interview, giving your best imitation of someone who is calm, composed, and competent. ■

THE CENTRAL AND PERIPHERAL NERVOUS SYSTEM

When the stress of a situation like an interview makes you sweat, your brain is sending messages to the farther reaches of your nervous system. The brain and the spinal cord, which extends down the spinal column directly below the brain stem, compose the *central nervous system;* all the nerve fibers leading to and from the rest of the body are called the *peripheral nervous system.* The central nervous system relies on the peripheral nervous system to sense and act on the world (Andreassi, 1980).

The spinal cord is a cylinder of nerve tissue that extends from the brain stem about two-thirds of the way down the back. It conducts messages to and from the brain, but it also acts as a sort of subbrain, taking in messages from nerves throughout the body and sending out responses to them, without the brain becoming involved. These responses are *reflexes*, or unlearned, automatic action patterns, such as the knee jerk in response to a tap on the tendon below the knee, or blinking in response to a puff of air.

The network of nerves in the peripheral nervous system connects the brain and spinal cord to all other parts of the body. It has two major jobs: through it the sensory (or afferent) system brings information from the outside world or from inside the body to the central nervous system, while the motor (or efferent) system carries messages from the central nervous system to muscles and glands.

The motor system is also divided into two subsystems. The *somatic system* carries messages to the skeletal muscles that help us perform voluntary actions like throwing a ball. The *autonomic nervous system* directs the so-called involuntary muscles of the body—those which, like the heart or the muscles in the walls of the blood vessels, seem to be beyond our conscious control. Both the ancient practices of body control among yogis and the modern advances of biofeedback have shown that these autonomic functions can, with training, be influenced by conscious control (Miller, 1969).

The autonomic nervous system also breaks down into two parts. The *sympathetic* system mobilizes the body; the *parasympathetic* system puts it at rest. Both systems operate in an intricate balance, each having an opposite effect on organs, glands, and muscles. Some are controlled only by one system—the sweat glands, for example, are entirely under sympathetic control. Most, though, are under dual regulation. The sympathetic system, for example, speeds the heart rate, dilates the pupils, and inhibits digestion; the parasympathetic system slows the heart, constricts the pupils, and stimulates digestion (Noback and Demarest, 1972). The sympathetic system swings into action under stress and in emergencies when the body's energies must be channeled into quick responses. The sweat on your brow during an important interview, then, tells you your sympathetic nervous system is on the job.

SUMMARY

Although the main parts of the brain and their functions have been identified, researchers have barely begun to map its more intricate workings, and many details remain a mystery.

Neurons. The brain and nervous system depend for their functioning upon neurons, special coordinating cells that transmit messages to each other by means of their axons and dendrites.

The neuron's membrane is electrically excitable, and a sudden voltage change in the membrane to the action potential can cause the neuron to "fire," transmitting a message to an adjacent neuron in the form of a chemical neurotransmitter. The neurotransmitter's path takes it across the synapse at the junction of two neurons.

Some neurotransmitters excite neurons, making them fire, and others are inhibitors, shifting the neuron's electric charge away from its firing threshold. Firing causes a chain reaction of neurotransmitters from cell to cell, thus sending a string of messages throughout the body.

Only certain types of neurotransmitters can activate their corresponding neurons. Few of the various types have been positively identified. Known excitatory neurotransmitters include noradrenaline, adrenaline, dopamine, and serotonin. Gamma amino butyric acid (GABA) is the single inhibitory neurotransmitter identified to date.

There are many types of neurons. The three main categories are afferent neurons, which transmit sensory information to the brain; efferent neurons, which send messages from the brain; and interneurons, by far the largest category, which serve as conductors that pass information from one neuron to another. The messages for reflexive actions are passed more quickly from neuron to neuron than messages for nonreflexive behaviors, which follow more complex pathways.

The endocrine system. Hormones, secreted by the endocrine glands and carried by the circulatory system, regulate some of the same activities as those regulated by neurotransmitters. But they act in a slower and more diffuse fashion, and control different aspects of the activities. Hormones and neurotransmitters are both classifed as neuroregulators. In general, hormones regulate the metabolism.

Brain structure. Structures toward the bottom of the brain are shared by most species; those at the top are found only in higher, more evolved animals.

The topmost brain layer, the cortex, is the center of the mental abilities, such as perception, cognition, and movement. Composed of compressed multiple fissures, the human brain's actual surface area is huge. Some of the fissures mark the boundaries of the four major lobes.

The motor and sensory cortexes run in the form of strips across the top and down the side of the cerebral cortex.

The majority of the cortex consists of association areas that coordinate and integrate motor and sensory cortexes. The association areas seem to bring together inputs from all the senses. The more advanced an animal is, the larger the percentage of its brain devoted to association areas.

Each cortical hemisphere controls and monitors the opposite side of the body. The corpus callosum transmits impulses across the fissure between the two halves.

Each hemisphere is somewhat specialized for different abilities. In general, the left hemisphere analyzes things into their parts, and the right integrates patterns and relations.

The limbic system lies below the cortex and regulates a wide spectrum of feelings, including anger and pleasure. The structures that compose the limbic system are found in the brains of the lower animals. Surgical alteration of these structures in humans to control violent outbursts has been tried, but is highly controversial.

Brain function. The activity of the brain is orchestrated by groups, nets, and chains of cells that work together for specific tasks. A study of responses in cats' visual cortexes found that cells there were highly specialized to respond only to certain visual patterns. The total effect of the individual responses was coordinated to form the impression of the image being seen.

Neuroanatomists have proposed that cells localized in specific parts of the brain control specific functions. But localization theory fails to explain why some brain-damaged people recover functions from areas thought to be destroyed. Statistical configuration theory posits that brain functions are located in several sites throughout the brain, but that some sites are more important than others for any given function.

Luria mapped functional units in the brain, each of which integrates a complex mosaic of limited cell activity into a coordinated whole. He proposed that the brain has three major units, all working together throughout the brain. The first regulates the arousal level of the cortex; the second analyzes, codes, and stores information; and the third programs, regulates, and verifies all conscious activity.

Central and peripheral nervous system. The central nervous system, which includes the brain and the spinal cord, relies on the peripheral nervous system—all the nerve fibers leading to and from the rest of the body—for information to sense and act on.

Reflexes are automatic responses acted on at the spinal cord without involvement of the brain.

The peripheral nervous system both brings in information (through the sensory system) and sends out commands (through the motor system).

The motor system is divided into the somatic system, controlling voluntary muscles, and the autonomic nervous system, directing the so-called involuntary muscles, like the glands and heart.

The sympathetic and parasympathetic systems of the autonomic nervous system mobilize the body's organs and put them at rest. They act reciprocally, each balancing the other's actions.

GLOSSARY

Action potential A sudden voltage change in a neuron's membrane.

Adrenal glands Endocrine glands, located one above each kidney, that secrete noradrenaline.

Afferent neurons Neurons that transmit sensory information to the brain.

Agonist A substance that acts like another substance.

Antagonist A substance that blocks the effects of another substance.

Association areas Cortical zones that integrate information gathered by the senses with directions to the muscles.

Autonomic nervous system The part of the nervous system that directs the so-called involuntary muscles of the body and visceral organs.

Axon The long projection of a neuron that transmits messages to other cells.

Brain The part of the nervous system enclosed in the skull.

Brain stem The thick cordlike structure at the base of the brain from which the reticular formation reaches up to the cortex and down to the spinal column.

Central nervous system The brain and spinal cord.

Corpus callosum A bundle of nerve fibers that transmits impulses between the cortical hemispheres.

Cortex Topmost layers of the brain in which are located the distinctly human mental abilities.

Dendrite The projection of a neuron that receives messages from adjacent neurons.

Efferent neuron A neuron that transmits information from the central nervous system to the periphery.

Endocrine glands Organs that secrete hormones carried throughout the body in the bloodstream to regulate activities such as sleep, emotion, and sex.

Functional units Brain units that integrate a complex mosaic of cell activity into a coordinated whole.

Hemispheres The two halves of the cortex.

Hormones Chemicals of the endocrine system carried in the bloodstream that regulate the activity of the body's organs.

Impulse A wave of excitation transmitted through nerve tissue.

Interneurons Neurons that conduct information from one neuron to another.

Limbic system A series of brain structures rising from the brain's base toward the cortex; involved in emotions and motivation.

Localization theory The idea that specific parts of the brain control specific mental activities.

Motor cortex A strip that runs across the top of the cortex and down each side; controls the muscles.

Neurons Cells of the brain and nervous system that transmit information between each other.

Neurotransmitter Chemical messenger that passes between neurons to regulate brain activity.

Orienting reflex General cortical alertness and preparedness to react, regulated by the reticular formation.

Parasympathetic nervous system The part of the autonomic nervous system that regulates visceral organs; its activity tends to inhibit them.

Peripheral nervous system All nerve fibers external to the brain and spinal cord.

Reflexes Unlearned, automatic reactions to stimuli.

Resting potential The difference in electrical charge between the inside and outside of a neuron at rest.

Reticular formation Series of structures originating in the brain stem, spreading upward to connect with parts of the cortex and extending down to the spinal cord.

Sensory cortex Strip located behind the motor cortex; receives all messages from skin and other sensory receptors.

Somatic system The part of the nervous system that carries messages to the skeletal muscles.

Statistical configuration theory The idea that brain functions are distributed throughout several regions of the brain, but that some regions contribute more than others to any given function.

Sympathetic nervous system The part of the autonomic nervous system that mobilizes the body by exciting various visceral organs.

Synapse Gap at the junction of two neurons, across which the neurotransmitter passes.

Threshold The critical level at which a shift in a neuron's electric charge causes it to "fire."

6

SENSATION

COMMON MYTHS

MANY PEOPLE BELIEVE THAT ...	ACTUALLY ...
The eyes see and the ears hear.	The eyes and ears receive and send messages on to the brain, where they are interpreted as vision and hearing. Seeing and hearing occur in the brain.
Sensory deprivation drives a person crazy.	The effects of sensory deprivation can be positive or negative, depending on a person's motives, expectations, and inner resources.
People with red/green color blindness cannot tell if a traffic light is red or green.	While the red and green colors look the same to a person with red/green color blindness, they differ in position and brightness, and so can be told apart.
There are five senses.	The body has many more than five ways to sense the information it needs to function normally—there are, for example, three different senses that deal with balance and movement.
The "phantom limb" pain of people who have an arm or leg amputated is imaginary.	Their pain is real; part of the brain responds as though it were receiving pain messages from the missing limb.

Man is nothing but a bundle of
sensations.

PROTAGORAS, 450 B.C.

The mind sees and the mind hears.
The rest is blind and deaf.

EPICHARMUS, 450 B.C.

How do we know about the world around us—
through our senses, or through our thoughts?
This dispute is one of the oldest in philosophy.
Since at least the fifth century B.C., one school has
argued that without sensation there would be no
thought: images, memories, and ideas are just rep-
licas or combinations of sensations. The counter-
argument has been that thought is the critical
factor in knowing the world, not the senses in and
of themselves. After 2,500 years, the modern resolution is that neither sensation nor thought is
more important, but that both interact to shape
the world we experience.

SENSORY EXTREMES

Evidence of the importance of the senses was obtained unexpectedly when volunteers were placed
in environments of total *sensory deprivation,*
where there is minimal stimulus of any sort (Heron, 1957). The results partially bore out both positions: to some degree, experience was diminished,
but it certainly did not cease with the deprivation
of stimulation.

In the first such study, in the 1950s, William
Heron had student volunteers lie for as many
days as they cared to stay on a bed in a cubicle
provided with equipment to isolate them from
sight, touch, and sound. Plastic lenses over their
eyes permitted diffuse light but not patterned images. Cotton gloves and cardboard cuffs restricted their touch. A foam pillow and the continuous
hum of an air conditioner masked sounds. The environmental monotony was interrupted only by
breaks for meals, trips to the bathroom, and tests,
for which the students sat on the edge of their
beds.

Knowing that they would be free from distractions during the experiment, the students thought
it would be a fine time to review course material
or to plan papers or talks. But, rather than concentrating on work, they soon became "content to let
the mind drift." Shortly after entering the cubicle,
most of them went to sleep and on waking showed
signs of increasing restlessness and irritation.
Their need for contact with a normal, varying environment became apparent.

Some began to have hallucinations, involving
touch and hearing as well as vision, which they
found unpleasant and disturbing. At first the visu-

al images were dots of light and geometrical patterns, but they then developed into scenes such as prehistoric jungle animals or complex and colorful designs. Such reactions have also been experienced by airline pilots and drivers who on long, monotonous trips have reported seeing images like these.

While these results seem to affirm that we need a certain level of stimulation and variation in order to function and feel well, sensory isolation need not always be unpleasant. Heron's 1957 article was titled "The Pathology of Boredom"; Suedfeld's 1975 reevaluation of sensory deprivation, on the other hand, was called "The Benefits of Boredom." The experience of sensory isolation in a soundproof saltwater tank built for the experience, Suedfeld reported, can be restful and therapeutic rather than upsetting (Suedfeld, 1975). Indeed, in various cities around the country it is possible to rent time in a sensory isolation tank.

What seems to make the difference in the effects of isolation is the person's motive, expectations, and inner resources. If you want to try an isolation tank, expect a pleasant time, and enjoy solitude, you're more likely to have a positive experience than if you try it unwillingly, expect distress, and fear isolation.

If understimulation can be hard to take under certain conditions, so can overstimulation (Frankenhaeuser, 1978). Too much stimulation (for example, at a disco) causes an *information overload*, where the brain's ability to discriminate and respond appropriately among incoming stimuli is impaired. The result for many people is tension, fragmented thought, and impaired judgment. Noise, air, or odor pollution can also produce psychological discomfort (e.g., Cain, 1978, Cohen *et al.*, 1980). In short, extremes of stimulation, whether too much or too little, can impair and distort a person's sensory abilities.

Isolation tanks provide people with the experience of sensory deprivation. The tanks are soundproof, and people float naked in a saltwater solution that suspends them comfortably on the water's surface. Many people report the experience to be a deeply relaxing one. (Courtesy, Lee Leibuer/Samadhi Tank Co.)

PSYCHOPHYSICS

Imagine that you're having some friends over for dinner tonight, and you've decided to prepare your famous minestrone soup. Most of them have arrived, and are hanging out with you in the kitchen while you finish cooking.

"What do you think, Walt," you say, handing him a ladle of soup to taste. "Too bland? Need more salt?"

"Oh no—too salty," he says after a sip.

You ask another friend to taste and advise. "Needs more salt. Definitely more salt," she says.

The ladle makes the round of all six guests. The final vote is a split: three for more salt in the soup, three saying too much already.

That settles it for you—it's just right. ■

When your friends taste the soup to see if it's salty enough, salt molecules in the soup interact with nerves in their tongue to create the sensation of "salty." For there to be a taste of saltiness at all, there must be enough salt molecules in the soup to reach the range of energy that the person experiences as saltiness. The *stimulus threshold* is the minimum intensity that must be reached if a person is to experience the stimulus (see Figure 6.1). If there were no salt in your soup at all, or just a grain or two, the stimulus threshold would probably not have been reached, and everyone would have agreed that the soup definitely needed salt. The technical definition of the stimulus threshold is that stimulus that the subject can detect half the number of times it is presented.

If you had somehow made a ghastly mistake and dumped a cup of salt into the soup, you probably would have surpassed the *terminal threshold*, the upper limit of stimulus intensity beyond which increasing the salt no longer increases the taste of saltiness and may conceivably damage the receptor and cause pain. High-frequency noises beyond the range of the ear will fail to elicit a response; too bright a light can produce pain; too loud a noise can damage the eardrum. All these are cases of surpassing the terminal threshold.

A *just noticeable difference* (jnd; also called the difference threshold) is the smallest difference in

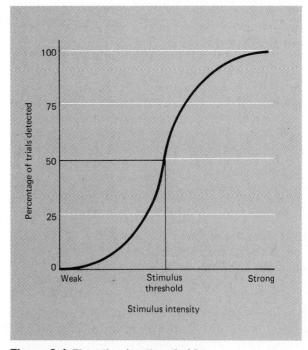

Figure 6.1 The stimulus threshold
The stimulus threshold is the minimum intensity that a person detects on at least 50 percent of trials.

Extremes of stimulation can be stressful. (© Joel Gordon 1979)

TABLE 6.1 **APPROXIMATE STIMULUS THRESHOLDS FOR THE FIVE SENSES**

Vision	A candle flame seen from fifty kilometers on a clear, dark night.
Audition	The tick of a watch from six meters in a very quiet room.
Taste	One gram of salt in 500 liters of water.
Smell	One drop of perfume diffused through a three-room apartment.
Touch	The wing of a bee falling on your cheek from one centimeter.

intensity between two stimuli that will allow a person to notice a difference. When you add a pinch of salt to the soup and can just barely tell it's saltier, you've changed it a jnd. The technical definition of a jnd is the smallest difference between two intensities of a stimulus that a person can discern half the number of times the two stimuli are presented. In soup, the jnd for salt is, say, just a pinch.

Fechner's law

The first scientific studies of the jnd were done in the middle of the nineteenth century by Gustav Fechner. Fechner concluded that all sensations, such as loudness, brightness, or saltiness, change in intensity according to a single principle. His equation, known as Fechner's law, states that in order for sensations to increase in intensity (from soft to loud, dim to bright, bland to salty, etc.) in equal steps, the stimulus itself must be increased in larger and larger doses in logarithmic steps. If the stimulus is very low in intensity, a slight change will be noticeable; if it is very high in intensity, then it takes a large change to be noticed (see Figure 6.2).

This law is sometimes called the Weber-Fechner law, because Fechner drew on the earlier work of Ernst Weber. Weber found that in order for a person to be able to tell that the intensity of a stimulus such as a light or sound has been increased, its physical intensity had to be changed by a fixed proportion of its starting value. Weber's law stated that this proportion was constant for each mo-

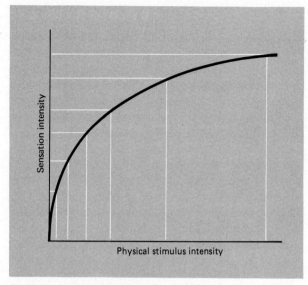

Figure 6.2 Fechner's law
It takes larger and larger increases in the intensity of a stimulus in order for a person to perceive that it has increased. Thus for a change in a strong stimulus (e.g., loud rock music) to be discernible requires a much larger increment than would be needed for a discernible change in a weak stimulus (e.g., a bee's buzzing).

dality (though measured, of course, in different units—sound in one way, light in another, tastes in still another). Weber's law was only partly true: it does not work for either very strong or very weak stimuli. S. S. Stevens (1975, Stevens and Marks, 1980) has more accurately explained the relationship between stimulus intensity and how we perceive it. According to "Stevens' power law," this relationship follows a consistent ratio over a wide variety of stimulus intensities. But the relationship between intensity and sensation differs for each sense. For example, when you double the amount of light coming from a bulb, your sensation of brightness increases by about one-quarter; when you increase the intensity of a sound three times, you hear it about twice as loud.

Signal detection theory

Our perception depends on more than simply the intensity of a stimulus; a host of psychological factors can sway and distort it. Studies of people whose duty during World War II was to watch radar screens for a sign of enemy planes—a task that required constant vigilance for hours on end—revealed that factors like motivation and attention play a key role in perception (Lachman, Lachman, and Butterfield, 1979).

Suppose a radar operator's job is to signal an alert whenever he sees a "blip" of light on a screen. Some of the blips are strong, others faint. The operator's dilemma when a faint blip appears is to decide whether or not he actually saw something. The decision is important: an unreported enemy plane could cost lives. On the other hand, reporting imaginary blips could cost his job. Over and above what he actually perceives, then, he will have to weigh the costs of misses against false alarms in reporting a faint blip. If his criterion for reporting is too lenient, he will probably not miss an enemy plane, but will turn in many false alarms. On the other hand, too strict a criterion would mean few false alarms, but poor warnings of enemy aircraft.

The radar operator's dilemma has been dealt with by *signal detection theory*, the study of how psychological factors affect perception (Green and Swets, 1966). This research has shown that there is a psychological component in the perception of thresholds, even for apparently simple and objective stimuli. Some of these studies have used the phenomenon of flicker fusion: if a light is turned on and off rapidly enough, the flickers appear to fuse into one steady light. A threshold of visual fusion is the rate of flickers at which the fusion into continuous light takes place.

For example, it was discovered that mental patients tested on flicker fusion were more likely than nonpatients to report that a flicker had fused. However, the reason was not a defect in their nervous system, but rather their assumption about how they ought to see it to be considered normal. The patients did not want to seem to be hallucinating a flicker that wasn't there, because signs of hallucinations could mean they might be kept longer in a mental hospital. Nonpatients, of course, did not feel this threat. When the flickers were presented so that there was less ambiguity about whether or not the light had fused, there was no difference between patients and nonpatients (Clark and Brown, 1966). The original difference was entirely the result of the patients' mental set.

Imagine that you've come in from a freezing cold day and decide to take a hot bath to warm up. As the water comes from the tap, you test it with your hand—it seems boiling hot. While you're running the bath, you stand over a heater.

By the time the bath is drawn, you're already toasty from the heater. As you lower yourself in the bath, anticipating being partly boiled, you're dismayed to find the water now seems lukewarm.

What happened? ■

Sensory adaptation

The water's temperature did not change; your body's temperature—and its sensitivity to heat—changed instead. The judgment of sensory intensities, such as temperature, depends on the state of the one who judges. If you come into a hot tub from a cold day, it seems boiling; if you warm yourself first, the water no longer seems so hot. Such a shift in the degree of sensitivity to a stimulus is due to *adaptation* of receptors, as when our eyes adapt to a dark room.

As you ease yourself into a hot tub, you'll slowly get used to the temperature. If it seemed boiling hot at first, it will slowly seem bearable. The longer we are exposed to a constant, unchanging stimulus, the less power it has to evoke a response in us. When we are no longer able to feel the touch of clothes on our skin or notice a boiling tub, we have adapted to these stimuli.

THE SENSES

Which sense is most important? Most people consider sight and hearing their most important channels of communication with the outside world. Each has specific advantages. Hearing is usually superior to seeing whenever the timing of events is to be discriminated, and sounds are more likely to be detected than sights when an observer is otherwise distracted. Hearing is particularly flexible in the kind of information it can receive with a minimum of searching and selecting; a voice, for example, is easily heard among a multitude of other sounds. Most important, congenital or pre-lingual deafness seriously handicaps the develop-ment of language, so basic to being human.

On the other hand, seeing is generally superior to hearing for spatial discrimination. With sight, more or less simultaneous comparisons can be made in searching for a particular element in a set, such as picking out the reddest apple from a basket.

The importance of smell in our sensory experi-ence is shown by the ease with which odors readi-ly trigger memories of past experiences. Like pain, taste and smell may have more value in emo-tion and the motivation of behavior than as chan-nels of information (Engen, 1980).

The importance of our senses is perhaps most apparent when we contemplate what life would be like in their absence. Imagine what it might be like to be blind or deaf from birth. It is not as simple as closing your eyes or turning off the sound on the TV set—deafness and blindness have far more

serious consequences than these temporary simu-lations could reveal.

For example, if you were born deaf or are pre-lingually deaf (that is, became deaf before you learned language), your ability to develop normal speech and language would be significantly af-fected. Without hearing, language development begins later and is extended over a much greater period of time than with hearing, resulting in de-lays in cognitive development and acquired skills such as reading.

Take, for example, the fact that word order is essential to specify the actor and the recipient of the action in a sentence such as "John kicked the teacher". While the deaf person can learn this, variations on word order are more difficult to master. Thus if the same information were put in the passive voice—"The teacher was kicked by John"—a deaf person might understand this as meaning that the teacher kicked John. This sort of error occurs because children generally learn the distinction between active and passive sentence structure by hearing such sentences and noting from the situation the differences in meaning they

Helen Keller, though blind and deaf since infancy, learned to communi-cate through touch. (© Karsh, Otta-wa 1978/Woodfin Camp & Assoc.)

HOW MANY SENSES ARE THERE?

■ We all know there are five senses—sight, hearing, touch, taste, and smell. Are those all?

That list of senses dates back at least to Aristotle, but the ancient Greeks knew nothing of how the brain receives sensory information. A modern conclusion is that there are more than twice as many senses than Aristotle listed, and that they can be grouped into major clusters called "perceptual systems" (Gibson, 1966). They include:

System	Senses	Respond to
Auditory system	hearing	sound
Visual system	sight	light
Basic orienting system	vestibular	gravity and acceleration
Haptic system	touch	contact with objects
	kinesthetic	movement of skin, muscles, joints
	pain	overstimulation
	thermal	temperature change
Savor system	smell	
	taste	chemicals
	touch	

Some of these perceptual systems are no surprise, for example, the auditory and visual systems. But the others may seem puzzling. The savor system, for example, includes smell and taste—both obviously appropriate for savor. But why the tactual, thermal, and pain senses as well?

We know that there is an intimate connection between what affects both taste and smell receptors in the nose and mouth: most of what we call "taste" is really smell. But eating involves more than that—it also involves touch, for example, which tells us about the texture of food, and can also detect dangerous objects, such as a pebble among our rice. The thermal sense tells us the temperature of food, and also warns us if it's too hot. And the pain sense tells us loud and clear if we're smelling or eating something dangerous.

These last three senses—pain, thermal, and tactual—are shared with the haptic system, the mode for perceiving what we touch and contact. The kinesthetic sense informs us of our body's movements, while messages about pressure let us know how intensely what we contact presses against us. All these varieties of sensory messages work together to perceive how we move, what we touch, and what the consequences may be—whether pressure, heat, or pain.

The basic orienting system is more commonly known as the sense of balance. Its main sense is vestibular—the mechanism in the inner ear that reacts to acceleration and monitors the direction of gravity. But the visual system also perceives important cues, such as the horizon, to help us balance. And the kinesthetic sense's information about body movements rounds out the perceptions necessary to keep the body oriented properly. ■

carry. A deaf child does not have the chance to do this.

Another drawback to deafness is great difficulty in learning to produce the sounds of the language. People commonly describe deaf people as "deaf and dumb", which implies being unable to hear and speak. But hearing loss does not entail the inability to speak; it simply means that the deaf person has difficulty learning to produce normal-sounding speech. Since deaf people don't have

the chance to learn to pronounce words by hearing how they sound, their speech often sounds muffled, hollow, or flat, and can be difficult to understand.

A similar range of disabilities happens to those born blind. Loss of other senses, such as the ability to feel pain, can also have serious drawbacks. But sight and hearing are the ones we depend on most for social interaction, and so their loss carries special personal and social costs.

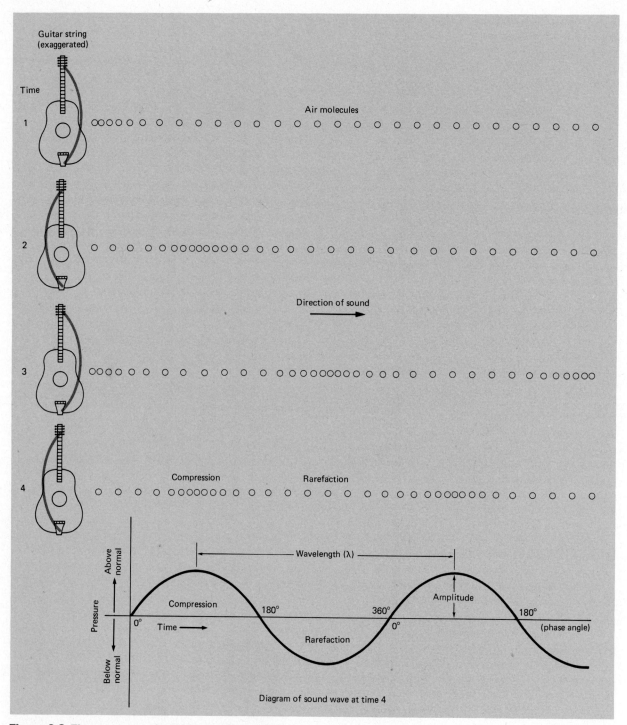

Figure 6.3 The waves produced by a guitar string

The lower part of the figure shows the guitar string producing a single wave, or pure tone, but this is not actually the case; the guitar, like all other instruments, owes its unique sound quality to the combination of frequencies it produces.

HEARING

Imagine that a tree falls to the ground in an isolated forest. There is not a person or animal within earshot.
Is there a sound? ■

Yes and no. When the tree falls, it creates a set of physical vibrations that travel through the air. But the vibrations may not be considered sound until they stimulate an ear. The auditory system transforms physical vibrations into sound. What is heard, though, is not the same as the physical stimulus, but rather is derived from it.

All sounds, whether a tree falling in a forest or a whispered "I love you," are caused by vibrations transmitted through air, water, or other media. Sound moves at about 1,100 feet (one-fifth of a mile) per second through air, its usual medium. As the vibrating object, such as a string on a guitar, moves out from its resting position, it compresses particles of the surrounding air. When the string moves back, particles of air expand, or rarefy. Each vibration causes compression and rarefaction, and a series of these form waves traveling away from the source. These waves, as produced by a guitar string, are illustrated in Figure 6.3. Sounds produced by single waves rather than a combination of different waves are called *pure tones*. The pressure variation generated by the tuning fork is similar to the simple, harmonic back-and-forth motion of a swing.

Wavelength is the distance from one wave peak to the next. The *amplitude* of a wave is the height the wave reaches at its peak, the highest strength the wave pressure reaches. The pressure of waves is usually expressed in terms of a unit called a *decibel* (dB), one-tenth of a unit named after Alexander Graham Bell, inventor of the telephone. The range of sounds the human ear can detect extends all the way from those made by the movement of the body's muscles and joints to loud, jarring sounds like a sonic boom, intense enough to be felt throughout the body.

The *frequency* of a wave is the number of peaks that pass a given point in one second, expressed in cycles per second, usually called Hertz (abbreviated Hz) after German physicist Heinrich Hertz. The shorter the wavelength, the greater the frequency. Frequencies below about 20 Hz and above

TABLE 6.2 **THE INTENSITY AND FREQUENCY OF SOME COMMON SOUNDS**

Sound	Intensity (dB)
	200
manned spacecraft launch (from 150 feet)	• 180
pain threshold	• 160
loud thunder; rock band	• 140
	120
shouting	• 100
conversation	• 80
	60
soft whisper	• 40
	20
threshold of hearing at 1,000 Hz	• 0

Sound	Frequency (Hz)
lowest note on piano	27.5
lowest note of bass singer	100
lowest note on clarinet	104.8
middle C on piano	261.6
standard tuning pitch (A above middle C)	440
upper range of soprano	1,000
highest note on piano	4,180
harmonics of musical instruments	10,000
limit of hearing for older persons	12,000
limit of hearing	16,000–20,000

about 20,000 Hz—called "ultrasound"—cannot be detected by the human ear. Some animals have a much wider range of hearing than humans; the bat, for example, can hear sounds up to 80,000 Hz and beyond.

The sound produced by the human voice box, or larynx, as well as most other natural sounds of significance to us, are never as simple as the pure tones of tuning forks. The sound of a simple bell, for example, consists of one wave of relatively small amplitude and high frequency superimposed on another wave of relatively large amplitude and low frequency. Speech sounds are even more complex.

The frequency of sound waves is what the listener would describe as the *pitch* of the sound, the changes in amplitude or pressure are experienced as changes in *loudness*. With different combinations of waves, the listener hears differences in sound quality, or *timbre*—i.e., the difference between the sounds of a trumpet and a cello.

The ear

The principal functioning parts of the ear are shown in Figure 6.4. Entering through the outer ear, sound waves are directed from the outer auditory canal to the eardrum, or tympanic membrane. In the middle ear, tiny bones, called ossicles, are attached to the eardrum and connect it with the oval window of the inner ear.

The vibrations of the eardrum are first transmitted through the three ossicles. One of these little bones, the stirrup, is attached to the membrane of the oval window, the entrance to the cochlea, a bony, snail-shaped structure attached to the vestibule. The cochlea is made up of chambers filled with fluid and separated by thin membranes. One of these chambers contains the organ of Corti, named after an Italian anatomist. It includes cells with tips that look like hairs. These "hair" cells are the receptors for hearing. The sound waves that pass through the outer ear channels and make the eardrum vibrate affect the organ of Corti to produce hearing (von Békésy, 1957). The stirrup acts like a piston on the oval window, increasing the pressure of the cochlear fluid twenty-two times. These vibrations set up traveling waves through the liquid in the cochlear canal, making a thin membrane in the cochlea vibrate, which in turn moves the hair cells.

This force on the cell membranes of the hair cell depolarizes it, creating a nervous impulse. The impulse then travels from the receptor cells to a nerve that leads to the cortex. The greater the amplitude (or pressure) of the sound, the more the membrane is deformed. This causes more receptor cells to respond more often with neural impulses, increasing the loudness of the sound sensation.

Imagine that you're just leaving your home when you hear a phone ring. Is it yours or a neighbor's? You can't quite tell. As you tilt your head this way and that to place the source of the ring, you decide it's yours.

You rush in, pick up the receiver, and hear a dial tone.

It was your neighbor's. ■

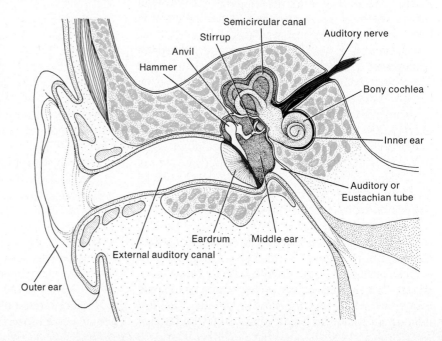

Figure 6.4 The ear

The auditory receptors are the hair cells, located in the bony structure of the cochlea. Sound vibrations are transmitted to the cochlea through the eardrum and the ossicles: the hammer, anvil, and stirrup.

Sound localization

How can you tell where a sound comes from? We locate sounds by means of tiny differences in their arrival times, phase, or intensity at the two ears. Our ears can discriminate differences of five ten-thousandths of a second or less in sound arrival time (Rosenzweig, 1961). The sound stimulates the closest ear first, then the other ear. This order helps us tell where the sound comes from. Deafness in one ear thus makes localization very difficult. A sound is often confusing if it comes from directly behind or in front of us, for then it strikes both ears at once. However, slight movements of the head will improve localization. That's why you automatically tilt your head in different ways when you're trying to tell if the ringing phone is yours or your neighbor's. The need for sound localization has led some motorcyclists to object to laws that require them to wear helmets. They claim a helmet interferes with localization of other vehicles, and so endangers them.

SIGHT

We sense the electromagnetic spectrum in the form of light. But only a small part of this spectrum is visible to the human eye (see color insert, this chapter). We are aware of other parts of the same spectrum through the skin, in the form of heat, and still other portions of the electromagnetic spectrum can be detected by mechanical means: radio and television "perceive" portions of the spectrum out of range of the human eye. However, we are "blind" to most of the spectrum.

Imagine that you've decided to repaint your bedroom, now a dull mustard yellow. You want to match one of the colors in your bedspread, a rich, autumny rust. In the basement there are a dozen or so half-used cans of paint, so you set to work mixing them to get the exact color you want. An exasperating hour later you've managed to make mud—a shade of gray.

You head for the paint store, bedspread in hand. You show the color you want, and the clerk begins mixing it for you. Minutes later you leave with a gallon of just the color you wanted. ■

Hues

The colors in the visible spectrum range in a rainbow from violet to blue, green, yellow, and red. These *hues*, or colors of sensed light, each correspond to different bands of wavelengths of the electromagnetic spectrum. Any color in this spectrum can be matched by a mixture of three primary wavelengths: blue, green, and red. But these three wavelengths must be "mixed" in a special sense, called additive mixture—a kind of color combination different from mixing paints.

There are two kinds of color mixture. When we mix lights—for example, projected on a screen with different projectors—the mixture is additive. Then all wavelengths projected will be reflected from the screen to the eye. But mixing paint is a subtractive process, for paint pigments actually absorb light and reflect only some of it. For example, blue may reflect only short wavelengths and absorb medium and long ones. Green, though, only reflects the medium, and yellow only the long waves in its part of the spectrum. When the three pigments are mixed, short, medium, and long wavelengths are all absorbed, and the paint looks muddy.

Adding three such lights with projectors produces a white light, because that is a mixture of samples of the whole visible spectrum. When a light consists of a single wavelength, it is spectrally pure, like a pure tone from a tuning fork. Such a pure light is *saturated*, free from whiteness. As white light is added to this pure light, the hue becomes less saturated—pure red, for example, turns pinkish and finally approaches white. The intensity of radiant energy determines the visual brightness we sense. Intensity varies with the rate at which a source emits energy. The relationship between the intensity and brightness of a color is analogous to the relationship between the amplitude and loudness of a sound.

The eye

Light enters the eye through the cornea and the pupil of the lens. The light is focused by the lens and falls upon the retina, which consists of many layers of different cells and lies at the back of the eye (see Figure 6.5). Changes in the curvature of

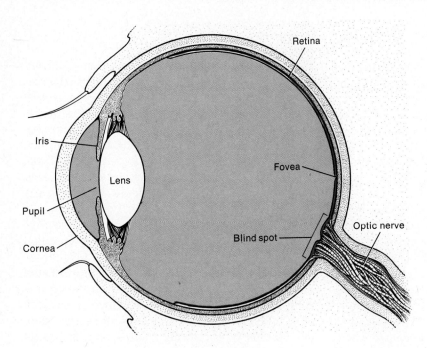

Figure 6.5 Cross section of the human eye

the lens focus the light projected on the retina in a sharp but inverted image, but we see it, of course, right side up. Whether this is an innate or learned ability is not clear.

The photosensitive receptors are behind other transparent layers of cells in the retina. There are two types of receptors, *rods* and *cones*. Rods, which are more numerous, are longer, thinner, and cylindrical; cones are thicker and tapered. Rods and cones serve different visual functions: rods mediate night vision, and cones, daylight vision. Owls and other nighttime animals have only rods, while chipmunks and other daytime animals have only cones. Still other animals, including humans, have both. People who have no rods are "night-blind"; they are functionally blind at night, but see well during the day. People with no cones are "day-blind": they see no color, have poor vision, but manage well at night.

The human retina contains over 100 million rods and cones. The fovea is in the center of the retina, where the image is projected in bright daylight vision. It contains only cones, which are essential for sensing color. Rods, located in the periphery of the retina, are used in night vision. They are sensitive to low illumination, but they don't distinguish colors. Rods are more likely to be stimulated when the pupil opening is large.

There is a blind spot on the retina, where the bundle of nerve fibers connected to the receptors leaves the eye. The viewer is not aware of the blind spot in ordinary seeing because the two eyes receive slightly different views of an object. What is missed by one eye is seen by the other. Our binocular vision also gives one of the most important cues in perception of depth and three-dimensionality. This is demonstrated by the stereoscope, in which two flat pictures of the same object taken from slightly different angles are presented separately to the two eyes but appear as one three-dimensional image. As in seeing the world right side up, whether such perception of depth is an inherent ability or is learned from experience is not clear, but in either case it depends on not only the structure of the eye, but also the organization of information in the brain (Frisby, 1980).

Night vision

Chemicals sensitive to light have been discovered in the visual receptors. The rods contain a chemical called rhodopsin, or visual purple, which absorbs light and is bleached by it. This changes rhodopsin to retinene, and this change generates the nerve impulse. Under the control of enzyme catalysts, retinene is changed to vitamin A and then back to rhodopsin again. This recycling is demonstrated when a person becomes dark-adapted—for example, when you walk into a darkened theater, and gradually begin to see clearly. When a person is in the dark, the light-sensitive chemicals in her eyes are not being stimulated, rhodopsin is regenerated, and she becomes more sensitive to light occasionally flashed on. The ability to detect lower and lower intensities of illumination improves for at least a half hour, by which time the person is maximally sensitive to low levels of illumination (see Figure 6.6). The fact that lack of vitamin A impairs night vision confirms its role in recycling.

Color vision

Night vision, dependent mainly on the rods, is largely in shades of white, gray, and black. Daylight vision, mediated by the cones, is in full color. No one explanation of color vision is yet generally accepted. The Young-von Helmholtz or *trichromatic theory* proposes that colors are sensed by three kinds of cones, each maximally sensitive to light of wavelengths corresponding to the color sensations of blue, green, and red, the primary colors. As mentioned, by adding corresponding wavelengths in different proportions, any color in the spectrum can be matched. The trichromatic theory suggests that color sensations are based on stimulation in various proportions of the three different kinds of cones. Evidence supports the existence of cones with varying responses to different wavelengths. The theory accounts for the ability of normal observers to match colors of the same wavelength correctly. The corresponding inability of color blind observers may be explained as the lack or alteration of one or more kinds of cones such that their absorption spectra are changed (see plate 3—color insert, this chapter).

A second view of color vision, the *opponent theory*, posits two basic processes composed of pairs of opposite colors, namely, red-green or blue-yellow, in addition to a black-white process. These processes probably operate higher in the visual system than in the receptor cells. Each member of a pair is antagonistic to the other. This means that the production of the color sensation red is associated with the breakdown of its opponent, the process accounting for green, and vice versa. If you look at a bright red light for some time and then look at a white screen, the screen will look greenish. The prolonged viewing depletes the red process, and the opponent green process dominates in a manner analogous to dark adaptation. If both opponents are stimulated equally by a mixture of wavelengths, they cancel each other, and you sense only grayness. If you look at a gray spot on a bright red background, for example, the spot will appear more green than on a white back-

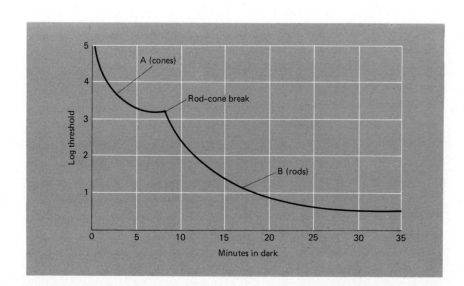

Figure 6.6 The dark adaptation curve

In the dark, the sensitivity of the eye changes. Dimmer and dimmer light marks the stimulus threshold as the eye becomes more sensitive. There is a point in adaptation to the dark at which the cones become fully adapted and the more sensitive rods take over vision.

ground. If the background is white, the gray spot will look darker than against a black background. Color plate 6 (color insert, this chapter), indicates how backgrounds affect colors.

Opponent color theory can account for many features of color vision, as can trichromatic theory. In fact, the theories seem to supplement each other. The trichromatic theory probably offers the best description of activity at the level of the receptors, whereas the opponent theory accounts best for the various interconnections beyond the receptor level in the brain. Although color sensations must be based on neural impulses varying in frequency and arriving over different nerve fibers, exactly what happens in the brain when we see colors still remains a mystery.

A defect in color vision, commonly called "color blindness," can manifest itself in several ways. People who have no cones and so see no color are extremely rare. The most common form of color deficiency is "anomalous color vision," an alternation or change of one cone such that its absorption spectrum is altered. A person with this defect will see all the colors of the spectrum, but will disagree with a person with normal color vision about what color a certain wavelength is.

Another color vision defect exists when only one type of cone functions. Such people, called "monochromats," see only black and white; they have difficulty telling colors apart. People who have only two types of cones working are "dichromats"; they can tell the difference between some,

but not all, colors. Dichromats differ by virtue of whether their color deficiency involves cones that are most sensitive to the red, blue, or green regions of the spectrum.

In addition to the alternation of receptor cones, dichromancy may also involve change at the opponent level such that a red-green color deficient person would see things in shades of yellow and blue. This creates a problem when red-green is a crucial distinction, for example, at traffic lights. Luckily, the ability to discriminate brightness is not affected in all such dichromats, and red and green traffic lights differ in brightness as well as color. However, for some red-green dichromats, brightness discrimination also suffers. Such people can only tell the difference between red and green traffic lights by their position.

TASTE AND SMELL

Imagine that you've discovered a sensational French restraurant, and want to take your friend there to celebrate her birthday. It's expensive but you figure it's worth it just once a year. Besides, the food tastes extraordinary.

The waiter has just brought your friend her order of *filet mignon*. You wait until she takes a bite, then ask, "Well, how do you like it?"

"I don't know," she replies. "I have a cold. Can't taste a thing." ■

Figure 6.7 A taste bud
Clusters of these spindle-shaped structures are located in the mouth, mainly on the tongue. Each cluster contains several sensory cells.

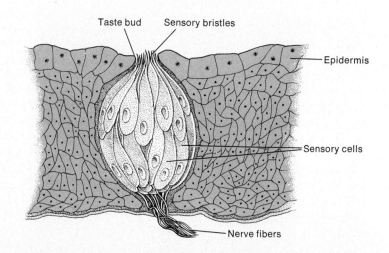

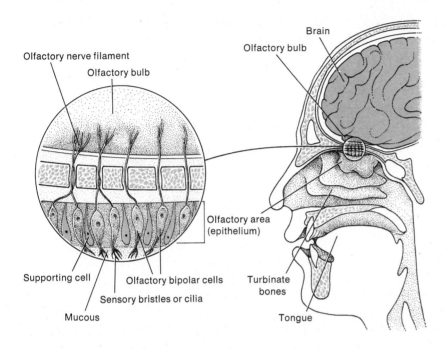

Olfactory nerve filament

Olfactory bulb

Brain

Olfactory bulb

Olfactory area
(epithelium)

Supporting cell

Olfactory bipolar cells

Sensory bristles or cilia

Turbinate
bones

Mucous

Tongue

Figure 6.8 The olfactory system in cross section
The epithelium with its receptors has been magnified.

A cold interferes with a person's ability to taste because the receptors for smell are located in the mucous membrane of the upper nasal passages and a stuffed-up nose prevents the odorous molecules from reaching the receptors. When your friend said she couldn't *taste* a thing, actually she could still taste—she just couldn't *smell.* Complete taste is a blend of stimulation of the physiological systems of *gustation* and *olfaction,* sensations of taste and smell respectively.

The basic tastes are sour, salty, bitter, and sweet. Substances found in varying proportions in our foods account for their taste. Sourness is elicited by the hydrogen ion in acids, saltiness by chlorine and sulfate salts, sweetness by sugars, and bitterness by alkaloids.

Exactly how these substances stimulate the taste receptors on the tongue and mouth is not known. Taste specificity may be determined by the nerve cells with which the receptor cells connect, or by the pattern of stimulation of receptors, each of which may respond to more than one qual-

ity. The region of the cortex that registers taste is close to the areas for facial touch and near the auditory cortex. The regulation of taste in the brain seems to be closely related to other senses, and to the centers for the motor activities of chewing and swallowing. There appear to be no areas of the cortex devoted exclusively to taste or smell.

Imagine that you've gone for a drive in the country, and bought some freshly picked artichokes from a vegetable stand. An avid artichoke fan, you rush home and eat half a dozen, dipping each leaf in mayonnaise.

Although you didn't notice, the mayonnaise had started to turn bad. Within an hour or two you feel desperately nauseated.

The next day, recovered from your mild bout of food poisoning, you see the rest of the artichokes in your refrigerator. The sight of them makes you ill. You throw them out. ■

Taste preferences

Taste seems especially easy to associate with illness, producing a learned distaste through classical conditioning. As we discussed in Chapter 2, this method has been used effectively with wolves to discourage their attacking herds of sheep: when wolves ate meat treated with lithium, a noxious element, they became sick and acquired an aversion for sheep (Garcia *et al.*, 1976). In another program, coyotes were kept away from sheep by first giving them meat spiked with synthetic tabasco sauce, then spraying the same sauce on sheep. In humans a similar phenomenon has been called the "sauce béarnaise effect." This occurs when a person eats a meal and then becomes sick afterward; frequently the most distinctive taste from the meal (such as sauce béarnaise or artichokes) will be distasteful thereafter.

People often report developing aversions to foods they happened to eat just before becoming ill (Garb and Stunkard, 1974). A study with children who were receiving chemotherapy for cancer showed that the nausea induced by the drugs they took did indeed cause them to acquire a distaste for food eaten during the treatment (Bernstein, 1978). Children taking these drugs were given a new flavor of ice cream called "mapletoff," a popular blend of black walnut and maple. One group ate the ice cream just before taking the nausea-producing drug, another had the ice cream but then had a drug that didn't cause nausea, and a third group had the nausea-inducing drug, but got no ice cream. Three weeks later all the children were given the choice between mapletoff or playing a game. Only 21 percent of the children who had mapletoff and then the nausea-inducing drug chose mapletoff; around 70 percent of children in the other groups chose the ice cream.

Positive food preferences also seem to be acquired. Even young children in Mexico come to like the very strong—and irritating—taste of chili peppers (Rozin and Schiller, 1980). Food preferences can often override what is best for the body. For example, too much salt in the diet is associated with hypertension. Even so, young children learn to like both salt and sugar. At birth, children seem to have a relative distaste for salt (Crook, 1978). But by age two, they tend to prefer salted over unsalted pretzels. Children nine to fifteen years old preferred the taste of a salt solution more than did adults, and black children preferred the strongest solution (Desor *et al.*, 1975); rates of hypertension are highest among blacks.

What tastes good is also determined in part by what needs to be eaten to maintain body metabolism. When their adrenal glands are removed, animals excrete great quantities of salt, which must be replaced if they are to survive. These animals do eat large amounts of salt or salty food when such foods are available and maintain themselves in good health. Physicians have reported similar reactions in patients. For example, a three-year-old boy whose adrenal gland was diseased kept himself alive on his own by eating large amounts of salt. When he was placed in a hospital for evaluation, however, and was unfortunately put on a regular diet, he died from salt deficiency (Wilkins and Richter, 1940).

Thus, metabolic needs in part determine our food choices, but they are not the sole factors. And, children free to do so will not necessarily choose a nutritious daily diet.

Smell

A person's nose has roughly 10 million olfactory, or odor, receptor cells, which are spread over an area of about 1.5 square inches. Dogs are thought to be more sensitive to smell because they have even more of these receptors. A neural response is initiated in these receptors by physical or chemical attributes of molecules of gas that contact the receptors, but the exact mechanism is not known.

The human sense of smell can distinguish among and remember a vast range of different odor qualities. The olfactory system is also more sensitive than physical instruments for detecting substances; that is why people act as odor detectors in chemical laboratories. Obese people seem to be particularly responsive to the sight and smell of foods (Rodin, 1977). A new treatment for obesity teaches the ability to monitor these responses and so better regulate one's eating habits (Stunkard, 1978).

THAT SMELL'S FAMILIAR

■ "Nothing revives the past so completely," wrote novelist Vladimir Nabokov, "as a smell that was once associated with it." Experimental evidence supports this claim for the unique capacity of odors to prod our memory.

In a study of odor memory, Engen and Ross (1973) presented close to 200 people with a series of smells. The odors ranged from familiar household items, such as onions and vinegar, to perfumes like Fabergé and unfamiliar chemical compounds. Their aim was to compare the curve of forgetting—the rate at which people are unable to recognize an item—for smell with that for other senses. After only a short wait, the subjects could recognize only 70 percent of the odors. When they were tested thirty days later, though, they could still recognize 70 percent. In fact, when fifteen of them were retested after a full year, they could still recognize 65 percent of the odors.

Figure 6.9 Memory for odor and for pictures compared

When asked which of two items had been presented in an earlier part of the experiment, subjects had poorer initial memory for odors, but as time went on, their memory for odors was much better than for pictures.

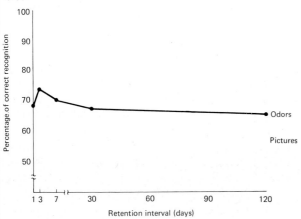

The comparable rates for recognizing a series of pictures is much poorer: immediate recognition is at 100 percent, but after three months it dwindles to chance (Shepard, 1967). Memories for sounds follow a similar curve of forgetting. In short, the nose remembers far better than the eyes and ears.

The tenacity of odor memory may be due to the way the olfactory system is wired in the brain (Engen, 1980). Other senses send their messages to the cortex indirectly, through the thalamus. The nose has a more direct route. Nerve fibers run from the nasal passage directly to the brain's emotional center, the limbic system. The interlinking between the olfactory system and the emotional center is greater than for any other sense, which may be a clue to the unusual potency of odor memory. The web of connections between the limbic and the olfactory systems makes it much easier for associations to form between a given odor and the rest of what we are experiencing at that moment.

Odor may have been given this role in the brain because, far more than any other sense, it tends to be a distinct, unitary perception. For example, visual images have far more distinguishable parts, some of which may be crucial for recognition, others utterly irrelevant. But a single odor is hard to break down into many of its parts. That may be why, for example, the odor of your mother's kitchen can recreate a whole situation far more effectively than most anything you might see in it.

Perhaps because of its greater power to evoke the past, odor may have played a role of special significance in the brain's evolution. The limbic system in primitive species like reptiles is purely olfactory; in such species, that part of the brain is called the rhinencephalon—Greek for "nose brain." But the higher a species is on the evolutionary ladder, the

THAT SMELL'S FAMILIAR (Cont.)

"SURE HE 'MEMBERS YOU... HE NEVER FORGETS A *SMELL!*"

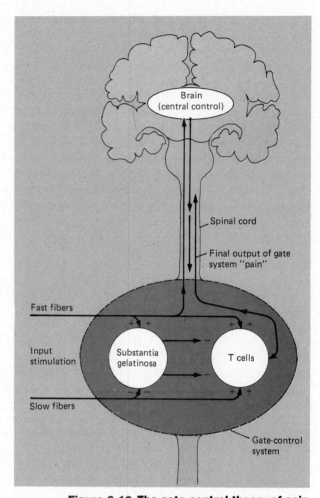

Figure 6.10 The gate-control theory of pain
Fibers with large diameters are quick in their transmission;
those with small diameters are slow. Plus signs (+)
indicate excitation, and minus signs (−), inhibition.

more the rhinencephalon is diversified to control a broad range of emotion and behavior. In humans, the limbic system reaches the peak of its complexity and importance.

One speculation is that the close links between the olfactory and limbic systems enhanced the abilities of a species to survive. Pegging experience to smell (e.g., the previous encounter with a particular dinosaur) freed an animal from responding to situations solely on the basis of genetically fixed reflexes (e.g., trying to fight). By calling on a pertinent past encounter (e.g., the time it outran the dinosaur), it could give a more adaptive, learned response instead (e.g., running like mad). Odor, then, was the memory cue that allowed an animal to learn from experience—and so survive better. ■

TOUCH AND PAIN

The general term for the skin receptors is the *cutaneous senses*, which include pain, warmth, and cold. *Somesthesis* includes the cutaneous senses plus some sensations from internal organs of the body, for example, the feeling of fullness after a large meal. These senses are organized to receive and transmit information to the brain much like the other senses. Although mostly located in the skin, some of the cutaneous receptor cells are also found inside the body in the viscera (making possible, for example, stomach aches).

One of the more puzzling of the cutaneous senses is pain. For one thing, pain has complex ties to other sensory systems; for another, a person's psychological state can radically alter the pain sense. Unlike the other sensory systems, pain receptors do not respond primarily to a single type of stimulus. Instead, any form of injury—whether mechanical, chemical, thermal, or electrical—can activate pain receptors.

The sense of pain differs greatly from person to person. People born without the sense of pain teach us its great importance to survival. Melzack (1973) reports the case of Miss C., a young Canadian girl born with congenital insensitivity to pain. As a child, she suffered accidents like radiator burns simply because she had no warning that her body was being harmed. Her body felt no pain from strong electric shock, nor did she show any other physiological change to stimuli such as burns or an ice-bath. Unfortunately, this pain defect led to severe medical problems. Her knees, hip, and spine needed corrective surgery because she failed to shift her weight while standing, or even to turn over in her sleep. Her joints became inflamed because she failed to assume postures that normally would have prevented the condition. She died at twenty-nine of massive infections resulting from the injuries a sense of pain would normally have prevented.

On the other hand, medical annals report some people who suffer spontaneous, unbearable pain with no known physical reason. Another curious problem is the pain often experienced after amputation in a so-called "phantom limb," when patients report sensations in the missing limb. The idea that such persons are describing only imaginary pains is not consistent with the evidence. This pain is most likely associated with spontaneous activity of nerve cells in the brain previously connected with the receptors of the amputated limb.

Such unusual phenomena have given rise to the *gate-control theory* of pain. According to this theory, a number of "gates" may be open, partially open, or closed in the pathways to and from the brain, the spinal cord, and the body (see Figure 6.10). These gates may facilitate or inhibit the transmission of pain signals. The gates can increase, decrease, or even stop pain, or refer it to areas of the body other than those actually injured (Wall and Melzack, 1965).

Some of the differences between people in their sensitivity to pain may be due to the way their

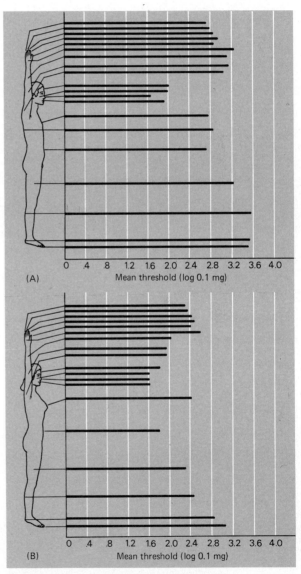

Figure 6.11 The detection thresholds for pressure at different parts of the body
Men and women differ in the degree of sensitivity of different parts of the body. In general, women are more sensitive to touch throughout the body than men.

nervous system reacts to excessive stimulation of all kinds. It is speculated that some people's brains act to reduce sensations at high-intensity levels, making them "reducers"; the brains of others enhance the intensity of sensations, making them "augmenters" (Buchsbaum, 1978). Reducers are presumably less sensitive to pain, while augmenters overreact to it (Petrie, 1979). Women, who have greater sensitivity to pain, tend to be augmenters. Alcohol and aspirin may turn augmenters into temporary reducers. Age could make a difference, too: children up to ten tend to be augmenters, people over forty are more apt to be reducers. Drugs that block endorphin, a brain chemical that lessens pain, turn pain-tolerant reducers into pain-sensitive augmenters (Buchsbaum, 1978). Possibly these differences in sensitivity to pain are due to variations in the level of endorphin in the brain.

Long ago, Titchener pointed out that there was a difference between the sensation of pain and the feelings it arouses. The sensation of pain in an aching tooth is localized in the tooth, but the feeling of unpleasantness associated with this pain encompasses all of the person's conscious awareness. When pain becomes keen enough, it tends to dominate and motivate all a person's behavior. A person may be unable to do anything but pace back and forth, holding his jaw and groaning. The effects of prefrontal lobotomy, in which the prefrontal lobes of the cortex are separated from the rest of the brain, provide evidence for the distinction between pain as a sensation and the feeling it causes. After a lobotomy, patients often report that they are experiencing pain but that it no longer bothers them. Certain drugs used to relieve pain have a similar effect.

The sense of pain is greatly affected by experience and by cultural norms of what is painful (Melzack, 1961). For example, the extent to which childbirth is judged painful varies greatly in different cultures. Similarly, memories of earlier pain can modify the degree of pain sensed, implying that the higher brain centers must be able to modify the neural impulses caused by injury through pathways originating in those higher centers. These centers may be those in which memories of earlier injuries and pains are stored and which affect the person's psychological state at the time of injury.

THE UNITY OF THE SENSES

Imagine that you're at the top of the Empire State Building, even though heights make you a bit queasy. You edge toward the observation window, eyes riveted straight out over the rooftops of Manhattan. Then, for a split-second, your gaze goes downward, to the street eighty-six stories below. For a moment you have the distinct feeling of falling. You quickly return your gaze skyward. ■

While we think of the senses as separate channels of information, each sensitive to a different variety of energy, the senses also have much in common (Marks, 1978). The senses often assist each other in perceiving an event, as when the kinesthetic message of falling adds its dramatic message to your view of the street far below. Or, take the experiences of someone paralyzed from birth. Such a person could not, for example, "see" that a surface is smooth. Such a perception depends on prior experiences of touching such a surface; our total perception of smoothness combines both the sight of the smoothness and the memory of the feel of smoothness. This unification of sensory messages into a total perception during information processing occurs in the sensory cortex. There the simultaneous messages from the senses are integrated in a meaningful whole.

SUMMARY

Sensory extremes. The importance of the senses has been illustrated by experiments with sensory deprivation that caused distortions in subjects' experiences. But sensory isolation may be restful and therapeutic, depending on the person's motivations, expectations, and inner resources.

Information overload can also impair and distort a person's sensory abilities.

Psychophysics. Sensory stimuli are felt within the limits of the stimulus threshold and the terminal threshold. The amount of change in a stimulus that will make a just noticeable difference has been determined for all five senses.

Fechner's law states that in order for there to be a detectable difference in sensations, the stimulus itself must be increased in larger and larger doses. Fechner drew on the work of Weber, who found that for a difference in stimulus to be perceived, its physical intensity had to be changed by a fixed proportion of its starting value, a proportion that was constant for each sense.

Signal detection theory proposes that there is a psychological component in the detection of stimuli.

Sensory adaptation causes changes in the judgment of sensory intensities.

The senses. Sight and hearing are perhaps the most important senses especially for social interaction and cognitive activities.

Hearing serves to discriminate the timing of events and is particularly flexible in the kind of information it can receive with a minimum of searching and selecting. Without it, the acquisition of conventional language is seriously impaired.

Sight allows spatial discrimination and simultaneous visual comparisons.

Hearing. Sound waves can be described in terms of wavelength, amplitude, and frequency; they have varying pitch, loudness, and timbre.

The more intense the sound, the greater the activation of the hair cells, the receptors for sound.

Sound localization is achieved as we perceive the tiny differences in sounds' arrival times, phase, or intensity at the two ears.

Sight. We sense the electromagnetic spectrum in the form of light. Each hue corresponds to different bands of wavelengths of this spectrum. Color mixtures are of two kinds, additive and subtractive.

The intensity of radiant energy determines the visual brightness we sense. Binocular disparity gives one of the most important cues in perception of depth and three-dimensionality.

There are two types of visual receptors, rods and cones. Rods mediate night vision and are sensitive to low illumination. They allow visual adaptation to darkness. Cones mediate daylight vision and are essential for color perception.

There are two theories of color vision, the trichromatic theory, focusing on the nature of cones, and the opponent theory involving processes at a higher level than the cone. The two theories may be complementary.

Color blindness can be monochromatic or dichromatic; people who see no color at all are extremely rare.

Taste and smell. Taste is largely determined by smell; there appear to be no areas of the cortex devoted exclusively to taste.

Taste aversions and preferences can both be acquired; what tastes good may also be determined in part by what the body needs.

The nose has approximately 10 million receptor cells and seems especially well suited for remembering a vast range of odor qualities.

Touch and pain. The cutaneous senses include receptors for pain, warmth, and cold. Somesthesis is the combination of the cutaneous senses with sensations from the internal organs.

Pain is one of the more puzzling somesthetic senses. A person's psychological state can radically alter the pain sense, and pain differs greatly among individuals.

Gate-control theory proposes that the transmission of pain signals may vary in many ways according to whether "gates" in the pathways to and from the brain, spinal cord, and body are open, partially open, or closed.

People who are "reducers" and "augmenters" react to pain in different ways, possibly because of differences in the amount of endorphin present in their brains.

There is a difference between the specific sensation of pain and the general feelings it arouses. Lobotomy and certain drugs allow the sensation and the feelings to be separated. Experience and cultural norms can also affect the intensity of pain felt.

Unity of the senses. Senses often work together in the perception of an event. The unification of sensory messages into a total perception occurs in the cortex, where simultaneous messages from various senses are integrated.

GLOSSARY

Adaptation The lessening ("fatigue") of sensitivity of sensory receptors to a stimulus.

Amplitude Intensity at the peak of a soundwave.

Cone A type of photosensitive receptor in the retina that mediates daylight vision and is essential for color vision.

Cutaneous senses General term for the sensations of pain, warmth, cold, and touch.

Decibel The unit used to express the pressure of sound waves.

Fechner's law States that, in order for sensations to increase in intensity, the stimulus itself must be increased in larger and larger steps logarithmically.

Frequency The number of peaks of a wave that pass a given point in one second, expressed in cycles per second.

Gate-control theory A theory of pain: a number of "gates" may be open, partially open, or closed in the pathways to and from the brain, the spinal cord, and the body, controlling the transmission of pain signals.

Gustation The sensation of taste.

Hues Colors of sensed light.

Information overload An excess of stimulation, causing impairment of the brain's ability to discriminate between and respond appropriately to incoming stimuli.

Just noticeable difference (jnd) The smallest difference in intensity between two stimuli that will allow a person to notice a difference half the number of times the two stimuli are presented.

Olfaction The sensation of smell.

Opponent theory A theory of color vision that posits pairs of colors (such as red-green) are in opposition; stimulation of one color sensation entails the weakening of the other.

Pitch Characteristic of sound caused by frequency of the sound waves.

Pure tones Sounds produced by single waves rather than a combination of different waves.

Rod A type of photosensitive receptor in the retina that mediates night vision and is sensitive to low levels of illumination.

Saturated Light from a single wavelength, free from whiteness.

Sensory deprivation A situation in which a person receives minimal stimulation of any sort.

Signal detection theory Deals with the effect that psychological factors have on detection of stimuli.

Somesthesis The cutaneous senses along with sensations from internal organs.

Stimulus threshold Minimum intensity that must be reached if a person is to experience a stimulus.

Terminal threshold The upper limit of stimulus intensity, beyond which increasing the stimulus no longer makes a perceptual difference and may damage the receptor and cause pain.

Timbre Characteristic of sound caused by specific combination of waves.

Trichromatic theory A theory of color vision: colors are sensed by three kinds of cones, each maximally sensitive to light of wavelengths corresponding to the color sensations of blue, green, and red.

Wavelength Distance from one wave peak to the next.

7

PERCEPTUAL ORGANIZATION

COMMON MYTHS

MANY PEOPLE BELIEVE THAT ...	ACTUALLY ...
Seeing is believing.	Optical illusions demonstrate that you can't always believe your eyes.
The speed of reading is limited by the time required to decipher each letter.	Rapid readers don't decipher each letter—they read whole words and lines at a glance.
Extrasensory perception (ESP) has been proven to exist.	There is still no certainty whether or not ESP is possible.
Talking too fast makes it impossible for other people to understand what you're saying.	People can understand speech at a rate of four or five times the normal rate.
Absentmindedness is a sign of weak concentration.	An absentminded person may be keenly concentrating on his or her own thoughts, although inattentive to external events.

Once a man, having taken a bath,
stepped from the river onto a wet rope,
which he mistook for a snake.
Overcome with horror and fear, he
pictured in his mind all the agonies that
the snake's bite would bring.

Then he saw that it was not a snake
but a rope. His horror disappeared.
Once he knew the true nature of the
rope, he was flooded with relief.

The cause of his fright was not the
rope, but his wrong perception of it.

GOTAMA BUDDHA, SERMON AT BENARES

We all have such moments now and then. At the time, we are convinced of their reality; later, when we discover our mistake, we call them "illusions." Illusions occur because of the way we sense and perceive the world. Our subjective world is as our senses tell us it is, a premise the seventeenth-century philosopher Thomas Hobbes stated as: "There is no conception in man's mind which hath not at first, totally or by parts, been begotten upon the organs of sense." Without our senses, the world would not exist for us.

Faith in the trustworthiness of our senses is built into the fabric of our reality. "Seeing is believing," the saying goes, but, unfortunately, the world as we perceive it does not always conform to external reality. The snake can be a rope.

HOW REAL IS "REAL"?

Stop to consider how you know anything about the world around you. The answer begins with your senses. If not for your senses, your brain would be trapped inside your skull like a prisoner in solitary confinement. Your world would be a si-

lent, dark void, without feeling, taste, or smell. Your brain relies on information brought to it by your senses. Your world is as your senses tell you it is.

Figure 7.1 The impossible stairway
The stairway appears to go up and up (or down and down) in an impossible fashion—an optical illusion, of course.

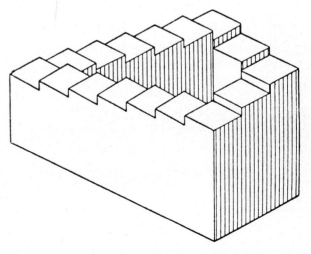

But how well does the world portrayed by your senses correspond to external reality? Faith in our senses is built into our lives; yet while seeing may be believing, what we see is not an absolutely accurate portrayal of the world. No perception can give you direct knowledge of the world around you, for what you know of the world is a mental end-product, not a direct portrayal.

Indeed, quite complex processes occur as a light wave strikes the cornea of the eye and an image registers in the mind. Seeing, for example, first requires that the brain translate physical wave forms into rhythms of neuronal firing, the brain's own language. Then there are subtle distinctions, classifications, comparisons, contrasts, and multiple decisions before the data of our senses become interpreted in our awareness.

The sensory organs simply receive and transmit messages that are processed further. It is how the messages are organized in perception that gives them meaning, not the raw sensory facts themselves. To understand how we perceive the world around us, we need to know more than just what the principles of psychophysics tell us about sensation—we need to understand perception.

The whole process whereby we register, interpret, and understand the world is called *information processing*. The first phase of information processing is *sensation*, the stimulation of sense organs. Sensation includes processes such as those whereby the eye registers light, the ear reacts to sound waves, or the skin registers the quality of a surface. The next phase in information processing is *perception*, the organization of sensations to create awareness of objects, relations and events in the world around us.

Perception determines how we form an accurate representation of what is sensed—is that long thin object I stepped on a snake or a rope? The final phase in information processing is *cognition*, understanding what has been sensed and perceived. If it's a snake, I jump; if a rope, I'm relieved.

LEARNING AND PERCEPTION

Our perceptual habits are learned, although we notice the role of learning in perception mainly in those cases where it is deficient. One researcher,

■ You saw it with your own eyes. But is seeing remembering? How sure can you be of what you've witnessed? Elizabeth Loftus (1980) has done research to determine what factors influence perception and memory, from the time one witnesses an event to the time one recounts it. Eyewitness testimony, of course, plays a key role in our legal system.

Loftus made up a crime in which a store owner and his daughter were robbed and killed. She presented it to 150 student "jurors." Some of the jurors were told no one had seen the crime, a second group was told that there had been an eyewitness, and a third group was told that the witness hadn't been wearing his glasses and therefore could not possibly identify the criminal. Of the group that thought there were no witnesses, 82 percent voted not guilty. But 72 percent of the group told there was an eyewitness voted guilty. And 68 percent of the third group voted for conviction, even though they were told the eyewitness was unreliable. The weight of eyewitness testimony—even when untrustworthy—is convincing. But is it always trustworthy?

According to Loftus (1975), when we remember something, we piece together the event from a

for example, has reported that people who have vision restored, after being almost completely blind from birth because of cataracts, reveal unexpected perceptual problems (Hebb, 1966). Although by touch they know the shapes of a triangle, a cube, or a square, and the faces of familiar people, these patients find it difficult to recognize and remember these forms visually after they have had the opportunity to identify them visually. The ability to perform this apparently simple task of recognition evidently requires time and practice.

Hubel and Wiesel (1963) deprived kittens of normal visual experience for two months after birth.

WITH MY OWN EYES

combination of what we actually recall plus inferences drawn later. For example, in one experiment she showed a film of a car accident. Afterward she asked groups of students different questions to see how the language she used affected their memories. Half the students were asked "Did you see *a* broken headlight?" The other half were asked "Did you see *the* broken headlight?" Using the word "the" implies there was a broken headlight. Using the word "a" makes no such assumption.

Loftus found that the group with the question containing "the" was more likely to report that they had seen something that wasn't there than the group with "a" in their question. Fifteen percent of the former group reported that they had seen the broken headlight (there was none in the film) while only 7 percent of the latter group made that error. Witnesses who were asked "a" questions were more likely to say "I don't know" than witnesses who were asked "the" questions. Changing one seemingly trivial word can greatly influence eyewitness reports.

In another experiment in which a film of a traffic accident was shown, Loftus asked witnesses afterward "About how fast were the cars going when they *hit* each other?" She substituted the words "smashed," "collided," "bumped" and "contacted" for the word "hit" in posing the question to different groups. Though these words all refer to the coming together of two objects, they all imply different speeds. The witnesses questioned with the word "smashed" estimated the highest speed (about forty miles per hour), while the witnesses questioned with the word "contacted" estimated the lowest speed (about thirty miles per hour).

A week later the witnesses, without seeing the film again, were asked if they had seen any broken glass (there wasn't any in the film). Twice as many witnesses who had been questioned with the word "smashed" said yes, they had seen broken glass, compared to those questioned with the word "hit." Thus key words like "smash," which implies a severe accident, can influence one to "remember" details that didn't actually occur.

How a question about an event is worded can greatly influence the way a witness "remembers" it. A question with a false implication can lead a person to reshape his or her actual memory in accord with the faulty inference. Thus eyewitness testimony can be altered by the way questions are asked—a fact not lost on judges and lawyers. ■

They did this by putting shields, which transmitted diffuse light but no patterns, over their eyes. The cells connecting the visual receptors with the cortex of these kittens failed to develop. After the shields were removed, the kittens fell off tables, stepped in their milk dishes, and displayed other evidence of perceptual abnormalities. Studies such as this show that the brain's perceptual system requires normal stimulation to develop and to function normally in the adult animal. Early experience is essential for development of the normal brain structure that is the basis for perception.

Similar perceptual deficiencies were demonstrated by chimpanzees who were reared in complete darkness to simulate the conditions of blindness (Riesen, 1950). When they were brought into light and tested on perceptual problems, the chimpanzees were very slow in acquiring normal perceptual responses. Studies of other sense modalities, such as touch, have yielded similar results.

Such deterioration can apparently occur later in life, long after childhood. For example, inmates on Devil's Island, a French penal colony near South America, were sometimes put for years at a time in solitary confinement, a situation of extreme sensory deprivation. Such unfortunate inmates showed degeneration of visual receptors as the result of their long periods in dark dungeons (Walls, 1951). Without stimulation, perception can atrophy, just as without learning, proper perceptual skills can fail to develop.

PERCEPTUAL CONSTANCIES

Imagine that you've pulled up to a stop sign, waiting to cross a busy street. It's dusk, and not all the cars have their lights on.

Clear on the right side. You look left, and see a car approaching down the street. Plenty of room for you to cross. A quick look right, glance left, as you edge out.

Wait—the car on your left is much closer than you thought. You brake quickly, reverse, pull back out of its path. ■

The world we perceive is constantly in flux, as are the organs through which we perceive. Your eye, for example, makes two to four small movements per second. As you scan the street, objects fleetingly appear and disappear in your visual field. As a car approaches you, your retinal image of it grows larger. A first impression can be misleading, but a closer look will help you to accurately gauge the car's distance.

The sensory world is full of myriad shifts, appearances and disappearances, shrinking and growing Alice-in-Wonderland style. Yet you do not consciously experience these changes. The world as you perceive it has far more stability than the sensory apparatus through which it filters. This stability is created through *perceptual constancies*, whereby the attributes of an object do not seem to change even though the physical stimuli perceived change. It is an effect of perceptual constancies, for example, that an approaching car somehow appears closer rather than just larger, or a door looks rectangular from different angles (see Figure 7.2).

There are several kinds of constancies. *Color constancy* makes the perceived color of an object seem the same, even under variations in lighting. A green leaf looks the same green in the shade or in the sun, and when a face is illuminated with red light, it still seems the ordinary color of flesh.

Size constancy allows an object to keep its perceived size whether it is near or far. A distant car is not perceived as the size of a matchbox and, up close, immensely larger. Nor does a pilot on landing see the runway as increasingly larger; just closer. The perceived size stays the same.

Brightness constancy keeps objects seeming to

Figure 7.2
Perceptual constancy
Although the images that the two doors project on the retina are quite different in shape, in real life both are seen as rectangles. There is constancy of shape, just as for color, size, and brightness.

be the same brightness regardless of the actual amount of light energy they reflect under different conditions. A piece of coal on a white paper will seem black and dark and the paper, white and bright—even in strong sunlight where, in fact, the amount of solar energy reflected by the coal is much greater, which ordinarily makes objects appear brighter.

One theory of constancies suggests that they are the product of our experience; perceptual constancies mean that what we have learned about the world we perceive overrides variations in how we sense it. The perceived attributes of familiar objects stay constant because we have a perceptual model of them in the mind; it is the model of memory that we perceive rather than an actual sensory experience. For example, even though a hallway in visual perspective seems narrower in the distance, we know it is the same width along its whole length, and so we perceive it that way.

There are objections to this hypothesis of familiarity, though. For one, there are constancies in objects never seen before. For another, the absence of distance cues, for example, makes it hard to compare the size of two different objects, supporting the idea that cues of distance, rather than unconscious inferences about the sizes of objects based on familiarity with them, are responsible for perceptual size constancy.

ILLUSIONS

Which of these lines is longer?

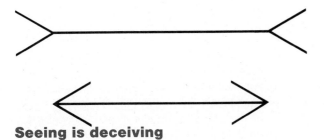

Seeing is deceiving

Although the top line appears longer, both are actually the same size. Perceptual constancy, whatever its true explanation, makes it possible for people to judge the nature of objects correctly. But our senses can be fooled. Illusions reveal the discrepancy between the real world of physics and the world as we perceive it (Frisby, 1980). A small can of sand, for example, will feel heavier than a large one filled with the same amount of sand.

Perhaps the most common illusion is the moon illusion: the moon looks larger on the horizon than high in the sky. This moon illusion has puzzled people through the ages. The moon actually seems about one-and-a-half times larger when it is viewed on the horizon than when it is directly overhead—yet it does not appreciably change its size or distance from the viewer. The amount of sky the moon covers does change slightly as the moon varies its distance from the earth during the course of its elliptical orbit, but this small change in distance cannot explain the large change in the moon's apparent size.

The moon illusion has been simulated in a laboratory, using artificial terrain and using prisms and mirrors to move the moon through its orbit from the horizon to high in the sky (Kaufman and Rock, 1962). This research found that the key to the illusion was the relationship of the moon to the horizon. If the terrain is masked, the illusion disappears, and the moon at the horizon and high in the sky looks the same size. With the terrain high in the sky, the moon looks larger than it did at the horizon with the terrain removed. The horizon gives the viewer distance cues.

We use distance cues in accord with our experience. We have all observed that, usually, the more things there are between ourselves and any object, the farther away it seems. Unconsciously, we use this inference to gauge the distance of the moon. The false inference that the moon on the horizon is farther away causes us to exaggerate the size of the same circumference in our mind. The moon high in the sky does not seem farther away, and so, according to this theory, we see the moon of identical circumference as smaller.

Such illusions may also arise from mechanisms of information processing that ordinarily make the world easier to comprehend. Under certain circumstances, these usually helpful perceptual habits lead to illusions (Coren and Girgus, 1978). For example, when a person looks at the moon, sensory information is relayed to the brain. There the information is organized according to the most appropriate model or principle for understanding it, say, distance cues. The mind cannot store a unique

THE ESCALATOR ILLUSION

■ Look at these pictures either out of the corner of your eye or as you sweep your eyes back and forth across the bottom of this page.

Did you see them "move"?

When 678 subjects were asked to look at these figures with their peripheral vision, about three-quarters said they saw a smooth, continuous rotation. The rest saw only slight, jerky motion, or no movement at all (Fraser and Wilcox, 1980).

This effect, called the "escalator illusion," is unusual in that certain people see the illusion, while others do not. When the figures were rotated at a low speed while subjects looked at them, those who at first could not see the effect with fixed figures finally could. The inability to see the escalator illusion, then, is in the person's degree of sensitivity; it is not a case of being "blind" to it.

In general, optical illusions are obvious to all viewers. But because some people can see the escalator illusion better than others, research has been conducted on the possibility that susceptibility to such visual effects may be inherited, and that this factor may also guide people to some degree in their choice of college major and even career.

For example, when Fraser and Wilcox (1980) tested parents and their offspring on the escalator effect, there was a strong correlation: children of parents who saw the escalator effect also tended to see it. While this may mean that the ability to see illusions such as this is inherited, it might also be the case that family environment rather than heredity is responsible. ■

Seeing is deceiving. Did it take a second glance to notice what seems out of place in this picture? (© Joel Gordon 1980)

model for every object; instead it seems to store information about classes of objects. Illusions of any sort seem to occur when the model does not somehow quite fit the particular object—for example, usual inferences about distance don't apply to the special case of the moon. Illusions, then, could be due to the imperfect nature of the categories we apply to make sense of objects in a complex sensory world.

There is evidence that being raised in one culture or another can lead people to develop learned differences in perception. People from some non-Western cultures, for example, may be less susceptible to the Muller-Lyer illusion (the deceptive lines on p. 163) than are Westerners (Segal, Campbell, and Herskovitz, 1966). Greater exposure to "carpentered" environments that have right angles to cue for depth and size may also influence susceptibility to this illusion (Wagner, 1977).

Perceptual adjustment

Turn this book upside down and try reading the rest of this paragraph, noting what happens as you read line after line. After a few lines, you will easily identify most of the brief words like "the," "and," and "of." In 1897, G. M. Stratton did a classic experiment on the effects of learning on the perceptual skills involved in moving about. Stratton wore prisms over his eyes, turning his whole visual world topsy-turvy, so that the ground seemed to be up and the sky down. Similar experiments were also conducted more recently by Köhler (1962).

When prisms are first worn, perception and motor abilities are profoundly disturbed. Familiar things such as faces, and even colors, look different. Gradually the upside-downer learns to move about in his strange world. For example, he requires days of practice learning to do anything complicated like riding a bicycle. Even though he still sees the world as inverted, he can, with practice, ride. After this adjustment to the upside-down world, when the prisms are removed, considerable time is required to adjust again to the right-side-up world. These experiments suggest that it is not necessary that we see the world as we are used to seeing it. We could learn to live in an upside-down world.

Figure 7.3

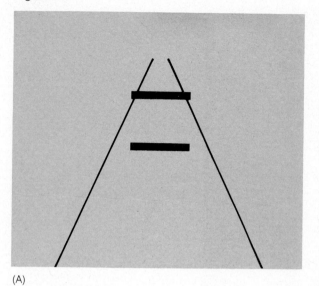

(A)

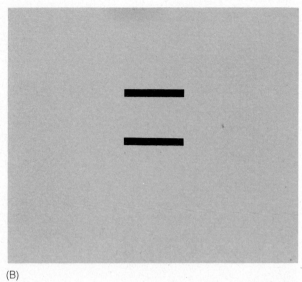

(B)

The Ponzo illusion. The identical bars in B seem to take different sizes in A and C, where the other lines lend the impression of perspective.

(C)

Figure 7.3 (cont.)

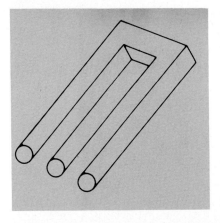 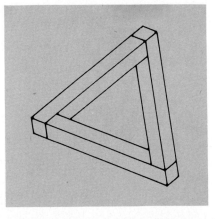

Where you fix your eyes determines the pattern you see in this illusion (far left). Is it three columns, or a U-shaped figure?

This impossible triangle (left) seems consistent part-by-part, but is non-sensical overall.

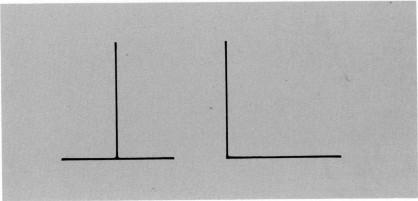

The vertical/horizontal illusion. Although the horizontal and vertical lines are actually equal in length, the vertical line appears longer, especially in the upside down T.

Figure 7.4
Keeping the book right side up, look at this figure with your head upside down between your legs. If you do, you will see the other face even though it is right side up. This is because faces are recognized on the basis of a right-side-up orientation in the retina.

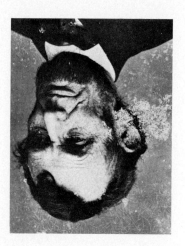

Do you recognize this face? While the stimulus itself is very familiar, its upside-down orientation makes it difficult to recognize familiar cues. This face of Lincoln is from a famous photo by Matthew Brady; it was used for the engraving on the five-dollar bill. (Library of Congress)

Imagine that you're at a noisy, packed party, talking to a new neighbor.

"Where are you from?" you ask her.

The raucous laugh of a man about four inches from your ear blocks some of what she tells you, which sounds like "I'm from . . . ain."

"Oh, I just love Europe," you reply.

As she shoots back a puzzled look, you realize she said "Maine," not "Spain." ■

Phonemic restoration: a helpful illusion

Illusions are not only visual; they can also occur in hearing. While our ability to infer what a person has actually said to us can fail from time to time, more often than not we correctly fill in missed words or sounds in a sentence. This capacity is called *phonemic restoration*, where such a missing speech sound is "heard" as clearly as any of the sounds actually present (Warren and Warren, 1970). This ability to extract information about missing sounds depends on inferences based on the verbal context. This skill is highly developed in professions such as telegraph operator: old-time Morse code operators did not write down a word until six to twelve words later in the message, making use of the whole meaning to confirm their deciphering of a given word. We all do the same to guess the meaning of words or sounds that we happen to miss in a sentence.

When part of a taped sentence was cut out, and then a cough replaced the missing phoneme, listeners clearly heard the missing sound (Warren and Warren, 1970). The sound was reconstructed on the basis of context: it made sense that it be there, and so the brain registered it as though it were there indeed. In another experiment, Warren and Warren constructed a sentence that left ambiguous the context that a listener would need to reconstruct the missing sound. They presented the sentence: "It was found that the __eel was on the _____ ." "Axle," "shoe," "orange," or "table" was used at different times to complete the sentence. The choice determined whether the listener "heard" as the missing sound "wheel," "heel," "peel," or "meal," respectively.

People seemed to store the incomplete information until the necessary context revealed what it should be, that is, until a model was decided upon. When no context was supplied, they had no clue. Information processing, then, includes a series of rules that allow us to supply missing information on the basis of inference from the context.

GESTALT: PSYCHOLOGY OF THE WHOLE

The percept

A "percept" consists of sensations elicited by physical stimuli.

The way in which percepts are organized in awareness was studied more than half a century ago by the gestalt school of psychology. The motto of this school is "the whole is greater than the sum of its parts." *Gestalt* means "form," "pattern," or "configuration" in German, and gestaltists proposed that the whole, integrated percept was the basic datum of psychology (Köhler, 1929). Depth perception—our ability to see the relative distance of objects—is a case in point. The retina of each eye obtains a flat, two-dimensional picture of the world, yet we see it as though it were three-dimensional. Each eye alone gives no clue to depth and distance; both together do. There is no clear explanation of how this greater perceptual whole comes about, but the gestalt psychologists described the principles of organization involved.

Figure 7.5 Figure and ground
You may see either profiles of two faces or a vase on a dark background, but not both at the same time.

Gestalt principles

The gestaltists sought answers to questions such as why things look as they do. The answer they proposed was that organizing rules give rise to how we perceive, over and above the pure sensory input, or percepts, that we register. The principles whereby percepts are organized into wholes are the main contributions of the gestalt school (Wertheimer, 1959).

One of the most basic gestalt principles is the figure-ground relationship, which is always present in our perception. The *figure* is any pattern, object, or shape we notice; the *ground* is its background. If you look at Figure 7.5 you will see either a white urn against a blue background or a pair of blue faces against a white background. Without any previous experience or training, we seem to perceive objects as standing out against a background. This is not a problem of detection, because in Figure 7.5 all the elements required to see either figure are clearly above your visual threshold. One aspect of the picture cannot be said to be more or less noticeable than the other. Figure-ground distinctions probably characterize all the sense modalities. In hearing, for example, a voice may represent the figure, and all other sounds affecting the ear may be the noise, or ground.

Among the rules of perceptual organization gestalt psychologists propose are

☐ Similarity. If several elements with similar

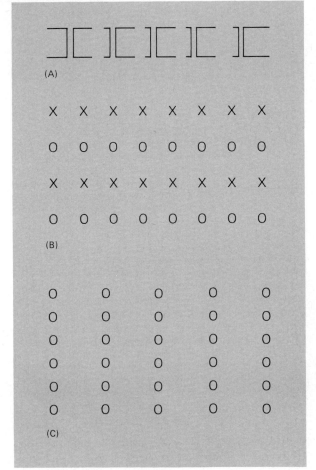

Figure 7.6 Gestalt principles
The gestalt principles of (A) closure, (B) similarity, and (C) proximity.

An example of visual closure.

characteristics are present in a perceptual field, they will be seen as though grouped together. When you watch a football game, you may see the players in one kind of uniform "together," despite the scrambles they get into with players from the other side.

☐ Proximity. Elements of the perceptual field located near one another tend to be seen as a group. When the football players are lined up for the hike, the players on the front lines may be seen as one group (regardless of team), those in the backfields as others.

☐ Closure. An incomplete figure is perceived as complete (see above drawing). Similar to phonemic restoration, closure works when you don't hear part of a sentence, but fill in for yourself what's missing. It also may explain why it is difficult to proofread, as we shall see.

PERCEPTION AND LANGUAGE

Imagine that you've just gotten back a term paper you wrote on "The Psychology of Perception," but you're chagrined to see your instructor has circled a word in the title: you spelled it "Psycology," without the h.

You know you proofread the paper carefully. How could you have made such an obvious error? ■

Reading

The average college student can read about 300 words a minute, or 1,500 letters. Each letter has a form that must be discriminated from twenty-five others in the English language by means of such physical properties as roundness, linearity, or zig-zaggedness (Künnapas, 1968). If each letter had to be discriminated, taking about 0.2 seconds, only 300 letters or 60 words could be read in a minute. Reading is much faster than this because it is based on perceptual organization of the letters into whole words, rather than on discrimination of the geometric characteristics of individual letters.

Because of perceptual organization we can learn to read by understanding the meaning of whole words and phrases. Expert readers perceive a whole line at a glance, although two or three glances are usually necessary, with minute jerky saccadic eye movements across a line. Only a slow or poor reader studies letters. There is roughly 50 percent redundancy in language, so letters and whole words can be skipped without any loss in meaning (Weaver, 1955). Similar duplication occurs within words themselves. In English, for example, the letter q is nearly always followed by the letter u, except in a handful of words derived from Arabic. The letter u could be left out entirely without any problem in conveying information.

If words or letters are actually left out, the reader usually fills the gaps in automatically, illustrating the gestalt principle of closure. For example, when you see a sign with a letter missing, you probably fill it in automatically. The context gives the information about the missing part and determines to a large extent what the reader perceives. Proofreading is difficult because of this same perceptual tendency, especially if you are proofreading material you have written yourself. *Psychology* spelled as "sychology," "psycology," or "pyschology" conveys about the same information. A mistake may be missed by even the best speller if the reading material is familiar.

Speech perception

One of the puzzles of perception concerns how we understand phonemes, the smallest sound units that distinguish one speech sound from another.

There are about forty phonemes in English. While there are twenty-six English letters, many of them can have several sounds, and some sound alike in certain uses—for example, *k*, and the *c* in "could"—and so represent the same phoneme. Other phonemes are compounds like *sh*. The mystery is how we can keep the phonemes straight when we hear them in so many different combinations and contexts. We are able to sort out the distinctive sounds of the phonemes no matter how we hear them.

The sounds a person makes when speaking are not at all as neatly organized as a written sentence. There is no punctuation in speech, no spaces between the words. Speech is more like a continuous, varying blur of sound, with few breaks or clearly separated segments of sound (Clark and Clark, 1977). When someone says "Hey—look over there!" it actually sounds more like "Heylook-overthere!"

Another problem with speech is that there is vast variability in its sounds. A printed *l* looks the same no matter what word it appears in. But a spoken *l* is pronounced differently depending, for example, on the word it is in (the *l* in "lip" and in "ill" is a different sound), the voice and accent of the person speaking, and the way it is spoken—in a whisper, in a shout, or through a mouth full of food, for example. Given the variation in how sounds are actually spoken, it is a minor miracle of perception that we can decode them so easily.

We not only pick out speech sounds with uncanny accuracy, but can do so much more quickly than with any other kind of sound. We ordinarily speak at the rate of twelve units (or distinct sounds) per second. But we can understand speech speeded up to rates of about fifty units per second, about four or five times faster than normal speech (Foulke and Sticht, 1969). Nonspeech sounds, though, give us more trouble. For example, people can only determine the correct order of nonspeech sounds at the rate of less than one unit per second. We seem to have special talents for detecting the sounds of speech.

We recognize speech sounds through the perception of auditory patterns, picking out certain key features of sounds from the blur of speech. Auditory perception, then, seems to work in a way

Figure 7.7 A spectrograph
The frequency of a voice speaking a sentence is plotted over time with shades of darkness representing the intensity of the sound.

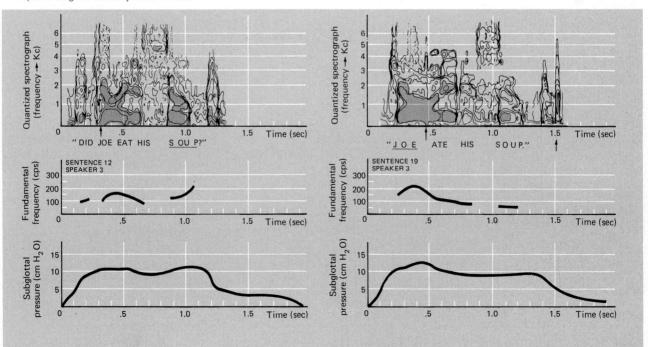

parallel to vision, where certain cells are attuned to respond to specific visual cues such as right angles (Abbs and Sussman, 1971). Unfortunately, it is easier to isolate the features we respond to in the case of vision than it is for speech.

Doyouseewhatwemean?

COGNITIVE FACTORS

Imagine that you're expecting a visit from your Aunt Lucy. She doesn't come by often, but you dread her visits when she does. Aunt Lucy is extremely finicky, and always lets you know that your place isn't as neat and clean as it should be—no matter how much energy you put into cleaning up beforehand.

It's been a hectic week, and the place has gotten pretty messy. You're frantically throwing odds and ends into a closet when the doorbell rings.

You open the door with your defense in full swing: "I'm sorry about the mess, Aunt Lucy, but . . ."

You do a double take: it's your next-door neighbor, Alice. "Oh, it's you. Thank goodness! I can relax." ■

Schemata

How we perceive an event is guided by what we expect. Your expectations about Aunt Lucy made you act accordingly when you opened the door;

when you saw your neighbor, you changed how you acted. Such an organization of perception and action is called a *schema* (plural: schemata) (Neisser, 1976). A schema is a sort of mental plan for finding out about something, storing what you've learned, using that information to deal with that something in the future, and adding to or changing your plan according to experience. Your schema for dealing with Aunt Lucy made it important to clean up your place or apologize for the mess; your schema for dealing with your neighbor made neatness irrelevant.

We have innumerable schemata stored in our minds, each with a different domain of applicability. For example, how to act on a tennis court could be one, how to act in a classroom discussion another. How to drive your car, make a cup of coffee, or look something up in a card catalog are still others. A schema is a pattern for action, but it is also responsive to perception: new information will change it. A given schema filters out information that is not pertinent—for example, your "Aunt Lucy" schema is not affected by what happens with your neighbor. But a schema will collect relevant information and modify itself accordingly. For example, if your cousin informs you one day that what really matters to Lucy is how much dust there is on tables, next time she comes you'll give special attention to table dusting.

Perceptual activities such as looking, hearing, and feeling seem to be controlled by schemata (Niesser, 1976). We see what we look for, and ignore the rest. Schemata tell us what to look for, and so organize visual perception. For example, if you are looking for somewhere to eat in a strange

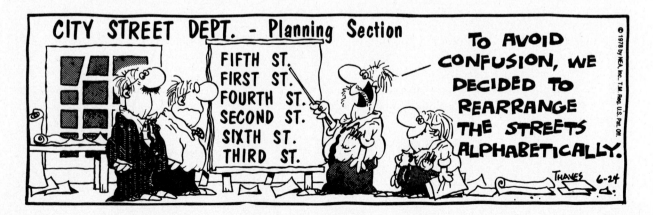

DARTMOUTH VS. PRINCETON, 1951

■ Everyone agreed that the football game was a rough one. Referees seemed to be blowing their whistles constantly, each team was penalized several times, and numerous players were hurt. But who was to blame? As might be expected, each college held the other responsible, and the school newspapers fanned the flames of partisan feeling. Princeton's victory began to seem almost incidental, especially since its star, Dick Kazmaier, had been injured.

What interested psychologists was this question: What had people actually *seen?* They designed a questionnaire, which was given to students at both schools after they had watched a filmed version of the game. Nearly all Princeton students judged the game to be "rough and dirty"; not one of them found it "clean and fair." And they saw the Dartmouth team commit over twice as many infractions as were seen by Dartmouth students.

As for the Dartmouth viewers, many agreed that the game was "rough and dirty," but over a third characterized the encounter as "rough and fair." The majority of Dartmouth students felt that both sides were to blame for infractions, and that

charges of foul play were being leveled at their school because of Kazmaier's injury. (Whether or not students had actually attended the game made little difference in their responses.)

According to the investigators:

It seems clear that the "game" actually was many different games and that each version of the events that transpired was just as "real" to a particular person as other versions were to other people. . . . In brief, the data here indicate that there is no such "thing" as a "game" existing "out there" in its own right which people merely "observe". . . .

From this point of view it is inaccurate and misleading to say that different people have different "attitudes" concerning the same "thing." For the "thing" simply is *not* the same for different people whether the "thing" is a football game, a presidential candidate, Communism, or spinach. . . . We behave according to what we bring to the occasion, and what each of us brings is more or less unique.

Albert H. Hastorf and Hadley Cantril, "They Saw a Game: A Case Study," *Journal of Abnormal and Social Psychology,* 49, 129–134 (Jan. 1954). ■

part of town, you will pick out visual cues that might guide you to food. You'll ignore other shops on the block while you scan for a restaurant. But if you need to get your watch repaired, then you'll look for jewelers and ignore the other stores, including restaurants. At each moment we hold schemata for specific kinds of information—the precise category depends on what matters most to us at that moment.

One kind of schema organizes our physical environment for us so that we can move about effectively. This sort of spatial schema is called a *cognitive map.* If we suddenly feel we don't have an adequate schema of this sort to orient us to our

surroundings, then we say we are "lost." A cognitive map functions as an orienting schema. The mental images we have of our surroundings are one sort of cognitive map. Visualize, for example, the route you take between home and school. That would be part of your cognitive map for your environment. You have similar maps of your bedroom, medicine cabinet, trunk of your car, and the neighborhood (or neighborhoods) you grew up in. Like other schemata, cognitive maps are structures for actively seeking information. As time goes on and you notice more information about any of these places, your cognitive map changes accordingly.

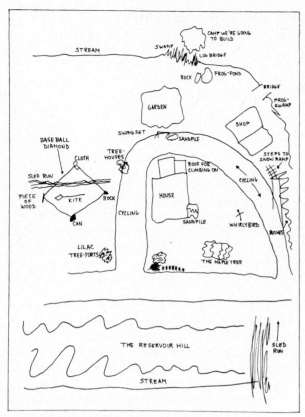

A child's map of his neighborhood highlights those spots that are meaningful in his scheme of activities. (From "Children's Experience of Space" by Roger Hart © 1979 by Irvington Publishers Inc.)

Imagine that you're at a noisy party, listening to someone you don't know very well expound on a subject that doesn't interest you much. Then, in a conversation between two people somewhere behind you, you hear your name mentioned.

Suddenly you zoom in on that conversation, eavesdropping, while continuing to pretend to listen to the one you're in. ■

Attention

This phenomenon, known as the "cocktail party effect," is an example of the flexibility of *attention*, the ability to focus on specific sources of information and ignore others. Attention directs

perception. The information you attend to can be in any of the sense modes, or simply your own thoughts. We are constantly being bombarded by a simultaneous array of sights, sounds, smells, touch. But we can only handle so much of this information at once. The brain regulates the flow of attention so that focusing on one kind of information puts a damper on other kinds. When you eavesdrop, your attention picks up the relevant sounds, and reduces the volume of other sounds, whether background laughter and music or the words of your conversational partner.

This purposeful focus is *selective attention*, which allows full focusing on a particular source of information and a rudimentary focus on others. You use selective attention in a class when at times you listen carefully to a lecture, and at other times tune it out while you think about other things. Or take the case of an "absentminded professor." He crosses a street blissfully unaware of the cars swerving to miss him. This state of self-absorption—which we all experience from time to time—is simply a case of deploying attention inward, to our thoughts (Reed, 1974). All outer sources of information, meanwhile, are damped down. If a car honks at the professor, he will almost certainly notice and respond. Contrary to common belief, absentmindedness is not a lack of concentration, but rather an instance of selective attention: an intense, inner-directed concentration.

In a classic study of selective attention, subjects wore a set of earphones through which they heard two different messages, one in each ear (Cherry, 1953). The subject's task was to "shadow" one of the messages by repeating it word for word. This meant they had to ignore the other message, a task they did easily. Later, though, they were tested on their recall and recognition of the message they didn't shadow. While they didn't remember most things about it, they did recall some aspects: whether the voice was a man's or a woman's, if their own name was mentioned, and if any of it was relevant to the shadowed message. But they didn't remember such obvious things as whether the nonshadowed message was words or nonsense syllables, the language it was in, or any of its content. (See Figure 7.8.)

One of the first explanations of our ability to tune in and tune out was the filter theory of atten-

In a crowded situation like a cocktail party people tune out conversations nearby in order to focus on the one they are part of.(© Elliott Erwitt/Magnum)

Figure 7.8 Shadowing

In "shadowing," a person is asked to repeat the information presented to one ear. Afterward the person is asked about information presented to the other ear, or even to another sense modality, such as vision.

HERMANN EBBINGHAUS

(Bettman Archive)

■ At the turn of the century, Germany was the center of psychology, which was then an abstract philosophical field rather than a science. Psycholo-gy was considered the study of the soul, and direct observations of man were seen as petty or even wicked.

It was Hermann Ebbinghaus who, because of an accidental discovery, helped to change psychology into a scientific discipline. One day, while browsing through a second-hand bookstore in Paris, he found a copy of Fechner's *Elementen der Psychophysic*, a pioneering application of experimental methods to perception, in which Fechner used himself as the subject of study. Ebbinghaus set out to apply Fechner's technique to the study of memory.

For the next five years—and completely on his own, without laboratories, funding, or support from universities or teachers—Ebbinghaus conducted carefully controlled studies of his own memory. His main method was to memorize lists of words, and then later test himself to see how well he remembered them. For this experiment he invented over 2,300 nonsense syllables, like *gok* or *wox*, which eliminated the possibility of contaminating effects from meanings associated with real words.

His discoveries about memory include the "curve of forgetting"—that forgetting is very rapid in the first few minutes, but slows down over the next few

---

tion proposed by Broadbent (1958). He proposed that the nervous system can be seen as a single channel of limited capacity; its capacity is smaller than the combined capacities of the senses that flow into it. This single channel is thus a bottleneck of sorts. To prevent its overloading, information passes through a selective filter that passes on some information and excludes the rest. Broadbent proposed as criteria for selection such features of messages as intensity or physical source, but he neglected a major one: meaningfulness. It is this criterion that allows you to tune in to the conversation about yourself.

Another change in Broadbent's model is that the filter does not fully exclude irrelevant information, but merely attenuates it (Treisman, 1960). This means that you monitor that other conversation in a vague way, until your name pops up. Then you tune it in, and tune out your own. The information that is not given full attention does

EXTRASENSORY PERCEPTION

Imagine that you haven't thought about your cousin Millie in years. Yet this morning you wake up thinking about her. You wonder where she is these days, what she's been doing. Then the phone rings. For some reason you're sure it's her.

You pick it up. It's Millie. ■

Your premonition about Millie may be a case of *extrasensory perception* (ESP for short), the perceiving of an event by means inexplicable in terms of the known limits of perception. *Parapsychologists* (*para* meaning "beside" or "beyond") do not believe that our perceptions are limited to responses to physical stimulation. People often report strange incidents in which, without using their ordinary senses, they seemed to perceive what another person was thinking or experiencing (mind reading), or directly communicated with others through thoughts alone (telepathy), or knew of events occurring at a distance (clairvoyance), or could move objects using their mind alone (telekinesis). While the meaning or mechanism for the "extra" has not been defined, there are many hypotheses about possible mechanisms that are currently under research (Wolman, 1977).

Events experienced through ESP could be based on unknown sensory modalities that are nevertheless similar to those already investigated. Or, as parapsychologists believe, the experience could be totally different from ordinary sensory and perceptual experience. The former idea is a hypothesis within the usual rules of science. The latter notion of experience of some other nature cannot be considered to be within the framework of science, and it has produced great controversy. Certainly the conception of *precognition,* or knowledge of events in the future, seems to preclude operation of any traditional sensory channel. Mind reading and telepathy could possibly be based on an as-yet-unknown sensory ability. But most psychologists do not believe that the hypotheses of an undiscovered sense, or of a totally different sort of perceptual experience, are tenable.

hours, and slows down even more in the next few days. His research led him to adopt statistical techniques used in physics to measure the accuracy of his observations, a methodological approach to psychology that has been *de rigueur* in the field ever since.

Ebbinghaus was by nature an original, independent thinker, unaffected by current scholarly theories. This independence enabled him to see the weaknesses in psychological study, and improve it. Of the rather philosophical, unscientific nature of psychology in his time he remarked, "Wherever the structure is touched, it falls apart."

An extremely systematic man, Ebbinghaus regulated his personal habits to ensure accurate data in his research on himself. Day after day he would follow the same unvarying schedule. Once he memorized some stanzas from Byron's *Don Juan,* and relearned the stanzas twenty-two years later to test his memory retention over long periods of time.

Ebbinghaus is remembered for setting psychology free from the hold of philosophy. In his words, "From a most ancient subject we shall produce the newest science." And that is precisely what he did. ■

not seem to be totally rejected. Rather, it is reduced, so that while most of it does not register, any significant, meaningful messages do reach a person's awareness (Treisman, 1964). Selective attention is not an all-or-nothing process, but a matter of modulating the volume of various sources of information. The main job of attention in organizing perception, then, is as a gatekeeper, selecting which sensory messages will be allowed into awareness, and filtering others out.

Parapsychologists claim to have obtained experimental evidence of ESP. A typical experiment involves the ability to predict the symbols on cards without looking at them. A special deck of cards with five symbols (circle, plus sign, wave, star, and rectangle) is used. The cards are presented to a subject face down and in random order, with instructions to identify the symbol on each card. Nobody can do this without error, and most students do no better than chance (one in five, or 20 percent). But some subjects have done much better than this. Parapsychologists claim that only certain people have ESP ability, and even those people do not have it to the same degree, or all the time; it depends on their attitudes, interests, and other personality attributes. Even if an ideal card experiment were designed, it would probably not be a simple matter to decide how many correct judgments—short of a perfect score—would be required to demonstrate the reality of ESP. A tally of correct answers (obtained purely by chance) for a large number of trials by one subject, or one trial each by a large number of subjects, should show an orderly distribution of scores. One in five (20 percent) should be the most frequent and average score, with progressively lower frequencies for higher and lower scores. What is taken as evidence for ESP is that subjects have obtained scores that are higher than the average, although experiments reporting results in support of ESP have presumably eliminated all perceptions based on physical stimuli.

Tart (1976) developed a machine that gives feedback on the correctness of a subject's guess during an ESP test. Those subjects who had higher-than-average ESP abilities to begin with seemed to have learned to increase significantly their ESP accuracy. If such results were to be widely duplicated by many researchers, the hypothesis of the existence of ESP would be hard to reject. All scientific relationships are a matter of probability, of course, so such statistical problems are not peculiar to the study of ESP. What sets ESP data apart from data usually considered adequate for establishing a phenomenon is their relatively low reliability, apparently too low to be useful in gambling (Churchman, 1966; Murphy, 1958). Yet this too is a matter of degree, and ESP remains an intriguing problem—and a matter of heated controversy (e.g., McBurney, 1980).

While ESP may exist, there may be much less of it than incidents such as your cousin Millie's phone call suggest. There is a tendency for people to remember the "hits" and forget the "misses," especially with nebulous phenomena like ESP (Weil, 1974). How many times might you have thought about Millie and forgotten about her when she did not call? Instead, you're much more likely to remember the one time your thoughts coincided with her call—and conveniently forget all the others.

Also, it might not have been a real coincidence in the first place. Perhaps it was her birthday, which you used to celebrate together, and on which it's natural for each of you to think of the other. Perhaps that day's newspaper carried an obituary of a movie star that you both idolized as kids—the obit reminds each of you of the movie star, then of the movies you used to see together, then of each other. Independent environmental events can set off such parallel trains of thought, and neither party need be aware of the process. Thus when the phone call is made, it seems truly mysterious. Not all psychologists take this skeptical view. Jung, for example, called such apparent coincidences "synchronicity," and assigned them an almost mystical significance. Many people seem to cherish the feeling of mysterious forces, which such experiences can bring. But before going overboard into the occult, it's worth checking around the everyday environment for that possible independent event.

SUMMARY

How real is "real"? Our subjective world is what our senses tell us it is, but our perceptions do not always conform to external reality.

In information processing, the brain registers, interprets, and understands the world through three phases: sensation, perception, and cognition.

Learning and perception. Perceptual habits are learned. This fact is best seen in cases of perceptual deficiencies caused by sensory deprivation in youth. Perceptual abilities in adults can also deteriorate through extreme sensory deprivation.

Perceptual constancies. Perceptual constancies allow stability in the perception of an object even though the physical stimuli related to the object may vary.

There are several kinds of perceptual constancies, including color, size, and brightness. It is not known whether constancies are innate or the product of experience.

Illusions. Our senses can be fooled. Illusions reveal the discrepancy between the real world of physics and the world as we perceive it. They seem to arise from mechanisms of information processing that ordinarily make the world easier to comprehend, but that are misleading under certain circumstances.

Culture, age, and schooling can make a difference in people's ways of perceiving and their susceptibility to certain illusions.

Experiments have shown that it is possible to learn to function in a visually topsy-turvy world.

Phonemic restoration is the helpful illusion that we have heard a missing sound or word, when actually we have filled it in by inference from the verbal context.

Gestalt: psychology of the whole. The gestalt school emphasized the whole, integrated percept as the basic datum of psychology. A basic gestalt principle is the figure-ground relationship, which probably characterizes all the sense modalities. Other gestalt rules of perceptual organization are similarity, proximity, and closure.

Perception and language. Because of perceptual organization, we gradually develop the ability to read by understanding the meaning of whole words and phrases, rather than by looking at individual letters. If words or letters are left out, the reader usually fills in the gaps, unconsciously using closure.

Another example is how we understand spoken phonemes when we hear them in so many different combinations and contexts, and when there is such great variation in speech sounds.

Cognitive factors. A schema is an organization of perception—for example, a mental plan for finding out about something, storing what has been learned, using the information to deal with it in the future, and adding to or changing the plan according to experience.

Innumerable schemata are stored in our minds; they include cognitive rules. Schemata organize perceptual activities such as looking, hearing, and feeling, as well as relevant actions.

Attention directs perception, and is flexible and selective; the brain regulates the flow of attention so that focusing on one kind of information puts a damper on other kinds.

Broadbent proposed a filter theory to explain selective attention, seeing the nervous system as a single channel of limited capacity that excludes irrelevant information. Modifications of this theory posit that the filter dampens irrelevant information, but does not totally exclude it.

Extrasensory perception. Parapsychologists believe that our perceptions are not limited to responses to physical stimulation, but may include information totally different from ordinary sensory and perceptual experience. ESP data have relatively low reliability, however, and people may give disproportionately heavy emphasis to what seems to have been an ESP experience.

GLOSSARY

Attention The ability to focus on specific sources of information and ignore others.
Brightness constancy Perceptual constancy that allows objects to seem to be the same brightness regardless of the actual amount of light energy they reflect under different conditions.

Cognition The processes involved in learning, thinking, problem solving, and organizing psychological events.

Cognitive map Spatial schema that organizes our physical environment for us so that we can move about effectively.

Color constancy Perceptual constancy that makes the perceived color of an object seem the same, even under variations in lighting.

Extrasensory perception The ability to perceive events without using the or inary senses.

Figure A gestalt concept: any pattern, object, or shape we notice.

Gestalt A German term meaning form, pattern, or configuration.

Ground The background of the gestalt figure.

Information processing The process whereby we register, interpret, and understand the world.

Parapsychologist A psychologist who deals with extrasensory perception.

Perception The organizing of sensations into objects, relations, and events in the world around us.

Perceptual constancies The stability of perception whereby the attributes of an object do not seem to change even though the physical stimuli perceived have varied—for example, in size or position.

Phonemic restoration The capacity to "hear" a missing phoneme, as clearly as any of the sounds actually present, by inferences based on context.

Precognition The knowledge of events in the future.

Schema An organized pattern of perception or behavior.

Selective attention The ability to focus fully on a particular source of information, and rudimentarily on others.

Sensation Experience resulting from the stimulation of sense organs.

Size constancy Perceptual constancy that allows an object to keep its perceived size whether it is near or far.

8

STATES OF CONSCIOUSNESS

COMMON MYTHS

MANY PEOPLE BELIEVE THAT...	ACTUALLY...
A hypnotized person can perform feats of strength he or she could not do ordinarily.	With the proper encouragement, people who are not hypnotized can do everything they do when they are hypnotized.
Many people never dream.	Everyone dreams, although many people do not recall their dreams.
Mental activity ceases while we are asleep, except during dreams.	Forms of mental activity continue through all stages of sleep.
LSD makes a person temporarily psychotic.	The altered state produced by LSD is not the same as psychosis.
The symbols in a dream have a universal meaning in "dream language."	The meanings of symbols in dreams depend on the dreamer.

> We all recognize as different great classes of our conscious states. Now we are seeing, now hearing; now reasoning, now willing; now recollecting, now expecting; now loving, now hating; and in a hundred other ways we know our mind to be alternately engaged.
>
> WILLIAM JAMES

If you take a few moments to reflect, you will see that what James called the "stream of consciousness" is constantly shifting. This shift is in both the object of your awareness—*what* you think about and perceive—and the nature of your awareness—*how* you think and perceive. The "how" is a *discrete state of consciousness*, a distinct pattern of awareness created by the sum total of psychological factors (Tart, 1977). These factors include cognition, alertness, sensing, selecting perceptions, memory, and emotions, among others. There are great numbers of discrete states: for example, a dream, morning grogginess, the alertness coffee brings, or self-absorption while driving a car.

Each person has a finite, but large, repertoire of such states that he or she commonly experiences over the course of a day. People differ according to which states are ordinary for them, which are unusual. A creative artist can be very familiar with a daydreamlike state in which her mind explores fanciful possibilities; a no-nonsense accountant may rarely, if ever, experience the same state. The creative reverie would be a baseline state of consciousness for the artist and an altered state of consciousness for the accountant (Tart, 1977). Technically, an *altered* state is any discrete state that varies from a given *baseline* state of consciousness. Baseline states are those that a person ordinarily experiences. In this chapter we will review a range of familiar discrete states, including some varieties of normal wakefulness and the stages of sleep and dreams, as well as altered states produced by hypnosis, meditation, and drugs.

WAKING STATES

Imagine that you were up much too late last night. Now, sitting in a lecture, trying to take notes, you notice your mind wandering. You force yourself to pay attention, to jot down what the professor is saying.

At the end of the hour, you find you have a page of illegible notes and two pages of doodles. ■

The spectrum of arousal

Among the psychological factors that change our state from moment to moment is alertness, which varies with our level of brain *arousal*. Like a rheostat on consciousness, brain arousal varies from maximum levels during panic or intense excitement to lows during deep sleep. The states we experience range from sharp alertness at one extreme to drowsiness at the other.

In full wakefulness, we are capable of flexible, focused attention, and so can concentrate on items of interest, ignore others, and shift our attention when necessary. We can recognize significant patterns in our environment, understand their meaning, and react to events as we need to (Hartmann, 1973). If you are in this state at a lecture class, you follow what is being said, your mind wanders little, and you take good notes. While tired, though, we find it hard to pay attention for long, are easily distracted, often fail to notice important cues, and our performance suffers (Mackworth, 1970). Sitting through a lecture in this state can be agony—you lose the thread of thought easily, are distracted by people and things nearby, and take poor notes.

While our level of arousal determines one aspect of consciousness, the pattern of *deployment of attention* creates another. Attention is like a searchlight of awareness; just as a beam of light can sweep through the skies or pick out a single object, cast a narrow or large beam, so our attention follows similar patterns of deployment (Broadbent, 1958). How we cast the beam of attention is a prime determinant of our state of consciousness. When we are alert, we can focus finely on a single object with minimal distractions. When we are drowsy, we are easily distracted, and our attention makes wide, undisciplined sweeps.

Daydreams

Like an absentminded professor, the daydreamer is deeply absorbed in her own thoughts, oblivious to her surroundings. In a study of the daydream habits of 500 college students, Singer (1975) found that almost all engaged in some form of daydreaming every day. Because daydreams require one to ignore one's surroundings, most people daydream during quiet, private moments, such as just before bedtime. Some people daydream much, others almost not at all.

Singer found four patterns of daydreams.

■ During surgery, part of the ceiling of the operating room caved in. The surgeon, though, was so absorbed in the operation that he continued as though nothing had happened. Puzzled, he asked afterward what the plaster was doing on the floor.

The surgeon's highly concentrated state—totally oblivious to distractions yet performing complex surgery with skill—is called "flow." The flow state has been studied extensively by Csikzentmihalyi (1976) through interviews with people like surgeons, composers, rock climbers, chess players, and athletes. They all engage in challenging tasks that demand total attention in order to do well, and these seem to be the conditions under which flow is most likely to arise.

The feeling of flow is characterized by intense feelings of pleasure, a sense of losing oneself in the activity at hand, a heightened awareness of this activity, and intense concentration on it. Almost any activity—from studying for an exam to rock dancing—can be the occasion for flow. But for flow to emerge, a specific set of conditions needs to prevail.

The first is that your skills fit the challenge at hand. If you are too skilled for the challenge—say playing racquetball with someone far poorer than yourself—then the challenge is too easy. You'll be bored. But if the challenge is too tough for you—playing with someone far better—then you'll be anxious. But when you're up against someone whose skills just match your own, then the game is at its most exciting and involving. Flow is far more likely; it occurs in the domain between boredom and anxiety.

"Anxious distractibility" in daydreams is characterized by fleeting, loosely connected fantasies filled with worries and doubts. In "guilty, negatively toned daydreams," striving for achievement and heroic acts are accompanied by fear of failure and resentment of others, and there is a strongly ethical tone and frequent self-questioning. In

FLOW: A NATURAL HIGH

Another condition for flow is that you focus total attention on the task at hand. People in flow find themselves centering their attention almost automatically. Nothing can distract them; their concentration on what they are doing—the sensations they experience, what to do next—is unwavering. If something should intrude and distract them, they would lose the flow state.

One sign of this total absorption is an altered sense of time. Focusing on the present seems to produce a time distortion: things seem to take much longer or go much more quickly than usual. The person is lost in the activity and may be oblivious to the true passage of time.

A final prerequisite for flow is a direct, immediate contact with the activity at hand. A person in flow responds immediately to feedback—whether it be an opponent's chess move, the rebound of a racquetball, or the sound of a composition—without stopping to evaluate how to respond. Response is automatic. There are no thoughts such as "Am I doing well?"—self-consciousness destroys flow.

Flow typically emerges when people perform at their best—no matter what the activity. It seems to be the psychological state that accompanies peak performance.

Activities that offer fast and direct feedback are more likely to produce flow. This, suggests Csikzentmihalyi, may be the appeal of games. The rules are clear, the level of challenge is easy to estimate, and it is obvious if you're faring well or poorly. ■

In the state called "flow" people are operating at peak performance. (© Seth Resnick 1980)

"positive-vivid" daydreams, fantasy is used for pleasant anticipation of the future and for entertainment; the "happy daydreamer" uses fantasy to solve problems and for pleasure. Closely related is the "controlled daydream," where the daydreamer programs his fantasies for active, orderly planning.

SLEEP AND DREAMS

While we can easily observe changes in our consciousness while we are awake, most people think of sleep—except during dreams—as a period when consciousness stops. For those people who claim they don't dream at all, sleep seems to be the exact opposite of waking consciousness. In the past thirty years, though, psychologists have made discoveries about sleep that show that these assumptions are wrong. Some kind of mental activity goes on during all or most of sleep, and everyone dreams, although most people have trouble recalling their dreams after awakening (Dement, 1978).

Falling asleep

There is a transitional "twilight" stage between wakefulness and sleep in which we sometimes experience dreamlike or *hypnagogic* images and sensations. Lasting up to ten minutes, this zone of consciousness just preceding actual sleep is marked by looseness of thought and disjointed, vivid images.

The first moment of sleep marks a sharp shift in a person's state of consciousness. Subjects in a sleep laboratory were asked to lie in bed with their eyes taped open while six inches from their face a bright strobe light flashed in their eyes every second or two (Dement, 1978). The subject was told to press a switch in his hand every time the strobe flashed. Suddenly he would stop pressing, though

the light continued to explode before his open eyes. Sleep had begun, and the sleeper was totally unaware, his eyes functionally blind. At the moment the perception of a person falling asleep ceases, his eyes will drift slowly from side to side, and this is another reliable sign of the onset of sleep.

The stages of sleep

One of the most revealing indicators of what happens to consciousness during sleep is the brain's level of activity. A person's brain waves go through consistent changes as he or she drops from wakefulness through light to deep sleep (see Figure 8.1). Brain waves are measured in cycles per second; beta waves are the fastest at fourteen or more per second, alpha waves fall in the range between eight and twelve per second, theta are five to seven, and the slowest waves, delta, are four or under. The brain wave record of a person who is fully awake and alert, eyes open, usually displays a predominance of beta waves. A person who is awake, but relaxed with eyes closed, on the other hand, typically displays a predominance of alpha waves. As a person falls asleep, she enters

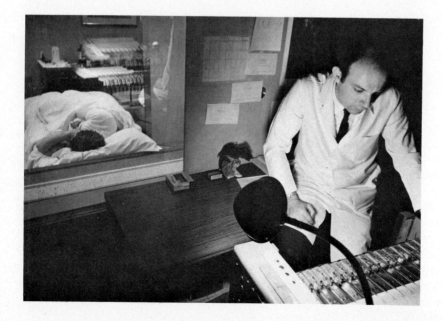

Sleep researchers monitor their subjects' patterns of response all through the night they are tested. (Ken Heyman)

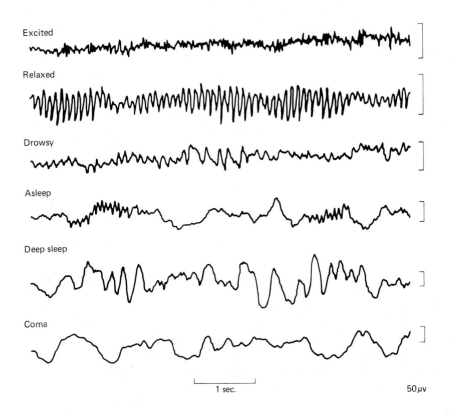

Excited

Relaxed

Drowsy

Asleep

Deep sleep

Coma

1 sec. 50 μv

Figure 8.1 Brainwaves and arousal
Electroencephalogram (EEG) patterns for the spectrum of arousal from excitation to coma.

ports that sleeptalki
among college stud
find people who ha
in their life that they

Unlike night terror,
any one period of s
studied in a sleep l
about 80 percent o
nonREM sleep, les
or "dream" sleep.
percent of the slee
sleeptalking is eve

What people say i
single word like "
tire paragraph. Mc
few seconds, but
more. While many
mumbled, much o
sometimes it is wh
be punctuated by
were in a convers
range of types of
ious to singing; m
nary conversatior

far less freque
ing upon how
much nonREM
ing, unstructu
Soaring thro
winged horse i
in a dream. On
seventy the a
150,000 dream
fascinating ad
tive recall for
exciting ones,
sleeper is aw
asked what sl

stage 1 sleep; her brain still shows a large proportion of alpha waves, but mixed in with them are some theta waves, with occasional bursts of high-frequency beta waves. As sleep becomes progressively deeper, in stage 2, the alpha pattern disappears; delta waves begin to dominate the record in stage 3 sleep.

In deep sleep, stage 4, the very slow delta waves occupy more than half of the brain wave record. For this reason, this stage is sometimes called "slow wave sleep." During stage 4, which occurs early in a night's sleep, the sleeper's muscles are relaxed, and her heart rate and breathing are slow and regular. The nature of consciousness in this stage is a puzzle; it is extremely difficult to wake someone in stage 4—the person seems to be almost in a coma. By the time the sleeper is awakened, it is unclear whether what she reports actually occurred during stage 4 or while she was coming awake. Yet some sort of mental activity clearly occurs, since most episodes of sleepwalk-

ing, sleeptalking, and intense nightmares happen during stage 4, as well as the neighboring stage 3.

During a night's sleep, a person does not merely fall into progressively deeper sleep and then gradually wake up. Instead her brain waves show a regular cyclical pattern that recurs about every ninety minutes. First, the person falls into deeper and deeper sleep, but then she gradually returns to a stage 1, or "waking" pattern. At this point, though, the person does not wake up as might be expected. Instead, she remains sound asleep and she enters another stage where her eyes move rapidly back and forth under her closed eyelids. This stage is known as *REM (rapid eye movement) sleep*. The average person has about four or five episodes of REM sleep each night, totaling about 25 percent of total sleep time, from 1½ to 2 hours. Other stages of sleep are collectively called *nonREM (or NREM) sleep*. The difference between REM and nonREM marks the sharpest contrast in the discrete states of sleep.

NIGHT

■ Have you e
state of terror?

If so, then you
especially inte
Night terrors a
cally and subj
Indeed, during
what may be
possible in hu
in rate in as li
Fisher, and E

The garden v
curs during R
hand, are mo
4, and do no
all. One theor
arousing just
sleep; the ph
vide a buffer
the intense h
terrors.

When twelve
in a sleep lal

Dreams

Imagin

ture hall, tak
notice that y
answers. Pa
your exam b
thing you kn
through a cl
island. You'r
pressing aga
Suddenly
sound, com

unteers, and left a control group of volunteers alone. Those who were sprayed reported more dreams about water. This incorporation into dreams of environmental stimuli may protect sleep itself. Volunteers in a British sleep laboratory were awakened during REM by a gradually increasing "white noise." When they awoke they told what they had just been dreaming. Those whose dreams somehow included the noise were able to stay asleep longer, while the noise increased to higher intensities (Bradley and Meddis, 1974). Even though incorporating potential disturbances into a dream may make a sleeper harder to wake, dreams do not protect her or him from waking up at some point.

Sigmund Freud formulated for modern psychology the view that dreams express the hidden needs and desires of the subconscious. Freud distinguished between the *manifest* and the *latent* content of a dream. The manifest content of a dream is derived from the events of the day, sensations during sleep (such as bladder tension), and early memories. The latent content is unconscious wishes, primarily from unresolved early psychosexual development. These hidden meanings are interpretable in terms of *dream work,* by which the manifest content veils the unconscious wishes in symbolic images that are more acceptable to the dreamer. Freud noted three key mechanisms of dream work through which latent content can be deciphered: condensation, displacement, and symbolism. For example, in *symbolism* terms and contents are given concrete reality. For Freud, objects such as sticks, tree trunks, and umbrellas stood for the penis; boxes, cupboards, and ovens for the uterus.

Over the years, Freud's insights into dreams have been modified; only the most ardent psychoanalysts follow his method of dream interpretation to the letter. Some therapists have abandoned the search for latent content in favor of direct meaning: the student who dreams about his disappearing ink the day before a test is simply worried about the upcoming exam, not trying to resolve some childhood conflict. The dream is not saying one thing and meaning another. The source of the dream is believed to be more fruitfully sought in the current concerns of the dreamer, not his or her remote past (Hall, 1971). The rigid interpretation

of symbols has also given way to the recognition that similar objects or events have different meanings for various people.

HYPNOSIS

Imagine that the scene is a nightclub, with ten volunteers sitting in straight-backed chairs. A stage hypnotist is saying, "I want you to relax your body, become comfortable as I talk. Just relax and become limp . . . you find yourself becoming warm, at ease, more comfortable . . . now you will become drowsy and sleepy, drowsy and sleepy. . . ." As she goes on in a soft, reassuring tone of voice, the volunteers one by one close their eyes and lower their heads.

When everyone is still, the hypnotist tells them, "Now clasp your hands together tightly . . . as though they were locked together by a band of steel . . . Try as you might, you can't get them apart . . . try to open them; you can't . . ."

Volunteers strain to pry open their interlocked fingers, but they cannot take them apart! But when they are told "Stop trying and relax . . . your hands are no longer locked together . . . you can take them apart . . ." the straining stops and their hands easily separate. Fingers cramped just a moment before now twitch slightly. Some of the volunteers flex their fingers to see if they still work properly. ■

Hypnotic susceptibility

Not everyone would be a fitting volunteer for such a nightclub act. One estimate is that about one person in twenty is particularly susceptible to hypnosis, but about nineteen in twenty can be hypnotized to some degree if they want to be and if they trust the hypnotist. The ability to spot a person who can be easily hypnotized is the key to success for a stage hypnotist. One trick, for example, is for the stage hypnotist to tell her audience that she will show them how easy it is to relax through the power of suggestion alone. After telling them repeatedly to relax and close their eyes, she then suggests that they will find it difficult to open their eyes. Next she goes through the audience and picks those who have still not opened their eyes to go up on stage (Barker, 1976).

Psychologists measure the trait of hypnotic susceptibility more systematically through tests such as the Stanford Hypnotic Suggestibility Scale. In this test, after a brief introduction, the hypnotist makes a series of suggestions to the subject, such as that his left arm will become rigid, or that he will be unable to say his name when asked. If the subject is unable to bend his arm more than two inches in ten seconds, or speak his name for ten seconds after being asked, his response is scored as susceptible. When 533 college students were tested with the Stanford scale, about 10 percent were identified as highly susceptible (Hilgard, 1965).

People are fairly stable in their degree of hypnotizability. Attempts to make people more hypnotizable through encounter groups, behavior modification, sensory deprivation, and even giving electrical shocks for inattention to a hypnotist's words have all proved of little value; none of these methods made hypnotic virtuosos out of low-scorers (Davidson and Goleman, 1977).

Why would a person want to become more easily hypnotized? The trait of hypnotic susceptibility is more positive than one might first think. It does not mean a weak-willed acquiescence to pressure from a stronger person. People who score high on this trait have been found to be able to become spontaneously absorbed in experiences like reading a novel, listening to music, or appreciating the beauty of nature (Bowers, 1976). Highly susceptible people are more likely as children to have had a history of daydreaming and imaginary companions (Hilgard, 1970). It seems that people who are easily hypnotized have developed in childhood the fantasy skills that make them susceptible to hypnosis as adults.

Is there a hypnotic state?

There is controversy over the question of whether hypnosis is a discrete state of consciousness. To date, no single objective measure has been found to correlate with hypnotic trance. Psychophysio-logical measures such as brain waves and heart rate vary according to the hypnotist's instructions: if he suggests relaxation, they show a slowed metabolism; if alert activity, they show a speedier one. There is no specific set of physiological changes that are sure signs that a person is hypnotized. Some, like Hilgard (1977), take the position that this simply means we have yet to find the appropriate measures.

Even though there are no certain measures of the hypnotic state, Hilgard (1977) lists the changes in behavior that hypnotists have long recognized as signs that a subject has been hypnotized. These include: increased suggestibility; enhanced imagery and imagination, including visual memories from early childhood; avoidance of initiative and compliance with the hypnotist's instructions; and reduction in reality testing. Such changes, suggests Hilgard, help the subject convince himself he is hypnotized as well as let the hypnotist recognize that he is.

Others object that these changes do not indicate the person is in a special state of consciousness because all of them can be induced outside hypnosis. Barber (1972) claims that with nonhypnotized subjects, brief instructions, exhortations that they try their hardest, and assurances that the tasks to be performed are easy have the net effect of allowing people to perform the same "feats" (e.g., lying stiff with the head on one chair, feet on another) as a hypnotic induction procedure. In short, Barber contends that everything done under hypnosis can also be done in a person's ordinary state. Orne (1959), however, offers evidence that hypnosis brings about a discrete state that is genuinely different from ordinary consciousness. Orne compared people who were hypnotized with people purposely faking hypnosis. The hypnotist did not know which were which and found it difficult to guess correctly. Orne, as well as other investigators, found that people who fake hypnosis can do virtually all the supposedly superhuman feats that hypnotized people can do, if they are strongly motivated.

But Orne also found some important differences between the two groups. The hypnotized group showed what he called *trance logic*. Using trance logic, a hypnotized person may readily perceive hallucinations suggested by the hypnotist

Under hypnosis a person can perform striking feats, but many claims made for hypnosis are unfounded. (Brown Brothers)

and, without making any attempt at logical consistency, may mix these hallucinations freely with perceptions of real objects and events. For example, in Orne's experiment the hypnotist told the subject there was a third person sitting in a chair next to him that was actually empty. The third person was, in fact, standing *behind* the subject. When the subject turned around and saw the third person, he acted surprised and said he saw two images of the same person. In contrast, when people who were faking turned around, they said either that they saw no one or that they did not recognize the person they saw. Their faking was exposed by their own efforts to respond in a consistent or logical way.

THE SELF-REGULATION OF CONSCIOUSNESS

Imagine that a yogi sits in an Indian laboratory with his legs crossed and eyes closed, deep in meditation. A team of Indian psychologists intently watch as a polygraph shows the yogi's brain to be emitting a steady flow of rhythmic alpha waves. The experiment begins. A psychologist strikes a tuning fork and holds it next to the yogi's ear. The alpha waves stream on unbroken—a sign that his brain has not recorded the sound at all.

A Zen master in a Japanese monastery sits with his eyes open, staring blankly, engrossed in meditation. An EEG records his brain waves while a psychologist makes a steady series of tapping sounds. Normally, a person's brain waves would show that by the eighth or tenth tap the brain no longer responded, but the Zen master's mindfulness lets him note the thirtieth tap as strongly as the first. ■

These studies, both done in the early 1960s, opened the door for a wave of research on the ways people might regulate their own consciousness (Schuman, 1980). Some changes in consciousness, for example, the changes produced by the sleep and waking cycle, are largely beyond our control. Also beyond our control is the influence exerted by a hypnotist, through her suggestions. In meditation and biofeedback, however, the person himself is in control of the changes he undergoes. Self-regulation techniques such as meditation and biofeedback allow us some control over the changes we undergo.

Meditation

There are many kinds of meditation. Despite the vast differences in beliefs and other details, they all share one common definition: *meditation* is a retraining of attention (Goleman, 1977). The specific effects vary according to the attentional specifics of meditation: the Indian yogi whose brain did not respond to sounds or touch was in *samadhi*, a state of intense concentration on a single thought or object (Anand, Chhina, and Singh, 1961). On the other hand, the Zen master who responded to each tap in a long series as though it were the first was practicing *zazen*, a meditation technique that cultivates mindfulness of each successive moment of awareness (Kasamatsu and Hirai, 1966).

Although there are hundreds of meditation techniques, most Americans hear of only three:

Human Behavior, March 1977. © Sidney Harris.

TM, yoga, and Zen (Goleman, 1977). TM (short for "transcendental meditation") was developed by the Maharishi Mahesh Yogi from classical Indian techniques, and is at base a method for the passive focusing of attention. What is popularly called "yoga" is actually not a meditation at all, but a series of stretching and bending exercises that were designed millennia ago in India as a relaxing prelude to meditation. "Zen" is the name of a Buddhist group in Japan who practice *zazen*, a set of meditation techniques designed to make the meditator more fully aware of each moment.

Most forms of meditation involve sitting quietly with eyes closed and focusing attention on one thing. In TM, the object of attention is a *mantra*, a short sacred sound from Sanskrit. In one form of zazen, the meditator simply notices the normal flow of her breathing, without trying to control it in any way. In still other schools of meditation—such as Tibetan Buddhism—the meditator visualizes an elaborate portrait of a deity or teacher, each detail of which has a special meaning. Other common objects for meditation are short prayers (the early Christians used *Kyrie Eleison*), a sacred picture, a candle flame, or various bodily sen-

Zazen is one of many kinds of meditation, all of which entail retraining attention. (Rene Burri/Magnum)

sations. Whatever the object of meditation, the learner's task is always the same: to let go her normal thoughts and feelings as they intrude on her attention.

Physiological Changes. The meditator's body undergoes a number of changes, all of which indicate a slowing of the metabolism and relaxation. Wallace and Benson (1972) recorded these changes during TM. Oxygen consumption fell markedly, breathing and heart rates slowed, skin resistance rose abruptly, and blood pressure dropped. Taken together, these measures indicated a *hypometabolic state,* a slowing down of bodily processes due to a reduction in the rate of energy the body uses. Reviewing the typical changes in these measures during sleep and hypnosis (where they vary according to the suggestions given), Wallace and Benson concluded that meditation produces a unique state, which differs from both sleep and hypnosis.

While meditation is deeply relaxing, the state it produces is also unlike that of simple relaxation (Schuman, 1980). Although the meditator undergoes physical changes similar to relaxation (Woolfolk, 1976), the difference is seen in the brain wave patterns of the meditator. The relaxed person shows no marked brain wave changes; the meditator's brain wave can reveal an altered state.

The brain state of the meditator depends to a large extent on the kind of meditation practiced, as we saw with the yogi in samadhi and the mindful Zen master. In another study of Zen meditators, Kasamatsu and Hirai (1966) found that monks practicing *zazen* had alpha waves in their EEG as soon as they started, even though their eyes were wide open. Alpha is normally found in large amounts only in people whose eyes are closed. As the meditation session progressed, the alpha waves changed systematically to a slower theta wave—very unusual in a person with open eyes. Other researchers have found different EEG patterns during other kinds of meditation, such as a distinctive wave pattern indicating intense concentration during TM (Banquet, 1973).

The effects of meditation seem to extend beyond the meditation session itself. Goleman and Schwartz (1976) found that, compared to control groups, both long-term meditators and people meditating for the first time in their lives recov-

■ Have you ever wondered what it would be like to die?

For obvious reasons, each of us will never really know until we do it. But until then, the best evidence comes from people who have returned from the brink of death. Moody (1975) collected reports from 150 people who had been resuscitated after being pronounced clinically dead, had come close to death through accident or illness, or had been with people who told them of their experiences as they died. From these records of brushes with death, Moody pieced together a composite description of the points that commonly recurred. While the account does not duplicate any one particular person's experience, it is a representative account:

A man is dying and, as he reaches the point of greatest physical distress, he hears himself pronounced dead by his doctor. He begins to hear an uncomfortable noise, a loud ringing or buzzing, and at the same time feels himself moving very rapidly through a long dark tunnel. After this he suddenly finds himself outside his own physical body, but still in the immediate physical environment, and he sees his own body from a distance, as though he is a spectator. He watches the resuscitation attempt from

ered more quickly from the physiological arousal produced by threatening movie scenes. They proposed that meditation training is an antidote to stress because it allows the meditator to get over its adverse effects more quickly. Apart from a more rapid stress recovery, meditators seem also to undergo a range of beneficial personality changes, including lower anxiety levels, increased sensitivity to environmental cues, increased self-actualization, and an improved ability to focus attention (Shapiro, 1980). Some researchers, however, suggest that these differences are not the result of meditation, but rather that they are characteristics of the kind of person who chooses to meditate and stays with it for a long period (Otis, 1976).

WHAT IS IT LIKE TO DIE ?

this unusual vantage point and is in a state of emotional upheaval.

After a while, he collects himself and becomes more accustomed to his odd condition. He notices that he still has a body, but one of a very different nature and with very different powers from the physical body he has left behind. Soon other things begin to happen. Others come to meet and to help him. He glimpses the spirits of relatives and friends who have already died, and a loving, warm spirit of a kind he has never encountered before—a being of light—appears before him. This being asks him a question, nonverbally, to make him evaluate his life, and helps him along by showing him a panoramic, instantaneous playback of the major events of his life.

At some point he finds himself approaching some sort of barrier or border, apparently representing the limit between earthly life and the next life. Yet, he finds that he must go back to the earth, that the time for his death has not yet come. At this point he resists, for by now he is taken up with his experiences in the afterlife and does not want to return. He is overwhelmed by intense feelings of joy, love, and peace. Despite his attitude, he somehow reunites with his physical body and lives. (Moody, 1977, pp. 5–6)

An independent study of over 500 cases of death-bed testimony in India and America found many of the same elements Moody reported (Osis and Haraldsson, 1977). The most common was the vision of a human figure. But for the Americans, the figure was usually a loved one; for the Indians usually a Hindu deity. This suggests that while the processes that bring about deathbed visions may be organically determined, the specifics of what is seen are subjectively determined.

The basis of these experiences on the edge of death may lie in the biology of dying. The body does not die all at once—the moment of death is actually a sequence of events. Different organs and cells expire at their own rate (Veach, 1976). When the heart stops beating, the brain begins to be starved of oxygen. But several minutes elapse before the brain dies completely of oxygen starvation.

It is this period between the cessation of the heartbeat and the brain's death that is the most likely explanation of the near-death experiences that people report. The brain during this period is being slowly starved of blood, a condition conducive to an altered state of consciousness in which visions, dissociation from the body, and the like could occur. ■

Biofeedback

While biofeedback is mainly used as a therapy (e.g., to help people gain self-control over physical symptoms like high blood pressure), it has also been tried as a means to alter consciousness. Some early claims made for the effects of biofeedback on consciousness have failed to hold up, most notably those made for alpha biofeedback (Miller, 1974). In the popular press, the alpha state, which people enter through brain wave biofeedback, was touted as a calm, blissful altered state. Subsequent research, however, showed that people could be in an "alpha state" and still feel anxious rather than blissful (Orne and Paskewitz, 1974). What's more, there is evidence that biofeedback cannot teach a person to generate more alpha waves than he would normally produce by relaxing and closing his eyes. In one study (Orne and Paskewitz, 1974), control groups received either no feedback or false feedback for their alpha rhythms, while an experimental group received proper feedback. The biofeedback group did no better than either control group; the investigators suggested that the apparent increases in alpha production found in earlier studies simply reflected gradual relaxation as subjects became accustomed to their situation over the course of the experiment.

In general, biofeedback is a much more specific procedure than meditation, and so does not produce the global "hypometabolic" changes seen during meditation. This is because a person is controlling only one function during biofeedback, such as heart rate or muscle tension. Other physiological functions may or may not change along with the one being monitored; if they do, it is usually as part of a general relaxation response. But relaxation, while a discrete state of consciousness, is not an altered state.

While alpha training has proved disappointing in this regard, biofeedback for theta waves is more promising. Budzynski (1976) has used theta biofeedback to teach people to stabilize their consciousness in the "twilight" state we normally experience only briefly as we slip off to sleep. The twilight state is a deep reverie in which vivid images can appear, a dreamlike reality predominates, and one is more open to the unconscious.

This highlights a more general problem in evaluating the effectiveness of self-regulation techniques like biofeedback or meditation. It is difficult to separate all the elements involved and say with certainty which are responsible for the observed effects. In biofeedback, for example, factors such as the person's beliefs and expectations, general relaxation, and the beneficial effects of taking control over part of one's life may each contribute their share.

DRUGS AND CONSCIOUSNESS

Imagine that you're at the dentist, anxious about the tooth he's about to drill. You hate the very thought of how the drill sounds, let alone how it feels. His assistant starts to give you nitrous oxide—"laughing gas."

Suddenly your anxiety dissolves. You don't mind his probing at all—you're too absorbed in the soothing sound of the drill. ∎

A "drug" is any substance that can alter the functioning of a biological system. Many substances fall within this broad definition, ranging from aspirin, antibiotics, and vitamin C to heroin. The drugs of interest for the study of consciousness are those that interact with the central nervous system to alter a person's mood, perception, and behavior. Such *psychoactive* drugs range from the caffeine in coffee and cola drinks, to powerful consciousness-altering substances like marijuana, alcohol, amphetamines, and LSD—and the nitrous oxide some dentists use as a relaxant.

People take most psychoactive drugs for medical reasons, to treat a physical or psychological disorder. Indeed, the tranquilizers (with brand names such as Valium and Librium) are the single drug most often prescribed in America today, outselling even antibiotics. Many psychoactive drugs, though, are—like alcohol—taken simply for the altered state they bring about.

Alcohol

The action of yeasts on natural vegetable sugars causes them to ferment; a by-product of this process is ethyl alcohol, a psychoactive chemical. Without doubt alcohol is the number-one drug of choice among Americans. Alcoholic drinks date back at least 6,000 years; no one knows where or by whom wine was first made from fruit juices, beer from malted grains, or mead from honey.

Alcohol acts to depress the central nervous system, particularly the cortex and reticular formation. It slows down the higher brain centers first; because their action is in the main inhibitory, alcohol's initial effect appears stimulatory, releasing tensions and inhibitions. The peripheral nervous system becomes more active: blood vessels dilate, circulation improves, appetite increases. People typically feel more relaxed and sociable. Tests given to people during the course of a party revealed that the more they drank, the freer they became in expressing their need for power (McClelland, 1975). The overall freedom from inhibition that alcohol brings may explain the increasing impulsiveness of people who are drinking.

The more alcohol a person drinks, the more his entire central nervous system becomes depressed. His ability to discriminate between stimuli and his judgment in general suffers. Coordination, speech, vision, and balance are impaired. One special danger in the state of drunkenness is that the person's ability to judge his level of competence is impaired early on; even though his actual performance ability suffers, he may be convinced that his ability to perform is unchanged or even improved (Poley, Lea, and Vibe, 1979).

Very high levels of alcohol blunt pain; as the nervous system slows further, the drinker may become sedated and drift into sleep. Extremely high levels of alcohol can be lethal. Death from drinking is due to depression of the centers in the lower brain that control breathing, but this is quite rare.

In general, the greater a person's body weight—especially if muscle rather than fat—the more alcohol the person can hold. Larger bodies metabolize alcohol faster. One rule of thumb is that a 150-pound man can drink a five-ounce glass of wine once per hour without accumulating alcohol in his body (see Figure 8.2).

Alcoholics, who drink large quantities of alcohol regularly, can do so without showing the usual signs of drunkenness. Many alcoholics can accu-

Alcohol can induce an altered state that makes routine activities like driving dangerous. (Courtesy, U.S. Department of Transportation)

Body weight (lbs.)	Number of drinks*											
	1	2	3	4	5	6	7	8	9	10	11	12
100	.038	.075	.113	.130	.168	.225	.263	.300	.338	.375	.419	.450
120	.031	.063	.094	.125	.156	.168	.219	.250	.281	.313	.344	.378
140	.027	.054	.080	.107	.134	.161	.188	.214	.241	.268	.285	.321
160	.023	.047	.070	.094	.112	.141	.164	.180	.211	.234	.258	.281
180	.021	.042	.063	.083	.104	.125	.146	.167	.188	.208	.229	.250
200	.019	.038	.056	.075	.094	.113	.131	.150	.169	.188	.208	.225
220	.017	.034	.051	.068	.085	.102	.119	.138	.153	.170	.188	.205
240	.016	.031	.047	.063	.078	.094	.109	.125	.141	.156	.172	.188

Under .05	.05 to .10	.10 to .15	Over .15
Driving not seriously impaired	Driving increasingly dangerous (.08 legally drunk in Utah)	Driving dangerous (legally drunk in many states)	Driving VERY dangerous (legally drunk in any state)

*One drink equals 1 ounce of 100 proof liquor or 12 ounces of beer.

Figure 8.2 Alcohol consumption and intoxication
The larger one's body, the more alcohol it takes to make one drunk.

rately perform complex tasks after a number of drinks that would cause the average person to do poorly. The reason is that their central nervous system seems to develop a tolerance, adapting to alcohol. The brain, for example, becomes less sensitive to the depressing effects of alcohol. This means that larger and larger amounts are needed to become intoxicated (Poley, Lea, and Vibe, 1979). Alcoholics also seem to develop strategies for coping with familiar situations while drunk (Whitter and Leonard, 1980).

While the alcoholic's brain may adapt to alcohol, his liver—which bears the brunt of removing it from the body—does not fare as well; liver disease is the primary cause of alcohol-related deaths in alcoholics. Brain tolerance has its limit, too. There comes a point in the progression of alcoholism where tolerance for the substance disappears, and a small amount of alcohol is once again enough to make the person drunk.

Marijuana

Before 1960, marijuana use was common in America only among certain subcultures, such as jazz musicians and artists in big cities. By the mid-1960s, however, other people had discovered marijuana, and since then its rate of usage has increased by a factor of perhaps ten thousand. According to government figures, about one out of every seven Americans over the age of fifteen uses marijuana in any given week.

The active ingredient in marijuana is a complex molecule called tetrahydrocannabinol (THC), which is found naturally in resin exuded from the female plants of the common weed *Cannabis sativa*, or Indian hemp. Although the effects of the drug vary somewhat from person to person and also seem to depend on the setting in which it is taken, there is considerable consensus among regular users on how it affects them (Tart, 1973). Most sensory inputs are greatly enhanced or augmented—music sounds fuller, colors are brighter, smells are richer, foods taste better, and sexual and other experiences are more intense. Users become elated, the world seems somehow more meaningful, and even the most ordinary events may take on a kind of extraordinary profundity. The time sense is greatly distorted. A short sequence of events may seem to last for hours. Users may become so entranced with an object that they sit and stare at it for many minutes.

As many users of marijuana have discovered, the drug can heighten unpleasant as well as pleasant experiences. If a person is in a frightened, unhappy, or paranoid mood when she takes the drug, she stands an excellent chance of having these negative experiences blown out of proportion, so that her world, temporarily at least, becomes very upsetting.

In a study of the effects of marijuana, seventeen college students volunteered to smoke it and be tested on the results (Weil, Zinberg, and Nelson, 1968). Nine of them had never smoked marijuana before; the other eight had smoked it many times. They smoked one of three types of cigarette: the first contained a high dose of marijuana, the second, a low dose, and the third, none at all. The participants were not told which type of cigarette they were smoking. The experienced marijuana smokers were tested only on the high-dose cigarettes.

Among the inexperienced participants, only one actually got high (that is, reported the typical euphoria), but all showed impaired performance on tests of both intellectual and motor skills soon after smoking marijuana. In many cases, the heavier the dose, the greater the impairment. However, regular users of marijuana (all of whom got high during the sessions) showed *no* impairment either of intellectual function or of motor skill on the tests.

A more general concern has been with psychological effects of chronic marijuana use. Some professionals feel strongly that prolonged use makes a person apathetic, impairs judgment, and leads to focusing one's existence on the drug experience. More recent studies, however, have failed to support these concerns (Dornbusch *et al.*, 1976). For example, a study of Costa Rican men who had smoked marijuana daily for from ten to twenty-eight years found that, compared to matched controls, they had no differences in testosterone level or sexual function, no immunological deficits, and no psychological abnormalities (W. J. Coggins *et al.*, 1976). The one consistent finding of adverse effects is an increase in respiratory ailments, which may be due to smoking rather than marijuana per se.

Cocaine

The active ingredient in the coca plant, cocaine, is a *stimulant,* one of a class of drugs that provide energy, alertness, and feelings of confidence. Once easily available in various remedies, cocaine was one of the active ingredients in Coca-Cola for a number of years (now caffeine is the only psychoactive drug in Coke). These days, cocaine is both expensive and illegal. It is taken in the form of a fine white powder that is inhaled, or "snorted," through the nostrils, where it is absorbed into the bloodstream through the mucous membranes.

While there has been little laboratory research on the effects of cocaine, Grinspoon and Bakalar (1977) have studied its effects through interviews with users. A moderate dose of cocaine produces a euphoric state that can last for thirty minutes to an hour. It improves attention, reaction time, and speed in simple mental tasks, and so can be helpful for work that requires wakefulness, a free flow of associations, or the suppression of boredom and fatigue.

However, the euphoria that cocaine brings can make the user overestimate his capacities or the quality of his work. And since it does not replenish energy stores, the user will pay the price in physical exhaustion after the drug wears off when his body "comes down" or "crashes." Large doses of cocaine or long-term use can have more negative effects. Repeated use can irreversibly damage the mucous membranes that separate the nostrils. Psychologically, cocaine taken in large doses can cause delusions of grandeur or paranoia.

Hallucinogens

Hallucinogens—so-called because one of their effects is to produce hallucinations—are found in plants that grow throughout the world, and have been used for their effects on consciousness since earliest human history (Schultes, 1976). These drugs are also called "psychedelic" because they demonstrate potential ways in which the mind can function. Among the more familiar hallucinogenic plants are belladonna, henbane, mandrake, datura, a species of morning glory, peyote cactus, many kinds of mushrooms and, of course, cannabis. We still do not know the exact chemical effects of hallucinogens on the brain, though some contain chemical compounds that seem to mimic the activity of certain neurotransmitters, the chemical messengers that regulate brain cell activity.

LSD (lysergic acid diethylamide) is the most potent of the hallucinogens, and it is one of the most powerful drugs known. LSD is 100 times stronger than psilocybin, which comes from a Mexican mushroom, and 4,000 times stronger than mescaline, which comes from the peyote cactus. A dose of a few millionths of a gram has a noticeable effect; an average dose of 100 to 300 micrograms lasts from six to fourteen hours. LSD is the best-known and most extensively studied of the hallucinogens.

Extensive LSD research in the fifties and sixties was spurred by the hope that LSD was a "psychotomimetic" drug, mimicking the effects of psychosis. This research path was a dead end: the LSD "trip" did not prove similar to a psychotic episode.

During an LSD trip, a person can experience any number of mood states, often quite intense and rapidly changing. The person's "set"—expectations, mood, and beliefs—and the setting in which LSD is taken can affect the kind of experience that will be had, enjoyable or frightening. Perceptual hallucinations and distortions are very common with LSD. A typical progression of hallucinatory activity begins with simple geometric forms, progresses to complex images, and then to dreamlike scenes (Siegel, 1977). The user may find an absence of familiar form in objects or distortions in form that make familiar objects unrecognizable. For example, a wall may seem to pulsate or breathe; sounds may be "seen," and visual stimuli may be "heard." Time may be experienced as slowed down or accelerated.

As measured by the ability to perform simple tests, the LSD-user's thinking is impaired; however, he may feel that he is thinking more clearly and logically than ever before. Lifelong problems may seem to be suddenly resolved, or the need to solve them may seem absurd. The person often experiences the "great truth" phenomenon—that is, he feels that previously hidden and ultimate inner truths have been revealed to him. When the trip is over, the magnitude of these discoveries shrinks, and the solutions may turn out to be untenable.

After three to five hours, the experience begins to become less intense and often stabilizes; after six hours, the hallucinations and illusions disappear—if no complications occur.

Panic reactions are the most common of the unpleasant side effects, and they may be terrifying. Persons who experience panic and later describe it often say that they felt trapped in the experience and were afraid that they would never get out or that they would go mad. At this point, they would try to ignore, change, or otherwise rid themselves of the effects of the drug—and then panic when they could not succeed. The best treatment, if the panic is not too severe, seems to be the comfort offered by friends and the security of pleasant familiar settings (Grof, 1979).

SUMMARY

Our stream of consciousness is constantly shifting. Everyone has a large repertoire of discrete states of consciousness.

Waking states. The level of brain arousal in waking states varies from sharp alertness to drowsiness. Full wakefulness is characterized by flexible, focused attention and appropriate reaction to events. Tiredness makes it hard to concentrate and perform well.

Deployment of attention is affected by the level of arousal. When alert, we can narrow or widen our area of attention as necessary. When drowsy, the deployment of attention tends to be made in wide, undisciplined sweeps.

Daydreaming involves ignoring one's surroundings and focusing on an inner reverie. Some people daydream a lot, others almost never. One study found four common patterns of daydreams: anxious distractibility; guilty, negatively toned daydreams; positive-vivid daydreams; and controlled daydreams.

Sleep and dreams. Some kind of mental activity goes on during all phases of sleep. Just at the point of falling asleep we may experience dreamlike or hypnagogic images and sensations, marked by disjointedness. In the first moment of sleep, the state of consciousness shifts markedly.

There are four stages of sleep, which are reflected in progressively slower brain wave rates. These rates show a regular cyclical pattern that recurs about every ninety minutes. In the deepest sleep, stage 4, the sleeper almost appears to be in a coma; yet most episodes of sleepwalking and talking and intense nightmares occur during this stage, as well as in stage 3.

Rapid back-and-forth eye movement (REM) under the closed lids characterize REM sleep, in which dreams most often occur. REM sleep is also called paradoxical sleep because of its puzzling combination of brain wave alertness with coma-like muscle relaxation.

Many dreams are quite prosaic. Some incorporate data from the sleeper's immediate environment, perhaps to protect the sleeper from waking.

Freud hypothesized that dreams are expressions of the unconscious. The manifest content of the dream, drawn from various kinds of factual material, does the dream work of veiling the latent content—unconscious wishes connected primarily with early psychosexual development.

Some modern therapists feel that dreams may be more fruitfully interpreted as direct expressions of the dreamer's current concerns.

Hypnosis. The hypnotic state is characterized by increased suggestibility, enhanced imagery and imagination, avoidance of initiative, and reduction in reality testing. Yet the hypnotized person's brain waves are not different from his normal waking state.

Some researchers doubt that hypnosis is an altered state of consciousness, claiming its characteristic changes can also be induced through brief instructions, exhortations to try hard, and assurances that the tasks to be performed are easy.

Defenders of the hypnotic state point to the existence of trance logic, in which a hypnotized person freely mixes hallucinations with perceptions of real objects and events in a manner that people faking hypnosis could not reproduce.

The self-regulation of consciousness. Meditation and biofeedback both allow people to regulate their own consciousness to a degree.

The many kinds of meditation all involve a retraining of attention. Most forms involve sitting quietly, focusing on one thing, and letting go of the normal flow of thought.

During meditation the metabolism slows and the muscles relax, producing an altered state marked by changes in brain wave rates. Meditators seem to undergo a range of beneficial changes in their lives.

Since biofeedback involves concentration on only one bodily function, it does not usually produce the global changes characteristic of an altered state of consciousness.

Some early claims for biofeedback, especially those related to alpha wave production, have proved overoptimistic. Theta wave biofeedback yields a more pronounced consciousness change.

Drugs and consciousness. The psychoactive drugs that alter a person's mood, perception, and behavior range from caffeine to LSD.

Marijuana causes the enhancement of sensory input and of mood—it can magnify both pleasant and unpleasant feelings.

Cocaine, a stimulant, causes a euphoric state and improves attention and reaction time, though it may also cause the user to overestimate his or her performance and result in physical exhaustion after the drug wears off.

Of the many hallucinogens, LSD, by far the most potent, produces intense auditory and visual hallucinations and feelings of profound insight. Panic reactions are occasional side effects.

GLOSSARY

Altered state of consciousness Any discrete state that varies from a baseline state of consciousness.

Arousal The level of brain activity that determines degrees of alertness.

Baseline state of consciousness State of consciousness ordinarily experienced by a person.

Biofeedback Process that, through electronic technology, gives the subject a continuous flow of information about the "involuntary" bodily processes, which she or he may then learn to control.

Deployment of attention The manner in which attention is focused.

Discrete state of consciousness Distinct pattern of awareness created by the sum total of psychological factors operating at a given moment.

Dream work According to Freud, the process by which the manifest dream content veils the latent content.

Hallucinogen A type of drug that produces hallucinations, among other psychological effects.

Hypnagogic images The dreamlike state just before sleep, marked by looseness of thought and disjointed, vivid images.

Hypnosis A state characterized by increased suggestibility, enhanced imagery and imagination, avoidance of initiative, reduced reality testing and trance logic.

Hypnotic susceptibility The capacity to be hypnotized.

Hypometabolic state The slowing down of bodily processes by a reduction in the body's rate of energy use.

Latent dream content Unconscious wishes, according to Freud, primarily from unresolved early psychosexual development.

Manifest dream content Material derived, according to Freud, from the events of the day, sensations during sleep, and so forth; veils the latent dream content.

Mantra Short sacred sound from Sanskrit, used in such techniques as transcendental meditation (TM).

Meditation A retraining of attention, usually involving sitting quietly and focusing on one thing.

NonREM sleep (NREM) The deep sleep of stages 2 through 4, in which rapid eye movement and dreaming do not often occur.

Paradoxical sleep Another term for REM sleep, because of its puzzling combination of brain wave alertness with comalike muscle relaxation.

Psychoactive drugs Drugs that interact with the central nervous system to alter mood, perception, and behavior.

REM (rapid eye movement) sleep Stage 1 sleep, in which the eyes move rapidly back and forth, and most dreams occur.

Samadhi A state of intense concentration on a single thought or object.

Stimulants A class of drugs that provide energy, alertness, and feelings of confidence.

Symbolism A form of dream work in which, according to Freud, terms and contents are symbolized by concrete objects.

Trance logic The free mixing of hallucinations with perceptions of real objects and events by a person under hypnosis.

Zazen Meditation technique that cultivates mindfulness of each successive moment of awareness.

NATURE AND NURTURE

APPLYING PSYCHOLOGY / THREE

WHERE DO WE GET OUR TRAITS?

The limits of learning ■ The politics of genetics

PRINCIPLES OF GENETICS

Genes: blueprints for a person ■ Predicting inheritance ■ How traits develop

SOCIOBIOLOGY

The case of colors ■ The unselfish gene ■ The double standard: a smart genetic bet?

WHERE DO WE GET OUR TRAITS?

Assume that your mother is small-boned and has a natural talent for music, while your father is large-boned and is a whiz at learning languages. You are small-boned and can play practically any instrument, while your sister is large-boned and superb at learning languages.

Have you each inherited these traits from your parents?

In the nineteenth century, most scientists would most likely have answered this question in the affirmative: people's traits are inherited from their parents. The excitement over Darwin and genetics led them to see heredity underlying most human traits, from body build to special talents, and even as the explanation for why some people are criminals. The rise of Watson, Skinner, and the behaviorists in the early part of this century, however, brought a new emphasis on learning as the cause of individual traits. Thus a behaviorist would most likely have said that your build was inherited, but your sister's language skills and your musical abilities were the product of learning, not heredity.

Now the pendulum has begun to swing in the other direction. The general view in *behavior genetics,* the study of the influence of heredity on behavior, is that heredity sets the limits for what a person can accomplish or what personality traits will develop, while learning determines whether that potential will be fulfilled (Gottlieb, 1976). In this view, then, you and your sister each inherited a potential capacity for your respective talents, but it also took learning on your part to be as good at these skills as your heredity would allow.

The limits of learning

What we have learned makes us who we are, but we are not simply the sum total of what we have learned. There is much about us that learning cannot alter. Each of us has a unique biochemical profile, a specific metabolic pattern, a particular biological constitution. These are givens, and learning never changes them. If your genes and diet determine that you will be five feet nine at the peak of your growth, nothing you have learned can make you taller or shorter.

Although you may learn to become a proficient

basketball player, your height will always be a fixed constraint on your performance, whether an advantage or a drawback. Such genetically determined limits and capabilities are called *inborn capacities*. At birth each person has a set of inborn capacities that limit how much and how fast he or she can learn any given skill, behavior, or response.

Many simple behaviors are genetically determined. Nature provides newborns with a great variety of automatic reflexes, from the knee jerk to the "Babinsky reflex"—the automatic curling up of an infant's toes when the sole is stroked. Babies seem to have an inborn fear of falling, and adults and babies alike react with a startle to a sudden, loud noise. Though necessary for survival, these built-in reflexes have little overall effect on who we become as we grow and learn. But in most other animals, whole ways of life seem determined by a genetic blueprint, with little room left for learning to shape a unique being. Birds, for example, follow inborn patterns in singing, feeding, courting, nest building, and rearing their young.

In humans, though, as well as most animals, behavior is the product of both learning and inborn capacities. The earthworm flees automatically from light, yet it can also learn the path to follow through a maze. A baby crawls unaided by her parents, but she cannot learn English without hearing others speak it. The part of behavior that is fixed by a person's genetic endowment is the result of *nature*, and the part that learning affects is the result of *nurture*. The vast range of human behavior is an interplay of both nature and nurture.

The politics of genetics

The issue of whether people are the product of nature or nurture is debated under many names. Sometimes the question is put in terms of whether a behavior is "innate"—a biological given—or learned. Others ask whether a person's behavior is shaped more by heredity or environment, by genetic factors or experience. The "nativist" view is that behavior is innate, due to heredity; in other words, genetic. The opposing "empiricist" view is that it is learned, shaped by the environment, or

by experience. "Naturism" and "empiricism" are terms that refer back to classical philosophical debates on the matter.

The implications of this debate are social as well as philosophical. Are we masters or victims of our fate? If our behavior is fixed by genes, then we have little freedom; if it is shaped by learning, then we have more control. The latter position is a more optimistic outlook, in keeping with American values of democracy. The idea that people's fate is stamped in their genes does not fit with the ideal that anyone can rise to the top, given the right situations. Perhaps it is because it fits so well with American social values that the nurture position of Watson's behaviorism had such strong appeal for many American psychologists. And perhaps that is why in those areas where heredity has been considered of particular importance, some of psychology's most heated arguments have flared.

But to adopt the nurture stance is not to deny entirely nature's role. The question can be restated as: which is more important for what behaviors? The weight of evidence is that virtually every psychological trait is the product of an *interaction* between nature and nurture. A person's hereditary endowment allows possibilities for—and sets limits on—development; the person's experience and learning then determine the degree to which these genetic possibilities are fulfilled. Thus, a person may have a combination of genes that would allow her to be a great musician, but if she never learns any musical skills, that potential will go unfulfilled.

As D. O. Hebb put it, asking whether heredity or environment is more important is like asking which contributes more to the area of a rectangle, length or width. Obviously, both are essential: there is no rectangle without both length and width—and there is no behavior not rooted part in nature and part in nurture.

PRINCIPLES OF GENETICS

Genetics, the study of the laws of heredity, shows us that nature plays a large role in determining a person's anatomy, abilities, and predispositions.

The classic investigations of heredity were performed by an Austrian monk, Gregor Mendel. (He published his findings in 1866, but they did not receive attention from scientists until the turn of the century.) Mendel was not the first, of course, to notice that physical characteristics seem to repeat from generation to generation. People had long realized that if a father or mother had red hair or crossed eyes or a receding chin, the children and grandchildren might be blessed or cursed with the same trait.

Lacking the longevity to wait for three or four generations of humans, Mendel carried out his experiments with garden peas. In growing different varieties, he discovered that certain traits appeared to dominate in each new crop. When he crossed purebred tall plants with purebred short plants, the new generation was always tall, not half tall and half short or another distribution. Mendel therefore designated the factor for tallness as "dominant" and for shortness, "recessive."

Figure C.1 Mendel's laws of heredity
Mendel's principle of dominant and recessive traits allows a prediction of the likelihood that the children of a couple will inherit certain traits, such as hair color.

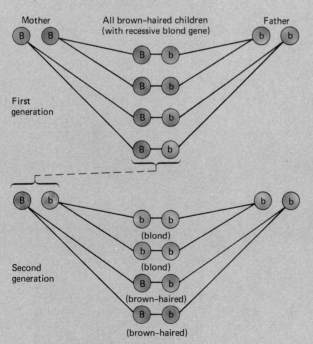

Mendel's studies discovered a principle of genetics: in colloquial terms, what you see isn't necessarily what you'll get. That is, the physical appearance, or *phenotype*, of a new generation will be a predictable consequence not of the appearance of the parents but of their genetic make-up, or *genotype*.

Genes: blueprints for a person

Genetics has come a long way from Mendel's garden peas in unraveling the mysteries of human heredity. At conception, the person-to-be is but a single cell formed when the spermatozoon (male germ cell) penetrates the ovum (female germ cell). Yet, this one tiny cell contains the entire building plan for a new individual, in the form of twenty-three pairs of microscopic *chromosomes* in the cell nucleus. This blueprint is coded in long molecules of deoxyribonucleic acid (DNA), which makes up the chromosomes. The double helix configuration of this DNA molecule permits it to replicate again and again as cell division occurs.

Each new cell formed contains precisely the same configuration or number of chromosomes as the original fertilized egg. The only exception to this rule is the male and female sex cells themselves. Each of these contains only a single member of each pair of chromosomes—that is, twenty-three in all. When two sex cells combine in the process of fertilization, they give the embryo its full complement of forty-six chromosomes, half from each parent.

In twenty-two of the pairs of human chromosomes, the two members are identical. In one pair normally found in the male, however, one chromosome (X) is noticeably larger than the other (Y). This so-called sex chromosome is thus known as XY in the male and XX in the female. Since a male's sperm has only one of the pair of sex chromosomes, it can be either an X-sperm or a Y-sperm, while the female's ovums are all Xs. If an X-sperm fertilizes the ovum, the result is a girl (XX). If the Y-sperm does so, the result is a boy (XY).

The term *gene* is used to indicate any part of a chromosome that specifies any given characteristic. A chromosome contains hundreds of genes,

Twin studies are important to psychology. By studying identical twins raised in different families, researchers are better able to tell which traits are due to environment and which to heredity. (© Michael Goldstein)

each responsible for a given aspect of development. It is the genes that produce differentiation of body cells into skin, muscle, and other tissues, and into groupings that become the body organs such as the heart, lungs, and eyes. It is not surprising, therefore, that many genes are common to all members of a species—for example, the genes that cause people to develop arms rather than wings.

Other genes determine the individuality of each member of a particular species, whether marigold, mouse, or human being. Millions of unique beings walk the earth, and even brothers or sisters are clearly different from each other. The only exception is identical (or monozygotic) twins, who are the product of a single fertilized egg split into two organisms. There is so much variation among people because of the billions of cells in the body, which make the number of possible hereditary combinations enormous. Even if we were to as-

sume that in a given person only two gene pairs in each chromosome were different, that person would still be capable of producing more than 19 trillion genetically different eggs or sperms.

Predicting inheritance

One way that characteristics are transmitted from generation to generation is through single-factor inheritance, where a trait is attributed to a single dominant or recessive gene. Over 300 traits have been linked to a dominant gene, many of them related to defects or abnormalities, such as cataracts or extra fingers. More than 250 human traits can now be attributed to a single recessive gene; these include albinism, deafness from birth, and cretinism. A fourth defect inherited in this way is phenylketonuria (PKU), the inability to metabolize properly the amino acid phenylalanine. This condition can lead to mental retardation. Fortunately, it is an easily detectable defect for which newborn infants are now routinely tested. With early diagnosis and a corrective diet, PKU-caused mental deficiency can be prevented.

The sex chromosomes, X and Y, carry a number of genes not directly related to an individual's sex. Over sixty so-called sex-linked characteristics have been identified. Many of them are carried by the X chromosome and are passed on by the mother, though she herself may not exhibit the trait. One example is color blindness, often called Daltonism after the famous English scientist John Dalton, who used to startle his colleagues with the wildly mismatched color combinations of his clothes. Another sex-linked characteristic is hemophilia, a condition in which the blood does not clot, causing the sufferer to be in almost constant danger of bleeding to death. Common among the ruling families of Europe, hemophilia was probably transmitted by, among several royal mothers, the otherwise irreproachable Queen Victoria.

Using Mendel's principles of dominant and recessive genes, many traits that hinge on a single gene can be predicted. The prediction is given in terms of the likelihood that a child will bear the trait in question. With some inherited abnormalities, such as albinism, the prediction can be relatively definite—the probability of a child of an albino also being albino is 50 percent if the other parent is a carrier of genes for albinism. With other inherited traits, such as sickle-cell anemia, prediction is more difficult.

How traits develop

The mechanisms of single-factor inheritance are complex enough, but for *polygenetic* inheritance—that is, inheritance involving more than one gene pair—prediction is vastly more difficult. A vast array of human traits are probably inherited in this way. Polygenetic traits are highly influenced by a person's experience.

For example, schizophrenia, a severe mental illness, is far more common in blood relatives of schizophrenics than in the general population, and even more common in identical twins of schizophrenics. At first, it was assumed that similar environmental factors could explain this pattern, but

Some medical disorders are inherited. Queen Victoria passed on to her children not only royal titles, but also the genes for hemophilia. (Brown Brothers)

later studies demonstrated that schizophrenia occurred almost as often in twins reared apart as in twins reared in the same household. On this basis, some researchers conclude that genetic factors play a role in schizophrenia, the inheritance of which might be polygenetic (Crider, 1979). Simply knowing that schizophrenia may be polygenetic, though, has not helped researchers to understand much about the missing half of the equation: what sort of environment might trigger the genetic potential for schizophrenia, and what sort might leave it dormant.

In general, then, a baby is endowed with a certain genetic potential for development. However, its experience or environment may support this genetic plan—or sabotage it. For example, no matter what great potential genetic endowment may exist for your musical talent or your sister's language ability, without the right opportunities— music lessons or language classes—these skills could not flower.

SOCIOBIOLOGY

Over the millions of years during which our species evolved, those men and women whose traits had more value for survival tended to live longer, have more children, and so contributed more genes to the species than those with less adaptive traits. Some of the genes they contributed may have been for the very traits that gave them a better chance at survival; these traits show up as invariant patterns of behavior in people.

These are among the basic assumptions of *sociobiology*, the study of the impact of natural selection on social behavior.

Learning theory, sociobiologists point out, has a limited domain of applicability: it can explain some kinds of behavior, but not all (Barash, 1978). For example, if a dog is on a leash tangled once around a pole, straining at food just out of reach, it will keep straining. Put a squirrel in the same fix, and it will untangle the leash, then go after the food. Does this mean squirrels are better learners than dogs? Not at all, according to a sociobiological view. Squirrels have evolved while living in trees, in a three-dimensional world where they have had to learn, for example, to hunt around for branches that touch in order to go to the next tree. Quite simply, those squirrels survived who learned to go away from a goal (the next tree) in order to reach it—a test dogs in their evolutionary past never had to pass very often. Thus the ability to detour was favored by natural selection in squirrels, giving them in this special predicament a talent that has nothing to do with their ability to learn.

The main theorist of sociobiology, Edward O. Wilson (1975), claims that there is a "human biogram," a pattern of potentials built into the heredity of the human species. He points to behavior patterns that are universal as signs of this biogram. These include some facial expressions, the incest taboo, male dominance, a sexual division of labor, and spoken language—though not the details of language. Wilson acknowledges that in most traits people vary. But people are not totally

flexible: we operate within biological limits, passed down in our genes.

The case of colors

Take colors as an example. Have you ever wondered if people all over the world see colors the same way? Different cultures have different ways of classifying colors; some ignore parts of the color spectrum that others name. For this reason, color naming has been considered by some a learned and arbitrary scheme. Whorf (1964) theorized that people first learn the categories of their culture for naming colors, and then organize their perception of color accordingly. Yet the sensory system has physiological constraints that would seem to make everyone's color perception basically the same, although we name colors differently (Bornstein, 1979). This school of thought holds, in keeping with sociobiology, that our sensory systems preordain how we see colors, and we name them accordingly.

When chips of various colors are shown to English-speakers, they label four basic categories: red, green, blue, and yellow. A cross-cultural study found that these same four color categories appear first in almost any language. Although cultures vary in the complexity of their system for naming colors, they always name first black and white, then the four primaries, and any elaborations after that (Berlin and Kay, 1969). Even the Dani, a culture whose color-naming system is organized by brightness rather than hue, could recognize the basic primary colors with no difficulty (Rosch, 1973).

Another bit of evidence comes from infants who are too young to know names for colors. A test found that newborns partition the spectrum into the four primaries, and thus bring into the world a set of innate proclivities. These innate demarcations of colors serve as basic guidelines for how languages organize colors (Bornstein, 1979). Thus while cultures differ in the specifics of color names, they all begin with the same basic, innate building blocks. Color perception rests on a basic biological foundation (like Wilson's "biogram") that is common to all humans rather than dependent on particulars of language and culture (Marler *et al.*, 1980).

The unselfish gene

Such constraints on human behavior evolved over the millions of years that our ancestors lived as hunters and gatherers. No understanding of human behavior, says Wilson, is complete without studying these most general laws of social behavior. Wilson and his followers have gone much further afield than color perception in searching for signs of the human biogram. Sociobiology has sought, for example, to explain acts such as altruism in terms of its benefits to the survival of the species. Altruism is any act that increases the well-being of another person at the expense of one's own, like taking the risk of jumping into a lake to save a drowning person. Self-sacrifice for someone not closely related to you does not promise to increase your own contribution to the gene pool. But it seems to have another payoff, for the species as a whole—it contributes to their overall survival. So while there is no immediate evolutionary gain for the altruistic person, these "genes for unselfishness" may have endured because they perpetuate the survival of groups rather than individuals (Densberry, 1977).

The double standard: a smart genetic bet?

Sociobiologists have probed sexual behavior, too. For example, the sexual double standard holds that while it is "natural" for a man to want to have sexual relations with many women, the same yearnings in a woman are reprehensible. Could this double standard—held in our culture for many centuries, and common throughout the world—be rooted in some deep biological predispositions? Probably, contends Robert Trivers (1972), who points out that these differing strategies are the best way for men and women to assure the most representation of their genes in the gene pool of the next generation. In most species, a female's investment of time and energy in raising offspring is greater than a male's. In humans, a woman can bear an offspring about once a year, while there is no such limit to the number of offspring a man can father with different women. Since a woman becomes pregnant for nine months, and raises a child for one or two decades,

A single pair of parents can make a substantial contribution to the genetic pool by having many children. (Ergun Cagatay/Liaison)

survival to have children with several women, rather than being monogamous. By impregnating many women he can have far more offspring—in theory—than if he impregnated only one.

This may indeed have been true for the 99 percent of human history during which we were wandering hunters and gatherers, although it is obviously less true in these days of single-parent families and working women. Even so, these behavioral tendencies may have come about in humans through evolutionary processes that rewarded men for one strategy, women for another (Densberry, 1977).

Sociobiological explanations such as this one for the double standard have been attacked by many social scientists. One ground for criticism is that this sort of explanation of human behavior hinges on extrapolations from observations of other animal species and from unprovable speculations about the course of human evolution.

Wilson himself, however, is sensitive to one of the potential misuses of sociobiology: to justify social inequities or biases. Feminists, for example, would take issue with the implications of Trivers' theory of the double standard, should anyone invoke it to justify male adultery, or deny equal sexual freedom to women. Any explanation that human behavior is fixed in a person's makeup from birth can be twisted into a justification for social inequities. But such scientific findings should not be misapplied, in Wilson's view, "to pass a value judgment or to deny that a great deal of the behavior can be deliberately changed if individual societies so wish" (1976).

she needs to find a single man whom she can depend on for help—and who can impregnate her again when she is ready. A man, according to Trivers' theory, does better in terms of genetic

GLOSSARY

Behavior genetics The study of the influence of heredity on behavior.

Chromosomes The microscopic structures present in a cell nucleus that contain the genetic "blueprint" for a person.

Gene Any part of a chromosome that specifies a given characteristic.

Genetics The study of the laws of heredity.

Genotype The genetic makeup of a new generation.

Inborn capacities The genetically determined limits and capacities that determine the rate at which a person can learn any given skill, behavior, or response.

Intelligence The capacity to learn.

Nature The part of a person's endowment fixed by heredity.

Nurture The part of a person's capabilities that learning can affect.

Phenotype The actual physical characteristics of a new generation.

Polygenetic The term that describes any inheritance involving more than one gene pair.

PART FOUR

MOTIVATION AND EMOTION

9

MOTIVATION

THE NATURE OF MOTIVES

Basic definitions ■ Basic issues ■ Understanding people's motives ■ Incentives ■ Extrinsic versus intrinsic reward ■ Pressure ■ Optimal drive ■ Intensity of motives

BIOLOGICAL FACTORS

Hunger ■ Overeating ■ Thirst ■ Pain ■ Pleasure ■ The need for stimulation ■ Sex ■ Parental care ■ Aggression

PSYCHOLOGICAL FACTORS

Anxiety ■ Locus of control ■ Goal-oriented motives ■ The TAT ■ Achievement and affiliation ■ The trappings of power ■ Self-actualization

COMMON MYTHS

MANY PEOPLE BELIEVE ...	ACTUALLY ...
We are born with the set of needs that motivate everything we do.	Many motives are learned, not innate.
Sexual behavior is instinctive.	While the sex drive is biological, how it is expressed is determined by learning.
Anxiety harms performance.	Anxiety actually helps performance up to a point; only if anxiety increases beyond the optimal level does it harm performance.
Money is the best motivator.	People may be more highly motivated when the work they do is for their own pleasure than when it is for money.

A man always has two reasons for doing anything—a good reason and the real reason.

JP MORGAN

Why would one person take up parachute jumping as a sport, while another becomes a chess buff? Why does one mother sacrifice a career for her children, while another abandons them? Why does one teenager grow up to be a Ph.D., while her sister becomes a dropout? Why did banker JP Morgan hoard his wealth, while steel magnate Andrew Carnegie became a great philanthropist?

As Morgan himself observed, our motives—the reasons we do what we do—are by no means always obvious. Some needs, such as hunger and thirst, are innate. They swing into action when our bodies are deprived of essentials. Other motives, such as the need to do well, seem to be learned. But there is often no clear-cut distinction between motives that spring from our biological nature and those we acquire. Take being a parent: the species requires that some people take up the role of parenthood, and there is certainly a biological basis to this urge. But people vary greatly in their commitment to the role. Such motives seem to be a combination of innate urges and acquired tastes. Both biological and psychological factors play a role in the *why* behind most everything we do.

Motives are complex, and so there are many different theories of their nature. Some theories deal with the most basic motives, like thirst. As part of

his psychoanalytic theory, Freud proposed that sex and aggression are basic human motives. More humanistic theories, like those of Carl Rogers and Abraham Maslow, propose that people are motivated by the need for psychological growth and the fulfillment of their human potential. Another view has it that much behavior is the result of people seeking the most comfortable level of stimulation for themselves. Other theorists, like David McClelland, posit the existence of needs for achievement, power, and affiliation. Still another view of why we do what we do holds that the way people perceive their own actions and those of others also shapes motivation. Each of these theories of motivation can explain some of the reasons that impel us to act, but none of them can explain the whole range of behavior in all its complexity.

THE NATURE OF MOTIVES

Basic definitions

A *motive* is the force that impels a person to move toward a certain goal. There are several varieties of motive; the main ones are needs, drives, and in-

THANES © 1980 by NEA., Inc. T. M. Reg. U.S. Pat. O88.

centives. Internal factors that move a person to act are called *needs*. Some, like the need for food, are physiological; others, like the need for affection, are psychological. The state of arousal that stems from a need is called a *drive;* a drive is a feeling that directs a person to move toward a goal. When you feel hungry, you seek food; when you need affection, you seek a lover.

Incentives are the rewards a person seeks in satisfying a need. A hamburger satisfies hunger, finding a mate satisfies the desire for affection. When needs are satisfied and drives are satiated, there is a stable inner state called *homeostasis*. The pleasant feeling of fullness after a hamburger, or the peaceful contentment you feel as part of a couple are both kinds of homeostasis; in this placated state you have no sense of urgency to fulfill these same needs, no drive to do so, no interest in further incentives of the same sort. Neither another hamburger nor another potential lover interests you.

Needs can be present and, in fact, intense, without actually affecting behavior, as when a swimmer in a long race overrides her need for more air and water with her need to win the race. Also, an increase in need arising from increased depriva-

tion, such as a major loss of body fluids, does not always result in an increase in drive, for the organism may be so weakened by the need that it cannot act. Finally, although physical needs, such as the need for food, often do result in drives, sometimes the same drives arise when there is no biological need. The sight of a table loaded with your favorite foods is often enough to make you feel hungry, even when your stomach is not empty. Presumably, such a reaction is a conditioned response.

Basic issues

One of the major issues in thinking about motivation is whether the origins of motives are innate or learned (Arkes and Garske, 1977). The earliest theorists saw motives as inherited traits of the human species. They thought the whole range of activities—from writing a play to frying an egg—could be explained in terms of a few basic human drives. Later theorists dealt in the main with nonbiological motives, such as the need to achieve; they saw these motives as learned, not inherited.

Another issue has been whether people respond

in a mechanical, automatic way, or whether people's thoughts and attitudes determine how they act out their motives. Freudian theory saw unconscious thoughts about instinctual drives as motivating our behavior, often in highly disguised forms. Thus Freud saw the creativity of the artist as the sexual instincts in disguise. Humanistic theorists, on the other hand, saw people as consciously aware of the thoughts that moved them to act.

Imagine that in a discussion in a class on human sexuality, your friend Barbara told this story:

Looking back on my first sexual encounter, I have to laugh at my naivete. I'd been interested in boys for several years by the time I managed to overcome my shyness of them. When I finally met Ralph at my friend Jane's party, I liked him immediately. I went to every track meet to root for him, and finally he noticed me enough to ask me out.

We dated for a half year, getting more and more intimate sexually. Finally, the night of the Junior Prom, the two of us were in my parents' front room about 1 A.M. He was leaving for a summer job in a week; this might be our only chance to make love before he left.

We hadn't dared before. Just as we were starting to undress, I asked him, "Did you bring any contraceptives?"

"Oh my gosh!" he said. "I forgot." At that moment we heard footsteps from my parents' room, and my mother's voice call, "Is that you, dear? Are you home?"

Mortified with fear, I answered, "Yes, Mom, we're just saying good night!" We hurriedly straightened up our clothes, mumbled a quick good night, and Ralph was gone.

I never heard from him again. ■

Understanding people's motives

The situation is common enough, the motives simple—at first glance. A closer analysis, though, reveals a complex interplay of needs, drives, and motives in the story of Barbara and Ralph. There

are certain conditions that make satisfaction more likely in such cases. If the conditions aren't present, needs and drives will be thwarted—as Barbara and Ralph discovered. Specifically:

1. The drive itself should be strong enough to arouse the person to action. The sex drive increases in intensity as the reproductive system matures but declines, for example, during illness. Barbara's interest in the opposite sex, and Ralph's, presumably, was intense enough to get them together as a couple.

2. A person's degree of maturity and experience affects how well and in what ways he or she can satisfy a need. Before puberty, boys and girls tend to cling to all-boy or all-girl groups. As they mature, they learn how to interact socially with the opposite sex. Inexperience in such situations can be a powerful inhibitor to fulfilling the sex drive. Barbara had to overcome her shyness before she could go to the party where she met Ralph.

3. Appropriate incentives should be present. In Barbara's case, the original incentive was the chance to meet a boy at Jane's party. Later it was the possibility of dating Ralph that brought her to the track meets. And still later in the relationship, it was petting on dates.

4. Some probability of attaining or at least approaching the goal should be apparent, or other activities may eventually be substituted for it. For example, the thwarting of intercourse may have led one or both members of the couple to masturbate later that night. There are other, less direct channels for the sex drive: sports, hard physical work, or intense studying can all be alternative channels for sexual needs.

5. Conflicting motives should not be too strong. If they are, they may lead to indecision, or turning away from the goal altogether. Barbara might have been seeking affiliation, not sex; she may have been all too glad for the interruption by her mother.

6. Inhibiting feelings should be absent, or weaker than the drive itself. Feelings of fear, anxiety, inadequacy, bashfulness, or shame can interfere with the sex drive. The voice of Barbara's mother no doubt aroused several of these feelings in the hapless couple. Also, even if Barbara's

mother hadn't intervened, the failure to have contraceptives on hand may well have led to their deferring intercourse because of the fear of pregnancy.

In short, most significant situations in life do not spring from a single motive, but involve a complex interplay of factors.

Imagine that summer approaches, and you seem to have only unpleasant choices: summer school with courses you don't want to take, or a boring summer job on an assembly line. How depressing, you think.

Then an old friend calls up. She's leading a tour of high school kids through Europe. They need another counselor to come along. Are you interested?

Sign me up, you tell her, without a second thought for summer school or the assembly line.

But all the next week you constantly think about how badly you need to take those summer school courses. Finally you call your friend and, sadly, tell her you can't go. That day you enroll in summer school.

And all summer you constantly think about how you'd rather be leading that tour. ■

Incentives

Incentives—what's in it for you to behave in one way or another—interact with drives. Negative incentives (like the prospect of a dull summer in school or at work) lead to attempts to avoid or escape a situation. Positive incentives, or rewards (like a summer abroad), have quite the opposite effect: they keep you involved and interested. Positive incentives can reduce a drive by satisfying a need; the incentive of good grades and getting into graduate school can keep you studying hard at dull courses.

Incentives are sometimes mixed, with both positive and negative qualities: a trip to Europe may be pleasant, but shepherding teenagers through strange countries may be a hassle. Incentives can intensify drives: the sight of pastries in a bakery window can make you feel hungrier than you were. Negative incentives, on the other hand, can also lessen drives: if you can't stand seafood, the sight of it may make you feel less hungry.

Because incentives can be positive or negative, conflicts can develop in situations in which several different incentives exert opposite influences. One theory is that such conflicts fall into three basic categories: approach-approach, avoidance-avoidance, and approach-avoidance (Lewin, 1935). An *approach-approach conflict* confronts a person with two attractive choices: say, a trip to Europe or a new car for the same money. In theory this is the easiest kind of conflict to resolve since, as a person moves toward one or the other incentive, it increases in attraction for her or him, and the pull of the other lessens. It's easy to forget the car when you're lying on a beach on the Riviera.

An *avoidance-avoidance conflict* is a toss-up between two things you don't want to do—say, summer school or the assembly line. This is said to be a harder choice to make, since the negative force of each alternative becomes stronger as you approach it, making vacillation more likely.

An *approach-avoidance conflict* is one where you are both attracted and repelled at the same time by the same prospect—a job pays well but bores you, a loan from parents helps with the bills but comes with strings attached, or Europe is great, but the kids on the tour are a pain. This sort of conflict is the most difficult to resolve.

Extrinsic versus intrinsic reward

The power of inner satisfaction may be greater than the promise of an external reward. For example, children in a nursery school who showed an interest in drawing with colored marking pens were put in one of three groups: in the expected-reward condition, they agreed to play with magic markers in order to gain a reward; in the unexpected-reward condition, they played with the pens but did not know they would get a reward; and in the no-reward condition, they neither expected nor received a reward. The children who expected a reward showed the least interest in or enthusiasm for drawing of any of the groups. In short, an activity that was already of intrinsic interest was made less enjoyable by offering an inducement for its performance (Lepper, Greene, and Nisbett, 1973).

This finding questions the wisdom of programs that routinely offer inducements like gold stars, grades, or special privileges for activities that children would enjoy doing anyway. If a student is

motivated to learn a subject without any special promise of a reward, he or she may be more likely to learn with enthusiasm. Inner rewards can be more powerful motivators than outer rewards for already-satisfying tasks. But when there is less incentive to do something—like wash the dishes—then a reward increases motivation.

The same principle seems to apply in incentives on the job. *Intrinsic motivation* is the inner enjoyment brought about by what one does. A person has a high degree of control over such rewards, and they are intrinsic to the task itself, for example, the opportunity to be creative or to develop interpersonal skills, or the pleasure of doing something well. *Extrinsic motivation* is a reward other than the task at hand and is controlled by someone else, for example, pay, promotion, fringe benefits. A review of studies that compared the effect of intrinsic and extrinsic motivations on work found that—contrary to popular assumptions—one consequence of extrinsic motivation may be the reduction of intrinsic motivation (Notz, 1975). When the work is originally rewarding in and of itself, giving people external rewards for what they already enjoy may lessen their pleasure in the work (DeCharms, 1968).

Pressure

External pressures may not be all bad. Under certain conditions, job pressures can be to a person's advantage. Hall and Lawler (1977), in a study of job performance in research laboratories, found that some kinds of pressures enhanced a person's

job performance and enjoyment. Foremost among these was quality pressure, the feeling that the competent performance of one's work is critical to the overall success of the organization. Others are job challenge, the feeling that one's work is a test of one's abilities, and financial responsibility, the sense that one's job performance has a direct bearing on the financial success of the organization. Counterproductive pressures, on the other hand, include interpersonal conflict and unreasonable demands.

Optimal drive

In 1908 Yerkes and Dodson proposed a general rule that relates the intensity of drive to the efficiency of performance. Known as the *Yerkes-Dodson law*, it posits that the relationship between drive and efficiency is an inverted-U: on easy tasks, people perform best when their motivation is very high; on difficult tasks, they perform best when their motivation is lower (see Figure 9.1). The reason too high motivation does not lead to good performance of difficult tasks is that it becomes disruptive. Past an optimal level, the higher a person's drive, the less efficient his performance. In short, easy tasks are done best when motivation is strong, hard ones when it is weak. When the pressure is on and the challenge is great, being too keyed up to perform—that is, having high drive—leads to anxiety, which can interfere with performance.

Intensity of motives

Psychologists look for objective measures of the intensity of motivation, rather than relying on subjective reports, which are often undependable (Young, 1973). As measures of intensity, they have used increases or decreases in the speed of movement during a minor task like sorting objects, in the power of muscular contraction as measured by hand grip on a dynamometer, in rapidity of learning, and in precision and coordination of movements. The quantity and quality of work performed per unit of time can also be taken as indications of how strong motivation is. You

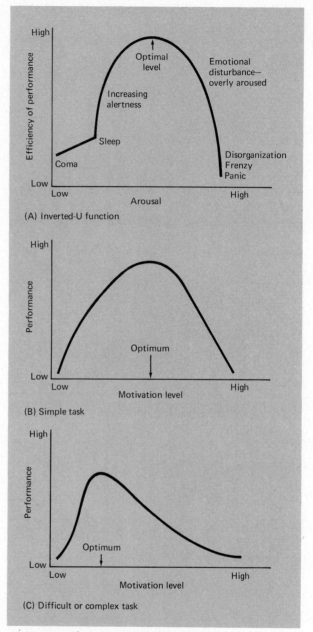

Figure 9.1 Arousal and performance

A) The spectrum of arousal ranges from the lows of coma and sleep, through increasing alertness to high arousal, and finally disorganization, frenzy, and panic. The most efficient performance in general occurs when arousal is in the mid-range, with alertness at a peak, but before emotions become disturbing. The optimal level of arousal (or motivation) is higher for a simple task (B) and lower for a more complex one (C).

may have a strong drive to get unpleasant work done quickly, for example, and so you will work hard and fast at it.

Much of what we know about the intensity of motivation is learned from laboratory studies of animals. A number of different measures have been used in the laboratory. In the "activity" method, the strength of a drive is judged by the amount of restlessness and activity the animal exhibits when deprived of a goal-object, such as food, water, or a mate. This activity level can be measured mechanically in cages that are so delicately balanced they record every movement of the animal; or it can be determined by the amount of running the animal does in a revolving exercise drum and its speed while running. Another method uses rate of performance as a measure; this measure is already familiar to you as a favorite of students of operant conditioning. It can be applied to a single response or to a complex task that has already been learned—e.g., a pigeon pecking at an array of discs to get food. The rate at which the response or task is performed can be used to gauge the subject's motivation. The criteria here are usually how long the animal takes to respond to a stimulus, and how often and how speedily it performs the responses that will reduce its drive.

BIOLOGICAL FACTORS

Imagine that you've accepted a friend's challenge to swim the length of a pool underwater. Years ago you were on a swim team, but you're nowhere near in the shape you used to be.

"Oh well," you think as you head off, "it can't hurt to try."

Halfway down the pool you start to have your doubts—it *can* hurt to try. Your desire to breathe builds into a desperate urge. But it's just a few more feet to the end . . .

Your effort ends abruptly as you burst out of the water, gasping for air. ■

Your body has a biological need for oxygen that you can't ignore, no matter how intent you are on swimming the pool's length. You *have* to breathe—you can't stop yourself. After your gasps for air bring enough oxygen into your body, the drive is reduced; you can relax and breathe normally. The need for oxygen is one of many biological motives. Others are hunger, thirst, the need for sleep and for proper body temperature, and the need to escape pain.

Those motives that are biologically based, like the sex drive, are *primary. Secondary*, or acquired, motives are learned; the need to achieve or excel is an example. Acquired motives largely build on primary motives. For example, we learn to like the sight and smell of food because of its pleasant association with the satisfaction that follows eating, which satisfies the primary motive of hunger. Primary motives are innate, and the need to fulfill them is caused by a homeostatic imbalance (like thirst or hunger). Acquired motives, like the need to achieve, are largely learned, and are often activated by reinforcers; for example, the pleasures of doing well in school may lead someone to get a Ph.D.

Hunger

The simple physiological response to being deprived of food is hunger. Although its function is to regulate eating so that the organism gets enough food to satisfy its needs for energy, growth, and tissue repair, there is a psychological side to hunger as well.

The hunger drive is aroused by a complex network of factors. Hunger pangs show some correlation with stomach contractions, but not precisely. Sensations of hunger are connected to receptors in the mouth and stomach, substances in the blood such as blood sugar, and perhaps more. The fact that food ingested by mouth reduces hunger more than food injected directly into the stomach proves that receptors in the mouth contribute to our sense of having eaten enough.

The concentration of blood sugar and other substances in the blood somehow signals satiety to the brain, which then reduces the hunger drive. The center in the brain where this occurs seems to include part of the hypothalamus, called the ventromedial nucleus (Teitelbaum, 1967). If an animal is given a surgical lesion in the side region of the hypothalamus, it won't eat at all. However, if the animal is lesioned in the front region of the hypothalamus, it will eat voraciously. In short, this part of the brain seems to be a "satiation center" that regulates hunger. These cells detect when the level of fat and glucose in the body gets too low. When the level is low, they stimulate hunger.

Studies of infant eating habits have shown that differences in eating patterns may develop at a very young age. When fat and normal babies just two to four days old were given a sweetened solution, the fat babies ate 28 percent more at the feeding than the amount they usually ate, while the normal-weight babies increased their intake by only 8 percent (Nisbett, 1972). This raises the possibility that abnormal sets may already be established at birth, affecting the hunger drive. We do not yet have a full explanation of the hunger drive, but undoubtedly it is partly a physiological mechanism, and partly something learned and reinforced through experience.

Overeating

Overweight people may react to food in much the same way as animals with lesions in the front region of the hypothalamus: they eat regardless of whether their bodily needs have been satisfied. Stanley Schachter (1971) reviewed findings about obese, lesioned rats and then showed parallels with humans by comparing normal and obese people. The parallels included the following: on the average, overweight people eat more of good-tasting food and less of bad-tasting food than normal weight people; overweight people eat more per meal, eat faster, and are more emotional but less physically active. Schachter cites the case of one woman who happened to have a brain tumor that destroyed the front section of her hypothalamus; like the similarly lesioned rats, she ate immense amounts of food, and became very obese and highly emotional.

The theory of overeating that Schachter proposes is that in obese people, the brain regulator of hunger is malfunctioning (although there is no evidence of an actual lesion or other damage). Instead of eating according to their body's physical

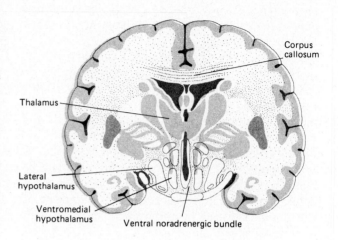

(A)

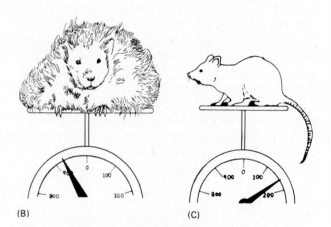

(B)   (C)

Figure 9.2 Brain lesions and obesity

A lesion in (A), the ventromedial area of a rat's brain, produces (B), an obese rat. Compare the obese rat with (C), a nonlesioned, normal rat.

needs, overeaters eat according to whether or not appealing food is available. In short, normal-weight people are motivated to eat when their inner bodily signals tell them they are hungry and to stop when they feel full. Overweight people's eating is externally controlled: when food is present, they will eat; they overeat because their internal cues for satiation do not tell them when to stop.

tween obese and normal weight people in a simple experiment. He gave subjects the chance to snack on almonds, either unshelled or in the shell. Obese people ate many more almonds than normal weight people when the almonds were already shelled, but if the almonds were unshelled, they weren't interested. In another experiment, scheduled to take place around dinner time, researchers put rigged clocks in the laboratory. All subjects sat for fifty minutes, until 5:50 P.M., while galvanic skin response and heart rate readings were taken (the ostensible purpose of the study). However, those who were in the room with a slow clock thought the experiment finished at 5:35, and those who had a fast clock thought the time was 6:20 when it ended, or past dinner time. Coming in to release the subjects, the experimenters offered them crackers. Obese subjects ate much more when they thought it was 6:20 than when they believed it was only 5:35, while subjects who were not obese ate the same number of crackers regardless of the time on the clock (Schachter and Gross, 1968).

Being overly responsive to external cues for eating does not itself explain obesity; there are many people of normal weight who are overresponsive to food, and many overweight people who are not especially responsive (Rodin and Slochower, 1976). Furthermore, losing weight does not change a person's predisposition: overweight women who lost more than 15 percent of their weight in a reduction program did not change in the degree to which the sight of food prompted them to eat (Rodin, Slochower, and Fleming, 1977). And formerly overweight people were more responsive to the taste of food than they had been before their weight loss, eating more than normal-weight people of foods that taste good, and less of those that don't.

One possibility is that the tendency to overeat tasty food regardless of appetite stems from an internal change in the endocrine system that controls how the body metabolizes and stores food. In our evolutionary past, humans underwent regular periods of feast and famine, especially during winters. A sudden weight loss from, say, dieting, might simulate the effects of famine. A brain chemical called beta-endorphin seems to stimulate the body to prepare for food shortages by encouraging overeating and the storage of fat. One researcher suggests that a disorder in the body's balance of beta-endorphin may trigger obesity (Margules, 1979).

Thirst

A dry mouth alone is not enough to drive a person to drink. Like hunger, the feeling of thirst arises when brain centers sense that there is too little liquid in the body. The body loses water constantly—through sweat, urine, even breathing. Short-term regulators in the brain monitor the body's water; they determine when there is too little fluid, and immediately drive us to drink. Long-term regulators don't have an immediate effect on thirst; in-

LOSING WEIGHT WITHOUT A DIET

■ A motivational approach may be the best method for many overweight people to lose weight, according to obesity expert Albert Stunkard (1975) of Stanford University's Eating Disorders Clinic. Many of Dr. Stunkard's patients, discouraged with traditional diets, have managed to lose weight and not gain it back, with a success rate some 50 percent better than that resulting from conventional means.

Stunkard's method is a form of behavior modification, which in this case emphasizes a person's reasons for overeating and helps him or her learn to overcome unwanted habits. A typical obese patient first learns to keep a written record of every bite of food eaten, as well as the conditions surrounding the eating—the patient's mood, the time of day or night, and the company, if any.

Studying such a record can be quite revealing. One woman realized for the first time how often she ate when she was angry, another how she dived for sweets when she was depressed. As might be expected, several people faced up to the fact that the nightly television ritual, with its snack accompaniment, was their undoing.

Patients are not put on prescribed diets (going on a diet automatically implies that you can go off a diet, says Stunkard). Instead they are encouraged to change their behavior. For instance, the woman who ate when she was angry learned to stay out of the kitchen when she felt her temper flaring.

Another key is eating slowly. It takes about twenty minutes for the body's signals that the stomach is full to become effective. Stunkard believes that obese persons eat so rapidly that such signals are not effective.

In true behaviorist fashion, Stunkard rewards his patients for chewing slowly, for waiting two minutes between bites, and for stopping to count the number of bites necessary to consume a meal. Though the patient is free to buy a chocolate sundae with the reward money, he or she more often buys new clothes—in a smaller size.

A one-year follow-up of the first 108 people to complete the weight-loss program showed that many, but not all, patients maintained their weight loss (Jeffrey, Bender, and Wing, 1978). The average weight for men before treatment was 257 pounds; for women, 209 pounds. The group lost an average of 12.8 pounds during the program, and almost half continued to lose weight during the following year. But there was extreme variation in weight loss: from eighty pounds lost to eighteen pounds gained.

What made the difference? The best predictor of success was a change in thinking about food. Those who were most able to understand the emotional needs that motivated their overeating, for example, were best able to change their eating habits, and so lose weight.

The single technique that correlated most highly with weight loss was self-monitoring—simply noticing when, why, and under what conditions you eat. This technique was more effective than trying to stick to a diet, which in the long run was no help at all. ■

stead they control fluid levels in the cells and circulatory system.

The most immediate signs of thirst are a sense of dryness or stickiness in the mouth and throat and parched, dry lips. This dryness is undoubtedly part of the short-term regulation of drinking, but it is not the sole determinant of thirst. People who have been lost on the desert and have undergone severe water deprivation go on drinking long after their mouths and throats are soaked. Someone who is thirsty remains so even if experimenters anesthetize his or her mouth by spraying it with cocaine. In some experiments, scientists actually severed nerves in the mouths and throats of

Intense physical activity—such as sparring—causes the body to lose fluids through sweating, which in turn creates thirst. (Courtesy, The Seven-Up Company)

dogs—and it had no effect on the amount they drank. The local theory, then, which holds that the need to drink is derived solely from the condition of the mouth and throat, is disproved by such observations (Cofer, 1972).

The short-term and long-term regulator of water intake is thought to be in the hypothalamus. Scientists theorize that the thirst mechanism operates this way: When the fluid concentration in the blood is diminished, less blood flows to the kidneys, which then secrete a chemical called angio-

tensin and release it into the bloodstream. Angiotensin acts on the areas of the brain that produce thirst (Anderson, 1971). Short-term and long-term thirst regulators seem to be independent of one another, for damage to one does not affect the other, though both are affected by widespread destruction of the hypothalamus.

The brain seems to respond with thirst to two kinds of signals from the body, osmotic signals, which monitor fluid in cells, and volemic signals, which monitor fluid around cells. Each apparently involves different receptors. Whether they both transmit their messages to the same part of the hypothalamus or not, we don't know yet. Another unsolved puzzle about thirst is the fact that people often drink when they are not thirsty, when they see others drink, or because a preferred drink is handy—suggesting that factors other than strict monitoring of fluid levels can also lead us to drink.

Imagine that you're seeing a doctor for a serious sore throat. A throat culture has confirmed you have strep. The treatment: a hefty shot of antibiotic.

As the nurse approaches with the syringe, you instinctively draw back—even though you know the shot won't really hurt much at all. ■

Pain

Your pulling away from the syringe to avoid the anticipated pain of a shot—even though you tell yourself the pain isn't so bad—is a combination of reflex and learned pain response. Because pain is so closely connected with harm to the body, the drive to avoid or escape it is as necessary for survival as the drives like thirst and hunger that keep the body in homeostasis. Pain is so basic to the body's survival that it leads to many reflexive responses, like automatic pulling back from the syringe, but the circumstances that elicit it, like anticipating a shot, are to a great extent learned.

The drive to escape pain is goal-directed in the sense that the goal is to achieve a situation in which there will be no pain. When a person succeeds in doing this, his or her behavior is operant-

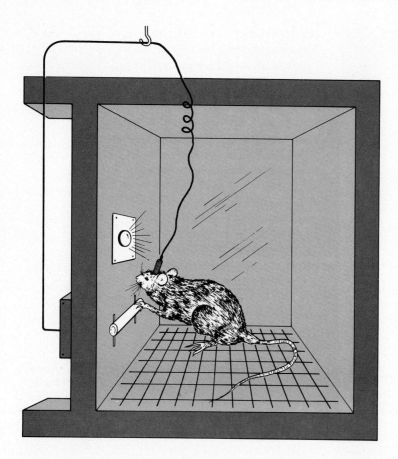

Figure 9.3 A rat with an electrode implanted in its "pleasure center"
It can press a lever in order to receive a pleasurable small electric current through the electrode.

ly conditioned and will probably be repeated. For example, an experiment with rats showed that an animal can be taught to be fearful in a particular situation and to have a strong desire to reduce its fear (Miller, 1948). Rats were placed in a white compartment with a grid floor, through which they were shocked. They squealed in terror, ran around in great agitation, and quickly learned to escape through a door into a gridless black compartment. They also learned a strong fear of the white compartment and a drive to escape it, both of which persisted for hundreds of trials *after* the shock was turned off. The black compartment had become an incentive, and the reduction of fear was apparently reinforcement enough.

Pleasure

Just as pain can move us to act, so can pleasure. The biological basis for pleasure as a motive has been dramatically shown in studies in which rats

had electrodes implanted in areas of the lower brain near the hypothalamus known as the "pleasure centers." These rats quickly learned that pressing a particular bar would deliver a weak shock to the pleasure center through the electrode (Olds, 1956). Given a choice between eating and stimulating the pleasure center, hungry rats invariably chose to press the bar and thus receive the stimulation. Some pressed the bar as often as 5,000 times an hour, for twenty-four hours without rest (Olds and Milner, 1954).

The pleasure center is part of the *limbic system,* a series of brain regions that also includes the hypothalamus. The limbic system seems to be involved in all reward systems, including hunger and thirst. Not all parts of the limbic system produce pleasant sensations, however. When electrodes are placed in other limbic areas, they activate displeasure. Animals with electrodes in these centers will do everything possible to avoid stimulating the centers (Delgado, Roberts, and Miller, 1954).

Imagine that you're driving from the East Coast to California by yourself. Pressed for time, you've decided to drive all night. It's been almost eight hours of flat, endless interstate through Nebraska and Wyoming, and your radio hasn't worked for the last day.

You can't stand it. The monotony is killing you, and there's not so much as a diner open anywhere.

Finally you spot an all-night truck stop. You pull up and spend the next two hours listening to every song on the jukebox. ■

The need for stimulation

As you found on your monotonous trip, all animals, including people, seem innately disposed to seek the right amount of stimulation. For example, rats placed in mazes with plain walls and in mazes with walls painted with designs of increasing complexity at first showed individual preferences for one type or another. But as time passed, they all came to prefer wall designs of greater complexity (Dember, Earl, and Paradise, 1957). Monkeys will push open doors in compartments to look out and increase their stimulation; their drive to explore is strong (Butler, 1954). Investigators have called this drive a "curiosity" or "exploratory" drive, a "manipulative" or "competence" drive, or an "investigative" or "activity" drive. Perhaps it can be most simply identified as a general need for stimulus variability, whatever the behavior through which it is expressed.

Varied stimuli are also attractive—most people enjoy new experiences. However, experiments have shown that complexity is more rewarding than novelty alone. In one study, a red metal box with a lever that could be moved up and down was placed in a playroom. To the preschool children in the room it was novel, and they played with it for a time and then forgot about it. Then the box was redesigned so that each time the lever was moved the box would make a buzzing sound or numbers on a counting device would change. With this added complexity, the children kept playing with the box for five sessions (Hutt, 1966).

Why do we have a need for sensory stimulation? One possible explanation is that such stimulation activates the reticular formation. One

function of the reticular formation is to keep the cortex generally active and responsive to the great variety of nerve impulses that come flooding into it. In evolutionary terms, one can see how an inborn drive to obtain information from and about the environment might be helpful in adjusting to it and might even be necessary for survival. The need for stimulus variability is apparently basic. On the other hand, overstimulation, because it can be confusing, tiring, or disturbing, may be aversive. Both humans and animals need to find the optimum level of stimulation.

Imagine that you're sitting in a hamburger joint near campus, overhearing a conversation at the next booth. Two men are bemoaning the difficulty of meeting girls.

"If I don't find a girlfriend," says one, "I think I'll die."

"I know what you mean," says the other. "If we needed sex like we need air, I'd have suffocated long ago." ■

Sex

Unlike other biological drives, like thirst, hunger, or the need for air, sex is not essential for a person's survival. We need air, food, and water, but we can get by without sex. The species, however, could not survive without sex. Hunger and thirst are the result of body deficits, but there is no such body deficit that sex replenishes. It requires an output of energy but, unlike eating, does not replace it. Finally, sexual activity is as much stimulated by its objects—an attractive partner, for example—as it is a drive to reduce internal needs.

In many animals, experience and learning are not necessary for adequate sexual behavior. Young rats and birds raised in isolation are capable of normal sexual behavior; however, monkeys raised in isolation are not. In fact, when male and female monkeys raised in the absence of other monkeys are paired during the female's fertile period, they will fight violently, rather than mating (Seay, Alexander, and Harlow, 1970).

Learning, experience, and psychological factors play far larger roles in people's sexual behavior

THE SENSATION SEEKERS

■ Do you dive right into a swimming pool, or enter gradually as you get used to the cold water? Would you like to try parachuting, or would you never jump out of a plane? These are some of the questions Marvin Zuckerman (1978) asked over 10,000 people, to collect data on what he calls "sensation seeking"—the urge for stimulation and varied experience. Zuckerman feels sensation seeking is a basic human need, at times a cause of both creativity and destructiveness.

Zuckerman first became interested in sensation seeking as a result of experiments done in the 1960s on sensory deprivation. Volunteers were isolated in rooms or water tanks with minimal distractions for up to two weeks. The subjects' emotions ranged from boredom to panic. One-third couldn't stay in isolation rooms for more than two days and hardly anyone could stay in a water tank for more than ten hours.

Zuckerman developed the sensation-seeking scale to see how the level of novel stimuli one seeks relates to one's reaction when deprived of stimuli. He found that people who search for excitement became extremely restless when confined to an isolation chamber, while people who were low in the need for sensation felt uncomfortable in more intense situations, such as having music or another person in the room.

Zuckerman expanded his research to include the types of experiences sensation seekers were having. In the early 1970s, he found sensation seekers (at least among college students) were likely to use drugs extensively, especially marijuana, amphetamines, and psychedelics; low sensation seekers generally avoided both drugs and liquor. High sensation seekers were also more sexually adventurous. In the early years of college they had more sexual partners and a greater range of sexual experiences (e.g., oral-genital sex) than did the lows.

Women high in sensation seeking reported frequent intercourse, masturbation, and multiple orgasms far more than women low in sensation seeking. Even if highs and lows engage in the same risky activity, their appraisals will differ: the high sensation seekers anticipate pleasure; the lows, anxiety.

Zuckerman found four factors common among highs:

□ Thrill and adventure seeking—they sought excitement in risky pursuits such as parachute jumping and driving fast—or said they would like to do so.

□ Experience seeking—they sought stimulation through a range of experiences such as travel, unusual friends, or a freer lifestyle.

□ Disinhibition—they found an escape from day-to-day pursuits through activities with others like social drinking, parties, and a variety of sexual partners.

□ Boredom susceptibility—they shared a low tolerance for long periods with little stimulation, becoming restless and bored.

Although there may be a biological basis for sensation seeking, it is difficult to tell if it is an inherited trait (Zuckerman, Buchsbaum, and Murphy, 1980). Parents who provide challenging activities for their children may be high sensation seekers themselves. If their children turn out similarly, it could be the result of either heredity or the experiences and models the parents provided.

Highs and lows may sometimes have trouble understanding each other. Those who seek adventure may see people who don't as prudish and inhibited. Those low on the sensation-seeking scale may feel the highs are foolish, reckless, and even crazy. The gulf between a high sensation seeker and a low one could be especially troublesome if, for example, they happen to be parent and child, or husband and wife. ■

People differ in their need to seek stimuli. Some people would never dare take the risks that others enjoy. (Susan McCartney/Photo Researchers)

than in animals'. For example, there is much more variety in the way the sex drive is manifested in humans than in lower animals. Unlike females in other species, who are sexually receptive during estrus only (i.e., when "in heat"), women are receptive to intercourse throughout the menstrual cycle. The conditions under which sexual relations take place, the positions assumed for the sex act, and other customs and attitudes toward sex vary tremendously. While the sex drive itself is biological, its expression is largely a matter of learning.

Imagine that you've never had children and never been especially interested in them. But one day your old friend Frank visits you and brings his three-year-old daughter along.

You all decide to go out for an ice cream. As you walk down the street, you feel a tiny hand reach up and take hold of yours. You're amazed to find yourself delighted, thinking, "Wouldn't it be nice to have a kid of my own?" ■

Parental care

The urge you felt to be a parent—to care for a small child—is not necessary for the survival of the person who feels it, but is obviously essential for the survival of the human species. Many species of animals—especially mammals—are strongly motivated to care for their young. Mother rats will surmount obstacles and endure pain to reach their infants, and this drive is apparently stronger than many others.

The physiological factors that affect maternal behavior are not completely known, but the hormone prolactin seems to be one of them. It causes the secretion of milk, and when virgin female rats or even male rats are injected with prolactin, they will begin nest building and will care for young rats. However, prolactin cannot be the sole factor involved, since mother animals whose mammary glands have been removed, so that they are no longer producing prolactin, will still try to suckle their young.

There may also be an innate, or physiological, component in human parenthood, though the evidence is not clear. Babies do many things that arouse a parent's response—such as cry, cling, and suckle—without being taught. They also smile, at an early point in their development; even babies born blind and deaf smile at about the same age as sighted infants. For the mother or father who has been through a long and difficult period of having to tend almost constantly to the needs of a completely helpless infant, that smile may be an important reinforcement. The parent's caring and affection will also be reinforced by close body contact with the baby and by the way the baby's hunger cries stop when feeding begins.

Learning, however, also plays a part in the parental drive, in humans and among monkeys. Some of the monkeys mentioned above that were raised in isolation eventually had babies, but because they had had no contact with other monkeys, there was no opportunity for them to learn mothering, and with their own infants they were indifferent or even hostile. All avoided the baby and refused to nurse it; some bit the infant, crushed it to the floor, and actually endangered its life. However, a smaller group of females who had as infants been allowed some contact with other young monkeys proved to be adequate mothers. Even the first group became less hostile to their babies with time, and some went on to have another baby and, apparently having learned from experience, provided normal monkey mothering the second time around (Seay, Alexander, and Harlow, 1970).

Aggression

Harming others—or the intent to do so—is aggression, said by some to be an innate human motive. Freud postulated a death instinct and aggressive drives that would build up a rising head of pressure within the individual if they had no release. Ethologists observe that the human is a predatory animal and one of the few species in which individuals frequently set out to destroy one another; in other animals, combat rarely leads to fatal injuries. Lorenz (1970) believes that modern man is in great need of safe outlets for his innate aggressive urges.

The *frustration-aggression* hypothesis (Dol-

lard, *et al.*, 1939) holds that when an individual is frustrated or blocked from achieving his or her goals, aggression is often the result. Originally, the hypothesis insisted that frustration always leads to aggression and that the cause of aggression is always frustration. This would seem to be an oversimplification, however, since frustration can also lead to despair and withdrawal, and aggression can be only a means to an end. Police officers, for example, may subdue suspects not because of frustration but because it is their job.

Another theory holds that humans *learn* aggressive behavior (Bandura, 1969). They learn it because they are rewarded for it (a boy who is bullied and defends himself with his fists is likely to gain the respect of his peers), or they learn it through imitation (e.g., watching violent TV shows). There are many different kinds of rewards in our society that may encourage aggression. In some instances there is social approval—for the acts of soldiers and the police, for example; there are also the rewards of successful self-defense and the aggrandized self-images that aggressors may acquire.

Experimental evidence suggests that the very sight of a gun may encourage aggressive responses. In one study, subjects were given an opportunity to give an electric shock to another person, actually a confederate of the experimenter (Berkowitz and LePage, 1969). Some of them had been humiliated by this person during an earlier phase of the experiment; some had not. The table where the subjects sat to deliver the shocks was in one condition empty; in another, badminton racquets and shuttlecocks were laid out; and in the third condition, the table held a shotgun and a revolver. The experimenter casually shoved the badminton equipment or the guns aside, explaining that they were left over from another experiment. As predicted, the subjects who saw the guns gave more shocks and longer ones, and the humiliated subjects who saw the guns were the most punishing of all.

The *why* of aggression is important. The view that aggression is an instinct—a biological drive as basic as hunger or thirst—hardly bodes well for the future of humankind. If aggression is learned, we may be able to forestall the learning; and if it results from frustration, we can concentrate on alleviating the frustrations, especially the very basic ones, such as poverty and discrimination.

PSYCHOLOGICAL FACTORS

Imagine that it's your first day on the job in a busy copy center. There are long lines of customers waiting for service; you're one of three people operating a copier full blast.

As you tend your machine, you notice you're very nervous, afraid you'll make some dumb, expensive mistake. At the same time, you look forward to the chance to get to know the other people working there; they seem very nice. And you hear that this copy center makes lots of money, and that employees who stay on for more than a year get a share of the business. You hope you'll do well . . . you could sure use the extra money that a share of the profits would bring. . . .

Just then your reverie is broken as you realize you've set the copier for 100 instead of 10 copies. ■

The thoughts that cross your mind as you tend the copy machine are clues to your motives. Your worries about making a mistake reflect anxiety. Your hope of making friends reveals a need for affiliation. And your dream of doing well and earning a share of the business indicates a need for achievement. All these—anxiety, affiliation, achievement—are some of the basic psychological motives that a given situation can call into play.

People's motives are not only varied, but changeable. Sometimes, however, people continue to do something long after the original motive has disappeared. This illustrates the principle of *functional autonomy*. Functional autonomy is the term for behavior that becomes independent, or autonomous, of its original function. (Allport, 1937). A man who struggles to become wealthy for years, for example, may continue long after he is rich to save his money and work very hard.

Anxiety

Freud regarded fear, shame, and guilt as different forms of anxiety produced in situations likely to be dangerous for us in some way. Objective anxiety, he said, is fear and arises from real, external dangers; social anxiety is shame, resulting from the criticisms of others; guilt is anxiety originating in one's conscience.

Anxiety is part of the apprehension a person feels when he or she faces a threat (Lazarus, 1980). In such a situation, the anxiety a person feels is both a signal of impending threat and a motivator to mobilize resources to cope with the threat. Anxiety, in this view, is not necessarily unhealthy, but rather a necessary part of the process whereby people mobilize themselves to handle dangers, threats, and challenges. If you felt no anxiety before an exam, you might not get around to studying for it enough or in time. The anxiety you feel, then, mobilizes you to take the necessary action—studying—that will prepare you to handle the threat that the exam poses. If, however, the anxiety you feel is too great, you may be unable to concentrate on studying or may panic during the exam and so do poorly. In this case—when anxiety cripples rather than mobilizes your ability to cope with stress—it is neurotic anxiety.

Imagine that you have to choose which of the following pairs of statements you agree with more:

I strongly believe that:	or that:
Promotions are earned through hard work and persistence.	Making a lot of money is largely a matter of getting the right breaks.
There is usually a direct connection between how hard I study and the grades I get.	Many times the reactions of teachers seem haphazard to me.
The increasing number of divorces indicates that more and more people are not trying to make their marriages work.	Marriage is largely a gamble.
When I am right, I can convince others.	It is silly to think that one can really change another person's basic attitudes. ■

Locus of control

If you agreed more often with the statements on the left, you may see yourself as able to control the things that happen to you. If you agreed more with those on the right, you may feel that you are at the mercy of forces you cannot control. Using a scale of twenty-nine statements very much like these, Julian Rotter (1972) assessed the degree to which people are *internals*, who see the locus of control of their lives inside themselves, or *externals*, who see the locus of control outside. This continuum ranges from those who are fatalistic—who believe that no matter what they do, it will make no difference—to those who see themselves largely in control of their fate.

Internals perceive rewards as contingent on their own behavior, and so would be motivated to act when they believe their skills can matter. Externals, on the other hand, are more likely to give up when they meet failure, believing nothing they do will make much difference. DeCharms (1968) points out that internals feel that they are the origin or source of what happens to them in their lives. They are more likely to see a difficult situation as a challenge, and so be motivated to try to meet it. Externals, by contrast, feel they are pawns, unable to control what happens to them. They are more likely to see difficulties as threats, and so be less likely to try to overcome them. Can you guess the different ways in which internals and externals would react to the loss of a job? A divorce? A poor grade on a midterm?

Goal-oriented motives

A great deal of human behavior cannot be explained in terms of simply satisfying biological drives like hunger and sex or negative forces like the need to reduce anxiety. These other motives are goal-oriented. A group of such motives has been studied extensively by David McClelland (1975): *affiliation*, the need to associate with others, *achievement*, the need to excel, to accomplish a goal, and to be recognized, and *power*, the need to influence or have an impact on others. While most people have all these motives, one or two tend to be stronger in any given person. Each of them seems to arise in childhood as the result of a particular sort of upbringing, and each of them leads to particular tendencies in adult life.

People will act very differently in the same situation depending on their needs. For example, in a ring-toss game, people who are high in the need to achieve prefer to make moderately risky bets on how well they will do, while people high in the need for power make extremely risky bets. Those with high power needs seem to care more about making an interpersonal impact with a flashy bet than about how well they will actually perform on the game (McClelland and Watson, 1973). People high in power needs prefer games of chance, while those high in achievement needs prefer games of skill. The incentive for the achievement need is doing well, while for the power need, it is having a big impact (McClelland, 1975).

The TAT

One often-used test of which motives are at work in a person is the Thematic Apperception Test (TAT), in which people write brief stories to explain what is going on in ambiguous pictures

Figure 9.4 What is going on here?
One of the TAT pictures used to assess motivation. The person is asked to make up a story about what is happening in the picture.

(McClelland, 1971). The TAT was originally developed by Henry Murray to measure a wide range of human needs. In an early experiment using the TAT, three groups of men who had not eaten for one, four, or sixteen hours wrote stories to a set of TAT pictures. As hunger increased, the stories dwelt more and more on hunger and getting food. From tests such as these, the TAT's ability to measure the intensity of a given motive was established (Atkinson, 1958).

Because the ambiguous nature of the TAT pictures allows a person to tell a vast range of possible stories, it also measures the degree to which different motives preoccupy a person (see Figure 9.4). After a person has written stories to half a dozen or so TAT pictures, the stories are scored for the number of thoughts that deal with a particular need. The scoring codes are spelled out so that independent raters would mark a story the same way. The achievement motive, for example, is indicated by someone in the story who wants to do something better. The affiliation motive is indicated by someone who wants to be with someone else for mutual friendship. The power motive is shown when someone in the story desires to have impact or make an impression on someone else (McClelland and Steele, 1972). By totaling the points for each, the TAT scorer gets a profile of the relative intensity of these motives for the person who wrote the stories.

Achievement and affiliation

Investigators have found that children with a high achievement need, more often than children with a low need, have mothers who praise them for accomplishment and require them to be independent (Winterbottom, 1953). First-born children tend to score higher on the need to achieve than those born later (Sampson and Hancock, 1967). When people with a low achievement need are matched with people of equal ability with a high achievement need, those with a high need do better on mathematical and verbal tasks (Lowell, 1952) and on intellectual problems (French, 1958). In fact, those with a high need generally do better academically in high school and college (Sadacca, Ricciuti, and Swanson, 1956) and are more likely to be upwardly mobile in society, moving above the social class of their parents (Crockett, 1962). Furthermore, they tend to be more realistic than others in estimating and taking risks, factors that seem to lead to success (McClelland, 1961).

THE FEAR OF SUCCESS

■ That people fear failure should surprise no one. But fear of *success*? Yet research shows that some people do, indeed, fear success. At one time it was thought that the fear of success was more common among women than men. Later findings, however, revealed that factors like the sort of success being measured mattered more than sex in determining whether a person feared it or not.

Investigators first discovered a kind of reverse achievement motive, the fear of success, in women. Female college students were to complete a story that began "After her first-term finals, Anne finds herself at the top of her medical school class . . ." (Horner, 1968). It was found that the brighter the woman, the more she tended to denigrate Anne's achievement: Anne was said to be an acne-faced bookworm, or she was simply lucky, or she was a code name for a nonexistent person created by a group of students who did her work for her.

On the other hand, when men were asked to complete a story about a successful medical student named John, they generally felt good about his achievement. Some bright women, apparently, are caught in a double bind. They are afraid of failing, but they are also afraid of too much success, since the traditional stereotype is that women are not supposed to compete with men, or to achieve too much (Bloom and Arnold, 1979).

Women vary greatly in the degree to which they fear success, and they do not always fear it more than men (Tressemer, 1974). One important factor seems to be whether the woman's mother worked or not. If she did, then her daughter is less likely to grow up with a stereotyped model of the woman's role as housewife (Hoffman, 1977). When female high school seniors completed the story about Anne, the medical student at the top of her class, those whose mothers worked had much less fear

---

The roots of affiliation are deep; infants in their helplessness are dependent upon the affiliative feelings of their parents. Whatever its source, first-born children are more likely to have a high need for affiliation than their younger siblings (December, 1964). This may be in part because parents focus more attention on their first-born.

Anxiety can increase the need to affiliate. In one study, a group of college women taking part in an experiment were warned (falsely) that they would be given severe electric shocks (Schachter, 1959). Given the choice of waiting their turns alone or in the company of others, 63 percent preferred company and only 9 percent chose to wait alone; the rest said they didn't care. Another group of women were told they would be given mild, painless shocks; only 33 percent preferred company while they waited.

Imagine that you're at a bar, where you meet Fred, a grad student in business school. As you order drinks, he asks for a very expensive

brand of scotch, and insists on paying for yours. The two of you start talking. After a half hour or so, it turns out that you've stuck to one topic: Fred.

He's told you a saga about how he had his several successes in business ventures and how he was offered important jobs with large companies before going into the master's program, how he owns his own condo, and what a wonderful car his Alfa Romeo is. He says when he has his own company, he'd like to offer you a job.

"Boy," you think, "this guy's really on a power trip." ■

The trappings of power

You're right—Fred is on a power trip. At least from this first impression, he gives every sign of having a strong need for power (the power motive is also called "n Power"). The need for power essentially is the desire to have an impact on others, for example, through aggression, persuasion, get-of success than those with nonworking mothers (Gibbons and Kopelman, 1977). Women who hold to more traditional views of sex roles tend to have lower career aspirations (Peplau, 1976).

Women, however, do not fear success in jobs that are traditionally feminine: when women were told a story about a successful student in nursing school, they were positive about her success (Feather, 1975). In fact, the sex-typing of jobs works both ways: college men were found to fear success in nursing more than women (Janda, O'Grady, and Capps, 1978).

Since the higher-paid and more prestigious careers in our society are stereotyped as ''men's'' jobs, women who have high achievement strivings may be more likely to run up against this sort of fear than men. The less traditional among them, though, should fare better. ■

ting an emotional response, displaying signs of prestige, and so on (Winter, 1973; McClelland, 1975). Fred was trying to impress you with his expensive tastes and possessions, his great accomplishments, and his ability to affect your life.

College students high in n Power display the trappings of prestige and potency (Winter, 1973). Like Fred, they tend to have more "prestige possessions," such as fancy stereos and cameras—even compared to students with the same income. They are more likely to put their names on the door of their dorm rooms. They also boast or exaggerate their accomplishments: when students were asked the lowest grade they had gotten in college, the high power group reported a higher grade than it was in reality.

The person high in n Power seeks to control people by impressing them. There are many avenues to this sort of control. A common one is the embellishing of what one has done. Winter (1973) found a subtle way that power was asserted in college classes: students high in n Power tended to hand in their term papers in impressive plastic covers with a plastic grip along the margin, the paper itself carefully typed. Other students turned in their papers in a variety of formats, most commonly poorly typed pages held together with a paper clip. To the degree that a paper is judged by its cover, the high power students would get a favorable first reaction.

Getting a reaction from people is important to those high in n Power. When Winter asked students "If you could say one sentence—any sentence—to *anyone*, anywhere in the world, in person and without fear of reprisal, what would you say?" the high need group was much more likely than the low to say something both negative and obscene—ensuring a strong emotional impact.

Winter found a link between n Power and sex. College men high in n Power reported having had intercourse while they were still in high school, while those low in n Power were less likely to have done so. Power-motivated men, Winter notes, either have their first sexual encounter at an earlier age—or claim to.

Self-actualization

Humanistic theorists are not interested so much in those motives that move a person to act out of desperation, but rather in those that aim at personal growth and fulfillment. Carl Rogers (1961) refers to this sort of motivation as an "actualizing tendency," one that serves to develop all a person's capacities in ways that are enhancing. It takes the form of *self-actualization*, the motive to behave so as to fulfill or enhance the self.

The concept of self-actualization was made part of a more total model of human motivation by Abraham Maslow (1970). Maslow (1954) tried to account for all human motives, arranging them in a hierarchy of needs according to their strength in influencing behavior. In this hierarchy, lower needs must be satisfied before the higher ones can be (see Figure 9.5).

Thus, physiological needs, the most basic, must be taken care of before a person can do much to satisfy safety needs, such as the need to be secure and to stay out of danger. Higher up the hierarchy, people strive for love needs: acceptance, affiliation, and belongingness. The next step comprises esteem needs, such as achievement, approv-

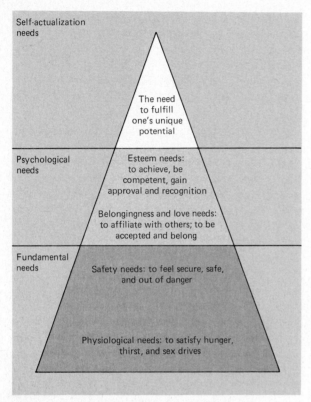

Figure 9.5 Maslow proposes a hierarchy of needs

Each level must be satisfied before a person can fulfill higher needs.

their talents. Among the characteristics of self-actualizers Maslow listed: naturalness, detachment, autonomy, deep interpersonal relationships, and an unhostile sense of humor. Such people also are more prone to "peak experiences," moments of intense awareness, ecstasy, rapture, and great joy.

The self-actualized person accepts herself and others and the realities of existence; she enjoys work and play, is spontaneous and creative, appreciates the arts, and has developed all her potential. Each of us, according to Maslow, is motivated toward self-actualization, unless deprivation or other adverse factors block the way.

al, and recognition. At the peak is the overarching need for self-actualization, the need to fulfill one's potential to the greatest possible degree.

In developing his theory, Maslow studied people he believed to be self-actualized: Lincoln, Thoreau, Eleanor Roosevelt, Einstein, and others whom he knew personally. Maslow felt that by studying the psychologically healthiest men and women, he could learn more about the upper limits of human potential. He called this group "self-actualizers," people who were relatively free of major personal problems and had made the best possible use of

Maslow's theory of self-actualization is based on studying the lives of accomplished people like Albert Einstein. (© Karsh, Ottowa/Woodfin Camp & Assoc.)

SUMMARY

Both biological and psychological factors play a role in the motives behind most everything we do; but not all motives are obvious. Motives are complex, and there are many different motivational theories.

The nature of motives. Motives impel a person to act. Internal motivating factors are needs; the state of arousal that stems from a need is a drive.

Early theorists saw all motives as inherited; later theorists, dealing chiefly with nonbiological motives, saw them as learned. Another issue has been whether or not people are conscious of the motives behind what they do.

Certain conditions make motives more likely to lead to satisfaction: strong drive; maturity and experience; appropriate incentives; possibility of attaining the goal; absence of strong conflicting motives or inhibiting feelings.

Incentives are sometimes mixed and lead to conflict. An approach-approach conflict confronts a person with two attractive choices. An avoidance-avoidance conflict is a toss-up between two things you don't want to do. An approach-avoidance conflict, the most difficult to resolve, involves a choice that includes both positive and negative aspects.

Intrinsic motivation, the enjoyment inherent in a task, may be reduced by extrinsic motivation, the offer of a reward for the task's performance. Reducing external motivation seems to enhance intrinsic motives.

Some kinds of pressure may also enhance motivation—quality pressure, job challenge, and feelings of financial responsibility. Interpersonal conflict and unreasonable demands, however, are counterproductive pressures.

The Yerkes-Dodson law posits that drive and performance are related in an inverted-U. On easy tasks, people perform best when their motivation is very high; on difficult tasks, lower motivation is better.

Much of what is known about measuring intensity of motivation has been learned from studying the behavior of laboratory animals when they are deprived of a goal-object. Measures of human motivational intensity include increases or decreases in the speed of movement during a manual task, power of muscular contraction, and speed of learning.

Biological factors. Primary motives are those that are biologically based and innate, although most include psychological, learned components. Primary motives are triggered by a homeostatic imbalance.

The hypothalamus seems to be the hunger regulation center. Overweight people eat more of good-tasting and less of bad-tasting food than normal-weight people. They also eat more per meal, eat faster, and are more emotional. Schachter pro-

poses that obese people's hunger regulators are malfunctioning. Their eating seems to be externally controlled. An imbalance in a brain chemical, beta-endorphin, may be the cause.

There are short-term and long-term thirst regulators: the former impel us to drink, and the latter control fluid levels in the cells and circulatory system. Mouth and throat dryness are not the only determinants of thirst, contrary to the local theory. Thirst regulators, like those for hunger, are located in the hypothalamus.

Pain, basic to the body's survival, leads to reflexive responses, but the circumstances that elicit pain are to a great extent learned. There is also a biological basis for the pursuit of pleasure. The pleasure center is part of the brain's limbic system.

All animals, including people, seem innately disposed to seek the right amount of stimulation, including novelty and complexity. Stimulation may activate the reticular formation, which keeps the cortex active and responsive.

While the sex drive is innate, its expression is learned. The urge to have a child, like the sex drive, is essential for continuation of the species.

The hormone prolactin may affect rats' maternal behavior. Evidence for a physiological component in human nurturing is not clear. Babies' innate behavior, however, tends to elicit nurturant responses.

Aggression may be an innate human motive. The frustration-aggression hypothesis holds that when an individual is frustrated or blocked from achieving his or her goals, aggression is often the result. Another theory holds that aggression is learned through modeling.

Psychological factors. Secondary, or acquired, motives are learned. They are often activated by reinforcers.

Fear, shame, and guilt are all forms of anxiety. Sometimes, anxiety can motivate a person to confront dangers and challenges rather than to escape an unpleasant situation.

Rotter's scale assesses the degree to which people are internals, seeing the locus of control of their lives inside themselves, or externals, seeing the locus of control outside themselves. Externals are more likely to see difficulties as threats, while internals are prone to see them as challenges.

The goal-oriented motives like affiliation, achievement, and power seem to result from one's upbringing. The Thematic Apperception Test (TAT) measures the extent to which each of these motives influences a person. Children with high achievement need have parents who encourage accomplishment and independence. First-born children are likely to have a high need for affiliation.

Anxiety increases the need to affiliate. People with high needs for power are concerned with having a strong impact on others.

Self-actualization is the motive to fulfill or enhance the self. Maslow arranged a hierarchy of human needs, with self-actualization at the peak; at the base of the hierarchy lie the physiological needs.

GLOSSARY

Anxiety The apprehension a person feels when faced with a threat.

Approach-approach conflict A conflict in choosing between two attractive incentives.

Approach-avoidance conflict A conflict caused by the presence within an option of both negative and positive aspects.

Avoidance-avoidance conflict A conflict in choosing between two unattractive possibilities.

Drive A state of arousal that stems from a need and directs a person to move toward a goal.

Externals People who see the locus of control of their lives outside themselves.

Extrinsic motivation Motivation stimulated by a reward separate from the task at hand and controlled by someone else.

Frustration-aggression hypothesis Holds that when an individual is frustrated or blocked from achieving a goal, aggression is often the result.

Functional autonomy The continuation of an activity long after the original motive for it has disappeared.

Goal-oriented motive A motive aimed to satisfy the need for affiliation, achievement, or power, directed at satisfying biological needs or reducing negative pressures.

Homeostasis A stable inner state of satiation reached when needs have been satisfied and drives extinguished.

Incentive The reward a person seeks in satisfying a need.

Internals People who see themselves in control of their lives.

Intrinsic motivation Enjoyment brought about by what one does, in and of itself.

Motive The force that impels a person to act toward a certain goal.

Need An internal factor that moves a person to act.

n Achievement The need to excel, accomplish a goal, and gain recognition.

n Affiliation The need to associate with others.

n Power The need to influence or have an impact on others.

Primary motive A motive that is biologically based.

Secondary motive A motive that is learned; usually built on a primary motive.

Self-actualization The motive to behave so as to fulfill or enhance the self.

Yerkes-Dodson law Posits that on easy tasks, people perform best when their motivation is very high; on difficult tasks, they perform best when their motivation is lower.

10

EMOTION

THE NATURE OF EMOTION

Definitions of emotion ■ The basic emotions ■ Motivation and emotion

THE PHYSIOLOGY OF EMOTION

Electrodermal activity ■ Respiration ■ Heart rate ■ Muscle tension
■ Brain waves ■ Emotion and the brain

THEORIES OF EMOTION

James-Lange theory ■ Cannon-Bard theory ■ Activation theory

EMOTIONAL AROUSAL

Cognitive factors in emotion ■ Emotion versus reason ■ Situational factors

EMOTIONS: INNATE OR LEARNED?

Innate emotional reactions ■ Do we learn fear? ■ Social influences ■ Hormones and moods

EMOTIONS AND HEALTH

EMOTIONAL RESPONSES

Facial expressions ■ Body language

COMMON MYTHS

MANY PEOPLE BELIEVE ...	ACTUALLY ...
There are only five or six emotions.	There are many emotions. There is no general agreement on exactly how many.
All fears are learned.	Certain stimuli, such as the dark, strange animals, and insects, seem to be innately fear-arousing.
Reason and emotion are opposites.	Many "reasonable" decisions are based on emotions.
People can read a person's emotions from facial expressions.	While the face often mirrors a person's feelings, people's emotions do not always show on their faces.
Facial expressions are used in the same way the world over.	Although people from different cultures agree on the emotional meaning of facial expressions, cultures differ on the appropriateness of various expressions to a given situation.

How does it feel
To be on your own,
A complete unknown,
So far from home
Like a rolling stone?

BOB DYLAN, "LIKE A ROLLING STONE"

Our feelings are a key feature in how we experience ourselves and the world. Feelings make the difference between a good day and a bad one, a pleasant time or a horrible one, well-being or illness. How we feel about other people—and how they seem to feel about us—determines how we treat them. Feelings make us human: the one feature lacking in the Vulcan Mr. Spock of *Star Trek* is emotion.

THE NATURE OF EMOTION

Imagine that you're driving in heavy city traffic. An impatient young man in a sports car behind you keeps driving up so close he is practically in your back seat. To make way for him to pass, you change lanes. But a minute later he darts up beside you and then cuts in front of you.

To avoid hitting him you step on your brake and swerve right—almost smashing into a taxi. You screech to a halt, your heart pounding, thinking thoughts of murder as you watch the sports car disappear down the street. ■

Definitions of emotion

In a situation like this, the emotion you feel is anger. But what does that feeling consist of? Is it the pounding of your heart, the tension in your muscles—the internal body responses? Is it your knowledge that the other driver behaved outrageously—is the anger, in other words, a mental experience? Is it the scowl on your face? Is it the particular action you decide to take—for example, blowing your horn vigorously? Or is it all of these things together?

Various definitions of "emotion" have emphasized each of these aspects. Psychologists have not yet arrived at a generally accepted definition. Plutchik (1980) reviews eighteen definitions, each of which emphasizes different aspects of emotion. P. T. Young (1973), for example, notes emotion is disruptive: "it is a perturbation, a departure from a normal level of non-emotional activity." Skinner (1953) defines emotion in terms of the strength of a response. Arnold (1960) sees emotion as the physiological changes that accompany attraction or aversion. Brenner (1974) defines emotion as a combination of sensations and thoughts. Perhaps the most generally acceptable definition takes all

241

these factors into account: Lazarus (1966) defines *emotion* as a complex disturbance that includes a person's subjective feelings, bodily arousal, and the impulse to respond.

Imagine that you drive on after your near-accident, and a few blocks later, stop at a red light. There in front of you is the thoughtless young man in the sports car.

The light changes to green, and the sports car is slow to start. You find yourself honking your horn impatiently, pleased to have an outlet for your anger. ■

The basic emotions

The British psychologist William McDougall listed seven basic motivating instincts. He believed that each gives rise to a corresponding primary emotion, and that all other emotions derive from these primary ones. His list reads: the instinctive motive of flight is accompanied by the emotion fear; repulsion accompanied by disgust; curiosity by wonder; pugnacity by anger; self-abasement by subjection; self-assertion by elation; and parental care by tenderness (McDougall, 1929). To illustrate the instinct for self-assertion, for example, McDougall cites the way animals display themselves: the peacock fans its tail, the pigeon puffs out its breast. As for humans, he noted that the emotion generated by successful self-assertion is elation, as any politician, valedictorian, or local Ping-Pong champion will be likely to confirm.

More recent attempts to classify emotions have come up with a list close to McDougall's. Plutchik (1980) distinguishes eight basic emotions: anticipation, anger, joy, acceptance, surprise, fear, sorrow, and disgust (see Figure 10.1). He believes that all other emotions can be accounted for in two ways: either as more or less intense versions of the basic emotions (terror is extreme fear; timidity, slight fear); or as blends of the basic feelings, just as a taste can be a blend of sweet, sour, bitter, and salty. While watching an exciting football game, for example, you might feel a mixture of joy, anticipation, and surprise. Those who have tried to classify emotions have usually agreed on most of the basic ones but not all of them.

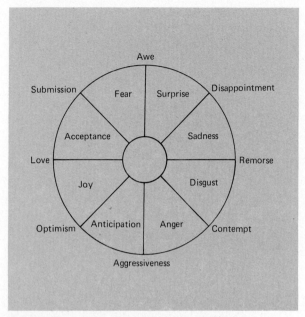

Figure 10.1 Plutchik's eight basic emotions and the emotions formed by combinations of adjacent pairs
Note that the emotions across the wheel from each other are opposites.

Charles Darwin (1890) was among the first to note a seeming continuity in emotions and their expression from lower animals to humans. He saw the bared fang of a wolf, for example, as related to the human sneer. He theorized that emotions increase the chances of survival for a species, since they are appropriate reactions to emergencies and signals to others of their species.

Following Darwin's lead, Plutchik (1980) proposes that the basic human emotions are part of fundamental patterns of adaptation that have been essential to the survival of our species. Joy he sees as the emotional effect of the reproductive urge; disgust as the emotion linked to rejection (for example, of bad food); anger is linked to attack. Reproduction, rejection, and attack are all essential patterns for species survival; joy, disgust, and anger are the feelings that arise from them.

Motivation and emotion

Although feelings and motives are not the same, emotions *can* motivate us. There are other connections between emotions and motivation. Any rough description of what emotion is will usually acknowledge that it involves subjective feelings, called "affects," physiological reactions, and observable behaviors. A description of motivation would focus on the same three elements. When the motivation is hunger, you feel the hunger drive: Your body experiences physiological reactions such as stomach contractions and the effects of low blood sugar, and you seek a goal—food.

Most psychologists distinguish between emotions and motives on several grounds. (1) The subjective experiences are different, as our language reflects. Usually we say that we *feel* angry or loving but that we *are* hungry or thirsty. Furthermore, we recognize anger and love by facial expressions and gestures, but there is no such obvious body language that expresses hunger or thirst. (2) Emotions *usually* result from external stimulation; motives, from internal conditions. Thus, horror (an emotion) may be aroused by the sight of an accident (external), but hunger (a motive) is associated with a low level of blood sugar (internal). We learn what another person's motives are by what she says and sometimes by what she does: someone who eats ravenously reveals her hunger. Since emotions are most often triggered by external factors, we can also infer them from a situation. When a woman has her handbag snatched, it is safe to assume she is angry. (Of course emotions can also arise from inside—for example, from the memory of an accident or the thought of having a purse snatched.) (3) Emotions are generally pleasant or unpleasant; love is pleasant, fear is not. Motives tend to be affectively neutral. (4) Though emotions are often motivating, they are not always motivating. Nor are they always expressed in behavior. You might feel great tenderness as you sit reading a love story. However, what you feel may not show on your face, and it may not result in any strong drive to act tenderly with those around you.

THE PHYSIOLOGY OF EMOTION

All emotional reactions are based in physiological changes in the body, though there is not always a clear-cut connection between a given emotion and a specific physiological change (Candland, 1977).

In a shift from one specific emotion to another—say from elation to sadness—investigators have not yet found an identifiable physiological change that precisely corresponds to the emotional one. When emotional states change, the accompanying physiological changes are general rather than specific. Furthermore, individual reactions differ greatly: the same situation may make one person's heartbeat increase, while another person's decreases. Even so, recent research has aimed at determining the physiological profile of major emotional states through measuring the norms in a large group of people that are associated with a specific emotional state (Davidson, 1978).

The body's internal responses are mainly under the control of the autonomic nervous system. Its two divisions, the sympathetic and the parasympathetic, tend to have opposite effects. The sympathetic system goes into action when we encounter an emotion-provoking situation. Breathing becomes faster, the pupils widen, the skin may become moistened, and hairs on the skin may bristle. As emotional arousal fades, the parasympathetic system takes hold and begins to decrease physiological responses. Any strong emotion generates certain physiological changes in the body, and most of these changes are measurable in a laboratory.

Electrodermal activity

The degree to which we are aroused by an emotion is reflected in small changes in the amount we sweat (Edelberg, 1972). This change in sweat level on the skin, called *electrodermal activity*, is measured by attaching small electrodes to either of the palms or to a finger to record the difference in the way the skin conducts electricity as a result of differences in the amount we sweat. The best-known measure of electrodermal activity is an abrupt rise and fall in sweating, the *galvanic skin response (GSR)*, famous for its use in lie detectors. The GSR ranges from low during nondreaming sleep to high when we experience strong emotions such as fear and anger.

Most recent research on electrodermal activity, however, uses slightly different measures: skin conductance level, a measure of the general, nonspecific sweat response, and skin conductance response, a measure of short, specific changes in direct response to a stimulus. After a loud noise or a threatening sight, the skin conductance response shows several abrupt peaks, which gradually diminish in frequency as the emotional response passes. At the same time, the level might show a sustained rise that stayed high while the person remained alert for the possibility of more emotionally arousing stimuli.

Respiration

The ancient Greeks, recognizing that the emotions are intimately related to respiration, believed that the diaphragm is the seat of the emotions. When we smile or laugh spontaneously, there is a slight forced expiration of air from the lungs, which is barely perceptible with a smile but is more obvious in laughter. Breathing changes also occur with other emotions; think of sobs of grief, the quickened breathing of love. Emotional stimulation usually increases the respiration rate, and some other kinds of stimulation have a similar effect. Infants presented with an odor, for example, begin to breathe more quickly (Engen, Lipsitt, and Kaye, 1963). A special feature of respiration is that it is easy to control voluntarily, despite the fact that it is normally automatic. Many yoga exercises designed to induce relaxation and peaceful emotions involve the control of breathing (Shapiro, 1980).

Heart rate

Although the ancient Greeks considered the diaphragm the seat of the emotions, the heart has more often been assigned that role. Increased heart rate generally indicates an increase in emotions. However, a decreased rate is also significant, for sometimes it is as if the body slows some of its internal processes in order to concentrate on others and get more efficient performance from them. For example, when an individual is waiting at an intersection for a traffic signal to change, his heart rate may decrease just before the light goes green, speeding up again afterward. It has also been shown that those who have such a de-

crease tend to be the quickest in reaction-time experiments. The heart rate decreases most in response to unpleasant stimuli (Kleinman, 1973). In association with lowered breath rate and increased sweating, a heart rate decrease seems to indicate a general *orienting response*, whereby a person becomes more alert and vigilant, as if prepared for an emergency (Sokolov, 1963).

Muscle tension

The patterns of muscle tension in the body change constantly. While many of these changes are due to shifts in position or particular physical efforts, others reflect changes in emotional states. In general, when we feel relaxed our muscles are too; when we feel tense, so do our muscles (Budzynski *et al.*, 1973). Facial muscles are keenly attuned to reflect changes in emotional states. Using electrodes to monitor the forehead muscle (which tenses when a person frowns), psychologists can detect when a person is feeling a negative emotion—even when there is no visible shift in facial expression (Schwartz, *et al.*, 1974). In the same way, monitoring muscle tension in the cheek muscle that tenses during a smile reveals when a person is feeling positive.

Brain waves

Because brain waves, as measured with an electroencephalogram (EEG), reflect such a vast array of mental activity, there is very little direct relationship between emotions and EEG. In general, the complexity of EEG activity corresponds to the level of mental activity, ranging from the slow, rhythmic theta waves seen when a person is on the verge of sleep, through the slightly faster alpha rhythm seen during quiet repose, to the rapid, desynchronized beta waves of alert mental activity. Within this range, there is no particular link to a person's emotional state. There may, however, be a clue to the link between brain activity and emotion in a recent finding: a higher ratio of activity on the left front of the cortex than the right indicates that a person is having an emotional response—although the particulars of the emotion can range widely (Davidson, *et al.*, 1979).

Emotion and the brain

Researchers have found that the hypothalamus is involved in evoking emotions, as is the limbic system (Leshner, 1977). In evolutionary terms, these are among the oldest parts of the brain in mammals; they developed much earlier than the outer cortex. The limbic system plays a role in conditioning and contains a number of the pleasure centers of the brain. As we have seen in the preceding chapter, the stimulation of some parts of this system is highly rewarding for animals: when allowed to stimulate themselves with a weak electrical current through electrodes implanted in the pleasure centers, they will continue to do so until exhausted, ignoring the hunger, thirst, and sex drives.

Paul MacLean (1968), who forty years ago coined the term "limbic system" for those brain structures most closely involved in emotions, suggests that at an earlier point in brain evolution this part of the brain played a primary role in essential human survival functions such as hunting, homing, mating, and breeding. The limbic system, which is common to species from the reptiles on up, is much older than the human cortex, a very recent addition to the brain from an evolutionary perspective. MacLean suggests that such basic emotions as desire, anger, fear, sorrow, joy, and affection—emotions that play an important part in the survival of the species—trace their roots in human behavior to this primitive part of the brain. The cortex, however, makes the experience and expression of these basic feelings more complex than their original manifestation in the primitive survival programs of the limbic system.

New evidence shows that the brain's hemispheres react differently to emotions. In most people the left frontal region is more active during positive emotions, the right frontal during negative emotions. The right hemisphere also is more responsive to changes in heart rate that reflect emotional arousal (Davidson et al., 1980). These differences in hemispheric responses may possibly indicate that, in the course of evolution, the right hemisphere was more involved in rejection and withdrawal, the left in acceptance and approval (Kinsbourne, 1980).

THEORIES OF EMOTION

James-Lange theory

In his famous *Principles of Psychology* (1890) William James suggested that behavior determines emotion, not the other way around. According to the traditional view held in James' time, a person perceives a situation, reacts with an emotion, and then takes action. James held that the real sequence is perception, response, and then emotion: Your car goes into a skid, you swing the steering wheel and pump the brake, and then you feel panic. You feel panic because you react to the skid; you do not react because you feel panic. Obviously, some prior learning and an appraisal of the situation are necessary (a young child riding in the car who did not know the danger of a skid might be simply curious), but James' point is that the emotion follows the body's responses: first come the visceral reactions and then the emotion. "We feel sorry because we cry, angry because we strike, afraid because we tremble," James wrote. Because Carl Lange, a Danish physiologist, had a similar idea independently, this approach is called the *James-Lange theory* of emotion.

But the theory has been challenged on several counts. For one thing, the visceral changes appear to be similar for different emotions—so similar, as far as we can tell, that if James and Lange were right, we would not be able to distinguish between many of the emotions that we perceive as different. For another thing, when people are injected with adrenaline, which is present during both fear and anger, they do not experience genuine fear or anger but report feeling "as if" they were having such emotions. Last, there are people with injuries that interfere with their awareness of internal changes during emotion (for example, a broken neck that causes paralysis and no sensations below the fracture), and they nevertheless report that they experience normal emotions (Cofer, 1972). Also, the viscera react too slowly to explain the speed of emotional reactions.

Cannon-Bard theory

Another theory of emotion, referred to as the *Cannon-Bard theory*, was based on the work of Cannon (1927) and extended by Bard (1934). It pro-

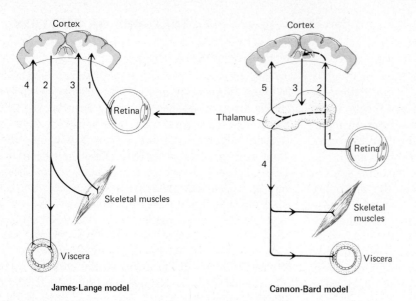

James-Lange model

Cannon-Bard model

Figure 10.2

The James-Lange and Cannon-Bard theories of emotion. The James-Lange theory holds that emotion occurs when messages from the viscera reach the cortex. The Cannon-Bard theory argues that emotion occurs when the thalamus sends signals to the cortex, the viscera and the muscles.

posed a sequence of events more consistent with the traditional view that emotion precedes, rather than follows, a motor response (see Figure 10.2). When a person perceives an emotion-provoking situation, the thalamus, regarded by Cannon and Bard as the seat of emotion, is activated. The thalamus, a structure at the top of the midbrain between the cortex and the spinal cord, in turn triggers the sympathetic system to prepare the body for an emergency response, and also sends signals to the cortex where the emotion is produced. Unlike the James-Lange theory, the Cannon-Bard theory holds that physiological arousal is a by-product of emotion, not its cause. The body's reactions are simply a side effect of emotion.

Activation theory

Some psychologists have suggested that activation or arousal is actually the principal characteristic of emotions. It has been proposed, in fact, that psychologists discard the term "emotion" and substitute "activation" for it (Lindsley, 1951; Duffy, 1962). According to activation theory, emotion is not a special psychological state; it is merely a reflection of an individual's level of *activation*, or energy mobilization. It can range from complete

relaxation or sleep to extreme disturbance or agitation.

The degree of activation can be measured by recording brain waves with an electroencephalograph (EEG), or by other physical indices such as heart or breath rate. Some critics have said that this approach fails to provide measures that adequately differentiate among the different emotions, since physiologically they are very similar (Davidson, 1979). That is, since a person's level of activation is a global response (most measures rising or falling roughly together), emotions as subjectively diverse as rage and excited pleasure seem the same when measured. While the body's level of activation may affect the intensity of an emotional state, general activation does not explain the discrete and unique nature of the emotions we feel.

EMOTIONAL AROUSAL

Imagine that as you drive on, you see that same sports car swerve through traffic, oblivious to other cars. You're getting angry again, thinking that drivers so dangerous shouldn't be allowed on the road.

At the next red light you manage to pull along-side the sports car, intending to give the driver a piece of your mind. But as you look over, you're surprised to see that the young man at the wheel seems very upset, almost on the verge of tears. No wonder his driving is so bad, you think; he's so distraught it's a wonder he can drive at all.

Your anger changes to concern—you wonder if there's some way you might help him. ■

Cognitive factors in emotion

Appraisal—how a person construes an event—can determine the emotions it arouses (Arnold, 1970). When you were outraged at the sports car driver, you were angry; when you realized he was driving so poorly because he was upset, your feelings changed from anger to concern. The degree to which a change in people's thoughts about a situation could change their interpretation of their feelings was demonstrated in a well-known experiment by Schachter and Singer (1962).

In a series of studies, groups of subjects were given epinephrine injections to arouse their visceral reactions (Schachter, 1971). Some subjects were told what symptoms the injection would cause (a faster heart rate, hand tremors, flushing); others were told nothing; and still others were deliberately misled and told to expect numbness and itching. While waiting for the drug to take effect, the subject shared a room with a confederate of the experimenter, who pretended to be another subject. The confederate either shammed great euphoria or faked anger over a questionnaire he and the subject had been asked to fill out.

The more misinformed the subject, the more likely he was to share the confederate's elation or anger. Those who were not told what physical reaction to expect from the injection tended to become elated or angry (along with the confederate), perhaps because their experiencing an emotion helped explain their physical symptoms. Those who were misled were even more apt to take on the confederate's mood, whereas those who had been told accurately what to expect were less likely to do so. These results suggest that the way an individual appraises a situation plays a key role in his or her emotional response.

The importance of cognitive factors like appraisal in *evoking* emotions has led to criticism of the Schachter and Singer model that a state of physiological arousal *precedes* emotion. In daily life rarely is there a strong state of arousal that precedes the emotion-producing event. Virtually always there is an event that is appraised one way or another, and an emotional response that arises as a result (Averill and Opton, 1968; Cordland, *et al.*, 1977).

Imagine that as you mull over what to do about the upset young man in the sports car, you realize that the shape of his face and sweep of his hair remind you of your father. You remember a time when you were very small, and saw your father crying. You wanted desperately to help him then, but had no idea how to begin.

Suddenly you feel very helpless and vaguely frightened. ■

Appraisal is not the only cognitive process that molds emotions. Another is memory. Your memory of your father crying tinges how you react to the man crying in the next car. An event can stir up not only your memories of similar experiences, but also their attendant emotions: you not only recall the scene of your father crying, but re-experience the emotions you felt then. Or, for example, the smell of chalk may revive memories of schoolrooms long ago and the emotional aura that went with them. The back of a woman's head may trigger a feeling of intense dislike if it resembles the head of someone you once knew and hated.

Because of generalization, the present stimulus need not even be exactly the same as the one it recalls; a single aspect of a situation can arouse a whole, complex emotional mood and you may not understand where your feelings come from. You may never realize that it is one person's slight resemblance to your hypercritical father that makes you feel gauche and uncertain with someone you have just met. Psychoanalysis uses the method of free association to take advantage of these features of memory. The associations of the patient are not really free, but hark back to earlier emotional conflicts that may have been repressed.

These can now be reconstructed by the patient with the assistance of the therapist.

Cognitive factors besides memory can generate emotions. Empathy is an example. When you empathize with a friend, you feel what she is feeling; you share her pain or her joy. We empathize with other people in everyday life, and sometimes with the characters in a good novel, play, or film.

Another cognitive process we engage in is projection: we attribute our emotions to other people. This is often a way to avoid acknowledging what we feel. For example, a young woman unable to admit that she is angry with her father may decide that it is he who is irritated with her. In a now classic study, Murray (1933) showed that fear influences one's tendency to perceive others as malicious. Before and after playing a frightening game called "Murder," little girls were shown pictures of people. The people seen after the game were perceived as more malicious (threatening) than those viewed before the girls had been frightened. Murray called this "complementary projection": seeing in others personality traits that justify one's personal emotions. In other words, a frightened individual tends to project onto others the attributes that cause his or her own fear.

Imagine that as you watch the man weeping in the next car, you're seized with the conviction that he needs your help. As he drives off, you follow.

When he turns right at the next corner, you do too, even though it's not at all the direction you were going.

What on earth am I doing? you think to yourself. Still, despite your doubts, you feel compelled to follow. ■

Emotion versus reason

Your emotions in this instance may have overcome your reason. But is our reason always so reasonable? Our reason may be more swayed by our feelings than we realize, except in obviously extreme situations in which we do become aware of their effect, as in your following the upset young man in the sports car. Traditionally, emotions have been said to be the opposite of reason. Supposedly, reason organizes behavior and controls it; strong emotion disrupts it. In a violent rage, a man is said to be "out of his mind" or "unreasonable." When we are "prey to our own emotions," it is thought that we are neither safe drivers nor efficient thinkers. Actually, though, reason and emotion are not simple opposites; emotion is always involved, even in what seems to be the most rational choice (Zajonc, 1980). The ambitious student who decides to pursue law rather than medicine may well be influenced by his own squeamishness in the face of physical illness. He may take into account the way he prefers to spend his time and the kinds of dealings he likes to have with other people. All these are legitimate considerations.

Likes and dislikes constantly influence behavior. Many people firmly believe that one must learn to control one's emotions, particularly those that are destructive. However, B. F. Skinner may be correct when he claims that we lack truly vol-

Drawing by D. Fradon; © 1980 The New Yorker Magazine, Inc.

*"No, I don't want to work on my anger with you.
I want to pop you one!"*

Drawing by William Hamilton; © 1979 The New Yorker Magazine, Inc.

untary control over our emotions and behavior. Advertisers assume that we act largely on the basis of our emotions; politicians, even when they seem to appeal to our reason, attempt to arouse our emotions. In fact, the emotional and rational components of behavior seem thoroughly tangled. Though some emotions, like rage, are largely destructive, others guide behavior constructively. A father's love for his child may lead him to plan years ahead for a college education. In his view, emotion, reason, and other cognitive processes work hand in hand.

Situational factors

Many events, both internal and external, can stir our emotions. A stubbed toe, a social snub, a happy memory, or a tough upcoming exam all have their emotional impact. Among the common situations that evoke an emotional reaction are those of frustration, conflict, and tension.

Frustration, one of the chief causes of aggression and anger, occurs when people are thwarted in pursuit of their goals. Both the anger and the aggression that follow on the heels of frustration are useful: they often lead to efforts to overcome

or at least diminish the frustration. But when individuals can find no outlets for their anger, they will sometimes *displace* it, aim it at a substitute object by directing it onto other people or things. For example, a student who fails an exam may pick a fight with his roommate. Sometimes when anger is displaced, it is turned against the self in the form of depression (Arieti and Bemporad, 1979).

Psychologists, investigating frustration and aggressive behavior among preschool children, have found that there are a number of variables that determine just how aggressive a child will become in a frustrating situation. Among them are the extent to which aggression is permitted or punished in the situation, just how frustrating the situation is, the child's anxiety at the prospect of expressing his aggression, and his frustration tolerance (Barker, *et al.*, 1941).

Conflicts also give rise to emotions, especially in situations where motives clash or goals are both desired and feared. You may long to try skydiving, yet feel panicky when you think about the risks involved. Or you might want to run for office in an organization, yet fear public speaking.

As tension builds in conflict situations, one experiences disturbing emotions. The release of tension, as conflicts are resolved or frustrations overcome, also generates emotions. People dance for joy or weep. Relief from tension is often expressed in smiling, laughing, and other signs of joy (Young, 1973). However, tension relief is sometimes unpleasant—when the worst fears are confirmed or when an individual feels like laughing and crying at the same time, as two people may do after a long separation.

EMOTIONS: INNATE OR LEARNED?

Innate emotional reactions

There are some stimuli that seem to produce the same responses in every member of a species, indicating that innate mechanisms may be involved. For example, there is an automatic aggressive reaction to painful stimulation. Many animals, including humans, will fight with their own kind or

BURN-OUT

■ At Christmastime, a woman went to see a poverty lawyer for help. She explained that she was so poor she couldn't buy presents for her children. "So, go rob Macy's," snapped the lawyer. "And don't come back unless you need me to defend you in court."

The lawyer was a victim of "burn-out," a syndrome among those in the helping professions in which they begin to lose concern for the people they work with (Maslach and Jackson, 1979). A burned-out person suffers from both physical and emotional exhaustion. Some of the other symptoms he might exhibit include: he no longer has any positive feelings or sympathy for his clients, he becomes cynical and often feels that the troubled people he's working with are getting just what they deserve. Consequently, the clients he is serving receive poor-quality care.

Maslach (1978) has studied the causes and symptoms of burn-out. She surveyed a range of people in the helping professions, including social workers, doctors, lawyers, child care workers, teachers and police officers. All of them reacted in similar ways to stress on the job.

One common technique they used was to put a distance between themselves and their clients through dehumanizing phrases such as "the poor" or "my case load." Professionals on the way to burn-out also psychologically withdraw from their clients by minimizing eye contact, communicating in form letters, and spending increasingly less time with them. Keeping relationships with clients on an impersonal level seems to create a protective emotional buffer.

Certain factors in the work situation heighten the risk of burn-out. One of these is client/worker ratio. A child care worker who takes care of twelve children will feel more frustrated than a child care worker who only works with four. The number of hours a worker puts in and the number of breaks he is able to take also affect his chances of burning out.

When a worker is burned-out, the quality of service he provides deteriorates. Often the burn-out victim blames himself ("I should have been able to handle it") or his clients. But as Maslach (1976) sees it, the situation, not the individual, is to blame. She feels that one of the reasons professionals blame themselves is that they have too high expectations of themselves and won't admit that the daily stresses are getting to them. Sometimes a worker will feel he is the only one who can't take it, and so put on an "I'm OK" front.

Because people in the helping professions see people at their worst—when they need help—it is easy for them to fall into a negative attitude toward their clients. People who seek help focus on some negative aspect of themselves, such as an illness or psychological problem. When the problem disappears, so does the client; the helper rarely has the chance to see clients in a positive light. The situation itself, then, reinforces a cynical, negative attitude.

What can one do to prevent burn-out? One thing Maslach suggests is to spend time alone. Just getting away from clients and administrators and cooling off seems to help. Maslach recommends a "decompression routine" in which the worker does some solitary activity such as jogging on the way home from work. After such a time-out, the worker will be more ready to face people again.

The alternative to solitude is using people to relieve stress. Other people, whether family or peers, can offer support, put a situation in perspective, and offer positive feedback to a worker who lacks such reinforcement on the job. ■

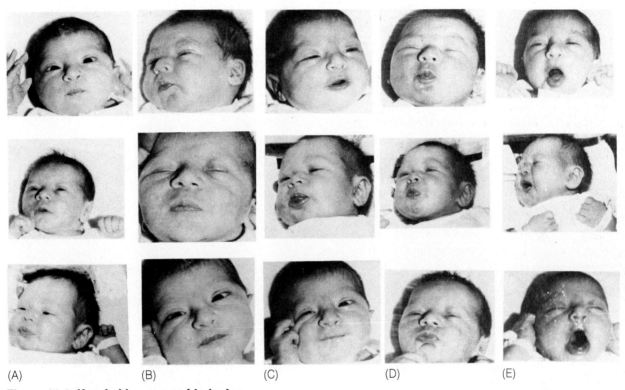

(A) (B) (C) (D) (E)

Figure 10.3 How babies respond to tastes
(A) resting; (B) distilled water (a neutral taste); (C) the sweet taste of sugar; (D) the sour taste of lemon; and (E) a bitter taste, like quinine.

The similiarities of expression among these three babies when reacting to the same tastes suggests some facial expressions are innate. (Courtesy, Steiner)

with a member of another species if in pain—as when a wounded lion or grizzly bear charges a by-stander. If excessive stimulation of any of the senses produces pain—loud noise, for example, or a blindingly bright light—an animal will either retreat in fear or fling itself forward in anger and aggression.

In the nineteenth century, Charles Darwin (1890) tried to categorize the innate human emotions. He analyzed the way emotions are expressed by animals, infants, primitive peoples, and the insane, because he felt that these individuals were least likely to try to control or repress the expression of their feelings. For the same reason, he also studied the painting and sculpture of the great masters. Darwin found it "difficult to determine, with certainty, what are the movements of the features and of the body, that commonly characterize certain states of mind." However, Darwin's observa-

tions that infants express emotions without inhibition has inspired many studies of children. After working with large numbers of infants and young children, from under one month to two years of age, Katharine Bridges (1931) proposed a checklist for describing the way a child's behavior reflects his or her emotions. Her list includes such items as:

The child has or has not, when required to do something disliked:
Lain on the floor and kicked.
Pouted and drooped lips.

The child has or has not:
Clapped hands in delight at things or events.
Laughed at his own mistakes (Bridges, 1931).

From his studies of infants, John B. Watson concluded that they have three innate emotional mechanisms: they respond to loud noises or loss of physical support with fear, to physical restraint with anger, and to stroking or handling with love (Watson, 1919). As we described in Chapter 1, Watson believed that all other emotional responses are conditioned, just as Albert was conditioned to fear furry objects after they were paired with loud noises.

However, Watson has been accused of attributing adult emotions to infants. The behavior he identified as fear looks very much like the Moro reflex, which is seen in infants, and the startle reflex of adults. Infants typically display the Moro reflex when they are dropped or in a less dramatic way experience loss of support: they bow their heads and extend their arms out and forward, as in an embrace, and at the same time flex their legs against their body. It is at least possible, then, that what Watson saw as fear and rage were simply the Moro reflex—an undifferentiated response to a strong, unpleasant stimulus. In addition, other studies have demonstrated that infants are sometimes quieted rather than enraged by swaddling, although extreme restraint does make them restless and tearful.

Aggression may originate in the baby's inborn tendency to protect itself in aversive situations. Lipsitt found that an infant who is physically restrained or who is choking or smothering responds with a particular pattern of activity: among other things, he waves his head, arches his neck, and thrusts out his arms; his face flushes and, of course, he cries. This looks like a rage reaction, and it is seen even in infants suckling at the breast, if they are inadvertently smothered and find themselves for a few seconds unable to breathe (Lipsitt, 1971).

Watson's belief that some emotions are innate is in conflict with Bridges' idea (1932) that newborn infants have no specific emotions but instead respond to stimulation with general agitation or excitement. From this original response, Bridges contends, "slowly appear the well-known emotions of anger, disgust, joy, love, and so forth. They are not present at birth in their mature form." Unpleasant distress and pleasant delight first develop from this original response of primal excitement. Then from distress come fear, dis-

gust, and anger, while delight becomes differentiated into elation and affection (Bridges, 1932).

Do we learn fear?

Some research suggests that humans and animals may be more prone to develop some fears than others and that a *readiness* to fear certain things may be innate.

Evidence for this innate component in fear was provided by a study by C. W. Valentine, an English psychologist, in 1929. Using his own young child as a subject, he tried to condition her (as little Albert was conditioned) to fear a pair of opera glasses. Each time she reached for the glasses, he blew a loud blast on a whistle; however, she showed no signs of alarm. Later, she was presented with a live object, a fuzzy caterpillar to which she had a mixed reaction, pulling away a little, but watching it with curiosity. Just then Valentine blew the whistle, and the child shrieked with fear. Though the whistle had not alarmed her before, now, in conjunction with the caterpillar, it terrified her. Valentine concluded that her attitude toward the caterpillar had been a very unstable one and that the loud noise was just enough of a shock to convert it into fear.

This experiment and later unsuccessful attempts to condition young children to fear blocks and bits of cloth suggest that the white rat used in the conditioning of little Albert was not a totally neutral stimulus. It seems possible that humans have an innate readiness to fear strange animals and insects, since such fears would be biologically useful to the species. Fears of darkness, of lonely and exposed places, and of violent strangers would also be useful for survival; the more common human phobias seem to derive from such fears. Phobics most frequently panic over specific animals or insects, heights, closed-in or open spaces, and strangers (Seligman and Hager, 1972).

Another common human fear is manifested in the nervousness many people feel at the sight of someone who is mutilated. One investigator discovered that even chimpanzees share this fear, and he has suggested a neurological explanation for it. In his study, a chimp was lured to the front of its cage with a tidbit of food. Next the experimenter opened a box that contained an object. When the object was an anesthetized motionless chimp or an ape's severed head, the animal exhibited fear. The investigator theorized that through past experience, the chimp had developed certain expectations: he expected other chimpanzees to move, and he expected a body whenever he saw a head. Consequently, the sight of the head started a sequence of neural events, which was disrupted because the body was missing; thus there was a disorganization of cerebral processes, and the result was fear (Hebb, 1946).

Imagine that you've followed the weeping man in the sports car for several blocks now, and you're beginning to have second thoughts. What on earth would you do, even if you could? Pull up beside him and say, Pardon me, but I saw that you were crying, and I wondered if I could help you . . . ?

No; on second thought, it seems pointless to follow him. Very inappropriate. Enough of this foolishness, you think.

When he turns, you keep going straight. ■

Social influences

Social factors—such as our idea of what's appropriate—shape how we express emotions.

For example, seeing the display of a given emotion can induce the same emotion in you. A fire in a crowded theater is a particularly dramatic example of a direct emotional response to a social situation. Panic spreads through a crowd at a cry of "Fire!" In theater fires, people have been known to trample one another in their rush for exits. The excitement of a crowd at a ball game is infectious, as is the weeping of mourners at a funeral.

Even though people tend to react with the same emotions in a social situation, there are differences from person to person in the freedom with which a person can express feelings (Mandler, 1968). Some are cautious and unexpressive; men,

Emotions are contagious—especially in an excited crowd. (Ellis Herwig/Stock, Boston)

in general, are less able—or encouraged—than women to display emotions that reveal feelings of helplessness, such as crying (Jourard, 1964).

Imagine that heading once again toward your own destination, you realize you've been in a mellow mood most of the day, despite your unsettling encounter with the young man in the sports car.

You whistle a tune as you drive on. ■

Hormones and moods

Moods form a special class of emotions; they often have no clear-cut cause, and they tend to be diffuse rather than directed at a specific object or person (Gaylin, 1979). We all go through numerous short-lived mood changes during the course of the day. Our moods have a strong effect on the intensity of our emotional reactions. If you're in a carefree, euphoric mood, casual disturbing events can be taken lightly. If, on the other hand, you're feeling down, casual effects can make you feel very depressed (Candland, 1977).

While most moods are hard to pinpoint because of their fleeting nature, researchers have been able to study the cyclic mood changes that occur over the course of a woman's menstrual cycle. While the evidence to date is inconclusive, there is a strong argument to be made that cyclic shifts in women's moods are due to the hormonal rhythms that regulate menstruation (Leshner, 1977). Many women report feelings of depression, anxiety, or irritableness just before the onset of their periods, a condition commonly called "premenstrual tension" (Parlee, 1973). About half of a group of healthy young women reported feeling their lowest—depressed, tense, and irritable—during their premenstrual phase, while 40 percent felt their worst during menstruation (May, 1976). Accidents and suicidal thoughts also increase during these two phases of the menstrual cycle.

In one study, college women in various phases of their menstrual period were asked to teach another subject, whom they observed on a video monitor, how to do a card-sorting task (Schonberg, *et al.*, 1976). The women were to instruct the "learner" by giving an electric shock that varied in intensity from weak to strong whenever he made a mistake. Actually the women saw a videotape in which the subject failed to learn the task. Although they believed they were giving shocks to the subject, nothing they did could affect his

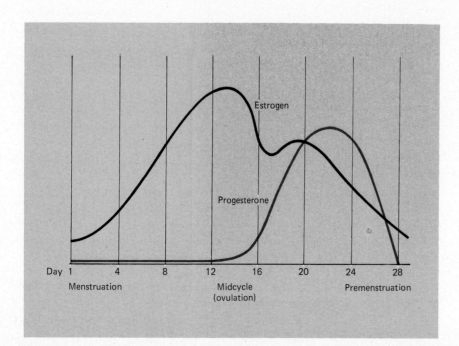

Figure 10.4 Hormone levels during the menstrual cycle
Estrogen levels peak at midcycle; progesterone a few days before menstruation.

learning ability. The women who were premenstrual—within five days of beginning their period—gave more and stronger shocks than did the other women. In short, premenstrual women are more aggressive than women in other phases.

The mood fluctuations women experience over the course of the menstrual cycle are thought to be due to changes in the levels of estrogen and progesterone, female sex hormones (Bardwick, 1971). During the middle of the menstrual cycle, estrogen levels are high; presumably this is the hormonal basis for the feelings of well-being women generally report for that phase. Levels of estrogen and progesterone plunge during the premenstrual phase, and this drop may explain the tension and anxiety felt then. Continuing low levels are thought to account for negative moods during menstruation (Englander-Golden, et al., 1977).

To test whether a hormone regulates any behavior, including moods, researchers can remove the gland that secretes the hormone to see if that will lessen the behavior, and then whether administering the hormone reactivates the behavior. This technique has been used to show the relationship between testosterone, one of the male sex hormones, and aggression (Sheard, 1979). For example, male mice begin to fight each other between thirty-five to fifty-five days after they are born, the time they become sexually mature. If they are castrated before puberty—and so never secrete testosterone—they don't fight other males at the age that would have been puberty. If they are injected with testosterone, though, they will fight like other males.

As is often the case, the relationship between testosterone and aggression in humans is more complex than in animals (Sheard, 1979). In one study, high levels of testosterone in young men correlated with feelings of both hostility and depression, inviting the speculation that depression is "hostility turned inwards" (Doering, et al., 1974). High levels of testosterone have been found in violent teenagers (Kreuz and Rose, 1972), prison inmates convicted of assault and manslaughter who continued to be violent in prison (Ehrenkranz, et al., 1974), and hockey players who get in frequent fights (Sheard, 1979). Even so, higher levels of testosterone do not always produce aggressive moods in people, nor is aggression always accompanied by higher levels of the hormone. While this hormone may contribute to violence and hostility in some people, it does not in and of itself account for aggression.

EMOTIONS AND HEALTH

While life completely without emotions would be dull and unsatisfying, the prolonged effects of extreme emotions can ruin a person's mental and physical health (Pelletier, 1977). Persistent unpleasant emotions, such as anxiety and depression, constitute emotional disorders that require clinical attention and treatment. *Psychosomatic illness* is caused in part by unpleasant emotional reactions. Among the common disorders thought to be psychosomatic are asthma and gastric ulcers; hypertension (high blood pressure) may be caused in part by psychological factors (Harrell, 1980). There is sometimes a direct link between the particular emotion at cause and the specific disorder that develops. Chronic worry, for example, can persistently increase muscle tension levels in the face and scalp, making a person susceptible to tension headaches (Lance, 1975). Feelings of anger, hostility, guilt, or worry may increase acidity in the stomach to the point where ulcers develop. While such emotional factors can lead to the development of one or another symptom, biological susceptibility also depends on genetic factors. Emotions do not cause disease, but they can alter one's susceptibility to it.

Perhaps the most striking demonstration of the impact of emotions on health is the phenomenon of *sudden death*, a fatality brought on by an emotional reaction to a trauma (Engel, 1977). An investigation of 275 cases of sudden death found that they generally occurred within minutes or hours of a major event in the person's life. Most often the person was in good health at the time, or if ill, not at all in any imminent danger of dying. The most common immediate cause was the sudden loss of a loved one, or simply the anniversary of such a loss. Other causes include danger, struggle, or attack; loss of status, self-esteem, or defeat; or even jubilant moments of personal triumph. While the physical reasons underlying such deaths are still unclear, one possibility is that the sudden emotional event mobilizes a person's emer-

BRAIN ATTACKS

■ Holmes and Masuda (1974) have shown that psychological stressors such as bereavement, marital insecurity, large mortgages, and moving are all associated with an increased susceptibility to a range of medical problems. Some evidence points to a biological link: the pituitary gland reacts to stress by releasing the hormone ACTH, which in turn inhibits the body's immune system and thereby increases the body's vulnerability to viral and bacterial infection.

But this mechanism does not explain stress-caused heart attacks, especially those perplexing cases where an otherwise healthy person suddenly "drops dead." The immune system is not involved and, while stress has been shown to increase heart rate and blood pressure, these factors alone cannot produce a heart attack. Recent research by James Skinner (1980) has identified the missing piece of the puzzle: under extreme stress, the brain's frontal lobe abolishes its role as regulator of heart rate, sending the heart muscle into what can be a fatal fibrillation, beating more than five times its normal rate.

The only known medical explanation for sudden death in otherwise healthy people is fibrillation. Electrocardiograms made in ambulances during medical emergencies have verified that this lethal cardiac arrhythmia is the cause for death of "heart attack" victims.

Cardiac pathology, such as a clot in a coronary artery or other heart disease, can explain many of these deaths. Such pathology causes an insufficient blood supply to reach the heart muscle, a situation called "ischemia" that leads to ventricular fibrillation in many cases.

But not all people with cardiac ischemia succumb to ventricular fibrillation. More importantly, 15 percent of the "heart attack" victims studied in several large-scale projects showed no pathology whatso-

gency coping systems, which bypass physiological limits, putting a fatal stress on the person's body.

While negative emotions can lead to disease or death, positive emotions can have the opposite effects. For example, Norman Cousins (1980) reports how he cured himself of a degenerative disorder of the nerves and muscles for which there was no known medical remedy. Cousins checked out of the hospital where he was under treatment, went to a hotel, and there set up a movie projector on which he watched reel after reel of Marx Brothers films and other comedies. After several weeks, his medical condition began to improve, and finally cleared up completely.* While a single case is no proof (Cousins' cure may have

*A more complete account can be found in Cousins' book, *Anatomy of an Illness As Perceived by the Patient: Reflections on Healing & Regeneration.* New York: Norton, 1980.

been a coincidence); it does suggest that a person's mental attitude can affect healing.

Hans Selye (1978) points out that the identical situation—for example, a promotion or a move—can be construed by a person as either a challenge or a threat. These different appraisals have very different emotional consequences: to construe an event as a threat can lead to debilitating emotions such as fear and anxiety. To see it as a challenge, however, can elicit what Selye calls "eustress," a state of exhilarated physical mobilization that is positively toned, rather than negative.

Richard Lazarus, another stress researcher, has shown that changing a person's appraisal can be a highly effective way to minimize emotional response to a threat. For example, when people were told beforehand that a disturbing film that they were about to see was just a fictional portrayal by actors, they were less emotionally

ever during extensive post mortem examinations. This led Skinner to ask, could psychological stress, without the presence of ischemia, lead to ventricular fibrillation directly, through the brain centers that regulate the heart?

Walter Cannon, who in the 1920s proposed the concept of a "flight-or-fight" response to stress, described how, in a self-defense emergency, centers in the higher regions of the brain can take over the autonomic nervous system, pushing internal organs into a pattern of activity that overrules their usual, carefully balanced, homeostatic rates. Heart rate and blood pressure, for example, can shoot up drastically to help mobilize the body for the muscular effort that fight or flight might demand. Cannon did not know, however, just where in the human brain this center might be located.

Skinner has been able to identify a region in the "frontal cortex" as the site of Cannon's cerebral defense system. This brain center seems to adjust the heart rate to fit the external situation. If there is a threat, it will increase the heart rate accordingly. The frontal cortex regulates the heart by sending messages to the brainstem, from where signals go to the autonomic nerves, including those that control heart rate.

When Skinner blockaded this nerve pathway in laboratory animals that had surgically induced arterial disease and then exposed the animals to stress, they did not have a fibrillation. But when other researchers directly stimulated the frontal cortex in animals that had nothing wrong with their cardiovascular system, their heart rate went awry, and some went into a fatal fibrillation.

The weight of evidence, Skinner believes, points to the frontal cortex as the area in the brain that can trigger a heart attack in people under acute stress—even among people who are healthy. ■

aroused by it than those who were not given this mental preparation (Nomikos, Opton, and Lazarus, 1973). Lazarus (1980) has found that people use a wide range of cognitive strategies to handle stress, ranging from outright denial of danger to vigilant attention to the exact nature of the threat. All such cognitive approaches are, in his term, "emotion-focused"; each is effective for handling certain kinds of stress, and each serves to soothe the emotional impact of stress.

EMOTIONAL RESPONSES

The varieties of ways in which we express our feelings are just as rich and varied as the stimuli that produce them. There is no exact count of how many emotions there are; they are so varied that people do not agree on how to describe and name feelings, nor how to recognize them in another person. When, in one study, people were shown thirteen photographs of faces and were asked to name the emotions expressed, they responded with 365 different terms (Allport, 1969).

While psychologists generally believed that infants could not imitate facial expressions of emotion before they were between eight and twelve months old, new evidence shows that the onset of this ability has been underestimated (Meltzoff and Moore, 1977). An experimenter presented his face for fifteen seconds to infants only fourteen to twenty-one days old. While the infant sucked on a pacifier, the experimenter either stuck out his tongue or opened his mouth. Then the pacifier was taken out of the infant's mouth; more often than not the infant made the same facial gesture as the experimenter (see Figure 10.6). This facial imita-

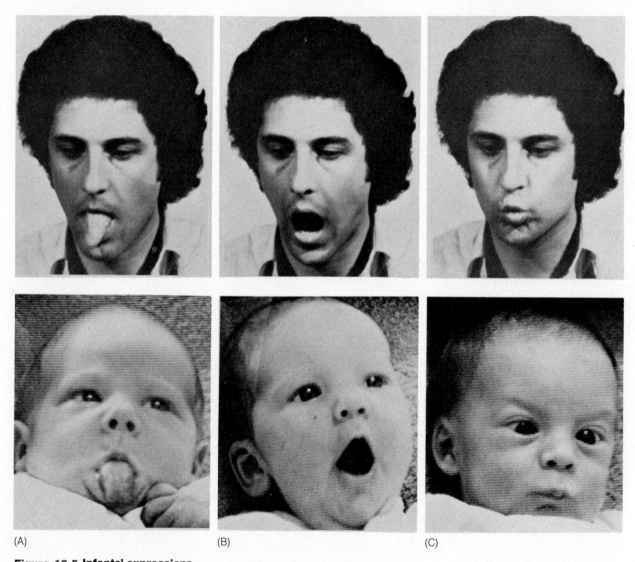

Figure 10.5 Infants' expressions
Infants only 2 to 3 weeks old imitate the facial expressions made by an experimenter: A)
sticking out tongue B) opening mouth, C) protruding lips. (Meltzoff, A. N. & Moore, M. K.,
"Imitation of facial and manual gestures by human neonates". *Science*, 1977, *198*, 75–78.)

tion seemed to occur in a newborn infant only an hour old. The experimenters concluded that the infant's imitation of facial expressions was due neither to conditioning nor to innate mechanisms, but rather to its ability to actively learn facial expression by matching in its own behavior what it witnessed in another's. The language of the emotions, then, seems to be acquired in part through imitative learning rather than either an innate genetic program or simple conditioning alone.

Imagine that as you drive on, you think about the young man in the car who seemed so upset. You wonder what he was so worked up about. As you think it over, you realize you're not quite sure he was *crying* exactly—you never really got that clear a look at his face.

On second thought, you realize that he could have been feeling any number of emotions, from intense anger to ecstatic laughter. ◼

Facial expressions

Your puzzlement over the meaning of the expression you saw on the young man's face reflects the uncertainty of the language of the emotions. You cannot always tell what people are feeling by looking at their faces, although facial expression is one of the major sources of information about a person's feelings. While babies seem to learn some facial expressions by imitation, other expressions may be innate; by and large, babies seem to learn the same set of expressions for the same basic emotions (Ekman, 1980).

Monkeys and apes announce their intentions and their attitudes toward one another by assuming particular postures and by displaying certain facial expressions. In this way they threaten or appease as well as invite another animal to groom

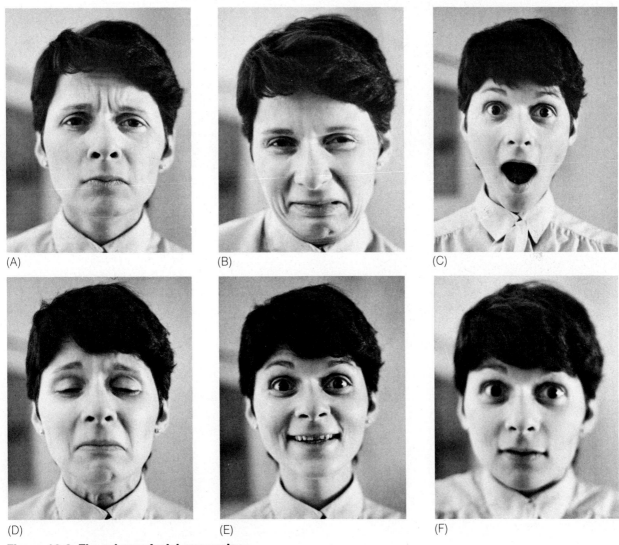

(A) (B) (C)

(D) (E) (F)

Figure 10.6 The primary facial expressions
Can you identify them? (Answers below.)

(A) anger (B) disgust (C) surprise (D) sadness (E) happiness (F) fear.

WILLIAM JAMES (1842-1910)

(Culver Pictures)

■ After several decades, the work of William James is receiving new attention. James, proponent of the James-Lange theory of emotion, was a prolific thinker who, at the turn of the century, was grappling with issues and topics that spanned the spectrum of psychology.

While no single theory James proposed has survived unchallenged, many of his writings anticipated later research. His notions of learning are similar to Skinner's behaviorist theory, his philosophical concerns were further developed in existential psychology, his thinking on cognition and attention affect current work on information processing, and his reflections on the nature of the self sound very much like the Rogerian self-concept. The recent interest in states of consciousness could well have taken as its motto James' (1910) words:

Our normal waking consciousness . . . is but one special type of consciousness, whilst all about it, parted from it by the filmiest of screens, there lie potential forms of consciousness entirely different. . . . apply the requisite stimulus, and at a touch they are there in all their completeness, definite types of mentality which probably somewhere have their field of application and adaptation. . . . they forbid a premature closing of our accounts with reality.

The eldest of five children of a wealthy New York–born father, William James spent much of his youth attending scores of different schools in Europe and America in search of what his father hoped would be a superior education. He was the star of the family, overshadowing his brothers and sister, even the next oldest, Henry, who was to become a famous novelist.

But William went through an extended period of personal turmoil and several shifts in direction before finally finding his true course. After brief flirtations with art and chemistry, physiology caught his interest, and he enrolled in Harvard Medical School.

Soon after he finally completed his medical degree, the death of a favorite cousin in the spring of 1870 precipitated in James a sudden breakdown that left him agonizingly aware of a ''pit of insecurity beneath the surface of life.'' The experience was strikingly similar to one that had befallen his father years earlier. The elder James had eventually found solace in the writings of the Swedish mystic, Emanuel Swedenborg. William, too, discovered a source of comfort and hope in a philosophical document—an essay on free will by Charles Renouvier. Inspired by the French philosopher's words, he decided that ''my first act of free will shall be to believe in free will. . . .''

In 1872 there came a turning point: he was asked to teach half of a new physiology course at Harvard. The subject matter of James' teaching went through a slow evolution. By 1875 he was labeling his offering ''The Relations Between Physiology and Psychology.'' In 1878 he began to teach psychology—one of the first psychology courses in America.

Just as he was beginning to teach his first pure psychology courses, James contracted with a publisher to write a psychology text. He promised to complete it in two years, but it was more than ten before the two enormous volumes of *The Principles of Psychology* were at last published. The exhausted author wrote his editor that the book was a testament to the fact ''that there is no such thing as a *science* of psychology.'' The assessment was at the time correct, nevertheless, the work quickly became a bestseller and is still a pleasure to read today. ∎

them or to play. Ethologists estimate that nonhuman primates have about thirteen different facial expressions, similar in all species. For example, an open-mouthed grin with no teeth showing is a universal invitation to play (Argyle, 1969).

Charles Darwin (1890) believed that with human beings and other animals, emotions automatically produce a particular facial expression. Studies of blind children tend to support Darwin's theory. Psychologists have found that all babies produce a social smile at about the age of five weeks, including babies born blind and therefore unable to imitate the faces of those around them. Blind youngsters also laugh, pout, cry, scowl in anger, and show fear and sadness with the same facial expressions as sighted children (Eibl-Eibesfeldt, 1970).

From about 1914 to 1940, psychologists tried without success to prove that people really can reliably judge emotions from facial expressions (Woodworth and Schlosberg, 1954). Typically, researchers would provide subjects with photographs of actors conjuring up different facial expressions and ask them to name the emotions being conveyed; those tested agreed only about 60 percent of the time. Or the researchers would put experimental subjects into situations calculated to generate particular emotions and then photograph them, hoping to capture recognizable expressions of emotion. The problem is that not everyone reacts the same way to the same situation. Pornographic photographs, for example, disgust some and titillate others—and some people become stolid with self-consciousness when they feel that their reactions are being observed (Ekman, Friesen, and Ellsworth, 1971).

Cross-cultural studies show that there *are* universal facial expressions with meanings that are recognized in every culture. Psychologists, using photographs of faces exhibiting the emotions that they felt were the primary ones (joy, surprise, fear, anger, sadness, and disgust-or-contempt), asked people in the United States, Brazil, Japan, New Guinea, and Borneo to identify the expressions. The subjects were in agreement on the whole. The psychologists tried the same photographs on the Fore, a neolithic New Guinea tribe isolated from the modern world until quite recently and obtained from them the expected identifications.

However, the researchers concluded that although the basic expressions themselves may be much the same the world over, there are "display rules" in every culture that specify which expressions are appropriate in a particular situation. The rules may call for an expression to be played down, exaggerated, disguised, or suppressed entirely. In Japan, for example, etiquette demands a smile in more situations than in America (Ekman, Friesen, and Ellsworth, 1971).

Imagine that you finally arrive at your destination—a friend's house where you're going to exchange class notes to study for an exam. Your conversation with her is quite matter-of-fact, concerned only with the notes—yet somehow you get the feeling she's angry with you.

There's something about her manner, her expression, the tone of her voice, and even her body movements. But you can't quite pin it down. There's an abrupt, aggressive quality to her gestures, a slight but tense frown on her face; when she handed you her notes, she seemed to pull away too quickly and she avoided your eyes.

Yet nothing was said that could give you a clue to her feelings. As you leave you're absolutely convinced she was angry, but can't say exactly why you think so. ∎

Body language

The nonverbal part of communication—a person's tone of voice, body movements, facial expression—often communicates feeling indirectly.

Working with projectors that can slow a film down until it can be analyzed frame by frame, researchers have found that emotional overtones are often conveyed nonverbally. It was just such an unspoken emotional overtone you sensed in your friend. The signals that let us know when someone likes us also seem clear. When a man is with someone he likes, he is apt to stand closer than he otherwise might, face the other squarely, make eye contact frequently, wearing an interest-

THE BODY LANGUAGE

∎ While body language can differ from culture to culture, there are some nonverbal expressions that seem the same the world over. Flirting, for example, may be universally similar in many details according to a review of research by Davis (1973). In six cultures—Samoa, Papua, France, Japan, Africa, and among Indians in South America—the basic interaction in flirting is the same. A two-man team went to each culture, one to smile and nod at women, the other to film what went on. The women's response to a flirtatious smile was essentially the same in each place: a smile, a quick lift of the eyebrows, followed by lowering the head or turning it away, eyes turned downward and eyelids partly closed.

The coyness of the women's response may have its roots in our evolutionary past. Among animals, courtship frequently has two stages: first, attracting a sexual partner, and second, overcoming the other's fear of intimate contact. The male risks attack if the female isn't receptive; if it's the female who approaches first, she needs to reassure the male that she's no threat.

A common solution to the problem of reassurance is to imitate the young. The male woodpecker finch, for example, mimics the gestures of a nestling begging for food in order to entice a female into his nest. Courting hamster males imitate the call of a baby hamster to attract a sexual partner.

While the risks aren't physical among humans, there are definite emotional risks to courtship. The coy childlike gestures of courtship and flirtation, Davis suggests, seem to serve the same reassuring functions among humans as among animals.

Similar gestures happen in noncourtship situations where one person seeks to reassure another of rapport. Called "quasi-courtship," these gestures occur in a wide variety of situations: at parties and meetings, between parent and child, doctor and patient, or teacher and student. Quasi-courtship is typified by the coy gestures of true courtship, and

OF COURTSHIP AND QUASI-COURTSHIP

Warm gestures

Looks into his eyes

Touches his hand

Moves towards him

Smiles frequently

Works her eyes from
his head to his toes

Has a happy face

Smiles with mouth open

Grins

Sits directly facing him

Puckers her lips

Nods head affirmatively

Raises her eyebrows

Licks her lips

Uses expressive hand gestures
while speaking

Has eyes wide open

Gives fast glances

Cold gestures

Gives a cold stare

Sneers

Gives a fake yawn

Frowns

Moves away from him

Looks at the ceiling

Picks her teeth

Shakes her head negatively

Cleans her fingernails

Looks away

Chain smokes

Pouts

Picks her hands

Looks around the room

Plays with her split ends

Cracks her fingers

Figure 10.7 "Cold" and "warm" gestures

by "matching": repeating some nonverbal action or gesture of a partner at the identical pace or in the same manner. But the connotation of quasi-courtship is not sexual; it is a means of getting attention.

Analysis of videotapes from psychotherapy sessions show that its functions in a conversation are quite different from courtship. For example, it can be used to keep people involved in an interaction when their attention seems to be flagging. In a therapy session with an entire family, for instance,

a teenage daughter seemed to be losing all interest in the proceedings. At that point, the therapist locked eyes with her and—even though he was talking with her father—began to drag on his cigarette in perfect synchrony with her. She stayed involved after that.

In short, Davis concludes that quasi-courtship is an effort to create or sustain moments of rapport or involvement, and is also a sign of alertness, well-being, and excitement—none of these necessarily related to sexual attraction. ■

ed or pleased expression as he does so, lean toward the other, and share postures with his friend—both may sit with knees crossed, for example, and hands clasped behind their heads (Davis, 1973). How many of these signals an individual uses in a situation is a sign of how intimate the relationship is—or sometimes, of how intimate one partner would like it to become. If, in fact, two people who are not intimates are forced to stand closer together than they like (for example, in a crowded elevator), they may studiously avoid making eye contact or smiling (Argyle, 1969).

Courtship signals are body movements that reflect the fact that two people are attracted to one another. Some of these signals seem to be simply signs of intensified intimacy. Like good friends, courting couples most often stand close and face each other squarely. They also trade long looks and flirtatious glances. They are apt to use arms and legs to block out outsiders or to emphasize their togetherness: sitting side by side, for example, talking to a third person, they'll form a closed circle with their legs, knees crossed from the outer sides in, so that their toe tips almost meet. They may cock their heads and, if standing, tilt their pelvises. A woman will usually tip her pelvis forward and up; a man may push his back (Scheflen, 1965).

People are, evidently, enormously aware of and responsive to the body movements of others. In moments of rapport, they are apt to assume similar postures, or one person may pick up the rhythm of another's movements and move with her or him. In films projected in slow motion, they look almost as if they were dancing to the same beat (Condon, 1968). Sometimes one individual will mirror another's gestures in unconscious imitation. In one film of a family in therapy, the mother frequently made a kind of juggling motion with her hands when she was feeling indecisive, and her adolescent son often used the same gesture even when his mother was not around—physical evidence of imitations and perhaps of the psychological process of identification (Davis, 1973).

Nonverbal communication must always be understood in its specific cultural context. A Frenchman moves like a Frenchman and an American like an American, and there are significant differences. In many parts of the world (South America, Spain, Italy, and the Arab countries, for example), people in conversation like to stand closer together than Americans do, and to touch each other more often. Sociologist Edward T. Hall (1979), who studies the importance of nonverbal communication across cultures, notes, for example, that the comfortable distance for talking in Arab cultures is closer than in America: two feet versus five. One difference this makes is that at the closer range Arabs are better able to read another person's facial expression as it changes—even to the point of noting small changes in pupil dilation (enlarged pupils may reveal excitement or interest, contracted pupils disinterest)—and so get more information on the other person's emotional response to what is being said.

SUMMARY

The nature of emotion. Psychologists have not yet arrived at a generally accepted definition of emotion, though many attempts have been made. One useful definition views emotion as a complex disturbance that includes subjective feelings, bodily arousal, and the impulse to respond.

Emotions can motivate us, and they share with motives the capacity to affect subjective feelings, physiological reactions, and observable behaviors. But there are distinctions to be made between the two. Subjectively, they are experienced differently: emotions usually result from external stimulation, motives from internal factors; motives are more affectively neutral than emotions; emotions do not always result in behavior, as motives do.

Attempts have been made to identify the basic emotions, but no general agreement has been reached.

The physiology of emotion. All emotional reactions are based in physiological changes, though the connection between the two seems to be only a rough one, and individual reactions differ widely. Recent research has aimed at determining the physiological profile of major emotional states through patterning of responses.

The Cannon-Bard theory proposes that signals from the thalamus simultaneously activate emotion and bodily responses; the responses are a side effect of the emotion, not a cause. Activation theory views emotions as on a single continuum of arousal, varying in intensity from complete relaxation to extreme agitation.

Emotional arousal. People's appraisal of a situation can determine the emotions they feel about it. Other cognitive factors also influence emotions, for example, memory, empathy, and projection. Reason and emotion are not simple opposites; even in what seem to be the most rational decisions, emotion is involved.

Many situations can stir our emotions—frustration, conflict, and tension, among others. There seem to be some stimuli that produce the same responses in every member of a species, indicating that some emotional reactions may be innate. In humans, frustration tends to cause an aggressive reaction.

Emotions: innate or learned? Studies of infants by Watson indicated that they have three innate emotional mechanisms in response to certain stimuli: fear, anger, and love. Bridges, however, believed that newborns have no specific emotions, but instead respond to stimulation with general agitation or excitement.

A readiness to fear certain things—strange animals and insects, darkness, lonely and exposed places, violent strangers—may be innate. Common human phobias seem to derive from such fears.

Social factors shape our expression of emotion. People tend to react with the same emotions in many social situations.

Moods, a special class of diffuse emotions, may be caused by hormonal changes. Plunges in estrogen levels in premenstrual women may make their moods more negative. Higher testosterone levels in men may lead to hostility and aggression.

Emotions and health. Prolonged extreme emotions can ruin emotional and physical health. The most striking demonstration of this is the phenomenon of sudden death brought on by an emotional reaction to a trauma. Positive emotions like amusement, though, may contribute to physical well-being.

Emotional responses. Facial expressions are in part learned, in part innate. Some facial expressions are recognized universally, even though the rules for displaying certain expressions can vary from culture to culture.

Body language communicates both negative and positive feelings nonverbally. Positive signals include facing the other squarely, frequent eye contact, and posture sharing. How many of these signals an individual uses is a measure of the intimacy of the relationship. Courtship signals include the usual positive signals and others too, like the use of arms and legs to block off outsiders, tilting the pelvis, and touch.

Slow-motion films have shown that people in moments of rapport share the rhythm of each other's movements and mirror each other's gestures.

Nonverbal communication does differ in certain ways from culture to culture. Conventions vary, for example, on how close two people normally stand when talking.

GLOSSARY

Activation theory Assumes that emotion is a reflection of an individual's level of activation, not a special psychological state.

Appraisal The way a person construes an event.

Cannon-Bard theory Holds that the body's reactions are simply side effects of emotion, not its cause.

Displace To aim an emotion at a substitute object.

Electrodermal activity A change in sweat level on the skin, reflecting the degree to which a person is emotionally aroused.

Emotion A complex disturbance that includes a person's subjective feelings, bodily arousal, and the impulse to respond.

Galvanic skin response (GSR) An electrical measurement of abrupt changes in the sweat level in response to a stimulus.

James-Lange theory Posits that the body's responses precede emotion.

Moods Transitory, diffuse emotions, probably affected by changes in hormonal levels.

Orienting response Increased vigilance in preparation for a possible emergency.

Psychosomatic illness Medical problems caused in part by emotional reactions.

Sudden death phenomenon Fatality brought on by an emotional reaction to a trauma.

11

HUMAN SEXUALITY

BIOLOGICAL ROOTS OF SEXUALITY

Male anatomy ■ Female anatomy

SEXUAL AROUSAL

The physiology of arousal ■ Physiological measures of arousal ■ Sources of arousal ■ The psychology of arousal ■ Sex fantasy ■ Familiarity ■ Sexual attitudes ■ Pornography and sex crimes

HOW SEXUALITY DEVELOPS

Childhood ■ Adolescence ■ Sexual issues: gratification or relationship?

SOCIETY AND SEXUALITY

Sexual norms and deviation ■ Cultural restrictions

THE RANGE OF SEXUAL BEHAVIOR

The Kinsey report ■ The Hunt survey ■ Sex and the college student

HOMOSEXUALITY

Homosexual men ■ Homosexual women ■ Bisexuality

SEX IN MODERN SOCIETY

Changing sex roles ■ Sex, love, and marriage

COMMON MYTHS

MANY PEOPLE BELIEVE ...	ACTUALLY ...
Children do not have sexual feelings.	Children can have sexual feelings, including arousal.
Masturbation is harmful.	Masturbation does no harm.
The United States is one of the most sexually permissive societies in the world.	Many societies are more permissive than the United States.
Homosexuals are easily identified by their appearance and mannerisms.	Homosexuals do not necessarily differ in appearance at all from heterosexuals.
Bigger men have bigger penises.	There is little or no relationship between the size of a man's body and the size of his penis.

The brain is the primary sex organ.

ANONYMOUS

Although sex is a biological necessity for the survival of any species, in humans the complexity of sexual behavior is far greater than in any other species. Its degree of complexity seems proportional to the greater development of our brain, and our psychology. Not just a single, stereotyped response in our species, sex is shaped by many factors.

Sexuality, the whole of a person's sexual behavior, is governed by both biology and social learning. Sexual behavior is at once a social event and a very private affair.

Added to its inherent complexity is the rapid rate of change in our society of the norms for the expression of sexuality: sexual behavior that was unthinkable (or, at least in polite society, unspeakable) a decade or two ago is openly treated in books, movies, and even on television. Part of the new sexual candor is the result of a general transition of social norms in our culture; part is spurred by social movements such as women's rights and the political activism of groups like homosexuals; and part is augmented by news coverage of phenomena like sex change operations.

How we behave sexually is the result of our attitudes toward sex and our experiences with it.

These attitudes and experiences can give us feelings of guilt and shame on the one hand, or self-confidence and fulfillment on the other. Freud contended that sexuality is among the major human concerns, and the constant reminders of sexual themes in the media underscore his point.

BIOLOGICAL ROOTS OF SEXUALITY

Sexuality is a mix of biological givens and the effects of what we learn. Our bodies are designed for sexual activity; fundamentally, sex is a biological process with reproduction as its purpose. Yet sexuality is more complicated than biology alone demands: there are innumerable variations in what causes sexual arousal, what emotions are connected with sex, and what is satisfying.

Among lower animals, sexual behavior is regulated largely by the sex hormones. The main male sex hormones in both animals and humans are testosterone and androsterone, both secreted by the testes. In females, estrogen is the basic sex hormone. In rats, for example, when the female has

THE SWEET SMELL OF SEX

■ Commercials encourage us to cover up our body odors with deodorants, powders, or perfumes in order to be more attractive. Yet these efforts may be misplaced in terms of the subtle odors that cue a sexual response in members of the opposite sex.

Studies of pheromones—chemicals that serve as sexual attractants in the animal world—show that in many species smell is a powerful sexual cue. A male moth can pick up the scent of a female moth's pheromone a mile away and respond to its call. Female dogs, cows, pigs, and goats secrete a pheromone to alert males that they are in season. But do humans also excrete—and respond to—pheromones?

In 1952 J. Le Magnen found that women were very sensitive to exaltolide, a musky fragrance used in many perfumes. Furthermore, a woman's ability to detect the odor is strongest around the time of ovulation, when conception is most likely to occur. This implies that nature may have meant males to attract females, rather than vice versa.

Odors may play a role in regulating other reproductive cycles, such as menstruation. Research shows that the "old wives' tale" that women who live together menstruate together is indeed the case. McClintock (1971) questioned 136 college dormitory residents and found that as the school year progressed, the menstrual cycles of roommates became more and more similar. She proposed that this synchrony was coordinated by pheromones.

Most human sweat is odorless, except for that produced by apocrine glands under the arms and in the genital area. The activity of these glands is attuned to our sex lives; they begin functioning at puberty, peak with sexual maturity and decline in old age. Russell (Hassett, 1978) conducted an experiment in which a woman with regular menstrual periods wore cotton pads under her arms every day. The pads were chemically treated to retain their scent. Later eleven other women were daubed just under their nostrils with the scent extracted from the pads.

In time, the menstrual periods of these women became more similar to that of the donor. This suggests that the similar timing of women's menstruation may be triggered by a smell in their sweat.

The search for human pheromones is a recent development, sparked by studies of how animals communicate through pheromones. Richard Michael of Emory University School of Medicine has studied the role of odors in primate sexuality. He observed that spayed female monkeys were ignored by male monkeys. When their bottoms were painted with vaginal washings from estrogen-treated females, however, the males were anxious to mount them. Michael called the chemicals involved "copulins."

Michael went on to study copulins in humans. He analyzed tampons worn by women throughout their menstrual cycle (not just during their periods) and found that 97.5 percent of the tampons showed at least a trace of the volatile fatty acids Michael calls copulins. The researchers Morris and Udry (1978) have found that sexual intercourse occurs most frequently during the ovulation period of the menstrual cycle. Since Michael found that the level of copulins is also highest at this time, Morris and Udry thought that pheromones might be responsible for the increase in sexual activity.

They asked sixty-two married women to rub four different perfumes on their chests every night before going to bed. One of these perfumes contained copulins. Husbands and wives filled out questionnaires in the morning describing the previous night's sexual activities. However, the different perfumes didn't seem to affect sexual desire or activity one way or the other.

No one as yet has established a direct link between a specific smell and human sexual behavior—but neither has one been ruled out. ■

high estrogen levels she becomes receptive to sex, becoming more active and presenting herself sexually to approaching males. Sexual readiness in the male rat varies with its testosterone level.

Sex hormones act directly on the brain. When synthetic estrogen is injected into a key area of a female rat's brain, she becomes sexually receptive; injections in other parts of the brain and under the skin produce no such effect. In both male and female rats, if a male hormone is injected into that same key area of the brain, the result is sexual behavior typical of males—even in females (Beach, 1951).

Sexual behavior in all species is more than just copulation. Each species has its own specific variations on attracting a mate, courtship, foreplay, nest building, and caring for offspring. Sexuality includes this complex pattern of behavior. While hormones can turn indifference into sexual assertiveness, even animals have to learn some parts of sexual behavior. Male rats and chimpanzees reared in isolation, for example, are ineffective—though willing—in their sexual performance.

While sex hormones affect humans as they do lower animals, more of human sexuality is programmed psychologically than biologically. Castration, for example, does not destroy a man's sex drive once he has matured, although it does decrease it (Shope, 1975). He will still have sexual interests despite the absence of sex hormones. If, however, he takes artifical male sex hormones, his sex drive will increase.

Male anatomy

The external male sexual organs are the penis, testicles, and scrotum. The main internal organs are the vas deferens, seminal vesicles, and prostate gland (see Figure 11.1). During sexual arousal, the penis undergoes tumescence, or *erection*, when hollow spaces within its shaft become filled with blood and it swells in size. There is no particular relationship between penis size and body dimensions; a small man can have a large penis, a large man a small penis. Erections, while usually

Figure 11.1 Male reproductive system

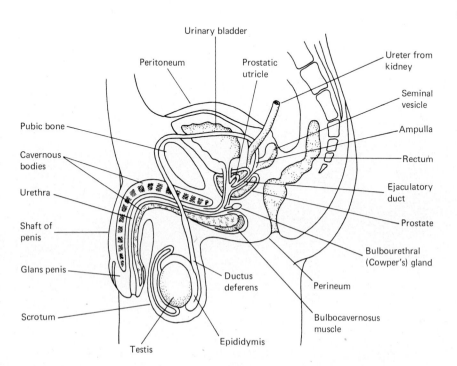

caused by sexual arousal, can also be caused by the need to urinate, heavy lifting, or irritation. A man's penis reaches its full size by the end of his full growth; after that nothing is likely to increase penis size. Sexually active men, however, are believed to have less loss of size during the general body atrophy of aging (Shope, 1975).

Female anatomy

The main external female sexual organs are the major and minor labia and the clitoris; together these are called the *vulva*. Internally a woman's main sexual organ is the vagina; the reproductive organs such as the uterus, fallopian tubes and ovaries are not directly involved in sexual activity (see Figure 11.2). The *minor labia*, "lips" that protect the vaginal opening, are sensitive to sexual stimulation. The main source of sexual responsiveness in a woman, though, is the *clitoris*, a shaft at the top of the vaginal opening which, like the penis, engorges with blood during sexual excitement. The vagina, which receives the penis during intercourse, emits a lubricating fluid during sexual arousal. Since the vagina itself has few receptor cells for sensation, it does not seem to be a major source of sexual stimulation.

(A)

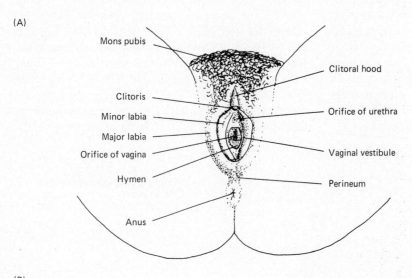

Figure 11.2 (A) External genitals of the female (B) Internal view of the female reproductive system

(B)

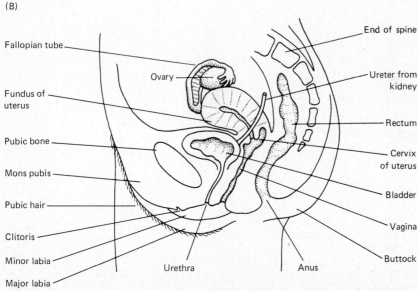

SEXUAL AROUSAL

The physiology of arousal

Beginning in 1959, William Masters and Virginia Johnson (1966) studied orgasms during intercourse and masturbation (sexual self-stimulation) in 694 participants, men and women ranging in age from eighteen to eighty-nine. From this research, Masters and Johnson determined the natural cycle of physiological response to erotic stimuli. While there are minor variations between people, the basic pattern follows the same phases of arousal: excitement, plateau, orgasm, and resolution (see Figure 11.3).

In men, the first physiological response to sexual excitement is erection, swelling and lengthening of the penis, and a rise in its angle from the body. The Kinsey (1948) report found that young boys also reported having erections during sports, emotionally charged events (such as being chased by police), and even sitting in church. By the late teens, though, erection occurred in response to more selective stimuli—direct stimulation or erotica.

In women the excitement phase begins with a moistening of the vaginal lining by a lubricating fluid. As arousal proceeds, the vaginal walls continue to "sweat," providing a lubricating film that

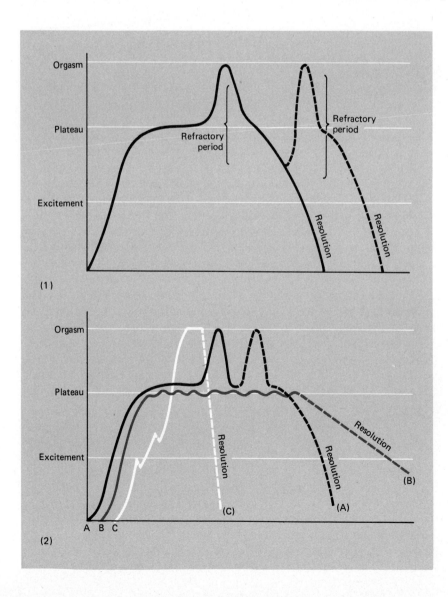

Figure 11.3 Masters and Johnson's portrayal of the cycle of sexual arousal in men and women

(1) Most males were found to have a single type of sexual response cycle in which excitement built rapidly, entered a relatively brief plateau stage, peaked at orgasm, and then returned rather rapidly to the preexcitement state in the resolution phase. Right after orgasm, males tend not to be responsive to continued stimulation, and this is called the refractory period. When that period is over, further stimulation can lead to a second orgasm (shown in dotted lines) followed by an even longer refractory period.

(2) Among females, three basic types of sexual response cycles were found. Type (A) depicts an excitement, plateau, and orgasm pattern much like males except followed quickly by a second orgasm without a refractory period. Type (B) shows a plateau phase characterized by a long series of small orgasmic responses and a very slow resolution phase. Type (C) shows a somewhat slower and irregular excitement phase that bypasses the plateau phase and reaches a quick, extended orgasm followed by a very rapid resolution phase.

readies the vagina for the penis. Like the erection of the penis, the vaginal lubrication results from an increased blood flow and engorgement of the vaginal tissue. During this phase, women's (and some men's) nipples become erect, and the breasts swell.

During the plateau phase, a man's testicles swell in size by half, and pull up into the scrotum. The changes in a woman are much more diverse. The most dramatic is the development of an *orgasmic platform*, the swelling of the tissues in the outer third of the vagina, so that it grips the man's penis. At the same time the inner part of the vagina balloons to make a cavity, and the uterus enlarges. The clitoris, meanwhile, retracts from the vaginal entrance. Although the retracted clitoris has less direct stimulation from the penis, it continues to rub against a covering hood that extends from the vaginal lips; as the labia move, the hood stimulates the clitoris.

In a woman, orgasm begins with a spasm of the orgasmic platform, which is followed by a series of rhythmic contractions. A mild orgasm might have as few as three contractions, an intense orgasm as many as twelve. Along with these contractions of the outer third of the vagina, the uterus also contracts in a manner similar to the contractions of birth, though not nearly so strong. Masters and Johnson checked especially to see if there existed anything like a sucking action that might draw sperm into the cervix; while this idea is commonly held, they found no evidence for it.

A man's orgasm follows the same pattern as the woman's in many respects. The main event is a series of throbbing contractions of the penis. In both men and women these contractions during orgasm occur initially at intervals of four-fifths of a second, with the interval lengthening as the intensity of the contractions lessens. At each contraction of the penis, semen is ejaculated under great pressure; if uncontained, the semen may shoot more than two feet from the penis.

Orgasm in both men and women is a moment of intense pleasure. The whole body response is one of extreme muscular tension and release. Pulse rate, blood pressure, and breath rate reach a peak; a blushlike "sex flush" may cover parts of the body. The person's face may tighten in a grimace, and muscles of the neck, legs, and arms contract in a spasm. The body may stiffen, toes curl in or

flare out, hands clench. The entire body may uncontrollably convulse in synchrony with genital throbbing. At the moment of climax, a person may sometimes pant, groan, scream, laugh, or cry.

Resolution is marked by a relaxation of all the tension that has built during orgasm. Pulse, blood pressure, and breath rate return to normal. Muscles rebound from peak tension to deep relaxation. A man in this phase enters a *refractory period*, when, for the span of several minutes or even hours, he cannot respond to sexual stimulation with an erection and orgasm. Women do not have such a refractory period; they can follow one orgasm almost immediately with another.

Physiological measures of arousal

The fact that erection of the penis is such a reliable indicator of sexual arousal has led to the development of the *penile plethysmograph*, a device that attaches to the penis and measures changes in its circumference. The penile plethysmograph is used in research on male response to sexual stimuli. For example, in a study of the effects of distractions on sexual arousal, male volunteers listened to an erotic tape of a woman's voice giving explicit descriptions of a sexual scene, including foreplay, oral-genital sex, and intercourse (Geer and Fuhr, 1976). The degree of their erections were recorded by plethysmograph (see Figure 11.4). In one condition, they heard the voice in one ear, while in the other a random number was spoken every three seconds. In another, they wrote down the random numbers; a third group had to add them in succession; the fourth group had to class each pair as more or less than fifty, odd or even. The greater the cognitive distractions, the less the arousal. The penile plethysmograph data for the last group, who had the most complex task, showed they weren't aroused by the story at all.

The discovery by Masters and Johnson that vaginal blood flow increases during sexual arousal in women led to the development of the *vaginal plethysmograph*, an acrylic vaginal probe that uses a light sensing device to detect blood volume changes. Just as with men, the plethysmograph for women is a sensitive detector of arousal in

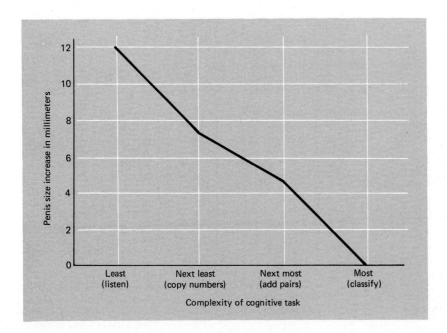

Figure 11.4 Arousal level of males listening to an erotic story while carrying out one of four types of cognitive tasks
The more complex the task, the more it interferes with arousal.

women. When volunteers were shown a nonerotic film and an explicitly sexual movie, the vaginal plethysmograph readings showed that the sexy film produced blood volume increases, while the neutral one did not (Geer, Morokoff, and Greenwood, 1974). Women who volunteered to masturbate showed a dramatic increase in blood volume during orgasm (Geer and Quartanaro, 1976).

Imagine that two men are talking about the dates they had the night before.

"Well," says the first, "I took your advice with Jane. I kissed her behind the ear while we were necking."

"It's incredible, isn't it? It just drives Ellen crazy. Did she love it?"

"Not exactly. She laughed. She's ticklish there." ■

Sources of arousal

The primary source of arousing stimuli during lovemaking is tactile. *Erogenous zones* are the sensitive areas of the body especially susceptible to sexual arousal. In men the primary zones are the tip and underside of the penis (but not the shaft); in women, the clitoris and the minor labia

(but not the vaginal canal). In both men and women, erogenous zones include: the area between the anus and genitals, the anus, breasts (particularly nipples), mouth, earlobes, buttocks, and inner thighs. Many other areas can respond erotically to touch, however, including the neck, palms and fingertips, soles and toes, abdomen, and lower groin. While knowledge of the erogenous zones may enhance one's skills as a lover, they vary greatly from person to person: what drives one person crazy may not be noticed by another (Katchadourian and Lunde, 1975).

The other senses—vision, hearing, smell, and taste—are less important avenues of erotic arousal since, unlike touch, they do not operate reflexively. With these senses, erotic responses are learned. There is wide individual and cultural variation, for example, in what parts of the body, style of dressing, cosmetics, or scent is "sexy." Even so, once learned, sexual associations in sight, sound, smell or taste can be quite powerful erotic stimuli.

The psychology of arousal

A fundamental factor in sexual stimulation is emotion. Some emotions, like affection and trust, enhance sexual feelings; others, like fear, anger or anxiety inhibit them. Despite a person's sexual artistry, the response evoked in a lover depends greatly on the other's feelings. The ability to arouse another person sexually does not, for example, depend on looks, as sexual encounters with beautiful but frigid women or handsome but unloving men reveal.

Loving, caring, and trusting are the most common emotional contexts of lovemaking. In order to feel comfortable enough to make love, most people need at least a minimal degree of trust and affection for the other person involved. Indeed, for many people, the greater the intensity of loving feelings, the more easily they can be aroused. Even so, for others there is not a necessary relationship between emotional intensity and sexual gratification.

Experiences during lovemaking can alter a person's sexuality. If a woman is repeatedly made to feel cheap and used in her sexual encounters, she may eventually become unresponsive sexually. If a man is made to feel sexually inadequate, he may eventually start to perform poorly. A heart attack suffered during intercourse can lead to an intense fear of sex. But a relaxed, intense sexual orgasm may lead a previously unresponsive woman or self-conscious man to be more open and sexually confident.

People differ in the ways they express affection, and in which preludes to lovemaking they find most stimulating. Despite the uniformity of romantic scenes in the cinema, there is no stereotyped way of initiating lovemaking; spontaneity and responsiveness to one's partner are the only guidelines that seem to apply across the board. Some couples enjoy wrestling and chasing each other, others prefer a quiet, subdued mood, and still others bother with little prelude at all to intercourse.

One of the functions sex serves for adults is that of a form of play (Katchadourian and Lunde, 1975). Some people enjoy enacting sexual scenarios that fulfill their sexual fantasies, for example, enacting a "rape" scene, a spanking, or pretending to be strangers (Comfort, 1972). Such sex games, though, must be enacted by mutual consent and must be enjoyable for *both* partners in order to be arousing.

Sex fantasy

If, as the apocryphal saying goes, the brain is the ultimate sexual organ, then the mind is the primary erogenous zone. One of the main sources of sexual arousal is not located anywhere in the body, but in the mind. That source is imagination and fantasy. The power of the mind to arouse suggests to some researchers that differences among people in "sex drive" are really differences in their ability to fantasize sexually (Baron and Byrne, 1977). When married couples were asked to look at erotic pictures, read sexy passages, or imagine exciting scenes, those who simply used their imaginations were much more sexually aroused than those given erotic material (Byrne and Lamberth, 1971). In another laboratory study, men and women volunteers were asked to sit in a comfortable chair and "turn themselves on" by imagining a sexual scene. Most were able to produce changes in vaginal blood flow or penis size—indicating sexual arousal—within two or three minutes (Geer, 1974).

The person fantasizing is almost always the "star" and lovers, acquaintances, or people known from afar most often play the other roles. Sometimes, though, fictitious people or movie stars figure in fantasies. The scripts possible in sexual fantasy are only as limited as a person's imagination. Often people express in fantasy desires that they would not allow themselves to realize in real life: homosexuality, sadomasochism, orgies, and the like. For this reason people sometimes find their fantasies embarrassing or a source of guilt.

Sex fantasies serve several functions (Katchadourian and Lunde, 1975). First, they are an easy source of pleasure. Second, they can serve as a wish fulfillment for unattainable satisfactions, such as a distant honeymoon, an inaccessible lover, or an embarrassing sex act. But the person may not always want the wish to come true in real life. This is especially so when the fantasy is a disguised replay of some childhood conflict, such as Oedipal desires (sexual attraction to the opposite-sex parent and fear of the same-sex parent). Third, sex fantasies, like any other daydreams, can be a helpful rehearsal for a real-life future situation.

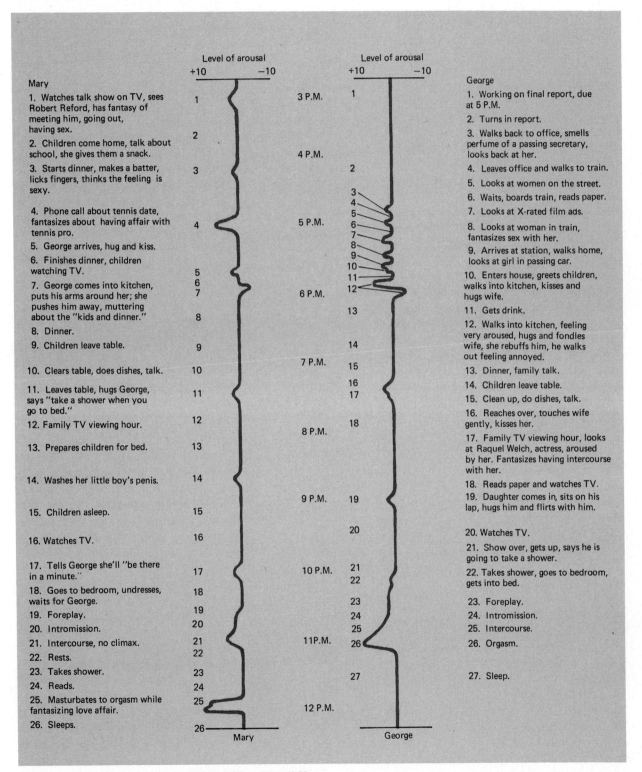

Mary

1. Watches talk show on TV, sees Robert Reford, has fantasy of meeting him, going out, having sex.

2. Children come home, talk about school, she gives them a snack.

3. Starts dinner, makes a batter, licks fingers, thinks the feeling is sexy.

4. Phone call about tennis date, fantasizes about having affair with tennis pro.

5. George arrives, hug and kiss.

6. Finishes dinner, children watching TV.

7. George comes into kitchen, puts his arms around her; she pushes him away, muttering about the "kids and dinner."

8. Dinner.

9. Children leave table.

10. Clears table, does dishes, talk.

11. Leaves table, hugs George, says "take a shower when you go to bed."

12. Family TV viewing hour.

13. Prepares children for bed.

14. Washes her little boy's penis.

15. Children asleep.

16. Watches TV.

17. Tells George she'll "be there in a minute."

18. Goes to bedroom, undresses, waits for George.

19. Foreplay.

20. Intromission.

21. Intercourse, no climax.

22. Rests.

23. Takes shower.

24. Reads.

25. Masturbates to orgasm while fantasizing love affair.

26. Sleeps.

George

1. Working on final report, due at 5 P.M.

2. Turns in report.

3. Walks back to office, smells perfume of a passing secretary, looks back at her.

4. Leaves office and walks to train.

5. Looks at women on the street.

6. Waits, boards train, reads paper.

7. Looks at X-rated film ads.

8. Looks at woman in train, fantasizes sex with her.

9. Arrives at station, walks home, looks at girl in passing car.

10. Enters house, greets children, walks into kitchen, kisses and hugs wife.

11. Gets drink.

12. Walks into kitchen, feeling very aroused, hugs and fondles wife, she rebuffs him, he walks out feeling annoyed.

13. Dinner, family talk.

14. Children leave table.

15. Clean up, do dishes, talk.

16. Reaches over, touches wife gently, kisses her.

17. Family TV viewing hour, looks at Raquel Welch, actress, aroused by her. Fantasizes having intercourse with her.

18. Reads paper and watches TV.

19. Daughter comes in, sits on his lap, hugs him and flirts with him.

20. Watches TV.

21. Show over, gets up, says he is going to take a shower.

22. Takes shower, goes to bedroom, gets into bed.

23. Foreplay.

24. Intromission.

25. Intercourse.

26. Orgasm.

27. Sleep.

Figure 11.5 A day in the sexual life of George and Mary

WHATEVER TURNS YOU ON

■ Sex fantasies seem to be part of a normal mental life, but the variety of fantasies among ordinary men and women sometimes surprises people.

In a survey, 75 percent of men and 80 percent of women reported having fantasies of intercourse with a lover (Hunt, 1974). But for nearly half the men and a fifth of the women, sex fantasies also included people other than lovers, in a wide range of sexual encounters. Some of the more daring fantasies included intercourse with strangers (47 percent of men, 21 percent of women), sex with several members of the opposite sex at once (33 percent of men, 18 percent of women), being forced to have sex (10 percent of men, 19 percent of women), forcing someone to have sex (13 percent of men, 3 percent of women), and homosexual encounters (7 percent of men, 11 percent of women).

While there is a common belief that women are more aroused by portrayals of romantic situations than of explicit sex, research does not bear this out (Heiman, 1975). Volunteer college students listened to erotic tapes while their sexual arousal was measured with a penile or vaginal plethysmograph. The tapes varied in degree of romanticism and sexual activity, as well as in whether the more active person was the man or woman. The majority of both men and women were more aroused by the sexual tapes than the romantic ones, women rating them even more arousing than the men. The single most arousing tape for both men and women was one in which a woman initiated the lovemaking encounter.

People seem most aroused by sexual acts that they themselves might engage in—or would like to. To find exactly which sexual acts were most arousing, Schmidt and Sigusch (1970) made a series of movies with the same man and woman; in each movie they engage in a different set of sexual acts. When the movies were shown to groups of men, some acts proved more arousing than others. The least sexy movie was one in which the couple partially undress while petting, but do not reach orgasm. The most arousing movie depicts the couples engaging in many different sexual acts in-

---

Sex fantasies commonly occur during simple daydreams, masturbation, and sexual intercourse. Psychotherapists have sometimes taken the view first expressed by Freud (1908) that "a happy person never phantasies, only an unsatisfied one." Holders of this negative opinion of fantasies—especially those during lovemaking—interpret them as revealing sexual inhibitions, an escape from taking responsibility for sexual excitement, or as a psychological withdrawal from the partner. More recent research, though, suggests an opposite interpretation (Hariton and Singer, 1974). One hundred forty-one suburban housewives answered a questionnnaire about their daydreams and fantasies during intercourse and at other times. The researchers concluded that erotic fantasies during intercourse were quite common, and do not indicate psychological disturbances.

Familiarity

There is some evidence that familiarity dims the appeal of sexual stimuli—especially for males. With rats, for example, the male after intercourse is sexually unresponsive for a period. If, however, an unfamiliar female is introduced, the male rat will engage in renewed sexual activity (Clemens, 1967). The reverse pattern does not seem to hold; female rats seem to prefer familiar partners to new ones.

In humans, too, familiar sexual stimuli lose their power to arouse. For example, in one study male volunteers were left in a room with porno films and sexy pictures and magazines for ninety minutes each day for ten days straight (Barclay, 1970). The level of sexual arousal dropped steadily over the ten-day period. Toward the end, some of

cluding oral-genital sex and having intercourse in many positions.

To further analyze the same movie, Miller, Byrne, and Fisher (1976) made a set of slides from them, presenting the slides in various order to groups of men and women undergraduates. There was no strong difference in arousal impact between men and women—both sexes were about equally turned on, and by more or less the same scenes.

A review of studies assessing the arousal strength of various sexual themes on men and women found both sexes aroused by sexual intercourse, genital petting, and oral-genital sex (the single most arousing for women) (Baron and Byrne, 1975). Both sexes were least aroused by sadism, homosexual acts, and clothed members of the same sex. Women were least turned on, however, by a picture of a nude man. When people have a special sexual preference, of course, that changes what they prefer: homosexuals were most aroused by depictions of homosexual acts (Abel, *et. al.,* 1975). ■

the men were preferring the *Reader's Digest* to the sexual material. Then, on the eleventh day, new erotic material was added, and the arousal level rose once again. Presumably the same would happen with women, although none were tested in this study.

Imagine that in a haircutting salon for men and women there is a large selection of magazines for the use of patrons while they wait. One morning a young man is reading *Playboy* while he waits for his haircut.

As he's reading it, a young woman his age walks in and sits down. He hurriedly puts down the *Playboy* and thumbs through the selection, settling on a *Newsweek*.

The young woman, meanwhile, picks up a copy of *Playgirl* and starts reading. ■

Sexual attitudes

From early childhood, a boy or girl hears parents express negative, ambivalent, or positive feelings toward sex. Parents also vary in the amount and accuracy of the information they pass on to their children about sexuality. A child whose parents are open, honest, and relaxed about sexuality is apt to have the same attitudes, while a child whose parents are closed, disapproving, and repressive toward sex is likely to adopt those attitudes (Martinson, 1968).

Each of us has learned to associate different aspects of sexuality with positive or negative feelings. In one study, for example, people were classified as sexual liberals or conservatives on the basis of their attitudes (Wallace and Wehmer, 1972). When shown a series of erotic pictures, both groups became sexually aroused. For the liberals, the most arousing pictures were seen as entertaining. For the conservatives, though, the most arousing pictures were seen as offensive.

Sex guilt is the tendency to become anxious whenever sexual standards are violated in deed or in thought. People vary widely, though, in the standards they've learned. One person may feel guilty at getting an erection while kissing a girl, while another may feel sex guilt only at the thought of cunnilingus (Mosher and O'Grady, 1979). High sex guilt leads people to avoid sexual thoughts and actions.

For example, college men who volunteered for an experiment were rated on a scale as high or low in sex guilt, feelings of shame, or anxiety about sexual activities (Schill and Chapin, 1972). When left in a waiting room with a variety of magazines, those low in sex guilt were likely to read *Playboy* or *Penthouse*. Those high in sex guilt chose to leaf through *Outdoor Life* or *Newsweek*.

Sex play, the sexual experimentation that children engage in, is also an arena for learning sexual attitudes. If a child learns to exchange sexual favors for social rewards such as attention, the pattern may carry over into adulthood in the form of exploiting sex for social gain. If sex play is en-

WHAT'S IN A NAME?

■ Question: Do you know what "bunny," "pocketbook," and "Christmas" all have in common? How about "peter," "peenee," and "poo poo?"

Answer: They are all terms people use for sexual organs—the former, female; the latter, male.

According to a study of Gartell and Mosbacher (1979), both boys and girls know more about male anatomy than about female. Children often learn no name at all for a woman's genitals, while most of them know the word "penis" by age eleven.

The two researchers gave out 500 questionnaires to adults in the Boston area to find out how men and women differed in learning about sexual anatomy. Over a three-month period, 223 questionnaires were returned.

Forty-four percent of the women surveyed learned no names at all for their genitals during childhood, while 43 percent learned only euphemisms or nicknames. Only 8 percent—one out of twelve—remembered being taught the right words while they were growing up. In comparison, 40 percent of the men who responded said that they learned the correct words for their sexual organs as boys, while 42 percent learned euphemisms.

Although both boys and girls knew the word "penis" by age eleven, "vagina" was learned, on the average, by the early teens and "clitoris" by the midteens. Women were often taught the correct words for male genitals before they knew the proper name for their own. Three women who responded said that they learned the right terms for their own sexual anatomy from labeled diagrams in the questionnaire.

There was a marked contrast between the nicknames given to male and female genitals. Cute names ("bunny," "toy-toy"), secret names ("down there"), and evil names ("nasty") more often represented the vaginal area, while the nicknames for the penis were very close to the correct word ("peter," "peenee"). A boy, presumably, would make the transition from child to adult language more easily than a girl who grew up referring to her genitals as "my nasty."

Though the data collected represents attitudes of the nineteen-forties, fifties, and sixties, (the periods when the adults surveyed were growing up), respondents who were now parents themselves indicated that children of both sexes still know more about male sexual anatomy than female. Parents gave many reasons for this. First of all, the penis is there to see and touch, while women's genitals are mostly hidden. Parents sometimes labeled body parts according to function, in which case the names they gave "penis," "vagina," and "bottom" were often in reference to going to the bathroom.

The clitoris, which has no function in the excretory system but is involved in a woman's sexual arousal, is often unacknowledged by name until late

gaged in with a feeling of guilt, then this attitude may carry into adulthood. On the other hand, if the experience is one of companionship and pleasure, then the result may be positive feelings toward sexuality.

Pornography and sex crimes

In 1970 the federal government's Commission on Obscenity and Pornography estimated Americans spend over $600 million each year on *pornography*—books, magazines, and movies depicting explicit sexual acts. Many people object to pornography on the grounds that it leads people to commit sexual crimes, such as rape. There does, however, seem to be an *inverse* relationship between exposure to pornography and likelihood of becoming a sex criminal. Convicted sex offenders, for example, were found to have had *less* exposure to pornography during their adolescence than nonoffenders (Goldstein, Kant, and Hart-

adolescence. Many parents saw no need to name sexual organs at all until their children reached puberty.

A study of the sexual names that college students use bears out the notion that men are more at ease with sexual language than women. Sanders and Robinson (1979) asked students to write a word or phrase they would use to name the sex organs and sexual intercourse. They were asked what word they would use when talking with others of the same sex, with a lover or spouse, with mixed company, and with their parents.

Men had a larger variety of terms than women, and varied them according to the people they were with. College women were more "rigid and reserved" in the language of sex than college men. For example, 41 percent of women had no response at all when asked what name they would use for their genitals when with a man, while 65 percent could name male genitals in mixed company. Fifteen percent of women had no term they would use for their own genitals in the company of other women.

Gartell and Mosbacher conclude that naming the body parts that give sexual pleasure allows children to identify and acknowledge those feelings. To teach young children the correct words for their sexual organs, they propose, will make it easier for them to accept their genitals as healthy and normal parts of their body. ■

Should pornography be outlawed? Many people think so, but when pornography was legalized in Denmark, rates of sex crimes plummetted. (Owen Franken/ Stock, Boston)

man, 1974). In fact, sex offenders seem on the average to be more reserved on sexual matters than most people; they have heard, seen, and talked less about sex than comparable nonoffenders (Eysenck, 1972).

There does, however, seem to be a correlation between pornography and the rate of sex crimes: it is associated with lowering rates. At least that seems to be the lesson to be learned from the case of Denmark. In the 1960s, that nation began to allow the sale of all forms of explicit sexual material. Instead of an increase in sex crimes in the following years, Denmark had a dramatic decline, including rates of rape, Peeping Toms, and homosexual offenses.

Although pornography may serve as a "safety valve" for sex crimes, it may also have a limited impact as a model for trying new kinds of sexual acts (Athanasia, 1980). In one study, male and female undergraduates were exposed to either a scene where a massage was used during foreplay to intercourse or a scene where one partner was tied down during intercourse (Miller and Byrne, 1979). The first scene was found to prompt people to consider imitating it themselves, but not the second, which was seen as a taboo sexual act. In short, explicit depiction of sexual scenes may prompt imitation to a degree, but in most people it does not seem to encourage the breaking of social taboos.

HOW SEXUALITY DEVELOPS

Childhood

Children cannot be sexual in the same way as adults. For one, their sexual organs have not reached the stage of development at which they can be stimulated sexually in the same way an adult's can. For another, they lack the language, symbols, and concepts that lend adult sexuality its flavor. Even so, observations of infants reveal that at least some can experience sexual arousal as intense as that of the adult who masturbates or has intercourse—although many people find it hard to acknowledge sexual behavior at such a young age (Martinson, 1980).

Because in childhood stimulating the genitals is a source of pleasurable sensations, such stimulation becomes a powerful reinforcer. A little girl, for example, may become sexually aroused riding a bike or rubbing on a mattress. While she may not know why she felt pleasant sensations, she may try to have them again by doing the same thing. The pleasure so obtained is a positive reinforcer for the sexual activity. If she continues to elicit it, then she will have learned to masturbate, to stimulate herself sexually.

A similar learning process may occur in a boy. Sometimes a boy or girl will learn to masturbate from a friend. Whichever is the case, masturbation—or simply spontaneous sexual arousal without orgasm—can lend stimuli associated with it an erotic significance. If a certain activity such as sports, bathing, or bedtime is *eroticized*, that is, takes on sexual associations by stimulating sexual arousal, then things associated with the activity itself can cause arousal. If a girl masturbates in the shower, then the wetness of the water, the warmth, and even the smell of the soap or shampoo may arouse her. If she becomes sexually aroused while horseback riding, then she may later feel a sexual excitement from just being around horses.

Sexual pleasures are a rich occasion for learning, and they can become complex responses. For example, the attitude toward masturbation in a boy or girl's family has a strong influence. If a child is discovered masturbating, the parent's punitive reaction may add a burden of guilt to the child's feelings about sexual pleasure. If a girl learns that touching her genitals is unclean and shameful, she may try to deny her feelings of sexual arousal, rather than feel "worthless" or "dirty."

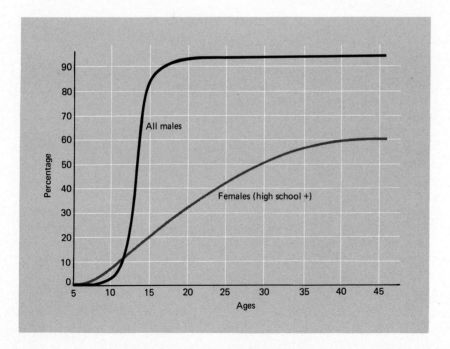

Figure 11.6 Incidence of masturbation to orgasm for males and females of different ages

Adolescence

The physical changes that occur during adolescence herald the biological maturity of a person's sexuality. Yet in our culture those changes are often accompanied by internal conflict (Shah and Selnik, 1980). One source of discomfort brought on by these changes is self-consciousness. A young teenage boy, for example, may pass through an early-adolescent fat period that makes him look somewhat less masculine. His perception of his looks and the unflattering comparisons he makes with his peers may make him embarrassed about his appearance and, perhaps more important, may make him concerned about his masculinity (Stolz and Stolz, 1951). Similarly, a girl who suddenly develops large breasts while still in grammar school may feel awkward and shy, or may feel social pressure to engage in more sexual activity than she cares to.

Sexual reveries are extremely common during adolescence. The teenager rehearses romantic and sexual scenes in the safe theater of the mind, often repeating favorite fantasies or variations on favorite themes. The sexual fantasy life that a person begins in adolescence usually continues throughout the life span, even into old age (Butler and Lewis, 1976).

Conflicts about sex can be intensified by the length of the adolescent period. On the one hand, information about sexual activity is given more freely than in the past. Birth control devices are widely available. Movies, books, magazines, and television programs parade a variety of sexual stimuli before the adolescent. Yet social custom requires that adolescents wait for years after reaching sexual maturity before they can enjoy approved sexual relations.

Frequently it is adults who intensify the conflict. First, they assure adolescents that sexual impulses are natural and healthy, certainly nothing to be ashamed of. But they also tell them that these impulses must be suppressed. To young people, who are unused to such fine but real distinctions, these instructions sound like flat contradictions. The frustration engendered by adults' "yes-but-no" advice may even lead to an exaggerated emphasis on sex—particularly since the frustration only adds impetus to an already high-powered drive.

Imagine that a teenage couple are having an argument.

"All you care about is sex," complains the girl. "You have no romantic instincts at all."

"Sure I do," he says. "When I see you wearing that sexy dress, it makes me feel romantic."

"What do you mean 'romantic'?"

"Well, I want to make out with you."

"See," she replies, "that's just what I mean. No romantic instincts." ■

Sexual intimacy is an increasingly common part of teen-age dating. (© Joel Gordon)

Sexual issues: gratification or relationship?

While adolescent boys and girls both have sexual impulses, they can often have different orientations toward sexual activity. Is sex for physical gratification, or part of a romantic relationship? Ausubel (1954) noted that boys seem to incline toward the "psychobiological orientation," that sex is for physical gratification. Girls tended toward the "psychoaffectional orientation," which stresses the emotional relationship that evolves out of sexuality. Thus an adolescent boy may see no connection between physical gratification and a tender emotional bond, while his girlfriend can't imagine one without the other. Because of this difference in orientation between the sexes, the seductive behavior that a girl hopes will evoke a tender, loving reaction may instead provoke a more direct physical response. While this issue may begin in adolescence, it is also common in adulthood.

SOCIETY AND SEXUALITY

Sexuality varies from culture to culture and even from one social class to another (Fisher, 1980). Indeed, the social environment plays a decisive role in the formation of sexual norms as well as their attendant difficulties. It is not biological development but cultural expectations about sex that often make adolescence a trying period in highly developed civilizations. Numerous nonliterate cultures permit more sexual freedom than most of today's developed countries, and in those societies adolescence seems to be a much less troubled phase in human development. For example, the Ba-ila people of northern Rhodesia regard sexual contact between boys and girls as a form of play. No shame is assigned to these activities, for adults consider them a form of immaturity. In fact, they tacitly encourage such play as preparation for adulthood.

Sexual norms and deviation

Society has a strong voice in what sorts of sexual behavior we deem pleasurable or acceptable. Each generation passes on to the next a set of attitudes about what kind of sexual activity is allowable, what kind is not; for example, the idea that intercourse between a married couple is good, while outside marriage it is bad. Often parental attempts to prevent "bad" sexual activity leave a child feeling all sex is bad. Thus, even today a large proportion of college students believe masturbation is harmful and shameful, despite all scientific evidence to the contrary (Abramson and Mosher, 1975).

Social norms for condoned sexual behavior define what will be labeled "deviant" in any given culture. Many behaviors considered deviant or abnormal in one culture, for example, homosexuality or oral sex, may be considered acceptable or commonplace in another (Ford and Beach, 1951). The official diagnostic manual for psychiatry lists a range of deviant sexual behaviors, but this list is shaped by the social norms of our society, which change: in 1973, homosexuality was changed from a sexual deviance requiring treatment to an acceptable sexual orientation requiring treatment only if a person wanted it.

In the past, treatment for sexual deviance assumed that if a person could be treated so that the object of his desire (e.g., another man) was no longer sexually arousing, then a "normal" heterosexuality would emerge and blossom (Gagnon and Davison, 1973). Recent research challenges this view. Brownell and Barlow (1980) maintain that reducing homosexual sexual arousal does not in and of itself guarantee an increased heterosexual responsiveness. Nor does therapy that allows a homosexual man to become aroused by a woman necessarily reduce his desire for other men.

Brownell and Barlow propose that there are four areas of sexual functioning that can deviate independently from norms; effective treatment begins by diagnosing which of the four present problems for a person. Sexual arousal is deviant, for example, if, as in a *fetish*, the object that stimulates it is inappropriate, for example, an inanimate object (such as a woman's shoe). Another example of sexual deviance involving inappropriate objects is *transvestism*, dressing in clothing of the opposite sex. A second problem area is the inability to become sexually aroused by an appropriate sexual contact with the opposite sex. A third component of deviant sexuality is a deficiency in

Social norms change. What was considered modest and proper attire on an American beach at the turn-of-the-century would seem odd today. And, of course, today's proper beach attire would have been shocking back then. (Culver Pictures)

social skills with the opposite sex. A man who is aroused by children, for example, may not have any social confidence when he is with an adult woman—although he may be aroused by her, too; therapy in this case would aim to extinguish arousal to children, encourage arousal to women, and teach the social skills needed to have a relationship with a woman (Barlow, *et al.*, 1980). The fourth component, gender role deviation, exists when a person consistently prefers to feel and behave like a member of the opposite sex.

Because attitudes toward sexuality have been changing so rapidly in this century, different aspects of society are sometimes at odds with each other over what sexual behavior is acceptable. There are several sorts of *norms*, sets of standards that apply to sexual behavior. The statistical norm simply tells us how common a given act is, for example, petting among teenagers or premarital sex. The medical norm judges whether the act is healthy. The moral norm judges whether it is ethical. The legal norm determines if it is within the law. Frequently a sexual act once judged unhealthy and uncommon—say oral-genital sex—

has come to be seen as statistically and medically acceptable, but the negative moral and legal judgments linger on.

Imagine that two men are talking about their children, who are away at college.

"My daughter tells me," says the first, "that lots of girls in her dorm have sex with their boyfriends."

"My son tells me the same."

"What do you say to him?"

"I tell him to be careful not to get someone pregnant. What do you tell your daughter?"

"I tell her that if I catch any jerk trying to have sex with her, I'll have him thrown in jail." ■

Cultural restrictions

Using anthropological records, Ford and Beach (1951) classified close to a hundred societies according to how restrictive of sexuality they were. They found that as a rule, restrictive societies kept children from learning about sex and repressed their sex play. In most of such cultures, female virginity was highly valued, although a sexual double standard prevailed that allowed more latitude to young men. They typically enforced rules on premarital sexual behavior through warnings, chaperones, and segregation of the sexes. Among the cultures categorized as restrictive was the United States.

Most cultures fell into the semirestrictive category: although they formally disapproved of premarital intercourse, they made little effort to check it. If pregnancy resulted, the couple were pressured into marriage. If Ford and Beach were to look at the United States now, close to thirty years after their original study, they might classify our society in this category.

There is little chance, though, that the United States could be classed as a permissive society. While such societies prohibited certain sexual activities, they were quite lax toward childhood and adolescent sex play. Among some cultures in the Pacific Islands, for example, boys and girls openly masturbated and in their play imitated intercourse. In some cultures, adults explicitly instructed children sexually, teaching them, for example, how to masturbate. Adult Trobriand Islanders showed boys and girls how to engage in intercourse.

Such sexual openness is a far cry from contemporary American norms. When college students were asked to make guesses about their parents' sexual activities, their response showed that the younger generation is in some ways as reserved about sex as their parents (Pocs and Godow, 1977). Many students were repelled at the very thought of considering their parents' sexuality. When asked to guess their parents' sexual activity before and since marriage and to estimate the frequency of intercourse, the students consistently rated their parents as less sexually active than research data suggest they would be.

THE RANGE OF SEXUAL BEHAVIOR

The question of who does what in sexual behavior was addressed most methodically by the research of Alfred Kinsey (1948; 1951). This survey of the sexual histories of thousands of men and women was the first, and—after thirty years—is still the most complete depiction of the sexual behavior of people in our society. Although Kinsey's interviews were from volunteers, and so do not represent a random sample, they still give us the best idea of patterns of sexual behavior. A more recent study by Morton Hunt (1974) surveyed over 2,000 people in twenty-four urban areas, a sample roughly matching the national population. Hunt's findings compared with Kinsey's give us an idea of current sexual trends.

The Kinsey report

When, in the late 1940s and early 1950s, Alfred Kinsey published the results of his survey of American sexual practices, many people were shocked at what his statistics revealed (Brecher, 1969). Kinsey and his associates interviewed more than 10,000 men and women, recording intimate details of their sexual history. Among the then-shocking findings of the Kinsey survey was the fact that, among women unmarried at the time of the interview, 40 percent had reached their first orgasm through masturbation, 24 percent during petting, 10 percent during premarital intercourse, 5 percent during an erotic dream, and 3 percent during a homosexual experience. Only 17 percent of married respondents reported their first orgasm during marital intercourse. So died the myth of the sexually innocent bride.

Among the main findings in the Kinsey survey were that 85 percent of married men and 48 percent of married women had engaged in premarital intercourse. About half the married men reported *extramarital sex*, intercourse outside their marriage, and one-fourth of the married women reported it. About 60 percent of the men had engaged in oral-genital sex, either *fellatio*, where the woman takes the penis into her mouth, or *cunnilingus*, where the man kisses and licks the woman's vulva; 43 percent of the women had engaged in oral-genital sex. Among men, 37 percent had a homosexual experience, a sexual encounter with another man, while 28 percent of women reported having had a homosexual experience. For both sexes, the higher the level of a person's education, the greater the range of sexual experience.

Women also varied drastically in how frequently they had orgasms. Some reported having none their entire lives, while others reported an orgasm during virtually every sexual encounter. Masturbation proved a surer route to orgasm for women than did intercourse; women who masturbated reported orgasm from it 95 percent of the time, while wives reported orgasm with their husbands only about 75 percent of the time. There was also a huge sex difference in sexual experience prior to marriage; men, on the average, had experienced 1,523 orgasms (not the same as sexual encounters) before getting married, women only 223 (these figures, now more than thirty years old, would certainly be different today; the numbers for both sexes would be more equal).

Among the rarer variations in sexual behavior discovered by the Kinsey survey were homosexual relations, contacts with animals, voyeurism, and fetishism. The Kinsey data showed clearly that many Americans did privately what they would never admit publicly. For the general population, Kinsey found about 2 percent of women and 4 percent of men were exclusively homosexual, though the statistics for men and women who had at least one homosexual encounter were much higher. About 15 percent of men and 10 percent of women were bisexual, having had sex partners of both sexes. Close to 20 percent of men and 12 percent of women were aroused by sadomasochistic fantasies. And 8 percent of men and 4 percent of women had erotic encounters with animals.

The Hunt survey

Twenty-five years after the Kinsey survey, the Playboy Foundation commissioned Morton Hunt (1974) to do a similar report in order to find how the nation's sexual patterns had changed in the intervening years. One of the main changes was in the occurrence of premarital intercourse. While Kinsey found only half the unmarried women under twenty-five in his survey had had intercourse, the figure in Hunt's survey was 75 percent. The percentage of males having premarital intercourse—85 percent for Kinsey—increased only slightly. Hunt also found more people having sex-

ual experience sooner in their lives: more than 50 percent of the college-educated men had had intercourse by age seventeen in his sample, while for Kinsey the figure was only 25 percent.

Not all the trends were upward, despite the decade's slogans of sexual liberation. Use of prostitutes in the Hunt survey was only half that reported by Kinsey's men—probably because freer options for partners made them less necessary. But married couples in Hunt's sample also reported more fidelity, at least among the men: rates for infidelity were down about 10 percent among husbands (to 41 percent) while for wives it was the same as in Kinsey's day (25 percent). Sexual activity among divorced men and women was much higher. Divorced men in Hunt's sample had an average of eight sexual partners a year; divorced women, 3.5.

One of the strongest changes was the greater number of men and women who had experience with oral-genital sex, up to 66 percent for men and 72 percent for women. Along with the general increase in sexual activity has come an increase in sexual responsiveness: more of the women in Hunt's sample usually experience orgasm during lovemaking (53 percent, up from Kinsey's 45 percent). One of the few figures to decline was the incidence of sex with animals—only 3 percent—probably because fewer people live on farms.

Sex and the college student

While the last decade has heard a lot about a "sexual revolution" among young people, the research findings suggest that the changes are more on the order of a gradual evolution. Sexual standards are steadily loosening, and sexual behavior is becoming less inhibited, but the change is not dramatic. A review of surveys of college students' sexual attitudes and behavior in the early 1970s found, for example, that between 50 percent and 80 percent of college men approved of premarital sex—but only 65 percent had actually experienced intercourse (McCary, 1973). For women, 70 percent approved premarital intercourse if in love; between 35 and 50 percent of college women have experienced intercourse (Kaats and Davis, 1970). The best estimate is that by age twenty-five, about 80 percent of the women now in college are likely to have had premarital intercourse, up from 47 percent in Kinsey's day. The rates for men are likely to increase in the same way. For both men and women, the greater change will probably be in the lowering of the age of first intercourse; in a 1970 survey, half the sexually experienced college men had had intercourse before attending college (Kaats and Davis, 1970).

HOMOSEXUALITY

One way to classify sexual behavior is by one's choice of a sex object: people who are sexually attracted by a member of their own sex are *homosexual;* those attracted by members of the opposite sex are *heterosexual;* and those attracted by people of both sexes are *bisexual* (Masters and Johnson, 1979).

Public opinion surveys show that about two-thirds of the American population views homosexuality as an illness and as "obscene and vulgar" (Weinberg and Williams, 1974). Despite popular stereotypes, researchers have been unable to find any personality characteristics that distinguish homosexuals from heterosexuals, apart from their choice of sex partners. As mentioned earlier, until the 1970s, homosexuality was designated by psychiatrists as a mental disorder, but in the latest revision of the psychiatric diagnostic manual, homosexuality is seen as a disorder only if it causes anxiety or other problems in adapting.

While some cities, like San Francisco and Provincetown, Massachusetts, are known for high concentrations of homosexuals, the estimated 2 to 4 million Americans who are exclusively homosexual are spread fairly evenly throughout the population. Homosexuals, like heterosexuals, have a wide variety of lifestyles. Some are secretive about their preference, while others live openly as couples. Some *lesbians*, homosexual women, live and raise children (often from former marriages) in family-style communes (Wolf, 1979).

The Kinsey Institute surveyed about 1,500 homosexuals living in the San Francisco area (Bell and Weinberg, 1978). Homosexuals were found to be about as sexually active as heterosexual peers in terms of frequency of sex. But almost half the male homosexuals estimated that they had had at least 500 different sexual partners during the course of their homosexuality. Many homosexual men preferred to "cruise" homosexual hangouts for sexual contacts, while most lesbians preferred a single, stable relationship.

Those homosexual men and women who were part of a stable couple tended to have more sexual activity, fewer sexual problems, and less regret about being homosexual than those without such stable relationships. More than a third of the lesbians had been married, but only a fifth of the men; many of those who had been married did not know of their homosexual preference before the marriage. Most homosexuals, they found, were satisfied with their sexual preference, the women even more than the men. As a group, the homosexuals appeared to be as well-adjusted as heterosexuals.

Homosexuality does not seem to have become more prevalent in the thirty years since the first Kinsey survey, but it has become more visible—especially in large cities. Even so, it is still illegal in about thirty states. Many people have a homosexual encounter at one time or another in their lives without becoming exclusively homosexual. People can also have both homosexual and heterosexual affairs at the same time. Some married men, for example, occasionally have secret homosexual affairs. Homosexuality is also more likely in situations of isolation from the opposite sex, such as the armed forces, boarding school, or jail.

Homosexual men

While "homosexual" is the term for a person who prefers a partner of the same sex, many homosexual men call themselves *gay*, a term that indicates a rejection of the negative cultural stereotype of the homosexual. Gay men are more accepting of their sexual preference and more likely to *come out*, or openly announce their homosexuality (Morin and Miller, 1975). *Latent homosexuals* are men who repress their homosexual impulses. When the impulses break into awareness, they

Homosexuals have been more open about their sexual preference in recent years. The annual Gay Liberation Parade in San Francisco draws tens of thousands of participants each year. (© Joyce R. Wilson 1978/Photo Researchers, Inc.)

may succumb to them with great feelings of guilt. Sometimes the conflict caused by homosexual impulses creates a *homosexual panic*, an episode of intense anxiety and personality disorganization.

A small proportion of homosexuals, called "drag queens," dress as women in public or adopt highly effeminate dress and manners. While this type may conform to the common stereotype, most homosexuals look and act as other men do. Some, in fact, go to extremes to fit the cultural image of masculinity, becoming body-builders with formidable physiques.

Homosexual women

Most lesbians, like male homosexuals, are not noticeably different from the general populace on any dimension except their choice of sex partner. Lesbians have an advantage over homosexual men in that—in part, because of the wider latitude society allows women in dress and physical contact with each other—they are noticed (and harassed) less: a female couple can live together for years and not attract attention, while a male couple living together may become conspicuous.

Many lesbians prefer to live in couples, and roles are often divided along traditional sex role lines, one masculine, the other feminine (Wolf, 1979).

Lesbians who play the part of extreme sex roles are either "butch" or "femme." The butch (sometimes called "dike") wears men's clothes, wears her hair short, and is masculine in manner. The femme is typically feminine in dress and manner, and is the more passive of the two. A more usual pattern, though, is for lesbian couples to live together without adopting extreme roles. Lesbians tend to focus their social life on other lesbian couples or activities.

Many homosexuals, men as well as women, prefer the term "homophile" to "homosexual." Removing the "sexual," they point out, is more in keeping with the facts of their lives: they are people with full lives like anyone else. Their sexual preference is one of many parts of their life, not the totality.

Imagine that a couple have met at a dance. As they walk off the dance floor, a very attractive woman catches their attention, though neither says anything about her.

"Thanks for the dance," says the man, intending to ask the beautiful woman for a dance.

But when he finds her, he's shocked to see she's already dancing—with the woman he just left! ■

Bisexuality

Sometimes referred to as "ac/dc" (for alternating and direct current), bisexuality is surprisingly common. Kinsey reported that 33 percent of men and 26 percent of women were bisexual to some degree and pointed out that sexual behavior, like most things in the living world, involves a continuum. This is especially true of sexual preferences: while some people are exclusively homosexual or heterosexual, some are somewhere in-between, preferring neither men nor women exclusively. Over the years, for example, many people may have a temporary period of bisexuality, during

which they have a lover of the same sex (or opposite sex, if their main preference is homosexual).

Traditional theories of sexuality have viewed bisexuality as an indication of arrested psychosexual development, or as a transitional stage between homosexuality and heterosexuality. Another view is that bisexuality is a step "beyond" heterosexuality, whereby a person can respond sexually to another regardless of the other's sexual identity. There is no sure answer; little research has been done to date on bisexuals (Money and Wiedeking, 1980).

SEX IN MODERN SOCIETY

Changing sex roles

The movement against the social tyranny imposed by sex role stereotypes, such as the dependent, passive woman and the dominant, assertive man, has had some impact on sexual behavior. As these stereotypes weaken, they allow both men and women more freedom in how they will behave sexually with each other. Men, for example, can be gentle and yielding at times, while women can be assertive.

Even so, these stereotypes are slower to change than the publicity given to the women's liberation movement suggests. Many men, for example, are aroused by the idea of a woman being sexually assertive, while women themselves feel that such behavior is undesirable (Allgeier, 1976). One of the changes that *has* come is in the Victorian idea that a woman's sexual activity is in the service of a man's needs. As more women assert their rights in the sexual arena, equal attention to the woman's sexual needs is more common (Katchadourian and Lunde, 1975).

Sex, love, and marriage

Within the last few decades, the proportion of men and women who engage in premarital sex has risen steadily. This change, nevertheless, does not indicate a loosening of all sexual bonds: the rate of indiscriminate sex with several partners has not increased. Instead, more and more serious couples are engaging in intercourse before marriage. Another marked trend is the eradication of the *double standard*, the idea that a man can have sex with many women, but a woman should remain faithful to one man. Men, if anything, are slightly less promiscuous after marriage, while the rate of premarital sexual experience among women is rising to match that of men (Hunt, 1974). The basic change is toward more sexual equality.

Within marriage, the quality of sexual activity seems to be improving, at least for some (Williams, 1980). A medical textbook in common use at the turn of the century, written by a onetime surgeon general of the United States, asserted that women felt not the slightest pleasant sensation during intercourse; frigidity was assumed to be

the norm for women. Sexual pleasures were thought to be a man's prerogative, not a woman's. By Kinsey's time that had changed for many married couples. He found, for example, that the frequency of orgasm during intercourse increased the longer a woman had been married. Hunt (1974), comparing the results of his survey with those of Kinsey twenty-five years before, found that the frequency of intercourse among married couples had risen significantly for all age groups. Other differences Hunt reported: more wives were sexually aroused by erotic stimuli, an increase in the variety of sex techniques used by couples, and an increased appetite for intercourse on the part of wives. In short, rather than threatening the institution of marriage, the increasing sexual openness in our society seems to make it more pleasant.

SUMMARY

Biological roots of sexuality. Among lower animals, sexual behavior is regulated mainly by the sex hormones, testosterone in the male and estrogen in the female.

The external male sexual organs are the penis, testicles, and scrotum; the chief internal organs are the vas deferens, seminal vesicles, and prostate gland. During sexual excitement the penis becomes engorged with blood, resulting in erection.

The external female sexual organs are the major and minor labia and the clitoris, which together are called the vulva. The main internal sexual organ is the vagina. The clitoris, like the penis, engorges with blood during sexual excitement.

Sexual arousal. Masters and Johnson studied the physiology of arousal and identified its phases as excitement, plateau, orgasm, and resolution. The physiology of sexual arousal can be measured by devices that monitor blood flow in male and female sex organs.

The primary source of arousal during lovemaking is the tactile stimulation of the erogenous zones, which can vary from person to person.

Emotion also plays a vital part in arousal. Some degree of caring and trust seem essential.

One of the main sources of arousal is imagination and fantasy. Fantasies are especially common in teenagers, but continue throughout life. Fantasies serve several purposes—as an easy source of pleasure, wish fulfillment, or rehearsal.

There is evidence that familiarity dims the appeal of sexual stimuli, especially for males.

People vary widely in their response to sex, depending on their experience. Guilt is a common attitude toward sex. Childhood experiences can shape an adult's attitudes toward sex.

Contrary to popular belief, there does not seem to be a direct link between exposure to pornography and the likelihood of becoming a sex criminal. When pornography was made freely available in Denmark, sex crimes declined rather than increased.

How sexuality develops. Children cannot be sexual in the same way as adults because they are not fully developed physically or cognitively. Nonetheless, even infants can experience sexual arousal, and many children learn to masturbate. Masturbation can lead to the eroticization of activities or sensations associated with it.

The physical changes that occur during adolescence affect to some extent the perception of an individual's sexuality. Parental attitudes and the information parents pass on are influential in shaping adolescent sexuality.

Our culture lengthens the adolescent period, forbidding intercourse long after sexual maturity has been reached, which intensifies conflicts about sex.

Boys and girls tend to have different orientations toward sexual activity, with boys emphasizing physical gratification, and girls the emotional relationship. This conflict in outlook can occur in adult couples, too.

Society and sexuality. The social environment plays a decisive role in the formation of sexual norms. Many nonliterate cultures permit and even encourage sex play among the young.

Society has a strong voice in what sorts of sexual behavior will be deemed pleasurable or acceptable. Because of the rapidity of current attitude change, sometimes one aspect of society (e.g., medicine) will condone a certain behavior while another (e.g., the law) will disapprove.

The United States, once labeled restrictive, is today semirestrictive of sexuality; for example, premarital sex is formally disapproved but not actually prevented. If pregnancy occurs, however, the couple is frequently pressured into marriage.

Despite increasing sexual openness, a study of American college students showed a reluctance to think realistically about their parents' sexual activity.

The range of sexual behavior. Kinsey's study of sexual behavior, conducted thirty years ago, still depicts general patterns with some accuracy. His findings included a high rate of premarital sex, fairly common extramarital and oral-genital sex, and homosexual experience among one-quarter to one-third of the population. The higher the educational level, the greater a person's range of experience.

Women varied dramatically in how frequently they had orgasms.

Contacts with animals, voyeurism, and fetishism were among the rarer practices.

The Hunt survey, twenty-five years after Kinsey, found a substantial increase in the occurrence of premarital intercourse as well as a trend toward earlier sexual experience. Use of prostitutes and male infidelity were down. Sexual activity among the divorced had increased, along with oral-genital sex. There was also an increase in female sexual responsiveness.

Surveys of college students have found that sexual standards are slowly but steadily loosening. The greatest change to come is probably a lowering of the age of first intercourse.

Homosexuality. Researchers have been unable to find any personality characteristics that distinguish homosexuals from heterosexuals, apart from their choice of sex partners.

Frequency of sexual activity seems to be similar for homosexuals and heterosexuals, but one study indicated that some male homosexuals have a much wider variety of partners. Homosexuals in a stable relationship seemed happier sexually than those who chose to "cruise."

The term "gay" is used to express positive feelings about one's homosexuality. Latent homosexuals repress their impulses; conflict over such impulses sometimes causes homosexual panic.

Lesbians are noticed and harassed less than homosexual men. Many prefer to live in couples and focus their social life on activities with other lesbians. There has been relatively little research on lesbians.

Bisexuality is fairly common—Kinsey reported that 33 percent of men and 26 percent of women were bisexual to some degree.

Sex in modern society. Sex role stereotypes are being modified to some extent, but this is happening slowly. More and more serious couples are engaging in intercourse before marriage, and the double standard is fading. Within marriage, the quality of sexual activity seems to be changing for the better.

GLOSSARY

Bisexual Having sexual partners of both sexes.

Clitoris The shaft at the top of the vaginal opening that engorges with blood during sexual excitement; main source of sexual responsiveness in a woman.

Come out To openly announce one's homosexuality.

Cunnilingus The act of kissing and licking the vulva.

Double standard The unspoken understanding that a man can have sex with many women, but that a woman should remain faithful to one man.

Erection The tumescence of the penis during sexual arousal, when the hollow spaces in its shaft fill with blood and it swells in size.

Erogenous zones Sensitive areas of the body especially susceptible to sexual arousal.

Eroticized Having acquired sexual associations.

Estrogen The basic female sex hormone.

Extramarital sex Intercourse outside marriage.

Fellatio The act of taking the penis into the mouth.

Fetish Sexual arousal to an inappropriate object, such as a shoe.

Gay The term used by homosexuals to express positive feelings about their sexuality.

Heterosexual Attracted to people of the opposite sex.

Homosexual Attracted to people of the same sex.

Homosexual panic An episode of intense anxiety and personality disorganization brought on by conflict over homosexual impulses.

Latent homosexual One who represses his or her homosexual impulses.

Lesbian A female homosexual.

Masturbate To stimulate oneself sexually.

Minor labia The lips that protect the vaginal opening and are sensitive to sexual stimulation.

Orgasmic platform During sexual arousal, the swelling of the tissues in the outer third of the vagina so that the vagina grips the penis.

Penile plethysmograph A device that attaches to the penis and measures changes in its circumference.

Pornography Books, magazines, and movies depicting explicit sexual acts.

Refractory period A span of minutes or hours after intercourse during which the male cannot respond with an erection and orgasm to sexual stimulation.

Sex guilt The tendency to become anxious whenever sexual standards are violated in deed or in thought.

Sexuality The whole of a person's sexual behavior.

Testosterone The basic male sex hormone.

Transvestism Dressing in clothing of the opposite sex.

Vaginal plethysmograph A vaginal probe that uses a light sensing device to detect blood volume changes.

Vulva The major and minor labia and the clitoris.

UNDERSTANDING POWER, THE BLUES, AND INTIMACY

APPLYING PSYCHOLOGY / FOUR

Power. Feeling down. Being a couple or breaking up. These issues affect us all. Recent research in the fields of motivation, emotion, and sexuality can shed light on these issues. David McClelland has described the link between the need for power and the way hypertension may develop in some people. Aaron Beck assessed why college students get depressed. And Ann Peplau, with a group of colleagues, detailed the balance of power in dating couples, and what leads them to break up or stay together. An insight into the dynamics of these issues may help you better understand and deal with those of them that matter in your life.

ISSUE # 1: POWER

The costs of power

High power needs may have deadly consequences. David McClelland (1979) suggests that the behavior pattern of people with high power needs can lead to high blood pressure, which, in turn, carries the risk of death from heart attack or stroke.

There are strong similarities between the profile of those high in n Power, and the "Type A" behavior pattern identified by Friedman and Rosenman (1974) as a cause of heart disease. The Type A person is hard-driving, always in a rush, pushes herself to capacity, and is ambitious and competitive. A Type A person, for example, is likely to set deadlines or work quotas for herself, over and above what school or the job realistically requires. Understandably, Type A students earn more academic honors than others.

Type A people are particularly concerned with being in control, according to Glass (1977). While they do not ordinarily have higher blood pressures than others, if they are thwarted, their blood pressure shoots up rapidly. If their hostility is repeatedly aroused by frustrations, then they come to be at risk for hypertension, chronically elevated blood pressure.

This same pattern of blood pressure rise when power strivings are thwarted is found in those with high n Power, according to McClelland (1979).

High power drive alone, however, is not sufficient for this chain to develop. The power drive must be inhibited, either by the situation or by the person herself. Top executives, for example, have lower blood pressure than urban blacks. This may be so, contends McClelland, because the executive has lots of opportunity to express his power needs, while blacks—who have higher unemployment and face the frustration of discrimination— more often confront obstacles they can't change, and they have to inhibit their hostility and anger.

To test the relationship between inhibited power needs and high blood pressure, McClelland (1979) did three studies. In the first, German men were given TATs, which were scored for n Power and for "activity inhibition"—the number of times the word "not" is used. Activity inhibition is an index of the extent to which people control their actions (McClelland, 1975). Their scores were then compared with blood pressure readings. A second test of 235 Harvard freshmen used the same procedure. The third test scored TATs taken by Harvard men around 1940, and then in midlife, and compared their scores with blood pressure readings taken twenty years later.

In all three cases, activity inhibition with high power needs correlated with raised blood pressure. One interpretation is that the inhibition of power needs leads to suppressed hostility, which in turn plays a role in the development of high blood pressure. These results agree with other evidence of how high blood pressure develops (Eisler, et al., 1977). Anger elevates a person's blood pressure by activating the sympathetic nervous system. If anger is felt but cannot be openly expressed, blood pressure stays higher than if an outlet is available. When suppressed hostility becomes a persistent reaction pattern for a person, the result is chronic activation of the sympathetic nervous system, which leads to hypertension.

The mix of motives

Men with other dominant motives—the need to achieve and the need to affiliate—have lower blood pressure than the high power, high inhibition group. This may be, McClelland suggests, because they prefer activities like spending time with others or doing things well and efficiently, which might reduce the stresses in their lives. The nature of the power motive seems to lead people to stressful encounters.

But, as McClelland points out, motives like the need for power are learned, as are the habits that lead to chronically blocking the expression of anger. What is learned can be changed. People's motive patterns can be altered, for example, by a traumatic life experience, by changes in lifestyle such as a new job or marrying, or by special efforts to avoid tension.

Each of us has a mix of motive patterns, and these shift over the course of our lives. In college the need to achieve and to affiliate may be higher than the need for power, while at the start of a career the need for power may outpace both the need to achieve and to affiliate. At different phases of life, each of these motives may be a valuable, useful means to attain specific goals in life. But to the degree they have hidden costs— such as hypertension—an awareness of the price we have to pay may allow us to make better choices in what makes us run.

ISSUE #2: THE BLUES

Imagine that lately you've been feeling down. You're sleeping much less than usual at night, and find yourself taking long naps during the day. You don't go out with friends as you used to, you've lost your appetite, and you feel lonely.

You can't get around to doing your work, no matter how much you prod yourself. You haven't been doing badly in school, but you feel like a failure and that your future is hopeless. Though you can't pin down the exact reason, you feel very, very sad. ■

The blues

If you have sometimes felt like this, you're not alone. At any one time, about one quarter of the national population of college students suffers some symptoms of depression such as these (Bumberry, Oliver, and McClure, 1978). While most people go through a cycle of emotional ups and downs, depression is different from a normal low: it is more intense, has a greater variety of symptoms, and they last longer. For example, someone who is in a low mood can manage to get started on work that needs to be done; someone who is depressed often can't work at all.

Depression

The college years seem to be particularly risky ones for depression. Pressures on students to meet their private (or parents') academic standards, the need to decide on career goals, and loneliness that results from the absence of old friends and family can all contribute to depression.

Research by Aaron Beck (1976) suggests that the cause of depression of the sort that students experience is not in the pressures and stresses themselves, but rather in the way the stresses are *perceived*. Academic life is full of challenges, difficulties, and temporary setbacks. An exam may be harder than you were prepared for, too many term papers due the same week may mean that none gets as much attention as you'd like to give it, a low midterm grade may upset you. But a single bad grade isn't a disaster.

Depression can start with the exaggeration of setbacks, for example, when a single bad grade *does* seem to be a disaster. A "D" is not the end of the world, but it may make a student who is bent on doing well feel as if her world is crumbling. A premed student, for example, may be convinced that a low grade in a science course may make medical school admission—and her dream of becoming a doctor—impossible.

When a single failure blots out the memory of past successes, it signals that a cycle of misinterpretation of events, anxiety, and unrealistically low self-evaluation begins. The downward spiral ends in depression. The depression then interferes with the student's performance. As the spiral becomes more vicious, the student misinterprets her academic difficulties as proof of intellectual incapability, instead of recognizing them as a sign of emotional stress.

One reason that college students may be more prone to depression is that, for many, college is a time of meeting countless new situations for the first time without the supports available at home. A student who as a high school senior may have been a prominent leader or an honor student has a much different status as a college freshman. In addition, small choices can have weighty consequences: the decision to take one course rather than another can, over the long term, mean choosing one career rather than another. Students whose families are making financial sacrifices to send them to college or those on scholarships may feel an extra obligation to do well; if they don't meet their own standards of performance, they are prey to self-blame. Many students feel a conflict between studying hard and taking the time to make new friends.

Another reason some students may be prone to depression is the atmosphere of competition for grades—especially if a student has hopes of graduate or professional school. Since competition *is* great, a lapse in grades can have damaging long-term effects. The depression-prone student, though, is likely to take a setback even harder than reality calls for. One response to depression has been to withdraw from school: a study of dropouts found that one-third had gone through a serious depression just before leaving (Beck and Young, 1978).

Only the lonely

Another prime cause of depression in college is loneliness. Students who were used to a close circle of friends developed over the years can find themselves far away, in a new community, and among strangers. It may take years to develop again a close network of friends. In the process, the almost inevitable result is feeling lonely.

Another trigger for loneliness can be the ending of a relationship that a person has depended on for companionship, intimacy, and support. Loss of a girlfriend, for example, can make some men feel deserted and alone. Here again, misperception can make the facts seem even worse than they are: a young man may think that this rejection means that no one will ever love him again.

Loneliness, like feeling down, can be a temporary episode or a persistent state. Loneliness can lead to social paralysis: fear of meeting people, going to class, making new friends. This social withdrawal, of course, only worsens the situations that made the person feel lonely in the first place.

Beck (1978) describes four types of loneliness:

☐ *Exclusion*, the belief that you are left out of a group to which you would like to belong;

☐ *Feeling unloved*, the sense that people do not accept you as you are;

☐ *Constriction*, the sense that your feelings are bottled up inside, with no one to talk to about them;

☐ *Alienation*, the feeling of being totally different from everyone else around.

When any or all of these factors lead a person to be cut off from meaningful relationships for a long period, then loneliness is likely to be severe and chronic. A person may feel bitter about people, an attitude that reinforces the pattern of social isolation.

This is far different from the everyday feelings of loneliness that pass as soon as someone shows an interest in us, calling or stopping to talk. Severe loneliness involves the same sort of misinterpretations that underlie depression: the person assumes that a minor rejection means everyone dislikes her—when in fact she has satisfactory friendships.

"Cognitive distortion" is Beck's term for misinterpreting or exaggerating the importance of unpleasant events. It is, according to his theory, a key cause of loneliness and depression. For example, when students who were sad and lonely were asked about their friends, they reported they had no one at school to depend on who really cared about them or loved them. They felt like outsiders who wanted to be liked more than they were. They blamed this state of affairs on their own inadequacies. But when they listed specific friends, students who were lonely had the same number of close friends as those who were happy, and they said that their close friends really *did* care about them (Beck and Young, 1978). Their feelings of loneliness, in short, did not fit the facts.

The cognitive cure

Beck (1972; 1976) has developed a program that changes how depressed or lonely people think about their situation. The key is replacing cognitive distortion with realistic perceptions.

Beck's approach includes:

☐ a daily activity schedule, where the student plans useful activities that will fill up the whole day. This directly counters a major symptom of depression: listless inactivity. Once depressed people start accomplishing useful tasks, like studying or even doing the laundry, they feel a sense of pleasure and accomplishment. They realize they are not totally incompetent and can still enjoy themselves.

☐ a dysfunctional thoughts record, in which the student describes the situation that led to a sad or anxious feeling, and the thought that accompanied the feeling, whenever such feelings occur. Then, usually with a therapist, she figures out a rational retort to the upsetting thought. For example, the thought "This low grade on my quiz means I'm just wasting my time in school" could be countered with the reply "Just because I got one low grade on a quiz doesn't mean I can't do better next time."

☐ rehearsal and training for better academic or social skills. Someone who wastes time and studies ineffectively would be taught how to schedule time efficiently and develop more useful study habits (for example, using some of the principles in the minichapter "How to Learn"). A shy and lonely student might practice real-life social situations with a therapist, such as starting a conversation with a stranger.

While these methods were devised by and for use with therapists, they don't have to be used in therapy. Beck and Young (1978) point out that these techniques can be used by anyone in a position to help someone who is depressed—dormitory counselors, teachers, or just good friends.

ISSUE #3: INTIMACY

Imagine that a couple are trying to decide where to go on a date. "I'd like to go to the basketball game tonight," he says. "It's a big game."

"I hate basketball," she says.

"Well, there's a great movie playing downtown. Woody Allen."

"I never did like Woody Allen movies."

"I suppose we could go see the play they're putting on at the campus theater. It's a musical."

"That's a wonderful idea! I love musicals!" ■

The balance of power

Who is more powerful in this relationship—the man who proposes what to do, or the woman who accepts or rejects the proposals? In this instance, she is. But the balance of power within a couple is more intricate than a single decision may reveal. Often one partner is more powerful in certain domains, such as where to go or what to do, while the other holds sway in other areas, such as having sex.

The traditional formula in our society is that the man should take the initiative, making plans, paying bills, and the like, while the woman should look up to him and support his decisions. This model of the balance of power, however, may be on its way out: most college students support an egalitarian balance of power, where each partner has an equal say in decisions (Peplau, 1978).

The balance of power in intimate relationships was studied in 231 dating couples from four colleges in Boston. The couples were interviewed and answered questionnaires several times over the course of two years (Peplau, Rubin, and Hill, 1976). Assessing the balance was not easy. For example, a woman who seemed to be in control by deciding what to do on dates, which friends the couple should see, and even selecting her boyfriend's clothes, may not be the boss. It could turn out that her boyfriend was a busy student in law school who felt all these decisions were trivial, and so left them to her. He would have veto power, but never have to use it, because she would carefully cater to his preferences in what she suggested in the first place. In this case, he would have the greater power, although he delegated his decision making to her.

All in all, despite the fact that most of these couples espoused equality, fewer than half reported equal power in their own relationship. When power was unequal, it was more often in the man's favor—the traditional pattern. To assess the true balance of power, couples were asked which partner had more say in five key areas:

what they did for fun, what they talked about, sex, how much time they spent together, and what they did with other people (Peplau, 1978).

How the balance tips

Peplau (1978) found a set of factors that could tip the balance of power one way or the other. Traditional sex role attitudes, for example, were more common among couples where the man held the power; couples that had equal partners were also more likely to hold nontraditional attitudes about sex roles, for example, believing a woman's career is as important as a man's.

Imbalances of involvement tip the balance of power. The more involved a person is, the more eager to defer to the partner's wishes. If one partner is passionately in love, and the other mildly interested, the commitment is not equal. The "principle of least interest" means that the partner who is less involved will have greater control. A corollary is that the more attractive one partner seems to the other, the more power the attractive partner will have. Attractiveness is not only physical—money, social savvy, or prestige can also be sources of attractiveness and power.

Another index of the balance of power is the attitude both partners hold toward the woman's career. Traditionally men and women divide their goals, women giving higher priority to family, men to careers. There was a strong relationship between the balance of power and the woman's career plans. When the women didn't even plan to finish college, 87 percent of couples also reported the man had more power. But in couples where the woman had plans for an advanced degree, only 30 percent said the man had the power. The higher the woman's career goals, the more equality in power.

Does the balance of power in a relationship determine how satisfying it will be? Apparently not. During the two years the couples were studied, Peplau (1978) found no difference on measures of satisfaction, closeness, or breaking up between couples with equal power and those where the man held the reins. Neither sex, though, was as satisfied in couples where the woman had more say. Peplau concluded that the traditional male-dominant couple or the newer pattern of equality seems easier to accept than one in which the woman is dominant.

But no matter what the balance of power, the factor that overrides all others is consensus. If both the man and woman agree that their particular pattern is satisfactory, then they will most likely have a durable relationship.

The end of an affair

Another part of the Boston study of couples focused on what brought about breakups (Hill, Rubin, and Peplau, 1976). Over the two years, 103 couples broke up. Several factors predicted a couple would break up. Foremost among these were their degree of involvement: couples who at the outset said they felt less close, saw less likelihood of marrying each other, and dated others were much more likely to split up. But couples who were quite intimate on these measures of involvement didn't necessarily survive either. Being in love with each other predicted staying together; liking each other did not. In addition, the woman's love for her boyfriend was a better predictor than the man's. Living together or having intercourse had surprisingly little relationship to the survival of the couple. While couples who have sex or live together may be closer, they also have more chance for friction, for example, over who does household chores.

Breakups were often tied to the school calendar: May–June, September, and December–January were the most likely months for breakups. This may be because these key turning points demand that a couple make decisions (such as whether to live together, spend vacations apart, or accept a job elsewhere) that lead them to reevaluate how committed they are to the relationship. A separation caused by a vacation, for example, may present a good pretext for the less involved partner to call it quits.

There are two sides to breaking up. When partners who have split up are asked the reasons and the effects, they don't always agree. For example,

the rejecting lover, who initiated the split, often feels less depressed and lonely, freer, and happier—but also more guilty—than the rejected partner. The rejecter generally feels relief; the rejected, regret.

The breakup is more often initiated by the woman; while men seem to fall in love more readily than women, women seem more likely to fall out of love. Women were also more sensitive to problems in the relationship—and so are more likely to speak up first when things go wrong.

One reason women may fall out of love more easily is that they seem to be more pragmatic about relationships. Contrary to the prevailing stereotype of the romantic, sentimental woman, women may have to be more canny about their choice of mate, if only for simple economic reasons. Even now, in most marriages the wife's status and income depend more on her husband's than her own. To be blunt, her choice of a mate is also a choice of a standard of living. Men can more easily afford to be romantic in their choice of mate.

These breakups may actually be for the better. The cost of breaking up before marriage—both emotionally and economically—is much less than that of a divorce. These breakups prevent marriages that would otherwise end in divorce—and the best divorce, an old saying goes, is the one you get before marriage.

One lesson learned from this research was that openness—whether it leads to breakup or marriage—seems the best course for any couple (Rubin, *et al.*, 1979). If both partners can disclose their true feelings and thoughts to each other, their relationship is more likely to survive and be healthy. But self-disclosure should come in steps, as the relationship deepens. It needn't be immediate, nor made in a spirit of obligation. Each partner should be free to decide what to reveal and when to reveal it. And there is no need to bare the darkest regions of one's soul, even in the most intimate of relationships—each person should be allowed areas of privacy. But a marriage based on openness seems more likely to thrive.

PART FIVE

HUMAN DEVELOPMENT

12

INFANCY AND CHILDHOOD

THE PRENATAL PERIOD

The fetus ■ Malformations ■ The mother's emotional state and health

THE NEWBORN

Prematurity ■ Reflexes ■ Infant learning ■ Individual differences

MATURATION

Environmental deprivation ■ Overcoming cognitive deficits ■ Environmental enrichment ■ Physical growth and motor development

PERCEPTUAL DEVELOPMENT

Visual discrimination ■ Depth and distance perception

COGNITIVE AND MORAL DEVELOPMENT

Piaget's theory of intellectual development ■ Sensorimotor stage ■ Preoperational stage ■ Stage of concrete operations ■ Stage of formal operations ■ Moral development

PERSONALITY DEVELOPMENT

Infancy ■ Feeding ■ Attachment ■ Toddlerhood ■ Preschool ■ Middle childhood

COMMON MYTHS

MANY PEOPLE BELIEVE . . .	ACTUALLY . . .
One-year-old infants are especially attached to their mother and hardly aware of their father.	One-year-olds are equally attached to both father and mother, preferring their company to that of even a friendly visitor.
A "difficult" newborn will be hard to raise as a child.	Difficult babies often no longer seem so at six months, and are by no means inevitably problem children.
Babies cannot tell the difference between people's faces until they are at least a year old.	Infants only five months old can distinguish between faces.
An infant deprived of stimulation will be retarded.	If a stimulation-deprived infant is put in a normal home, by later childhood it can make up for most early handicaps.
Parents who are firm in their rules and allow no disagreements have the best results in child rearing.	Parents who combine firm control with respect for their children's independence raise the most self-reliant and responsible children.

I don't know when I grow,
I'm always with myself.
I'm not mad when I'm bad,
I'm always with myself.
I can't see that I'm me.
I'm always with myself.
It's strange that you change,
You're always with yourself.

GWEN MILLER, AGE SEVEN

Children change. Of the hundreds of changes children go through as they grow and develop, some, such as the first step or first word, are milestones; others, such as the ability to pick up small objects, are less noticeable hallmarks of development. *Developmental psychology* is the study of all the changes that the growth process brings through the entire life cycle, from the womb to the tomb.

Three major concerns of developmental psychology are: (1) The sequences that children and adults pass through as they grow and develop; for example, the course of language development in children or changes in mental abilities through adulthood. (2) The individual differences between people as they pass through these sequences; for example, one child may start speaking very early, another later; one elderly person may become senile while another of the same age is mentally alert. (3) The influences of different cultures on these developmental sequences; for example, normal sexual development in one culture may seem slow or precocious in another. In short, developmental psychology studies how behavior emerges and changes over the course of a person's life, focusing on the interaction of heredity and environment. Developmental psychologists are concerned

too with major crises encountered at every phase of a person's life, including events such as career shifts and divorces—passages that until recently have received little research attention (Baltes, Reese, and Lipsitt, 1980).

The course of a person's life spans a series of eras, stages of life that have specific developmental tasks and typical psychological issues. There is no specific age when these eras begin and end for any given person, though on the average we can gauge when they occur for most people. Erikson's life stages, for example, mark off eras in terms of the psychological issues a person faces, but he gives no set ages when they occur, merely rough approximations.

The major eras of the life span, as assessed by Daniel Levinson (1978), last roughly twenty-five years each. They partially overlap, so that there is a transitional period between them, with the old era ending and the new one beginning. The major eras are: childhood and adolescence (roughly birth to age twenty-two); early adulthood (seventeen to forty-five); middle adulthood (forty to sixty-five); and late adulthood (sixty to death). These eras include several developmental stages, but they provide the overall framework in which the

305

developmental issues are worked out. They are the "macrostructure" of the *life cycle*, the overall sequence of growth and development through which every person passes over the span of life.

THE PRENATAL PERIOD

Imagine that a friend of yours is pregnant. For months she's been excited about the feeling of her baby stirring in her belly. For several weeks now you and she have gone through the same routine: You're sitting together talking when suddenly she says excitedly, "It moved! I can feel it! Here, put your hand right here—you can feel the baby move!"

You put your hand exactly where she points, and feel—nothing.

Today it's the same story, with a difference.

When you put your hand on her belly, you feel a slight poke from inside. "Migosh—I can feel it!" you exclaim with delight.

"Oh, you're just trying to humor me," she says. ■

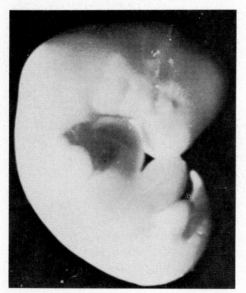

(1) Five weeks (Dr. Landrum B. Shettles)

(2) Eight weeks
(Dr. Landrum B. Shettles)

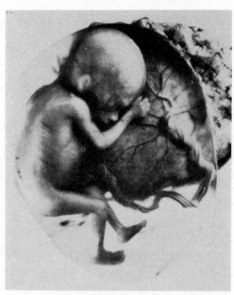

(3) Sixteen weeks (Edith L. Potter, *Fundamentals of Human Reproduction*)

(4) Twenty–four weeks (Dr. Landrum B. Shettles)

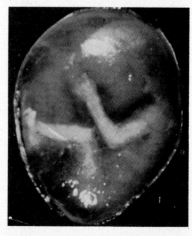

From the moment of conception until an infant is born, the fetus goes through a remarkable transformation. Within four weeks after conception, the embryo is about one-fifth of an inch long—10,000 times larger than the original egg. After eight weeks, when bones start to form, the fetus is more than an inch long, and is clearly human. At sixteen weeks it is about six inches long, and its head is enormous compared to the rest of its body; the fetus looks like a miniature baby. By six months the fetus has developed the capacities—such as the ability to breathe—that will allow it to survive if cared for properly.

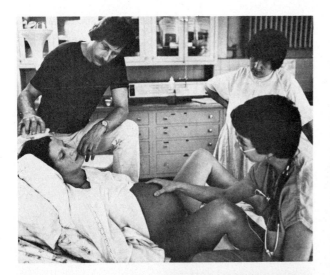

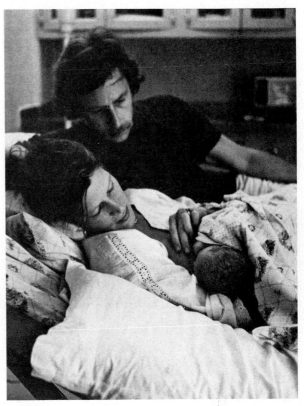

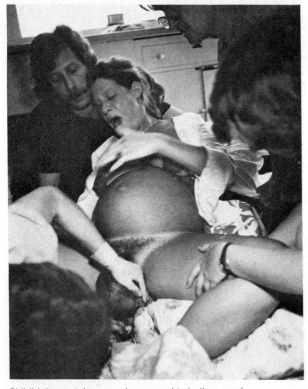

Childbirth can take many hours, and is both a grueling and joyous experience for the mother. Many hospitals encourage the father to be with his wife during labor, both to share in the experience himself, and to give his wife emotional support. (Photos © Mariette Pathy Allen)

The moment of birth is not the dawn of a person's history. As you found, a fetus has an active life *in utero*, in the womb. Any mother-to-be past the fifth month of pregnancy can attest to the sudden spurts of activity on the part of her unborn child. Indeed, fetuses may even start sucking their thumbs *in utero*. As good historians, developmental psychologists begin their investigations with the prenatal period, from conception to birth.

The fetus

The average gestation period for the human infant is 266 days. A single cell is formed from the fusion of two germ cells, an ovum from the mother and a sperm cell from the father. In the next two weeks, this cell is transformed into a *blastocyst*, or hollow sphere with an inner cell mass at one side. It is from this cell mass that the baby will form. In the next six weeks, the infant's rudimentary anatomy begins to take shape. At this stage, the developing organism is called an *embryo*. By the end of this six-week period, the baby-to-be has arms and legs, fingers and toes, as well as humanlike facial features. The endocrine system has formed, but no visible differences between the sexes can be observed yet.

At the next stage, the embryo is known as a *fetus*. During the fetal period, structures that have been barely sketched in at the embryonic stage grow and become elaborated. By ten weeks, the fetus can make breathing and sucking movements, and usually by the twelfth week, an expert can determine its sex.

Some time before the sixteenth week, reflex swallowing begins, and small amounts of amniotic fluid are ingested. Between the twentieth and twenty-eighth weeks, the heart begins to beat. It is at this time that the mother experiences fetal movement. Twenty weeks is the midpoint of pregnancy. By now the discomfort that many mothers experience during pregnancy (for example, a form of nausea called morning sickness) has passed.

Toward the twenty-fourth week, the baby-to-be opens and closes her eyes. Four weeks later, the fetus weighs about 2.5 pounds and has developed enough to have a fair chance of surviving birth. During the last weeks of pregnancy, the mother continues to feel healthy, but she also experiences some discomfort—for example, she must adjust to a new distribution in weight. Such discomforts make her see the coming event somewhat as a liberation (Stone and Church, 1979).

Malformations

Many factors influence prenatal development. Agents that cause malformations in the fetus are called *teratogens*, from the Greek work *teratos*, meaning "monster." The type of malformation a teratogen causes depends on which embryonic tissues are in their critical period of development—developing most rapidly—when it attacks (Thompson and Thompson, 1966). The most familiar teratogens are viruses, radiation, and drugs. Many enter the bloodstream of the fetus from that of the mother through the semipermeable membranes of the placenta and umbilical cord.

The most notorious instance to date of teratogenesis by drugs occurred in the early 1960s, when hundreds of women who had taken thalidomide early in pregnancy to counteract morning sickness gave birth to infants who were either stillborn or missing segments of their arms or legs.

Drugs such as heroin, morphine, and methadone can also cause birth defects. The babies of mothers who are addicted to heroin or morphine are born addicted to the same drugs and go through withdrawal symptons—such as vomiting, trembling, and rapid breathing—in the first few days of life. Sometimes the baby dies. Sadly, the same symptoms occur with women who use methadone, a heroin substitute used to help addicts get off the drug (Soyka and Joffe, 1979). With all these drugs, the severity of the baby's symptoms are directly related to the amount of the drug the mother uses; the greater the drug use, the greater the withdrawal. Other addictive substances, such as tobacco and alcohol, can also cause birth defects. Women who smoke during pregnancy, for example, are more prone than nonsmokers to have babies of low birth weight (Lubenchevco, 1976). And a malformation known as "fetal alcohol syndrome," where the infant shows physical defects, heart malfunction and, often, mental retardation, is found among children of mothers who drink alcohol daily during pregnancy (Jones, *et al.*, 1973).

The mother's emotional state and health

When a person is anxious or emotionally upset, additional adrenaline enters the bloodstream, increasing heart rate and blood pressure. When this state exists in a pregnant woman, a parallel reaction takes place in the fetus, and a number of studies show that the effect may be detrimental. For example, infants of mothers who are tense and anxious in the last weeks of pregnancy have a high incidence of irritability and tend to eat and sleep poorly. The mechanism at work is thought to be sensitization of the infant's autonomic nervous system by the chemical changes in the mother's body (Kagan, *et al.*, 1979). Mothers who are very anxious during pregnancy have more difficulties during labor and delivery than less-anxious women (Davids and DeVault, 1961).

It is also possible, however, that the anxious state of the mother continues after delivery and affects the way she cares for and handles the infant, thus making the child more irritable. Davids and Holden (1970) used psychological tests to explore the mother's state of mind during pregnancy and eight months after the birth of the baby. Scores on such variables as hostility, control, and negative attitudes toward child rearing tended to remain constant from pregnancy to the later testing date. Mothers who during pregnancy had negative attitudes toward child rearing were more anxious and depressed and did not interact well with their babies eight months after birth. Possibly women who showed a change in their maternal attitudes were influenced by the kinds of infants they had. A sickly and fussy infant could make a dismayed mother feel more negative about child rearing; on the other hand, an unusually attractive and responsive baby could make a pessimistic and hostile mother feel more nurturant. The need for adequate nutrition during pregnancy—and in both parents before conception of the child—cannot be overemphasized. A definite correlation exists between malnutrition in pregnancy and risk to the child, whether miscarriage, stillbirth, prematurity, or neonatal death (Pasamanick and Knoblock, 1966). If the infant is malnourished in early life, there is evidence that the number of neurons in the brain will be reduced. The earlier the malnutrition occurs, the more severe the effects on the number of brain cells (Winick and Rosso, 1969).

The probability that an infant will be born with congenital defects increases with the age of the child's mother (see Table 12.1). For example, women over thirty-five have a higher probability of giving birth to an infant with the chromosomal abnormality that causes Down's syndrome, or mongolism, in which severe retardation is accompanied by abnormal physical characteristics.

THE NEWBORN

Prematurity

Usually defined as being born before term, but now more broadly defined as weighing under 5.5 pounds at birth, *premature* or low-birth-weight infants start life with a handicap. They may have an uphill battle just to survive. And, if they succeed, they are far more likely than normal-sized infants to become ill or to have permanent physical handicaps, often in the form of neurological defects (Kennedy, 1971; Baumgartner, 1962). Some premature infants also tend to show significant impairment in IQ (Caputo and Mandel, 1970).

Low birth weight carries psychological burdens as well—for both mother and child. The infant is usually separated from the mother and immediately placed in an incubator, where, except during brief periods of feeding and diapering, she may have almost no human contact for weeks or even months. At the same time, the mother may be upset by the separation. She may blame herself for the infant's situation or, frustrated by the separation, she may vent her anger on the hospital or even on the baby. When the infant finally goes home, she may not seem like the mother's baby at all, and the normal mother-child relationship may not come easily (Lamb, 1978).

TABLE 12.1 **RISK OF DOWN'S SYNDROME BY MATERNAL AGE**

	Risk of Down's syndrome in child	
Age of mother	At any pregnancy	After the birth of a Down's syndrome child
−29	1 in 3,000	1 in 1,000
30–34	1 in 600	1 in 200
35–39	1 in 280	1 in 100
40–44	1 in 70	1 in 25
45–49	1 in 40	1 in 15
All mothers	1 in 665	1 in 200

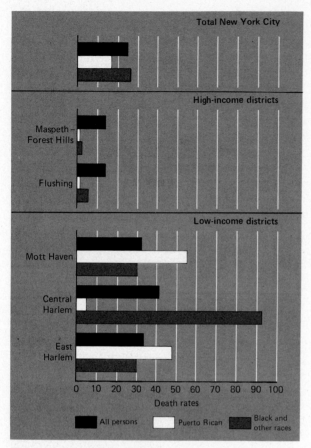

Figure 12.1 Infant mortality
Infant mortality is higher among low-income families, especially among minority groups. Infant mortality rates for different areas of New York City are shown by income, race, and ethnic group. (Death rates are per 1,000 live births.)

child during a premature infant's hospitalization increases the probability of child abuse later.

One of the effects of poor mother-infant bonding is sometimes *failure-to-thrive*, a disorder where an infant or young child fails to grow with no apparent medical reason; the child can also show other symptoms such as refusing food, vomiting and diarrhea, social withdrawal, and apathy (Roberts and Horner, 1979). The single main cause of this disorder seems to be either a physical or psychological absence that causes a lack of contact with the mother. Common factors in such cases include a mother who is hospitalized, working, depressed, alcoholic, or who has deserted the family. The physical needs of the infant are often ignored or handled poorly, including feeding, diapering, warmth, comfort, and medical health. There is often little cuddling of the infant, and its emotional needs are ignored (Lipsitt, 1979).

In light of these findings, one new approach to separation now instituted at several hospitals seems promising: these institutions provide the early contact required for normal mothering to develop (Klaus and Kennell, 1976). Under strictly controlled conditions, the mother cares for her low-birth-weight infant. The experiment benefits

Emotional bonds

There is a special attachment period in the human mother—the term "maternal sensitive period" has been proposed—immediately following the birth of the child, and long separation from the child during this time may affect later mothering abilities (Klaus and Kennell, 1976). The implications for mothers of low-birth-weight infants are clear; there may be an absence of mother-infant *bonding*, the formation of ties of caring and attachment between parent and child. Stern (1973) reports that prolonged separation of mother and

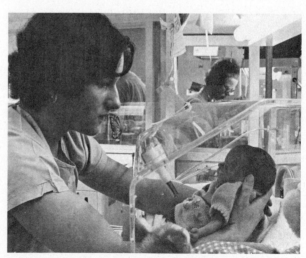

A mother visits her premature baby in its incubator. Premature babies, born before the full term of pregnancy is finished, have a higher risk of developmental problems in infancy, such as greater susceptibility to illness. (Suzanne Wu/Jeroboam)

THE CRIB DEATH PUZZLE

■ Every year 10,000 American infants die in their sleep from unknown causes. These deaths are due to the sudden infant death syndrome (SIDS), commonly known as "crib death." These deaths typically occur in infants within the first six months of life; it is the leading cause of mortality after birth in the first year of life. Yet there has been no satisfactory medical explanation for the causes of crib death.

A new theory proposed by Lipsitt (1979) suggests that crib death may be the tragic side of a usually normal stage of infant development. Lipsitt's theory is based on piecing together many bits of research evidence. If he is correct, his theory may lead to an effective program to prevent crib death (Lipsitt, 1980).

Lipsitt notes that the age of maximum risk of crib death is between two and four months. This is also the age of transition from reflexes to learned responses. The fact that crib death coincides with this developmental transition is the key clue in Lipsitt's theory.

A review of studies of crib death victims reveals a profile suggesting that they come into life with a series of developmental handicaps. Such infants are more likely to be premature or small at birth, to have young mothers, and to have more complications at birth. Often they have a history of respiratory difficulties from birth, or have required resuscitation in the delivery room. Their parents also tend to describe them as more lethargic and unresponsive than their other children. Lipsitt's conclusion: they may suffer a central nervous system deficit that lessens their ability to fight off trouble in breathing.

Typically, if a young infant has trouble breathing due to mucous or a similar cause, it will react by shaking its head or flailing its arms—a useful response. Such reflexive reactions to breathing difficulties are gradually replaced by learned responses such as clearing the throat and blowing the nose. But infants who fail to display a strong reflexive response against blocked breathing are also less likely to learn more developed ones.

Studies have shown that the period between two and four months marks a significant neuromuscular transition: the infant shifts from reflexive to learned reactions. During this time, the infant's neurological system is temporarily disorganized, even in completely normal infants. But those infants who are susceptible to crib death, Lipsitt proposes, are especially vulnerable during this period. Because of their earlier history of developmental difficulties, they may be slow learners during this critical transition. In short, when such infants have trouble breathing during the night, they may fail to move their head, cry, or do whatever else a normal infant would to breathe adequately. The result: lack of oxygen may overtake them, leading to death.

Lipsitt proposes that infants who are possible risks for crib death can be identified by a simple test. Putting a light gauze pad over an infant's face usually elicits a struggle; those infants who are more lethargic may be more at risk. But any movement that is appropriate to the threat of respiratory blockage—for example, shaking the head or crying—can be reinforced through a touch or other pleasing stimulus. This simple program of operant conditioning may prevent crib deaths by teaching infants at risk the simple skills they must master in order to weather this threat to their life. ■

both mother and infant: the mothers feel greater self-confidence, and the babies gain more weight and cry less frequently than the average incubated infant.

Imagine that your friend has had the baby, a boy. You go over to see the baby when he's just five days old. You're not used to being around such small infants, and you don't quite know what to do when she asks you if you want to hold him.

You can't very well refuse, but you're not thrilled by the thought. The kid, you think as you hold him, looks like a prune.

Tentatively, you stroke his tiny hand with your finger. Immediately he grabs hold of your finger, as tight as he can. He likes me, you think with delight. You know, he's pretty cute after all. ■

Reflexes

The newborn's grab for your finger is one of a set of reflexes that every infant is born with to help it survive. The fawn, calf, and colt can stand just a few hours after birth, but human infants are to-tally dependent on those who will care for them. It will take the average child more than two years to walk and run with ease. Of all mammalian young, the child has the longest period of dependency. But the length of this period does not reflect weakness or backwardness; on the contrary, it is required by the greater complexity of the learning task facing the infant and the higher level of development it is destined to attain.

There are several reflexes operative at birth that either have protective or survival value or help the newborn gratify some primary needs. Oral reflexes direct the infant toward food. And, during the first four days of life, an infant stops moving if a nipple is inserted into its mouth—even when no nutriment can be obtained by sucking. When the nipple is withdrawn, the infant starts

TABLE 12.2 **REFLEXES IN THE NEWBORN**

Name of reflex	Testing method	Response	Developmental course	Significance
Blink	Light flash	Closing of both eyelids	Permanent	Protection of eyes from strong stimuli
Biceps reflex	Tap on the tendon of the biceps muscle	Short contraction of the biceps muscle	In the first few days it is brisker than in later days	Absent in depressed infants or in cases of congenital muscular disease
Knee jerk or patellar tendon reflex	Tap on the tendon below the patella or kneecap	Quick extension or kick of the knee	More pronounced in the first two days than later	Absent or difficult to obtain in depressed infants or infants with muscular disease; exaggerated in hyperexcitable infants
Babinski	Gentle stroking of the side of the infant's foot from heel to toes	Dorsal flexion of the big toe; extension of the other toes	Usually disappears near the end of the first year; replaced by plantar flexion of great toe as in the normal adult	Absent in defects of the lower spine
Withdrawal reflex	Pin prick is applied to the sole of the infant's foot	Leg flexion	Constantly present during the first 10 days; present but less intense later	Absent with sciatic nerve damage
Plantar or toe grasp	Pressure is applied with finger against the balls of the infant's feet	Plantar flexion of all toes	Disappears between 8 and 12 months	Absent in defects of the lower spinal cord
Palmar or automatic hand grasp	A rod or finger is pressed against the infant's palm	Infant grasps the object	Disappears at 3 to 4 months; increases the first month in, then gradually declines; replaced by voluntary grasp between 4 and 5 months	Response is weak or absent in depressed babies; sucking movements facilitate grasping

moving again. The baby does not have to learn how to suck; the *sucking reflex* is elicited by any appropriate stimulus placed on the mouth (Kessen and Leutzendorff, 1963). As you found with your friend's baby, his hand automatically grasps an object that touches his palm. If we surprise him with a loud noise, he cries immediately, but this *startle reflex* usually subsides when he is picked up. He has an *orienting reflex*, turning his head toward a novel visual or auditory stimulus, and he automatically withdraws from painful stimuli.

Even a fetus of eight and one-half weeks responds to tactile stimulation. By twenty-eight weeks, basic tastes and odors can be differentiated, and visual and auditory reactions occur (Carmichael, 1954). And, before they are even a day old, newborns react to stimuli in their environ-ment. For example, their eyes can follow a moving light (Cohen, DeLoache, and Strauss, 1978).

The average male newborn is about twenty inches long and weighs about seven pounds; the female, slightly less. The head is disproportionately large, accounting for 25 percent of the length, and has soft spots, called *fontanels*, which allow expansion of the skull to accommodate the enlarging brain. The newborn will spend most of its first weeks sleeping, but this sleep will be punctuated by frequent jerks and tremors and by the rapid eye movements that occur in dreaming.

Infant learning

We know from recent research that the newborn infant is capable of several kinds of learning (Lip-

(Continued)

Name of reflex	Testing method	Response	Developmental course	Significance
Moro reflex	(1) Sudden loud sound or jarring (for example, bang on the examination table); or (2) head drop—head is dropped a few inches; or (3) baby drop—baby is suspended horizontally and the examiner lowers his hands rapidly about 6 inches and stops abruptly	Arms are thrown out in extension, and then brought toward each other in a convulsive manner; hands are fanned out at first and then clinched tightly; spine and lower extremities extend	Disappears in 6 to 7 months	Absent or constantly weak moro indicates serious disturbance of the central nervous system
Stepping	Baby is supported in upright position; examiner moves the infant forward and tilts him slightly to one side	Rhythmic stepping movements	Disappears in 3 to 4 months	Absent in depressed infants
Rooting response	Cheek of infant is stimulated by light pressure of the finger	Baby turns head toward finger, opens mouth, and tries to suck finger.	Disappears at approximately 3 to 4 months	Absent in depressed infants; appears in adults only in severe cerebral palsy diseases
Sucking response	Index finger is inserted about 3 to 4 centimeters into the mouth	Rhythmical sucking	Sucking is often less intensive and less regular during the first 3 to 4 days	Poor sucking (weak, slow, and short periods) is found in apathetic babies; maternal medication during childbirth may depress sucking
Babkin reflex	Pressure is applied on both of baby's palms when lying on his back	Mouth opens, eyes close, and head returns to midline	Disappears in 3 to 4 months	General depression of central nervous system inhibits this response

(A)

(B)

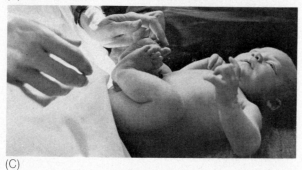

(C)

(D)

(E)

Infant reflexes include:

(A) the rooting reflex, where touching the side of an infant's mouth causes it to turn and try to find something to suck. (Hans Namuth/Photo Researchers, Inc.); (B) the sucking reflex, when the mouth or cheek is touched by a nipple, the newborn sucks rhythmically approximately 5 to 25 sucks a single burst. The sucking reflex is essential for survival in the first weeks of life. (© Erika Stone/Photo Researchers, Inc.); (C) the withdrawal reflex, where the infant's legs flex when the sole of the foot is stroked. (Suzanne Arms/Jeroboam) (D) the moro reflex, where the infant thrusts out its arms when it suddenly loses support for its head and neck. (Dr. David Prechtl and Donald Beintema); (E) the grasping reflex, where the infant grabs and holds on to a finger placed in its hand. (© Elizabeth Wilcox 1972/Photo Researchers, Inc.)

sitt, 1977). For example, Lipsitt and Kaye (1964) have demonstrated that a newborn's responses can be changed through classical conditioning. By first pairing a fifteen-second tone (the conditioned stimulus) with the insertion of a nipple into the baby's mouth (the unconditioned stimulus for the sucking reflex), they were later able to elicit sucking in the baby simply by presenting the tone.

Operant conditioning techniques have also been successfully applied with infants. One researcher was able to reduce an infant's crying habits by rewarding him by rocking him in a hammock at a very high rate (DeLucia, 1971). When he was rocked only as a reward for the cessation of crying, the infant cried much less frequently. Head turning (that is, the orienting reflex) has also been changed using operant methods (Siqueland, 1968).

Newborns can smell and taste. For example, they will turn away from an obnoxious smell, and are able to locate the direction from which smells originate. The smell sensitivity of the infant increases with age (Lipsitt, Engen, and Kaye, 1963), but newborns show a remarkable, obviously useful talent: they can distinguish between the smell of their own mother and someone else (Macfarlane, 1975). In a study done in England, one-week-old infants were presented with two recently-used breast pads, one from their own mother, one from another mother. The infants turned toward their own mother's breast pad more often than toward the strange mother's. Newborns also seem to

have a rudimentary appreciation of tastes: they will slow their rate of sucking in order to savor the taste of a sweet solution (Crook and Lipsitt, 1976). The earlier sensory sensitivity develops, the longer it seems to last: smell, which develops very early, does not decline even in old age, while sight and hearing, both of which mature later, decline more easily.

What the infant learns, it seems to remember. Three-month-old infants who were trained in two fifteen-minute sessions to kick in order to make an overhead mobile wiggle, were tested after two days in intervals up to two weeks. They remembered the response well up to the first week and several retained it at the two-week mark (Sullivan, Rovee-Collier, and Tynes, 1979).

Imagine that as you hold your friend's newborn son, she says proudly, "Isn't he sweet? I think he's really darling."

At that moment he looks up at you and starts to cry at the top of his lungs. ■

Individual differences

Parents typically see their baby as special and unique, with its own individual qualities and personality from birth. Research generally bears this

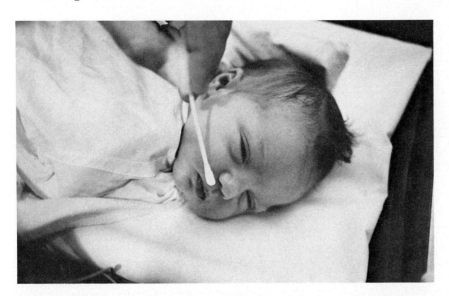

Newborn infants can be tested for perception of smell by placing a cotton swab dipped in an odor-producing substance under their nose. Although sensitivity to smell increases with age, newborns are able to discriminate remarkably between certain smells. (© Jason Lauré 1978/Woodfin Camp & Assoc.)

TABLE 12.3 **THREE TYPES OF CHILDHOOD TEMPERAMENTS**

Type of child	Regularity (of hunger, sleep, excretion)	Approach or withdrawal (in presence of a new object or person)	Intensity of responses	Mood (pleasant and joyful as contrasted with unpleasant and unfriendly)
"Easy"	very regular	active approach	low or moderate	positive
"Slow to warm up"	varies	partial withdrawal	low	slightly negative
"Difficult"	irregular	withdrawal	intense	negative

out: newborns show differences that will affect the quality of their interactions with people through infancy and beyond.

One such difference is the infant's *activity level*, individual differences in autonomic functions that may exist even in the first days of life. Brown (1967) believes differences in activity level reflect constitutional differences in the ability to maintain homeostasis, the body's chemical balance. Whatever its cause, we know that activity level influences both the nature and the intensity of an infant's responsiveness to stimulation. Even within the first five days of life, newborns react very differently to stimuli such as sights, sounds, and people (Birns, 1965; Lipsitt, 1977). *Signalability*, the infant's tendency to cry to attract attention and to smile to ensure interaction, is another index of individual differences. An infant whose signals are more powerful has better control over the environment than one who emits weak signals. Individual differences in signalability during the first six months increase still further with age (Tautermannová, 1973).

There also appear to be constitutional differences between the sexes. For example, the pain thresholds of girls and boys are different. Even during the first four weeks of life, girls make greater responses to a slight electrical shock delivered to a toe, showing a lower threshold to pain (Lipsitt and Levy, 1959). Activity level also appears to differ between the sexes: boys take a longer time to begin moving toward their mothers following presentation of a stimulus (a noise, for example) which suggests that boys have lower

arousal levels and are less prone to flee (Maccoby and Jacklin, 1973). Another possible reason for boys' slower reaction may be their slower maturation rate.

Parents often acknowledge their belief in such differences when they refer to an "easy baby" or to a "difficult child." A study of children observed from birth to age ten by a team of physicians (Thomas, Chess, and Birch, 1970) reports three distinct types of temperament as early as twelve weeks. "Easy children" comprised 40 percent of the sample. As infants they ate and slept regularly, and they reacted positively and with low or moderate intensity to new situations. As children they readily played new games and took up new activities, and they adjusted well in school. At age ten, only 18 percent had problems requiring psychiatric attention.

Ten percent of the sample were "difficult children." As infants they ate and slept irregularly, cried a lot, and adjusted slowly to new circumstances. As children they tended to be negative, moody, and slow to adapt to change. Their responses were intense, typified by loud laughter, crying, and violent temper tantrums. At age ten, 70 percent of these children needed psychiatric help.

Children described as "slow to warm up" both in infancy and in childhood comprised 20 percent of the sample. This group had a low activity level and a low-keyed reaction to new situations. In the remaining 30 percent, no general pattern of traits was evident (see Table 12.3).

The way parents and teachers handle a child

should vary with the child's temperament. The researchers who found these differences in types of children concluded that a harmonious interaction between the child's innate temperament and the way he or she is treated can make a crucial difference in adjustment (Thomas, Chess, and Birch, 1970). A child slow to adapt to change, for example, should be given a chance to get used to differences in routines.

The infant's temperament affects the mother's behavior as well (Ainsworth, 1979). As one investigator points out, the infant, too, has a caretaking role. By crying, he elicits appropriate patterns of maternal behavior such as picking him up, feeding and burping him, and changing his diapers (Bell, 1971). The easy infant is thereby quieted, reinforcing the mother's behavior. On the other hand, the difficult child may constantly fuss, frustrating the mother's need to feel competent. She, in turn may vent her frustration on him, setting up a vicious cycle of destructive behavior. The infant's temperament, then, is crucial in eliciting appropriate social behavior in the mother.

A note of caution: an infant identified as "difficult" by its mother at five weeks may no longer be seen as such at six months. Nor does the mother of a "difficult" child necessarily feel put upon. In short, difficult babies aren't inevitably problem children (Kronstadt, Oberklaid, Ferb, and Swartz, 1979).

MATURATION

Imagine that your friend's baby is six months old now. For the last two or three weeks your friend has been telling you she wonders if he's normal. She read in a book, she tells you, that most infants can sit up between twelve and twenty weeks. Hers is twenty-four weeks old, and still he doesn't sit up. She's worried.

You call her to wish him a happy six-month birthday. "Guess what," your friend tells you on the phone. "He sat up today all by himself. I guess he's okay after all." ■

Like your friend, parents are understandably concerned that their babies develop normally. There are tables of developmental norms (e.g., Gesell, 1954) that are based on the growth and performance of many children, but these are statistical averages, and don't hold for a specific child. Any given child has his or her own unique rate of development, determined by the interplay of the child's heredity, environment, and learning.

Strictly speaking, *maturation* is the process by which physical changes after birth cause the infant to develop biologically into an adult in fulfillment of its genetic potential. More than mere growth is involved; the process includes changes in body proportions as well as the hormonal changes of puberty. All these changes occur in an unvarying sequence; only an environment that is seriously awry will disrupt them. Learning shapes and controls the child's behavior and is basic to the mastery of many skills, but a child cannot learn a task until the neuromuscular structures needed to perform it are sufficiently mature. Children, for example, cannot learn to walk until they are able to stand.

Environmental deprivation

A child's early environment is considered "deprived" if there is a deficit in sensory experience, general stimulation, or social interaction. Research on sensory deprivation in young animals shows that their nervous systems need early stimulation to begin functioning. In their work with infant rhesus monkeys, the Harlows demonstrated that isolation for the first six months of life permanently impaired social and sexual behavior. Baby monkeys who were given a terry cloth covered wire monkey equipped with a baby bottle reacted to their artificial mother as though it were alive. But monkeys raised with terry cloth surrogates did not grow up to be entirely normal (Harlow and Harlow, 1966).

Lack of mothering for human babies can cause short-term and long-term intellectual deficits and emotional disturbances (Goldfarb, 1945; Bowlby, 1951; 1960). In the 1940s Renee Spitz (1945) did a now-famous study of the ill effects of deprivation on orphans in an institution. The conditions were appalling: babies lay in beds with sheets between them so they couldn't even see another child; their only human contact was with a hurried caretaker during feeding or cleaning; they had few if any toys, bottles were propped by their sides, and they received practically no individual attention. The results on development were profound: as they grew, these children had either little interest in forming relationships with other people or a desperate craving for affection, and an IQ deficit proportional to the length of stay in the institution. Even as adolescents they were marked by impulsiveness, antisocial acts, and aggression (Casler, 1967).

Overcoming cognitive deficits

While it was once thought that intelligence and other cognitive skills changed little from early childhood through adulthood, more recent studies find little correlation between IQ scores in infancy and those in later childhood (Kessen, Haith, and Salapatek, 1970; Pease, Wolins, and Stockdale, 1973; Honzik, 1976). Children who as infants suffer the ill effects of deprivation are not necessarily doomed to suffer developmental handicaps later in life (Kagan, Kearsley, and Zelazo, 1978).

In a cross-cultural study of the effects of deprivation on development, two groups of Guatemalan children were observed, one from an isolated Indian village in the highlands and the second from rural Spanish-speaking villages (Kagan and Klein, 1973). All these children spend the first year of life in small, dark huts, usually close to their mothers. They are rarely spoken to or played with and are not allowed to crawl around. At the age of fifteen months, they leave the huts during the day and receive a more normal amount of stimulation. This child-rearing pattern is typical of their culture.

Compared to American infants, these babies are extremely passive and quiet. Observations suggest that the infants are four months behind the American norm for intellectual development and five months behind in showing anxiety at the sight of a stranger. The appearance of speech in these infants seems to be even more retarded. Yet tests of recall of familiar objects, recognition, and perceptual abilities show that by the time they are eleven years old, rural Guatemalan children and American children perform comparably. In other words, the retardation that was seen in infancy

and early childhood is no longer evident at eleven. Even so, these findings do not mean that deprivation in infancy has no ill effects, only that such effects need not always be irreversible (Lipsitt, 1979).

Environmental enrichment

Just as deprivation and isolation seem to hurt development, an enriched environment seems to help it. In one experiment, some infants were handled frequently, had patterned sheets on their cribs and mobiles above them, and were placed on their backs to view people moving around their room. These "enriched" babies were able to reach for and contact objects in their visual field after about two weeks, while infants who did not have this enriched environment took five months to reach for and touch objects (White, 1969).

Many other studies show gains from enriched environments. One researcher (Skeels, 1966) compared young children who were raised in a barren orphanage and children who were taken from the orphanage at an early age and placed in an institution for the mentally retarded. This latter group of youngsters entered a more varied and stimulating environment, with adult mentally retarded women serving as mother substitutes and giving them much loving attention. When tested at later stages of their lives, many of the youngsters who were reared in the drab, unstimulating orphanage continued to be mentally retarded, while those who had been mothered by the retarded women obtained much higher IQ scores and went on to live normal, productive lives.

Imagine that your friend's son is fifteen months old now, and you're baby-sitting as a favor. He's an Olympic-level crawler these days, and you're run ragged keeping him from destroying the place.

You look up from the kiddie show the two of you are watching to see him halfway across the room, about to attack a lamp. As he slowly walks toward it, you jump up and race across the room to head him off. Your leap turns out to be faster than his teeter—you scoop him up and seat him firmly back on the couch.

When his mother returns and asks if everything was OK, you assure her it was "just fine, nothing unusual, no problems."

It nevers dawns on you that you've just been the sole witness to her son's first steps. ■

Physical growth and motor development

Motor development, the appearance and mastery of movement skills, begins soon after a baby is born. The whole process is gradual; there are few landmark moments such as a baby's first step. Bone, muscle, and nerve all mature gradually according to a genetic blueprint for timing and sequence.

The muscle fibers present at birth will weigh

forty times as much at maturity. The growth of the nervous system proceeds more rapidly. The newborn's head has already reached 60 percent of its ultimate size. By the age of six, the child's nervous system has almost achieved full maturity. Although motor development is aided considerably by the exercise of motor skills, it is basically dependent on maturation. A study of motor coordination in Russian infants whose freedom of movement had been restricted by the ancient custom of swaddling soon after birth illustrates this dependence. When first unwrapped, swaddled infants had poor coordination of arm and leg movements. But after a little time and some practice, their coordination equaled that of the control infants, and there appeared to be no permanent damage (Orlansky, 1949).

The ability to walk develops in late infancy. Most children learn to walk by fifteen months of age, but if an infant a few weeks old is held up-

Figure 12.2 Norms for the development of posture and locomotion in infants

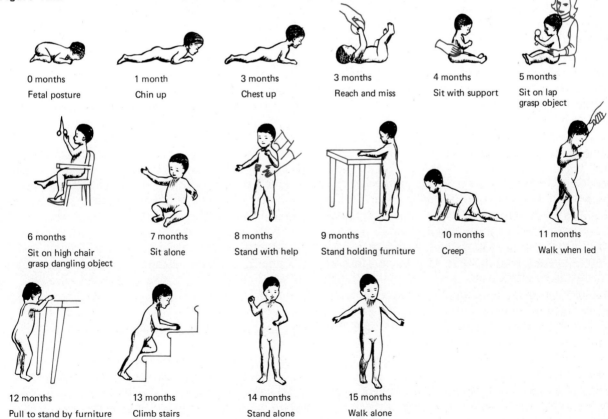

0 months — Fetal posture
1 month — Chin up
3 months — Chest up
3 months — Reach and miss
4 months — Sit with support
5 months — Sit on lap grasp object
6 months — Sit on high chair grasp dangling object
7 months — Sit alone
8 months — Stand with help
9 months — Stand holding furniture
10 months — Creep
11 months — Walk when led
12 months — Pull to stand by furniture
13 months — Climb stairs Steps
14 months — Stand alone
15 months — Walk alone

right with its feet touching a flat surface, its legs will make walking motions. This is known as the "walking reflex" and normally disappears when the child is about eight weeks old (Bayley, 1969). But infants given daily walking exercises in the first eight weeks begin to walk earlier than those not exercised. This is a case in which early enrichment of a type not usually given is able to speed up development by making use of the infant's readiness to learn (Zelazo, Zelazo, and Kolb, 1972).

PERCEPTUAL DEVELOPMENT

Around the turn of the century, William James called the infant's sensory world a "blooming, buzzing confusion," but the evidence accumulated since his day contradicts this view. Measuring infants' reactions to stimuli reveals that they are responsive to a much greater degree than had been supposed (Lipsitt, 1977). Researchers who have tracked eye movements of newborn infants report that they can follow the outlines of geometric patterns (Salapatek and Kessen, 1968). When they hear certain sounds, their activity increases and their heart and breath rates speed up (Bridger, 1961).

Visual discrimination

Infants have several early visual preferences on the basis of contour, contrast, and movement. For example, they favor patterned, more complex stimuli to unpatterned, simple stimuli (Fantz, 1961). From four days to six months of age, a baby prefers looking at a drawing of a human face or a distorted face to a blank gray oval (Fantz, 1961), probably because the stimuli are more complex. By the age of four months, familiarity becomes important; infants who are shown drawings that vary in how well they resemble a human face attend most to those that clearly resemble faces (Kagan, 1970).

One of the special visual talents of the young infant is response to faces. Infants only three to five weeks old will look at a face about one-quarter of

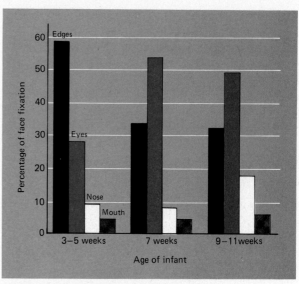

Figure 12.3 What infants see in faces
As infants develop from three to eleven weeks, they are better able to notice facial features, such as eyes.

the time it is presented; by the age of nine to eleven weeks, infants look at the face 90 percent of the time, and spend more time gazing at the eyes (Haith, Bregman, and Moore, 1977). Infants only five months old can distinguish between dissimilar faces (Cohen, DeLoache, and Strauss, 1978). This rapid development of facial responsiveness in the infant makes possible the child's awareness of people, and it is certainly a factor in bonding between parent and child. Interestingly, even though a mother's face may hold an infant's gaze, a study found that three-month-old babies looked at a doll's face longer than at their mother's face (Field, 1979). The probable reason: the rapid changes in the mother's face may have presented the infant with more information than it could handle in one dose, causing it to look away more often than from the unchanging doll's face.

Depth and distance perception

Soon after birth, infants' eyes begin to develop the ability to focus and perceive depth. Depth perception usually is achieved at six months and sometimes, in rudimentary form, even earlier. The ability of infants to perceive depth is demonstrat-

Figure 12.4 The visual cliff
Though covered by a sheet of glass, the abrupt drop
seems a real danger to infants about one year old
and younger.

Figure 12.5 Kitten-powered gondola
This apparatus was used to test the effects of experience on perceptual development.

ed in the *visual cliff response*, in which they stop
at what seems to be the edge of a cliff (see Figure 12.4). This phenomenon has been studied by
means of an apparatus that creates an illusion of
a cliff, although there is only a flat surface. Even
when encouraged by their mothers to cross over
the supposed cliff, infants six to fourteen months
old refuse (Walk and Gibson, 1961). At the sight of
the cliff, infants under six months, who could not
crawl, had decreases in heart rate typical of people of any age in new situations (Campos, *et al.*,
1970), suggesting the ability to perceive depth is
present from the earliest weeks of life.

Experience affects perceptual development. For
example, experimenters raised ten pairs of kittens
in total darkness for the first ten weeks of life
(Held and Hein, 1963). After ten weeks in the
dark, for three hours a day each pair of kittens
was placed in a box that had striped sides and contained the device shown in Figure 12.5. One kitten
from each pair was carried around the box in a
basket; the other could move around the box in a
harness. Within ten days, the kittens that had
walked around the box had normal perception.
But the kittens that rode passively in the basket
were perceptually retarded; for example, they
failed to stop short when they came to a visual

cliff. It seems that active interaction with the environment is needed in order for motor skills guided by visual perception to develop properly.

COGNITIVE AND MORAL
DEVELOPMENT

Imagine that your friend's son, now
two, has dropped by your house with his father.
You two grownups are talking, and he's wandering
around, looking for something to play with. He disappears into the kitchen, and doesn't reappear for
several minutes. He reappears shoving a pear
along the floor, making sounds as though it were
a toy car. ■

By the age of two, a child is able to treat objects
in symbolic terms: a pear can stand for a car. This
ability to treat objects as symbolic of something
else is one of several landmarks in the development of cognitive skills. The development of cognitive processes starts shortly after birth. Though
their first efforts are rudimentary, infants who

are only a few hours old are already beginning to store, retrieve, and interpret sensory data from which they will fashion knowledge and understanding of the world (Lipsitt, 1979).

Piaget's theory of intellectual development

Children are not miniature adults. Their thought processes are not merely less efficient versions of adult thought processes; they are qualitatively different. No psychologist devoted more time or energy to the study of the cognition of children than Swiss-born Jean Piaget. For more than half a century, he carefully observed and recorded the behavior of children—including his own—from infancy through adolescence (Singer and Revenson, 1979).

The infant inherits physical structures and automatic behaviors, such as reflexes, but for Piaget these play only a minor role in cognitive development. Instead, Piaget maintains, the infant tends to organize her thought processes into coherent systems. For example, the infant coordinates the structures of looking at a mobile over her crib and grasping the mobile into a system of visually directed reaching.

The child also adapts to his environment; that is, he modifies his understanding of it. Two processes, assimilation and accommodation, make up adaptation, and they go on continually. The child *assimilates* new information into his existing cognitive structures. Alternatively, he can *accommodate*, or adjust, his mental structures—and thus his behavior—in the light of new information. An infant given a cup of milk for the first time might suck on it as though it were a bottle, thus trying to assimilate it into his understanding of a bottle. After a time, though, he might learn how to drink from the cup, and so accommodate his understanding to this new source of fluid.

Assimilation and accommodation work together in an equilibrium—a balance between cognitive structures and incoming information. In this way, new mental structures are created out of old ones, and then combined to form coherent patterns. The functions of organization and adaptation are always the same, but the structures used to meet

TABLE 12.4 **PIAGET'S STAGES OF INTELLECTUAL DEVELOPMENT**

Stage one	the sensorimotor stage (0 to 24 months)
Stage two	the preoperational stage (2 to 7 years)
Stage three	concrete operations (7 to 12 years)
Stage four	formal operations (age 12 onward)

these ends change throughout the child's development in a regular and invariable series of stages (see Table 12.4).

Sensorimotor stage

In this stage, which lasts from birth to two years, the infant first depends on her inborn reflexes. But even then she uses information from her environment to organize these reflexes into patterns of behavior called *schemata*. For example, the sucking reflex combines with bringing the hand to the mouth to create the pleasurable thumb-sucking schema.

It is also during this time that the first signs of curiosity and imitation appear. One of the more important events is the development of *object permanence*. When we think of an object, we know it has a reality of its own. A cup does not change shape or move of its own accord. Mother is herself no matter how many times she changes her clothes; she does not disappear from the world when she is out of our sight. During the *sensorimotor stage*, the infant develops an awareness of the permanence of objects and people; she progresses, for example, from the passive acceptance of the disappearance of an object to an active search for it.

Preoperational stage

During the *preoperational stage*, which extends from two to seven years, several new capacities develop. Between the ages of two and four, *symbolic functions* appear. The child can now use an

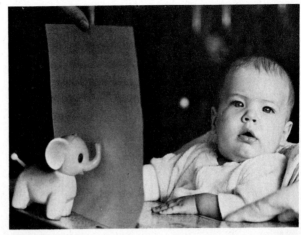

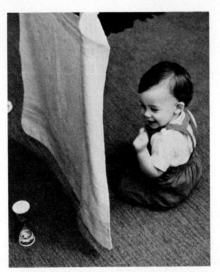

The child at the top has not yet developed object permanence. She is interested in the elephant when it is in front of her, but when the screen blocks it, she does not seem to know it is still there.

The older infant at bottom understands object permanence. When the toy is put behind a towel, he knows it is still there, and he crawls under the towel to get it. (George Zimbel/Monkmeyer Press Photos)

object or a word to represent something that is not present. Much of her speech reflects her *egocentrism;* unable to adopt the other person's point of view, she speaks as if she were talking to herself. Only gradually will her speech become more communicative. Her egocentric thought is expressed in her "animism"; she believes, for example, that objects like the sun and the moon are alive. As she grows older, she will come to recognize points of view other than her own.

Stage of concrete operations

From ages seven to eleven, the child is in the *concrete operational stage;* that is, her operations, or mental processes, involve concrete objects. She can now sort objects according to class and can order an array of sticks by length and match the members of two such arrays. She has also grasped the concept of *conservation,* the principle that, despite a change in its appearance, the total quantity of a substance remains constant. The idea of conservation of substance is acquired first; by age six or seven, children know, for example, that if two identical balls of clay are changed in shape, they still contain the same amount of matter. By nine or ten, children have an understanding of conservation of weight; they know that if there are two identical balls of the same weight and one is changed in shape, it is still the same weight as the other.

Thus, the operational child's thought has *reversibility*. She realizes, for example, that marbles poured from a short jar into a tall one, then poured back again, remain the same number of marbles. Her thought is *dynamic:* she is attuned to change in her environment and can see it happening.

Stage of formal operations

From eleven or twelve onward, the child's operations are no longer tied to the present; they can incorporate memories and symbols. She can analyze a problem by means of *formal operations,* reducing it to its components and testing one hypothesis at a time. After observing the results of

this testing, she can deduce an answer, using logical propositions. The child can consider several alternatives, and can assimilate and combine information from many sources. Her patterns of thought become increasingly flexible and abstract. Mental tasks as demanding as chess mastery and the deductive reasoning of a Sherlock Holmes are within her grasp.

Piaget's theory is the major, most well-elaborated model of cognitive development, even though recent findings have modified his views. Research in areas such as learning and perception in infants (e.g., Flavell, 1979) suggests that infants may be much more capable and advanced cognitively than Piaget believed. Bower (1976) presents evidence that some of the behaviors Piaget saw as showing progressive intellectual development do not in fact appear in a steady increment, but actually appear and disappear in an unsteady, inconsistent fashion. For example, infants at a very early stage may show signs of rather complex abilities—such as imitation of an adult and conservation of weight—that Piaget maintained only appear much later. Even so, although Piaget's theories may be altered by later tests, his work stands as the central framework for understanding cognitive development.

If these girls have grasped *conservation,* they will know that there are the same number of clothes on both lines, regardless of whether the clothes are close together or spread out. (© Burt Glinn/Magnum Photos)

Imagine that the sight of your friend's two-year-old smooshing a pear along your floor while pretending it's a car doesn't exactly delight you.

"It's not nice to smear pear on my floor," you say in a friendly voice. The two-year-old ignores you, and goes on smooshing the pear.

His father's voice booms, "You put that pear back right now or I'll tan your bottom!" The two-year-old jumps up and disappears into the kitchen to put back the pear. ■

Moral development

Your appeal to fairness was lost on the two-year-old, although it might have worked with an older child. His father's firmness was more effective with a two-year-old mind. One of Piaget's observations was that children's moral reasoning—their understanding of what is right and wrong, just and fair—changes through stages as do their cognitive abilities. Piaget (1932) interviewed children, asking questions about moral issues such as "Why should you not cheat when playing a game?" He found that from ages five through twelve, the child's moral judgment changes from a rigid, inflexible notion of right and wrong, regardless of surrounding circumstances, to a sense of equity that takes account of specific conditions. "Moral realism," in which a rule is sacred and obeyed blindly, is replaced with "moral relativism," in which the surrounding situation and the good of others is taken into account when making moral judgments.

Piaget's earlier theory has been expanded and refined by Lawrence Kohlberg (1964; 1969). Kohl-

TABLE 12.5 PIAGET'S STAGES OF MORAL DEVELOPMENT

Stage one   Justice subordinated to adult authority: "moral realism" (up to age 7 or 8)

Stage two   Egalitarianism and reciprocity: "moral relativism" (8 to 11 years)

Stage three   Egalitarianism tempered by sense of justice: "principled moral reasoning" (age 11 or 12 onward)

TABLE 12.6 KOHLBERG'S SIX STAGES OF MORAL DEVELOPMENT

Preconventional level

Stage 1: *Punishment and obedience orientation.* The physical consequences of an action determine whether it is good or bad. Avoiding punishment and bowing to superior power are valued positively.

Stage 2: *Instrumental relativist orientation.* Right action consists of behavior that satisfies one's own needs. Human relations are viewed in marketplace terms. Reciprocity occurs, but is seen in a pragmatic way, i.e., "you scratch my back and I'll scratch yours."

Conventional level

Stage 3: *Interpersonal concordance (good boy-nice girl) orientation.* Good behaviors are those that please or are approved by others. There is much emphasis on conformity and being "nice."

Stage 4: *Orientation toward authority ("law and order").* Focus is on authority or rules. It is right to do one's duty, show respect for authority, and maintain the social order.

Postconventional level

Stage 5: *Social-contract orientation.* This stage has a utilitarian, legalistic tone. Correct behavior is defined in terms of standards agreed upon by society. Awareness of the relativism of personal values and the need for consensus is important.

Stage 6: *Universal ethical principle orientation.* Morality is defined as a decision of conscience. Ethical principles are self-chosen, based on abstract concepts (e.g., the Golden Rule) rather than concrete rules (e.g., the Ten Commandments).

berg presented children of different ages with descriptions of moral dilemmas and asked them to explain what they would do in the same situation. In one, a man needs to obtain an expensive drug to save his dying wife. He does not have the money to pay for the drug and must decide whether to steal it or obey the law at the risk of his wife's life. Children are asked what they would do if they were the man.

Like Piaget, Kohlberg is concerned primarily with the child's moral judgments rather than with overt behavior. Kohlberg proposes three developmental levels of moral judgment: preconventional, conventional, and postconventional. Within each of these developmental levels, there are two distinct stages, resulting in the six stages of moral development shown in Table 12.6. According to Kohlberg, all children go through these developmental stages, although there are no specific ages at which the stages apply; adults too can, for example, be at stage two. Each stage is dependent upon previous ones and represents a reorganization and advance upon prior stages.

PERSONALITY DEVELOPMENT

Imagine that your friend's two-year-old, who has just disappeared into your kitchen to get rid of his half-mashed pear, comes running out again followed by your collie, Hilda. Hilda is bounding about happily, trying to lick his face; the little boy, certain he's going to be eaten up, is crying.

"Doggy! Doggy!" he yells, running over to the safety of his father's legs. Once he's clinging to a leg, he bravely says, "Nice doggy!" ■

It is quite normal for a two-year-old to seek the shelter of a parent when in danger. At a later stage of growth, though, he would certainly handle the crisis of the doggy differently; at an even later stage, there would be no crisis at all. The factors that influence how a child behaves at each age—and that finally shape adult personality—change as he or she passes from infancy through childhood to adolescence. The unique mix of genetic endowment and personal history that each child experiences at each stage of growth determines the nature of adult personality. Perhaps the most influential current theory of the critical experiences that each person passes through is that of psychoanalyst Erik Erikson (1968). Erikson proposes eight stages of psychosocial development, during each of which a person faces and resolves a "critical issue."

Infancy (birth to eighteen months)

In Erikson's scheme, the first developmental issue is "basic trust versus mistrust." The infant's experiences of being fed and of attachment to its mother will have special impact on the resolution of this issue. According to Erikson, the way in which this issue is resolved will set the tone for the rest of the child's life: whether he or she feels that the world is basically safe and trustworthy, or unsafe and insecure.

Feeding

Hunger is a primary physiological drive of the infant, and events during feeding will have a strong influence on the formation of basic trust. Rapid satisfaction of hunger will teach the child that people are reliable and that his own efforts—in this case, crying—can affect the world outside him and relieve his hunger. If hunger and other needs are not satisfied, the infant may develop a feeling of fear and suspicion, a general mistrust of others and the world in general.

Whether the mother feeds her child by breast or bottle, her mood at feeding is transmitted by many physical signs, including the way she holds the infant, the speed and tenseness of her movements, and her tone of voice. Whether the infant develops a sense of basic trust will depend to a great extent on the quality of the mothering he receives.

Attachment

At about seven months of age, infants separated from their mothers for temporary hospitalization begin to respond by crying and intervals of quiet, withdrawn behavior. Upon returning home, they have a period of readjustment during which they are insecure about their mother's presence and absence (Schaffer and Callender, 1959). These responses are evidence that an *attachment* has been formed between mother and infant. Attachment is a "meaningful bond with a mother-figure transcending separations of space and time" (Schaffer, 1971). Attachment is also formed to a father, of course, as well as to other adults who typically care for the infant (Bowlby, 1973).

Ainsworth and Bell (1970) report that when placed in a strange room, a one-year-old will explore it as long as his mother is present. When the mother leaves, however, the child stops exploring and begins to cry and look for her. The investigators believe that attachment and exploration go hand-in-hand; the infant needs both to survive.

During the latter half of their first year, infants show as much attachment to fathers as they do to mothers. Lamb (1977), for example, observed the reactions of infants in the company of their parents and a friendly visitor, and they approached or touched the mother and father equally. Both parents were preferred over the stranger, and there was no evidence to support the common belief that infants of this age prefer and are especially attached to their mothers.

The kind of time an infant spends with its mother and father is likely to differ greatly. Fathers are much more likely to play with an infant, mothers more likely to care for it; fathers, in fact, spend approximately five hours of playing with an infant for every one of actually taking care of it (Lamb, 1977). When mothers do play with infants, the way in which they play differs from fathers. Mothers tend toward verbal games like "peek-a-boo," while fathers' play is more rough-and-tumble. Moreover, when eighteen-month-olds were given a choice of play partner, they tended to prefer their father to their mother, possibly because roughhousing is more exciting (Clarke-Stewart, 1978). However, when infants of the same age were put in a stressful situation (introduced to a stranger) with both parents present, they preferred to retreat to the safety of their mother rather than their father (Lamb, 1976). In short, if all is well, the infant seems to prefer playing with the father, but in times of stress he or she prefers the mother, probably because the mother more often than not is the primary caretaker during early infancy.

Toddlerhood (eighteen months to three years)

Imagine that your friend's son is now almost three. He's tagging along while his mother visits you. You and she can hardly carry on a conversation, because he's into everything, poking around and generally messing things up. Now he's gotten out a football and is pretending it's a soccer ball, right in your living room.

His mother tells him to put it back—he's too young to play with a football. The more she tells him, the more determined to master its tricky bounces he becomes. Their dialogue, escalating by the moment, is broken off when the football bounces out of his hands and knocks over your coffee cup.

No longer defiant, he looks over at you and says contritely, "I'm sorry." ■

For Erikson this stage in the life cycle is best characterized by the phrase "autonomy versus shame or doubt." During this period, the child becomes fully mobile and active, developing muscular competence by constant practice and knowledge of objects by constant manipulation. The ability to walk and handle objects brings him into direct contact with the environment—and sometimes into direct conflict with his parents and other adults, as your friend's son learned. And here the struggle between autonomy and shame takes place.

If we follow the toddler around for an hour or two, we may see her open drawers and kitchen cabinets, spread utensils and toys all over the floor, open mail, or play with photographs or ashtrays. In general, there is a tendency for toddlers to get into everything. Although the toddler must be prevented from hurting herself or doing serious damage, the sense of autonomy and competence evolves out of this exploration—and even out of her negative reaction to discipline. If a mother is overprotective—if she becomes cautious and restrictive when her child tries to explore on her own—the mother may develop in the child a sense of shame or doubt about her own abilities to master the environment and control herself. On the other hand, if parents demand too much of the child, no accomplishment will seem sufficient to prove her worthy of independence.

More flexible parents restrict their children when necessary, but actively encourage independent action. In this way, the child learns that she can do some things by herself, such as getting a cookie or taking her jacket from a closet hook, and

she derives satisfaction because her actions are effective. She is encouraged to acquire new skills, to attempt harder tasks, and to discover how things in the immediate environment operate.

Socialization refers to all the processes that help mold a person's behavior to meet society's needs and expectations. Socialization comprises all the child's experiences with other people that affect the development of her motives, convictions, standards, and attitudes. One of the major steps in socialization is toilet training, often a child's first experience with stringent discipline. Here maturational level is important: children must be able to control their anal sphincter muscles and to signal when they are about to have bowel movements. Most children are ready between eighteen and twenty months. Training attempted too early can fail—an experience children may retain as an inability to live up to standards and as a generalized feeling of failure.

Good toilet training is not difficult for most parents. If mothers encourage children to use the toilet and praise them when they do, they will feel they are performing an important, successful action. Psychoanalytic theory maintains that such a feeling may be reflected in later productivity and creativity.

Preschool (three to six years)

At age three, the child is on the verge of truly phenomenal changes. In the next three years, given proper conditions, his new language ability will allow him to learn to behave in socially acceptable ways, to relate to and imitate his peers, to further identify with one sex, and to make moral judgments. Erikson has characterized the period from four to six in terms of "initiative versus guilt."

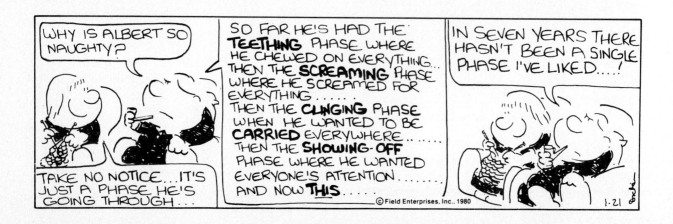

329 INFANCY AND CHILDHOOD

CHILD-REARING: AS THE TWIG IS BENT

■ ''As the twig is bent,'' the saying goes, ''so grows the tree.'' Most people would agree that the way that parents raise a child will shape to a great degree what sort of person she will become. But just how *should* a child be raised?

While developmental psychologists don't totally agree about how to best answer this question, they do agree that it matters. The atmosphere parents create in the home and the child-rearing methods they use are crucial to a child's personality development and socialization.

One of the more detailed studies of how children's treatment at home affects their behavior elsewhere was done by Baumrind (1967, 1971). Her observations of children at home and at school led her to propose that three main child-rearing practices have distinct effects on children's personality.

Authoritative parents showed a combination of high control and positive encouragement of the child's independence. These parents were warm and loving, communicated well with their children, and respected the child's independence, while standing firm in their own positions. Children of authoritative parents were the most competent, self-reliant, friendly, and assertive.

Authoritarian parents, on the other hand, were less sympathetic and warm, were highly arbitrary in their rules, highly controlling of their children, and did not encourage independence or disagreement from the child. Their children were somewhat self-reliant, but also discontented, insecure, and distrustful.

Permissive parents were warm but uncontrolling. They demanded little of their children and did not encourage self-reliance or independence. Their children were highly dependent, withdrawn, less self-reliant, and lacked self-control.

Only the authoritative parents, according to Baumrind, serve as models for responsible behavior. Neither authoritarian control nor permissiveness gives the child the kind of experience needed to learn social responsibility and independence. Even though authoritarian parents seek to establish social responsibility in their children and permissive parents say they want their children to be independent, their child-rearing practices are unsuccessful in achieving such goals.

Since learning to control aggression is perhaps the child's most essential step toward socialization, studies of child-rearing styles as they relate to aggression are of special interest. One study of boys reveals that punitive, rejecting parents involved in conflicts of their own and unable to control their child furnish the pattern for the child's own behavior. In contrast, boys are not aggressive whose parents adjust well to society, warmly support their child, establish clear rules, and conform to social norms (McCord, McCord, and Howard, 1961).

In another study, boys whose parents dealt with aggression by physical punishment alone conformed in the home but behaved aggressively outside it (Bandura and Walters, 1963). Parents who use physical punishment to curb aggression seem to provide the child with a model of the very behavior they are trying to extinguish and at the same time fail to allow the child to develop inner control. Both parental conflict and inconsistency in discipline seem to make children more prone to aggression and delinquency (Heatherington, Cox, and Cox, 1978). ■

The child who is allowed to move toward independence gains in self-confidence and skill by handling a variety of tasks and situations unaided. Without this encouragement toward self-assertion and competence, according to Erikson, he develops a sense of guilt about activities he initiates, and this feeling will recur in later stages of his life.

THE ELECTRONIC PARENT: CHILDREN AND TV

■ The average American home has the television set on 6½ hours a day. Nursery- and grammar-school-age children spend an average of three hours per day watching TV. By age sixteen, most American children have spent more time watching television than going to school (Liebert and Poulos, 1975); one estimate is that the average American child watches over 20,000 commercials per year.

Parents—and many psychologists—have become concerned over the effects of television, sometimes called "the third parent," on the development of children. Much research has sought to assess what these effects might be, focusing on three areas: the effects of TV violence on children's social behavior, the effects of children's shows on cognitive skills, and the gullibility of children as viewers of commercials.

Much research has focused on the negative effects of television, especially as a model for aggression. In a typical study, children between the ages of five and nine viewed excerpts from actual TV programs depicting either violent or nonviolent scenes; they were then placed in a free play situation. Children exposed to the aggressive programs engaged in longer attacks against other children than those exposed to the nonaggressive programs. The aggressive programs also elicited a higher level of aggressive play than the nonaggressive ones, particularly among the younger-aged boys taking part in the study (Liebert and Baron, 1972).

Perhaps the largest dose of violence on TV occurs not during prime time, but on Saturday mornings in programs designed for—and heavily watched by—children. Surveys of the content of programs have found that an average hour of cartoons has about three times as many violent episodes as the average adult program (Gerbner, 1972; Greenberg, *et al.,* 1977). Even so, not all studies of the effects of violent cartoons on children's behavior have shown them to increase violence.

In surveying these studies, Hapkiewicz (1979) points out the sort of difficulties that plague all studies that attempt to show the impact of TV on children's lives: the situations where children's violence is to be assessed are seen by the child as contrived, or have in them a strange adult, and so the child feels inhibited. Another factor: different sorts of children respond differently to what they see on television. For example, boys displayed more aggression after watching cartoons, while girls became better behaved. And children from about eight on are able to evaluate critically the information in commercials, although this ability to be a critical consumer of TV advertising can be improved (Feshbach, Dillman, and Jordan, 1979).

There is, however, a positive side to television viewing: it can be an effective teacher. For example, a study of youngsters who watched *Sesame Street* found that both lower-class and middle-class children showed gains in skills such as identifying body parts, letters, numbers, and geometric forms; sorting and classifying objects; and even in reading ability. The more the kids watched the show, the greater their improvement (Ball and Bogatz, 1972).

The socializing effects of TV can be beneficial too. Youngsters that watched shows emphasizing kindness were more helpful to other children (Sprafkin, Liebert, and Poulos, 1975); in another study, those who watched a generous adult on TV were more generous in making donations to needy children than were a group who watched stingy role models on TV (Friedrich and Stein, 1975). Shows like *Mister Rogers' Neighborhood* and *Sesame Street* have also been shown to instill positive social attitudes in preschool children (Tower, *et al.,* 1979). ■

Middle childhood
(six to eleven years)

Imagine that your friend's son is six now. He's staying the night with you while his parents are away. He's reluctant to sleep on the front room couch by himself, so you're letting him sleep on your bedroom floor in a sleeping bag.

You've set your alarm for six-thirty so you can have plenty of time to get him ready for school and yourself off to work. But in the morning, you're awakened by sunlight on your bed, not the alarm. It's clearly much later than six-thirty. What happened, you think groggily.

Then you see him, screwdriver in one hand, half-dismantled alarm clock in the other. "What on earth are you doing?" you demand.

"I just wanted to see how it works," he says. ■

The years of middle childhood, roughly six to eleven, are a time when children are fascinated by what makes the world work. Erikson believes that the years of middle childhood are best characterized by the phrase "industry versus inferiority." Children are now concerned with the way things are made, and they have general curiosity about everything. If they are supported and reinforced in their attempts to do and to make practical things, they develop a sense of industry. If their efforts are played down or ridiculed, a sense of inferiority is likely to predominate.

During these years the child's world expands, and peers, teachers, and even the media become socializing agents in addition to parents. Many changes occur in middle childhood. The child's sex role identification is being reinforced, and her self-concept is developing. Now she sets standards of achievement, competence, success, and failure. Performance in school and the desire to win the respect of peers will be fresh sources of anxiety, but she will also strengthen the defenses she has already acquired to cope with these new anxieties.

As the child enters elementary school, her social world enlarges dramatically. Even so, children generally bring to the schoolroom habits learned at home; for example, they seem to regard the teacher as a mother-substitute (Biller, 1974), and so treat the teacher much as they do their mother. If the teacher is a man, the children presumably treat him as they do their father. The school acts in some ways as an extension of the home, especially in shaping children's moral values, their aspirations for achievement and occupation, and even their patterns of thought and cognition (Walberg and Rasher, 1977; Glick, 1975).

At this age a boy usually identifies strongly with his father and rebels against his mother, and so is less influenced by his female teachers, presenting greater discipline problems than a girl (Kagan, 1968). A boy whose father is absent is particularly likely to have learning difficulties in the "feminized" classrooms found in most elementary schools (Biller, 1974); for example, boys taught by men do better in reading than those with female teachers (Shneidling and Pederson, 1970).

Interaction with peers allows school-age chil-

JEAN PIAGET (1896-1980)

(Yves de Brains/Black Star)

■ Jean Piaget studied and wrote about the development of children for close to half a century in Geneva, Switzerland. His theories are among the most influential in the study of cognitive development. Yet they are relatively recent arrivals to American psychology: it was not until the 1950s and 1960s that there was much interest in transla-

tions of his work in America, a full twenty-five years after he published what have become some of his most influential studies.

Piaget was cut out for a career in science from childhood. His first scientific apprenticeship was in his early teens, as a part-time assistant to the curator of a local museum of natural history. The curator was a specialist on mollusks, and Piaget—a serious student—became internationally known as an expert on mollusks by his late teens. By nineteen he had published twenty-one articles on the subject. One museum, on the basis of his articles, offered him a job as curator of mollusks. Piaget had to decline—he still had two years of high school to complete.

Piaget's godfather, trying to keep the young student from becoming too narrowly specialized, introduced him to philosophy. Piaget became intrigued by the branch of philosophy called "epistemology," the study of knowledge. The fundamental questions of epistemology—such as, How do we think? How do we know?—were later to be the focus of his research.

After receiving his doctorate, Piaget worked for a time in the Zurich clinic of a psychiatrist and friend of Freud. While there, Piaget learned the methods of clinical interviewing that he was to put to his own uses in studying children.

Piaget earned his doctorate studying mollusks, not children. But soon after completing it in 1918, he took a position with Theodore Simon who, at the time, was developing for France intelligence tests

dren to make a more realistic evaluation of themselves, which in turn shapes their changing self-concepts. Peers serve as both models and reinforcers, effects which increase as children grow older (Heatherington and Parke, 1979). Peer-

reinforcement—in the form of attention and approval—has strong effects on a child, as does the chance to observe and imitate other children's behavior.

As children grow older, their self-concepts grow

of the sort that had recently been pioneered in England. This first job turned Piaget's interests from shellfish to children, the focus of his research and writing for the next half century.

Piaget became intrigued by the reasons children *failed* to answer questions correctly on intelligence tests. To better understand these failures, he began to interview children about their mistakes. He patterned his questioning on a psychiatric interview, aiming to uncover the reasoning processes that went into their right—and especially their wrong—answers. In the course of this questioning, he chanced upon the discovery that was to preoccupy him for the rest of his career: certain kinds of reasoning are beyond the capacity of younger children. In short, cognitive abilities vary with age.

Piaget dedicated himself to studying how children understand the world, and the means by which their thought processes change and mature from infancy to adulthood. He published his first results in 1921, and shortly after that took the position of director at the Centre International d'Epistémologie Génétique in Geneva, where he remained until his death.

Piaget's main method was built on his earlier training in the natural sciences: careful observation. He systematically observed, for example, how children meet specific problems, and the ways in which they grapple with their solution.

All his professional life, Piaget continued to add to his theory. In his words, he was the ''chief revisionist of Piaget.'' ■

rejected, they feel inferior (Ruble, Feldman, and Boggiano, 1976). While the effects of childhood can leave a lasting mark on personality, they are not decisive in forming adult character (Sears, 1980). There are many later stages in development, many more chances to change and grow.

SUMMARY

Developmental psychology is the study of how behavior emerges and changes during a person's lifetime. The course of life comprises distinct eras, stages of life that have specific developmental tasks and typical psychological issues. Everyone goes through the same overall sequence of growth and development over the life cycle, although each person encounters different experiences along the way.

The prenatal period. The unborn child has an active life in the womb. Prenatal development may be affected by many external factors, for example, various drugs ingested by the mother and the mother's emotional and physical health.

Premature or very small infants run a high risk of illness, disabilities, and IQ impairment. Long-term hospitalization of such infants can also interfere with mother-infant bonding.

The newborn. Of all mammalian young, the human child has the longest period of dependency, because of the complexity of the learning tasks he or she faces.

Infants are born with several reflexes that help to satisfy their needs and ensure survival. Among them are the reflex of sucking, the grasping reflex, the startle reflex, and the orienting reflex.

Experiments have shown that newborns can learn through classical and operant conditioning, can be taught to make discriminations, and can become habituated to stimuli. Some responses to smell and taste are fairly well developed.

There are innate differences in individual infants' activity levels. One study has posited three temperament types: easy, difficult, and slow to

more stable. If their self-esteem is high, they have positive self-concepts. Moreover, they are more likely to accept others and to be accepted by them. If children are admired by their peers, they gain self-esteem and confidence in their own worth; if

warm up. The infant's temperament affects the mother's behavior toward her.

Infants differ in their degrees of signalability. There also seem to be constitutional differences between the sexes.

Maturation. Each child has a unique rate of development, determined by the interplay of heredity, environment, and learning; but a behavior cannot be learned until the appropriate maturation has been reached.

Early maternal deprivation can cause short- and long-term deficits and disturbances, but cognitive deficits can be overcome in later childhood. Enriched environments have been found to speed development.

Physical growth and motor development. Motor development is gradual. Bone, muscle, and nerve all mature according to a genetic blueprint of timing and sequence.

Most children learn to walk by fifteen months. By age four, the child has usually mastered a variety of complex and fine motor tasks. At six, the child's nervous system is almost mature.

Perceptual development. Very early, infants favor patterned, complex visual stimuli to unpatterned, simple ones. Infants only five months old can distinguish between dissimilar faces. Depth perception is usually achieved at six months or earlier. As with all maturing skills, active interaction with the environment is necessary for the development of visual perception.

Cognitive and moral development. Children's thought processes are qualitatively different from those of adults. The child's constant adaptation to her environment is achieved through thought organization, assimilation, and accommodation. Jean Piaget has described the cognitive development of the child as a four-stage process.

In the sensorimotor stage, the infant organizes her reflexes into schemata, shows signs of curiosity and imitation, and develops an awareness of object permanence.

Symbolic functions appear in the first part of the preoperational stage, but the child is egocentric and animistic. In the concrete operational stage, the seven- to eleven-year-old can sort objects into classes and concepts. He also understands the idea of conservation of many attributes of objects and situations, including substance, weight, and volume.

From eleven to twelve onward, the child can perform formal operations, reducing a problem to its components and testing hypotheses one at a time. Her thinking is becoming flexible and abstract.

Children's moral reasoning, like their cognitive abilities, goes through stages. Kohlberg has proposed six stages, each built on the previous one.

Personality development. Erikson's stages of psychosocial development assume that a critical issue is to be resolved at each stage. In infancy, feeding and parental attachment experiences influence basic feelings of trust or mistrust, setting the tone for the rest of the child's life.

Toddlerhood, during which the child becomes fully mobile and active and develops muscular ability, knowledge of objects, and a sense of autonomy and competence, marks the struggle of autonomy versus shame or doubt. Socialization takes place through interaction with the parents.

During the preschool years, the child learns socially acceptable behavior, relations with and imitation of his peers, sex identification, and moral judgment. Initiative versus guilt is the critical issue. Parents must now support the child's autonomy and provide behavior models.

In middle childhood, there is a fascination with what makes the world work. The critical developmental issue is a sense of industry (from attempts to make and do practical things) versus inferiority (which develops if these attempts are ignored). Important socializing agents are peers, teachers, and the media.

GLOSSARY

Accommodation The child adjusts mental structures and behavior in the light of new information.

Activity level The rate of autonomic functioning, which may vary among infants.

Assimilation The child integrates new stimuli into existing cognitive structures.

Attachment The establishment of a meaningful emotional bond with a parental figure.

Blastocyst Hollow sphere with inner cell mass at one side from which embryo will form.

Bonding The process of forming ties of caring and attachment between parent and child.

Concrete operational stage The cognitive development stage in which the child can sort objects according to class, understand concepts of inclusion and conservation, and think dynamically.

Conservation The principle that, despite a change in appearance, the total quantity of a substance can remain constant.

Conventional level In moral development, the emphasis on conforming to the rules of the existing social order.

Developmental psychology The study of all the changes that the growth process brings through the entire life cycle.

Dynamic thought During the concrete operational stage, the child's ability to see changes happening in the environment.

Egocentrism In the preoperational development stage, the inability to adopt the other person's point of view.

Embryo The prenatal stage of life from the second to the eighth week after conception, in which rudimentary anatomy begins to take shape.

Failure to thrive A disorder in which an infant or young child fails to grow with no apparent medical reason.

Fetus The prenatal stage of life from the eighth week after conception to birth, in which features grow and become elaborate until the fully formed child is ready to be born.

Fontanels Soft spots in the newborn's skull that allow for expansion to accommodate the enlarging brain.

Formal operations stage The cognitive development stage in which the child can incorporate memories and symbols and perform formal operations, reducing a problem to its components and testing one hypothesis at a time.

Grasping reflex When stimulated by an object touching its palm, the infant grasps it.

Life cycle The overall sequence of growth and development through which every person passes over the span of life.

Maturation The process by which physical changes after birth cause the infant to develop biologically into an adult.

Motor development The appearance and mastery of movement skills.

Object permanence In the sensorimotor stage, the concept of the permanence of things and people.

Orienting reflex Head turning in newborns stimulated by a novel sight or sound.

Pain threshold The point at which a person reacts to a painful stimulus.

Postconventional level In moral development, the determination of morality by one's own principles and conscience.

Preconventional level In moral development, behavior to avoid punishment and obey rule makers.

Prehensile control The grasping ability.

Premature infant A child born before term or with a birth weight of less than 5.5 pounds.

Preoperational stage The period in cognitive development in which egocentric thought diminishes and symbolic functions emerge.

Reversibility In the concrete operational stage, the child's capacity to understand the principles of conservation.

Schemata In the sensorimotor stage, the organization of reflexes into patterns of behavior.

Sensorimotor stage Cognitive development stage in which reflexes are organized into schemata, signs of curiosity and imitation appear, and object constancy develops.

Signalability The infant's tendency to attract its mother's attention by crying and smiling.

Socialization Processes that help mold a child's behavior to fit society's needs and expectations.

Startle reflex In newborns, a reflex stimulated by a loud noise or sudden touch.

Sucking reflex In newborns, a reflex stimulated by any appropriate stimulus placed on the mouth.

Symbolic functions In the preoperational stage, the ability to use an object or word to represent something that is not present.

Teratogen Any agent that can cause malformations in the fetus.

Visual cliff response A manifestation of depth perception, in which infants stop moving if they come to what seems to be the edge of a precipice.

13

ADOLESCENCE AND ADULTHOOD

ADOLESCENCE

Physical development ■ The role of maturation ■ Forming a self-concept ■ Drinking and drugs ■ Family ■ Peers

EARLY ADULTHOOD

Development ■ Marriage

MIDDLE ADULTHOOD

Physical changes ■ Mental and emotional changes ■ Midlife transition

LATE ADULTHOOD AND AGING

The final stage ■ Adjustment to aging ■ Retirement

COMMON MYTHS

MANY PEOPLE BELIEVE ...	ACTUALLY ...
Teenage boys are more sexually mature than girls their age.	Girls reach sexual maturity on the average two years earlier than boys.
It is abnormal for teenagers to be so preoccupied with their appearance that they spend hours gazing in the mirror.	Such mirror gazing is typical of the self-centered preoccupation normal in teenagers.
The romantic ideals of teenagers are unhealthy illusions that prevent them from becoming mature adults.	Such ideals become part of a teenager's self-definition and are helpful in forming an identity.
Bachelors are happier than spinsters.	Single men have poorer mental and physical health on the average than married men; single women are better off on these counts than married women.
Elderly people don't care about sex.	An active sex life continues in healthy people into old age.

All the world's a stage,
And all the men and women merely players.
They have their exits and their entrances;
And one man in his time plays many parts,
His acts being seven ages.

WILLIAM SHAKESPEARE, *AS YOU LIKE IT*, ACT II, SCENE VII

Life unfolds in stages. The developmental periods of childhood give way to those of adolescence, which in turn lead to the epochs of adulthood.

The shift from one developmental era to the next is marked by a transition period that—at least for the adult phases—seems to last as long as four or five years (Levinson, 1978). An era is marked by an overall pattern of living, not by any one particular aspect: adolescence, when one leaves behind childhood, sees great change in most aspects of a young person's life. The stage of early adulthood (when one is entering the adult world) is very different from late adulthood (when one is disengaging) although specific habits, duties, or involvements may be identical in both.

ADOLESCENCE

Imagine that your thirteen-year-old niece is bemoaning her fate to you: "Mom won't let me wear makeup to school, but all the other girls do. She says I'm not old enough. Then she tells me I've got to stay home and take care of my little brothers instead of going to the movies with my friends. Why do I have to take care of them? They're only six and eight, and I'm practically grown up," she says. "Being a teenager is a drag—all the duties of adulthood, and none of the privileges." ■

The teenager is neither child nor adult, a conflict in roles your niece's situation illustrates. Adolescence can be thought of as a halfway house between childhood and adulthood—a time of transition in human development corresponding roughly to the years from twelve to nineteen. Before the emergence of the term "teenager," the older world "adolescent," which derives from the Latin word meaning "to come to maturity," was commonly used. Over the seven- or eight-year span that constitutes adolescence, striking physical, emotional, cognitive, and social changes take place. As the adolescent leaves behind childhood roles, he or she attempts a task critical to this period—the formation of a positive personal identity. This, plus the establishment of one's own autonomy—that is, a sense of competence and independence—is the major goal of adolescence.

Although the young person attains physical ma-

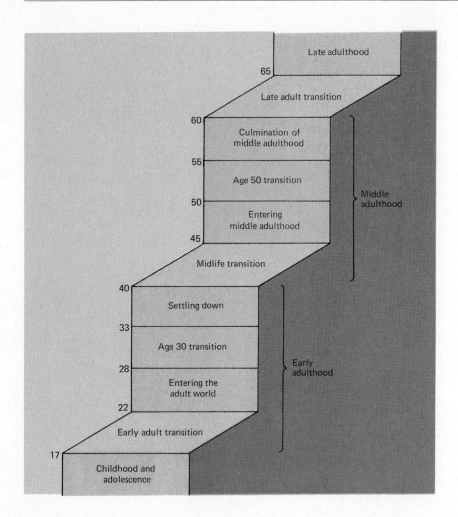

Figure 13.1 Levinson's eras of adult development

turity much earlier in our time than in the past century (Tanner, 1979), he or she usually lacks the emotional or social maturity to deal effectively with all the changes and situations likely to be encountered during the adolescent years. Frequently lack of social skills and experience can lead to abrasive or awkward incidents.

Concern with social status is only one aspect of the repeated search for personal identity that takes place during adolescence. During this stage in life, which Erikson describes in terms of "ego identity versus role diffusion," adolescents must successfully integrate many disparate images of themselves. They must establish some sense of continuity with their childhood past and family while also establishing a sense of themselves apart from childhood and family.

Imagine that your niece is still telling you her troubles. "Not only won't Mom let me wear makeup, what's worse is she won't let me date high school boys. I really like Bobby Williams—he's a senior in high school. But Mom says that since I'm only in the eighth grade, I shouldn't date anyone older than ninth grade. But these junior high boys give me a pain—they're *so* immature." ▪

Physical development

In early adolescence, the different rates at which boys and girls mature can create dilemmas like your niece's, where the social and physical development of the sexes is uneven. For example, most

TABLE 13.1 **ERIKSON'S AND FREUD'S DEVELOPMENTAL STAGES**

Erikson's psychosocial stages	Age	Successful resolution of crisis leads to	Freud's psychosexual stages
Basic trust vs. mistrust			
Consistent maternal care vs. negligence, irregular satisfaction of needs	first year	trust, optimism, warmth	oral
Autonomy vs. shame, doubt			
Assertiveness and physical self-control vs. dependency on parents and inability to be assertive	second year	sense of autonomy, pride of accomplishment	anal
Initiative vs. guilt			
Exploratory behavior and self-initiated activities vs. fearfulness and self-doubt	third to fifth years	development of conscience, self-worth, goal definition	phallic
Industry vs. inferiority			
Cooperation and competition vs. fear of failing and feelings of inadequacy	sixth year to puberty	competence, mastery of skills, self-confidence	latency
Identity vs. role confusion			
Integration of identity vs. role diffusion, lack of positive identity	adolescence	sense of continuity with one's past, present, and future; healthy sense of identity	genital
Intimacy vs. isolation			
Caring deeply for another person and vulnerability vs. shallow interpersonal relationships and fear of commitment	early adulthood	ability to form stable commitments and close relationships	
Generativity vs. stagnation			
Need to be needed and desire to contribute vs. self-absorption and early invalidism	middle adulthood	productivity, creative concern for the world and future generations	
Integrity vs. despair			
Reflection and evaluation vs. regret for past life and strong fear of death	old age	acceptance of mortality and of the human life cycle, sense of peace	

girls reach their adult height well before age nineteen. Because their period of maximum growth occurs later, boys frequently reach their full height later—by about twenty-one or twenty-two.

Until age eleven, boys and girls are generally about the same size. But the next two years or so, girls add height and weight faster than boys. Then at about age twelve or thirteen, boys move ahead and maintain their lead, continuing to grow heavier and taller than girls (Tanner, 1963).

Their accelerated physical growth does not mean, however, that boys mature before girls. On the contrary; definite social strains result from the fact that, on the average, girls reach sexual maturity two years earlier than boys. One important sign that the female has reached her growth peak is *menarche*, the onset of menstruation. Contemporary data suggest that about half the girls in the United States reach menarche between ages twelve and fourteen, 80 percent between

Figure 13.2 Rates of growth
There is a dramatic growth spurt in early adolescence, at about twelve for girls and about fourteen for boys. Growth rate then tapers off until full adult height is reached.

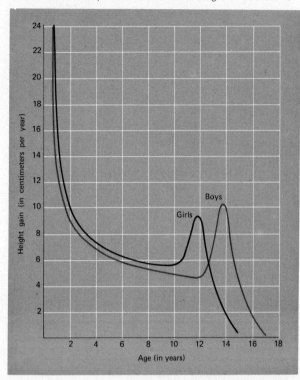

11½ and 14½, over 95 percent between ten and sixteen, and fewer than two percent before ten or after sixteen (Grinder, 1973).

For the last century or so, the age of menarche has been decreasing. In the United States, the average age in 1900 was 14.2; today it is 12.5. The age of menarche has declined an average of four months per decade for the last century. The most likely reasons for this drop are the marked advances in nutrition and health of the last hundred years in this country.

Sexual development in males begins with the increased growth of the testes and scrotum, and about a year later penis growth also accelerates. Although this sequence may begin soon after age ten, there are great variations in the age at which sexual development in males begins. In both males and females, secondary sex characteristics also appear during adolescence. Hair begins to grow in the pubic area around the sex organs as well as in the armpits. Boys also find that they now have more facial hair and that their voices are deepening (see Figure 13.3).

In early adolescence, the years of greatest growth disparity between the sexes, girls—like

Teenagers undergo different rates of physical development. The physiques of teenagers at a given age can vary dramatically. (© Jim Anderson 1978/Woodfin Camp & Assoc.)

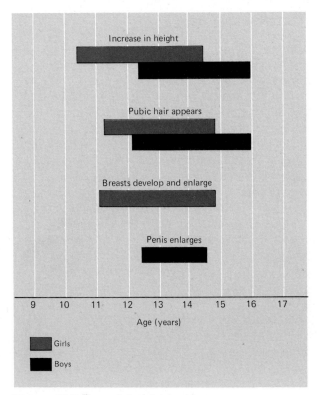

Figure 13.3 Sexual development

Girls begin developing sexual characteristics a year or two before boys.

covery, and further differentiation" (Erikson, 1968).

The role of maturation

We mature at different rates. Some of us are "late bloomers," others precocious. The experiences of early and late maturation both seem to have distinct effects on personality formation. Some research has shown that early maturers are more independent, confident, poised, and mature than late maturers. On a test of masculinity-femininity, for example, early-maturing boys obtained more traditional masculine interest scores than their late-maturing peers, who are described as having self-concepts that are less positive, and as being more tense (Conger, 1973). In addition, late-maturers are more interested in gaining the attention and acceptance of others and are usually more prone to rebel against parental authority (*Berkeley Adolescence Study*, reviewed by Eichorn, 1963; Mussen and Jones, 1958).

These findings seem predictable if we recall that the late maturer frequently has some difficulty in playing the same social roles as his peers. Although the physical inequalities of the late-maturing adolescent eventually disappear, some personality traits acquired as a result of slower development tend to be permanent (Jones, 1957). More specifically, in adulthood, the late maturers were found to be lower on traits of responsibility and dominance and to show less self-control.

Growth rate seems to have a different, less dramatic effect on the female personality. While early-developing girls tend to be shy and retiring during the first years of adolescence, they later become more confident about their femininity and their sex roles. In fact, one study suggests that early-maturing girls marry earlier (Buck and Stavraky, 1967). However, one researcher has said that late maturers may have greater advantages as they become older. It is possible, for example, that the experience of having been a late maturer in adolescence is related to having more insight, tolerance of ambiguity, selective awareness, and flexibility fifteen or twenty years later. At least for women, then, the late maturer may become more open-minded and adaptive (Jones, 1965).

your niece—are often interested in older boys who are their developmental equals. By late adolescence, the differences in the growth patterns of the sexes have been equalized by the male's development.

The slow journey into adulthood differs for each young person, depending on temperament, physical growth, and interpersonal relationships. But in all cases, adolescence remains a period of many changes, demanding proportionately many adjustments. In short, boys and girls entering the teen years are just beginning to discover who they are and where they belong on their own. They are, as Erikson (1963) has observed, moving into the first stage of an *identity crisis*. As used here, the word "crisis" does not connote impending catastrophe; it designates "a necessary turning point, a crucial moment, when development must move one way or another, marshaling resources of growth, re-

Imagine that your niece has just introduced you to her new boyfriend, Peter, who is 15. Since he's a tall, gangly youth who seems out of place in his own body, you try to make small talk to put him at ease.

"Do you play on any school teams?" you ask.

"Yes—"

"Don't tell me—let me guess. You're center on the basketball team."

Peter grimaces. "No, actually, I'm captain of the chess team." ■

Forming a self-concept

In the teen years, self-awareness can for the most part be equated with awareness of the body. Because of the major physical changes occurring in these years, this might be expected. A boy who is growing taller seemingly by the week must, like Peter, reconcile his new, more adult body with his self-image.

The new timbre in his voice as well as his tall, lean body will frequently prompt adults to tease him or make unflattering comparisons, especially if he happens to be clumsy or shy. As the rapid changes of adolescence occur, he must arrive at a balance between how he believes he looks and how he believes he should look and act. The balance between his self-perception and the ideal image that he creates for himself is an important determinant of his self-esteem.

Teenagers increasingly appreciate abstract ideals such as honesty, love, and courage, and these can become part of their *ideal self*, qualities to which they aspire. There is an increasing tendency throughout adolescence to answer the question "Who am I?" with an emphasis on relationships, moods, beliefs, and a concern for humanity at large (Montemayor and Eisen, 1977).

By the late teens, normally, adolescents have formed consistent self-images that integrate the many ways in which they see themselves. If the identity crisis of adolescence has been resolved and a secure sense of self established, the person can progress to young adulthood—the next developmental stage—and achieve true intimacy, the ability to care about and share with another person.

Drinking and drugs

The strongest influences on the drinking and drug-taking habits of teenagers are the examples set by their parents and the standards of their community (Schell and Hall, 1979). Teenage drinking patterns, for example, follow those of the community at large: boys drink more than girls, city kids drink more than those in the country, and middle- and upper-class teens drink more than those in the working or lower classes.

A recent report of changing patterns of teenage drinking and drug use shows that alcohol and drug use are becoming more common among high school students, although by no means all approve (Bachman and Johnston, 1979). A survey of a national sample of high school seniors conducted every year since 1975 found, for example, that by their senior year in high school, more than one-third had used at least one illegal drug other than marijuana. During the 1970s, the proportion using marijuana rose substantially; by the end of the decade, six in ten high school seniors had tried it, and one in ten used it regularly. The proportion who report daily drinking has held steady, at around 6 percent, as has the proportion who regularly use illegal drugs other than marijuana (Johnston, Backman, and O'Malley, 1977).

Daily drug use is twice as high for non-college-bound teenagers as for their college-bound peers; alcohol use and cigarette smoking are also higher in those not headed to college. Even though there is more use of illegal drugs in this generation than in the preceding one, the majority of high school students are conservative in their views of drugs. More than three-quarters of seniors disapprove of experimenting with drugs more serious than marijuana, believing them harmful. Even marijuana, if used regularly, is viewed as harmful by two-thirds, despite the fact that an increasing minority use it daily.

Largely because of the need to conform, experimentation with drinking and drugs is an increasingly common rite of passage among teenagers (Barnes, 1977). While in the 1960s (when drug use first became widespread) there was a generation gap that made for adult intolerance, adults have become better informed—especially about marijuana—and their fears have decreased somewhat.

Nevertheless, research to date has found that smoking marijuana may be as much as three times as damaging to lung tissue as regular cigarettes (National Institute on Drug Abuse, 1980). There may be other adverse physiological or psychological effects from marijuana, but as yet none have been definitively established.

Imagine that your friend's seventeen-year-old son is about to start a local college. The son wants to move out of the house and get his own apartment closer to school. He's willing to get a part-time job to help pay the extra expense. Your friend isn't sure that her son is up to taking care of himself on his own. What's really bothering your friend, though, is the fear that independent living will end the close relationship she has with him. ■

Drawing by E. Opie; © 1978 The New Yorker Magazine, Inc.

Family

Your friend needn't fear: when children move out on their own to go to college, their new independence can strengthen their emotional ties to their parents. Two groups of young men and their parents were tested: in one, sons were leaving home for college; in the other, they stayed at home and commuted to college (Sullivan and Sullivan, 1980). The group who moved away to college felt more independent, showed increased affection toward their parents, were more satisfied with them, and had better communication after moving out than the group that stayed at home. Thus the initial separation of leaving for college seems to further the developmental goal of becoming independent of one's family, while at the same time fostering strong emotional ties.

The social changes that take place during adolescence are rooted in family relationships. The turmoil of leaving behind childhood roles and growing into adult ones frequently puts teenagers at odds with their parents. The way teenagers relate to their parents will have long-term effects on how they relate to their friends, peers, and others in general.

For instance, a boy's behavior in adolescence of-

ten reflects the way his mother interacted with him at earlier stages in his development. Mothers whose child-rearing style tends to be rejecting produce boys who adjust poorly to adolescence. Having an adequate male model with whom to identify, usually the father, is very important to the young man's learning to behave in socially valued ways (Biller and Davids, 1973). Girls are equally sensitive to the influence of their mothers. For example, if the mother shows that she resents aspects of her own feminine role, the daughter may find it difficult in later life to develop a coherent sexual identity (Schaefer and Bayley, 1963).

It is not uncommon for an adolescent's relationship with his or her family to be strained by some conflict. Typically young people want more freedom or independence than their parents are willing to grant. Another recurring source of dissension is occasional reluctance to accept the responsibilities that accompany their new maturity. For example, a boy who wants an apartment of his own may be less than enthusiastic when it comes to washing his clothes, and he may bring his laundry home for his family to do.

Parental behavior affects the ability of adolescents to become more independent as they move into their later teens. If a mother and father are ambivalent about their child growing up, and if they were overprotective and denied him or her challenging experiences in childhood, they may well extend their overprotectiveness to the adolescent years.

Two other child-rearing styles clearly affect the development of independence. Parents who encourage their children to explore on their own and to develop a sense of autonomy usually have children who become confident, competent, and self-reliant as adults. Douvan and Adelson (1966) characterize such parents as "democratic." In direct contrast to them are authoritarian parents, who discourage their children's efforts to be independent. Adolescents from such households readily obey and submit to any order; even mildly stated suggestions take on authority for them. These adolescents are less competent, and despite their docile appearance, they may be deeply rebellious and hostile.

As important as independence is, few adolescents must struggle dramatically to achieve it. This is not to say that conflicts are nonexistent. Girls in their late teens report that when they were younger, they had small conflicts with their parents that loomed large at the time but have since diminished in importance. Asked about their relationships with parents, 57 percent of younger and older adolescent boys and girls interviewed felt they had a good relationship. About one out of every three adolescents admitted having some difficulty in communicating with parents (Yankelovich, 1973). Contrary to popular images of adolescence, though, as a group teenagers are not particularly in turmoil, opposed to the values of their parents, or rebellious (Adelson, 1979).

Peers

The peer group is a social setting in which adolescents first attempt to find a middle ground between the values imposed on them by adults during childhood and a world that is in part shaped by their own emerging values (Coleman, 1980). Peers exert a powerful influence. During the time a boy seeks acceptance by his peers, he acts in ways he believes they will approve. Once accepted by them, he will seldom risk their ridicule

or rejection. It is this need for the security the group can offer that leads to the formation of clubs, gangs, and cliques. Group members feel linked by allegiance to the group and make sharp distinctions between members and outsiders.

In early adolescence, boys may be primarily concerned with the group or gang and the security it provides, rather than with the personal traits of individual members. But by the middle teen years, the same boys often begin to place special value on many of the same traits that girls esteem: friendliness, cheerfulness, poise, physical attractiveness, agility, and a sense of humor. This merging of values between boys and girls reflects the growing social contacts that occur between the sexes in the midteen years, when they date and socialize casually, most often at school.

Among both boys and girls, the stability of the friendships they form is greatly affected by age level. In two studies, boys and girls from five to eighteen years of age were asked on occasions separated by two weeks to name their best friends. The results show that in the early years of rapid development, friendships change with corresponding rapidity; as children mature, they form increasingly stable friendships (Thompson and Horrocks, 1947: Horrocks and Buker, 1951).

Teenagers usually form at least a few stable relationships with their peers, but they would probably be surprised to learn that these friendships are in large measure influenced by their relationships with their parents. Close inspection of peer-group values reveals that in many ways they do not differ substantially from parental values. For example, for the most part, adolescents associate with members of their own social class. Therefore, parents and peers are likely to agree in their religious, economic, social, and educational views (Reiss, 1967).

There are exceptions. Some adolescents are almost exclusively peer-oriented. Investigators have found, however, that this focus is not necessarily desired by adolescents. It is lack of parental affection and care that can force teenagers to find comfort with their peers. Such adolescents usually view themselves and their friends more negatively than adolescents who are not neglected by their parents (Condry, Simon, and Bronfenbrenner, 1968). Conversely, adolescents whose parents are affectionate, patient, and understanding are less likely to set their parents' values in opposition to their friends' values. Such adolescents also find it easier to make and keep friends (Larson, 1970).

EARLY ADULTHOOD

Imagine that your brother has a buddy who's twenty-four but acts fourteen. You know he's been over recently, when you put sugar in your morning coffee and find someone switched it to salt in the sugar bowl. How on earth, you think, could anyone so old be so juvenile? ■

Most people view adulthood and maturity as one and the same. Yet the drawback to defining maturity in terms of chronological age is that you can come up with examples of people who, like your brother's friend, are far from mature, despite their age. Even so, the transition to adulthood begins largely in the late teens, and its first phase, early adulthood, extends into the late thirties (Levinson, 1978).

Some of those who are adolescents chronologically may in fact have assumed adult roles in their late teens, whereas others whose age clearly establishes their adulthood have never grown up. Erikson explains these failures to mature in terms of the stage in the life cycle at which a person is concerned with "intimacy versus isolation." In his view, the period for the development of intimacy extends from late adolescence to middle age. A young adult who has developed this sense of inti-

macy will be able to share experiences with and care for another person, whether as a marriage partner or as a friend. Intimacy, then, refers not only to sexual feelings but to feelings of friendship.

Development

In early adulthood, young men and women have the greatest physical capabilities they will ever possess. Body strength is great. The muscles are resilient and can endure fatigue and stress with considerable ease. Young adults move quickly. They can work long hours and still have energy to spare. The physical prowess of this age group is directly reflected in the records of athletes. Their skills, which rely on strength, speed, precision, and endurance, reach their peak between the ages of twenty-five and twenty-nine. Sexual interest and ability also continue to be high during early adulthood, the time at which most couples have their children.

By early adulthood a person's mental capacities are at their peak. Abilities such as memory, abstract thought, specific skills, and problem solving are fully ripened. If young adults are free of serious emotional conflict and self-doubt, they are able to use their intellects to the fullest. During this period, they graduate from "novice" in their field of work to full productivity.

According to one researcher, who attempted to determine the most productive and creative years in the lives of scientists, scholars, and artists, productivity begins to build significantly before age thirty, reaching its most fruitful period between

thirty and forty (Lehman, 1953). Another researcher reports that artists hit their stride in their twenties and thirties, whereas most scholars and many scientists reach their highest rate of output in their forties. The reason for such differences, he proposes, is that scholars and scientists require a longer period of preparatory study and data accumulation than artists, whose productivity depends on individual creativity (Dennis, 1966).

Women as well as men often experience their most intellectually productive period in their twenties and thirties. But this stage in the life cycle coincides with the time during which a woman usually becomes a mother. If she does have children, the greater part of her time will likely be spent at home, where she is preoccupied with caring for them as well as with the often tedious routines of cooking and cleaning. More and more women in this era of life are resolving the conflict between career and motherhood by deferring having children (or choosing to have none at all), by resuming a career soon after having children, or

simply pursuing both career and motherhood at the same time.

Marriage

Whether the culmination of a long-standing high school romance or the outcome of a quick and intense courtship, the choice of a marriage partner is a critical decision. While most first marriages occur in this early adulthood phase of life, so do many divorces: about 44 percent of all marriages in the United States end in divorce, and the probability of divorce peaks between two and four years after marriage (Kimmel, 1974). Reared in a culture that romanticizes marriage, many people are poorly prepared for its less glamorous aspects (see Table 13.2).

Lederer and Jackson (1968) proposed that for a marriage to bring satisfaction and well-being to both partners, it must have four basic elements: tolerance, respect, honesty, and a desire to remain

While newlyweds enter marriage with high hopes, the failure to resolve conflicts in the relationships leads many marriages to end in divorce. (© Eve Arnold/Magnum Photos)

TABLE 13.2 **TROUBLE SPOTS IN MARRIAGE**

Lear (1972) lists ten recurring sources of marital dissatisfaction:

1. Lack of communication
2. Constant arguments
3. Unfulfilled emotional needs
4. Sexual dissatisfaction
5. Financial disagreements
6. In-law trouble
7. Infidelity
8. Conflicts about the children
9. Domineering spouse
10. Suspicious spouse

Figure 13.4 What makes marriage work?
A majority of wives feel that love, respect, and friendship are the essential elements in their marriage. Sexual compatibility is desirable, but not essential. (From Redbook Magazine, June 1976.)

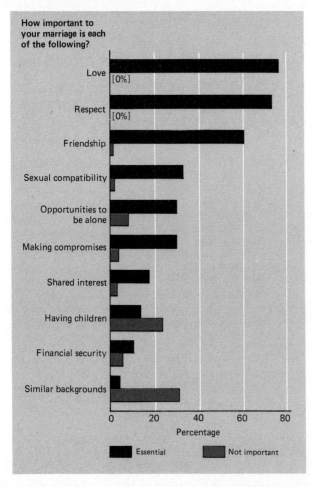

together for mutual advantage. One study reveals a positive correlation between disclosure of feelings and general satisfaction in marriage; wives are more prone to disclose their feelings than their husbands (Levinger and Senn, 1967). Other factors that seem to contribute to marital satisfaction are each partner's capacity and readiness to discuss mutual interests and personal problems, and the willingness of both partners to share responsibility and to grant each other a fair voice in decisions. Chances for happiness also increase if the husband and wife are from similar socioeconomic and educational backgrounds (Blood and Wolfe, 1968). Although people tend to choose spouses who are similar, they frequently assume a larger degree of similarity than really exists (Byrne and Blaylock, 1963).

Certain conditions make marital problems more likely. Couples who marry in their teens have a higher divorce rate, as do those who have a child early in their marriage. No one factor, though, is in itself a reliable predictor of marital unhappiness. Having children typically places more stress

Figure 13.5 Rising divorce rates
There were five divorces for every ten marriages in 1978. A decade earlier there were fewer than three divorces per ten marriages.

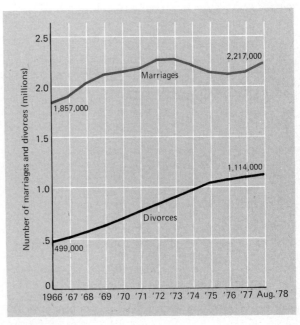

ALTERNATIVES TO MARRIAGE

■ More and more young adults are choosing to stay single, although the number who marry later is far greater. At any given time, about one-third of all adults are unmarried, separated, or otherwise on their own (Libby, 1977). Singlehood is increasingly popular: the number of people between twenty-five and thirty-five who have never married increased by 50 percent between 1960 and 1975, and the number of divorced people under thirty-five who have not remarried has doubled in the last decade.

Cohabitation, when an unmarried couple lives together, is also on the rise. Many couples who live together see it as a trial period to assess their relationship (Cole, 1977). Almost all agree that cohabitation allows greater freedom and flexibility than marriage, although typically the arrangement is a ''pseudo-marriage'': monogamous, sharing expenses and chores (Bernard, 1977). The emotional ties of cohabitation can also be as intense as those of marriage, making it just as stressful to end this kind of relationship as to divorce (Mika, 1979).

The single life does not fit common stereotypes, especially those of the carefree bachelor and the woebegone spinster. A comparison of married and unmarried men shows that bachelors have more mental distress, earn less money, and have higher crime and suicide rates (Bernard, 1977). Critics of this research argue that such men do not suffer from these conditions for want of a wife, but because they are simply unhappy men who have always been less well-adjusted—and in part for that reason have never married. In any case, widowed men also fare worse than married men with respect to mental distress, earning power, and crime and suicide rates (Bernard, 1977). Another study compared priests and other single clergymen to married men and discovered that married men live longer (Bernard, 1977). For men, the benefits of married life seem to far outweigh its limitations.

For single women, the statistics are quite different. Single women seem to have fewer mental problems and psychosomatic illnesses than married women; in fact, single women seem to have fewer psychological problems than married or single men. They often hold jobs that give them personal satisfaction and the opportunity to advance themselves. Generally, they maintain close family ties. Their sexual behavior tends to be conventional. Indeed, one researcher suggests that ''the psychological costs of marriage . . . seem to be considerably greater for wives than for husbands and the benefits considerably fewer'' (Bernard, 1977). ■

on parents, and this may be a major reason for the increased incidence of childless marriages. Couples who have raised children report even more satisfaction in life once their children are grown (Campbell, 1975).

MIDDLE ADULTHOOD

Imagine that your uncle is reflecting on his twenty-five years with the postal department: "You know, when I first started as a letter carrier, I thought I'd do it for a little while, then find something else that suited me better and I could make more money at. After the first five years, I got a little depressed that I was still walking the same route. After ten, I really got to like it: knowing all the people, being friendly with them. Last year when I was laid up with that back trouble for a couple of months, a lot of people missed me. Made me realize how much they liked me.

"And you know, looking back on it all, I don't regret any of it a bit." ■

In adulthood the pace of life levels off, gradually receding into retirement. This stage of *middle age,* roughly from the early forties to the early sixties, generally finds people more self-aware and reflective. By middle age most people have achieved some perspective on their past experiences and can review their lives with both insight and satisfaction. They frequently have a sense of competence, a quiet conviction that they've mastered the art of living.

Erikson has characterized this stage in the life cycle in terms of "generativity versus self-absorption." The concerns of "generative" people extend well beyond their own families. They are also interested in the welfare of future generations and in the nature of society. Erikson believes that if people do not develop this generative sense in middle age, they stagnate. Preoccupied with their own needs and comforts, they become totally self-absorbed. For many people, though, this phase of life is the most productive period, in part because they typically are at the peak of their power and responsibility.

Physical changes

For women, middle age holds one major physical change: *menopause,* which marks the end of the child-bearing phase; it occurs at different ages in different women. It is a period marked frequently by role conflicts: jobs versus mothering, family duties versus the need for one's own life, and so forth. Although most women view menopause as a significant event, they respond to the experience in different ways. Some are cool and determined to be unruffled. One woman said, "I just made up my mind that I'd walk right through it, and I did . . ." (Neugarten, 1970). Other women dread the so-called change of life and have varying levels of difficulty during this time. One woman recalled, "I thought menopause would be the beginning of the end . . . gradual senility, closing over, like the darkness . . ." (Neugarten, 1970). Despite such anxieties, many women feel a renewed interest in sex after they go through menopause, probably because their fear of pregnancy no longer exists.

Although men do not undergo a clear-cut physical change in middle age, they do experience what some writers have described as *male menopause.* From about age thirty on, there is a gradual decline in the body's level of testosterone, the male sex hormone; one result is that sexual drives may become less pressing, although by no means evaporate. The average frequency of intercourse among married people is 3.5 per week at age twenty; from age fifty on the rate is slightly more than once a week (Hart, 1973).

Mental and emotional changes

Although it is not yet upon them, middle-aged people are aware, at least dimly, of an approaching decline in their physical and intellectual abilities, especially in later years. At the same time, their social roles will be changing to suit their less-active position in society.

How successfully the middle-aged person adapts to these changes is, in effect, an index of his or her maturity. When we say that someone is mature, we imply more than competence, confidence, or, as we have said, chronological age. We mean a much more social development, a subtle grasp of how the real world operates and an understanding of human motivation and behavior. Mature persons should be more perceptive, noticing moods, nuances, and details that young people might miss or discount as trivial. They realize that their knowledge of the world is, of necessity, limited. Such perceptions help them to regard themselves with a sense of humor.

This is, of course, an idealized portrait, because how a given person ages is determined, to a large extent, by personality. For example, personality affects the amount of social activity a person needs to remain satisfied. Indeed, personality has been described as the "pivotal dimension" in any account of how and why aging persons behave and feel as they do. Researchers have found that personality characteristics endure, become more firmly established, and grow more closely related to overt behavior as people grow older. In short, if conditions permit, a person's personality becomes increasingly consistent over time (Leon, Gillum, Gillum, and Gouze, 1979).

MELLOW MIDLIFE

■ Midlife need not bring a crisis. In fact, one study has found that the quality of people's experience improves from adolescence onward, and peaks in middle age (Csikszentmihalyi, Graef, and Larson, 1979).

The method for this study was novel. One hundred seventy-nine men and women ranging in age from thirteen to sixty-five were recruited from schools and companies in the Chicago area. Each was given an electronic pager and a bound booklet of self-report forms, and instructed to fill out a form each time the pager beeped. They were beeped about eight times each day, at random times between seven-thirty in the morning and ten-thirty at night. The forms, which took about ninety seconds to fill out, asked what activity the person was engaged in at that moment, how involving it was, what mood he or she was in. and how alert.

Comparing different age groups, the older groups were generally more involved, alert, and invested in what they were doing. Specifically, older groups concentrated better on the tasks they were involved in throughout the day, and reported less desire to be doing something else. They also felt more alert, active, and strong. While some of these measures peak in the thirty-one to forty age group, others continue to increase between forty-one and sixty-five years of age.

Why should people experience life better in these ways at midlife? The investigators suggest that as people become more familiar with their roles at work and with their families, things get easier. Habit, if nothing else, might allow a person to concentrate better on what he or she is doing; familiarity might allow a person to feel a stronger sense of alertness and strength. Young people, on the other hand, are testing roles, are less sure of themselves, and find themselves in more unfamiliar situations, whether on a new job, or in forming families of their own.

A survey by Shaver and Freedman (1976) of the factors that make people happy or discontented with their lives may explain in part why people in midlife seem relatively more mellow than those at other stages. After reviewing the impact—or lack of it—on people's happiness of factors such as religion, therapy, sex, income, and education, the authors concluded:

Happiness has a lot to do with accepting and enjoying what one is and what one has, maintaining a balance between expectations and achievements. In 1890, psychologist William James proposed an equation for self-esteem. It was equal, he said, to the ratio of success to pretensions. One can raise self-esteem as much by lowering pretensions as by increasing successes. Wrote James: "How pleasant is the day when we give up striving to be young—or slender!" (1976, p. 75) ■

Midlife transition

Between thirty-five and forty-five, men and women reach a psychological turning point. This midlife transition links two major eras of life, early adulthood and middle age; although there is no specific event that marks it, turning forty is the time when many take note of the changes that are going on in their lives. While the midlife transition may be mild, if it is a time of emotional turmoil, it becomes a *midlife crisis* (Levinson, 1978). Essentially, this is a period of self-assessment and often discontent; the first signs of aging must be confronted.

The midlife transition is a "crisis" to the degree that there is a lasting and substantial shift in personality and in one's sense of identity, so that the framework of the person's earlier life is in question. At work, a person's career often plateaus, reaching about as high a level as it is likely to. This may mean the person reevaluates career aspirations downward to fit the reality, and also begins to worry about holding on to what has been achieved. During middle age the person may also reappraise in general how life has gone as compared to the dreams and hopes of youthful aspirations, which can lead to a feeling of malaise and failure.

LATE ADULTHOOD AND AGING

Imagine that you're at a birthday party for your aunt, who's just turned sixty-five. She tells you, "You know, I can remember reckoning my life by how many years it had been since I was born. Now I do it in terms of how many years are left." ■

As people age, they must anticipate certain changes in their lives—first, a decrease in the amount of social interaction, and, second, if they are working, the prospect of retirement. Finally, they must confront the inevitability of death.

The final stage

In later mature years, beginning in the early sixties, one passes through a final developmental phase described by Erikson as the stage of "integrity versus despair." In brief, Erikson contends that people who can reflect on their lives and find satisfaction in doing so experience a sense of integrity, a feeling that their lives have had direction and still retain some meaning. Those who review the better part of their life choices with regret, knowing it is too late to change anything, can feel only despair.

Adjustment to aging

Two theories attempt to explain how people adjust to aging. The *activity theory* contends that the

An active life can ward off the physical and mental deterioration of advancing age. (© Randolph Falk/1977/Jeroboam)

TABLE 13.3 **HOW LONG WILL YOU LIVE?**

This is a rough guide for calculating your personal longevity. The basic life expectancy for males is age 67, and for females it is age 75. Write down your basic life expectancy. If you are in your 50s or 60s, you should add ten years to the basic figure because you have already proven yourself to be quite durable. If you are over age 60 and active, add another two years.

Basic Life Expectancy   _____

Decide how each item below applies to you and add or subtract the appropriate number of years from your basic life expectancy.

1. Family history

Add 5 years if 2 or more of your grandparents lived to 80 or beyond. _____

Subtract 4 years if any parent, grandparent, sister, or brother died of heart attack or stroke before 50. Subtract 2 years if anyone died from these diseases before 60. _____

Subtract 3 years for each case of diabetes, thyroid disorders, breast cancer, cancer of the digestive system, asthma, or chronic bronchitis among parents or grandparents. _____

2. Marital status

If you are married, add 4 years. _____

If you are over 25 and not married, subtract 1 year for every unwedded decade. _____

3. Economic status

Subtract 2 years if your family income is over $40,000 per year. _____

Subtract 3 years if you have been poor for the greater part of life. _____

4. Physique

Subtract one year for every 10 pounds you are overweight. _____

For each inch your girth measurement exceeds your chest measurement deduct two years. _____

Add 3 years if you are over 40 and not overweight. _____

5. Exercise

Regular and moderate (jogging 3 times a week), add 3 years. _____

Regular and vigorous (long distance running 3 times a week), add 5 years. _____

Subtract 3 years if your job is sedentary. _____

Add 3 years if it is active. _____

6. Alcohol

Add 2 years if you are a light drinker (1-3 drinks a day). _____

Subtract 5 to 10 years if you are a heavy drinker (more than 4 drinks per day). _____

Subtract 1 year if you are a teetotaler. _____

7. Smoking

Two or more packs of cigarettes per day, subtract 8 years. _____

One to two packs per day, subtract 4 years. _____

Less than one pack, subtract 2 years. _____

Subtract 2 years if you regularly smoke a pipe or cigars. _____

8. Disposition

Add 2 years if you are a reasoned, practical person. _____

Subtract 2 years if you are aggressive, intense, and competitive. _____

Add 1-5 years if you are basically happy and content with life. _____

Subtract 1-5 years if you are often unhappy, worried, and often feel guilty. _____

9. Education

Less than high school, subtract 2 years. _____

Four years of school beyond high school, add 1 year. _____

Five or more years beyond high school, add 3 years. _____

10. Environment

If you have lived most of your life in a rural environment, add 4 years. _____

Subtract 2 years if you have lived most of your life in an urban environment. _____

11. Sleep

More than 9 hours a day, subtract 5 years. _____

12. Temperature

Add 2 years if your home's thermostat is set at no more than 68°F. _____

13. Health Care

Regular medical check ups and regular dental care, add 3 years. _____

Frequently ill, subtract 2 years. _____

psychological and social needs of older people do not differ significantly from those of middle-aged people. Thus, the decline in social activity that takes place in old age reflects a withdrawal from society. This theory concludes that old age is most satisfying when elderly people remain active as long as they can. Activity theorists therefore favor optional later retirement, partial retirement, or postretirement jobs (Havighurst, *et al.*, 1975).

A second view of adjustment in old age is called the *disengagement theory*. In this view, *both* society and the aging person withdraw, leaving a widening gap between them. Therefore, the withdrawal—as well as the accompanying decrease in social interaction—is a natural process (Cumming and Henry, 1961). This theory suggests that elderly people withdraw because of age-related personality changes, which increase their preoccupation with themselves and correspondingly reduce their interest in objects or other persons in their environment (Neugarten, *et al.*, 1964).

Other research suggests that neither of these theories alone represents the most accurate pattern for aging. How people age may depend largely on their earlier level of adjustment and lifestyle (Meltzer and Stagner, 1980). In most older persons, two forces seem to be at work—a desire to maintain a sense of self-worth by remaining active in society and a desire to withdraw to a more leisurely, contemplative style of life (Havighurst, *et al.*, 1975).

Retirement

Retirement can be a critical point as people age. When they give up the routines of their lifetime work, they separate themselves from an important source of satisfaction, self-esteem, and social contact. Today the proportion of retired people in the general population is growing as life expectancy increases, and studies show that retirement styles are quite varied. Some people want nothing more to do with their former work; they want to develop new interests, such as traveling. Others can accept retirement only if they find some way to use the job skills they have acquired over the years. One study found that whatever the retirement style, successful adjustment depends not on

how active people keep themselves but on whether their activity is a natural outgrowth of their long-term interests and needs (Reichard, *et al.*, 1962).

Especially in America, but in other Western societies as well, adjustment to retirement and old age is impeded by the cult of youth and its indifference to the elderly. The media, the fashion world, and the cosmetics industry all help to sustain this attitude. And it is not only the young person who disregards the aged. The middle-aged person often fails—or is afraid—to realize that, as the French novelist and philosopher Simone de Beauvoir points out, "his state tomorrow will be the same as that which he allots the old today" (de Beauvoir, 1972). Relegated to the role of second-class citizens, the elderly have become a forgotten segment of the population. De Beauvoir describes their situation accurately when she writes:

> Society looks upon old age as a kind of shameful secret that is unseemly to mention.... As far as old people are concerned, this society is not only guilty but downright criminal. Sheltering behind the myths of expansion and affluence, it treats the old as outcasts. (de Beauvoir, 1972)

Figure 13.6 The aging of America
The proportion of the aged in America has increased steadily since 1900.

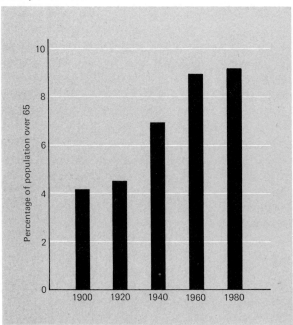

FACING DEATH

■ Just as people face each epoch of life in their unique way, so too do they face death with a distinctive stance (Shneidman, 1980). There is no "right way to die"—various cultures and religions offer different models. Even so, there seems to be a series of psychological stages through some or most of which a person may pass as he faces death. Psychiatrist Elizabeth Kubler-Ross (1970) interviewed close to 200 incurably ill patients, and identified five distinct reactions to the certainty of death. A person will often pass through all five stages as he copes with dying, although not necessarily in a fixed order. Each stage centers around a different defense mechanism:

1. *Denial* characterizes the first stage. The patient denies that he is going to die, saying or feeling "no, not me." This strategy helps him to keep the terrifying knowledge at a bearable distance while he attempts to collect himself and mobilize other, less radical defenses.

2. The terminal patient then turns to *anger,* the second stage. He is outraged. Every sign of life about him, in nature and other human beings, fills him with envy and resentment. "Why me?" he asks.

3. In the third stage, the patient tries *bargaining.* He tries to arrange an agreement that will salvage his life, gain a brief postponement, or perhaps just a few days without pain. Most of such bargains, which are usually kept secret by the patient, are made with God. At this stage, the person believes that if he is good and promises to do the right things, death can be postponed.

The plight of the elderly is intensified by the fact that they have little economic leverage and therefore no means of enforcing their rights. It is likely that as the proportion of elderly people grows, our society's attention to the problems of the elderly will also increase. In recent years, the elderly have become more active in agitating for their rights. A group called the Gray Panthers, for example, has taken the role of political advocate to protect and represent the elderly. Despite the negative factors associated with aging, older people report that—in spite of short-term declines, such as in health—they are satisfied overall with life (Miller, 1980).

An organization called SAGE (an acronym for Seniors Actualization and Growth Exploration) is a prototype of programs that aim to reverse the unnecessary human cost of negative attitudes toward aging. The premises of SAGE include (Luce, 1979): that old age is a time for personal growth, that many of the ailments of the aging are reversible, that people's attitudes can make them old before their time, and that old age can be a time for new beginnings. The SAGE program combines social activities with exercise, relaxation, nutritional awareness, and even play. The results are that participants frequently experience a renewed sense of vitality; programs modeled on SAGE are now available in many parts of the country (Dychtwald, 1978).

A physically active life is likely to help a person keep his or her wits throughout old age: the belief that people lose damaging amounts of brain cells as they age is unsupported by any evidence (Diamond, 1978). The critical factor is the health of a person's cardiovascular system. A healthy heart in old age guarantees ample blood to the brain, which in turn makes for mental alertness.

Despite its negative cultural image, old age can be a period of satisfaction in a person's life (Montagu, 1977). A study of people between seventy and seventy-nine years of age revealed that 75 percent of them were satisfied with their lives after retirement. Although some showed signs of

4. *Depression* fills the fourth stage. As illness destroys his body, the patient can no longer deny his imminent death. Anger and bargaining give way to a profound sense of loss, which manifests itself as depression. It is best for friends and relatives to allow the dying person freedom to express his sorrow, for it will prepare him for his final separation from the world.

5. The fifth and final stage is the *acceptance* of death. Assuming that the dying person has been able to pass through the four previous stages, he often can now await his death with some degree of quiet expectation. This is a time not of resignation but of numbness, an end to the struggle to live. Loved ones should offer their support, if only in the form of a look or a touch, but should be aware that the patient may prefer to be alone.

Even the dying person who passes through all these stages never completely gives up *hope*. A last-minute miracle, a wonder drug, a curative operation—they all remain possibilities, however remote. This hope sustains him during his illness and offers the possibility that his suffering has a meaning.

The dying have often been shut away because of negative attitudes in our culture. This, however, seems to be changing. There is an increasing awareness that dying is a meaningful part of a person's life, and that a person has a right to do it in accordance with his or her values and beliefs (Garfield, 1978). For some, it has meant choosing to die at home with loved ones, rather than in a hospital, or in a *hospice,* a special residence where the dying person is provided medical care in a homelike atmosphere. ∎

---

senility or mental disorder, most were active and not lonely (Neugarten, 1971). A common source of pleasure is grandchildren. The role of the grandparent has been called "pleasure without responsibility"; a survey of grandparents found that the majority found the role to be a source of comfort and satisfaction (Neugarten and Weinstein, 1975).

SUMMARY

A person's life spans an overlapping series of eras characterized by a general pattern of living, and a specific set of psychological issues to resolve.

Adolescence. During adolescence, striking physical, emotional, cognitive, and social changes take place. The establishment of one's own personal identity and autonomy are critical tasks. The adolescent is for a time suspended between past and future roles.

Some of the problems of the period are caused by the fact that it lasts longer than it used to. Also, physical maturity is attained earlier, but emotional and social maturity do not necessarily accompany it.

Erikson describes this stage in terms of the conflict between identity and role diffusion. Adolescents must integrate many different images of themselves.

Rates of physical development differ for boys and girls. Girls reach sexual maturity two years before boys; then boys' development moves ahead.

Full reproductive capacity does not arrive immediately with the onset of menarche in girls and the enlargement of the testes in boys.

In early adolescence, girls are often interested in older boys who are their developmental equals. In facing the tasks of personality development, adolescents must learn to deal with the results of their physical development and with the limits imposed on them by adults.

The rate of maturation influences personality development. Early-maturing boys tend to have more traditional masculine interests than late maturers, who may be tense and feel somewhat inferior. Early-maturing girls may be initially shy before gaining confidence about their sex roles, but late maturers may be relatively more insightful and flexible as they grow older. Formulating a self-concept centers around the teenager's perceptions of her actual self and her ideal self, and the attempt to strike a balance between them.

Drinking and drug taking generally follow the standards of parents, community, and peers. Social changes during the teens are usually rooted in family relationships. Young people may want more independence and less responsibility than their parents will give, but the majority of adolescents, especially girls, do not have serious conflicts at home.

Peer relationships—strong influences on behavior—teach the ground rules for adult behavior. Girls tend to value close friendships; boys tend to value the security of the group. But by the middle teens, boys' and girls' values become more similar.

Peer groups generally reflect parental values; most adolescents associate with members of their own social class. Heavily peer-oriented teenagers usually lack parental affection.

Early adulthood. Erikson terms the conflict of early adulthood "intimacy versus isolation," and sees the period for development of intimacy extending from late adolescence to middle age.

Young adults' physical capacities are at their greatest, and sexual interest is high. Mental abilities are also at their peak. Full work productivity is reached. Since these are the chief child-bearing years, women may feel a conflict between home and career.

Most first marriages and numerous divorces occur in early adulthood. Many young people are unprepared for the realities of marriage and the restrictions it may impose. Tolerance, respect, honesty, and the desire to remain together seem to be basics for a successful marriage. More and more young adults stay single or live together these days.

Middle adulthood. Erikson characterizes the middle adult years in terms of "generativity versus self-absorption." Healthy self-awareness and reflectiveness generate an interest in the welfare of future generations.

For women, menopause marks the end of the child-bearing phase. Some researchers have also identified a male menopause, characterized by declining testosterone levels.

The mature middle-aged person must adapt to the approach of a decline in his physical and mental abilities. Maturity in this stage implies an understanding of the world and of people and the capacity to confront the future with confidence.

Personality is a crucial determinant of the way a person deals with aging. An individual's personality tends to become increasingly consistent over time.

The midlife transition involves confronting the first signs of aging and mortality. Sometimes this causes emotional turmoil, discontent, and a significant shift in one's sense of identity—the midlife crisis.

Late adulthood and aging. Late adulthood brings the possibility of decreasing social interaction and of retirement. The inevitability of death must be confronted.

There are two theories on adjustment to aging, the activity theory and the disengagement theory. For the most part, two forces are at work in the elderly—the desire to remain active and the desire for a more leisurely life.

Adjustment is made difficult by the American emphasis on youth, but the elderly are becoming more vocal in demanding their rights and reversing their negative image.

Brain cells are not dangerously lost with aging, provided the cardiovascular system is sound. Nor do the elderly stop all sexual activity.

GLOSSARY

Activity theory Assumes that successful adjustment in old age depends on the elderly remaining active in society.

Adolescent Derived from the Latin, meaning "to come to maturity."

Disengagement theory Assumes that withdrawal from society by the elderly, and from the elderly by society, is a natural process.

Eras Stages of life that have specific developmental tasks and typical psychological issues.

Hospice A special residence where the dying are provided medical care in a homelike atmosphere.

Ideal self The qualities to which a person aspires.

Identity crisis The process whereby the adolescent's development begins to move in a definite direction.

Life cycle The overall sequence of growth and development through which every person passes over the span of life.

Male menopause The gradual decline of the testosterone level.

Menarche The onset of menstruation.

Menopause The physical change marking the end of the child-bearing phase of a woman's life.

Middle age The stage of life from roughly the middle forties to the early sixties, in which many people may develop heightened self-awareness, reflectiveness, and concern for future generations.

Midlife crisis The psychological turning point between early and middle adulthood; a time of self-assessment, emotional turmoil, and discontent.

CAREGIVERS: MOTHERS, FATHERS, AND OTHERS

APPLYING PSYCHOLOGY / FIVE

The times they are achangin' . . .

BOB DYLAN

One of the institutions hit hardest by the social changes of the last few decades has been the American family. Many sets of figures tell the story. Since 1960 the number of one-person households has doubled, so that they now represent more than 20 percent of all households in the country. While in 1960 three-quarters of homes were inhabited by a married couple, the figure was less than two-thirds by the end of the 1970s.

Not only are there fewer married couples, but family size is decreasing—a trend coupled with other signs that the family is on the wane: there are many more families headed by a single parent; the rate of divorce has doubled since 1960; by 1975 one couple divorced for every two who married.

More than one in six children lives in a single-parent family, usually a parent who works full time. While in the 1950s and 1960s most working women had no children, through the 1970s the greatest influx into the job market was made by mothers of small children (Farkas, 1977). More than half the mothers of school-age children work. For children under six, one out of three mothers works (Bronfenbrenner, 1979).

The basic family unit of mother, father, and children is eroding. More and more families are confronted with hard decisions about parenthood, divorce, and leaving young children while one or both work. Psychologists have been tracking these changes through research, and their findings have challenged some basic assumptions about the family, as well as giving some practical insights into the impact of the three fundamental forces confronting the family: working mothers, day care, and divorce.

WORK AND THE FAMILY

While at present about half of married women work, by 1990 that figure is expected to swell to two-thirds; the trend toward working will be even greater for women who have children (Smith, 1979). The housewife who stays home while her husband works is a vanishing breed. She is already in the minority: less than one-third of American wives are full-time homemakers raising children (*Providence Journal*, Sept. 25, 1979). By 1980, close to half of all children under age six are expected to have mothers who work. Among the implications of these changes are that, although family incomes are higher, families have less time together.

Mothers who work cannot be home with their children, but they can afford to have someone else look after the children while they work. In traditional cultures the extended family provided someone—a spinster aunt, a retired grandfather, an older cousin—who could look after young children while their mother worked. Increasingly in America that is done by a stranger—sometimes a babysitter, but more often workers at a day care center. What are the effects on children of having a mother who works?

The working mother

There is no simple answer; research has found several ways that a working mother affects a child's development (Hoffman, 1977). For one, a working mother offers a different model of what it means to be a mother. To the child who has two working parents, the roles of mother and father may seem more alike—not only because both parents are away working, but because their fathers are more likely to help out with household chores—duties the children of homemakers see their mothers doing. The net effect is that the children of working mothers see less stereotyped models of mothers and fathers, and so themselves have more egalitarian views of sex roles (Gold and Andres, 1978).

The impact of a working mother as a role model is greatest for daughters. Daughters of working mothers, compared to those of homemakers, more often see the woman's role as allowing greater freedom of choice, satisfaction, and competence (Broverman, et al., 1972). They also have higher self-esteem, more often intend to work themselves after they marry, and have greater need to achieve. The sons of working mothers see women as more competent and men as warmer and more expressive (Heatherington and Parke, 1979).

The effects on children of a mother's working depend a great deal on the mother's emotional state and attitudes. If the mother who works resents having to work, feels guilty about being away from her children, and dislikes what she does or works to escape her children, her children are more likely to suffer. On the other hand, if a working mother is pleased with her job, has made arrangements about child care and housekeeping

that prevent her from being overburdened by their demands, and is not guilty about working, then she can do as well as a nonworking mother. In fact, working mothers and nonworking homemakers who enjoy their role have more positive relationships with their children than do mothers who do not work but would like to (Heatherington and Parke, 1979).

The children of working mothers, compared to those of homemakers, become more self-sufficient and independent earlier (Hock, 1978). They are better able to fend for themselves, have higher achievement motivation, and feel more competent. The other side of the independence thrust on children of working mothers, though, is that the children spend less time with their mothers than they would if she didn't work. Whether a working mother can compensate for the amount of time spent away by increased quality—for example, with more special activities—is an open question.

It does seem that if the mother's absence means her children get poor supervision, they will suffer. Such children have difficulties in school, have less self-reliance, and do less well on achievement and intelligence tests than children of working mothers who have good supervision, or children of mothers who stay home (Woods, 1972). If a mother has to work, then, it is essential that her children be left with an adequate substitute. If not, the cost to their development may not be worth the extra income. If, however, the mother enjoys working and her children are well cared for in her absence, the effects may be beneficial all around.

The future is sure to see more and more working mothers. When seventeen-year-old girls in a high school class were asked to choose their preferred career, only 3 percent chose "housewife" as their first choice (Goodman, 1976). Indeed, a woman who had a mother who worked is much more likely to work herself. And when women in their sixties were asked if they had been satisfied with their job pattern over the course of their lives, the most satisfied were career women; the least, homemakers (Sears and Barbee, 1977).

Changing roles in work and family

When a national sample of high school students was asked whether women should be able to work, most said yes—and also felt the husband should help out with child care and housework (Herzog, *et al.*, 1979). Even so, many still felt that the wife should work only half-time or not at all. And if one of them had to stop working to care for children, the wife was clearly expected to be the one to do so. While the movement of women into the work force has demanded that the traditional division of labor by sexes within the family be overhauled, men generally have been slow to respond by more involvement in child care and housework (Pleck, 1976).

By and large it is the woman who seeks a more egalitarian division of household labor. In a survey of high school seniors, the boys were more traditional than the girls on every issue relating to home and work (Herzog, Bachman, and Johnston, 1979). More girls than boys objected to the conventional arrangement of a husband working full-time and wife not working at all. A sex role reversal, however, was just as objectionable: wife employed full-time and husband half-time or not at all was disliked by fully 85 percent of both sexes. When children enter the picture, both sexes feel the wife should stay home with the children, although more women than men feel she could hold a part-time job. When it comes to splitting care of the children and housework, most seniors felt these should be shared between husband and wife—but the girls preferred the split more strongly than the boys.

DAY CARE

While graduating high school seniors may still prefer the traditional family where Dad works and Mom stays home with the kids, the fact is that this arrangement is increasingly rare. More and more American children are cared for by people outside the family during the working day.

The effects of day care on children seem to vary greatly, depending on its quality. Some researchers have taken the view that proper development of a child depends on a mother's presence at home during the early years (Fraiberg, 1978). Others, though, contend that our culture's assumption that such a relationship is essential to a child's well-being does not hold up under scrutiny of the

evidence (Kagan, 1978; Etaugh, 1980). A study of the research, though, reveals a degree of truth in both positions.

Do children need mothers?

According to John Bowlby (1969), a warm, intimate, and consistent relationship with the mother fosters a child's emotional health. Unbroken mother love during the first two or three years of life is essential, according to Bowlby, if the child is to have the ability to form loving bonds later in life. Systematic studies, however, have not supported this view; children who were raised the first few years of life as infants in orphanages and then adopted did not reveal any great inability to form ties of affection (Tizard and Rees, 1975).

Even though long-term effects of maternal deprivation are hard to document, the immediate consequences are clear. If, for instance, the mother of a child who is between six months and five years old becomes ill, and the child is suddenly looked after by strangers, the results are traumatic (Schaffer, 1977). First there is a period of acute distress, when the child cries for her mother and refuses help from anyone else, then a period of despair and apathy, and finally a period of emotional detachment. While the child thus comes to terms with the separation, it is at the cost of her emotional tie to her mother and her ability to trust anyone else. If she is then returned to her mother, the child will for a time treat both her parents as coldly as strangers, later swinging to the extreme of overdependency, refusing ever to be left with strangers again.

While it is clear that total separation of mother from child under traumatic conditions is undesirable, that does not mean that day care need be such a trauma (Ragozin, 1980). For one thing, even as infants, children seem to form multiple attachments, not just one exclusive one to mother (Schaffer and Emerson, 1964). They are deeply bonded to older brothers and sisters, neighbors, grandparents, and, above all, fathers. "Mothering" can clearly be shared by many people without trauma to the child. The "mother" need not be the child's biological mother: it can be anyone of either sex with whom the child has a loving, caring relationship.

Consistency of care

While mothering can be distributed among many different people, it is essential that the care given to a child not be haphazard. The most common alternative to a mother's care is leaving a child at a day care center. Sometimes—especially in large commercial day care centers—the care is inadequate: there are often too many children, too few caretakers, and too little variety in activities. In such cases the child's development can be retarded, often seriously (Mussen, Conger and Kagan, 1979).

But when a day care center is well-run, leaving a child there can have distinct advantages, over and above allowing a mother to work. And leaving a child in someone else's care during part of the day does not mean the child will love the mother any less. This is a common fear among some mothers. On the contrary, studies of infants left in day care centers from less than six months old until they were $2\frac{1}{2}$ showed that, although they had warm bonds to the person who cared for them during the day, the infant invariably went to the mother for comfort when bored, tired, or distressed (Kagan, Kearsley, and Zelazo, 1977).

Further, when children in day care were compared with those reared at home, they did equally well on measures of attentiveness, memory, perception, and language. It seems that if a day care center is well run, there are no dangers: children develop as they would if they remained at home. Indeed, day care may have advantages over staying home. Kids in day care have the chance to explore a strange environment, play more with their peers, and be with a caring adult who may have more relaxed and accepting standards for cooperation, cleanliness, or aggression (Mussen, Conger and Kagan, 1979). This difference between home care and good day care may explain why children who have been in day care adapt more quickly to strange places and explore more and play more easily with peers.

While there is as yet no clear mandate for day care, the evidence so far shows that if it is adequate, being in day care may give a child everything he or she would get at home—and something more.

FATHERS

While the common presumption has been that mothering is essential to a child's healthy development, evidence is increasing that fathering, too, is needed for a child to blossom fully. Part of the evidence comes from studies of the effects of father absence. There are between 7 and 8 million American families headed by mothers alone; the absence of the father is typically due to death, divorce, or separation.

A review of the effects of father absence on children in these families shows that effects are more profound on boys than on girls, and vary with the age the absence occurred. To summarize (Lynn, 1974), for boys the adverse effects of father absence include: difficulty with conduct and poor adjustment to peers, hampered moral development, and—if the boy was two years old or younger, or between six and nine years old—difficulty delaying gratification. When a young boy loses a father, it frequently results in problems with his masculine identity (sometimes, for example, the boy expresses a "macho" masculine bravado). In older boys it can mean inability to accept male role models and rejection of the father as an ideal to follow. Boys may also be anxious about sex and courtship, and may become more feminine. In terms of cognitive development, father loss is associated with lower math skills, poorer verbal ability, and lessened motivation to achieve on mechanical tasks.

The effects of father loss on daughters are different (Lynn, 1974). While girls are not affected so strongly as boys, there is a pattern of adverse effects. Girls who lose their fathers find it more difficult in adolescence to interact appropriately with boys, sometimes becoming promiscuous. Father loss has also been found more common among women who fail to reach orgasm, are alcoholics, and attempt suicide.

SINGLE-PARENT FAMILIES

Some of these effects may be due to the stresses on families headed by a woman alone (Heatherington, Cox, and Cox, 1978). The single parent has to handle alone tasks that are typically full time for two adults. They are also usually under considerable financial strain: the mean family income of families headed by mothers is about half that of families headed by fathers; in 1974 more than half of such families had incomes below the poverty level (Bane, 1976).

Mothers in single-parent families often feel trapped, lonely, and frustrated—especially if they are divorced and have a misbehaving son or daughter. In a single-parent home there is only one parent to serve as both model of adulthood and disciplinarian. And there is no time out. There is no spouse to serve as a buffer, or to counteract the ill effects of a rejecting, incompetent, or unstable parent. The mother on her own, then, offers a more restricted array of attributes to model than does a two-parent family.

Most single-parent families, though, are so for a short time. Single parents marry fairly quickly; one in five divorced women and men remarry within the first year, and the average time between divorce and remarriage is about five or six years (Ross and Sawhill, 1975). Between 40 and 50 percent of children born in the 1970s will spend some time living in a single-parent family (Heatherington, 1979). While the most common reason is divorce, there is an increase in the percentage of children born to women during the disruption of marriage, and more children born out of wedlock entirely.

CHILDREN AND DIVORCE

While a couple who are locked in a terrible marriage may look forward to divorce as a relief, the children seldom welcome parents divorcing, even in the most troubled families (Wallerstein and Kelly, 1979). The needs of children and parents are not the same: mothers who recover most quickly from the divorce and report being happiest afterward were found to have gained their satisfaction at the cost of their children's well-being (Heatherington, 1979)—their children had more emotional problems both at home and at school, and these mothers were unresponsive to their children's suffering.

The course of divorce

Although a divorce may mean the end of a destructive family unit, most children find the first phase of divorce painful. Their early emotional responses are typically anger, fear, depression, and guilt. This emotional turmoil persists through the first year; a sense of well-being often doesn't appear until after that year. The child is reacting to the sudden loss of a parent, the discord of divorce, and an uncertain, disorganized home life. Most children, it seems, can adapt to these changes within a few years. But if stresses continue, there can be serious developmental disruptions.

A child whose parents have just divorced, for example, is more vulnerable to changes such as moving or lessened income than is a child whose parents have not gone through divorce. Life changes that would not otherwise be stressful to a child are, for the divorced child, upsetting events (Rutter, 1978). This means that changes in the life of a child whose parents have just divorced should be kept to a minimum; moves, for example, are better delayed until the child has adapted to the changes divorce brings. The first year after divorce is the hardest.

The child has to adapt to a broad series of changes after a divorce. These can include new relationships with each parent, the custodial parent becoming more important, the noncustodial parent less available. The parent the child lives with becomes a more important model, disciplinarian, and source of nurturance. Children are usually called on to take greater responsibilities for themselves and for chores around the house, to fill in to some extent for the missing parent. And very often the child has to adapt to a new set of changes should a parent marry: there is a step-parent, if not a whole step-family.

Divorce and development

A child's age at the time of divorce determines to a large extent what the long-term consequences will be. In general, the developmental tasks the child is engaged in at the time of divorce are most vulnerable. In preschool years, for example, a child may suffer in developing trust in interpersonal relations and in sex role identity. In grade-school children, the difficulty may be in dealing with authority or in academic achievement and feelings of competence. With adolescents, problems are more likely to crop up in dating, career goals, and becoming independent of family.

While some researchers propose that divorce is more difficult for younger children there is little clear evidence to this effect. Rather, it seems that the difficulty divorce brings depends on the child's character, and sex, as well as age (Wallerstein and Kelly, 1978).

Children of all ages undergo sadness and loneliness at a divorce. They particularly feel grief for the lost parent; anger and feeling rejected are also common. A young child is especially prone to blame him- or herself for the divorce (Tessman, 1978). Teenagers are best able to weather divorce, having more options to find supports outside home. This, too, may present problems, if the teenager does so to avoid contact with parents.

Young boys who had close relationships with their fathers before the divorce, and who then live with their mothers, show intense anguish at the separation. Boys whose parents divorce around the age of nine or ten, for example, are prone to explosive outbursts of anger and temper tantrums. In general, divorce is harder on boys than girls (Wallerstein, 1978; Porter and O'Leary, 1979). Boys from divorced families have more behavior problems at school, and get into trouble more often than girls. During a divorce, discipline is likely to become erratic, provoking more misbehavior on the part of boys—perhaps because a boy's relationship with his parents requires more discipline, and so deteriorates more quickly when the family is disrupted.

One study found that girls in families where the father had custody do less well than those who stay with their mothers, while the pattern is reversed for boys, who fare better when they stay with their fathers (Heatherington, 1979).

Custody and conflict

Perhaps the single most troubling aspect of divorce for a child is coercion by one parent to take sides against the other. During the turbulent conflicts that often precede—and sometimes follow—divorce, one parent may seek an alliance with a child against the other parent. This demand to reject one parent is not one a child is prepared to accept: the vast majority of children want to keep a strong relationship with both parents. When, for example, a child stays with his mother, and the mother is critical of the father, the child comes to view the father negatively. Such an alliance against the noncustodial parent can harm the child. For young boys it disrupts a healthy sex role identity as a male; for girls it disrupts good relations with the opposite sex in adolescence (Heatherington, 1979).

If a couple must divorce, the best outcome for the child seems to occur if the parents can keep their marital disagreements from sabotaging their parental roles. If a child stays with the mother, for example, the best adjustment occurs when the father is available, especially to a son (Hess and Camara, 1979).

When parents are able to overcome the conflicts that made them separate and work out a custody arrangement in their child's best interests, the optimal arrangement seems to be joint custody (Sander, 1980). In this arrangement, each parent continues to take equal responsibility for the development of the child and the child spends an equal amount of time with each parent (though this varies). The foremost advantage of joint custody is that it is most likely to prevent the profound sense of loss of a parent that divorced children often suffer. It further gives children the advantages of having two parents in their lives. The parents convey the message that both of them love and want the child; children are exposed to role models of both sexes; dangers of divided loyalties and fears of abandonment are reduced. For the parents, neither need undergo the sadness, loss, and loneliness that the noncustodial parent often feels (Benedek and Benedek, 1979).

Such an arrangement is only possible, though, when both parents want it, can focus on the child's best interests, and can cooperate. In that case, the adverse effects of divorce on children can be kept to a minimum.

PART SIX

NORMAL AND ABNORMAL BEHAVIOR

14

PERSONALITY

COMMON MYTHS

MANY PEOPLE BELIEVE ...	ACTUALLY ...
Freud's ideas have had little impact on fields outside psychology.	Freud's theories have influenced the outlook of people in a wide range of fields, including the arts, literature, and the social sciences.
Freud based his theories of childhood experience on his studies of children.	Freud's theory of the child's experience is based primarily on his work with adult patients.
Freud found that people were actually aware of the real reasons behind their actions, even the seemingly most inexplicable.	Freud found that people were often unaware of the real motives underlying their actions.
All personality theories have borrowed Freud's basic ideas.	Many theories of personality reject Freud's basic ideas.
There were no theories of personality before modern psychology.	There have been theories of personality for thousands of years.

'Cause you've got personality,
Warmth and personality,
Talk with personality,
Smiles with personality,
Charm with personality,
Love with personality . . .

LLOYD PRICE, "PERSONALITY"

We use the word "personality" with assurance, to mean many different things. We say that one person has "a good personality," another "personality problems," and still another "no personality." The most common usage refers to social skill: the "better" the personality, the more effective the person at getting along with others. Another common use is to label the overall impression people make with their most obvious trait; thus we say that Jack's personality is timid, Jane's cheerful, while Karen has an aggressive personality.

DEFINITIONS OF PERSONALITY

Personality theorists themselves offer a wide variety of definitions of "personality." When in 1937 Gordon Allport surveyed the technical literature on the subject, he culled close to fifty different definitions of personality. Today it is even more difficult to find a blanket definition of personality than it was in 1937. Based on their comprehensive review of theory and research, Hall and Lindzey (1978) conclude that there is no specific definition of personality that everyone will accept.

Some theorists emphasize its organizing function—how personality brings order to all the specific behaviors that make up a person's daily life. To other theorists, personality is an index of adjustment. Someone with a well-adjusted personality is able to function effectively. Many theorists define personality in terms of uniqueness, the characteristics and behavior patterns that set one person apart from others. When this orientation is taken a step further, personality is considered the essence of a person.

We will see in this chapter what each theorist means by his or her definition of the term "personality."

Imagine that you've been asked to describe something you did about which you felt very guilty, such as shoplifting or cheating on a test. Try to remember the details of the incident, such as the time of day, who you were with, and so forth.

Notice how resistant you are even to trying to think about such a memory, let alone recalling it in detail. ■

FREUD'S PSYCHOANALYTIC THEORY

It was this kind of unconscious resistance in his patients to facing the more unpleasant facts of the past that was keenly noticed by Sigmund Freud. Resistance was the sort of typical phenomenon that Freud knit together in his psychoanalytic theory, probably the best-known of all views of personality. Freud's insights have influenced every discipline that studies human behavior, from sociology and anthropology to most areas of psychology and psychiatry.

Freud stressed the role of hidden forces that motivate and guide much of our behavior; his main tool for probing those forces was psychoanalysis. *Psychoanalysis* is both a theory of personality development and a form of therapy. In psychoanalytic treatment, the patient reclines on the now-famous couch and free-associates—says whatever thoughts come to mind—no matter how bizarre, antisocial, or upsetting.

The major aim of psychoanalysis is to bring the patient's *repressed motives* (based on memories of traumatic experiences and infantile impulses that are submerged in the person's unconscious) to the surface, to release the repressed memories, and to resolve deep-rooted conflicts. Through the analyst's interpretations, the patient gains insight into his own motivations. As one patient put it, "I learn the ways I lie to myself."

Based on his work with neurotic patients, Freud developed a theory of psychiatric disorders and normal personality development. The root of all emotional difficulties, Freud concluded, could be traced to some traumatic or unpleasant childhood experience, often in early interactions with parents.

The case of Little Hans

One of Freud's most famous case reports is the study of horse phobia in a five-year-old boy, Little Hans (1909). His father, a physician friend of Freud's, reported that the boy, who was usually cheerful and unworried, began to have abnormal fears around the time that a new baby sister was born. During this period Hans focused much attention on his penis (which he called his "wiwimacher") and worried about masturbation. In addition, he could hardly go outside for fear that

"Good morning, beheaded—uh, I mean beloved."

STALKING THE ELUSIVE UNCONSCIOUS

■ None of us would ever claim that we can give a rational reason for everything we do. Even major decisions such as selecting a career or a spouse are often made on the basis of a hunch or inner feeling.

Such "irrational" decisions are, according to Freudian theory, products of the unconscious at work. While psychoanalysts have long regarded the existence of the unconscious as well-founded, others in psychology have been skeptical. Only recently has there been convincing experimental evidence that seems to confirm the Freudian theory of the role the unconscious plays in shaping people's behavior.

Psychoanalytic theory proposes that men may unconsciously inhibit themselves in competitive situations because winning has the symbolic connotation of defeating their father for their mother's love. This holdover from the Oedipal conflict operates unconsciously. If the Oedipal conflict is intensified by the message "Beating Dad is wrong," that should hamper performance. If the conflict is alleviated by the message "Beating Dad is OK," then performance should improve.

This was the rationale behind a study of college men in a dart throwing contest. To test the impact of the unconscious in this competitive situation, the men were exposed to one of two messages: either "Beating Dad is wrong" or "Beating Dad is OK." The messages were flashed subliminally—too rapidly to be read, but seemingly recorded out of awareness and presumably registered by the unconscious.

The results: the "OK" message improved their dart throwing scores, while the "it's wrong" message worsened their performance (Silverman, et al., 1978; Hayden and Silverstein, 1980). The results seem to confirm the psychoanalytic theory of the power of the unconscious to affect behavior.

Shevrin and Dickman (1980) have carried the pursuit of the unconscious a step further by studying the "evoked potential," a brain wave pattern that signifies that the brain is responding to a particular stimulus and that accompanies subliminal, unconscious processes. They measured the evoked potential while flashing subliminal messages.

For example, subliminally flashing a picture of a bee evokes a greater brain response than a geometric figure, presumably because the bee is more meaningful. If the person at the same time is free-associating—saying whatever words come to mind—then the bee will also yield more related words, such as "bug," "sting," and "honey." Shevrin (1980) believes that the greater evoked potential and relevant associations to meaningful—but subliminal—stimuli are further evidence that the unconscious is at work in shaping behavior.

A similar study done in Russia confirms Shevrin's results. The Russian researchers used words that had special emotional meaning for each subject, for example, a person accused of stealing would be exposed to the word "rob." Their subjects typically reported that they could not read the emotionally threatening words, but at the same time they had the greatest brain response to them. ■

a horse might bite him. Hans also fantasized about giraffes and their long necks and about an oversized plumber's borer in an overflowing bathtub. Freud saw these objects as phallic symbols representing Hans' sexual fears.

To Freud, Hans offered vivid evidence of the *Oedipus complex*. This reference is to the Greek king Oedipus, who, not knowing that they were actually his parents, murdered his father and then married his mother. Freud made use of the legend in explaining his belief that all children between the ages of four and six develop a sexual interest in their opposite-sex parent. A little boy's attraction to his mother brings with it strong negative feelings toward his father, whose role he wishes to usurp. But the child expects to be punished for his hostility, and he develops a form of *castration anxiety*, a fear that his father will cut off his penis unless he abandons his desire for his mother.

A comparable phenomenon, known as the *Electra complex*, occurs in women. The little girl desires her father and views her mother as a rival for his affection. Hostility toward her mother results in *penis envy*, the wish for a penis and the fear that her mother has already castrated her as retribution for her competitiveness. Critics of Freud point out that, rather than "penis envy," this may indicate envy of the superior position of males in many societies.

Both boys and girls must learn to relinquish sexual interest in the opposite-sex parent and to become more like the same-sex parent. The desire to look and act like the same-sex parent is in many ways an unconscious yet highly effective resolution to the Oedipus and Electra complexes.

Motives and development

Freud puzzled over the motivating force behind human activity, especially the manifestations of sexuality in infants and children. Since babies could not possibly have been taught about sexual functioning, he reasoned that their behavior must stem from a basic instinct. Freud viewed the basic instinctual energy, called *libido*, as sexual in nature and primarily directed toward obtaining satisfaction and pleasure. At first, a child is guided by the *pleasure principle*—concerned only with the immediate gratification of his desires. Later, through socialization, he learns to acknowledge the *reality principle*, so that he can delay his pleasure to work toward certain goals and tolerate the frustration that this delay implies.

Freudian theory divides personality development into five psychosexual stages that unfold in an orderly, predictable fashion (see Table 14.1). Libido shifts to a new focus at each stage, making a different part of the body an "erogenous zone," or source of pleasure. Unresolved problems at any of the psychosexual stages may result in fixation or regression. If the libido's energies remain fo-

TABLE 14.1 **PSYCHOSEXUAL STAGES**

Oral stage

Birth to eighteen months. The infant's most pleasurable activity is associated with the mouth. For about the first nine months, the infant's pleasure is derived primarily from sucking, a passive activity. Once the baby gets teeth, oral activities include such aggressive behaviors as biting and chewing. According to psychoanalytic theory, a person whose oral needs have not been gratified adequately in infancy is likely to become an oral character. As an adult, he or she tends to talk a great deal, to be overly dependent on others, and to overeat.

Anal stage

Eighteen to thirty-six months. The child's anal activities become sexualized—they acquire the ability to provide gratifying sensations. Since this is about the same time that toilet training begins, the child finds his excretory functions pleasurable just at the point when his mother and others think he should be limiting such functions to specific times and places. Involved here are problems of compliance, punctuality, order, and cleanliness. According to psychoanalytic theory, a person with an anal character, which results from unresolved conflicts at this stage, possesses the interrelated personality traits of obstinacy, stinginess, and orderliness.

Phallic stage

Four to six. The sexual organs have primacy as a source of both pleasure and anxiety. In this period a boy develops an Oedipus complex and a girl experiences an Electra complex. Anxiety resulting from the child's desires for the opposite-sex parent is reduced when the child relinquishes socially unacceptable drives and identifies with the same-sex parent. Rooted in the events of this period are problems in later life concerning heterosexuality, jealousy, hostility, and accommodation to authority figures.

Latency stage

Six through twelve. The child's sexual urges are suppressed, and energies are used to indulge curiosity by exploring the world. Motor skills such as bike riding and ball playing are learned rapidly, and hobbies are developed. Freudian theory views many of these activities as desexualized, sublimated expressions of libidinal energy.

Genital stage

Puberty through adulthood. The interests of previous psychosexual stages fuse. There is a renewed focus on sexuality, but it is no longer narcissistic, or self-loving. If conflicts in previous stages have been resolved, the adolescent progresses toward healthy, heterosexual relationships.

cused on activities appropriate to one of the early stages and the person seems unable to advance beyond this point, he or she is said to be *fixated*. More frequently, the person functions properly and experiences appropriately adult pleasures most of the time but reverts to an earlier stage during times of crisis. In this case, an individual is said to have *regressed*. People rarely show complete fixations, but they are apt to regress during stressful periods.

Imagine that you're working in an office supply store. One day the store gets a letter, with a money order enclosed. The letter explains that the sender had stolen several hundred dollars in goods from the store over a period of many years. Now remorseful, the anonymous sender enclosed a money order that covered the value of what had been stolen.

Why do you suppose a person would do something like that? ■

Personality structure

A Freudian interpretation of the letter-writer's motives might be that stealing represented the control of one part of his or her personality, while sending the letter was the work of another. Freud proposed three different systems that make up personality—id, ego, and superego—and these divisions can sometimes "war" with one another. Each segment of the personality has its own aims, functions, and concerns; sometimes they are in conflict with one another.

According to Freud, the *id* is the primitive and almost totally unconscious part of personality. It seeks immediate gratification for sexual and aggressive instincts. Concerned only with obtaining pleasure, it is impulsive, irrational, and unthinking. It might, for example, be the part of personality that leads a person to steal.

The *ego* is a conscious control system that is formed in the child as he or she becomes aware of social demands. A person with a strong ego has the ability to plan ahead, to tolerate frustration, to work for delayed gratification, and to adapt to social norms. The ego is the executive arm of the personality and follows the reality principle.

The *superego* consists of the social values and rules that a person has internalized. The dos and don'ts that were once imposed by parents and other authority figures now become part of one's own value system. The superego is the moral arm of the personality and is similar to the conscience, since it sets standards for behaving. It would be the part of personality that could be remorseful about stealing. But its influence is usually unconscious, influencing our actions far more than we realize.

A person does not always measure up to the demands of the superego. One is constantly working toward an *ego-ideal*, an aspect of the superego that reflects the kind of person one would like to be. This ideal is often modeled after a same-sex parent or another admired person—older sibling, grandparent, teacher, athlete, or even film star.

Defense mechanisms

The tendency to remember troubling events incorrectly is common in psychoanalysis. One will recall an event in a distorted fashion, remembering it in a way that makes one look better than would the actual facts if correctly recalled.

Of three systems of personality, it is the ego that controls most of our everyday behavior. The task of the ego is to reconcile (1) instinctual urges from the id, (2) internalized controls from within the superego, and (3) the demands of the outside world. The result of these internal conflicts is tension, anxiety, and discomfort. To ward off the anxiety created by these competing demands, the ego makes use of several unconscious techniques that have come to be known as *defense mechanisms*. In a reformulation of her father's work, Anna Freud (1937), also a renowned psychoanalyst, has identified several defense mechanisms (see Table 14.2, p. 376).

The original aim of defense mechanisms is to enable a person to live with himself and others in ordinary society. Defense mechanisms, all of which involve some distortion of reality, are used by everyone. When overused, however, they become as troublesome as the original unacceptable urges or behaviors. Defense mechanisms require energy to maintain, can lead to more serious distortions of reality, and can prevent a person from reaching constructive, reality-based solutions to conflicts.

TABLE 14.2 **DEFENSE MECHANISMS**

Repression

The energy and drives that would get a person into difficulty with society or would be upsetting are allowed no expression, and are forced back into the unconscious. Repression frequently occurs in combination with other defense mechanisms.

Reaction formation

A person behaves exactly the opposite of his or her true unacceptable inclinations; for example, expressing love for someone you really hate.

Projection

A person perceives in others unacceptable impulses and disturbing characteristics that he himself possesses. The classic example is the paranoid person who attributes his own hatred to others, seeing himself as an innocent victim of their hostility.

Displacement

Feelings are diverted from their original object to one that is similar but less threatening. For example, little Hans could not express his hostility toward his father or his fear of him, so he displaced these feelings to horses.

Rationalization

Giving oneself a ''cover story,'' offering plausible and socially acceptable reasons in order to protect one's feelings of self-esteem. Examples would be the job applicant who says that it would have been a terrible job anyway, after being told that someone else was selected over him, or the prospective college student who convinces herself that she did not want to go to that college anyway, after receiving a letter of rejection.

Denial

A person acts as though some upsetting or anxiety-provoking experience did not even occur. It may be obvious to others that something terrible is happening to the person, but she continues to ignore it and to act as though it did not exist. An example might be a person who is losing weight and showing many signs of serious illness, but who continues to act as though nothing is wrong.

Sublimation

Sexual and aggressive impulses are transmuted into behavior that is completely desexualized, socially approved, and of value to society. A good example is the surgeon, who engages in activity that in another context would be blatantly aggressive, destructive, and sadistic, but in the role of surgeon engages in these activities for socially valued purposes.

FREUD'S FOLLOWERS

Freud's emphasis on sexuality and traumatic childhood experiences led to disagreements with many of his initial followers. Whereas Freud saw unresolved conflicts behind most forms of neuro-sis, later analysts emphasized the role of social and cultural influences on personality.

Jung's analytical psychology

Carl Jung, almost twenty years younger than Freud, was for many years his disciple and close friend. By 1914, however, Jung had developed his own theory of psychoanalysis and methods of therapy, and he and Freud parted company. Jung refused to accept the libido (in its sexual sense) as the prime source of what he termed "psychic energy"—obviously a major disagreement with Freudian principles. In therapy, he felt it wrong to focus exclusively on past experiences; for him, a patient's current life situation and goals were of greater importance.

Carl G. Jung (Henri Cartier-Bresson / Magnum)

According to Jung, the conscious mind is the ego. He believed that each person is judged by the outside world according to his *persona*, the public mask he assumes to meet society's demands. The genuine self, the locus of all aspects of personality, straddles the gulf between the conscious and the unconscious.

For Jung the unconscious had two aspects: the *personal unconscious*, a submerged part of the ego consisting of repressed and forgotten material from personal experience, and the *collective unconscious*, a repository of myths and beliefs from our ancestral past. The collective unconscious is said to contain universal thought forms or ideas, called *archetypes*, genetically transmitted from generation to generation. Each person is born with archetypes—such as God, father, mother, child—and throughout his life they have considerable impact on his personality (Jung, 1936). The collective unconscious was one of Jung's most original—and controversial—ideas.

Jung's theory of personality grafted a typology onto psychoanalysis. Jung divided all people into *introverts* (shy, quiet, inhibited, centered within themselves) and *extraverts* (outgoing, sociable, talkative, uninhibited). Jung also proposed that there are four basic psychological functions: thinking, feeling, sensing, and intuiting. Individuals differ in their tendency to emphasize one of these functions in the personality. In Jung's scheme, it is possible to classify any person according to his or her major orientation (introvert or extravert) and one of the four characteristic modes of behavior.

Jung described two stages of personality development. The biological stage, from birth to about forty, encompasses growing up, learning a vocation, marrying, and having children. Some people never develop beyond this stage. The more mature, however, advance to the spiritual stage, which involves the ultimate fulfillment of the self through religion and dedication of one's energies to other social, civic, and cultural concerns.

Adler's individual psychology

Alfred Adler, another early collaborator, broke with Freud in 1911 and, like Jung, took issue with Freud's belief that sexuality was the all-important

Alfred Adler (Brown Bothers)

source of human motivation. Adler argued that mankind had social instincts that were equally pressing.

Originally, Adler perceived the aggressive drive and the *will to power* as the fundamental motives that shape human personality. He later extended and tempered this view by postulating a basic *striving for superiority* (1956). This striving is an attempt to compensate for the feelings of inferiority and inadequacy that all human beings experience when they are helpless infants. Adler felt that what he saw as their physical inferiority generated in most women a desire for masculine traits. He referred to their efforts to compensate for their disadvantages as "masculine protest."

Another important concept for Adler was "style of life," by which he accounted for the uniqueness of each human being. At an early age, each person develops a lifestyle out of the strategies he adopts in interacting with his family, and this style continues to influence him as an adult, both in his activities and his characteristic modes of response. Once formed, a lifestyle is highly resistant to change.

Adler also proposed that birth order is a deter-

BIRTH ORDER

■ Are you an only child? The first-born in your family? Youngest? Alfred Adler proposed that your place in the birth order of your family can have a profound influence on your personality.

The first-born, according to Adler, is likely to get a good deal of attention. But when the second child is born, the first-born is "dethroned" and must share the limelight with the newcomer. This experience, proposed Adler, may leave the first-born feeling insecure and fearful of reversals of fortune. But if the parents prepare the oldest child for the coming of a "rival," the first-born may become responsible and protective rather than insecure.

The second child, on the other hand, is ambitious, trying to outdo the first. Adler holds that the second-born is likely to be rebellious or envious, but better-adjusted than either younger or older siblings. The youngest child, like the oldest, is more likely to become a problem as the result of being "spoiled" as a child.

There have been hundreds of studies of the effects of birth order on personality over the last few dec-ades. Some have confirmed parts of Adler's theory. As discussed in an earlier chapter, Schachter (1959), for example, found that a person's birth order affected the need for affiliation. When college women in an experiment were waiting to receive what they were told would be an electric shock, they had the choice of waiting alone or with others. First-borns chose to wait with others, while later-borns were more content to wait alone. First-borns, then, had a higher need for affiliation under stress—perhaps a holdover from the tendency of parents to be overprotective toward their first child, and more relaxed about signs of distress in their later children.

First-borns stand out in another way: they tend to be high achievers. First-borns (which includes only children) are finalists for the National Merit Scholarships twice as frequently as children in other birth order positions. Twenty-one of the first twenty-three space astronauts were first-borns; first-borns are overrepresented in *Who's Who,* among Rhodes scholars, and among university professors, graduate students, and medical students; among stu-

minant of human personality. The term refers to the order of siblings within a family, such as the first-born child, or the youngest of three. Much research supports Adler's contention that the personality of the oldest, middle, or youngest child in a family develops in part because of differing social experiences due to birth order (Zajonc, *et al.,* 1979).

cial and interpersonal aspects of personality. The best-known of the Neo-Freudians are Erik Erikson, Karen Horney, and Harry Stack Sullivan. Each of them accepts some or even most of Freud's views, but drastically modifies the focus of thought in ways discrepant with orthodox psychoanalytic thought.

THE NEO-FREUDIANS

A number of the early members of the psychoanalytic movement—known as Neo-Freudians—modified Freud's basic theory to focus on the so-

Imagine that your friend Ellen is a junior this year, and has to declare a major. You're talking it over with her.

"Well," she announces, "I've decided to be pre-med. At least I think so. Maybe prelaw. I dunno . . . business school might be a smart idea. But

dents as a whole, first-borns have higher grade point averages than later-borns (Schachter, 1963).

Adler suggested that the drive to achieve in first-borns was due to a lifelong need for recognition and approval. An entirely different explanation for the success of first-borns is Zajonc's (1976; Zajonc and Bargh, 1980) model, which proposes that the first-born grows up in a family environment of higher average intelligence. Each successive child who enters the family lowers the average family intelligence, in effect, and so grows up in an intellectual environment that is poorer (Chapter 15 has a more detailed review of this model of family size and IQ).

A still different hypothesis is offered by Foster and Archer (1979). They propose that biology, not environment, explains the relatively greater success of first-borns. Their theory is that the immune system of a pregnant mother may actually attack the brain of her infant *in utero,* and that the probability and intensity of such an attack may increase with succeeding pregnancies. The first-born is at least risk for this sort of in-the-womb brain damage, while later siblings have a greater risk—and so are more likely to do more poorly in intellectual performance later in life.

Differences in hormone levels at birth may also have consequences for later competence and personality traits. Researchers gathered samples of blood from the umbilical cords of 218 infants and measured them for hormone levels. They found that first-born children and only children have higher levels of the hormones estrogen and testosterone (Maccoby, Doering, Jacklin, and Kraemer, in press). Hypothetically, there may be a link between higher levels of these hormones and behavioral differences that would make these children excel later in life—testosterone, for example, is thought to be related to aggressiveness (Parlee, 1979).

All these theories, of course, are highly speculative. If someone finally does convincingly demonstrate why birth order affects personality, it will be of interest to see whether he or she is a first-born, second-born—or youngest. ■

you know something? What I *really* want to do is drop out, get married, and have some kids. . . . Well, maybe not just now. I guess I'd like to just travel and bum around Europe for a couple of years . . ." ■

Erikson's theory of psychosocial development

Ellen's uncertainty could be a sign of an *identity crisis,* the confusion that often arises in late adolescence when a person has to decide who she really is and what to strive to become in the years ahead. Erikson accepts the importance of the sexual and aggressive drives as presented in the orthodox Freudian framework, but he focuses on the importance of *ego identity,* the person's perception of herself and her place in the world. Erikson's emphasis is on the ego's development and its role in human adaptation.

Erikson views ego development as a series of eight *psychosocial stages,* periods when a person must face and resolve distinct psychological issues, thereby shaping the personality. The five early stages (oral-sensory, muscular-anal, locomotor-genital, latency, and adolescence) follow the Freudian pattern, presenting crises of trust, autonomy, initiative, industry, and ego identity, respectively. The parents of the developing child are of crucial importance in helping her to resolve these crises and to acquire, in sequence, the basic virtue inherent in each of these five stages: hope, will power, purpose, competence, and fidelity.

Erik H. Erikson (Photo by Jan Erikson)

Freud considered personality completely formed at adolescence; Erikson, on the other hand, adds three more stages—young adulthood, adulthood, and maturity—in which the adult personality develops the basic virtues of love, care, and wisdom, respectively (see Table 14.3).

Horney's social psychological theory

Karen Horney radically revised Freudian notions of the instincts and focused instead on how culture shapes personality. While some of Freud's followers quarreled with his emphasis on the libido and aggressive instincts, she rejected these ideas altogether. Horney viewed aggression by both men and women as an attempt to protect themselves against a threatening environment. Moreover, she strongly opposed Freud's concept of penis envy in women, preferring to stress women's overdependence and lack of self-confidence.

Still, in the Freudian tradition, Horney (1945) accepted the notions of unconscious motivation and

TABLE 14.3 **A COMPARISON OF DEVELOPMENTAL STAGES ACCORDING TO THREE THEORIES OF PERSONALITY**

Erikson: eight developmental crises	Freud: five psychosexual stages	Sullivan: seven life periods
1. Trust vs. mistrust	Oral stage	Infancy
2. Autonomy vs. shame and doubt	Anal stage	Childhood
3. Initiative vs. guilt	Phallic stage	Juvenile
4. Industry vs. inferiority	Latency stage	Preadolescence
5. Identity vs. role diffusion	Genital stage	Early adolescence
6. Intimacy vs. isolation		Late adolescence
7. Generativity vs. stagnation		Adulthood
8. Integrity vs. despair		

Karen Horney (Jerry Soalt)

basic anxiety produced by childhood traumas. She described ten neurotic needs—for example, cravings for affection or for power—that individuals develop in attempting to resolve life's conflicts. Each of these needs reflects one of three basic social strategies: moving toward people (helplessness), moving away from them (isolation), or moving against them (hostility).

Normal personalities are able to integrate and make use of each of the three orientations; they have enough judgment and control to use the strategy most appropriate to a given social situation. For example, "moving toward" a lover, "moving against" a merchant that has cheated. In neurotic personalities, however, one of the three orientations may be used indiscriminately and inappropriately. Neurosis grows out of the basic conflicts among these three tendencies. Horney (1937) felt that people in our society are particularly susceptible to neurotic feelings of inferiority, which stem from the pressures of an overly competitive culture.

Imagine that you're talking to your friend Ellen again. She's talking about her relationship with her boyfriend, Pete.

"I don't know what to do. Pete wants me to drop out of school, marry him, and help put him through law school next year. I don't want to get swallowed up in his life—I want a career of my own. But whenever I try to tell him that, he takes it personally and starts sulking." ■

Sullivan's interpersonal theory

Ellen's problem with Pete is typical of the need to find a balance between intimacy with a mate and *autonomy*, a sense of one's own worth, independence, and identity. Striking this balance between intimacy and autonomy was a challenge of development that Harry Stack Sullivan saw as one of a series of crucial experiences that a person must undergo during the span of life.

While Sullivan's stages of development follow the Freudian model, they emphasize the social aspects of life experience, focusing on key relationships at each stage.

During infancy the first interpersonal experience occurs as the mother feeds the child. Infants develop a concept of the "good mother" or the "bad mother," based on how the mother handles the feeding situation, and from this they derive a self-concept. If she is affectionate and warm during feeding, she is the prototype of the good mother. The feelings of well-being the good mother arouses lead to the child's developing a self-concept of the "good-me," those aspects of him that are grounds for being loved. If the mother is angry or aloof—the "bad mother"—the child feels anxious. This anxiety is the basis of the "bad-me," those aspects of himself that in the child's eyes are the reasons others fail to love him. Finally, if a parent is brutal to a child, the resulting feelings of dread evolve into the "not-me," those aspects of himself that are so awful he wants to disown them.

With preadolescence, a need develops for a close friend of the same sex, a "chum." This intimate friendship is fundamental to adequacy in later human relationships. Early adolescence is ushered in by the increased sexual drive of puberty and by a

Harry Stack Sullivan (The Bettmann Archive)

shift in interest from a friend of the same sex to members of the opposite sex.

In late adolescence, if all has gone well in the developmental sequence, the person has a sense of security and autonomy and the ability to cope with anxiety while living harmoniously with members of both sexes.

According to Sullivan, by the time adolescents reach maturity, the final stage, they should have become truly human—largely through their interpersonal relations. Sullivan's theory emphasizes the fact that personality is not fully formed at an early age, but changes with an individual's interpersonal encounters throughout life.

HUMANISTIC THEORIES

While psychoanalytic and Neo-Freudian theories place great stock in the effects of the past in shaping a person's present situation, *humanistic* theorists emphasize the person's perceptions of the self and the potentials for fulfillment in the pres-

Carl Rogers (Photo by Nozizwe S., courtesy Carl R. Rogers, Ph.D.)

ent and future. Although humanists make some use of Freudian concepts, they do not view a person as at the mercy of primitive instincts. Instead, they place emphasis on what a person might become, and what factors in her present situation block her from fulfilling her greatest human potentials.

Carl Rogers, a major humanistic theorist, was a student of theology before becoming a clinical psychologist, and his perspective on personality reflects to some degree his unorthodox beginnings. Rogers, like Freud, developed a method of therapy first and then followed with a theory of personality (1961; 1977). His client-centered therapy is "nondirective"; the patient talks about whatever she chooses, and the therapist reflects back to her the feelings in what she is saying. Rogers believes that this method enables the client to see herself more deeply, to understand herself, and in this way to grow as a person.

From these therapeutic techniques, Rogers has expanded his views into *self theory*. His major concern is the interrelationships among the organism, the self, and the phenomenal field. The organism refers to the total person, the phenomenal field to all experiences the person has undergone, and the self to the sense of "I" or "me" that results from these life experiences.

As the child matures, social experiences teach her to separate the self (or self-concept) from the environment. Often this includes the incorporation of the attitudes and values of others. If these values and attitudes do not conflict with her own deeply felt values, this is a positive development. But if the values of others are forced upon her, the person begins to experience life in a distorted way. For example, she becomes so defensive or anxious about the disparity between her positive self-concept and the rest of her experience—for example, real or imagined rejections—that she rejects her own self-evaluation as worthwhile and sees herself as worthless.

The individual's proper goal is *self-actualization*, reaching a point of full functioning in which experiences and self-image are congruent. The self-actualized person sees and accepts herself as she is in reality. Such a person is unafraid of experiences, fully aware of reality, and in harmony with others.

EASTERN PERSONALITY THEORIES

■ Theories of personality did not originate with contemporary psychology; such theories have been part of the lore of civilization for millennia. For example, the Greek philosophers reflected on the nature of human behavior in their dialogues and writings.

Perhaps the most systematic ancient theories of personality to survive intact are those that were preserved as part of the great religions of the world, particularly Eastern religions. Along with their doctrines about the nature of the universe and other beliefs, most religions have included little-known, though thoroughly developed, personality theories (Murphy, 1968).

Typical of these theories is that of classical Buddhism. Called *Abhidharma* (''the ultimate doctrine''), it elaborates Gotama Buddha's original insights into human nature (Goleman, 1977). Abhidharma is still in use—as it has been for the last two thousand years—as an applied personality theory throughout Buddhist countries such as Thailand, Sri Lanka, Burma, and Tibet.

Like William James, the Buddhists see consciousness as a continuous flux of changing states, never the same from moment to moment. The Buddhist psychologists analyze the parts of the stream of consciousness that flow together from moment to moment into separate basic elements. There are 53 such mental factors, properties of mind that combine to flavor and define a psychological state.

While most of these factors are neutral in terms of personality, fourteen are called unwholesome, be-cause they have negative consequences, and a corresponding opposite set are called wholesome, because they are essential to a healthy personality. Among the unwholesome factors are delusion, agitation, greed, envy, and worry. The wholesome list includes factors such as insight, confidence, composure, impartiality, and adaptability. Personality types are based on the particular mental factors that dominate a person's mind most often. Thus a person who experiences the factor of greed more than others is called a ''lustful'' type; one who experiences aversion most often is a ''hateful'' type, and so on.

The positive and negative factors inhibit each other. For example, if impartiality dominates the mind, it keeps greed from arising; if composure dominates, it inhibits agitation. If all the healthy factors predominate, then none of the unhealthy ones arise in consciousness. A fully healthy person, according to Buddhist psychology, is one whose mind is dominated by the wholesome factors.

The name for such a person is *arhant,* which means literally one worthy of praise. A more common term for that level of development is ''enlightenment,'' a concept used in many Eastern religions to describe a totally healthy person. Among the personality traits listed in Buddhist psychology for an enlightened person are: equanimity in all situations, constant alertness and calm, strong feelings of compassion and lovingkindness, accurate perception, skill in action, and responsivity to the needs of others. ■

LEARNING THEORIES

Behaviorists explain behavior of all sorts in terms of the principles of learning. So it is with personality: behaviorist theories fit concepts of personality into models of learning that can be tested from observing behavior. This does not mean that behaviorists necessarily refute concepts such as those of the Freudians; indeed, one approach has been simply to translate Freudian concepts into the principles of learning. Stricter behaviorists, though, have proposed models of personality based solely on learning theory.

Dollard and Miller's stimulus-response theory

John Dollard, a sociologist, and Neal Miller, an experimental psychologist, formulated a theory that brings together Freud's psychoanalytic approach with stimulus-response learning theory (1950). According to their theory, drive, cue, response, and reward are involved in all learning. In order to learn, a person must want something (drive), see something (cue), do something (response), and get something (reward). In other words, drives provide the motivation, cues direct the behavior, and responses lead to reinforcement.

At first, infants seek only the primary rewards of food and physical comfort, but through social experience they soon learn to appreciate such secondary rewards as their mother's smile, a pat on the head, or, at a later stage, a gold star from the teacher. Dollard and Miller agree with Freud that infancy is the critical development period, since the baby is completely dependent upon others for rewards. They also accept the Freudian viewpoint that long-term problems may develop from mishandling of conflicts over feeding, toilet training, and control of aggression.

Through experience in these early learning situations, the individual child develops *response hierarchies,* which are habitual ways of behaving in response to a variety of stimulus contexts. With neurotic adults, the responses high in the hierarchy (i.e., the ones most likely to occur habitually in a given situation) are either inadequate or inappropriate.

Skinner's operant conditioning theory

B. F. Skinner's (1974) theory rejects Freudian assumptions about unobservable inner dynamics. Skinner explains personality in terms of operant conditioning, the effects of positive and negative reinforcement on behavior. He believes that a person's behavior is shaped by his environment. In a novel, *Walden Two,* Skinner (1948) outlines the social conditions that stifle initiative, creativity, and enjoyment and proposes utopian conditions that would improve human functioning. His model of communal sharing and programmed existence has been adopted by a few adventuresome individuals, although there is no research that evaluates its effects. Other applications of Skinnerian theory range from programmed learning and teaching machines in schools to the establishment of token economies and programs of behavior modification in prisons and mental hospitals.

Social learning theory

A more recent application of learning theory to personality development stems from the work of social learning theorists such as Bandura and Walters (1977a; 1977b) and Mischel (1973; 1979). Most social learning theorists agree that to explain social behavior we must go beyond the principles of classical and operant conditioning to include *modeling,* or imitation (sometimes called observational learning), as a way people learn new responses. Thus, personality is shaped not only by how a person is reinforced for the various behaviors she performs, but also by the behaviors she observes. Through *vicarious reinforcement—*

Neal Miller (Courtesy, Dr. Neal E. Miller)

Albert Bandura (Courtesy, Albert Bandura)

seeing others reinforced for a certain behavior—the likelihood that she will perform that behavior increases.

Self-efficacy, the belief in one's ability to cope with the demands of various situations, is a learned attitude that has many behavioral consequences (Bandura, 1977b). This sense of personal mastery is probably learned when one is a child, but it determines how one responds to challenges throughout life. People with little belief in their self-efficacy give up easily and tend to avoid situations in which they might fail. People high in self-efficacy, on the other hand, try their luck in novel situations and do not give up easily, even when defeated.

PERSONALITY: TRAITS OR SITUATIONS?

Imagine that Fred is tall and thin, Alec short and fat. One of them is a lover of comfort and sociable, the other is a socially inhibited loner.

Which of them would you guess fits which description? ■

Type and trait theories

This kind of attempt to match personality type with physique dates back centuries. Early theories grouped individuals by category, or *type*. The Greek physician Hippocrates classified physiques as short and thick or long and thin. He divided these types into four basic temperaments: choleric (irritable), melancholic (depressed), sanguine (optimistic), and phlegmatic (listless).

The attempt to relate body type to temperament has come to be known as "constitutional psychology." Its chief proponent has been William Sheldon, a physician as well as a psychologist, who proposed that we classify people according to three dimensions of physique: endomorphy, mesomorphy, and ectomorphy. When one of these dimensions predominates, we have an endomorph (fat and soft), a mesomorph (strong and athletic), or an ectomorph (tall and slender). Sheldon's work is little used today; the idea that body build dictates personality formation seems too limited for most theorists, who prefer to view personality as changing and developing throughout the life span.

To account for the variable quality of human behavior, trait theorists emphasize dimensions, or continua, along which individuals may be rated for any given personality trait. A person may be scored on a great number of scales—aggressiveness, shyness, curiosity, honesty—and from these data a trait profile may be assembled. The most notable trait psychologist is Gordon W. Allport, whose approach to personality theory is "idiographic"—that is, he focuses on case studies and other data that emphasize the uniqueness of the individual. This technique contrasts with "nomethetic" methods, which use statistical analyses of data from large groups of people.

While doing research on personality, Allport and Odbert (1936) found almost 18,000 words in the English language that could be used to differentiate one person from another.

According to Allport, cardinal traits are generalized tendencies that exert a pervasive influence on an individual's entire functioning, for example, a musician's passion for achieving excellence in her career. Central traits are less prominent influences in a person's behavior, but are still quite dominant, for example, introversion, self-reliance, dogmatism, or cooperativeness. Secondary traits

Gordon Allport (UPI)

are reflected in attitudes and in reactions to specific situations, for example, personal preferences for certain foods or music. In Allport's view, the sum of all these enduring traits produces the broad consistencies that define personality.

Imagine that
Henry is outgoing and talkative at work, but at parties he becomes a shy wallflower.

Barbara aggressively takes the initiative at school, and her classmates look up to her as a leader. But at home she asks her parents' opinions on every major decision, and always follows their advice.

Would you say Henry is sociable or shy?

Is Barbara aggressive or dependent? ■

(Plate 53 from *BERGGASSE 19:* Sigmund Freud at his desk, Vienna 1938; the photographs of Edmund Engelman. The photographs of Berggasse 19 © 1976 by Basic Books, Inc., Publishers, New York. Used with the permission of Basic Books, Inc. and Edmund Engelman)

The situation

Clearly the answers to these questions depend on the situation the person is in. Barbara acts differently at home and at school; Henry is not the same at work and at parties. Because people's behavior is not consistent in all situations, critics point out that personality traits have relatively little to do with how people may actually behave at a given time (Mischel, 1968).

Social learning theorists observe that behavior

SIGMUND FREUD (1856-1939)

■ Sigmund Freud is probably the best known of all psychologists. Freudian concepts such as the "unconscious," the "Oedipus complex," and the "ego" are part of our everyday language. The school of thought and therapy he founded has had a powerful influence on our culture and has permeated other fields, ranging from literature and drama to sociology and anthropology. Even so, there are relatively few strict adherents to the Freudian school of thought within psychology.

Freud was one of the first to confront directly areas of life—such as sexuality—that were taboo to his Victorian colleagues. In doing so, he challenged many prevailing viewpoints—especially in religion, medicine, and science—and breached both social and cultural proprieties.

Freud stood at a disadvantage from the outset in making such a challenge because of his Jewish background. Born in Czechoslovakia and raised in Vienna, Freud grew up in an anti-Semitic climate. The only professional careers open to Jews were law and medicine. At the University of Vienna he was treated poorly, as both "an inferior and an alien." This early adversity may well have prepared him to withstand the strong criticism his theories were later to draw from his medical colleagues.

Freud's first interest was in anatomy and neurology. He subscribed to the view that mental events could be reduced to physical and chemical processes in the brain. But the primitive state of the neurological sciences of his day led him to pursue other avenues to understanding human behavior.

An interest in psychiatry led him to study with a leading French hypnotist. There Freud realized that the symptoms of many patients did not make sense in terms of anatomy. In "glove anesthesia," for example, a person would have sensation in the arm and wrist but none in the hand, although this symptom pattern makes no sense in terms of how the nerves work. Freud saw that such disorders required a psychological explanation—and so began the lifetime enquiry that spawned his psychoanalytic theory.

At first Freud's theories met with sharp opposition from the medical circle in Vienna, but soon after the turn of the century, a group of interested students gathered around Freud, a professional society was established, and the psychoanalytic movement had begun. It was well on its way when Freud lectured in America in 1910.

The circle that gathered around Freud found a leader who could sometimes be fierce and even tyrannical. When his students—such as Carl Jung, Alfred Adler, and Sandor Ferenczi—ventured to offer their own refinements and changes in the theory and techniques of psychoanalysis, Freud banished them. His fear was that the changes they made would dilute the power of the methods he had developed and would distort his theory.

Freud's later years were difficult, although he continued to write prodigiously and revise his own theory until his death in 1939. From 1923 he suffered from cancer of the jaw; the thirty-three operations he endured did not dull the almost continuous pain he suffered. Yet he was able to keep a sense of humor in adversity. When in 1933 the Nazis burned a pile of his books in Berlin, he commented, "What progress we are making. In the Middle Ages they would have burnt me, nowadays they are content with burning my books." ■

is situation-specific: it varies with the particular situational factors at hand. Mischel (1973; 1979) criticizes personality theories that propose that people have constant dispositions or traits. He points out that a person's behavior depends more on the specific situation in which it occurs than on enduring traits. Thus a person like Henry may be outgoing at work but shy at parties; it would be misleading to label him overall either "shy" or "outgoing."

Bem and Allen (1974), while recognizing the weaknesses of trait theories, note that traits can also have value in understanding a person's behavior. They have shown that people are actually highly consistent on traits that are more meaningful to them, and much less so on those that don't matter much to them. For example, someone who prided herself on her outgoing nature would be more likely to be sociable in most situations with other people. In short, for any given trait, only some people will behave consistently no matter what the situation. Those who do not consider the trait relevant will be far less consistent from situation to situation (Epstein, 1980).

SUMMARY

Personality is a difficult term to define. Some consider it an integrator, others consider it an index of adjustment, others the essence of a person. There is no universally accepted definition of "personality."

Freud's psychoanalytic theory. Psychoanalysis is both a theory of personality and a therapy. It assumes childhood experience to be the root of all emotional difficulties. A central conflict to be resolved in childhood is the Oedipus complex in boys or Electra complex in girls.

Freud's view of development is based on the motivating role of the libido. He identified five psychosexual stages of child development. Sometimes people remain fixated at one stage, or regress to a previous stage under stress.

Freud divided personality into three aspects— id, ego, and superego. The id is the impulsive, gratification-seeking, primitive, and almost totally unconscious aspect. The ego is a control system, aware of social demands and following the reality principle. The superego consists of internalized social values and rules; its influence is mostly unconscious. The ego employs several defense mechanisms to lessen conflict between id, superego, and the world.

Freud's followers. Jung rejected the libido as the prime motivator and the past as the proper focus of therapy. He divided the mind into conscious and unconscious, and proposed two aspects of the unconscious, the personal and the collective, which is the repository for universal archetypes. He typed people as introverts and extraverts, posited four basic psychological functions, and saw two stages of personality development, the biological and the spiritual. Overall, Jung's approach, analytical psychology, stressed the intellectual and the spiritual.

Adler emphasized social instincts, the will to power and the striving for superiority. He thought that behavior is motivated by an individual's goals. He viewed individual lifestyles as unique and unchanging, and proposed birth order as an important personality determinant.

The Neo-Freudians. Neo-Freudians modified Freudian theory, focusing on social and interpersonal aspects of personality.

Erikson accepted the importance of the sexual and aggressive drives, but emphasized ego identity. He divided ego development into eight psychosocial stages from birth through adulthood.

Horney rejected Freud's ideas about the libido and aggressive instincts, but accepted the concept of childhood trauma as a personality shaper. She described ten neurotic needs, expressed through one of three basic social strategies—moving toward people (helplessness), moving away from people (isolation), or moving against people (hostility). Horney saw a strong relationship between culture and neurosis.

Sullivan proposed a developmental theory based on key relationships in each stage. He saw personality changing throughout a person's lifetime.

Humanistic theories. Humanism stresses perceptions of the self and others and fulfillment of human potential.

In his theory of behavior, Rogers emphasized the self-concept and the individual's life-long striving for self-actualization.

Learning theories. Behaviorists explain personality in terms of the principles of learning. According to stimulus-response theory, most behavior can be understood in terms of learned stimulus-response connections involving drive, cue, response, and reward.

Skinner accounts for personality in terms of operant conditioning, and maintains that behavior is shaped by environment. Social learning theorists regard modeling and vicarious reinforcement as major shapers of personality. Self-efficacy, a sense of personal mastery, is a learned attitude that has many consequences throughout a person's life.

Type and trait theories. Trait theorists classify people in terms of enduring personality traits. According to Allport, a person's trait structure—the pool of traits that appear in the person in unique variations and combinations—determines behavior and personality.

Critics of trait theories point out that a person's traits may predict little of his behavior, which can vary greatly from situation to situation. The more meaningful a trait is to a person, the greater will be his consistency in displaying it.

GLOSSARY

Anal stage Freud: second psychosexual stage of personality development, when anal activities become pleasurable.

Archetypes Jung: universal thought forms or ideas genetically transmitted through the generations, residing in the collective unconscious.

Autonomy Sullivan: sense of one's own worth, independence, and identity.

Castration anxiety Freud: boy's fear that his father will cut off his penis unless he abandons his desire for his mother.

Collective unconscious Jung: repository of myths, beliefs, and archetypes from humankind's ancestral past.

Defense mechanisms Freud: techniques used unconsciously by the ego to ward off anxiety created by competing demands of id, superego, and outside world.

Denial Defense mechanism in which person acts as if an uncomfortable or upsetting experience did not occur.

Displacement Defense mechanism in which feelings are diverted from their original object to one that is similar but less threatening.

Ego Freud: the executive component of the personality; reconciles id, superego, and demands of outside world.

Ego-ideal Freud: aspect of the superego that reflects the kind of person an individual would like to be.

Ego identity Erikson: person's perception of himself and his place in the world.

Electra complex Freud: little girl desires her father and views her mother as a rival for his affection.

Extravert Jung: personality type characterized by outgoing, sociable, talkative, uninhibited behavior.

Fixation Freud: state in which a person's energies remain focused on activities appropriate to one of the early psychosexual stages because of unresolved problems.

Generativity Erikson: in a mature adult, the capacity to share what one has acquired and nurture others in their own personal growth.

Genital stage Freud: fifth psychosexual stage of personality development, in which the focus is on sexuality in healthy, overt heterosexual relationships.

Humanism Emphasis on the person's perceptions of self and others and potential for fulfillment in present and future.

Id Freud: primitive, impulsive, irrational, almost totally unconscious part of personality that seeks gratification for sexual and aggressive instincts.

Identity crisis Erikson: personal confusion, often in late adolescence, over who one really is and what one should strive to become in the years ahead.

Introvert Jung: personality type characterized by shy, quiet, inhibited behavior centered within the person.

Latency stage Freud: fourth psychosexual stage of personality development, in which the child's sexual urges are suppressed and libidinal energy is used to learn and explore.

Libido Freud: basic instinctual energy, sexual in nature and primarily directed toward obtaining satisfaction and pleasure.

Modeling Social learning theory: learning through imitation—process by which new responses are acquired through observing behavior of others.

Neurotic needs Horney: unsuccessful attempts to resolve life's conflicts, reflecting one of the three strategies of helplessness, isolation, or hostility.

Oedipus complex Freud: the universal phenomenon of male children between ages four and six developing a sexual interest in the mother and rivalry with the father.

Oral stage Freud: first psychosexual stage of personality development, in which most pleasurable activity is associated with the mouth.

Penis envy Freud: little girl's fear that her mother has already castrated her as retribution for her competitiveness for the father.

Persona Jung: public mask each person assumes to meet society's demands.

Personal unconscious Jung: submerged part of the ego consisting of repressed and forgotten material from personal experience.

Phallic stage Freud: third psychosexual stage of development, in which the sexual organs have primacy as a source of both pleasure and anxiety.

Pleasure principle Freud: child's concern with the immediate gratification of his desires.

Projection Defense mechanism in which a person attributes to others unacceptable impulses and disturbing characteristics that he himself possesses.

Psychoanalysis Freud's theory of personality and a form of therapy in which repressed motives emerge through free association.

Psychosocial stages Erikson: development periods in which a person must face and resolve distinct psychosocial issues, thereby shaping the personality.

Rationalization Defense mechanism in which a person protects his self-esteem with a "cover story," offering plausible and socially acceptable reasons for his behaviors.

Reaction formation Defense mechanism in which a person behaves exactly the opposite of his or her true inclinations.

Reality principle Freud: ability to delay pleasure to work toward certain goals, and to tolerate the resulting frustration.

Regression Freud: a person's reversion to an early psychosexual stage during stressful periods.

Repressed motives Freud: motives based on memories of traumatic experiences and infantile impulses that are submerged in a person's unconscious.

Repression Defense mechanism in which the energy and drives that would get a person into difficulty with society or would be upsetting are forced into the unconscious and allowed no expression.

Response hierarchies Stimulus-response theory: habitual ways of behaving in response to a variety of stimulus contexts.

Self-actualization Humanistic psychology: full functioning in which experiences and self-image are congruent, and a person is unafraid of experiences, fully aware of reality, and in harmony with others.

Self-efficacy Social learning theory: the learned belief in one's ability to cope with the demands of various situations.

Self theory Rogers: general theory of personality based on interrelationships between the organism, the self, and the phenomenal field.

Sublimation Defense mechanism in which sexual and aggressive impulses are transmuted into behavior that is completely desexualized, socially approved, and of value to society.

Superego Freud: part of personality consisting of internalized social values and rules; its influence is mostly unconscious.

Traits Allport: enduring personality characteristics.

Types Grouping of individuals into discrete categories according to various characteristics.

Vicarious reinforcement Social learning theory: principle that when a person sees others being reinforced for a certain behavior, the likelihood that he will perform that behavior increases.

Will to power Adler: need for power, one of the basic motives that shape personality.

15

ASSESSMENT: INTELLIGENCE AND PERSONALITY

COMMON MYTHS

MANY PEOPLE BELIEVE ...	ACTUALLY ...
Children's IQ scores have little to do with how well they do in school.	There is a strong relationship between IQ scores and school performance.
Very bright children tend to be less well-adjusted than those of average intelligence.	Bright children are, in general, at least as well adjusted as those of average intelligence.
Creative people are often insane.	There is no evidence for a link between creativity and madness.
A person's IQ does not change.	IQ scores for a given person can fluctuate from day to day or over a period of years.
A good psychologist can tell all about your hidden motives and fears just by talking with you.	Psychologists use many different tests to assess various aspects of personality that an interview alone would not reveal.

In some ways every person
Is like all other people;
Like some other people;
Like no other person.

ADAPTED FROM CLYDE KLUCKHOHN
AND HENRY MURRAY

As you look around the room on the first day of a new class, you study your classmates. The most immediately striking differences among them are physical. People vary in height, weight, body type, sex, and facial features; in the color of hair, eyes, and skin. But as the term goes on and you get to know people, other kinds of differences become obvious: they differ in personality, interests, intelligence, and motivation. These psychological attributes of the people in your class are far more telling than their appearance: they reveal what is unique about them, what may draw you to them or leave you cold, intrigue you or turn you off.

Psychological tests evaluate such attributes by measuring a sample of behavior (Anastasi, 1976). Psychological tests must be judged by unbiased criteria so that they can be scored accurately, and results must be able to be compared from one person to another.

RELIABILITY AND VALIDITY

Imagine that you're taking a civil service exam for a job opening with the city as a part-time supervisor at a recreation center. The exam seems pretty easy: it asks general questions, and you finish quickly. You think you have a good chance for the job.

Three days later you get a postcard from the city notifying you that you passed the first screening and should take another exam.

When you go for your second test, you expect it to be as easy as the first. But you're dismayed to find it's nothing like the previous one—it's much harder, and asks lots of questions about sports, games, and child development that you haven't even a guess for. ■

Which test was the better one? From the city's point of view, the second test is the more useful: it is probably better able to place people more precisely on a particular continuum—in this case, people's qualifications as a recreation supervisor.

Reliability refers to the consistency of a test. One measure of reliability is *test-retest reliability*, the extent to which repeating the test on two occasions gives the same results. Suppose you had been given the same test the second time as the first. You would probably have done better on it simply because the first testing would have given you a chance to practice. To avoid this problem in retesting, two other ways of evaluating test reliability have been devised. In the *split-half* approach, the test is divided into two parts. A person's score on odd-numbered items of the test, for example, is compared with his or her score on even-numbered items on the same test. The second approach is to develop *alternate forms*, two or more versions of the same test in which each version is equivalent to but different from the other.

The *validity* of a test is the extent to which it measures what it is intended to measure. Validity can be determined by correlation, a statistical procedure that shows the degree to which one variable is related to another. A test's validity is high if test scores correlate well with a *criterion*, or standard for judgment. The criterion might be whether people who did well on the civil service test also performed well as recreation supervisors. When a test has high correlations between its scores and the criterion, then it has high *predictive validity*—it foretells accurately how a person will perform or behave.

INTELLIGENCE TESTS

Imagine that your friend Mark is an electronics whiz. In junior high he built his own stereo from scratch; in high school he concocted a computer.

But when he took an intelligence test for his high school guidance counselor, the results were average, and the counselor actually tried to discourage him from applying to college. ■

Your friend the electronics whiz has a talent that many intelligence tests might fail to measure. They usually assess a person's verbal and mathematical skills, but a creative genius in a field like electronics may have another kind of intelligence: the ability to visualize a creative mental image (Shepard and Meltzer, 1971). At best, only one part of most intelligence tests would measure this ability. The emphasis on verbal and mathematical skills in intelligence testing goes back to their historical beginnings.

The Binet tests

It was the famous French psychologist Alfred Binet who, around the turn of the century, stressed the importance of such aspects of intelligence as memory for short sentences, attention, reasoning, and other cognitive processes, including the ability to learn. In his tests, he tried to touch on all these areas. The intelligence test that resulted was extremely successful, and Binet's approach has been in use ever since.

In 1908, Binet introduced the concept of *mental age*, the average age at which subjects can answer a question or master a problem at a certain level of difficulty. For example, an eight-year-old who can master problems of the same difficulty as those mastered by the average twelve-year-old has a mental age of twelve.

Later, Wilhelm Stern, a German psychologist, suggested that intelligence be defined as the ratio of a person's mental age (MA) to his chronological age (CA). He called this ratio the *intelligence quotient (IQ)*:

$$IA = \frac{MA}{CA} \times 100$$

The ratio is multiplied by 100 simply to eliminate decimal points. The IQ of an eight-year-old with

"I have an enormous I.Q."

Drawing by Barsotti; © The New Yorker Magazine, Inc.

the problem-solving ability of a twelve-year-old would be calculated as

$$IQ = \frac{12}{8} = 1.50 \times 100 = 150$$

The IQ of a person who was actually twelve years old and passed the questions for the twelve-year-old level would be calculated as

$$IQ = \frac{12}{12} = 1.00 \times 100 = 100$$

An IQ of 100 thus becomes average, with IQs above 100 indicative of above-average intelligence and those below 100 of less than average intelligence. Although a child's mental age normally increases with chronological age, eventually a point is reached beyond which no further increase occurs. For adults, the age of sixteen is used as the maximum chronological age.

The Wechsler scales

During the late 1930s, David Wechsler, a clinical psychologist working with adult patients at Bellevue Hospital in New York City, developed an intelligence test for adults. The current version is

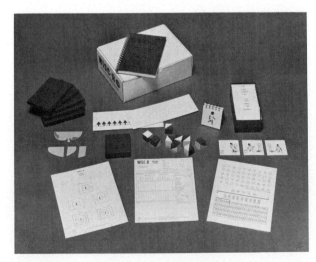

The WISC is an intelligence test designated for young children. It assesses their level of competence at a range of tasks, each reflecting a different type of intellectual skill. (Courtesy, The Psychological Corporation)

TABLE 15.1 **IQ CLASSIFICATIONS**

IQ	Classification	Percentage of people at each level
over 139	very superior	1
120–139	superior	11
110–119	high average	18
90–109	average	46
80–89	low average	15
70–79	borderline	6
below 70	mentally retarded	3

called the Wechsler Adult Intelligence Scale (WAIS). In the late 1940s, Wechsler developed the Wechsler Intelligence Scale for Children (WISC), an IQ test tailored for use with young children (see Tables 15.1 and 15.2).

To Wechsler, the concept of intelligence encompasses more than scholastic aptitude, which he considers to be merely the capacity to do schoolwork. Indeed, he was the first theorist to propose that intelligence involves some nonintellectual functions. He pointed out that two people can have the same test scores, but that one may be able to cope much more effectively with the demands of life than the other (Edwards, 1971). Given this orientation, it is not surprising that Wechsler defines intelligence in more general terms than most theorists. In his view, intelligence is "the aggregate or global capacity of the

TABLE 15.2 **SUBTYPES OF MENTAL RETARDATION**
The main disability in mental retardation is the excruciating slowness with which the retarded person struggles to learn. Those in the "mild" range are educable, and by late teens can master academic skills up to about the sixth grade; those in the severe and profound categories most often need total care.

Subtypes	IQ Levels
mild	50–70
moderate	35–49
severe	20–34
profound	below 20

individual to act purposefully, to think rationally, and to deal effectively with his environment" (Matarazzo, 1972).

In addition to verbal tests, the Wechsler scales include performance tests. In one performance test, the subject is presented with pieces of a disjointed object; the task is to put them together as rapidly as possible, thus forming the object. For another test, the subject is asked to arrange pictures in an order that tells a story. No words are necessary on either of these tests. Since the performance tests don't require spoken language, they allow the use of the Wechsler tests with the hearing-impaired or with non-English-speaking people.

Imagine that the morning you're due to take the Scholastic Aptitude Test (SAT), you come down with the flu. Weak, bleary-eyed, and aching, you bravely sit through the exam. When your scores come, they're disappointingly low. You immediately sign up to take them the next time they're scheduled. ■

Fluctuations in intelligence

People's intelligence, as tested at various points in their lives, can fluctuate. Temporary fluctuations—for example, factors such as anxiety or illness—can artificially lower IQ scores. Intelligence fluctuations seem to reflect broader changes in a person's life. For example, there are general trends in mental growth, with a period of rapid intellectual growth in childhood, slowing its rate during adolescence, peaking in early adulthood, and then showing slight decreases in some areas after the middle adult years (Brown, 1970). There are, of course, exceptions, both "late bloomers" and "early wilters."

Highly intelligent and well-educated people seem to maintain or increase their intellectual abilities over a longer period of their lives. But even among the highly intelligent, continued intellectual stimulation enhances intelligence later in life. A group of children who at around age twelve all had IQs of 135 and above were tested again in

their forties. Those who had continued their education longer (e.g., getting advanced degrees) had higher intelligence scores as adults (Sears, 1977).

Because intelligence can vary in a person from age to age, the capacity that intelligence tests measure does not seem to be the meaningful index it was originally hoped to be. Stability in intelligence in part reflects a relatively constant environment. The greatest changes in intelligence occur with the largest variations in experience. For instance, studies during the 1930s indicated that the IQ scores of children reared in barren orphanages tended to decrease. When similar children from the same institutions were placed in family homes, they showed remarkable increases in intelligence. Studies of this sort showed that a person's environment could affect IQ.

Today we know that injury, illness, severe emotional upset, or unstimulating family and social conditions may stunt the growth of intelligence or cause it to decrease. On the other hand, health, intellectual stimulation, or the relief of emotional conflicts can foster an increase in IQ—particularly during childhood, its period of most rapid change.

For several years educators have been bemoaning the decline of high school students' SAT scores (and, by implication, their IQs, which seem to have been dropping steadily since the early 1960s). Much has been made of the role of television in blunting the desire to read, the drive to create, even the ability to think. The permissiveness and antiintellectualism of the sixties have come in for their share of criticism. Some have blamed the tests themselves.

Undoubtedly there are kernels of truth in these explanations, but the root of the problem may well be a simpler one. Zajonc (1976) indicated that the intelligence of an individual is affected by the size of her family and by the order of her birth into the family. The higher both numbers, the lower the IQ (see Figure 15.1). This effect tends to be lessened when the births are widely spaced.

Zajonc proposes that the total intellectual environment of a household can be determined by summing and then averaging the intellectual level of all its members. Assigning adult parents an arbitrary thirty units, and a newborn zero, a first child would be born into an intellectual environ-

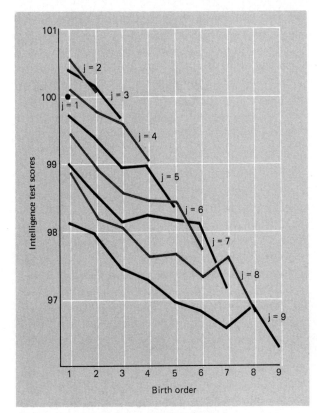

Figure 15.1 Family size and intelligence

Scores on an intelligence test vary with the size of a child's family, as well as a child's order of birth. The children born earlier tend to have higher scores than those born later; children in larger families tend to have lower scores than those in smaller families. The figure displays scores according to both birth order and family size. "J" indicates the number of siblings in a family. (From Zajonc and Markus, 1975)

ment of twenty units [(30 + 30 + 0) ÷ 3]. A second child, born when the first had attained a level of, say, four units, has an intellectual environment of only sixteen units [(30 + 30 + 4 + 0) ÷ 4]. A fifth child's environment would obviously be a great deal more intellectually impoverished.

The students whose SAT scores have been the focus of concern turn out to be the children of the baby boom that began in the late forties and continued to produce relatively large families into the early sixties (Zajonc and Bargh, 1980). By 1980 or so, the children of the smaller families that became typical after 1963 will be taking their SATs. Zajonc's prediction, already supported by the results of tests given these children in grade and junior high school, is that the scores will show an upward swing.

Imagine that your friend Mark, the electronics whiz, took his counselor's advice and did not go to college.

Now, you've just heard, he's become the vice president for research and development of the electronics firm he joined straight out of high school. ■

Intelligence and success

Do intelligence tests predict how successful a person will be throughout life? The evidence is mixed. Intelligence tests seem fairly adequate predictors of academic success, although variables other than intelligence are quite important in determining academic success too. A person with average intelligence who works very hard can get better grades than a person with above average intelligence who goofs off.

A group of 1,500 children with IQs that average about 150 have been followed for over fifty years, first by Lewis Terman, who designed the Stanford-Binet test, then by Robert Sears (1977). When, as adults, the records of the 150 most successful (in terms of career and income) and 150 least successful were compared, both groups were found to have the same average IQ, near 150. Thus IQ alone does not determine success; if it did, the more successful group should have had significantly higher average IQs. The critical difference between the groups seems to have been the need to achieve (Odem, 1968). Members of the successful group were more ambitious, even as children; they felt more parental pressure to get better grades, finish school quickly, and go to college. The ambition and drive of the successful group proved to be a constant theme throughout their lives, while the unsuccessful group, though of equal intelligence, was lacking in the drive (Goleman, 1980).

When people finish school and set out on their careers, then, achievement depends on many factors other than those measured by IQ tests. Christopher Jencks (1979) examined the social factors that positively influence success (as measured here by earnings and occupational status). In a national survey, the factors that were related to success included finishing college, family background, and having leadership skills (Jencks, 1979).

Because the factors that lead to later success are more complex than a single IQ score can predict, David McClelland (1973) has proposed that IQ tests be abandoned altogether. In their place he proposes substituting "competence tests," measures of performance skills and personality traits that are necessary in various occupations (McClelland and Boyatzis, 1980). McClelland notes that while IQ and achievement test scores predict school grades well, there is little relation between grades in school and occupational success. An alternative approach to testing that would predict occupational success is *criterion sampling*, a measure of the actual skills involved. Thus, if you want to know how well a person can drive a car (the criterion), give her a driving test, not a written test of general intelligence.

THE IQ CONTROVERSY

Early in this century, when intelligence tests were developed, psychologists thought intelligence was an inborn capacity that remained at a permanent level from infancy to adulthood. Some people were by birth brilliant; others would be dim-witted no matter what happened. For this reason, mentally retarded people were relegated to huge custodial institutions—human dustbins. But when retarded children were placed in enriched settings, their scores on intelligence tests often improved markedly. The view that intelligence is determined solely by nature—by a person's inborn endowments—had to be changed. Nurture—the experiences a person has throughout life—also clearly affects intelligence.

The battle over the heritability of intelligence has been going on ever since Galton (1869) found that the height of children was related to that of their parents and then went on to claim that nearly all psychological traits, including intelligence, are inherited. His emphasis on the inheritance of intelligence was criticized, of course, because the gifted people he studied were also from well-to-do

families and had been given great educational and cultural advantages.

More than a century later, the debate continues. Consider, for example, the following set of hypothetical statements. Would you consider them true or false?

1. If differences in mental abilities are inherited, and

2. if success requires superior mental abilities, and

3. if earnings and prestige depend on success, then

4. social standing will be based to some extent on inherited differences among people.

These statements, formulated by Richard Herrnstein (1971), constitute a valid hypothetical argument. Consequently, if the premises (the "if" statements) are true, then the conclusion (the "then" statement) must also be true.

If mental abilities such as intelligence are largely inherited, then, Herrnstein argues, following premises (2) and (3), the United States will become more and more of a meritocracy, with intelligence constituting the merit. Selected by intelligence tests and advanced by scholastic achievement, the successful people in all our cultural institutions will be the most intelligent and will ultimately rule society. Ours will be a caste system based on level of intelligence.

But are the premises of Herrnstein's arguments true? The truth or falsity of his first premise— that "differences in mental abilities are inherited"—is the subject of heated debate.

One educational psychologist who argues for the heritability of intelligence is Arthur Jensen. On the basis of results gathered from many studies of intelligence, Jensen infers that differences in IQ scores between blacks and whites, as well as between poorer whites and those from higher socioeconomic levels in our society, are genetically based. According to Jensen, about the same difference in average intelligence holds between poor whites and well-to-do whites as holds between whites and blacks. He argues that a genetic difference accounts for the apparent failure of special education programs to equalize the average IQ differences between whites and blacks as well as between whites of lower and upper socioeconomic levels (Jensen, 1973).

Jensen's position has been attacked on many grounds. Another survey of research on intelligence by Jencks (1972) concluded that it is only

CYRIL BURT'S IQ FRAUD

■ In the heredity-versus-environment debate, the work of Cyril Burt, the highly respected "father of educational psychology," has had a profound impact. His studies, several of them regarded as classics, provided what—until recently—many considered unassailable support for the theory that intelligence is determined chiefly by genetics.

Burt's career began in 1912, when he was appointed educational psychologist—the world's first—to London's schools. He held the post for twenty years. Later, in the 1930s and 1940s, as an educational adviser to the government, he was instrumental in setting up the "three-tier" system used throughout British schools: at the age of eleven, all children are permanently assigned, on the basis of their IQ scores, to one of three levels of coursework. Only the top-tier students have a good chance of getting a university education.

His best-known publications were a series of reports on sets of identical twins who had been reared apart from one another in sharply dissimilar environments. Burt wrote that, despite the differences in their upbringing, each pair of twins had remarkably similar IQs. In another study he presented the results of tests conducted on 40,000 fathers and sons in a typical London borough. The correlation between the level of the subjects' socioeconomic status and the level of their IQs was, Burt reported, very close. The poor had low IQs, the rich high ones. Burt used the results of these two studies to support his class-biased three-tier educational system.

In 1946 Burt was knighted—the first psychologist ever to receive that honor. Though the controversy he generated was fierce indeed, his defense of his work was equally fierce, and during his lifetime no one questioned the validity of his data—at least not publicly.

But in 1972 Leon Kamin read one of Burt's papers for the first time. Kamin's reaction: "The immediate conclusion I came to after ten minutes of reading was that Burt was a fraud." Closer examination of Burt's work revealed telling peculiarities. For example, Kamin found that the study of separated twins, published in three reports over a period of eleven years, with an increasing sample size each time, gave the correlation between the IQ scores of the pairs of twins as 0.771 each time—a wildly improbable consistency. There were other, similar coincidences. Kamin (1974) also noted a certain vagueness throughout Burt's writings: basic pieces of information like sex and age of subjects, identification of tests used, and so on, were frequently omitted.

Other inquiries into the validity of Burt's findings turned up further irregularities. D. D. Dorfman (1978) reanalyzed the statistics that Burt had used. Dorfman demonstrated that instead of testing his subjects, Burt had simply chosen numbers from a bell curve and assigned them to the "appropriate members of various social classes."

It seems clear now that the fabrication of data was Burt's general practice during a large part of his career (Samelson, 1980). Has the exposure of this fraud caused the collapse of the hereditarian viewpoint? Arthur Jensen of the University of California, whose article on race and IQ sparked a furor in 1969, thinks it has not. "This doesn't change my position at all," said Jensen (1978). "We now have a considerable amount of other data that support the heritability of IQ."

In 1980 Jensen published a massively detailed review of the topic in support of his—and Burt's—view. Nevertheless few psychologists share his view that blacks are by heredity less intelligent than whites. As Gould (1980) points out in a careful assessment of Jensen's latest book, Jensen has made fundamental mistakes in his reasoning, such as assuming that differences in IQ scores between blacks and whites are necessarily due to heredity, rather than differences in upbringing, nutrition, or other such factors. "The copious citation of numbers cannot salvage an argument grounded on invalid premises," Gould concludes. ■

minimally inherited from parents, environment having much more weight than genes. To explain the social and racial differences in success, Jencks contends that it is more useful to look at social factors in people's backgrounds then genetic factors. In a later survey, Jencks found that family background—including father's occupation and income, parents' education, and race or ethnic group—accounted for job success better than intelligence (Jencks, *et al.*, 1979). Jencks' conclusions challenge Herrnstein's second premise, that success requires superior mental abilities. Jencks also questions Jensen's conclusions that the failure of remedial education programs is due to racial and social differences in IQ; the reason they fail, says Jencks, is that they do nothing to change the financial and social inequities in students' family backgrounds, thus doing nothing to remedy these strong social handicaps.

Most opponents of Jensen—including Jencks—concede that intelligence is determined to some extent by heredity. The issue is how much by environment, how much by genes (Gould, 1980). If the amount contributed by heredity is high, then the intellectual destiny of people is mostly fixed at birth. There is little that can be done to improve their lot, and inequities in academic achievement, job status, and pay, for example, can be attributed to lower intelligence, rather than other social factors. If environment accounts for more than heredity, though, then social factors—like poverty and prejudice—can be seen to be holding people back from potential accomplishments.

Perhaps the most telling rebuttal to Jensen is the study by Scarr and Weinberg (1976) of transracial adoptees—130 black children adopted by well-to-do white families. They found that these black adoptees, whose natural parents had average educations, scored above the average IQ and school achievement level of both black *and* white children. The conclusion: given better rearing conditions, disadvantaged blacks can do much better on IQ scores. Scarr and Weinberg (1979) accept estimates that the heritability of intelligence is somewhere between 40 and 70 percent. But the variation that matters, they conclude, is social environment.

They further point out that, while genetics has a strong model of how characteristics are transmitted through genes from one generation to the next, there is no comparable model for environmental transmission. Yet all that we learn is transmitted to us through the environment. It stands to reason that, for example, the habits that lead a child to do well in school and on tests could be, in part, handed down from parent to child. To say, then, that intelligence "runs in the family" could refer to the social transmission of traits, not genetic transmission.

ACHIEVEMENT AND APTITUDE TESTS

Imagine that you're trying to fulfill a language requirement in Spanish without having to take the course. You sign up for an achievement exam in Spanish, and spend a few days brushing up on your high school course in it. When you get your test score back, it's only 450, too low to fulfill the requirement.

The next term you take Spanish. If you pass a full year of Spanish, the requirement is fulfilled.

But after just one semester you decide to try the achievement exam again.

This time it works: you get 630, well above passing. ■

Achievement and aptitude

For any given skill or ability we can distinguish between people's achievement and their aptitude. The Spanish tests measured your *achievement*, the level of performance you attained at a given level of training. Achievement tests cover a wide variety of subjects, and are used to assess knowledge and skills needed in many occupations.

Your general knack for learning languages is your *aptitude*, your potential capacity to master the skills involved before receiving specific training. The potential for certain skills is measured by intelligence tests and by exams such as the Scholastic Aptitude Test (SAT). Other tests measure mechanical, clerical, musical, and a host of other aptitudes.

THE CREATIVE PERSONALITY

■ What's your image of a creative person? Are creative people highly intelligent, like an Einstein? Are they mad, like a van Gogh? Such common impressions of the personalities of creative geniuses do not seem to be founded in fact.

MacKinnon (1962), who has carried on creativity research at the Institute of Personality Assessment and Research at the University of California, Berkeley, reports that beyond a required minimum level of intelligence there is no correlation between intelligence and creativity, except in mathematicians. He tested architects, creative writers, engineers, industrial researchers, mathematicians, and physical scientists. Another study offers evidence that, at least in school children, "creativity is a different type of cognitive excellence than general intelligence" (Wallach and Kogan, 1965).

Cronbach (1970) views the findings on intelligence and creativity in a somewhat different light, suggesting that the dutiful learning of school lessons may be incompatible with a free-ranging intellect. Below the IQ level of 120, suggests Cronbach, intelligence and creativity seem to go together, but above it the two are not necessarily related.

Apart from intelligence, though, there seems to be a constellation of psychological traits that characterize creative people. The first is their relative openness to both internal and external stimuli. People who are creative are less controlled, repressed, and defensive than others. And though they may seem disturbed and withdrawn during their creative work, they are not pathologically so (Barron, 1963). There is no evidence to support the claim that a link exists between madness and creative ability. On the contrary, creative people seem to have the patience and strength to give significant form to their work and to react to problems in a constructive way.

Creative people also tend to be independent in their attitudes and social behavior; their strong sense of their own identity and their self-acceptance permit them to disregard the reactions of others. They are further distinguished from others by their interests, attitudes, and drives. Although they are in frequent and perhaps necessary conflict with the status quo, creative people are nonetheless able to express themselves in fresh and significant ways in whatever sphere of human activity they may be immersed (Dellas and Gaier, 1970). ■

sample of creativity. Perhaps it is for these reasons that most tests of creativity are constructed, instead, to measure divergent thinking.

Divergent thinking is required in a testing situation when there are many possible solutions to a problem and the best one must eventually be chosen. Divergent thinking requires more fluency and flexibility than convergent thinking; it demands a free flow of ideas of the kind also called for in "brainstorming," an activity in which any and all ideas are encouraged. Tests of divergent thinking seem to come closer to measuring creative ability than tests of convergent thinking.

PERSONALITY ASSESSMENT

Imagine that you're at the bank because you've overdrawn your account. You've already deposited a check that should cover the overdraft, but it hasn't cleared yet. You're a bit nervous about asking them to cover your overdraft until your deposit clears.

As you approach the tellers' windows you see three lines. The teller at the first line is an older woman who has been gruff with you in the past. The one at the second window is a young man who seems surly and unfriendly. But the teller at the third window is a young woman who seems sympathetic and warm. You get in her line. ■

We all make such off-the-cuff readings of people's personalities in our daily lives. Whether it's guessing the traits of a bank teller, professor, or blind date, we can't help but form impressions of other people's personalities. Sometimes the accuracy of your impression doesn't matter much—say whether the waitress in a coffee shop is really sullen. Sometimes it can be very important, as when you're trying to decide if a prospective employer would be fair and interesting to work for or when you meet someone you might become romantically involved with.

The assessment methods that psychologists use to gauge personality are designed to give more ob-

jective and reliable evaluations than our ordinary impressions allow. There are two main ways to measure personality. In the direct method the psychologist uses objectively scored techniques to evaluate the person's behavior. This method includes questionnaires and self-rating scales. The indirect method uses projective techniques to probe unconscious factors in personality. A person often is unable or unwilling to directly report this kind of information, so psychologists use unstructured, ambiguous material such as perceptions of inkblots to observe how the person responds. The person's perceptions and interpretations reveal unconscious motivations and hidden personality structures.

Quickly read the following adjectives and put an X in the box beside each one that you consider describes yourself. Be frank—check those adjectives that describe you as you really are, not as you would like to be:

☐ absentminded	☐ wholesome
☐ active	☐ wise
☐ adaptable	☐ withdrawn
☐ adventurous	☐ witty
☐ affected	☐ worrying
☐ affectionate	☐ zany

Objective techniques

This is a sample of items from Harrison Gough's Adjective Check List, a booklet containing three hundred adjectives. Listed in alphabetical order, from "absentminded" to "zany," the sample includes words that would likely be used to describe a person. Such self-ratings are a simple, direct way to assess personality traits. Adjective check lists and self-rating scales reveal your own idea of what you are like. Because both desirable and undesirable traits are included in the list or scale, your self-concept can be measured quite readily—providing you are honest.

Such rating scales are frequently used by one person to rate the personality of another. Supervisors, for example, might use such a scale to rate employees. This kind of rating, however, is susceptible to *rater bias:* if the rater likes the person, he or she may stress good qualities and overlook less attractive ones. If the rater dislikes the person, the reverse can happen. The result is a "halo effect," where a positive (or negative) rating on one factor, such as sociability, spills over as a generalized positive (or negative) rating on other traits.

Personality inventories are questionnaires that provide a whole profile of several traits. The profile for a given person is given by comparing him or her on a variety of traits with norms for each that are based on results from giving the same test to large groups of people. The most widely used personality inventory is the Minnesota Multiphasic Personality Inventory, or MMPI. The MMPI measures a person's relative standing on a variety of psychiatric classifications. There are thirteen scales on the MMPI, the first four of which assess any factors that might invalidate or distort a person's reply. These include a scale that reveals a person faking responses to look good, and another that shows if a person is careless in answering questions. The remaining nine scales rate the person on traits related to abnormal behavior, such as hypochondria, or anxiety over health; depression, or feelings of worthlessness; paranoia, or delusions of persecution; schizophrenia, or bizarre thoughts and hallucinations; and mania, or emotional excitability.

The 550 statements on the MMPI, to which a person responds "true" or "false," include "I worry about sex matters," "I believe people are plotting to get me," and "I sometimes think about things that are best kept to myself." While the response to any particular item may not reveal much about a person, the responses to clusters of items can. Norms for item clusters have been established for large numbers of normal people and psychiatric patients, and a person's rating for each of these is compared to these norms. On any given item, for example, 90 percent of paranoids might indicate agreement, whereas only 10 percent of normal people will. For the person who answers "true," this response becomes part of the paranoid cluster.

Mark "true" next to those statements with which you agree, and "false" next to those with which you disagree:

TRUE	FALSE	
____	____	1. I enjoy social gatherings just to be with people.
____	____	2. The only interesting part of the newspaper is the "funnies."
____	____	3. I looked up to my father as an ideal man.
____	____	4. A person needs to "show off" a little now and then.
____	____	5. I have a very strong desire to be a success in the world.
____	____	6. When in a group of people I usually do what the others want rather than make suggestions.
____	____	7. I doubt whether I would make a good leader.
____	____	8. I tend to be on my guard with people who are somewhat more friendly than I had expected.
____	____	9. Usually I would prefer to work with women.

These items are randomly taken from the California Psychological Inventory, another widely used personality questionnaire. It includes in its 480 true-false statements many items similar to those on the MMPI, but was designed to assess normal personality traits rather than the pathological ones the MMPI examines. The traits measured by the CPI are those that we all have to some degree—sociability, dominance, self-control, self-acceptance, responsibility, and flexibility, among others.

Projective techniques

A projective test presents an ambiguous stimulus to which a person may respond with whatever perceptions and thoughts come to mind. The stimulus is vague and unstructured and so does not have a specific, correct response, and thus the person *projects* his or her personality in the responses given.

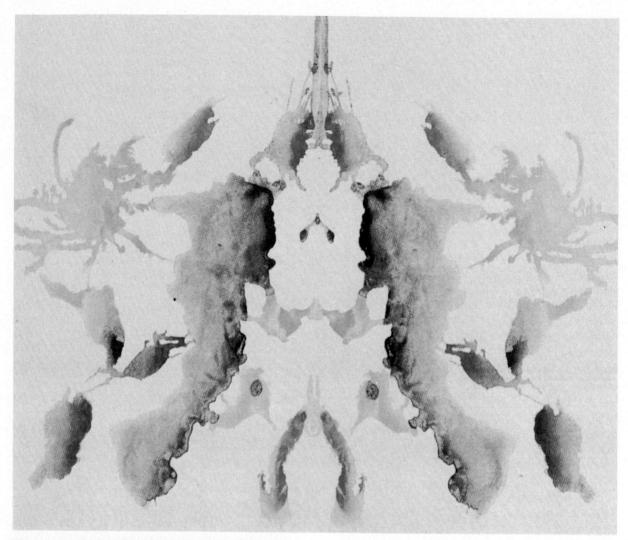

Figure 15.3 An inkblot used in the Rorschach test
The subject is asked to look at the inkblot and tell the examiner what he or she sees.

Projective tests elicit a person's projections, and then interpret them to assess unconscious aspects of personality. The *Rorschach test* is the best known and probably the most widely used projective technique. Developed in 1921 by Hermann Rorschach, a Swiss psychiatrist, the test consists of ten inkblot cards, some black and white and some multicolored. One is shown in Figure 15.3.

If you were to take a Rorschach test, you would be presented with the blots, one at a time, and asked to say what each one reminded you of, what

it looked like or could be. Because the blots are vague and indefinite, you would project aspects of yourself into your interpretations of them.

Look carefully at the picture on the next page, and make up a short story about it. What is happening? What led up to it? How will it turn out?

This picture is from the Thematic Apperception Test, or TAT, devised in 1935 by Christina Morgan and Henry A. Murray. (The personality assessment version of the TAT includes different pictures than the version used to measure motiva-

Figure 15.4 One of the pictures in the Thematic Apperception Test (TAT)
What is happening in the picture? What are the circumstances that have led up to this scene? How will the situation turn out? Subjects taking the TAT are asked to consider questions such as these.

tion, discussed in Chapter 9.) Each picture is purposely ambiguous, so that a person is free to interpret imaginatively what is happening. The TAT consists of four series of twenty pictures—for boys, girls, men, and women. The first picture in the series for boys, for example, shows a boy sitting at a table staring at a violin. The examinee is asked to make up a story about each picture, focusing on what led up to the present scene, what the person in the picture is thinking, feeling, and doing, and how the story will end. The assumption is that the storyteller identifies with the central figure in his tale and so through fantasy reveals a great deal about his own personal psychodynamics.

In the *word association test*, a person says the first word that comes to mind in response to a cue word. Originated by Carl Jung, the procedure is quite simple. If you were to take this test, you would listen while the examiner said a word; then you would give your immediate association with that word. For example, if she said "man," you might respond with "woman" or "friendly" or "kill" or any word that occurred to you. The speed of your reaction would be recorded, as well as the word itself, since being slow to respond indicates a significant emotional topic or area; later, the associations you made would be analyzed for content to identify your particular personality traits.

Drawing techniques require that the subject draw a picture, instead of asking her or him, as most tests do, to respond either verbally or in writing. In the most commonly used method, you might be presented with a pencil and a sheet of pa-

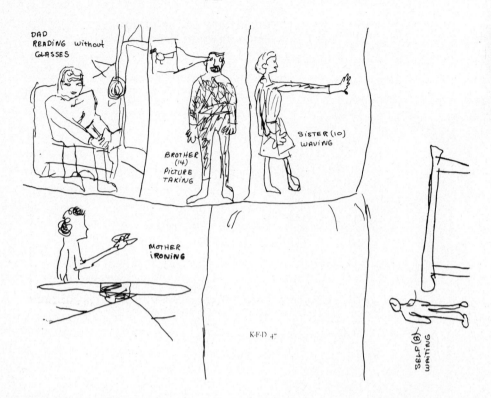

DAD READING without GLASSES

BROTHER (14) PICTURE TAKING

SISTER (10) WAVING

MOTHER IRONING

K·F·D 4˥

SELF (8) WAITING

Figure 15.5 An example of a child's drawing of his family from the Kinetic Family Drawings test

per and simply told to "draw a person." The psychologist would then analyze your drawing for such things as the sex, age, and size of the person you drew. She would note missing or accentuated parts of the body as well as the expression on the face and type of clothing, analyzing these simple drawings for such things as anxiety, aggression, sexual identification, and overall self-concept.

There are several variations of the draw-a-person procedure. Kinetic Family Drawings, where the subject is asked to "draw a family doing something," reveal information about family relationships. Child therapists who work with this test have found that there are certain recurring themes. Children who feel isolated will typically draw family members doing things alone in separate rooms, and in the drawings of children who feel neglected, the parents are generally busy going about their business—the mother cleaning house, perhaps, the father driving off to work. One seven-year-old clearly revealed his Oedipal fantasies when he drew himself as a boat, speeding through the water, dragging his mother—na-

ked—behind him. He used the back of the paper to draw his father, saving the whole front page for himself and his mother. Drawing tests are usually interpreted clinically to understand a person's psychodynamics.

Drawbacks of projective tests

Mischel (1977) points out that situational variables have not been given due consideration in using projective tests to predict behavior. His point is that behavior is specific to situations and that a person's responses even in highly similar situations are often quite different. Thus to expect responses to a projective test to be able to predict a person's behavior in a very different situation is quite unrealistic. According to this view, much more attention must be paid to the specifics of the social situation in which testing takes place.

Some studies have found a strong association between personality, as revealed by projective tests, and actual behavior in everyday life. Others,

however, have not (Anastasi, 1976). In any case, many psychologists maintain that this is beside the point: projective tests are designed not to predict behavior but to reveal a person's fantasies, conflicts, and unconscious processes.

The major disadvantages of projective tests are that they are time-consuming to administer and score, and require a highly trained psychologist to analyze the findings. And many studies have found these tests to have low reliability and validity (Anastasi, 1976). Nevertheless, projective tests continue to be widely used as tools in clinical assessment. Their reliability and validity seem to depend to a large degree on the skills of their interpreter.

BEHAVIOR ASSESSMENT

Imagine that you're applying for a managerial training job with a large corporation. The interview seems to be going well. The interviewer has offered you a cigarette, and you're starting to feel more relaxed as you smoke it.

You're about to flick the ashes, when you notice something: there's no ashtray in the room.

What do you do? ■

The interviewer may be watching to see exactly what the answer to that question will be. How you handle this minor situation may give her clues to

THE BARNUM EFFECT

■ Suppose an astrologer offered to do your horoscope for you. After finding out the exact time, date, and place of your birth, the astrologer would then plot the configuration of stars in the sky at the moment you were born, and then assess their influence in forming your personality. You might get back an astrological interpretation of your personality that reads something like this:

You have a great need for other people to like you and admire you. You have a tendency to be critical of yourself. You have a great deal of unused capacity that you have not turned to your advantage. While you have some personality weaknesses, you are generally able to compensate for them. Your sexual adjustment has presented problems for you. Disciplined and self-controlled outside, you tend to be worrisome and insecure inside. At times you have serious doubts as to whether you have made the right decision or done the right thing.

If you find this a fairly accurate portrayal of your own personality, it has nothing to do with your horoscope. This is a portion of a personality sketch that was used in a study of people's tendency to accept as true an assessment supposedly based on psychological tests they took.

When a group of college students completed a personality test, and then a week later received this sketch (which was supposedly derived from their results) they almost universally judged the interpretation to be an accurate portrayal of their own personalities (Forer, 1949). This common tendency to accept as true ambiguous statements that are supposedly based on personality tests is called the "Barnum effect," after the circus promoter P. T. Barnum (remembered for his famous saying "There's a sucker born every minute").

The last three decades have seen numerous studies of the Barnum effect, most of which have used the same procedure: subjects complete a personality test, then wait while the test is supposedly scored. They then receive an interpretation of their personality, purportedly based on the test they took, but actually the same for everyone. The subjects then rate how accurately they feel the interpretation fits their own personality (Snyder, Shenkel, and Lowery, 1977).

There is no single profile of the "gullible" person. Most people see global, ambiguous, Barnum-type descriptions as fitting them, and believe that the in-

many aspects of your personality and behavior relevant to the job you're applying for: how you react to stress, your social skills in an awkward situation, your poise or lack of it. This approach is typical of *behavior assessment*, the direct observation of how a person behaves in real-life situations.

Situational assessment

One standard technique of behavior assessment is the *situational test*, where a person is placed in a specially created situation and his or her behavior

observed in it. One of the best known situational tests was first described by Henry A. Murray, who directed the assessment staff of the Office of Strategic Services (OSS) during World War II. Murray and his staff conducted intensive psychological assessments of OSS candidates, since these men were to be assigned risky and important missions. The men took a battery of intelligence, personality, and achievement tests, and they were also subjected to situational tests, designed to study their ability to function under conditions of frustration and stress.

One situational test paired each candidate with two companions. The three men were given the

terpretation was written just for them. They fail to realize it fits just about everyone.

In fact, subjects not only accept Barnum interpretations, but even increase their faith in the skill of the people who give them.

Certain features make people most disposed to accept a Barnum interpretation; for example, it should be brief and ambiguous. It should not name ways in which the person differs from most other people. Not surprisingly, it helps if the interpretation reflects positively on the person who receives it (Snyder and Cowles, 1979).

Some researchers feel that Barnum-type personality assessments are particularly apt to be accepted uncritically by patients in a clinical setting, for a number of reasons (Snyder, Shenkel, and Lowery, 1977). For one, the assessment is given as though it were (1) tailored for the particular patient; (2) made on the basis of results from personality tests; and (3) interpreted by an expert. Studies with college students show that all these factors make people more accepting; the insecurity of patients is likely to amplify their readiness to accept a diagnostic assessment without reservations. ∎

task of building a bridge across a brook. They were supplied with the necessary equipment and allotted a relatively short amount of time to complete their mission. Though ostensibly all three men were OSS candidates, two were actually staff members who were there to frustrate the real candidate, to deliberately make his job difficult in order to discover how he would respond to stress.

Situational tests have been used in other comprehensive programs of assessment, more recently to help screen candidates for the Peace Corps, security agencies, and corporations. Student teaching is, in part, a situational test. Although such tests provide interesting information about a

person that could not be obtained in other ways, critics have questioned their reliability, validity, and ethics. Because situational testing is costly and time-consuming, it is not widely used.

Target assessment

Behaviorists are concerned with observable acts, not the fantasies, feelings, and motivations that many personality tests measure. They maintain that assessments should focus on the behavior that is a problem. Staunch behaviorists feel that it is a misuse of time and effort to probe the psyche with personality tests, making complex evaluations and assigning psychiatry's diagnostic labels. In their view, the most appropriate test is *target assessment*, direct observation and measurement of the behavior that is the focus of study or treatment. Target assessments conducted before treatment and again afterward (for example, before and after a course of behavior therapy) can show whether or not the treatment was effective.

For a program of behavior modification with psychotic children, Ivar Lovaas and his collaborators (1965) designed an apparatus with recording pens connected to push buttons. Each button was used to record a particular behavior—talking, running, hitting oneself. During observation periods, examiners simply held down the appropriate button to record the child's behavior. The apparatus thus recorded both the frequency and duration of the behaviors, giving precise information on how they changed over time. Elaborate recording devices are not, however, necessary for target assessment. In mental hospitals, staff sometimes sample the problem behavior (e.g., hallucinating or stealing) of patients at specified times of the day. The changes in these behaviors gauge whether the patient is improving.

ISSUES IN ASSESSMENT

There is considerable evidence that people can intentionally fake their responses to most personality questionnaires (Anastasi, 1976).

For example, when two groups of college students were tested by both direct and projective techniques, those in the first group, volunteers who believed they had nothing to lose by being honest, revealed the same personality traits on both kinds of tests. However, the students in the second group were hoping to be hired as research assistants and had been told that the researchers were looking for well-adjusted individuals. These students obtained scores revealing quite different personality traits on the direct and on the projective assessments. Compared with the first group, they appeared noticeably better adjusted, at least according to their self-ratings and their answers on straightforward personality questionnaires. But on the projective tests they revealed about the same amount of psychopathology as the first group (Davids and Pildner, 1958).

When the person taking the test has a lot at stake and is strongly tempted to present a favorable personality picture, the fact that faking is so easy may be a definite drawback. Some of the inventories, like the MMPI and the CPI, have items designed to reveal faking on the part of examinees. If a person obtains high scores on these validity (or faking) scales, then the entire performance is regarded as suspect.

An unintentional source of distortion and lack of validity is a *response set*, the tendency of some people to respond in a certain way to the test items regardless of their specific content. For example, the person may have a tendency to answer "yes" or "true" to the great majority of questions on the inventory without paying attention to the actual personal relevance of the item. Another factor influencing the accuracy of responses is the "social desirability" of the items. One experimenter (Edwards, 1957) has conducted extensive research on the ways in which the wording of items on personality inventories can strongly influence the tendency of examinees to answer either "yes" or "no," or "true" or "false." For example, sometimes the examinee can easily tell if it would be desirable, in terms of the values of our society, to answer in a certain way, and if she wants to present a socially attractive image, she will tend to answer accordingly.

Distortions are not the only problem with direct methods. Several of the theories of personality, as well as psychoanalytic theory, stress the fact that we all have certain traits, feelings, and motives that we cannot report or describe because we are unaware of them. Many people, for example, hide their hostility not only from the world but from themselves. For this reason, many psychologists maintain that projective tests and in-depth interviews are essential for a valid, comprehensive appraisal of personality.

Besides the possibility of conscious distortion and unconscious omission, another criticism often leveled against personality assessment concerns its accuracy. Almost all the assessment techniques described in this chapter have been attacked by critics at one time or another. It seems to be true that any test, administered alone, can produce misleading results. However, when a person is given a comprehensive battery of tests and the results form a clear pattern, a more reliable and valid picture of personality is obtained.

SUMMARY

Psychological tests are intended to give objective and standardized measures of people's unique attributes.

Reliability and validity. Tests must be reliable, that is, they must show consistency and reproducibility of results. Reliability can be measured by the test-retest approach, the split-half approach, or the alternate forms approach.

Tests must also be valid, that is, they must measure what they are intended to measure. The predictive validity of a test depends on how well it predicts a person's performance or behavior.

Intelligence tests. Binet stressed the importance of such aspects of intelligence as memory of short sentences, attention, reasoning, and the ability to learn. Binet introduced the concept of mental age, the average age at which subjects can answer a question or master a problem at a certain level of difficulty. Stern suggested that intelligence be defined as the ratio of a person's mental age to his chronological age, resulting in the intelligence quotient, or IQ.

Wechsler's intelligence tests compute a person's IQ relative to the average score obtained by persons of his age group. The Wechsler scales include verbal tests and performance tests designed to measure both intellectual and nonintellectual functions.

Intelligence can fluctuate, as a result of either temporary factors or general trends of mental growth. Thus IQs may not be the stable, unchanging index they were originally considered to be. Larger families may lower a child's IQ by lowering the level of a family's intellectual environment.

It is not certain whether intelligence tests can predict success in life. Social factors like finishing college, family background, and leadership skills count too.

The IQ controversy. The degree to which intelligence is a product of heredity or environment has been much debated. Jensen claims that the lower scores of blacks on IQ tests is genetically based. Jensen's critics point out that a change in environment can raise the IQ scores of blacks much more than Jensen's theory would account for, and note that social environment probably accounts for more variation in IQ than does heredity, although both play a part.

Achievement and aptitude tests. Achievement tests measure the level of performance attained in a subject at a given level of training. Aptitude tests measure one's potential or capacity to learn.

The distinction between aptitude and achievement is not always clear: current achievement can indicate aptitude, and aptitude can depend to an extent on one's previous experience.

Achievement tests are used to survey the performance level of a group, to diagnose a person's strengths and weaknesses, and to gauge a person's readiness for the next stage in training or school. Such tests have been criticized for reflecting norms for middle- and upper-income groups only, for relying too heavily on multiple-choice questions, and for being poor indicators of actual ability to perform.

Creativity. Convergent and divergent thinking are involved in different types of creativity. Convergent thought is the ability to find a specific answer to a problem; divergent thought entails inventing many possible solutions and picking the best among them.

Personality assessment. There are two ways to measure personality. The direct method uses objective evaluation of the person's own report or behavior. The indirect method uses projective techniques to probe unconscious factors in personality.

Objective techniques commonly use check lists or true-or-false items. Gough's Adjective Check List, the Minnesota Multiphasic Personality Test, and the California Psychological Inventory are widely used personality questionnaires. It is possible to fake responses to such tests, though some have items designed to reveal faking.

The Rorschach test is a widely used projective technique, along with the Thematic Apperception Test. Both have been criticized for lack of reliability and validity. Word association tests and draw-a-person tests also measure unconscious aspects of personality. There is disagreement over the reliability and validity of projective tests.

Behavior assessment. Situational tests involve placing a person in a specially created situation and observing his or her behavior in it. Behaviorists use target assessment, direct observation and measurement of the behavior being studied or treated, and assessment of the changes that have taken place after treatment.

Issues in assessment. Besides problems with distortion of responses, psychological tests have been criticized for inaccuracy, oversimplification, and test bias.

GLOSSARY

Achievement The degree of skill or performance attained at a given level of training.

Alternate forms Two or more versions of the same test in which each version is equivalent to but different from the others; used in checking test-retest reliability.

Aptitude The potential or capacity to master a specific skill before training.

Behavior assessment A direct assessment of how a person behaves in real-life situations.

Convergent thinking Finding the solution to a problem with a specified correct answer.

Creativity Showing originality, innovation, and ability to use familiar elements in novel combinations.

Criterion A standard or measure against which the success of a predictive test is verified.

Criterion sampling A measure of actual skills involved in a task.

Divergent thinking Inventing several innovative solutions to a problem and picking the best among them.

Intelligence quotient (IQ) The ratio of mental age to chronological age, multiplied by 100.

Mental age A scale proposed by Binet for use in measuring intelligence; the average age at which subjects can answer a question or master a problem.

Personality inventories Questionnaires that provide a whole profile of several traits, comparing the subject with norms for each trait.

Predictive validity The extent to which a test foretells accurately how a person will perform or behave.

Projective tests Tests that elicit a person's projections.

which the scorer then interprets to assess unconscious aspects of personality.

Psychological tests Objective and standardized measures of a sample of behavior.

Rater bias The possibility that a personality evaluater may allow one quality to color the whole of a rating.

Reliability The extent to which a test consistently and reproducibly measures what it should.

Response set The tendency to respond in a certain way to test items regardless of their specific content.

Rorschach test A projective test consisting of inkblot cards, with the subject asked to describe what he or she can see in the blots.

Situational test A person is placed in a specially created situation and his behavior is observed in it.

Split-half approach A method of checking test-retest reliability: one test is divided into two equal parts and the scores of a subject on the two parts are compared.

Target assessment The direct observation and measurement of the behavior that is the focus of study or treatment.

Test-retest reliability The extent to which a repetition of a test gives the same results.

Thematic Apperception Test (TAT) A projective test consisting of ambiguous pictures; the examinee makes up a story about each picture.

Validity The extent to which a test actually measures what it is intended to measure.

Word association test A projective test in which the subject says the first word that comes to mind in response to a stimulus word.

16

ABNORMAL BEHAVIOR

COMMON MYTHS

MANY PEOPLE BELIEVE ...	ACTUALLY ...
One single cause underlies all mental disorders.	Mental disorders are usually due to many factors working together, such as heredity, family life, and stress.
People can only become addicted to hard drugs such as heroin.	People can become addicted to any brain-altering substance, including alcohol and caffeine.
Paranoid schizophrenics are completely out of touch with reality.	Many paranoid schizophrenics are realistic about all subjects except a narrow range of delusions.
The odds of getting depressed are about the same for everyone.	Many more women than men are diagnosed as "depressed."
Hyperactive children will become even more active and excitable when given stimulant drugs.	Drugs that stimulate normal adults often have the opposite effect on hyperactive children, slowing them down and helping them concentrate.

"In *that* direction," the Cat said, waving its right paw round, "lives a Hatter; and in *that* direction," waving the other paw, "lives a March Hare. Visit either you like: they're both mad."

"But I don't want to go among mad people," Alice remarked.

"Oh, you can't help that," said the Cat: "We're all mad here. I'm mad. You're mad."

"How do you know I'm mad?" said Alice.

"You must be," said the Cat, "or you wouldn't have come here."

LEWIS CARROLL. *ALICE'S ADVENTURES IN WONDERLAND*

Each of us acts "mad" occasionally. Under the right circumstances, any of us could be overtly hostile, intensely anxious, or deeply depressed. From time to time we may withdraw from people, or avoid certain situations, or be confused and frightened. At these moments we may feel slightly "mad." But only when such behavior becomes a person's habitual way of dealing with life would we call it "abnormal."

ON "ABNORMALITY"

"Abnormal" means literally "away from normal." Broadly speaking, the ideal of normality is adaptive behavior, actions that promote the growth and well-being of a person and the society. Abnormal behavior, then, is that which is *maladaptive*, that is, causes personal discomfort and/or violates standards of socially acceptable behavior.

Thus not only personal distress, but also the customs and norms of a culture define normal behavior: the abnormal departs from cultural expectations. However, simply because a behavior is accepted in a culture or occurs commonly does not necessarily mean it is adaptive. For example,

schizophrenia—where a person may act bizarrely with delusions or hallucinations—seems to occur in all cultures. While some cultures tolerate it better than others, it is nevertheless maladaptive for those who suffer from it. Abnormal psychology deals with behavior so maladaptive that it causes discontent and psychological suffering to a person or those around him.

In ancient times, deviant people were thought to be possessed by the devil. Witches, shamans, and even priests were believed to have the power to exorcise the devil, and so cure a person's mental disorder. The scientific understanding of mental disorders has come only in the last hundred years. It was early in the nineteenth century with advances in the knowledge of human anatomy, physiology, and neurology, that scientists began to understand that physical disease was due to underlying organic disorder. The *medical model* of mental illness proposes that, like physical disease, all mental disorders have underlying organic causes. One advocate of the medical model argues that the current use of the term "disease" includes any gross deviation—whether physical, mental, or behavioral—from desirable standards (Ausubel, 1961). Thus people who have psychological problems are no more accountable for their abnormal behavior than people who are physically ill.

Others, such as psychiatrist Thomas Szasz (1960), challenge the medical model as a modern version of the notions of shamans or inquisitors of past eras. The medical model, says Szasz, is simply a convenient place to put the blame for our problems in living. Just as other societies blamed witches or demons for their problems, we blame germs or chemical imbalances. Mental disorder, according to Szasz (1974), grows out of the conflicts of living; it is misleading to explain mental disturbance by analogy to physical illness.

Criticisms such as these have lessened the influence of the medical model and given rise to *psychosocial models*, which explain mental disorder in terms of psychological and/or social factors. One of the first alternatives to the medical model was Sigmund Freud's psychodynamic theory. He proposed that people who suffer mental problems are driven by unconscious sexual and aggressive urges in tandem with the irrational forces of their defense mechanisms. Another view, presented by psychiatrist Harry Stack Sullivan (1953), holds that abnormal behavior stems from interpersonal conflicts. In the Sullivanian model, maladaptive behavior is the result of distorted communication.

The behaviorists, on the other hand, maintain that abnormal behavior is due to faulty learning. In their view, it can be accounted for by failure to learn adaptive behaviors and acquisition instead of maladaptive ones.

Of course there is a continuum of behavior from normal, effective functioning to abnormal, poor functioning. In general, most mental health professionals recognize behavior as abnormal on the basis of three characteristics. The first is extreme social deviance—behavior that disturbs other people, such as standing on a busy sidewalk and trying to collect a toll from passersby. The second is subjective distress, such as excessive fearfulness and anxiety, depression, or other emotional disturbances. A third criterion is psychological handicap—emotional problems that impair functioning in everyday social or work roles.

Violating social norms, personal discomfort, or handicap are not the only criteria of abnormal behavior, though. Statistical rarity or failing to match an ideal for adjustment are also grounds for judging abnormality—though clinicians rarely use these (see Table 16.1).

DIAGNOSIS AND CLASSIFICATION

The official classification system for mental disorders is a book called *The Diagnostic and Statistical Manual of Mental Disorders*, or DSM for short. This manual lists every psychiatric disorder, and gives an elaborate description of its symptoms. It enumerates such details as the disorder's essential features (those symptoms always seen), occasionally associated features, other complications that can occur, typical age at onset and course, predisposing factors, prevalence in particular groups and by sex ratio, and the common family patterns of patients. One section rates the degree of life stress that the person is undergoing. Two final sections for each disorder are most important in establishing a reliable diagnosis. One is *differential diagnosis*, which explains how a particular disorder can be distinguished from similar ones. The other offers *operational criteria* for diagnosis, the specific symptoms that must always be present before the diagnosis can be made.

DSM-III

The first DSM was put together by a group of psychiatrists shortly after World War II; the second was published in 1968. The third version,

TABLE 16.1 **CRITERIA FOR DEFINING ABNORMAL BEHAVIOR**

Norm violation	Substantial deviation from the society's norms, its standards for proper conduct.
Statistical rarity	Substantial deviation from the average behavior in the social group.
Personal discomfort	Behavior causes distress to the person.
Deviation from an ideal	Behavior falls short of a theoretical ideal of optimum psychological adjustment.

DSM-III, has only recently been approved as psychiatry's official diagnostic manual, after several years of testing by task forces of more than a hundred clinicians (American Psychiatric Association, 1980). It is designed to incorporate all known research findings on the more than 150 disorders it describes and classifies (Rakoff, 1977). A major improvement of DSM-III over its predecessors is the specificity with which it spells out the symptoms a person must display before a particular diagnosis can be given. In addition to the precision with which symptoms are detailed, another improvement in DSM-III is its "multiaxial" approach to diagnosis, allowing a patient's behavior to be diagnosed along four dimensions, or axes. One axis, for example, evaluates the amount of stress a person is undergoing; another axis assesses the highest level of a person's functioning (what she was like at her best) before the current disorder. The other two axes assess any relevant medical problems and any underlying personality disorders or problems in development.

Drawbacks of diagnosis

Accurate diagnosis can serve to improve the understanding of a patient's disorder and guide his or her treatment. It also facilitates research and is essential for accurate record keeping. But critics of diagnosis raise several objections. Some contend that the procedure is unreliable; one clinician may label a person's symptoms one way, while another would call them something else. In research on DSM-II, for example, a number of psychiatrists were asked to diagnose hypothetical cases to see how often they would agree. The range of reliability was from .2 (very poor) to .8 (respectable), with the average hovering around .5 (Beck, *et al.*, 1962). When the same kind of research was done on an early version of DSM-III, the range of reliability was from .6 to .9—a higher level of agreement (American Psychiatric Association, 1980).

Even if DSM-III proves more reliable than the version it replaces, however, some clinicians object to giving any labels at all. For one, such labels have long-lasting effects, well beyond the time a person might be in the hospital or in treatment. A diagnostic label can stay with a person for life. For example, in one study in which perfectly normal volunteers posed as mentally ill people and were committed to hospitals (see box, "On Being Sane in Insane Places," p. 420), despite the fact that they had never been mentally disordered in the first place, they were given the "schizophrenia, in remission" diagnosis on release (Rosenhan, 1973).

Such a label can harm the way a person feels about himself, and also lower the regard in which others hold him. When a psychiatric diagnosis received at one point in a person's life becomes a discrediting attribute, it has become a stigma (Goffman, 1973). The stigma of being identified as a mental patient at all can affect the way others perceive a person. In one study, for example, researchers showed a videotaped interview to two groups of psychologists, one behavioristic in outlook, the other psychoanalytic (Langer and Abelson, 1974). Half the psychologists in each group were told the interview was with a "patient," the other half that he was a "job applicant." The behaviorists did not show much difference in the way that they rated the person's adjustment, no matter which label they had been given. But the psychoanalytically oriented rated the person as much more disturbed when they thought they were watching a patient. A later look at the same data revealed that the behaviorists saw the "patient's" problems as a product of his environment, while the psychoanalytic therapists tended to place the blame on the "patient's" inner problems (Snyder, 1977).

Being identified as having a mental disorder can have damaging effects in a person's life. The stigma of being labelled a mental patient is likely to mean that people will regard a person unfavorably in general, and people's opinions are especially low of those whose mental problems have been so severe that they have had to be hospitalized (Farina, Murray, and Groh, 1978). Thus one criticism of DSM-III has been that it is overly inclusive in the range of behaviors for which it offers a diagnosis (Goleman, 1978). For example, such behaviors as drinking too much coffee, being overly shy, academic underachievement, and reading disorders are all included as psychiatric diagnoses. Any of these categories would mean that millions of people who have what most people would consider a minor problem could be given a psychiatric label. This is particularly objectionable to some

ON BEING SANE IN INSANE PLACES

■ How many sane people are there in mental institutions? How many people are there who would be sane outside a mental institution, but who, because of their surroundings, are now insane inside such an institution?

Questions of this sort are disturbing. The doubts they embody are strengthened by studies such as one by D. L. Rosenhan (1973). Eight pseudopatients, including Dr. Rosenhan, gained admittance to a total of twelve mental institutions. They each presented the same complaint: "I hear voices, unclean voices. I think they say 'empty,' 'hollow,' 'thud.'" Apart from this fabrication and altered identities, everything else they said was true and reflected their normal state of mind. In almost every case they were diagnosed as "schizophrenic."

Once admitted, the pseudopatients had no more symptoms and behaved naturally throughout their hospital stays, which averaged nineteen days. Their sanity was never detected by hospital personnel; it was spotted, however, by many of their fellow patients.

Pseudopatients took notes on their experiences (behavior seen as pathological by staff observers, one of whom wrote "patient engages in writing behavior"). Among the most revealing of their findings was the fact that those with the most power in

mental institutions—psychiatrists and other physicians—spent the least time with patients, while relatively powerless attendants spent the most. The latter sometimes abused patients verbally and physically, and often treated them as if they did not exist. When asked simple questions by pseudopatients (directions or times of meetings), only a fraction of the hospital personnel would even deign to reply. It was this depersonalization that Rosenhan and his fellow researchers found most disturbing: "Neither anecdotal nor 'hard' data can convey the overwhelming sense of powerlessness which invades the individual as he is continually exposed to the depersonalization of the psychiatric hospital" (1973, p. 256).

Rosenhan believes that depersonalization results partly from avoidance because of our ambivalent feelings toward the mentally ill: on the one hand fear and distrust, on the other, benevolent intentions. Another cause is the hierarchical structure of hospitals, where attendants and nurses model their behavior toward patients on that of physicians, trying to have as little contact as possible. The pseudopatients suffered intensely from the feeling that they were unworthy, if not invisible. The sad lesson they learned: once a person is labeled as a patient in a mental hospital, nothing he or she does there is likely to be considered normal. ■

---

critics in the case of reading disabilities, because it might stigmatize children so labelled for the rest of their lives by bringing "under psychiatry's wing deficits and disabilities that are not mental disorders" (Garmezy, 1978).

ORGANIC MENTAL DISORDERS

Imagine that there was a kind old man who lived in your neighborhood while you were growing up. He used to tell you stories about

his days as a sailor, and he was always friendly to you and your friends.

Now after several years you stop in to see him. You're shocked to find that his apartment, which was always spic-and-span, is a mess; tin cans strewn everywhere, piles of old newspapers, a stack of unopened mail. He hasn't shaved in days and he's still in his bathrobe and slippers, even though it's late afternoon.

When you tell him your name, he says, "I used to know a kid by that name." But he doesn't seem to realize you're that same kid.

He sits you down and immediately starts in on

stories from his seagoing days. You grow uneasy when he tells you the identical story three times in a row. When he accuses you, out of the blue, of stealing his Social Security checks, you know it's time to leave.

You get up to go, and as you're leaving he asks your name. You tell him, and he says, "Oh yeah, I used to know a kid by that name. . . ." ■

Your old friend displays the symptoms of "senile brain disorder," commonly called senility. Senility is one of the *organic brain disorders,* mental disorders that are due to temporary or permanent malfunction of the brain. They include a wide range of syndromes, ranging from the brain decay seen in the later stages of syphilis or alcoholism, to damage resulting from head injury or severe infections, to degenerative brain diseases like senile brain disorder. In order for any of these diagnoses

to be made, however, there has to be evidence of brain malfunction. Your old friend, for example, would almost certainly be the victim of arteriosclerosis, or hardening of the arteries of the brain, whereby the cranial blood supply is slowly constricted, relentlessly destroying brain cells (Diamond, 1978).

Although organic brain disorders always mean that a person has suffered damage of some sort to the brain, they are also commonly accompanied by emotional and cognitive problems. Psychological factors can influence the course of organic brain disease. For example, a person who realizes that his or her brain is not working as well as it did in the past is likely to view that situation as a serious threat or loss. This can lead to anxiety, depression, and shame. Some may attempt to cope by avoiding situations in which their deficiencies will be exposed. Some—like your old friend—may ac-

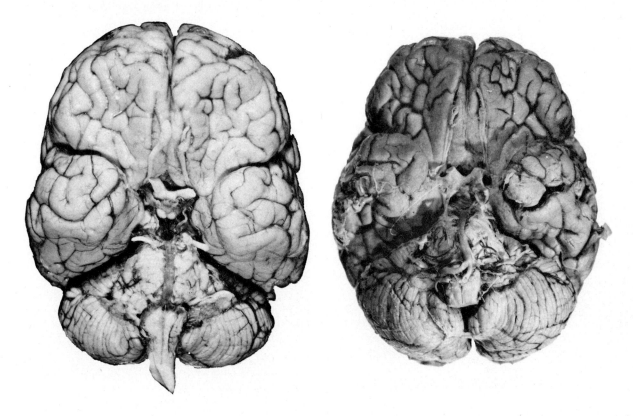

When seen next to a healthy brain (left), the damage done to the brain of a victim of syphilis (right) is clear. Such extensive damage occurs only after many years, when the syphilis goes untreated. (Armed Forces Institute of Pathology)

cuse others of maliciously misplacing or stealing their possessions, blaming others for their own deficiencies. As memory loss increases, he may try to conceal gaps by confabulation—making facts up.

Dementia is an organic brain disorder characterized by the deterioration of a person's memory, impulse control, and intellectual abilities to the extent that the person can no longer function socially. At the most advanced stages, memory deteriorates to the point where only basic facts like a person's birthday and details about immediate family are remembered. Senility, like your old friend suffered, is one type of dementia.

The deterioration of intellectual abilities in dementia shows up as difficulty with new tasks or things done under time pressure, and irritability and anxiety in such situations. In later stages the person has difficulty with logic and concept formation. Impaired impulse control often takes the form of coarse language and jokes, neglecting hygiene and appearance, and disregard for social rules. Often personality changes are so dramatic that others remark that the person is "no longer the same": a meticulous housewife may no longer clean her house, an avid concert-goer may become uninterested in going out at all. As dementia progresses, a person's characteristic traits can become marked, be it toward compulsivity, hysterics, impulsivity, cantankerous irritability, or suspiciousness.

SUBSTANCE ABUSE DISORDERS

Imagine that Jane is a capable but somewhat anxious office manager at the firm you work for. One night you're both working late, and as you're walking out of the building together she asks if you'd care to join her at the tavern across the street for some drinks.

You don't really enjoy her company that much—her uptightness makes you feel tense—but it's been a long day. As you both pull up a stool at the bar, you're surprised to see that everyone greets her as a regular.

You're on your second beer—and Jane's on her fourth gin and tonic—when you realize that she's a changed person. No longer the tense and businesslike office manager you're used to, Jane is ebullient, expansive, and the center of attention.

When you leave after your second beer, she's started on gin and tonic number five. She hardly seems to notice your exit, she's so busy trading bawdy jokes with her cronies. You suddenly understand why Jane sometimes doesn't show up at work for days at a time. ◼

Jane is well on her way to becoming an alcoholic, one of a series of addictions classified in DSM-III as *substance abuse disorders*, the habitual use of brain-altering drugs to the extent that they interfere with social functioning or cannot be stopped without causing an adverse physical reaction.

It is normal in our society to take drugs that modify our mood or behavior. Most adults drink alcohol socially and use caffeine in coffee, soft drinks, or tea as a stimulant. Even so, any form of drug addiction has been viewed in our culture as a sign of moral weakness and irresponsibility. A more enlightened view of drug dependence sees it as a self-defeating attempt to cope with the demands of living. The short-term gains, such as the reduction of anxiety, are offset in the long run when a person comes to rely excessively on drugs like alcohol. While it is quite normal to drink socially, excessive reliance on alcohol to cope with problems in living can create more problems, as was the case with Jane and her absences at work.

The drugs most common in substance abuse disorders are alcohol, heroin, amphetamines, barbiturates, and marijuana. A person can also become addicted to tobacco and caffeine, although these are not generally regarded as substances of abuse.

For a drug to be classified as abused, a person must use it consistently for at least one month. During this time it must disturb the user's social functioning—for example, so that she fails to meet important obligations to job, school, friends, or family—or cause her to develop erratic and impulsive behavior, such as the inappropriate display of aggression.

Psychological dependence occurs when a person has a compelling desire to use a drug and is unable to cut down or stop its use, despite the ab-

Controlled Substances: Uses and Effects
DRUG ENFORCEMENT ADMINISTRATION
UNITED STATES DEPARTMENT OF JUSTICE

	Drugs	Schedule*	Often Prescribed Brand Names	Medical Uses	Dependence Potential: Physical	Dependence Potential: Psychological	Tolerance	Duration of Effects (in hours)	Usual Methods of Administration	Possible Effects	Effects of Overdose	Withdrawal Syndrome
Narcotics	Opium	II	Dover's Powder, Paregoric	Analgesic, antidiarrheal	High	High	Yes	3 to 6	Oral, smoked	Euphoria, drowsiness, respiratory depression, constricted pupils, nausea	Slow and shallow breathing, clammy skin, convulsions, coma, possible death	Watery eyes, runny nose, yawning, loss of appetite, irritability, tremors, panic, chills and sweating, cramps, nausea
	Morphine	II	Morphine	Analgesic	High	High	Yes	3 to 6	Injected, smoked			
	Codeine	II III V	Codeine	Analgesic, antitussive	Moderate	Moderate	Yes	3 to 6	Oral, injected			
	Heroin	I	None	None	High	High	Yes	3 to 6	Injected, sniffed			
	Meperidine (Pethidine)	II	Demerol, Pethadol	Analgesic	High	High	Yes	3 to 6	Oral, injected			
	Methadone	II	Dolophine, Methadone, Methadose	Analgesic, heroin substitute	High	High	Yes	12 to 24	Oral, injected			
	Other Narcotics	I II III V	Dilaudid, Leritine, Numorphan, Percodan	Analgesic, antidiarrheal, antitussive	High	High	Yes	3 to 6	Oral, injected			
Depressants	Chloral Hydrate	IV	Noctec, Somnos	Hypnotic	Moderate	Moderate	Probable	5 to 8	Oral	Slurred speech, disorientation, drunken behavior without odor of alcohol	Shallow respiration, cold and clammy skin, dilated pupils, weak and rapid pulse, coma, possible death	Anxiety, insomnia, tremors, delirium, convulsions, possible death
	Barbiturates	II III IV	Amytal, Butisol, Nembutal, Phenobarbital, Seconal, Tuinal	Anesthetic, anti-convulsant, sedation, sleep	High	High	Yes	1 to 16	Oral, injected			
	Glutethimide	III	Doriden	Sedation, sleep	High	High	Yes	4 to 8	Oral			
	Methaqualone	II	Optimil, Parest, Quaalude, Somnafac, Sopor	Sedation, sleep	High	High	Yes	4 to 8	Oral			
	Minor Tranquilizers**	IV	Ativan, Azene, Equanil, Librium, Miltown, Serax, Tranxene, Valium, Verstran	Anti-anxiety, muscle relaxant, sedation	Moderate	Moderate	Yes	4 to 8	Oral			
	Other Depressants	III IV	Clonopin, Dalmane, Dormate, Noludar, Placidyl, Valmid	Anti-anxiety, sedation, sleep	Possible	Possible	Yes	4 to 8	Oral			
Stimulants	Cocaine†	II	Cocaine	Local anesthetic	Possible	High	Yes	2	Injected, sniffed	Increased alertness, excitation, euphoria, dilated pupils, increased pulse rate and blood pressure, insomnia, loss of appetite	Agitation, increase in body temperature, hallucinations, convulsions, possible death	Apathy, long periods of sleep, irritability, depression, disorientation
	Amphetamines	II III	Benzedrine, Biphetamine, Desoxyn, Dexedrine	Hyperkinesis, narcolepsy, weight control	Possible	High	Yes	2 to 4	Oral, injected			
	Phenmetrazine	II	Preludin	Weight control	Possible	High	Yes	2 to 4	Oral			
	Methylphenidate	II	Ritalin	Hyperkinesis	Possible	High	Yes	2 to 4	Oral			
	Other Stimulants	III IV	Bacarate, Cylert, Didrex, Ionamin, Plegine, Pondimin, Pre-Sate, Sanorex, Voranil	Weight control	Possible	Possible	Yes	2 to 4	Oral			
Hallucinogens	LSD	I	None	None	None	Degree unknown	Yes	Variable	Oral	Illusions and hallucinations (with exception of MDA); poor perception of time and distance	Longer, more intense "trip" episodes, psychosis, possible death	Withdrawal syndrome not reported
	Mescaline	I	None	None	None	Degree unknown	Yes	Variable	Oral, injected			
	Psilocybin-Psilocyn	I	None	None	None	Degree unknown	Yes	Variable	Oral			
	MDA	I	None	None	None	Degree unknown	Yes	Variable	Oral, injected, sniffed			
	PCP‡	II	Sernylan	Veterinary anesthetic	None	Degree unknown	Yes	Variable	Oral, injected, smoked			
	Other Hallucinogens	I	None	None	None	Degree unknown	Yes	Variable	Oral, injected, sniffed			
Cannabis	Marihuana, Hashish, Hashish Oil	I	None	None	Degree unknown	Moderate	Yes	2 to 4	Oral, smoked	Euphoria, relaxed inhibitions, increased appetite, disoriented behavior	Fatigue, paranoia, possible psychosis	Insomnia, hyperactivity, and decreased appetite reported in a limited number of individuals

*Scheduling classifications vary for individual drugs since controlled substances are often marketed in combination with other medicinal ingredients.

†Designated a narcotic under the Controlled Substances Act.

‡Designated a depressant under the Controlled Substances Act.

**Major tranquilizers such as phenothiazines, thiozanthenes, or butyrophenones are not now controlled substances.

sence of physical addiction. With prolonged use, a person may develop drug *tolerance,* which means that increasing amounts of the drug are needed to achieve the desired effect. In *withdrawal* there is a specific set of distressing or painful symptoms that follow the person's reducing or stopping the drug's use. While the effects of drugs per se do not lead people to criminal acts, the intense needs of addicts and their inability to work may lead them to crimes such as theft or prostitution to get money for drugs.

Roughly 9 million Americans can be considered alcoholics, chronic drinkers whose addiction severely impairs their lives. Alcohol acts as a depressant, inhibiting the higher centers of the cortex and lowering a person's control, so that he or she is more likely than normal to express emotion and less able to hold impulses in check.

Opium derivatives such as heroin and morphine produce an immediate euphoria lasting perhaps a minute, followed by a "high" lasting several hours. During the latter period, the addict is typically lethargic and withdrawn. An addict experiences withdrawal symptoms when another dose is not obtained within about eight hours.

Cocaine and the amphetamines are stimulants that speed up the action of the central nervous system (Grinspoon, 1977). Cocaine induces a euphoric state that can last up to several hours and may be preceded by dizziness, headaches, and restlessness. It produces psychological, not physiological, dependence—that is, there are no physical withdrawal symptoms. Physicians prescribe amphetamines for weight reduction or to relieve fatigue and maintain alertness, but when overused they may cause confusion, sleeplessness, tremors, and excitability. In extreme cases, they can cause psychotic behavior.

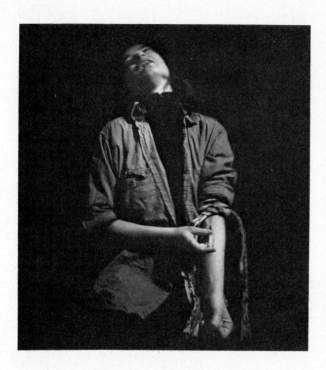

The "junkie", or drug addict, often takes up a criminal career in order to come up with the money needed to buy drugs in the shortest amount of time. For women, this can mean becoming a prostitute; for men, a thief. (Michael Weisbrot)

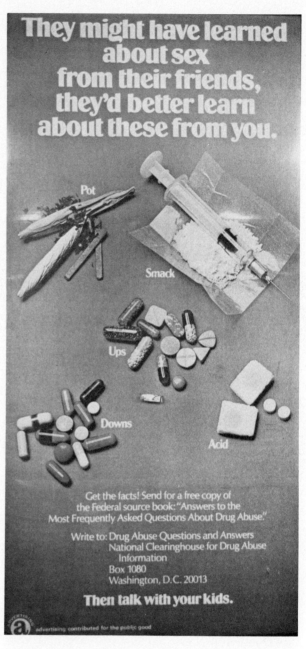

In recent decades drug abuse has become a major problem, especially among younger people. Some drug experts believe that better information about the dangers of drugs would prevent abuse. (Richard Frieman/Photo Researchers, Inc.)

Barbiturates, on the other hand, act as depressants, inducing relaxation followed by drowsiness. Excessive doses may be fatal, for they may cause paralysis of the brain's respiratory center. Barbiturates can produce both physiological and psychological dependence.

Psychedelic drugs, known as the hallucinogens, induce hallucinations and a range of "mind-expanding" states. People's reactions to psychedelics are highly unpredictable. LSD typically produces eight hours of varying, intense sensory perceptions. Sensations are out of proportion to the stimuli—objects appear brighter and sharper than they actually are, or slight noises become loud sounds; hallucinations are common. The psychedelics are not physically addicting, though people can sometimes become psychologically dependent on them. Naturally occurring hallucinogens, such as the peyote cactus, are used in religious rites among some Native Americans (Schultes, 1976).

The most commonly used cannabis-type drugs are marijuana and hashish. Marijuana is a mild hallucinogen, inducing a high with euphoria and intensified sensory perceptions. Its effects depend on the user's mood, personality, and past drug experience, as well as on the dosage and purity of the drug. Typically it produces a mild euphoria; occasionally it can induce a state of anxiety or depression (Tart, 1976). Although illegal in most states, marijuana is used socially—especially among young people—in the same fashion as alcohol. While cannabis, like the hallucinogens, is not physically addicting, people sometimes become psychologically dependent on it in a way akin to the alcoholic's use of liquor (Yankelovich, 1975). Many charges have been levelled against marijuana, for example, that chronic use causes an "amotivational syndrome," or loss of will (McGlothlin and West, 1968). A comprehensive review of research concluded that findings have been contradictory; more careful studies are needed before firm conclusions about the harmful or benign effects of marijuana can be made (Grinspoon, 1977).

SCHIZOPHRENIC DISORDERS

Imagine that you're riding a bus when an unkempt woman carrying a load of ragged clothes in two old shopping bags sits down next to you.

"They're after me again," she says, looking you directly in the eye, as though you had met before. "But they're not going to get me this time," she continues, her voice getting louder and more insistent, almost angry. "So you can tell your buddies at Interpol to take their tokens and go to hell. A handbasket, that's what you think I am. You can take your Easter lily hamburger and shove it."

She's practically yelling at you now. It's not your stop, but you feel so uneasy you decide to get off anyhow.

As the bus pulls away you see she's changed seats and started in on someone else. ■

Psychosis is the most severe form of mental disorder, in which a person loses contact with reality. This loss of contact with reality may be restricted to a specific range of situations, or may be so pervasive that the person can no longer care for herself. The two main subdivisions of psychosis are *affective disorders*, of which extremely elated or depressed shifts of emotion are the chief feature, and *schizophrenia*. The chief symptoms in schizophrenia include severe distortions of thought, perception, and mood, bizarre thoughts and hallucinations, and withdrawal from other people. Your unexpected companion on the bus was undoubtedly psychotic, probably a schizophrenic of the paranoid type.

A person suffering from schizophrenia undergoes a drastic loss of former levels of routine daily functioning such as work, relationships, and even in basics of self-care. Family and friends often notice that he or she is radically different, frequently in unsettling ways.

While no one symptom is invariably seen in every case of schizophrenia, certain features are typical. There is often a disturbance in the person's language abilities, such as making incoherent statements. In extreme cases, a person may speak in a "word salad," an utterly incomprehensible stream of words and sounds (e.g., "An oozy is an eel for a reel really eelly lee . . .").

A typical symptom is *delusions*, false beliefs about reality, such as that people are spying on or conspiring against one. This can also take the form of delusions of reference, where the person interprets unrelated events as of great personal significance, for example, thinking that a TV show is full of personal messages. Some other common delusions are that a person's thoughts are being broadcast from his head over the radio; that his feelings, impulses, thoughts, or actions are being imposed upon him by an external force; or ideas of overvaluation, such as that one is a messiah or great political leader.

Schizophrenic perception is often marked by *hallucinations*, perceiving things that aren't

there in reality. The most common hallucinations are auditory, frequently the sounds of voices. Sometimes the voices seem to be commenting on the person's actions, or making insults. A hallmark of schizophrenia is blunted or inappropriate affect, or expression of feelings. Blunted affect means that a person's emotional responses are severely reduced, so that he no longer responds with normal intensity. Inappropriate affect is seen when the person's feelings don't match the situation, for example, when a patient complains he is being tortured by conspirators, but smiles and laughs while saying so. Finally, the schizophrenic frequently withdraws from involvement in the external world, becoming preoccupied with fantasies and delusions.

Several studies have found that schizophrenics suffer from a deficit in attention (Oltmanns, 1978; Helmsley, 1975). They usually do poorly on tasks that demand close attention, fast reactions, or continuous vigilance (Kopfstein and Neale, 1972; Place and Gilmore, 1980). The schizophrenic seems less able to ignore distractions that might intrude on his awareness. This susceptibility to distractions has been proposed as an explanation for the odd language patterns of schizophrenics. Their speech seems to include associations, details, and random thoughts that normal people exclude (Maher, 1972).

Types of schizophrenia

The most common diagnosis among hospitalized mental patients, schizophrenia is also one of the most baffling of mental disorders. Although it

sometimes occurs in short episodes, schizophrenia is more often chronic. When its onset is sudden, with some obvious event triggering a breakdown, it is termed "reactive schizophrenia"; when it has a long, gradual course with no obvious precipitating event, it is called "process" schizophrenia. The age of onset typically ranges from fifteen to forty-five. It is not a disorder exclusive to advanced societies; it is found in all cultures around the world. Approximately one-quarter of all hospitalized mental patients are diagnosed as schizophrenic, but the diagnosis can cover a vast range of different symptom patterns.

In *hebephrenic schizophrenia*, the thinking of patients is blatantly disorganized. Their emotional reactions are shallow and inappropriate. Their unpredictable giggling and silly, regressive behavior (classic examples are refusing to wear clothes or insisting on eating with one's fingers) are typical. The bizarre quality of this psychosis comes through in the following dialogue:

Therapist: What do you like to do? Anything in particular?

Patient: I like to ride. I like to read. I like to ride on a bicycle. And I like to go to prayer service. I never went to prayer service.

Therapist: What kind of prayer service?

Patient: Prayer service at the North Pole prayer service.

(Later in the same interview.)

Therapist: What was the name of the town?

Patient: The town? It was, uh. I can't remember. It was, uh, Bemidji, is that all right? (Giggle) . . . I didn't see the comb. I wanted, I wanted to try to in the bathroom and then I died underneath in the bathroom (gig-

TABLE 16.2 **SUBTYPES OF SCHIZOPHRENIA**

Hebephrenic type	Characterized by incoherent speech and inappropriate affect, especially silliness and giggling
Catatonic type	Characterized by disturbed motor behavior—either violent hyperactivity or mute inactivity or both in alternation
Paranoid type	Characterized by delusions of persecution or grandeur, and/or by hallucinations on the same themes

gle), and it was hurting me so hard that anybody was watching my nose and I pointed right at my own nose, and I lost control of everything. . . . (Rosenbaum, 1970)

The disturbed motor activity so common in *catatonic schizophrenia* often alternates between two forms. Patients may become immobile, rigid and negativistic. They may be mute and appear to be in a stupor. In this phase they may exhibit "waxy flexibility," in which their legs or arms remain in whatever positions they have been placed. Then, without apparent reason, patients may suddenly become highly agitated, shouting and talking constantly. During these periods of excitement they may launch violent attacks on others or try to injure themselves.

Suspiciousness, delusions, and hallucinations are all symptoms common to *paranoid schizophrenia*. People with this disorder are frequently

Paranoid people see the world with mistrust, reading plots and deception into innocent events and encounters. Typically, they scan their environment for minor details that seem to confirm their delusions, such as that they are the target of a conspiracy. (Mary Ellen Mark/Magnum)

aggressive and sometimes extremely religious. In their delusions of persecution, they appear to be projecting on others characteristics they cannot accept in themselves. One middle-aged man diagnosed as a paranoid schizophrenic expressed the belief that "his thoughts were being 'captured' by radio and television for use by the enemy" (Swanson, Bohnert, and Smith, 1970); at one point he tried to phone the president in an attempt to get the secret service to protect him from his tormenters.

There is a related type of psychosis, called *paranoia*, in which the only sign of abnormality is the person's delusional system. The delusions may involve one's spouse, other family members, an employer, or even some larger "enemy" like communists or foreigners. Other than the elaborate and persistent delusions, the paranoid is not schizophrenic and is often able to function quite adequately in most areas of daily life.

Causes of schizophrenia

Schizophrenia of whatever type is exceedingly resistant to therapy. For this reason much research concentrates on discovering its causes with a view to eventual control or prevention. The conditions under which schizophrenia develops are complex, involving both biological and psychological factors. A number of studies show that a predisposition to schizophrenia can be inherited. For example, the joint incidence of schizophrenia is higher for twins than for siblings or half-siblings (Kringlen, 1967; Rosenthal and Kety, 1968). Having a close relative who is schizophrenic increases the odds of becoming schizophrenic. About 12 percent of children of a schizophrenic parent become so, while the risk to siblings is about 8 percent. The risk for the population at large is estimated at from 0.2 percent to 1 percent (Bernheim and Levine, 1979).

Imbalance in the levels of some neurotransmitters, notably dopamine, have been linked to schizophrenia. The "dopamine hypothesis" holds that schizophrenia is due to excess activity of those parts of the brain that this neurotransmitter regulates. Other chemicals, such as the amphetamine drugs, have been found to produce psychotic symptoms with prolonged use. But as yet there is no definitive evidence that establishes a clear biochemical cause for schizophrenia (Snyder, 1980).

Some researchers and therapists see the family as underlying the schizophrenic's problems. Family theorists explain schizophrenia in several ways (Scheflen, 1980). For one, the schizophrenic may actually hold together a family that is so riddled with hidden conflicts that it can only survive by uniting against him. This is "scapegoating," where one member plays out the hidden conflicts among the others in the family (Haley, 1959). Another view holds that a schizophrenic child may be protecting his parents by distracting them from their own problems (Haley, 1980). Gregory Bateson (1972) described the confusing nature of communication within schizophrenic families as a *double bind.* In a double-bind situation, the parent presents the child with conflicting messages. For example, a mother may tell her son "I love you," yet, when he approaches, her body language may say "get away from me." Such unhealthy patterns within the family might lead to schizophrenia in the child.

While certain patterns of family interaction may act as a source of stress in a schizophrenic's life, there is little evidence to support the theory that families directly cause schizophrenia (Bernheim and Levine, 1979). Both genetic and environmental factors seem to play a role in the onset of schizophrenia. The *diathesis-stress theory* takes this into account by proposing that schizophrenia occurs in people who have an inherited predisposition for it—the diathesis—who are also exposed to stress (Bernheim and Levine, 1979). The theory proposes that both a genetic susceptibility and life stress are required to induce schizophrenia. One condition or the other by itself will not. Still, despite all the research on these possible causative factors, there is no single adequate explanation of what makes a person schizophrenic.

AFFECTIVE DISORDERS

Imagine that you've just gotten a letter from Anne, a girl you knew in high school as friendly and outgoing. After her mother's death three years ago, she moved to a large city, and you hear from her occasionally. Her letter has you worried.

She's had periods of listlessness before, but the day she wrote you she was barely able to leave the apartment for her job as secretary in an advertising agency. She has broken up with her boyfriend, and since then she's come straight home, watched TV, and fallen asleep by 7 P.M. She hardly knows a person outside the office, and can't seem to bring herself to make any friends. She often broods about her life, and cries frequently. Sometimes, her letter says, she wishes she were dead. ■

The *affective disorders* are characterized by extreme disturbances of mood, either excessive depression or elation. Anne's listlessness, brooding, and fatigue are all symptoms of her depressed mood, which colors the whole of her life. Such disorders are often *episodic*, where the period of illness is clearly different from the person's typical mode of functioning before onset. They are called *chronic* if the disorder is long-standing—two years or more—and there is no clear onset.

The key feature of the affective disorders is a severe extreme of mood, whether positive or negative. When the dominant mood is sadness, the disorder is *depressive.* When the predominant mood is extreme, agitated expansiveness, the disorder is *manic.* When the person swings from one extreme to the other, it is termed a "bipolar" affective disorder.

Manic episodes

The manic syndrome is marked by a distinct period during which a person's mood is unusually elevated, with extreme hyperactivity. Often a person in a manic phase will become enthusiastically involved in activities without recognizing their potential for dangerous consequences, or even that they are risky at all. A manic person typically has pressured, rapid-fire speech, inflated self-esteem, little need for sleep, and is highly distractible. The manic's euphoric mood has an infectious quality, especially to strangers, but seems disturbingly out of character to those who know the person well. This expansiveness is often unceasing, and there is a nonselective enthusiasm for any and all people and things.

On the other hand, the manic can be highly irritable, especially when thwarted. The manic's hyperactivity leads to multiple projects, which take such forms as business ventures, political campaigns, religious evangelism, or sexual exploits. The manic in pursuit of these ventures will be demanding—for example, calling old acquaintances in the middle of the night—but is unable to acknowledge his intrusiveness. The manic's lack of judgment can lead to flamboyant or bizarre acts out of touch with reality, such as reckless driving, buying sprees far beyond the capacity to pay, or even distributing bread, candy, or money to passing strangers.

The manic's speech is often packed with jokes and puns, word plays, and irrelevancies. It is sometimes punctuated by snatches of song and theatrical mannerisms. If irritable, the manic is capable of angry tirades. The distractibility makes for "flight of ideas," abrupt changes from topic to topic based on loose associations. At its extreme, there may be "derailment," loosening of associations that makes speech incoherent.

Depressive disorders

Common signs of depression, apart from outright persistent unhappiness, are loss of interest or pleasure, restless or very prolonged sleep, dis-

The strong negative moods of a depressed person can have a devastating effect on those close to them. (James Motlow/Jeroboam)

SUICIDE

■ What city in America has the highest suicide rate?

As of 1980, Las Vegas, Nevada led the list, with 30.5 suicides per 100,000 of population, compared to a national average of 12 per 100,000 (United Press, April 23, 1980).

The average person who commits suicide in Las Vegas is between eighteen and thirty-five, and typically has no family life there. The rootlessness and absence of meaningful relationships within the floating population of Las Vegas may be at the root of its high rate: the despair of depression, compounded by the feeling that no one cares, seems to make a person a higher risk for suicide.

Depression in and of itself does not seem sufficient to cause suicide; in a study of 453 attempted suicide cases, Lester, Beck, and Mitchell (1979) found that the single best predictor of suicide was a sense of hopelessness, rather than any other aspect of depression. When the same group of patients admitted to a hospital for having attempted suicide was followed for up to six years after the admission, fourteen went on to kill themselves later. These fourteen people differed from the rest in three ways: (1) they were more serious about

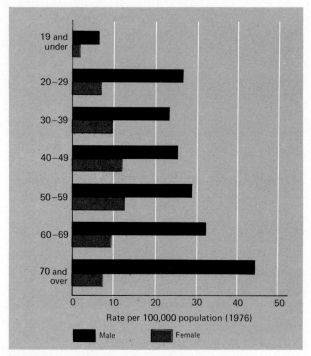

Figure 16.1 Suicide rates in 1976 by age and sex

Suicide is more common among men than women, although women are more likely to be diagnosed as depressed and to attempt to kill themselves. (Department of Health, Education, and Welfare).

turbed appetite (eating either significantly more or less than before), physical agitation or slowness, lethargy, feelings of guilt or worthlessness and, sometimes, thoughts of death or suicide. Typically the depressed person withdraws from family and friends, and loses interest in activities that were formerly pleasant. The depressed person's agitation can take the form of fitful sleep, pacing, hand wringing, or talking incessantly. Often, though, depressed speech is slowed, with long pauses, and is low and monotonous.

During episodes of depression a person may find it hard to concentrate or make decisions. Decreased energy makes the person tired even in the

absence of physical exertion. The sense of worthlessness can range from mild inadequacy to wholly unrealistic negativity to the point where even the smallest task seems difficult or impossible. Small failings are exaggerated, and the person clings to cues that confirm his or her negative self-evaluation. Suicidal desires are often couched in terms of the belief that others would be better off if the person were dead. When depression does culminate in attempts at suicide, men commit suicide about three times as often as women, though women account for three times the unsuccessful suicide attempts of men (Farberow and Shneidman, 1965).

their intent to die at the time of their first attempt (many people who unsuccessfully attempt suicide are ambivalent about wanting to die); (2) they were more depressed in general; and (3) they scored higher on a measure of hopelessness.

Bedrosian and Beck (in press, 1980) propose that hopelessness is the link between depression and suicide. While several million people become mildly or seriously depressed each year very few go on to commit suicide. Those who do seem to share a set of attitudes best described as "hopelessness": they view their situation as untenable, believe they cannot be helped by treatment or any other means, and see suicide as the only way out of a desperate situation.

Because suicide is so rare and unpredictable in the general population, research on it is difficult. But a survey of statistics and of the research that has been done shows that many common beliefs about suicide are wrong (Pokorny, 1968; Shneidman, 1973). For example:

☐ *People who talk about suicide will not kill themselves.* Actually, almost three out of four suicide victims have let others know they intend to commit suicide.

☐ *The motives for suicide are obvious.* We do not fully understand why people commit suicide; for example, a serious personal loss, such as the death of a spouse, may lead one person to suicide while most others weather such a loss much better.

☐ *People with terminal diseases are unlikely to commit suicide.* The awareness that one is about to die does not preclude suicide; some people with terminal illnesses commit suicide to spare themselves pain or to lessen the suffering of loved ones.

☐ *The tendency to commit suicide is inherited.* There is no good evidence that this is so.

☐ *People who commit suicide are insane at the time.* Although most suicidal people are depressed, they usually appear quite rational and in touch with reality prior to taking their lives.

☐ *Improvement in the emotional state of severely depressed people makes them less likely to take their lives.* Research shows that depressed patients are particularly at risk for suicide as their mood begins to improve, perhaps because they still perceive their situation as hopeless, but now have the energy to do something about it—escape by death.

Theories of depression

The cognitive viewpoint, exemplified by the theory of Aaron Beck (1974), holds that depression is the product of illogical, negative thoughts. The depressed person is seen as having a negative view of himself, the world, and the future that is not in keeping with the facts of his life. These negative thoughts lead to a depressed mood. It is not the events of life that lead to depression, but rather the way the person thinks about them. Depressed people show a special readiness to notice the negative side of events; not only do they have gloomy thoughts, but they seem to screen their percep-

tions to reinforce their negative viewpoint (Lloyd and Lishman, 1975). Depressed students have also been found to do poorly on measures of interpersonal problem solving (Gotlib and Asarnow, 1979). The inability to deal effectively with others could, according to Beck's theory, reinforce the depressed person's low self-esteem, making him still less confident in dealing with others and leading to a downward spiral of negativity.

An alternative theory, stated by Martin Seligman (1975), sees depression as "learned helplessness." When people learn that whatever they do will have no effect on their situation, they come to feel helpless. If as a child, for example, a person

Reprinted by permission of Chon Day. As appeared in Psychology Today Magazine.

undergoes inescapable hurtful experiences, these will instill a sense of helplessness that can evolve into depressed feelings. Critics of this viewpoint contend that situations of helplessness can lead to feelings other than depression, such as anxiety or hostility (Blaney, 1977).

Operant learning theory sees the depressed person's negative mood as the product of a low rate of positive reinforcement (Lewinsohn, 1974). The depressed person has led an inactive, unrewarded existence in which few events are reinforcing. Very little the person does results in a positive outcome. People who become depressed, for example, were found to participate in fewer positive activities than they did before the onset of the depression (Lewinsohn and Graf, 1973). This finding, however, may simply reveal two different facets of the same phenomenon: people who are on their way to depression may already have begun to withdraw from pleasant activities, so that their withdrawal is not a cause but a correlation of their negative mood (Blaney, 1977).

A psychoanalytic theory of depression (Arieti and Bemporad, 1979) holds that depression stems from the loss of a "love object," a real or fantasized person to whom one is especially attached. The loss needn't be actual, as when someone leaves or dies; more often it is symbolic, such as the withdrawal of approval and affection during a critical period of development. Such a loss then predisposes the person to react with depression to similar situations in life where there is the real or imagined withdrawal of love.

This theory is sometimes cited in explaining the reason that two to five times as many women as men are diagnosed as depressed (Scarf, 1979). Traditionally, women have received less encouragement than men to become self-sufficient; they are more likely to try to recover an early lost love object through a love bond in later life, while men are more likely to do so through the pursuit of a career goal. The rate of lost love bonds as a result of changes in relationships—for example, through divorce—is much greater than the rate at which career goals fail; one outcome may be that many times more women than men are depressed.

Several biochemical causes of depression have also been proposed. The most influential is that depression is related to an imbalance in the neurotransmitter MAO. But as is the case with biochemical theories of schizophrenia, the evidence at this point is too thin to firmly support a clear understanding of the biochemical factors that may underlie the disorder (Snyder, 1980).

ANXIETY DISORDERS

Imagine that Mitch, a distant cousin you've never met, is passing through town and gives you a call. You invite him over for supper.

You're just showing him into the living room when your new kitten, Oliver, bounces in. Starting to introduce this adorable ball of fluff to Mitch, you stop in midsentence at the sight of him cowering against the wall. "Help! Help!" he says in a tiny scream.

Hastily you grab Oliver and lock him in the bedroom. In the living room, Mitch is mopping the sweat from his brow. "I'm sorry," he manages to explain, "but I'm terribly afraid of cats." ■

Mitch's fear of cats marks him as having an *anxiety disorder*, a behavior pattern in which some form of anxiety is the dominant symptom. A person like Mitch with an anxiety disorder has a morbid fear of an object, act, or situation despite the awareness that no real danger exists, or a response that is out of proportion to any actual danger. Anxiety is frequently one of many symptoms found in numerous diagnostic categories; in anxiety disorders, however, an irrational fear is the primary problem. In some instances there is free-floating, generalized anxiety, that is, a feeling of anxiousness with no particular object. However, the two most common anxiety disorders are *phobias*, where a specific object or situation arouses immobilizing anxiety, and *obsessive-compulsive disorder*, where the person suffers from recurrent ideas that seem foreign to his nature, yet cannot be ignored. These disorders are relatively common: an estimated 2 to 4 percent of people have had one at some time, and an estimated 10 percent of patients who consult heart specialists suffer from them (American Psychiatric Association, 1980).

Phobic disorders

Many people avoid objects or situations that provoke irrational fear, such as harmless bugs or giving speeches. When this avoidance has only a trivial effect on a person's life, then it is not a psychiatric symptom. But in those cases where such fears—and the avoidance they compel—bring a person distress, then the diagnosis is "phobic disorder."

The most familiar phobic disorders are simple phobias, where there is a single object that provokes irrational fear. The most common of these specific phobias are fear of animals, particularly snakes, insects, and rodents. Others are claustrophobia (fear of enclosed spaces), acrophobia (fear of high places), hemataphobia (fear of blood), nictophobia (fear of darkness), and xenophobia (fear of strangers). Mitch's fear of cats is ailurophobia.

Another common phobia is *agoraphobia*, where the person is morbidly afraid of leaving familiar surroundings. Typically, the victim of agoraphobia experiences a panic attack in unfamiliar settings. Thereafter, in anticipation of helplessness while having such an attack, the person becomes reluctant to be alone while traveling or to be in such situations as crowds, closed spaces, busy stores, or tunnels or bridges. In its severest form, the person becomes housebound.

Obsessive-compulsive disorder

In this disorder a person has obsessions—recurrent, persistent thoughts or impulses that seem foreign to his nature—and/or compulsions, the compelling need to engage in certain behavior. Common obsessions are thoughts of violence (such as attacking a stranger) or doubts (e.g., that the person will fail at some familiar task) that seem senseless to the person. Common compulsions are ritualistic: hand washing, counting, or touching. If the person tries to resist a compulsion, tension mounts—and can only be relieved by acting on the compulsion. Even though the person is clear that the obsessive thoughts are senseless and the compulsive rituals unnecessary, he cannot keep from giving in to them.

Dissociative disorders

In this class of disorder a person's identity undergoes a sudden, temporary change. Sometimes this results in loss of memory for important events in a person's life, or in strange acts such as aimless wandering. There is a splitting off, or dissociation, of parts of the personality from each other. The most common attribute is a short-lived shift in identity, so that a new identity takes over while the person forgets his customary one. In cases of *multiple personality*, which are rare, the person is dominated by one or more distinct, alternative identities. Each is a fully formed figure, with complex memories, habits, and friendships (Watkins and Watkins, 1979). The transition from one personality to another is sudden, and often occurs in reaction to stress. One of the personalities will be dominant, and often each of them will have amnesia for the others. The formation of several alternate personalities, in some cases, seems to be a protective dissociation, allowing the person to remain immune to overwhelming threats such as brutality from parents (Winer, 1978). In one well-

SYBIL: A STUDY OF SIXTEEN SELVES

■ There were sixteen of her, each trapped within the same physical body. Sybil, the usual waking self, was a fragile, demure woman whose only chance of survival was to dissociate into fifteen distinct personalities. Vicky projected the self-assurance of an attractive, omnipotent woman who possessed knowledge and insight into the other selves. Peggy Lou expressed herself as assertive, enthusiastic, and often volatile, and Peggy Ann acted like a frightened child. The intensely emotional Marcia Lynn wrote and painted. Vanessa Gail was a highly dramatic, willowy redhead. Mary Lucinda, thoughtful and maternal, was plump and had long dark hair. Some of the other selves included Mike and Sid, Sybil's male counterparts; Nancy Lou, interested in politics; Ruthie, a perpetual baby; and five other female selves.

Sybil's usual self was oblivious of the memories and experiences of the alternating selves and so, of course, unable to recognize the incongruities their identities posed to her own. As a young woman, Sybil often found herself in strange places where Peggy Lou or Peggy Ann had taken her. At other times, Sybil discovered paintings she had not painted, clothes she had not bought, and friends she had never met. These amnesic experiences, in which she seemed to "lose time," were perhaps the most compelling factor that motivated Sybil to seek out Dr. Cornelia Wilbur (Schreiber, 1973).

Through psychoanalysis, Wilbur uncovered the causes of Sybil's dissociation. The sixteen personalities, Wilbur concluded, resulted from Sybil's being born into a family that was "restrictive, naive, and hysterical"—Sybil's schizophrenic mother inflicted ritualistic daily tortures upon her daughter; Sybil's aloof father provided no escape route; and her grandfather was a wrathful and hysterical religious fanatic. Because no escape from this family existed, Sybil dissociated into sixteen fragmented personalities in order to ensure her emotional and physical survival.

During the psychoanalysis, Dr. Wilbur had the opportunity of meeting all the other selves. Vicky, possessing the memories of Sybil as well as the

---

known case of multiple personality, the person had sixteen distinct, well-developed alternate personalities (see box, "Sybil: A Study of Sixteen Selves").

PERSONALITY DISORDERS

Imagine that your childhood neighbor, Fred, was always in trouble. He skipped school constantly, making up elaborate lies for both his teachers and his parents. His reputation as the bully of the block was well-earned: he stole money from smaller children and picked fights with just about anybody. Whenever windows were broken at school or playground equipment was damaged, everyone knew Fred was the vandal, though no one could ever prove it.

Although bright, he never did his schoolwork, and by junior high he was three grades behind in school. Not that it mattered: his fighting and smoking got him expelled.

Somehow it doesn't surprise you many years later to pick up a paper one day and find Fred has been arrested for robbing the local bank. ■

Fred's history of troublemaking marks him as an *antisocial personality,* a person who is constantly in conflict with society. The antisocial person belongs within the diagnostic category of *person-*

other selves, served as coanalyst. Wilbur engaged her support to probe into the initial traumas that caused each dissociation. The omnipotent personality of Vicky was also the essential link in the evolution of a new, "integrated" Sybil.

To achieve this integration, Wilbur recognized that she would have to analyze each personality as if he or she were a completely different person. Throughout the analysis, Wilbur's most agonizing task was confronting Sybil with her other selves and encouraging her to recognize their memories and experiences as her own. Only through acceptance of them would integration—normalcy—be possible.

After eleven arduous years of therapy that involved a variety of techniques such as hypnosis and pentathol (a barbiturate that aids in relaxation and hypnosis), Wilbur was able to consider her patient cured. The stolen memories, experiences, and feelings—so long ago dissociated—were returned to a new, whole Sybil. ∎

TABLE 16.3 **TYPES OF PERSONALITY DISORDERS IN DSM-III**

1. Paranoid personality disorder Pervasive and unwarranted suspiciousness and mistrust of others.

2. Introverted personality disorder Inability and lack of desire to form social relationships.

3. Schizotypical personality disorder Tendency toward schizophrenic-type language, thought, and misperceptions without any sign of psychotic break with reality.

4. Histrionic personality disorder (hysterical personality) Excitability, self-dramatization, attention-seeking, shallow, and lacking in genuineness, and frequently manipulative of others by suicidal threats, gestures, or attempts.

5. Narcissistic personality disorder Self-centered and with a grandiose sense of self-importance. Exhibitionistic, requiring constant attention and admiration. Lack of empathy for others and a tendency to exploit others for personal gain.

6. Antisocial personality disorder History of tantrums and chronic antisocial behavior (lying, thefts, vandalism, aggressive behavior, etc.), in which the rights of others are violated.

7. Borderline personality disorder Stormy personality who drifts into psychotic states under stress.

8. Avoidant personality Low self-esteem, hypersensitivity to rejection, social withdrawal.

9. Dependent personality disorder Low self-confidence, fearful of self-reliance, relies on others to assume responsibility for major areas of one's life. Intense discomfort when alone.

10. Compulsive personality disorder Shows signs of obsessive-compulsive neurotic actions (indecisiveness, preoccupation, etc.).

ality disorders, deeply ingrained maladaptive patterns of behavior and relations with others. These disorders seem central to the whole personality, rather than isolated symptoms, and interfere with a wide range of social and personal situations. There are several types of personality disorder, including, for example, narcissism, where a person is self-absorbed and unable to care about others. Personality disorders typically begin in adolescence or before, and continue through adulthood.

The antisocial person (one of many kinds of personality disorder) shows continuous and chronic disregard for the rights of others. Typical childhood signs are lying, stealing, truancy, and fighting. By the teen years, the antisocial person is unusually promiscuous sexually and likely to overindulge in drinking or illegal drugs. In adulthood the more flagrant of these behaviors diminish, but the person may never become self-supporting. The adult years of the antisocial person often reveal frequent job changes, long periods of unemployment or absenteeism, several marriages and separations, defaulting on debts, or traveling with no clear goal from place to place. Often this pattern culminates in crime and imprisonment. The antisocial person is frequently of above-average intelligence, but has never performed up to the levels expected.

Because this behavior pattern seems typical of many criminals, some criminologists have equated the antisocial person with the "criminal personality" (Yochelson and Samenow, 1978), though psychiatric critics point out that such a label obscures the social and economic factors that seem to underlie much of crime (Menninger, 1978). Other lines of research have sought to find psychophysiological or behavioral differences among antisocial people that would explain their frequent criminal behavior. Some investigators, for example, have sought to show that antisocial criminals have fewer emotional reactions than other people, and so could be more "cold-blooded" in their treatment of others (e.g., Hare, 1975). Others have looked for differences in brain wave patterns among this group (Knott, Platt, Ashby, and Gottleib, 1963). Neither approach has yielded definitive explanations of the antisocial personality type.

Another line of thought is that what sets the antisocial person apart is cognitive, not physiological. The remarkable indifference of antisocial criminals to punishment may be due to a quirk in their thinking: many seem to have a superstitious belief in their immunity and are therefore not deterred from crime by the threat of punishment, believing instead in their invulnerability to arrest. When punishment is uncertain (as when a person commits a crime but may not be caught), this belief in immunity prevails, but when punishment is certain, the antisocial person is deterred (Seigel, 1978).

PSYCHOSEXUAL DISORDERS

Imagine that you're sitting at a bar nursing a beer when a striking blond sits on the stool next to you. "Mind if I join you?" she asks in a low, throaty voice.

"Please do," you say. The blond is elaborately made up and dressed to kill. Quite striking. Until it suddenly dawns on you: she's a man. ■

Sexual behavior that departs from the sanctions of a given society is called *deviant*, but different cultures have different standards for what is deviant and what normal. In modern America, the man dressed as a woman in the bar would be considered deviant, while in other cultures a man dressed as a woman for certain rituals or celebrations may be following cultural norms. People

who deviate from the accepted norms for sexual behavior in this culture may have a *psychosexual disorder*, a psychological condition that compels them to engage in deviant acts or causes them distress about their sexual identity or behavior.

There are three major groups of psychosexual disorders. In *gender identity disorders* a person feels discomfort about his or her biological sex and prefers to act in ways typical of the other sex. In *paraphilia* a person is sexually aroused by objects or situations that normally do not arouse people, and is furthermore unable to have a loving sexual relationship. In *psychosexual dysfunction* the person does not undergo the expected changes of sexual responsiveness.

People with gender identity disorders feel an incongruence between their anatomical sex and their gender identity. A biological woman with a gender identity disorder would, for example, experience herself as a man, despite her social role as a woman. This disorder underlies *transsexualism*, the persistent discomfort with one's anatomic sex and the wish to live as a member of the other sex. Transsexuals are often uncomfortable wearing the clothes of their anatomic sex and frequently cross-dress in the clothes of the opposite sex. Their own genitals are often repugnant to them, and they frequently seek surgical or hormonal treatments to physically alter their sex.

The woman in the bar who turned out to be a man may have been a *transvestite*, one of the paraphilias in which a heterosexual male dresses as a woman to become sexually aroused. Transvestites may merely wear a single article of female clothing while alone or fully masquerade as a woman in public. Transvestism should not be confused with the cross-dressing of a transsexual. A transvestite cross-dresses for sexual excitement; a transsexual does so to identify with the opposite sex.

The paraphilias are a group of conditions marked by persistent sexual fantasies and stimulation of an unusual nature. Some of the more common paraphilias are: *fetishism*, a preference for an object—for example, a woman's shoe—to induce sexual arousal; *sadomasochism*, sexual activity that involves suffering or hurting; and sexual activity with nonconsenting partners, such as *pedophilia*, or the desire for sex with children.

The paraphilia diagnosis is applied only when these sexual tastes are so extreme that they impair the person's capacity for socially acceptable, affectionate sexual activity (Goleman and Bush, 1978). They are far more common in males than females. Some theorists suspect this is so because males are more easily aroused sexually, and so have more opportunity to pair sexual arousal with various objects or situations—thus acquiring an unusual sexual taste.

Psychosexual dysfunction involves hampered sexual appetite or physical responsiveness. Cases of frigidity or impotence fall into this category. In general, the person suffers an impairment in one or more phases of the sexual response cycle. The first phase is appetitive, and includes sexual fantasies and the desire for sexual activity. This leads to the excitement phase, feelings of sexual pleasure and accompanying physical changes, such as an erection in men and vaginal swelling and lubrication in women. Orgasm, the third phase, consists of the peaking of sexual pleasure with release of sexual tension. The final phase, resolution, is a sense of relaxation and well-being.

Homosexuality, the preference for a sexual partner of the same sex, is not in itself regarded as a psychiatric disorder. Instead, homosexuality is regarded as a disorder only when the person is distressed by this sexual orientation. If homosexuality causes other disorders—for example, anxiety—then these will be diagnosed and treated.

DISORDERS IN CHILDHOOD AND ADOLESCENCE

Imagine that your neighbor's kid is a holy terror. He's only five, but even the seven-year-olds on the block steer clear of him. For one thing he flies off the handle over the least slight, attacking anyone who happens to be in range. For another, he won't wait his turn in group games and always wants to be first at everything. If the other kids don't go along with his whims, he starts a fight.

His mother has often complained to you that she can't control him herself. "Ever since he could crawl," she bemoans, "he's ignored my orders. He won't follow instructions in kindergarten either. He can't seem to keep his mind on the same thing for more than a few seconds."

It was the memory of this conversation that was in your thoughts one day when she asked you if you might be able to babysit. "Sorry," you lied, "I've got a date." ■

The hard-to-take neighborhood terror fits the description of *hyperactivity*, overactivity with disorganized inattention. This disorder is one of the more common found among children and adolescents. Some children's disorders (including hyperactivity) clear up or fade in significance as the person grows into adulthood. Others—particularly psychosis—are much more serious when found in childhood, and will quite often continue throughout adult life.

Hyperactivity

The child who is constantly excited and on the move, bothering other kids and grownups, restless, and impulsive falls into the DSM-III category of "attention deficit disorder with hyperactivity." Difficulties with attention are virtually always present in hyperactive children and seem to be the key problem underlying their overactivity. In school, these children are found to have a short attention span, be impulsive, distractible, and inattentive, and have trouble following instructions. At home, they ignore their parents' requests, can't play a game for as long as others their age, and are constantly on the go. The quality of overactivity in such children is disorganized, haphazard, and disruptive. While it may not be obvious in a playground, it is clearly debilitating in a structured situation like school.

The effect of attentional deficits in hyperactivity is paradoxical. One speculative theory holds that such children suffer from a rate of brain activity that is too slow. They are neurologically understimulated, and crave stimulation from the outside; their extreme restlessness is the pursuit of this stimulation (Wender, 1971). This theory (as yet unproven) would explain why drugs that are brain stimulants for most people have the opposite effect on hyperactive children, slowing down their relentless motor activity: when their brain becomes stimulated, they no longer need to seek stimulation from their suroundings.

Infantile autism

While each child follows his or her own individual route to developing basic motor, social, and language skills, there are broad developmental norms that most follow. The *developmental disorders* are distortions in the usual timing and sequence of development, severely impairing many basic areas of a child's psychological skills. The best-known pervasive developmental disorder is *infantile autism*, where a child by age three shows a lack of responsiveness to people, is grossly impaired in communication ability, and responds bizarrely. Autistic children do not display the signs of attachment normally seen in infants; they do not cuddle, are indifferent or averse to affection and touch, and show no interest in other people. Often parents take this indifference as a sign of deafness. The child may never learn to speak, and may make only strange facial expressions and odd gestures.

The autistic child's bizarre responses can include fascination with movement or music and attachment to odd objects, such as always carrying a certain pencil, rubber band, or piece of string. Resistance to even minor changes in the environment can take such forms as screaming if the child's favorite chair is moved. Ritualistic behavior might include constantly repeating strange hand movements; an autistic child may stare for hours at a whirring fan. Oddly, autistic children often will have exceptional memory for details from the distant past, such as the exact license plate number of cars or the details of a train schedule, or even have the mathematical brilliance of an "idiot savant," who can perform incredible feats such as multiplying two twelve-digit numbers in his or her head, but would otherwise be considered mentally defective (Rimland, 1978).

Sometimes the parents of an autistic child do not realize there is anything unusual in its early development, particularly if it is their first baby. The problems become obvious when the child is in a group with other children. Very few autistic children make a full adjustment to adult life, the majority needing total care throughout their lives.

It was once thought that infantile autism could result from poor parent-child relations in the first months or years of the child's life. Evidence has failed to support this theory. While the causes of autism remain unknown, the best candidates seem to be biological or neurological in nature.

SUMMARY

Abnormal behavior is that which diminishes a person's personal and social well-being. The medical model proposes that all mental disorders have organic causes. Psychosocial models explain such disorders in terms of psychological or social factors or both.

DSM-III is an extensive diagnostic and classification system for mental disorders. Diagnosis has its critics, however, who contend it is unreliable and stigmatizes people.

Organic mental disorders. Organic disorders are caused by temporary or permanent malfunc-

tion of the brain, and are commonly accompanied by emotional and cognitive problems.

Dementia, one form of organic disorder, is characterized by deterioration of memory, impulse control, and intellectual abilities.

Substance abuse disorders. The drugs most common in substance abuse disorders are alcohol, heroin, amphetamines, barbiturates, and marijuana. To be identified as abused, a drug must be used over a period of at least a month and disturb the user's social functioning. Drug use can result in psychological dependency as well as physical addiction. Physiological tolerance can build up, requiring larger doses. Withdrawal symptoms accompany discontinuance of the abused drug.

Schizophrenic disorder. In psychosis, a person loses contact with reality and behaves in a bizarre, socially uncontrollable manner.

The different types of schizophrenic disorders have in common language disturbance, delusions, hallucinations, distorted affect, and withdrawal from the world. Schizophrenia is categorized into three main types: hebephrenic, catatonic, and paranoid.

Theories about the causes of schizophrenia include genetic, biochemical or environmental factors, or a combination (the diathesis-stress theory). Research has not yet definitively identified an origin for the disease.

Affective disorders. The affective disorders are characterized by extreme disturbances of mood, either depressive, manic, or bipolar. The cognitive theory sees depression as a result of negative thoughts. Behavioral theories see depression as the product of self-defeating attitudes, such as learned helplessness. The psychoanalytic theory sees depression triggered by loss of a love object. Biochemical theories include hormonal and neurotransmitter imbalances. As with schizophrenia, however, no simple adequate explanation has yet been found.

Personality disorders. Antisocial behavior is one of the personality disorders, which interfere with healthy functioning in a wide range of social and personal situations. The antisocial person, for example, shows continuous and chronic disregard for the rights of others, and his life seems constantly unsettled. Sometimes labeled the "criminal personality," such an individual may think differently from other people, for example, believing himself invulnerable to punishment.

Psychosexual disorders. There are three major groups of psychosexual disorders: gender identity disorders, paraphilias and psychosexual dysfunctions.

People who feel uncomfortable about their sexual identity have a gender identity disorder. Transsexuals prefer to act in ways typical of the other sex. Their feelings are so compelling that transsexuals often seek to change their sex through hormonal and surgical treatment.

The paraphilias include fetishism, sadomasochism, pedophilia, and transvestism. Psychosexual dysfunction involves hampered sexual appetite or physical responsiveness.

Childhood disorders. Disorders in childhood and adolescence include attention deficit disorders—with hyperactivity, impulsivity, and distractibility their hallmark—and pervasive developmental disorders, of which the best known is infantile autism.

GLOSSARY

Affective disorder Extreme disturbances of mood, whether depression or elation.

Agoraphobia A morbid fear of leaving familiar surroundings.

Antisocial personality A personality disorder characterizing a person who is constantly in conflict with society, does not feel guilt, and does not learn from experience or punishment.

Anxiety disorder A psychological problem in which some form of anxiety is the predominant symptom.

Catatonic schizophrenia A psychosis characterized by immobility, rigidity, and negativism, sometimes interrupted by periods of agitation and shouting.

Chronic disorder A long-standing illness for which there is no clear onset.

Delusions False beliefs about reality.

Dementia An organic brain disorder characterized by deterioration of a person's memory, impulse control, and intellectual abilities.

Depression An affective disorder characterized by negative mood.

Developmental disorder A distortion in the usual timing and sequence of a child's development with severe impairment of many basic psychological skills, such as the ability to concentrate.

Diathesis-stress theory Proposes that schizophrenia occurs in people with an inherited predisposition for it (the diathesis) who are also exposed to stress.

Differential diagnosis The ability to distinguish one disorder from similar ones.

Double bind A situation in which one person gives another conflicting messages; believed by some to be a causative factor in schizophrenia.

Episodic disorder A period of illness that is clearly different from the person's typical mode of functioning before onset.

Fetishism A preference for a particular inanimate object or part of the body to produce sexual gratification, to the exclusion of the person as a whole.

Gender identity disorder A condition characterized by a person's feelings of discomfort with the role of his or her own biological sex.

Hallucinations Perceptions of things that aren't there in reality.

Hebephrenic schizophrenia Blatantly disorganized thinking, shallow and inappropriate emotional reactions, and regressive behavior.

Hyperactivity Overactivity with disorganized inattention.

Infantile autism In children, lack of responsiveness to people, gross impairment of communication ability, and bizarre behavior.

Maladaptive behavior Abnormal behavior that diminishes a person's well-being and growth.

Manic An affective state of extreme, agitated expansiveness.

Medical model Proposes that, like physical disease, all mental disorders have underlying organic causes.

Multiple personality The domination of a person by one or more distinct, alternative identities.

Obsessive-compulsive disorder An anxiety disorder in which a person suffers from recurrent ideas or strong impulses that seem foreign to his nature yet cannot be ignored, such as the impulse to wash his or her hands every few minutes.

Operational criteria Specific symptoms that must always be present before a particular diagnosis can be made.

Organic brain disorders Mental disorders due to temporary or permanent malfunction of the brain.

Paranoia A psychosis in which the main sign of abnormality is a person's delusion of being persecuted.

Paranoid schizophrenia A psychosis characterized by suspiciousness, delusions, hallucinations, and aggressiveness.

Paraphilia A psychosexual disorder in which a person is unable to have a loving sexual relationship and is sexually aroused by objects or situations not normally considered sexual.

Pedophilia A paraphilia where a person seeks sex with children.

Personality disorder Deeply ingrained maladaptive patterns of relating to others.

Phobia An anxiety disorder in which a specific object or situation arouses immobilizing anxiety.

Psychological dependence The compelling desire to use a drug and inability to cut down or stop its use, despite the absence of physical addiction.

Psychosexual disorder A condition in which a person is compelled to engage in deviant sexual acts or which causes him distress about his sexual identity or behavior.

Psychosis A mental disorder in which a person loses contact with reality.

Psychosocial model Explains mental disorder in terms of psychological or social factors or both.

Sadomasochism A paraphilia characterized by sexual activity that involves suffering or hurting.

Schizophrenia A psychosis whose chief symptoms are disturbed thought, perception, and moods, and withdrawal from other people.

Substance abuse disorder The habitual use of brain-altering drugs to the extent that they interfere with social functioning or cannot be stopped without causing an adverse physical reaction.

Tolerance The physical condition in which increasing amounts of a drug are needed to achieve the desired effect.

Transsexualism Persistent discomfort with one's anatomic sex and the desire to live as a member of the other sex.

Transvestism A paraphilia in which a person dresses like a member of the opposite sex in order to become sexually aroused.

Withdrawal A specific set of distressing or painful symptoms that occur after a person stops or reduces intake of a drug upon which he or she has become dependent.

17

THERAPIES

COMMON MYTHS

MANY PEOPLE BELIEVE ...	ACTUALLY ...
All therapies are alike.	There are many therapies that have little or nothing in common.
The titles "psychologist," "psychiatrist," and "psychoanalyst" are interchangeable.	Each refers to a different kind of professional training.
A psychoanalyst knows specific universal meanings for the symbols in people's dreams.	The meaning of symbols in dreams is highly individualized; the same symbol in different people's dreams can mean different things.
"Behavior modification" refers to the use of shock to change a person's behavior.	"Behavior modification" describes a wide variety of therapeutic techniques, all of which derive from principles of learning theory.
Shock treatment is used primarily to cure various types of neurotic behavior.	Electroconvulsive therapy is most often used to treat acute psychosis, especially cases of severe depression.

Psychotherapy may be described as "an undefined technique applied to unspecified cases with unpredictable results." For this technique rigorous training is required.

VICTOR RAIMY

While psychotherapy is certainly not as ambiguous a procedure as Raimy's wry description suggests, it is also not as precise and well-defined as one might hope. For one thing, there is a therapy boom: the number of different therapies has proliferated to well beyond 250 (Herink, 1980). The range of techniques that call themselves "therapy" is so vast that there is little or nothing in common between many of them. Psychoanalysis and nude marathon encounter groups are very different, yet both are seen as "therapies."

The one commonality among *therapies* is that, though they may differ dramatically in specifics, they are all experiences that aim to change maladaptive behavior and help a person to behave in a constructive manner. A technical definition of therapy is as follows—"any intentional application of psychological techniques by a clinician to the end of affecting sought-after personality or behavioral changes" (Korchin, 1976).

Each therapist's method will be influenced by his or her theoretical bent. There are four main approaches to therapy. The *psychodynamic* model has as its goal self-knowledge, or insight. By helping the patient bring repressed, anxiety-causing memories into awareness, the psychodynamic therapist frees him for a more productive life. The *humanistic-existential* model has the therapist help the patient to assume more responsibility for his behavior through increased self-awareness and self-acceptance; the greater use of the patient's human potential is the goal. The *behaviorist* model holds that the therapist should use the principles of conditioning to change maladaptive response patterns, with little or no regard for the experiences that caused them. In the *medical* model, the therapist, who is usually a physician, tries to cure mental illness as she would any other malady, with such treatments as drugs, hospitalization, and even brain surgery.

The classic dichotomy in psychotherapy has been between the psychodynamic viewpoint that only insight and understanding can bring about lasting therapeutic change and the behaviorist stand that only actual change in behavior counts. In practice, though, few therapists take either of these extreme positions. Instead they combine a concern for understanding underlying causes with attempts to bring about specific behavioral changes (Messer and Winokur, 1980).

443

THE THERAPEUTIC RELATIONSHIP

Although every type of person can have psychological problems, certain types of people seek therapeutic help out of proportion to their numbers. Studies show that the overwhelming majority of people who seek psychotherapy—and can afford to pay for it—are sophisticated, verbal, and intelligent. They tend not to be seriously impaired, but regard psychotherapy as a valued and socially acceptable way to get help for their problems in living. These patients have been dubbed the YAVIS: "youthful, attractive, verbal, intelligent, and successful" (Schofield, 1964).

On the other hand, many severely distressed people who are virtually unable to function in daily life—who constitute most of the nation's mental health problem—rarely receive professional psychotherapeutic attention (Kennedy, 1978). These are the patients who come to the attention of therapists only in extreme crisis, or who end up in custodial institutions.

The type of problem the patient has determines—or should determine—the kind of therapy he receives. But the question of which type of therapy or combination of techniques is best for a given disorder is far from answered (Wolman, 1976). The research that has been done is often confounded by *spontaneous recovery*, the improvement of patients who have received no therapy at all (Bergin, 1980). For example, one study showed that people seeking therapy who are placed on a waiting list tend to improve as much as a comparison group of patients who go to therapy (Barron and Leary, 1955). A recent review of all such studies examined the contention that patients who receive therapy actually do worse than those who do not (Mays and Franks, 1980). The conclusion: there is no sound evidence to support that contention, although more and better research is needed in order to more fully understand and evaluate the effectiveness of therapy.

Another factor that confuses our understanding of the therapeutic relationship is the *placebo effect*, the improvement of a patient's condition due to the simple expectation that improvement will occur (Shapiro, 1978). The prerequisite for the placebo effect—or any other unexplained healing—seems to be the shared expectation between patient and therapist that improvement will be seen (Frank, 1979).

The positive effects of expectation of recovery can be used to advantage in therapy. In one study, female patients with a fear of snakes were given psychological tests before they were treated, then randomly assigned to one of three groups: no treatment at all; treatment but no test feedback; and both treatment and the report that tests showed they were ripe for therapeutic change. While the treatment-only group improved markedly more than those who were not treated, the group told they had potential for improvement outshone both (Halperin and Snyder, 1979). In other words, the belief that one can improve enhances one's chance of improving.

KNOW YOUR THERAPIST

■ There is no single standard for training, credentials, or outlook among the mixed bag of people who work as therapists. A therapist may be a psychologist (Ph.D. with clinical training), a psychiatrist (M.D. with further training in psychiatry), a psychoanalyst (usually, but not always, a psychiatrist with further training in psychoanalysis), a psychiatric social worker or other master's-level degree-holder, psychiatric nurse (R.N. with some training in psychiatry), or a nonprofessional whose only training is acquired in a special orientation or program that does not earn any academic credential.

The training and credentials of therapists are a clue to their experience and perspective, but these do not always guarantee the quality of therapy. The greatest factor in a therapist's effectiveness may be her own personality—not the type of training received or method employed. An extensive study of the traits of effective therapists identified three: (1) accurate empathy, the ability to put oneself in the patient's place and to understand his difficulties; (2) warmth, the capacity to like a patient without being possessive; and (3) genuineness, sincerity in dealing with the patient (Truax and Carkhuff, 1967).

The lines between different therapies as actually practiced are also becoming blurred (London, 1974). For example, all forms of "insight" therapy, such as psychoanalysis and the humanistic-existential, aim to discover the causes that underlie the patients' behavior. The assumption is that by understanding our motives and behavior, we will be better able to deal with them. In insight therapies, there is more emphasis on understanding symptoms, less on changing them. "Action" therapies, such as the behavior therapies, put less emphasis on talking and more on changing the symptoms for the better.

Of course, few therapists fit neatly into any of these categories. By borrowing from several or all of these models, each therapist evolves her own technique. Some say there are as many kinds of therapy as there are therapists.

The course of therapy is determined in part by the ideals and values of the therapist. A therapist, like anyone else, has his or her own preconceptions of what people are like, what they should be ideally, and what means of therapy will make them more like the ideal. Whether or not these preconceptions are ever openly stated by the therapist, they will guide what happens during therapy. Because the therapist's values influence what happens, Hans Strupp (1974) has raised the question of whose agent the therapist is: The patient's? The family's? Society's? The school system's? In no case is the therapist really "value-free."

Strupp goes on to argue that the therapist's influence is so powerful that the concept of a value-free or neutral therapy is a fiction. He also points out that the patient, far from being passive, is thinking and responding, and so, of course, also determines the course of therapy. In the last analysis, it is the patient's response to change that makes a success or failure of therapy. ■

Because the patient is a partner in the progress of therapy, and because questions of values can be a crucial factor in what the therapist does, some therapists are calling for a "participatory" psychotherapy (Coyne and Widiger, 1978). Rather than assume, as in the past, that patient welfare is best served by the therapist's exercise of control over methods, goals, and decisions, the therapist shares information with the patient so that they can jointly decide how to proceed.

There is little doubt that the therapeutic relationship is in transition. For one thing, less and less therapy continues for years, as it did originally in psychoanalysis. Patients are more frequently seen for short-term treatment to handle specific life crises, and participate on the average for eight sessions; 80 percent are out of treatment by twenty-five sessions (Koss, 1979).

THE CASE OF MRS. C.

Mrs. C. is the mother of six children: Arlene, 17; Barry, 15; Charles, 13; Debra, 11; Ellen, 9; and Frederick, 7. As the orderliness of her children's names and ages might suggest, Mrs. C. is an obsessive-compulsive. For the past ten years she has been plagued by a compulsion to wash. She washes her hands twenty-five to thirty-five times a day, five to ten minutes each time. Her two-hour-long morning shower entails elaborate ritual washing of each part of her body; if she loses her place in the order, she begins all over again. More than once this has meant that when her husband came home from work eight hours later, she was still in the shower. She also won't let anyone in her family wear a pair of underwear for more than a day, and often won't wash them. There are piles of unwashed underwear in every corner of the house. Mrs. C. has not bought any clothes in seven years, and her appearance has become ragged. She is also a hoarder, with closets filled with sheets, towels, and most of her clothes from the last twenty years.

Mrs. C., although willing to engage in intercourse to satisfy her husband, admits she has never been sexually excited in her life. In the last two years, though, sex has become so unpleasant for her that she has had intercourse only twice. Currently quite depressed, Mrs. C. swallowed a bottle of aspirin in a suicide attempt triggered by the thought that her therapist was giving up on her and her husband was going to send her to a mental hospital.

Her washing compulsions began ten years ago when a daughter came home with pinworms. Her physician had told her to boil her clothes, and be careful to wash the family's underwear to kill any pinworm eggs. Her preoccupations continued and built from that time.

Mrs. C. came from a strict home, dominated by a physically huge father. Her father would not al-

low the expression of anger, especially toward himself, and was puritanical about his daughter's behavior on dates. Mrs. C.'s mother was also compulsive and rigid and warned her daughter about the importance of cleanliness, and how disgusting sex was. ■

The case of Mrs. C., as reported by James Prochaska (1979), is based on an actual patient treated in a mental health clinic. A severe obsessive-compulsive disorder was diagnosed, with the prognosis that she would be difficult to treat. Mrs. C.'s case could be treated by any number of therapies. To better understand how each type of therapy works, we shall see how each of the major ones might go about helping Mrs. C.

PSYCHOANALYSIS

Imagine that Mrs. C. consults a psychoanalyst. In a typical session, Mrs. C. would talk freely about her problems and about any associations to them from her childhood, while the therapist would say little except for an occasional observation. When told to lie on a couch and say whatever comes to mind, she would resist letting her thoughts go where they would. Her anxiety would be due to fears of giving up control to the analyst and would take the form of returning, whenever she felt anxious, to the topic of her obsession with pinworms and washing. The analyst would point out this pattern when it occurred and interpret it for her by observing that she uses her obsession to keep herself from experiencing fears even greater than pinworms.

As Mrs. C. slowly became aware of the ways her symptoms defended her from feelings—particularly from the anger and sexuality her parents forbade her to express—she would begin to feel these very things toward the analyst. Just as her father and mother tried to control her aggression and sexuality but were themselves ungiving, she would become enraged that her therapist was also ungiving—yet she would also become aware of sexual impulses toward him.

With time Mrs. C. would realize the meaning

and causes of these feelings toward her therapist and at the same time gain insight into the causes of her symptoms. Finally, her obsessive-compulsive symptoms would drop away as she became able to express her anger and sexual impulses without panic (adapted from Prochaska, 1979). ■

The methods of psychoanalysis originated with Freud's theory of *abreaction*, overcoming traumatic experiences by bringing them into awareness. As Mrs. C. was able to remember the childhood trauma of her father's controlling her anger and her mother's attitude that sex was disgusting, this awareness allowed her to reshape her expression of these impulses more adaptively. Instead of being preoccupied with her obsessions with cleanliness, she was able to acknowledge her underlying feelings of anxiety and anger, and talk about them openly. Such an understanding of the childhood roots of maladaptive behavior is termed *insight*. Insight into repressed feelings allows a person to deal with them more effectively; the path to insight in psychoanalysis demands reexperiencing past traumas with all their emotional upheaval, a difficult task for most of us.

The patient in conventional psychoanalysis lies on a couch with the therapist out of view, relaxes, and focuses all attention inward. The main technique for achieving insight is *free association*, saying whatever thoughts or feelings come to mind. While free association sounds easy, most people find they do not seem to think of anything to say, or their thoughts seem too embarrassing or strange to say freely. Such hesitancies, or *resistance*, are exactly what the therapist is looking for. Any such signs of the patient's resistance to thoughts or feelings indicate that the latter are painful or threatening—and therefore important. Noting the kinds of topics that elicit resistance, the therapist can interpret their meaning, and so help the patient work through, or examine, the neurotic conflicts, dreams, and childhood memories that have appeared in a meaningful pattern during his or her life (Freud, 1939). *Interpretation*, making unconscious associations clear and understandable to the patient, is at the core of psychoanalysis.

What the patient says may not seem significant on the level of its *manifest* content, the obvious, surface meanings. The analyst's task is to uncover and explore with the patient the *latent*, or underlying, content. Dreams are a frequent vehicle for latent content. Because a person's defenses are lowered during sleep, forbidden desires or unac-

In psychoanalysis the therapist typically says very little, while the patient free associates. During traditional psychoanalysis the patient lies down with the therapist out of view. In other kinds of therapy patient and therapist sit facing each other.
(Sedwick/The Picture Cube)

ceptable motives can find symbolic outlets in dreams. Through such means as interpreting the meanings of the symbols in a patient's dreams—always a highly individualized matter—the analyst helps the patient lay bare the unconscious conflicts that plague his or her life.

Because he can elicit such disturbing, anxiety-laden memories, the therapist plays a unique role for each of his patients. At some point during the analysis, the patient develops an intense, emotional response, called *transference*, to the therapist; in fact, he transfers to the therapist all the characteristics of the principal figures remembered from childhood. He reenacts his unresolved childhood conflicts with this substitute figure. If, for example, he hated his father, he comes to hate the therapist. But now he can work through—examine—his feelings and finally understand his hostility and anxiety. As his unconscious motives are brought to the level of consciousness, his inappropriate defenses are cast aside, and—in theory—he can respond to the therapist and to others who are important to him in a more spontaneous and positive way. For example, the patient who learns with the therapist to understand the roots of his anger toward his father should finally be able to relate to his father realistically, without anger.

HUMANISTIC AND EXISTENTIAL THERAPIES

Humanistic therapists work toward the goal of self-understanding, striving to help patients become more truly "themselves," maximizing their sense of freedom. These therapies focus on a person's potential for health and happiness and capacity for responsible self-direction. Existential therapists encourage clients to take responsibility for their own symptoms and to consider such issues as alienation and meaninglessness that block them from achieving their full human potential.

Imagine that Mrs. C. consults a client-centered therapist. The therapist does not condemn Mrs. C.'s compulsive washing, or even suggest that she needs to stop.

This attitude of unconditional positive regard is far different from the feelings of worthlessness Mrs. C. got from her parents. In her childhood she was made to feel that her worth depended on being meek and nonaggressive, clean, and asexual. With her husband and family, too, she has found that caring is as rigidly conditional as in childhood: they tell her, don't wash and we will love you.

Now with her therapist she encounters someone who regards her as worthwhile because of who she is rather than what she does. She need not give up her one remaining source of self-esteem—her washing. Slowly she begins to feel that she is held in high regard whether she washes or not, whether she talks about washing or doesn't.

As she experiences the therapist's positive regard, she finds herself free to understand that she can love herself whether or not she washes. She begins to feel better about herself. One day Mrs. C. finds that she no longer washes compulsively (adapted from Prochaska, 1979). ■

Client-centered therapy

With a client-centered therapist, Mrs. C. finds herself talking to someone who does not attempt to find the unconscious meanings in what she does, but rather reflects back to her the feelings behind the things she says. Mrs. C. is free to talk about whatever she wishes, with full confidence that her therapist will be accepting and sincere, no matter what she says. The client-centered therapist is *nondirective*, allowing the client to discuss whatever he or she wishes to discuss. The therapist is simply a mirror, reflecting back the true feelings that underlie the client's words.

Developed by Carl Rogers (1961), client-centered therapy operates under the assumption that acceptance of the client by the therapist increases the client's sense of self-worth, giving him or her the strength to face denied or hidden feelings. As insight and self-confidence develop, the client can drop neurotic defenses and become more open to people and to new experiences. The improvement of the client's symptoms is part of a larger process of growth that is facilitated by the enhancement of the client's sense of self-esteem. Rogers prefers the term "client" to the traditional "patient" and sees client-centered therapy as more a process of enhancing personal growth than one of curing symptoms.

Existential therapy

There are many kinds of existential therapy, all of which stem from the concerns of philosophers such as Kierkegaard, Heidegger, and Sartre. They all emphasize man's freedom of choice and the responsibility that freedom brings. The emphasis is on the here-and-now rather than what happened in a person's past.

In an *encounter* between two unique people—patient and therapist—existential therapy requires that the therapist share herself so that the patient can respond to her as just another person. The therapist must see the world through her patient's eyes and confront him with questions concerning the meaning and purpose of his existence. Once the patient recognizes the destructive aspects of his lifestyle, his motivation to change will be renewed. According to this view he can then commit himself to action and to other people.

Gestalt therapy

Developed by Fritz Perls, gestalt therapy is one of the more popular humanistic techniques. Perls combined insights from his own psychoanalytic training with the thinking of gestalt psychologists. Perls' methods aim to bring one into full awareness of one's *gestalt*, the total pattern made by one's feelings, actions, and the situation at a given moment. Rather than looking into the past for causes, gestalt therapy aims to restore awareness of the here-and-now; the main task is to replenish the capacity for full awareness by helping people learn how they lose, avoid, or misuse awareness. The therapist confronts clients with the indirect ways they coerce others to satisfy their needs, and helps them learn to rely on inner resources and to approach others openly.

The curative instrument is awareness, not psychoanalytic-type insight. The key techniques include a series of "games" or exercises (Levitsky and Perls, 1970). One such is *role playing*, in

WELL...YOU'RE ON YOUR OWN FOR ANOTHER WEEK... GOOD LUCK !!

OR SHRINK

10-9 ©1979 Universal Press Syndicate

which the person enacts different roles, or parts, of himself or herself. For example, the person may become alternately the "top dog," that part of the self that is righteous, speaks in "shoulds," and corresponds to Freud's superego, and the "underdog," the part of the person that is submissive to the top dog's authority. A similar technique is used in the gestalt approach to dreams. Although Perls believed that dreams can reveal important truths about a person's inner life, the gestalt use of dreams is quite different from the Freudian search for hidden meanings in dream symbols:

> In Gestalt therapy we don't interpret dreams. Instead of analyzing and further cutting up the dream, we want to bring it back to life. And the way to bring it back to life is to relive the dream as if it were a story in the past, act it out in the present, so that it becomes a part of yourself, so that you are really involved. (Perls, 1969)

The assumption about dreams in gestalt therapy is that every element, whether human or not, represents some part of the person. The dreamer takes the part in turn of everything in the dream, whether a parent or a rock. Dream reenactment aims—as do all techniques in gestalt therapy—to help people fill in gaps in personality, become more fully aware, and finally take responsibility for their actions.

TRANSACTIONAL ANALYSIS: GAMES

∎ Transactional analysis (usually called TA for short) is a therapy developed by psychoanalyst Eric Berne (1964) and popularized in his best-selling *Games People Play* and in Thomas Harris' *I'm OK—You're OK* (1969).

In a modification of the Freudian concepts of id, ego, and superego, TA theory holds that in each person there are three ''ego states'' that operate: the Parent, the Adult, and the Child. Berne held that a person's primary need is neither sexual nor aggressive, but rather the need to be recognized by others. The basic unit of recognition is a stroke, any form of giving or receiving recognition, from a deep embrace to a simple ''hello.''

Early in life people develop a script, a pattern of thoughts about how to live so as to gain strokes. Each ego state has its own script. The Adult is rational and sees situations realistically. The Parent is a collection of parental attitudes and duplicates how a person's mother and father acted. The Child consists of feelings and ways of thinking from early childhood.

Some scripts are harmful, especially if formed very early. Such early scripts incorporate parental injunctions, programming that tells the now-grown person how to behave. The TA therapist helps one see how one's ego states and early scripts limit one's life. TA particularly emphasizes recognition of the ''games,'' or scripts, one employs to get strokes, and it assumes that people can become aware of the Parent, Adult, and Child ego states in their own behavior. As this awareness grows, people will be able to abandon behaviors that are messages from the Child or Parent, becoming more fully Adult. For example, say you're late for class because you had to wait in line for gas longer than you anticipated. As you walk in, your teacher says: ''Why are you late?'' You answer guiltily, ''It won't happen again. Sorry.'' The TA diagram would show a crossed transaction, with your teacher's Adult talking to your Adult, but your Child answering to her Parent.

BEHAVIOR THERAPY

Behavior therapy is the use of principles of learning to change nonadaptive behavior; it is based on the assumption that all behavior is learned, whether deviant or accepted, a problem or not. Behavior therapists reject the psychoanalytic theory that phobias, anxieties, and other personality problems are the result of hidden conflicts. Such problems, say behavior therapists, are the outcome of people's conditioning. They see no need to explore a person's past or unconscious for insights into the causes of these problems: the symptom itself is the problem, rather than a sign of more basic, underlying conficts (Wolpe, 1974). Behavior therapists work toward extinguishing nonadaptive behaviors and strengthening more useful ones (Farkas, 1980). Behavior change is the result of the therapist's systematic use of rewards and punishments.

Counterconditioning

Underlying the central concept of a number of behavior therapy techniques is *counterconditioning*, the notion that the power of a stimulus to affect a person will weaken if an incompatible response is also aroused. For example, it is hard to stay anxious if you are at the same time relaxed, sexually aroused, or assertive. This principle is applied in *systematic desensitization*, a method of replacing a person's anxious response to a stimulus with a relaxed one by training a person to re-

PEOPLE PLAY

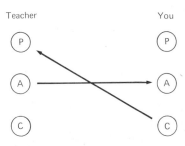

Teacher   You

Instead, the interaction might have gone: Teacher: "You're late." You: "Yes, I had to wait for gas longer than I had expected." The TA diagram would show this nonincriminating, nonguilty interaction as Adult to Adult:

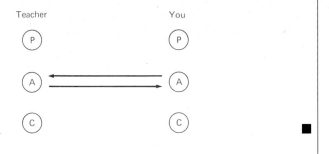

Teacher   You

■

main calm in circumstances that formerly produced anxiety.

In desensitization with a woman who is afraid of flying, for example, the behavior therapist's first step would be to train her in deep muscle relaxation. This state of deep relaxation is incompatible with anxiety. Muscle tension and relaxation stand in a relationship of *reciprocal inhibition:* where one is, the other cannot be (Wolpe, 1958). After teaching the patient how to become deeply relaxed, the therapist would join her in drawing up a list of all the conditions that elicit the anxiety, arranging them in a hierarchy from the least (1) to the most (10) anxiety-provoking conditions. Our patient's list might start with reading about a plane trip (1), proceed to hearing a plane overhead or driving near an airport (2), and work all the way

7-28 FAGAN

to sitting in a plane rocked by turbulence (10). In the desensitization sessions, the therapist assists the patient to become completely relaxed. Then the patient is told to imagine successive scenes from her anxiety hierarchy. The therapist calms her if any signs of anxiety develop and systematically leads her along the hierarchy. Therapist and patient meet about twice a week for successive short sessions, usually fifteen to thirty minutes long, in which the patient gradually works up to the most feared stimulus. The program may take several weeks or even months.

Imagine that
Mrs. C. goes to a behavior therapist who uses the counterconditioning technique called "implosion," or emotional flooding.

At the outset the therapist determines which conditioned stimuli Mrs. C. finds aversive, such as dirt, pinworms, dirty underwear. He sees her compulsive hand washing as a response to these fears that is reinforced because it reduces her anxiety about dirt. In accord with the counterconditioning principles employed in implosive therapy, the course of treatment is to have Mrs. C. face the anxiety-eliciting stimuli, remain in their presence, and finally experience the fact that she can survive this exposure, thus realizing the unrealistic nature of her fears.

The therapist first asks Mrs. C. to imagine one of the stimuli, such as pinworms. Then the therapist guides her in visualizing a scene far beyond her own fears: she imagines that pinworms are crawling on her arms; when she rushes to a sink, there is no water. Instead of water, more pinworms come from the faucet. They begin to burrow into her skin, crawl in her ears, eat at her eyes. They cover her body, destroying her flesh.

After this imagined scene, the therapist guides Mrs. C. through others that make it seem mild by comparison. These scenes evoke the most vivid images of dirt and filth, uninhibited aggression and raunchy sex. She becomes flooded with anxiety and aggression—the emotions she has always avoided—but her therapist will not allow her to rely on her habitual avoidance of these feelings. She faces what she fears most. In doing so she discovers that the things she had dreaded are not so fearsome after all. The anxiety they elicited in the past is extinguished as she endures and survives visions of horror far worse than these mild, real-life matters (adapted from Prochaska, 1979). ■

Implosive therapy

As Mrs. C. would find, *implosive therapy* does not use the gradual desensitization approach that slowly replaces anxiety with relaxation. Instead, the implosive therapist floods the person with anxiety by having her imagine in the most graphic terms the situation that is most feared (Stampfl and Levis, 1967).

If, for example, the therapist discovers that the patient is made anxious by thoughts of aggressive behavior, he will ask her to imagine various situations in which she is behaving aggressively. Then the therapist will suggest a scene and ask the patient to playact. He might go to the extreme of having the patient think about and act out the mutilation and killing of another person. If, on the other hand, the patient's anxiety stems from unresolved conflicts pertaining to sexual activities, the therapist might ask her to imagine and act out having incestuous relations or actively engaging in some form of homosexual practice. Through this rehearsal in a nonthreatening situation, the patient is forced to learn that her imagined fears cannot harm her.

Closely related to techniques like implosive therapy is *covert sensitization,* the eradication of an undesired response by pairing it in imagination with an obnoxious stimulus. Imagined discomfort instead of actual pain is often sufficient to extinguish undesirable behavior (Cautela, 1970). For example, an obese person who is trying to stop eating whenever he feels the urge might be told to imagine maggots or worms crawling all over the food he is thinking about. Or a person who wants to curtail his performance of oral homosexual acts might be encouraged to think about vomiting all over himself while visualizing himself in this activity. In other words, the person thinks about and imagines very undesirable consequences as a result of engaging in the behavior he wants stopped, but does not actually suffer actual physical pain or discomfort.

Modeling

Behavior therapists use modeling (learning through observing someone else) on the assumption that learning a new behavior is easier if a person can simply watch another person do it first, an important component of much of children's learning. Bandura (1969) found that children learned to act aggressively by watching an adult do so. He applied this principle to a more positive objective with people who are phobic of snakes. As they watched other people gradually moving closer and closer to snakes and finally handling them, the patients' fears were greatly lessened (Bandura, Blanchard, and Ritter, 1969).

Operant conditioning

Counterconditioning techniques such as desensitization and implosion attempt to extinguish negative undesirable behaviors. *Operant condi-*

AVERSIVE CONDITIONING

■ When self-defeating habits like overeating, smoking, or drinking are pleasurable, they require a special behavior therapy: aversive conditioning. In those disorders where the maladaptive behavior is itself positively reinforcing, aversive conditioning can be used to displace pleasure with punishment.

This approach is used most often in conditions that are self-reinforcing, like obesity, alcoholism, smoking, drug dependence, gambling, and sexual deviations. In each of these, the habit itself produces a pleasurable state, although the longterm consequences of the behavior make it a problem.

In aversive conditioning the therapist produces pain or discomfort either by removing positive reinforcers or by presenting noxious stimuli or conditions that become associated with the undesirable behavior so that its frequency decreases. For example, an aversive therapy treatment for alcoholics includes the following methods:

The behavior therapy takes place in a hospital treatment room resembling one's favorite cocktail lounge containing a bar, and related accoutrements, and consists of using as an unconditioned stimulus a powerful emetic (a drug that induces vomiting) which is injected by a nurse or physician while the patient is seated on a stool in the "bar." The patient is fixed his or her favorite drink which is left on the bar while the patient drinks several glasses of warm water. The therapist studies the neck and mouth muscles, the breathing, and flushing face for signs of imminent retching. Seconds before this occurs, the patient is asked to take a big gulp of his or her favorite alcoholic drink. A bout of retching into a large basin attached to the stool immediately follows the ingestion of the alcoholic drink if the therapist's timing is correct. The patient is then offered another, and then another drink, following the same sequence in this first treatment session. He or she is then returned to bed where more retching will follow. A day of rest in bed is allowed the next day. In five such treatment sessions, one repeated every other day, the patient is offered by the nurse or physician serving as bartender-helper, a full range of other beverages—wines, beer, liqueurs as well as one's first requested favorite drink. By the third treatment, patients seated on the bar stool in this complex *conditioned stimulus environment* are nauseous at the sight or smell of the *unconditioned stimulus,* alcohol in any form, and thus are showing a beginning conditioned response. By the fifth treatment, usually given on the tenth to fourteenth day after hospital admission, most patients show successful conditioning and return home, usually committed to a life of sobriety (research shows that some 60 percent still have not taken their first drink 12 months later). These patients do, however, return to the hospital for "booster" *reconditioning* sessions over the next twelve months, and as often as they feel they need to from that point on. (Matarazzo, in press)

The application of behavior modification techniques like aversive conditioning to institutionalized patients or criminals, who are not free to consent to or protest their course of treatment, is frightening to many people. Indeed, behavior therapy in institutions has been compared to the brainwashing of a captive population. Even when programs are voluntary, it is difficult to regulate such sanctions as reaction from the prison administration or parole boards to those prisoners who refuse treatment. The critics of aversive conditioning see it as only a step away from the nightmares described in *Brave New World* and *A Clockwork Orange.* ■

tioning, on the other hand, ignores undesired behaviors while rewarding desired ones that a person already engages in from time to time. One of the main applications of operant-conditioning-based therapy is the *token economy,* where each time a patient performs a desired act (e.g., making a bed) he or she receives a token that can be exchanged for a reward, such as cigarettes or time to watch TV. Token economies are used primarily with institutionalized patients, where there are full-time supervisors who can watch for the desired behavior and reward it with a token. Token

General

In exchange for the privilege of remaining together and preserving some semblance of family integrity	Mr. and Mrs. Bremer and Candy all agree to concentrate on positively reinforcing each other's behavior while diminishing the present overemphasis upon the faults of the others.

Specific

In exchange for the privilege of riding the bus directly from school into town after school on school days	Candy agrees to phone her father by 4 p.m. to tell him that she is all right and to return home by 5:15 p.m.
In exchange for the privilege of going out at 7 p.m. on one weekend evening without having to account for her whereabouts	Candy must maintain a weekly average of B in the academic ratings of all of her classes and must return home by 11:30 p.m.
In exchange for the privilege of going out a second weekend night	Candy must tell her parents *by 6 p.m.* of her destination and her companion and must return home by 11:30 p.m.
In exchange for the privilege of going out between 11 a.m. and 5:15 p.m. Saturdays, Sundays, and holidays	Candy agrees to have completed all household chores *before* leaving and to telephone her parents once during the time she is out to tell them that she is all right.
In exchange for the privilege of having Candy complete household chores and maintain her curfew	Mr. and Mrs. Bremer agree to pay Candy $1.50 on the morning following days on which the money is earned.

Bonuses and sanctions

If Candy is 1–10 minutes late	she must come in the same amount of time earlier the following day, but she does not forfeit her money for the day.
If Candy is 11–30 minutes late	she must come in 22–60 minutes earlier the following day and does forfeit her money for the day.
If Candy is 31–60 minutes late	she loses the privilege of going out the following day and does forfeit her money for the day.
For each half hour of tardiness over one hour	Candy loses her privilege of going out and her money for one additional day.
Candy may go out on Sunday evenings from 7 to 9:30 p.m. and either Monday or Thursday evening	if she abides by all the terms of this contract from Sunday through Saturday with a total tardiness not exceeding 30 minutes, which must have been made up as above.
Candy may add a total of two hours divided among one to three curfews	if she abides by all the terms of this contract for two weeks with a total tardiness not exceeding 30 minutes, which must have been made up as above, and if she requests permission to use this additional time by 9 p.m.

Monitoring

Mr. and Mrs. Bremer agree to keep written records of the hours of Candy's leaving and coming home and of the completion of her chores.
Candy agrees to furnish her parents with a school monitoring card each Friday at dinner.

Figure 17.1 A contingency contract between Candy, a delinquent girl, and her parents
The contract states clearly what is expected of both Candy and her parents.

economies have brought about striking improvements in chronic patients thought to be beyond hope. Many such patients have learned responses ranging from simply dressing themselves to performing hospital jobs daily (Ayllon and Azrin, 1968; Atthowe and Krasner, 1968). Token economies have also found success in homes for the retarded, in ordinary schools, and with parents trained in its use at home with their own children (Atthowe, 1976).

A closely related method is *contingency contracting*, where there is a written agreement that spells out the positive reinforcements a person will receive in return for fulfilling certain obligations (Krumboltz and Thoreson, 1969). The principle is a familiar one: most children know they must be home by a certain hour and do their homework if they don't want to be punished or lose privileges. Contingency contracting works well with disturbed children; their persistent behavior problems benefit from the specificity that contracting provides (Stuart, 1971).

Biofeedback

Another therapeutic application of operant conditioning principles is *biofeedback*, where a person uses electronically monitored signals of physiological changes to learn how to control these bodily processes. Electronic monitoring allows a person to note subtle internal changes that one would ordinarily never be aware of, such as blood pressure or brain wave activity. Using these electronic signals, a person can find which thoughts, images, or other mental activity will increase or decrease the function being measured. There are no sure recipes for controlling brain waves or blood pressure; each person must learn what will work for her.

The effectiveness of biofeedback stems from the principle that any symptom that is learned can be unlearned. Thus, in theory, a person whose body has learned to react to stress with dangerous rises in blood pressure can unlearn this unhealthy habit and instead learn to respond to stress without such a dangerous reaction (Pelletier, 1977). The range of applications for biofeedback has included irregular heartbeat, epilepsy, hypertension, migraine and tension headaches, Raynaud's disease (poor circulation in hands and feet), muscle reeducation following paralysis, stuttering, spastic colon, asthma, and vaginal blood flow (Rimm and Masters, 1979). In some conditions where anxiety and tension underlie the disorder, using biofeedback for relaxation training combined with psychotherapy is a more effective treatment than either relaxation training or the psychotherapy alone (Walker, 1979). However, while biofeedback training has proven effective in disorders such as tension headaches (Budzynski, Stoyva, and Adler, 1973), there is as yet no clear evidence that it is the most effective treatment for many of the disorders for which it has been used (Melzack, 1975).

COGNITIVE RESTRUCTURING

Cognitive therapy

In *cognitive restructuring* the therapist aims to relieve a person's symptoms by directly changing the inappropriate ideas that accompany them (Beck, 1980). The cognitive therapist takes the patient's reports of what is going on at face value, and works in an explicit and direct manner to change the attitudes that produce symptoms.

The basic assumption in cognitive therapy is that the personal meaning of an event causes a person's emotional response; it is the core of any emotional disorders that the person may have. In the course of cognitive therapy, the patient will learn such lessons as:

☐ a person's perceptions of reality are not the same as reality itself

☐ how you interpret reality depends on fallible processes of thought

☐ a person's beliefs are hypotheses that can be tested and changed.

Certain erroneous beliefs, or *cognitive distortions*, are typical of specific disorders. Compulsions, such as Mrs. C.'s hand washing, for example, are attempts to relieve obsessional fear through acts that the patient erroneously thinks will lessen the threat. Other sorts of common cognitive distortions include: overgeneralization, a blanket judgment based on a single incident; polarized thinking, the dividing of information into dichotomous categories such as success or failure, with no midground; "selective abstraction," the focusing on a petty detail so that the total meaning of a situation is missed; and "tyranny of the shoulds," where a person sets unrealistically high standards. Depressed and anxious patients are prime candidates for cognitive therapy (Beck and Kovacs, 1977).

Imagine that Mrs. C. has consulted a rational-emotive therapist.

His attitude is that what is important about Mrs. C.'s case is the irrational nature of her beliefs.

"You have created the horrible reality that makes you suffer," he tells her. "You have blown up the threat of pinworms and dirt beyond all reasonableness. It should be clear to you that the emotional consequences of your morbid dread of filth, and your incessant hand washing, are unbearable to you and everyone in your family. You will have to reexamine your beliefs, and understand that the pinworm infestation was a catastrophe only in your own mind. If you stop to think about the worst that can actually happen, you'll find it's not all that bad."

The therapist drives home his points by giving Mrs. C. homework assignments, such as listening to tapes that will show her how she harangues herself with "shoulds" and "ought tos"; her assignment is to practice substituting more realistic words such as "prefer" and "want to." She also completes such assignments as a paper on the actual dangers of pinworms; her husband is given his own homework to help him deal with her rationally, rather than giving in to her neurotic demands.

As Mrs. C. slowly becomes able to disagree with the beliefs that supported her obsessions and compulsions, she is able to enjoy more of her life, no longer a slave to her fears and fervent washing (adapted from Prochaska, 1979). ■

Rational-emotive therapy

This approach is typical of a host of therapies that focus on cognitive restructuring, the reshaping of a person's beliefs into a more adaptive outlook. One such therapy, the brainchild of psychologist Albert Ellis (1962), is called *rational-emotive therapy*. This method of psychotherapy recognizes that the emotional consequences of an event are largely due to a person's belief system. When these beliefs are irrational, the person's emotional reaction is maladaptive. The therapist intervenes by challenging these irrational beliefs; as the beliefs are disputed effectively, the disturbing emotional consequences cease (Ellis, 1979). This is exactly the tactic employed with Mrs. C. by the rational-emotive therapist: he confronted her with the irrational nature of her beliefs in order to undermine the disruptive emotional reactions that were ruining her life.

According to Ellis (1962), there are certain commonly held irrational beliefs that are the cognitive underpinning of many neurotic problems. They include such beliefs as:

□ "A person must be loved or approved by almost everyone,"
□ "To feel worthwhile I must be competent in everything I do,"
□ "When things don't happen the way I want, it is a catastrophe,"
□ "The best way to handle a threatening event is to worry about it,"
□ "There is always a perfect solution to my problems, and I must find it."

The revision of such irrational beliefs Ellis calls *rational restructuring*. The most direct method of rational restructuring is to change a person's "self-talk"—what you tell yourself about events—since irrational self-talk is tied to maladaptive emotions (Russel and Brandsma, 1974). For example, a person who held the belief that to feel worthwhile he must be competent in everything might tell himself things like, "I'm worthless because I did poorly on that test." Rational restructuring would help him to see that most people occasionally do poorly on exams, but such failures don't make them worthless people. Cognitive techniques have become increasingly popular among a range of therapists in recent years; many behavior therapists, for example, adapt methods of rational restructuring in their work with clients.

Multimodal therapy

Recognizing that no one therapy is tailored for every person's disorder, behavior therapist Arnold Lazarus (1973) developed *multimodal therapy*, a comprehensive treatment in seven modalities that covers the range of difficulties patients present. Lazarus coined the acronym BASIC ID for the modes his therapy brings to bear on a given person's disorder: behavior, affect, sensation, imagery, cognition, interpersonal relations, and drugs. Each of these represents a potential problem area for a given patient. The keynote in multimodal

Encounter groups use many kinds of exercises to make people more open and to demonstrate psychological issues that the group can discuss. Arm-wrestling, for example, is a springboard for the group members to discuss interpersonal power. (Richard Kalvar/Magnum)

therapy is flexibility: the therapist should use any and all techniques that will work, instead of being locked in to a single approach. If a therapist uses only one orientation for all patients, argues Lazarus, then there is the danger that too narrow a focus will lead to some of the patient's problem areas being overlooked.

GROUP THERAPY

There are many kinds of therapy situations that go under the name *group therapy*, but they all assume that disorders are due in part to a breakdown in a person's ability to relate to others and that the group is the means through which treatment can occur. The size, structure, and process of group therapy vary. Traditionally, group therapy began as a variation of one-to-one psychotherapy, where the same techniques were applied by a single therapist to patients in a group with an optimal size of eight or ten (Yalom, 1970; Berne, 1966). The specific techniques applied by the therapist can vary greatly, depending on his or her training background. Group therapy is undertaken in a wide range of settings, from ward meetings of psychotic patients, to groups of neurotics led by a psychoanalyst, to Alcoholics Anonymous, TA, and gestalt groups, to encounter groups of various sorts, including marathon and nude

groups, sensory awareness groups, and men's and women's consciousness-raising groups.

In contrast to formal therapy groups, which are often concerned with the problems of individual members, encounter groups focus on group interaction. The emphasis is on personal growth and self-actualization. Typically, one or two therapists, or leaders, are present; they function as models in helping members express their thoughts and feelings, and they also provide some safety valves. But encounter groups may also be leaderless gatherings. They may use interpretive dance, yoga, role playing in psychodramas, touching, or any number of imaginative techniques.

The main goal is to get people to drop their defenses so that open and authentic communication becomes possible. There is no fixed method for how this is to be accomplished. Such nonverbal techniques as eye-to-eye contact, trusting exercises, and group games are sometimes used. Nudity has also been tried as a gesture symbolic of dropping all roles and pretenses. Another technique is the marathon session, in which the fatigue of constant interaction over twenty-four to thirty-six hours serves to break down defenses.

There seem to be two basic shortcomings in encounter groups that create dangerous situations: (1) the lack of adequate screening to weed out participants who are mentally unstable, and (2) the lack of adequately trained leaders. The pain involved in self-disclosure and the risk of loosened emotional and sexual restraints can prove to be an explosive combination, but given proper supervision, this type of group interaction holds potential for individual growth and self-fulfillment.

FAMILY THERAPY

Imagine that Mrs. C. consults a family therapist.

The therapist meets with her entire family: Mrs. C., her husband, and all their children. The therapist does not talk only to Mrs. C., but to everyone there, taking a careful history of the family's past and its milestones. Then the therapist focuses on the pinworm incident, and Mrs. C.'s compulsive habits since then. The therapist asks each person in the family to describe the problems and interpret them. From listening to each member of the family and then inviting other members to respond to what is said, the therapist pieces together a picture of the family's typical communication patterns.

Mrs. C., the therapist points out, has handled any and all differences by eliminating the point of view of the other person in the family, whether it was her husband or any of the children. In the family communication system, her opinions prevailed, even though her obsessions and compulsions upset everyone else. Never mind the piles of underwear in the corners, never mind that her husband had no sex with her: Mrs. C.'s need to wash and wash again prevailed over every other family member's feelings.

During the course of therapy, the whole family brings out into the open hurts, angers, and frustrations that have never been allowed expression before. As she was confronted with the true situation in her family, Mrs. C. began to respond to the newly expressed feelings of her husband and children. She gradually became less focused on her own preoccupations, and could understand the distress her behavior had been causing them. Slowly she gave up her compulsive habits, replacing them with more helpful responses to her family's needs. ■

Family therapy treats the patient's entire family, viewing the patient's problems as symptoms of disturbed familial relationships (Guerin, 1976). The *identified patient* is the member the family has unconsciously chosen to represent its problems. The therapist emphasizes that the whole family is to be treated, not just the identified patient. This was the approach used in the example of Mrs. C.: she was the identified patient, but the

The family therapist deals with the entire family, seeing a particular family member's problem in the context of everyone else's needs. An "identified patient" may simply be manifesting a problem that is symptomatic of the whole family's pattern of interaction. (© Linda Ferrer Rogers 1980/Woodfin Camp & Assoc.)

therapist worked with the entire family as a single system. In this form of therapy, even little children are seen as contributing to the family pattern rather than as passive victims of it.

Family therapy can vary from brief crisis-intervention procedures, often designed to keep one member out of a mental hospital, to long-term sessions lasting for many months. (Andolfi and Zwerling, 1980). Treatment length varies with therapists, but in general it is more flexible than in individual therapy. The therapist knows that he is part of the family pattern during a session, and he carefully observes each member's behavior toward him. Hostility among family members is not seen as symptomatic of inner conflict but rather is interpreted positively by the therapist, often as protectiveness toward another family member. The aim is to change the defective relationships that cause the hostility. Sometimes sessions are recorded on videotape, and sometimes one or more members of the family are seen by the therapist separately to work out certain aspects of their relationships. The key realization resulting from family therapy is that the family is a social system, with its members filling a set of interlocking roles that influence one another.

Among the major facets of family life that create a disorder are habitual styles that interacting members adopt. Satir (1967) calls these *family system games;* they are the unspoken rules of interaction that family members follow in relating to each other. One such rule that can lead to pathology was at work in Mrs. C.'s family; this rule says that a person handles differences by "eliminating" himself or herself—that is, the person always agrees with other family members regardless of how he or she truly feels. Mrs. C. got everyone in her family to go along with her irrational fears of dirt by using such a rule to her advantage. One of the goals of therapy is to get such families to adopt a new rule, one that allows them to be open with each other about their true feelings, and to negotiate any differences between members, rather than hiding such trouble.

Many of the principles developed by family therapists have been used to treat the problems of couples, particularly troubled marriages (Framo, 1980). Typically, husband and wife are treated together in the same session, just as is the whole family in family therapy. They may also, however,

see the therapist individually (Olson, 1970). As in families, the problems of married couples are frequently the result of a breakdown in effective communication. For example, distressed couples will be in the habit of saying many more negative things to each other than positive (Billings, 1979). Nagging, complaints, and arguments typify their interactions. The therapist seeks to improve their ability to talk openly and frankly with each other and to negotiate any differences between them.

BIOLOGICAL THERAPIES

Chemotherapy

Treatment with drugs, or *chemotherapy*, is used frequently with people who are too agitated, disturbed, or unresponsive to benefit from psychological therapies. It is also used in many cases along with individual psychotherapy, and is even prescribed for "normal" people who are under psychological stress. Unfortunately, understaffed institutions frequently use drugs as the sole therapeutic device. Although medications have revolutionized the institutional scene, it is important to remember that other therapies may be needed for permanent improvement.

The most commonly prescribed classes of drugs are *tranquilizers*, *stimulants*, and *antidepressants*. The minor tranquilizers include such medications as Miltown (meprobamate), Librium (chlordiazepoxide), and Valium (diazepam). These drugs are prescribed to reduce tensions and anxieties in normal people and mildly disturbed patients, but they cannot alter the basic problems that make such persons unhappy. Patients may become overdependent on them, experiencing withdrawal symptoms when they are discontinued.

Whereas the minor tranquilizers are effective with normal individuals, the major tranquilizers, or *antipsychotic agents*, have been tremendously useful with severely disturbed patients. They are often prescribed to calm agitated or destructive people so that they can lead more normal lives. Reserpine, a derivative of snakeroot used for a variety of ailments as long as 2,500 years ago, was introduced as a tranquilizer in the 1950s. But it often produced the undesirable side effect of depression. Today phenothiazines such as chlorpromazine (Thorazine) are most commonly prescribed. These agents are helpful in reducing the frequency of delusions and hallucinations so common in schizophrenics. The relative calm and quiet that prevails in today's mental institutions is largely due to the administration of phenothiazines.

Stimulants such as Dexadrine (dextroamphetamine) and Ritalin (methylphenidate) have the opposite effect of tranquilizers. These mood elevators act as psychic energizers. Elavil (amitriptyline) and Tofranil (imipramine) are commonly used antidepressants. But these drugs also often have undesirable side effects, such as causing anxiety and agitation in depressed patients.

Chemotherapy offers the advantages of temporary reversible effects and dosages that can be tailored to individual needs. But the side effects of drugs are often difficult to control. And it must always be remembered that symptoms may recur once drug treatment is terminated.

While tranquilizers like Thorazine can bring calm to agitated patients—and to those who must care for them—by quieting the patients, many patients who are given these drugs have complained that they make things *too* calm (Vonnegut, 1975). The overly tranquilized patient, some complain, loses interest in daily activities, going around in a "fog" of indifference and apathy.

Another drug that many people have complaints about is the tranquilizer Valium, one of the most widely prescribed drugs in the world (Larned, 1975; Baldessarini, 1978). About 15 percent of Americans take Valium to help soothe their anxieties. Critics of the use of Valium point out that the very anxiety it dampens may well be a signal of psychological disorder that might be better—and more thoroughly—dealt with in psychotherapy.

Electroconvulsive therapy and psychosurgery

One of the more dramatic forms of biological treatment is *electroconvulsive therapy* (ECT), passage through the brain of an electric current that induces a seizurelike spasm of all the muscles (controlled with a muscle relaxant), momentary loss of consciousness, and changes in the ratios of brain chemicals (Salzman, 1978). The most common use of ECT is as an intervention in acute depression, which in many cases it alleviates—though no one knows exactly why this is so. One view suggests that ECT acts as a stimulant to increased neural activity (Kety, 1967). Another view suggests that it clears neural circuits and permits the patient to think better. But this is pure guesswork. Shock treatments cause generalized, often debilitating memory loss, and they frequently endanger the lives of patients who have other medical problems. Although shock treatments may effect rapid improvements or lessen the risk of imminent suicide, they do not necessarily reduce the chance of future depressions.

Psychosurgery refers to operations on the brain designed to relieve psychiatric symptoms (Fleming, 1978). The Freeman-Watts treatment, known as prefrontal lobotomy, involves severing the connections between the frontal lobes of the brain and the thalamus. The cut nerve fibers are those that seem to control the interplay of thought and emotion. During the 1940s and 1950s in the United States this operation was a widely used way to

TABLE 17.1 **PSYCHOACTIVE DRUGS AND THEIR EFFECTS ON BEHAVIOR**

Purpose	Chemical group	Generic name	Trade name
Minor tranquilizers	propanediols	meprobamate	Miltown, Equanil
	benzodiazepines	chlordiazepoxide	Librium
		diazepam	Valium
Major tranquilizers (antipsychotic agents)	phenothiazines	chlorpromazine	Thorazine
		trifluoperazine	Stelazine
		thioridazine	Mellaril
	butyrophenones	haloperidol	Haldol
	thioxanthenes	chlorprothixene	Taractan
Stimulants	amphetamines	dextroamphetamine	Dexedrine
	piperidyls	methylphenidate	Ritalin
Antidepressants	tricyclics	imipramine	Tofranil
		amitriptyline	Elavil
		doxepin	Sinequan
	monoamine oxidase inhibitors	phenelzine	Nardil
		tranylcypromine	Parnate

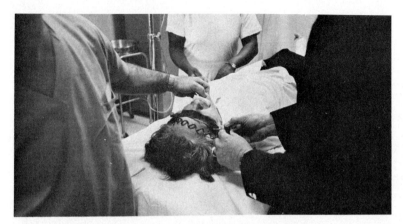

Electroconvulsive therapy has been shown most effective in cases of acute depression. Before tranquilizers were available, it was used to treat a far wider range of mental disorders. (Paul Fusco/Magnum)

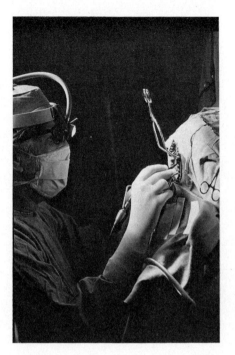

Psychosurgery, operations on the brain meant to relieve mental illness, was common in the 1940s and 1950s, before tranquilizers and other kinds of chemotherapy were discovered. Psychosurgery is now rare. (Allen Green/Visual Departures)

control anxiety or violence in hospitalized mental patients. Unfortunately, these lobotomies often resulted in seizures, indifference to people, and intellectual impairment, making the patient more dependent than ever on custodial care.

Because of its undesirable side effects, because this radical treatment is irreversible and does not always work, and most importantly because there is little medical research that supports its usefulness and safety, psychosurgery is the subject of heated debate on scientific, legal, and ethical grounds (Valenstein, 1980).

AN OUNCE OF PREVENTION: COMMUNITY MENTAL HEALTH

The disorders that bring people to therapists begin at home. By the time a person seeks professional help, a long process has already occurred during which various stresses and conflicts escalated and intensified. In the 1960s a movement began that sought to foster *community mental health,* fostering the well-being of people in order to prevent their developing mental disorders. Prevention occurs at three levels.

Primary prevention is the promotion of healthiness in people's general living conditions, with an eye toward enhancing their emotional, intellectual, and social competence. It can include the replacement of slums with good housing, programs such as Head Start, equal opportunities for jobs, or the provision of general health care (Matarazzo, 1980).

Secondary prevention occurs after a person has begun to show signs of a mental disorder. Its aim is early detection and prompt treatment. Among the programs typical of this kind of prevention are suicide "hotlines," "safe houses" for wives and children who are abused at home, and community mental health clinics where anyone can go to seek help.

Tertiary prevention is rehabilitation, the attempt to help people whose mental problems have led them to become inmates of a mental institution or other total care facility. Its aim is to prevent them from becoming chronic patients and to restore them to home and community. Halfway houses for mental patients are typical of such rehabilitative measures.

One great impetus for community mental health programs came from a widespread disillusionment with the inefficiency and abuses that prevail in large state mental hospitals. By the 1960s the watchword was *deinstitutionalization,* getting patients out of mental hospitals and back in their own communities (Macht, 1970). The philosophy of the federal government shifted to support community mental health centers rather than large state hospitals, and "neighborhood psychiatry" was envisioned as a means of treating people's problems at home rather than shipping them off to distant mental hospitals (Brown, 1963). While this national effort has succeeded in closing many state hospitals, community programs have not always filled the gap, resulting in the unfortunate situation—especially in large cities—of patients who formerly might have been in the chronic wards of hospitals now isolated in cheap hotels on government subsidies, receiving little or no treatment.

There has also, however, been an upswing in the range of emergency services available for people going through acute psychological crises. *Crisis therapy* holds that unusual pressures in a person's life can bring about a period of intense emotional upset and confusion that will pass in a matter of weeks (Caplan, Macht, and Wolf, 1969). *Crisis intervention* is any effort that aims to help a person weather the crisis period (Macht, 1970). Typical of such interventions are in-home counseling for people with terminal illness, suicide hotlines, or short stays in the psychiatric wing of a local hospital.

Because the police are available on a twenty-four-hour basis, they are frequently the first to ar-

Many family problems come to the attention of the police long before a therapist ever hears of them—if a therapist hears of them at all. (© Sepp Seitz 1978/Woodfin Camp & Assoc.)

rive on the scene of a psychological crisis, whether it be a suicide threat, a violent spouse, a helpless alcoholic, or a runaway child. One innovative project in an Ontario, Canada, police department created a special unit of mental health professionals whom police officers could immediately consult when confronted with such crises (Jaffe, Thompson, and Paquin, 1978). A follow-up study of the project showed that it both prevented the occurrence of future crises and aided people with potential psychological problems at a much earlier stage than would have otherwise been the case.

The closing of many mental hospitals has led to an increase in "shopping bag" ladies and others who wander the streets of larger cities. These people formerly were taken care of as longterm patients in mental hospitals, but they now find they have no place to live. (Jean-Marie Simon)

SUMMARY

Although the range of therapies is vast, they all have in common the goal of changing maladaptive behavior and helping people behave in a constructive manner.

There are four main therapeutic models: the psychodynamic, the humanistic-existential, the behaviorist, and the medical. Few therapists, however, fit neatly into only one of these categories. Many people who seek psychotherapy are sophisticated, verbal, and intelligent. Research on the effectiveness of therapy is confounded by both spontaneous recovery and the placebo effect.

Psychoanalysis. Psychoanalysis is based on Freud's theory of abreaction, overcoming traumatic experiences by bringing them into awareness. Psychoanalysis involves reexperiencing past traumas in order to gain insight into the roots of maladaptive behavior. Resistance during the process of free association is a sign that a significant area of feeling has been encountered. The therapist interprets the unconscious associations and latent content (common in dreams) of what the patient says. Through transference the patient reenacts his unresolved childhood conflicts with the therapist.

Humanistic and existential therapies. Humanistic therapies focus on self-understanding, the ability to control one's own life, and the potential for health. Existential therapies encourage clients to take responsibility and consider issues such as alienation that block their potential.

Client-centered therapy is nondirective; the therapist mirrors the feelings behind whatever the client chooses to say. The therapist's acceptance leads to insight and self-confidence on the part of the client.

Based on an encounter between patient and therapist, existential therapy confronts the patient with questions about the meaning and purpose of his or her existence.

Gestalt therapy aims to restore full awareness of the here and now by pointing out ways in which the patient misuses awareness and coerces others. Key techniques include games such as role playing different parts of oneself. Role playing is used also in working with dreams.

Behavior therapy. Behavior therapy makes use of the principles of learning to extinguish nonadaptive behaviors and strengthen more useful ones. Counterconditioning lessens the power of an anxiety-arousing stimulus by eliciting an incompatible response—such as relaxation—along with it. Systematic desensitization can be used to replace anxious responses to stimuli with relaxed ones.

Implosive therapy floods the patient with exaggerated anxieties about the feared situation. Rehearsal of anxieties in a nonthreatening situation forces the patient to realize that his imagined fears cannot harm him.

Covert sensitization uses imagined rather than real punishment, eradicating an undesired response by pairing it with an obnoxious stimulus in the patient's imagination. Behavior therapists also use modeling to teach patients appropriate responses.

Operant conditioning deals with undesired behavior by ignoring it and rewarding spontaneous desired behaviors. Token economies, based on this technique, are effective with chronic institutionalized patients, as well as with the retarded and with children in school and at home. Contingency contracting spells out the positive reinforcements a person will receive for desired behavior.

Biofeedback can be applied to many disorders involving a maladaptive physiological response to stress.

Cognitive therapy. The cognitive therapist aims to relieve a person's symptoms by identifying cognitive distortions and directly changing them. Depressed and anxious patients are prime candidates for this therapy. Patient and therapist may collaborate on identifying the problem and setting an agenda. Ellis' rational-emotive therapy uses cognitive restructuring to revise, among other things, a person's irrational "self-talk." Multimodal therapy addresses itself to seven modalities of common problems—the BASIC ID—using whatever approach is appropriate for each.

Group therapy. Group therapy assumes that disorders are due in part to a breakdown in a person's ability to relate to others. Encounter groups focus on open, authentic group interaction, with one or two leaders acting as models and safety valves.

Family therapy. Family therapy views the identified patient's symptoms as symptoms of the whole family's problems. The therapist treats the whole family as a social system and intervenes in family patterns of interaction. Family therapy aims to get families to adopt new rules that will allow more openness and negotiation about their troubles. Marital therapy treats husband and wife together, helping them communicate better to identify and solve their relationship problems.

Biological therapies. Chemotherapy uses tranquilizers, stimulants, or antidepressants to treat people too disturbed or unresponsive to benefit from psychological therapy alone.

Electroconvulsive therapy has been found effective in relieving depression, though no one knows exactly how it works, and it has been widely criticized.

Also much criticized, psychosurgery—operating on the brain to treat psychiatric symptoms—is sometimes useful, but its results are unpredictable, and it is now rarely used.

Community mental health. Community mental health aims to prevent emotional problems. Primary prevention concentrates on general environmental good health. Secondary prevention aims at early detection and treatment of mental problems, preventing them from becoming chronic. Tertiary prevention provides halfway houses, for example, in attempts to rehabilitate former mental patients. Community mental health programs also frequently provide crisis intervention.

GLOSSARY

Abreaction Overcoming traumatic experiences by bringing them into awareness.

Antidepressants Drugs that relieve feelings of depression. replacing them with a more positive mood.

Antipsychotic agents Tranquilizers used to calm severely agitated or destructive patients.

Aversive conditioning Extinguishes positively reinforcing but maladaptive behaviors either by removing reinforcers or by presenting noxious stimuli with the undesirable behavior.

Behavior therapy The use of principles of learning to change maladaptive behavior.

Behaviorist model Holds that the therapist should use principles of conditioning to change maladaptive behavior.

Biofeedback The use of electronically monitored signals of physiological change to aid in control of bodily processes.

Chemotherapy Treatment with drugs.

Cognitive distortions Erroneous beliefs about reality.

Cognitive restructuring Directly changing inappropriate ideas, thereby relieving a person's symptoms.

Community mental health Seeks to further the well-being of people in order to prevent their developing mental disorders.

Contingency contracting A written agreement that spells out the positive reinforcements a person will receive in return for fulfilling certain obligations.

Counterconditioning The concept that the power of a stimulus to evoke a given response (e.g., anxiety) will weaken if an incompatible response (e.g., relaxation) is aroused at the same time.

Covert sensitization The eradication of an undesired response as a result of pairing it in imagination with an obnoxious stimulus.

Crisis intervention Efforts aimed at helping a person weather a period of crisis.

Crisis therapy Holds that unusual pressures in a person's life can bring about a period of intense emotional upset and confusion that may be short-lived if treated promptly.

Deinstitutionalization Getting patients out of mental hospitals and back into their own communities.

Electroconvulsive therapy (ECT) Passage through the brain of an electric current; used chiefly to alleviate depression.

Encounter In existential therapy, the mutual open relationship between therapist and patient.

Family system games The unspoken rules of interaction that family members follow in relating to each other.

Family therapy Treats the patient's entire family, viewing the patient's problems as symptoms of disturbed familial relationships.

Free association In psychoanalysis, saying whatever thoughts come to mind.

Gestalt The total pattern made by one's feelings, actions, and the situation at a given moment.

Group therapy Assumes that disorders are due in part to a breakdown in a person's ability to relate to others and that the group is the best setting for treatment.

Humanistic-existential model Involves the therapist helping the patient to assume more responsibility for behavior through increased self-awareness and self-acceptance.

Identified patient In family therapy, the member the family has chosen unconsciously to represent its problems.

Implosive therapy The client is flooded with anxiety as a result of being asked to imagine in the most graphic and exaggerated terms the situation that is feared.

Insight Understanding of the childhood roots of maladaptive behavior, bringing unconscious material into awareness.

Interpretation Making unconscious associations clear and understandable to the psychoanalytic patient.

Latent content The underlying, significant meaning of what a patient says in psychoanalysis.

Manifest content The obvious, surface meaning of what a patient says in psychoanalysis.

Medical model An approach to therapy in which the therapist, usually a physician, tries to cure mental illness with medical treatments.

Multimodal therapy A comprehensive treatment in seven modalities that covers the range of difficulties patients present.

Nondirective therapy The therapist allows the patient to discuss whatever he or she wishes to discuss and mirrors the feelings underlying the patient's words.

Operant conditioning The rewarding of desired behaviors.

Placebo effect The improvement of a patient's condition due to expectation, rather than as the result of anything done to improve it.

Primary prevention The promotion, through community mental health, of healthiness in people's general living conditions, with an eye toward fostering emotional, intellectual, and social competence.

Psychodynamic model A model for therapy in which the goal is self-knowledge, or insight.

Psychosurgery Operations on the brain designed to relieve psychiatric symptoms.

Rational restructuring The revision of irrational beliefs.

Rational-emotive therapy Recognizes that the emotional consequences of an event are largely due to a person's irrational beliefs.

Reciprocal inhibition One state inhibits its opposite; for example, the relationship between muscle tension and relaxation.

Reconditioning The strengthening of a stimulus-response pairing by repeating it after some time has passed.

Resistance Hesitancy or refusal to express a thought during free association or therapy.

Role playing A gestalt game in which a person enacts different parts of herself or himself.

Secondary prevention Aims for the early detection and prompt treatment of mental disorders through community mental health programs.

Spontaneous recovery The improvement of patients who have received no therapy.

Stimulants Mood elevators that act as psychic energizers.

Stimulus environment In aversive therapy, an environment set up to evoke pleasurable but undesirable responses in the patient; paired with obnoxious stimuli, it becomes an aversive stimulus.

Systematic desensitization A method of replacing an anxious response to a stimulus with a relaxed one.

Tertiary prevention Aims to rehabilitate formerly institutionalized mental patients and get them back into the community.

Therapies Experiences that change maladaptive behavior and help a person behave in a constructive manner.

Token economy A system whereby each time a patient performs a desired act, he receives a token that can be exchanged for a reward.

Tranquilizers Drugs with calming effects, reducing tensions in mildly disturbed people and lessening agitated behavior and hallucinations in severely disturbed patients.

Transference In psychoanalysis, the patient's development of an intense, emotional response to the therapist, through which unresolved childhood conflicts are reenacted.

ADJUSTMENT TO STRESS AND TRANSITION

APPLYING PSYCHOLOGY / SIX

STRESS

The nature of stress ■ The costs of stress ■ Crisis

COPING WITH STRESS

TRANSITIONS

Leaving home ■ Living alone ■ Finding a job

Change is the essence of living. As you go through life you change your friends, your home, your work, your pleasures. The major transitions of life—for example, leaving home, marriage, starting a career—all demand a host of changes. You give up some parts of your past in order to step into new routines, new roles, new relationships. Each change means that you have to adjust to unfamiliar situations, demands, or people. Whether you find a given transition and the pressures it creates stressful depends to a great extent on your preparedness for it. If you are under stress, there are positive steps you can take to lessen its toll on you.

STRESS

Imagine that you've just transferred to a new school. You have to find a place to live and a new part-time job. You don't know anyone, and until you start to meet people your social life will be on hold. To top if off, the administration of your new school won't accept some of your transferred credits; they insist you repeat some courses you feel you've already taken equivalents for.

You feel frustrated, worried, and wonder if you've made the right move. ■

The nature of stress

Small wonder you're feeling upset: you're under lots of stress. The term "stress" refers to situations that present some sort of threat and the reactions such situations evoke (Monat and Lazarus, 1977). Stress is what occurs when demands exceed a person's ability to handle them. Even seemingly mild events can be stressful. Any situation that demands that you adapt to it can be stressful: finding a job, getting a roommate, preparing for an exam. Stress can arise from frustrations, conflicts, and pressures, or simply from unavoidable life events.

Take frustration. Your dispute with the administration over how many transfer credits they should accept is frustrating. They are thwarting you in your desire to finish college quickly, presenting you with a challenge that you can do little to meet. No matter what you do—whether it be getting upset and angry or writing letters and making appeals—you may end up stymied. The result: stress.

LIFE CHANGE AND PHYSICAL AILMENTS

∎ After studying the recent histories of people with medical problems, Holmes and Holmes (1970) have concluded that any number of illnesses, and not just the commonly recognized psychophysiological disorders, can be precipitated by the stress accompanying changes in one's life. To measure the impact of different kinds of changes, Holmes and Rahe (1967) have developed the Social Readjustment Rating Scale, which rates each kind of potentially stressful event in terms of "life change units" (LCUs).

The more LCUs you compile in a short period of time, the more prone you are to disease. In one sample Holmes found that of those who had more than 300 LCUs during a one-year period, 86 per-

Life event	LCUs	Life event	LCUs
Death of spouse	100	Son or daughter leaving home	29
Divorce	73	Trouble with in-laws	29
Marital separation	65	Outstanding personal achievement	28
Jail term	63	Wife begins or stops work	26
Death of close family member	63	Begin or end school	26
Personal injury or illness	53	Change in living conditions	25
Marriage	50	Revision of personal habits	24
Fired at work	47	Trouble with boss	23
Marital reconciliation	45	Change in work hours or conditions	20
Retirement	45	Change in residence	20
Change in health of family member	44	Change in schools	20
Pregnancy	40	Change in recreation	19
Sex difficulties	39	Change in church activities	19
Gain of new family member	39	Change in social activities	18
Business readjustment	39	Mortgage or loan less than $10,000	17
Change in financial state	38	Change in sleeping habits	16
Death of close friend	37	Change in number of family get-togethers	15
Change to different line of work	36	Change in eating habits	15
Change in number of arguments with spouse	35	Vacation	13
Mortgage over $10,000	31	Christmas	12
Foreclosure of mortgage or loan	30	Minor violations of the law	11
Change in responsibilities at work	29		

Or take pressures. You may feel obligated to get good grades to justify loans you've taken or money your family is paying to put you through college. Or pressure may come from the fact that you want to get into graduate school. No matter what the source, the pressure to do well will demand that you work harder than you otherwise might, pushing yourself to excel. The pressure will lead to stress.

The ordinary events of your life can also be stressful. Holmes and Rahe (1967) designed a scale that assesses the number of changes in a person's life that, taken together, indicate how much stress she is under. They ranked life events according to how stressful each was. At the top of the list is the death of a spouse, followed by divorce, marital separation, and then serving time in jail. Other items on their scale are more usual: marriage, pregnancy, changing jobs, beginning or ending school. Some hardly seem stressful, like

cent experienced some serious health problem, whereas health changes were found in only 48 percent of those who had scored between 150 and 300 (Colligan, 1975).

Imagine, for example, a woman in her senior year of college. In April, she is notified that the graduate school she wants to attend has not only accepted her, but is offering her a big scholarship (outstanding personal achievement: 28 LCUs). In May her father dies (death of close family member: 63 LCUs), and the trust fund he has established for her begins paying her a generous monthly income (change in financial state: 38 LCUs). In June she graduates (end school: 26 LCUs) and goes to Bermuda for a month in the sun (vacation: 13 LCUs). There she is arrested for marijuana possession, spends two nights in jail (jail term: 63 LCUs), and is deported. Returning home discouraged and depressed, she shies away from drugs, parties, and friends and spends the rest of the summer at home reading and keeping to herself (revision of personal habits: 24 LCUs). In September she leaves for graduate school (change in residence: 20 LCUs) and for the first time in her life takes an apartment of her own (change in living conditions: 25 LCUs). She starts classes (begin school: 26 LCUs), and by October she has fallen in love with a man who, as she soon discovers, is impotent (sex difficulties: 39 LCUs). Leaving her in the middle of her difficulties, we can now stop and total up her score for the last five months: 365 LCUs. According to Holmes, it's likely she'll need to see a doctor in the near future. ■

taking a vacation and Christmas. But each of these events demands adaptation, and so any of them can be stressful.

Each person's life situation makes her or him susceptible to particular sorts of stress. When a scale was designed to assess stress among college students, several special categories were added, such as becoming engaged or breaking an engagement, changing schools, entering college, changing dating habits, trouble with the school administration, changing majors, and working while going to school (Hart and Holmes, n.d.). Stress is a normal part of anyone's life.

The extent of a life change is not in itself the best measure of how stressful the change is; a truer picture would include the meaning of each event for the person (Lazarus, 1979). Some people with massive scores on the stress scale will nevertheless do fine. How an event is understood by the person experiencing it determines how stressful it is. If a person sees a given life change, such as changing schools, as a challenge rather than a threat, it will not be nearly as stressful. For one person a divorce may represent a great loss and tragedy, for another a much desired new start in life. Stress, then, is also a function of how a person appraises an event (Lazarus, Kanner, and Folkman, 1980).

The costs of stress

The medical understanding of stress is in terms of its wear and tear on the body; Hans Selye (1976), the pioneer in the study of stress, defines it as "the nonspecific response of the body to any demand." Because the body mobilizes its resources to meet demands, stress takes a physical toll.

Life changes can lead to illness. When Holmes (1978) developed his scale of life changes, it was in order to test the relationship between life's stresses and disease. He found that a wide variety of diseases followed closely after increases in a person's total life changes. The ailments Holmes found stress could cause range from backache, asthma, and psychiatric disorders to tuberculosis.

Holmes (1978) matched the magnitude of life change with how much illness occurred during the next half year. Thirty percent of people with a low degree of life change contracted a major illness during that period, but about half the people in the medium range of life change became ill, and of those in the high range, 80 percent became ill.

When 100 college football players filled out a life change scale at the start of football season, their scores were compared with the number of injuries they got during the three-month football season. Of those in the high life change group, 70 percent got injured (Bramwell, *et al.*, 1975). Holmes found a direct relationship between life change and illness: "The more change you have," says Holmes (1978), "the more likely you are to get sick."

While the cost of stress is often medical, it can also be psychological (Lazarus, 1966). The emotions stress produces can lower a person's ability to perform a task that under relaxed conditions would be effortless; examination jitters are one example. When stress makes a person fearful, anxious, or angry, her performance is certain to suffer. The sense of being threatened causes a person's perceptions to narrow, and cognitive processes become increasingly rigid. This makes it difficult to consider a range of alternatives or even to see a different perspective on things. Even if a response is getting nowhere, the person may be unable to find a different way of doing things—which simply compounds the problem.

Some people create their own stress. Friedman and Rosenman (1974) have identified the "Type A" behavior pattern, which is common among people who get heart disease. The Type A person is ambitious, competitive, and aggressive and is always racing against the clock. The "Type B" person, on the other hand, may be just as successful as the hard-driving Type A, but is more patient and easygoing and less preoccupied with competition. An extreme Type A person is a perfectionist who works tremendously hard and sees life as a deadly serious game that must be won at any cost. He watches the clock to avoid wasting time and to always be on time.

Friedman and Rosenman (1974) interviewed 3,500 men, classifying them as either "A"s or "B"s. Years later they compared the rates of coronary heart disease between the groups. Heart disease was two to three times greater among "A"s than among "B"s. The difference in heart disease does not seem to be related to any background differences between the two groups, but rather to the tense, pressured, frantic lifestyle of the "A"s. They seem to create their own ongoing state of crisis, and their health suffers as a result.

Crisis

Stress can differ in its intensity and duration. An extremely intense stress amounts to a crisis. Crisis theory holds that an unexpected event causes severe psychological discomfort that cannot be handled by a person's ordinary means. If new methods to handle the crisis fail, the result is anxiety, depression, helplessness, and a loss of self-esteem (Auerbach and Kilmann, 1978). The intense stress of crisis can be brought on by any number of tragedies: death of a loved one, a fire destroying one's home, or a serious diagnosis like cancer.

To better understand the nature of crisis, a group of patients undergoing surgery for cancer were compared with patients undergoing surgery for minor illnesses (Lewis, Gottesman, and Gutstein, 1979). They found that the course of crisis was more severe and prolonged for the cancer patients—they were in a crisis state marked by extreme feelings of anxiety and helplessness. As time went on, their inability to do anything to change their condition made them despondent; they lost faith in themselves. They could not adapt to the fact that they had cancer, although their anxiety and depression lessened after about two months. Their feelings of helplessness and worthlessness, however, continued for as long as half a year. An ongoing crisis, then, can take an emotional toll for many months. But crises that have a limited duration—like a heart attack or fire—seem to allow a better chance to adapt and recover.

COPING WITH STRESS

Imagine that you have an old acquaintance from high school who goes to your college. You don't enjoy his company at all, but he seems to dote on yours. He keeps calling you up and dropping by to see you. It's a hassle.

The last straw comes when you're giving a small dinner party for some close friends and he pops in unannounced. Seeing the dinner in progress, he clearly expects to be invited to join it.

You get furious. In desperation, you step outside and tell him point blank that he's not welcome to call or come by. As you go back in, you feel a flicker of guilt, and then great relief. ■

Roskies and Lazarus (1979) propose that there are two major strategies for dealing with stress: problem-solving coping and emotion-focused coping. Problem-solving coping involves an effort to change a troublesome situation. When you finally told your pesky high school acquaintance how you really felt, you solved the problem of a minor source of stress. Even a major crisis is more bearable if you can take steps to reduce its impact. A heart attack victim can change the demands he lets his job make on his time, or exercise regularly. A home fire victim can collect insurance and start rebuilding.

Emotion-focused coping is the method of choice when you can't change the stressful situation. The exam will take place whatever you do, or an operation is inevitable, or you have to find a new job. Since you can't do much to change the reality, the best thing to do is handle whatever emotions you find it arouses. There are a range of ways to do this, many of them tactics we use spontaneously. For example, you might try to ignore the stress or try to think of something else. You might joke about it or attempt to minimize its importance. Or you might take a tranquilizer. Each of these approaches may soothe your feelings.

Take, for example, the anxiety you may feel about an upcoming exam. If you feel threatened by the exam, then it is a source of stress. One way to cope might be to change the threat into a challenge and harness your anxiety to improve your performance. Your first tactic might be to notice what you're telling yourself about the exam that makes it threatening. For example, you may be saying to yourself something like: " This exam is going to be too tough; I've never really understood clearly the topic it's going to cover." You could change what you tell yourself to make it less threatening: "Most people get anxious before an exam; if I study enough, I'll be able to understand the material." You might use your anxiety to prod you to study for the exam. Of course, the final test of any stress coping method is how well it works in the actual demands of the situation.

Some people are generally more anxious than others, making them all the more vulnerable to stress (Speilberger, 1977). An anxious person is likely to meet minor happenings as if they are a threat. While anxiety can help a person marshal her resources to meet a challenge, constant, ongoing anxiety simply makes a person suffer more from stress in the face of life's inevitable changes.

Not everyone experiences anxiety in the same way. One person under stress may begin to sweat and tremble, while another becomes mentally fixated on the situation but shows no physical signs of stress. These represent two different aspects of anxiety, the somatic and the cognitive (Schwartz, Davidson, and Goleman, 1978). If one or the other reaction—cognitive or somatic—predominates in the way a person experiences anxiety, she can choose alternative techniques for relaxation that will be better suited for it.

For example, a person who suffers cognitive anxiety would be burdened by repetitive thoughts about a stressful situation. Often these thoughts are so worrisome that they intrude on other activities the person is engaged in; frequently this means sleeplessness, since the worrisome thoughts keep a person tense when she should be going to sleep. The methods that are the most direct antidote to cognitive anxiety are those that focus a person's mind on something else that is not anxiety-arousing. Doing a crossword puzzle, playing chess, or meditating are all effective antidotes to cognitive anxiety.

Somatic anxiety, on the other hand, is typified by physical symptoms. A person's heart races, stomach aches, or brow sweats in a stressful situation. The best antidote for such physical symptoms is almost any form of exercise. Jogging, tennis, swimming, or any activity that gives the person a thorough workout is the best way to soothe physical anxiety. Purely relaxing activities—like a hot bath, yoga, or deep muscle relaxation—can also have the same effect. For both cognitive and somatic worriers, a regular regime seems to lower day-to-day anxiety, making them less prone to suffer from stress.

Since life events are themselves stressful, Holmes (1978) gives several tips that will make them easier to handle. These include:

☐ Realizing that various life events require different amounts of change, and that such change can be stressful.

☐ Recognizing when you are in the midst of such a life event.

☐ Identifying the feelings you experience because of it, and finding the best way to adjust.

☐ Anticipating life changes and planning for them if possible.

☐ Taking your time to make decisions about life events.

☐ Being more careful about your health when undergoing life changes.

TRANSITIONS

Imagine that you know a woman who can't seem to leave home. She's almost twenty-eight, and she's gone to live with her parents again, the fifth time since she first left for college at eighteen.

Once she came back after dropping out in her freshman year, twice after losing jobs. Once it was a failing marriage that brought her home. And now she has mononucleosis. She figures that after a few months of good care from her parents, she'll be back on her own again. ∎

Leaving home

A natural life passage requires leaving home—getting established with friends of your own and finding a source of livelihood that frees you from dependence on your family. For most Americans this transition occurs sometime between the late teens and the late twenties. People vary greatly in how quickly they leave the family nest. Some people have their own apartment and a job before they finish high school; others may rely on family funds and a place to live at home to finance graduate study well into their thirties. From what we know about life events, the large number of changes that leaving home demands marks it as a potentially stressful life change.

There is no absolute standard by which to gauge how well this passage is progressing: subcultures and specific families have their own norms for how close children on their own will stay to their parents. For some it may mean a daily visit or phone call—or even a shared dwelling. For others contact may dwindle to a yearly Christmas card. The transition to independence from one's family is more readily measured by the alternative social and financial supports a person has. If someone has a social circle apart from the family and does not rely on it for support, then the person has "left home."

A young person has not left home to the degree that she relies on her family for a social life or for financial support. Your friend has a long record of turning to her family in situations where others might turn to friends or simply see things through on their own. Some people, says Jay Haley (1980),

make careers of failing in order to have their family rescue them—in effect, staying at home. Your friend is a prime example.

There are many ways people can fail, and so never leave home. Two extremes are to get into trouble or to be helpless and apathetic. Examples of the first sort might include a young woman who has a child out of wedlock or a young man who gets sent to jail or becomes addicted to drugs or drinking. The second sort of failure might include being unable to keep a job, never making friends of one's own, or becoming mentally ill. Any or all of these kinds of failure might ensure that one's family was continually needed to come to one's rescue.

Each family has its own criteria for measuring success and failure. For some, graduation from high school may mark a major success, while for others, success only begins after receiving a graduate degree. In each case, Haley points out, a young man or woman bent on failure can do fine until just before success is at hand. At that point one might fail to complete the last crucial bit of training that would make one self-sufficient—dropping out in the last term of high school, neglecting to take enough courses during the senior year to get a B.A., or never finishing a doctoral dissertation. If work rather than school is the arena of failure, one can act at job interviews so as never to be hired, or if employed, act so as to get fired. Simply staying in a job that one's family considers menial may constitute failure. Whatever the specifics, the pattern is the same: just as success and independence are about to come, one does something to sabotage them.

Why should someone want to fail at leaving home? Haley contends that people who fail to leave home do so, more often than not, to protect the family, especially their parents. Whether fully aware of it or not, they may sense that their parents are about to separate or harm each other psychologically. By making trouble—failing—they force the parents to put aside their disagreements and work together to come to their rescue. The function of failure, then, is to stabilize the family. The parents can focus on the young person's problems, and so ignore their own.

When Haley sees such a family in therapy, his goal is to get the child to leave home. Typically this means the parents must be made to exert authority that they have turned over to the child. He helps them set up a series of demands that the child start leaving, for example, going out every day at eight in the morning to look for a job. If the parents can stick to these demands, then the child neither gets any further benefits from failing nor feels the need to fail in order to save the parents.

Imagine that you run into an old friend, Jack, whom you haven't seen in years. Over drinks, he tells you that he and his wife have just divorced. The marriage was a disaster, and he's relieved to be done with it.

"It must be great," you say, "to start over. I'll bet you're having the time of your life."

"Well, I date now and then," he replies. "But I've never felt more lonely in my life." ∎

Living alone

People who live alone are not necessarily lonely, but for some, solitude is akin to isolation. Loneliness, according to Peplau and Perlman (1979) is a social deficiency that exists to the extent that one's network of relationships is smaller or less satisfying than one desires. Jack's sense of loneliness revealed the discrepancy between his actual level of social interaction and what he desired.

During the 1970s, the number of Americans living alone increased by 42 percent; by the start of the 1980s, an estimated one in five households will consist of just one person (Shaver and Rubenstein, 1979). Almost half the people living alone are over sixty-five, and almost two-thirds are women. And as more young people opt to stay single longer, the figures for one-person households are certain to increase.

To determine what life is like for people who live alone, Shaver and Rubenstein (1980) published a questionnaire in newspapers in five cities. The respondents were people who lived alone as well as people who lived with others. From the responses, they found that people who live alone are, on the average, more lonely than others—but many who live in solitude don't feel lonely in the least. The most lonely single group are those adults who still live with their parents; it may be that many in this group suffer from shyness or

have otherwise failed to carve a social circle outside the family.

But people who live alone are usually *not* socially isolated. Although they spend more time alone, they do not socialize less than other people. Moreover, they are less often bored than people who live with others. Men and women respond to living arrangements differently: married women are more lonely than married men, but single men (especially those who are separated, divorced, or widowed) are more lonely than single women.

The people who find life alone most painful are generally those who associate solitude with negative feelings like fear or anger. People who live alone but are not lonely react positively to solitude, associating it with feeling calm, creative, happy, and relaxed. Attitudes toward living alone also matter in another way: they are tied to health. There is no difference between the health of people who live alone and those who live with others—but there is a strong relationship between loneliness and health. Lonely people are more troubled by psychological problems; they report more feelings of despair and anxiety, more fears and crying spells, and more trouble concentrating. Loneliness, in short, is stressful—although living alone is not necessarily related to poor health or emotional upset.

Given that the transition to adulthood commonly means that a person will at some point live alone or in a strange town, how is loneliness to be avoided? Peplau and Perlman (1979) point out that it matters whether you attribute feelings of loneliness to your own failings or to the situation. If you feel the situation is the reason for loneliness, then you can take steps to change it.

The more direct ways to cope with loneliness are fairly obvious. One is to make efforts to meet people. Classes, a beach or park, volunteer work, an encounter group, or a laundromat are the kinds of places where new social contacts can start. All it takes is striking up a conversation. Another way to assuage feelings of loneliness is to lower your expectations about how much social contact you need. Perhaps you knew dozens or even hundreds of people in your old home town whom you considered friends—but now, you may realize, having only a small social circle can be just as satisfying.

If you have felt shy at some time in your life, you are not alone: 80 percent of people in one survey said they had been shy; 40 percent said they felt shy at present (Zimbardo, 1977). You can meet what you feel are social deficiencies head-on, whether it be shyness or feeling unattractive or unfamiliar with social graces. Clinics or therapists can help with severe feelings of shyness or awkwardness; a cosmetician or hairdresser can help with feeling attractive. In short, the more efforts you make to combat loneliness, the less likely you'll be to suffer from it.

Imagine that you're looking for a full-time job. One friend tells you that the best way to find a job is by answering classified ads. Another advises you to send out several dozen resumes to firms you might want to work for, hoping some will ask you for an interview. Still another friend suggests yet another approach: pick companies you'd like to work for and decide what you'd like to do for them; find out who would make the decision to hire you at each firm, and give the person a call.

Which technique should you use? ■

Finding a job

The third tactic—picking your employer—is the best approach, according to Robert Bolles (1979). Bolles points out that career choice and career change—and the job search they entail—are stressful life events. There is no ready place to acquire the skills it takes to find a job, yet the search for one can easily become frustrating and tension-filled or boring and unrewarding, or both.

Bolles reports that the average worker under thirty-five goes hunting for a job once every year-and-a-half; the average worker over thirty-five, every three years. Over a lifetime, the average worker will change careers three to five times; often the new field will be one in which his or her previous experience will not count much. One of the special dangers of the job search is what Bolles calls "rejection shock," the result of long and fruitless job hunting. The failure to find work can lead to the erosion of your self-esteem, especially if you take the failure to mean rejection of your worth. If the situation makes you feel there is something wrong with you, it can lower your ex-

pectations and lead to feelings of worthlessness, despair, or apathy. This point is particularly important to remember during a recession: if unemployment is high in general, it's not your fault. Finding work is harder for everyone.

The impact of irritability or withdrawal can spread to relationships with friends and family: divorce is a common consequence. Bolles cites a survey of 15,000 clients of an executive career counselor that showed that 75 percent of these job seekers were either facing, in the midst of, or just through with a divorce. Even finding a job may not end rejection shock if the job does not meet expectations. Settling for a job you don't want can be as desolating and dissatisfying as not finding the job you'd like.

Bolles identifies three common assumptions among job hunters that are self-defeating. One is that the job hunter should stay loose and vague about what she wants in order to take advantage of whatever jobs might become available. A second is that the job hunter should search out organizations anywhere in the country that might be interested in her and apply to them regardless of where they are located. The third is that potential employers only see people whose resumes are attractive and well written—and hardly any of those, at that.

In place of these self-defeating assumptions, Bolles suggests, the job seeker should operate from their counterparts. First, he advises, decide exactly what you'd like to do—don't be vague, but have a firm idea of the job you want. Next decide exactly where you'd like to do it, doing your own scouting to find potential employers in places you'd like to live. Then research these employers that interest you in detail, finding out exactly who has the power to hire you for the job you want—and approach that person directly.

Bolles backs up this strategy with data from a national survey that shows that the most effective method of finding a job was applying directly to the employer. This method was twice as effective as either using an employment agency or answering newspaper ads. In short, Bolles advises, you must decide for yourself what you want to do in this world: honestly assess your skills and talents, interests, motives, and how much money you want to make. Then aim for the best available rung of the job ladder you want to climb.

PART SEVEN

SOCIAL BEHAVIOR

18

ATTITUDES AND BEHAVIOR

COMMON MYTHS

MANY PEOPLE BELIEVE ...	ACTUALLY ...
Facts matter more than feelings in forming attitudes.	Feelings are as important as facts in forming attitudes—sometimes more important.
If you believe that someone is trying to persuade you of something, you are more easily swayed.	Knowing that someone is trying to persuade you is likely to make you resist being persuaded.
All stereotypes are inaccurate.	Some stereotypes are largely accurate, although many are not.
Experiencing prejudice against oneself makes a person more prejudiced.	Experiencing prejudice against oneself can make a person less prejudiced.
Women are more romantic than men.	Women are often more realistic about relationships than men.

A great many think they are thinking
when they are really rearranging their
prejudices.

EDWARD R. MURROW

Sad to say, facts do not always make much difference in how people make up their minds. Quite often a person's prejudices, feelings, and attitudes
about an issue override the facts. We frequently
make judgments on the basis of our likes and dislikes . . . rather than a careful analysis of pros and
cons. Opinions and biases often count as much as
objective fact in the outcome of elections, the exclusion or acceptance of people in groups, or the
attraction between two people.

ATTITUDES

An *attitude* is an enduring predisposition that
makes a person ready to respond in a predictable
manner to people, objects, or ideas. An attitude is
often connected with an emotion, and attitudes in
some instances—but not always—lead to acts
(Kahle and Berman, 1979). There are three components to an attitude: cognitive, emotional, and behavioral. The belief, or cognitive part, reflects
what you hold to be true about something. Your
feelings about the subject—liking or disliking it—
are the emotional part. Your beliefs and feelings

lead you to act in a predictable fashion; this is the
behavioral part.

How attitudes are formed

We get many of our attitudes from the people
around us, for the most part by observing them
rather than by hearing their opinions directly. In
general, as children we acquire a set of attitudes
from our parents by imitating them as models,
just as we learn other kinds of behavior (Bandura
and Walters, 1963). Parents and children tend to
have similar views about religion, economics, and
politics, as indicated by a nationwide survey of
high school seniors, which found that 76 percent
favored their parents' political party (Jennings
and Niemi, 1968).

While parents have great influence over their
children's attitudes early in life, from the time a
child starts school his peers have an increasingly
great influence on his attitudes. By the time you
reach high school, the way your friends dress,
drink, or dance may be far more important to how
you do these things than anything your parents
say about them.

479

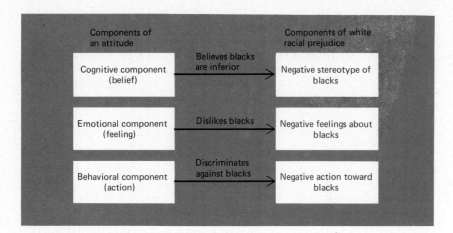

Figure 18.1 The anatomy of an attitude

The components of an attitude and their relationship to one attitude—racial prejudice.

Imagine that your best friend in high school used to complain to you about her parents. She couldn't stand her father's speeches about the virtues of the Republican party; her mother was always nagging her to watch less TV and get more culture into her life. She felt trapped at home; she was ready for freedom and change at college.

The summer after your freshman year, when you both meet again at home, you learn she's joined the Young Democrats and chosen to major in communications, with a specialty in videotaping for television. ■

Reactance

Why should your friend end up doing exactly the opposite of what her parents had urged her to do? The answer might lie in the ways her parents inadvertently shaped her attitudes. Direct modeling or imitation of someone else's attitudes is by no means the only or most frequent way attitudes are acquired. The very attempt to influence how a person thinks can backfire, especially if that person feels manipulated. In fact, a simple forewarning that you intend to persuade someone of something encourages the person to consider the counterarguments, especially if the listener is highly involved with the issue (Petty and Cacioppo, 1979). *Reactance* occurs when a person

perceives that another person is trying to influence her and sees it as a threat to her freedom to make up her own mind (Brehm, 1966). Your friend resented her parents' attempts to shape her political and cultural outlook; reactance led her to form attitudes opposite to those of her parents.

Attitudes and consistency

Can you hold two opposite opinions toward the same thing? Not comfortably, according to *balance theory:* people tend to change their discrepant attitudes to bring them into agreement (Heider, 1958). If you hold attitudes that don't agree with each other, you're likely to change one or the other so that your own viewpoints are harmonious. When two people are discussing an issue, there is the same tendency toward balance. If they disagree, each will try to sway the other; if one of them changes her opinion, then they are in balance.

This tendency to bring attitudes into agreement is sometimes termed the need for *cognitive consistency*, a condition in which one's beliefs are consistent with one another. Theorists who hold this view maintain that having attitudes that are in conflict makes a person uncomfortable, and so she changes them to be consistent. The state of tension that exists when a person holds two beliefs, ideas, attitudes, or opinions that are inconsistent with each other is called *cognitive dissonance* (Festinger, 1957). Because this state is unpleasant, a person tries to resolve the dissonance by changing one or another viewpoint (Higgins, Rhodewalt, and Zanna, 1979).

A chain smoker who knows that there is a strong link between smoking and lung cancer is likely to experience cognitive dissonance. On the one hand, she may believe smoking makes her more relaxed. On the other, she may hear of evidence that shows smoking will increase the likelihood of getting lung cancer. She can resolve the dissonance in one of two ways: stop smoking or find a way to refute or deny the evidence that smoking is harmful. Or, she may decide that the short-term gain of tension relief more than justifies the long-term risk of cancer. This kind of attitude adjustment is a common way to reduce cognitive dissonance. In short, if there is dissonance, we try to create consistency by changing our attitude, our behavior, or both.

Imagine that for weeks you tried to decide what kind of car to buy. Your choice narrowed to a foreign compact and a larger American car. On the one hand, the compact gets great mileage and doesn't need many repairs. On the other, the American car is safer and more powerful.

You finally decide to get the foreign car. After that, you notice that you only read ads for and reports about foreign cars—you ignore what anyone has to say in favor of American cars. ■

Dissonance theory

One way to reduce dissonance is by *selective exposure,* seeking out information that supports your own beliefs. In other words, people who are already decided tend to look only for evidence that they are right—as you did after you bought your foreign car. Although people often seek out both sides of an argument, they are more likely to expose themselves to information that confirms their own viewpoint, especially when the discrepancies between sides are great (Wicklund and Brehm, 1976).

Dissonant information threatens people (Zanna and Aziza, 1976). Whether or not a person will seek out information that might disconform her own view depends on how she deals with anxiety-evoking information generally. Repressors, who tend to deny or repress anxiety, avoid information that might disconfirm a decision they've made, while sensitizers, who generally seek out threatening information, do so even when it might invalidate their own viewpoint (Olson and Zanna, 1979).

When faced with dissonance—say, a strong argument that goes against their own attitudes—people can also reduce their discomfort by discrediting the argument itself or the person making it. The more the argument disagrees with a person's attitudes, the more likely it is that the person will try to discredit it (Aronson, *et al.,* 1963).

Dissonance theory holds that the harder you work for a goal, the more attractive it will seem to you. This is one reason that groups sometimes put new members through a difficult initiation: it makes the group seem more worth joining. For example, college women volunteered to join a group that met to discuss the psychology of sex (Aronson and Mills, 1959). Each was told that in order to join, she had to go through a screening to show that she could discuss sex freely and openly. One-third of the women had to recite aloud, in front of a male experimenter, a list of obscene words and read some lurid passages from novels. One-third went through a milder initiation, reciting a list of sexual words that were not obscene. The final third had no screening. Each then listened to a rather dull tape, supposedly a sample of the discussion from the group they wanted to join. The women who underwent no initiation or a mild one rated the discussion as dull. The group that had to read the obscene words, though, somehow convinced themselves that the discussions were interesting and rated them as worthwhile.

Dissonance theory also predicts that the greater the reward, the more likely people will be to comply with a demand, but the less likely they will be to change their attitudes about their task: doing it won't mean they like it. In a classic demonstration of this hypothesis, subjects were asked to perform a dull, difficult task (Festinger and Carlsmith, 1959). Afterward, they were paid to tell the next person waiting to participate that the task was in-

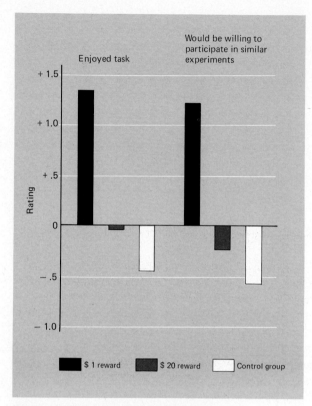

Figure 18.2 Rewards and attitude shift

The less the reward for engaging in behavior contrary to an attitude, the greater the accompanying change in attitude. The greater the reward, the less the change in attitude.

The need to reduce dissonance often underlies self-justification. For example, when Princeton University students were asked to write and record a speech in support of doubling the size of the freshman class—a policy they opposed—doing so led them to change their minds and favor the expansion (Goethals, *et al.*, 1979). This self-justifying attitude change was greatest for those who chose to give the speech knowing it might be sent on to the administrative board about to decide on the issue.

These studies point up some dangerous human tendencies: when we submit to the demands of authority against our own better judgment, we can justify performing acts that belie our own values.

Imagine that it's a warm spring day. You're on your way to Economics 101. The class is a huge lecture, the hall is always stuffy, and the professor's lectures have bored you lately.

Your friend Karen, walking with you, says, "Hey, listen—it's a beautiful day. That lecture hall is always too stuffy, and besides, this class bores me. I'm going over to the cafeteria for an iced tea. Want to come?"

You think it over for a second. "No," you reply, "I think it's wrong to cut classes. Besides I'm getting behind and can't afford to cut. See you later."

As she heads toward the cafeteria you pause a moment, then walk on.

Five minutes later, to your own surprise, you find yourself at a table in the cafeteria sipping iced tea. ■

teresting and pleasant. The payment ranged from only $1 for some subjects to up to $20 for others. At the end of the experimental session, the liars were asked by the researchers how much they had actually enjoyed the dull task. Subjects who had received large amounts and subjects in a control group who had not been asked to lie said the task was boring. Those who had been paid only $1 for lying said that they found the task enjoyable.

The subjects receiving $1 had less reason to lie than the higher-paid subjects, so to account to themselves for their behavior—and to reduce their increased dissonance—the members of the lower-paid group changed their attitude. They justified the lie by coming to believe it. In short, a person who has sufficient justification for lying does not change his true attitude to fit his lie. On the other hand, if the reward he receives is insufficient, he justifies his behavior by believing his own lies.

ATTITUDE CHANGE AND BEHAVIOR

Attitudes and behavior seem to be a two-way street. In some cases our attitudes shape our actions, in others what we have done may shape our attitudes. A review of thirty-one studies of the relationship between people's attitudes and their actions in such areas as race relations, job satisfaction, and cheating found that often what people did was not related to what they felt (Wicker,

1969). This fact of human nature is expressed in the adage, "Do as I say, not as I do."

Even so, there is a large zone of human behavior where attitudes and actions fit together (e.g., Fazio, Zanna, and Cooper, 1978). A better understanding of the fit between attitude and action can come from assessing the range of a person's attitudes toward a situation rather than a single opinion (Wicker, 1971). Take cutting classes. Students were asked how they felt about specific professors and about cutting. Then the number of times the students cut class were counted. Their feelings about cutting class were better predictors of how often they actually cut class than their attitudes toward the professors. But predictions of cutting were most accurate when *both* attitudes—toward the professor and toward cutting—were taken into account (Rokeach and Kliejunas, 1972).

Dissonance could be at work in the area of cutting: if you find yourself doing it, you may come to believe that it is all right to do it. Changing your attitude would, according to dissonance theory, make you more comfortable with your behavior. You could cut class happily rather than guiltily.

Not necessarily, though. A major objection to Festinger's theory of cognitive dissonance was voiced by Daryl Bem (1972), who challenged the assumption that dissonance produces an internal tension that must be resolved. Bem proposed that many of the attitudes and behaviors that had been seen as resolving dissonance were due to something else instead: people were *learning* about their attitudes by watching their own behavior.

Thus, in Bem's analysis, the students who lied may have thought about how they acted and the forces that made them lie. When there was a strong bribe—the $20—they could infer that they had lied about liking the experiment just to get the money. But when there was only a mild bribe to lie—in the case of the students who got just $1—they would conclude that they really *did* like the experiment, since the money they got was not enough to justify to themselves telling a lie.

Bem's theory holds that *self-perception*, the way one sees oneself, can shape attitudes. We judge ourselves just as others do, by observing our own behavior. We then shape our attitudes to fit our behavior. Bem's theory would explain your change of attitude toward cutting without having to resort to the idea that cutting had made you feel uncomfortably dissonant (e.g., that you really didn't feel cutting was so terrible). The singular advantage of Bem's theory over Festinger's is simplicity: it allows a more direct explanation of the same facts.

Imagine that you thought your term paper was the best you'd ever done, but it came back with a C. You're waiting for your professor's office hour to start. You feel sure you can convince her to raise your grade to a B at least, maybe even an A.

As you sit outside her door, you rehearse your arguments. You consider whether to mention that you've just been named to the honor roll for your grades last term. You wonder whether you should just give your plea or also mention some opposing arguments in anticipation of her objections. Finally you weigh the virtue of ending on a note of personal disinterest, asking only that she reread the paper, not demanding a better grade. You see her coming.

What should you say to her? ■

Persuasion

Your best bet would probably be to use all three tactics. Each of them exemplifies techniques known to increase the persuasiveness of an argument. Among the main factors in changing someone's attitude are the source and content of a communication and the nature of the listener.

By slipping the fact that you've made honor roll into the conversation, you might raise your prestige in your professor's eyes. A person's prestige can make his arguments more credible. Information about the prestigious nature of a speaker—for example, his age, intelligence, or social class—can all make his arguments more convincing. In a classic study, Hovland and Weiss (1951) had subjects read identical statements about controversial issues. Some people were led to believe the statements were from a well-known business magazine, and others thought they were from a Hollywood gossip columnist. The greater attitude change came in the subjects who believed the statements were from the business magazine.

But be careful about overplaying the honor role angle. When someone feels you are trying to impress her, it can backfire (Jones, 1965). To guard against this negative reaction, you can make your case more effectively by giving both sides—the arguments both for and against a better grade. Giving only one side of an argument works well when the audience is already sympathetic to that position. A "give-'em-hell" approach would go over at a political rally, but a two-sided argument appeals more to listeners who are well enough informed to know that there is more than one side to every issue (Hovland, Lumsdaine, and Sheffield, 1949).

Including some arguments against your self-interest should also help convince your professor. When listeners feel you are not simply out to con them, your argument seems more credible. For example, when criminals argued for curbing police powers, they had little sway on their audience; when prisoners argued for increased police power, however, their arguments were highly effective (Walster, Aronson, and Abrahams, 1966). People arguing *against* their own self-interest—or seeming to—have more credibility.

Seeming disinterested in changing a person's views also increases the potency of an argument. In a study by Walster and Festinger (1962), listeners who thought they just happened to overhear someone were more convinced by the arguments offered than were people who thought the communication was aimed directly at them. When you have no reason to believe someone is trying to persuade you, you give more credence to his or her opinions.

There are other factors that can increase the persuasiveness of an argument (Maddux and Rogers, 1980). For example, the more a speaker is liked, the more persuasive he can be. A famous actor claiming to like a beer or a high-fashion model endorsing a new perfume can change our attitudes toward the beer or perfume—not because of any new information, but because we find the people appealing. When college men listened to an attractive young woman give a speech, they were more apt to change their opinions than when the speaker was the same woman made up to look unattractive (Mills and Aronson, 1965).

Imagine that you happen to notice a sign painter putting up a huge billboard, a cigarette ad. You pause to watch him for a while, admiring the skill with which he works.

As you watch him skillfully paint the words on a cigarette package, "Warning: The Surgeon General has determined that cigarette smoking is hazardous to your health," it strikes you: he's been chain-smoking all the while. ■

Emotion and attitude change

Many public health campaigns try to arouse fear in people who continue habits such as smoking or overeating. Overall, this has been shown to be an effective approach—under certain circumstances.

For fear arousal to be effective, it should be kept within reasonable limits, and listeners should be given a specific alternative, something they can do to minimize the threat. Thus if the fears aroused are of cancer or heart attack, specific positive changes—for example, stop smoking, eat less, exercise more—should be suggested (Berkowitz, 1970).

In one study, a group of people were shown a brief film that depicted the dangers of smoking by means of a mechanical "smoking machine," with charts showing that death from lung cancer increases with cigarette sales. Another group saw the same film with some added scenes of an actual lung-cancer operation where the black and diseased lung of a cancer victim was removed. The operation scenes were so gory that some people left the room. The group that saw this film reported feeling more upset and afraid of getting cancer than the other group, and its members were more eager to quit smoking than those in the low-fear group (Leventhal, Watts and Pagano, 1967).

Thus both attitudes and actual behavior can be changed through appeals to fear. Of course it is possible to overdo such an approach, either by threatening such terrible consequences that they appear ridiculous or by making people so anxious that their defenses are mobilized to resist the threat. Moderate to high levels of fear seem most effective (Janis, 1967).

Fear is not the only emotional appeal that works; pleasant feelings can also increase the effectiveness of an appeal to change. Students who ate a snack while reading persuasive appeals on such issues as reducing the size of the armed forces were more persuaded than students who had no snack (Janis, Kaye, Kirschner, 1965). Another study used songs about social issues like water pollution and the plight of the aged to present a case for change. Some people heard only the spoken lyrics, some heard them sung without guitar accompaniment, and others heard them sung with a guitar. The group that heard the songs with guitar reported feeling the best and had the most change in their attitudes (Hendrick, 1972). The experimenters thought that the songs worked so well because positive feelings made people more receptive to new information, and so more likely to change their opinions.

The listener

"Some people," goes a common saying, "believe everything they hear." There is a grain of truth in this homily: while there are great differences between people in persuadability, people who are likely to change attitudes in one situation are more likely to do the same in another (Hovland and Janis, 1959).

One key characteristic of people who are easily

YOU'RE PROBABLY RIGHT

Ed Arno

Drawing by Ed Arno; © 1979 The New Yorker Magazine, Inc.

persuaded is low self-esteem; they place little value on their own opinions and are quick to give them up. Their negative self-image may make them attribute more prestige to someone who tries to change their mind. And if they are concerned about acceptance by a group, they may fear contradicting opinions of the majority.

In general, people who have high self-esteem are less easy to persuade. They stick to their own opinions more strongly. Such people, although not rebellious, are independent, can maintain their attitudes in the face of criticism, and are largely unaffected by external standards (Hovland and Janis, 1959). Presumably their ability to resist stems from having been rewarded in the past for maintaining their attitudes despite criticism.

Responding to criticism of your opinions makes you less likely to change them. *Inoculation theory* holds that, just as a small amount of virus immunizes a person against an illness, attacks against a person's opinions make him or her resistant to appeals to change them. For example, people were asked if they concurred with truisms such as "Everyone should brush their teeth after every meal if at all possible." They then heard their position attacked, at first mildly, and then later more strongly. Hearing the first mild attack made people better able to resist the later, strong attack (McGuire and Papageorgis, 1961). Anything that alerts a person to the possibility their attitudes may be attacked seems to prepare them to rebuff contrary opinions better (McGuire, 1969). But forewarning doesn't always last; as time goes on the "inoculation" can lose its impact, and the effect of the discounted argument prevails (Watts and Holt, 1979).

Imagine that in a physics class people are forming study groups for the first midterm. The one person left out of the study groups is Tom. The reason: Tom is blind.

No one wants to have to help him struggle through the physics review, let alone have to slow down for him to have everything read aloud.

On the day of the midterm, Tom is there with someone to read him the problems. As the class ponders the problems, Tom leaves about halfway through the exam period. "Too bad," several people think. "Must have been too tough for him."

When the grades come back, it's clear why he left first: Tom's grade was the highest in the class. ■

PREJUDICE

Tom was the victim of a *stereotype,* a rigid and oversimplified conception whereby all people in a group are seen as having the same characteristics, regardless of their actual differences. Tom's classmates erroneously assumed that he would need special attention and help, perhaps like other blind people they had seen in other situations. The classmates were displaying their *prejudice,* hostility toward a member of a specific group based on faulty generalizations. Except for a person to read to him, Tom needed no special help to master physics; in fact he could have helped others instead.

The generalizations that support prejudice often remain faulty because people do not give themselves the chance to check their bias against the facts. For example, 100 people advertising an apartment for rent were called to see if they would rent to a mentally retarded person who had been through a special training program (Trippi, *et al.,* 1978). Only one out of 100 agreed; fifty-two claimed the apartment was no longer available, while the remaining forty-seven tried to make it seem unattractive.

Avoiding contact with a stereotyped person—as the landlords did with the retarded renter or the class did with Tom—perpetuates the stereotype. If you keep your distance, you can't gather new information to make the category more accurate—such as, finding out that blind people vary greatly in their talents, abilities, and competence, as do the sighted. Common stereotypes such as the lazy black, the greedy Jew, the drunken Irishman and the emotional Italian can be maintained only if a person ignores the preponderance of hardworking blacks, generous Jews, sober Irishmen, and calm Italians. We all use stereotypes to some extent, simply because they simplify our view of the world and of others. Faulty stereotypes are reinforced by *selective perception:* people accept information that fits their stereotypes and screen out any that doesn't.

■ Research done in the 1950s suggests that a person with an "authoritarian personality" is more likely to have prejudiced and hostile attitudes (Adorno, *et al.,* 1950). Such people were identified on the basis of a questionnaire called the F scale (F for fascism), where they indicated whether or not they agreed with statements like: "An insult to our honor should always be punished" and "Obedience and respect for authority are the most important virtues children should learn."

People who agreed with statements like these tended to be unquestioning in their acceptance of authority figures within their groups, hence the name "authoritarian personality." Such people will change their attitudes in deference to someone in authority more often than others, even accepting a viewpoint contrary to their own. They also tended to dislike minority groups, to have unusually high national and ethnic pride, to believe in severe punishments for deviants, and to perceive interpersonal relationships in terms of dominance and submission.

Authoritarianism has also been linked to a need for consistency (Steiner and Johnson, 1963). Authoritarians seem to have a need for certainty that leads them to oversimplify things. They are particularly upset by inconsistent information. Their inability to tolerate ambiguity leads them to form black-and-white judgments. Since the world is actually shades of grey, they achieve clarity by ignoring or suppressing data inconsistent with their viewpoint. Stereotypes are particularly appealing to authoritarians, since they simplify complexity.

On the basis of interviews with eighty people who scored high on authoritarianism, researchers were able to assess the factors in childhood that may have shaped this attitude (Sanford, 1973). The "highs" saw their fathers as distant and stern and their mothers as morally restrictive. The "lows,"

THE AUTHORITARIAN PERSONALITY

The authoritarian personality is typical of members of neo-Fascist groups such as the American Nazi party. (© Leif Skoogfors 1980/Woodfin Camp & Assoc.)

though, saw their fathers as relaxed and mild, their mothers as intellectual and aesthetic—but not restrictive. The highs also tended to idealize their childhood, skipping or ignoring negative aspects of their parents. The high authoritarians were also more likely to have grown up in homes where discipline was harsh and rules conventional, while the lows tended to have parents who reasoned with them on the basis of moral principles rather than strict adherence to rules.

The interpretation of the researchers was that the authoritarians' harsh and unloving childhood made them hostile to their parents but afraid to express their anger openly. Instead they denied their hostility, directing it against people who differ from the middle-class norms they grew up to follow. The authoritarian person, then, uses these negative attitudes to ward off feelings of resentment toward his parents. Like all psychological defenses, this one has a cost: the authoritarian person must rigidly deny information that might show that his prejudices are wrong. Thus a defense against childhood hurts and angers leads to the typical authoritarian personality pattern, to prejudice, and to a rigid cognitive style.

This interpretation—and the research on which it was based—has been severely criticized as being too speculative about events in childhood and based on too few cases (Christie and Jahoda, 1954). But later research has borne out many of the original conclusions. For example, there is a high correlation between authoritarianism and harsh discipline in childhood (Martin and Westie, 1959), support for the attitudes of those in power (Izzett, 1971), and even a high regard for Archie Bunker, TV's most famous authoritarian (Capko and Lewis, 1975). ■

Scapegoating

Economic or political rivalry between groups often leads to prejudice. When ethnic groups are vying for the same jobs or fighting over the same land, their hostility predisposes members of each group to be prejudiced toward the other. Tensions of this sort can also lead to *scapegoating,* where anger or frustration is displaced onto an innocent party. A man who loses his job at a factory may displace his anger by yelling at his children or blaming a minority group: "It's those lazy Mexicans who ruin the assembly line. They make us all look bad."

Groups become easy victims for scapegoating when they have certain characteristics: (1) their physical appearance makes them easily identified, (2) they are accessible, (3) they can't retaliate, and (4) they have been scapegoats before (Allport, 1944). When Hitler blamed Germany's troubles on the Jews, all four elements were present. First, Hitler ordered Jews to wear badges to they would be visible. Since Jews lived throughout Germany, they were easily accessible. They were not armed and so were unable to retaliate. Finally, Jews had been blamed before for Germany's economic problems.

Imagine that one of the study groups from the physics class quickly asks Tom to join them, as soon as they find out he got the highest grade on the midterm. He does, but more in the role of tutor than student.

It turns out that Tom—though blind—is not only a physics whiz but a superb pianist. He also knows a lot of statistics and trivia about football.

By the time the term is finished, Tom has made two close friends: an aspiring concert pianist and one of the tackles on the varsity football squad. ■

Ending prejudice

Since prejudice thrives on overgeneralization, misinformation, and stereotypes, one way to reduce prejudice in someone is to expose him to the kind of person against whom he holds the prejudice. The pianist and football player would not have had a chance to meet and become friends with Tom if the study group hadn't invited him to join. Sometimes—not always—such close contact will show the prejudiced person how distorted his beliefs are and so change them. This is one of the arguments made for racial integration (Bem, 1970; Pettigrew, 1971).

Members of different groups working together for a common goal—e.g., on a sports team—is one sort of experience that has been found to lessen prejudice. (© Wendy Watriss/Frederick Baldwin 1979/ Woodfin Camp & Assoc.)

BLACK AND WHITE TOGETHER

■ At least in theory, when people from different racial and ethnic groups are together in friendly, cooperative situations, any prejudices between them are likely to weaken. When members of different groups live together in the same neighborhood, an ample opportunity is provided for prejudice to decrease.

But some social forces seem to be working against this prejudice-reducing possibility: according to a report by the Institute for Social Research (ISR), the marking off of neighborhoods as white or black is a prevailing trend (1979). One result may be that America is becoming two societies—white suburbs and black cities.

Racially segregated communities persist despite civil rights laws and the best efforts of integrationists. There are three major theories of why this should be so: the economic status of blacks, blacks wanting to be with other blacks, and the resistance of whites to integrated neighborhoods—but none explain the trend very well.

To better understand what else might have led to segregated neighborhoods, investigators surveyed people in the Detroit area to assess racial attitudes, economic factors, and the housing market (ISR, 1979). Instead of asking outright, "Would you object to a black on your block?" they showed a series of neighborhood diagrams representing different degrees of integration, from one black family in a neighborhood to a predominantly black population with a few white families. Respondents reported their willingness to live in each kind of neighborhood.

They found that while whites did not object to a few token blacks in their neighborhood, as the proportion of blacks increased, their willingness to stay decreased: they feared decreasing property values, increased crime, and feeling out of place with black neighbors.

Blacks, on the other hand, preferred to live in a neighborhood with an equal number of blacks and whites. They objected to all-black neighborhoods, but resisted even more being the only black family in a white neighborhood.

Thus, the most preferred pattern for whites—a few blacks among many whites—was the least preferred pattern by blacks.

Blacks are more willing to be the third black family to move to a white neighborhood than to be the first. Most felt that a family that was first was in danger from hostile neighbors. But almost a third of blacks were just as reluctant to move to an all-black neighborhood.

The investigators hypothesize that a neighborhood that is 70 percent white and 30 percent black is the most likely to remain stably integrated. When the balance tips more toward blacks, whites are likely to move out. That means the 50-50 balance preferred by blacks is not likely to stay such.

The picture the survey depicts is much different than it would have been had whites simply been asked "Would you accept a black on your block?" If that had been the question, the results would have undoubtedly depicted whites as being much more open to integration than they actually are. Most whites would probably have said "yes," meaning yes to *one* black on the block. But few would have said yes to many more than one. ■

But simply throwing together people who have prejudices about each other is not enough: desegregation of public schools does not seem to have decreased the prejudices of black and white students toward each other (Stephan, 1978). Other ingredients besides increased contact are needed to lessen prejudice (Cook, 1969). One of these is cooperation among people from antagonistic groups.

According to Allport (1954) prejudice may be reduced by equal-status contact between majority and minority groups in the pursuit of common goals. This is especially effective when the contact is supported by law, custom, or local atmosphere and is of a sort that leads group members to see common interests. Allport's suggestion could explain why, for example, there are fewer racial incidents among soldiers in combat zones than in peaceful areas.

Another way to lessen a person's prejudice may be to experience prejudice against oneself. Third-graders randomly chosen for a study were told that they were "superior"—smarter, cleaner, and better behaved than other children—and were given special privileges that their classmates, who were "inferior," did not enjoy. Then on another day the roles were reversed. Later when these children, all of whom were white, were asked whether they would attend a picnic with some black children (who are frequent victims of prejudice), 96 percent said "yes," while only 60 percent of third-graders who had not experienced being "superior" and "inferior" said they would (Weiner and Wright, 1973). Presumably having themselves been the object of discrimination made the third-graders in the experiment less prejudiced—and so more open to a picnic with black children—compared to those third-graders who did not experience discrimination.

Imagine that a headline in the campus paper tells you that a local candidate for mayor has come out in favor of legalizing marijuana. She's the first local politician ever to do so.

"Big deal," you think to yourself. "It's a college town, so lots of voters are young. She's just playing politics." Even though you favor legalization too, you're not impressed.

But you read on. A poll shows that in fact most of the local voters are conservative; they oppose legalization of marijuana by a 2 to 1 majority.

"She means it," you think.

Reading on you discover that she's young and that the local police chief condemns her stand.

You decide to register and vote for her. ■

ATTRIBUTION

When we have to guess why people act as they do, we apply a "commonsense" psychology, forming our own ideas about people and situations (Heider, 1958). To decide whether the candidate's campaign stand expressed her real self or whether she was just playing politics, you had to go through a series of steps that helped you discover her motivation. This process is described in *attribution theory*, which holds that our perceptions of and responses to another person's behavior are largely determined by the motives we attribute to her.

When people attempt to explain their own behavior, they tend to attribute its cause to the situation they are experiencing. When people watch someone else, however, they tend to attribute what they see to the other person's characteristics, such as personality (Jones and Nisbett, 1972; Snyder and Monson, 1977). If you're rushing to catch a bus so you won't be late for an important appointment, you may in your hurry push someone. Your own explanation for pushing would be the situation: you're in a great hurry. Someone who saw you pushing might consider you a "pushy" person. *Attribution* is the process of inferring people's characteristics from what they do.

When people form impressions of others, they tend to overestimate the extent to which a person's behavior is due to their traits, such as pushiness, and to underestimate the degree to which it's caused by situational factors, such as being in a rush (Mischel, 1968). This seems to stem from the fact that most of what we know about others comes from observing what they do and then inferring the motives or traits behind the actions (Jones and Nisbett, 1972). With our own behavior, such impressions are often self-serving: people tend to see the positive things they do as more consistent with their true dispositions than the negative things they do (Eisen, 1979).

Situation or disposition

In deciding whether a person's actions are due to situational or dispositional factors, there are patterns that we search for to help us decide (Kelley, 1972). One is consensus, the extent to which other people act in the same way as the person observed; another is consistency, the extent to which the person acts that way at other times in similar situations; and a third is distinctiveness, the extent to which the person acts differently in other situations. We are likely to conclude that an act is due to a person's disposition if there is low consensus (e.g., other people aren't pushing to get on the bus), high consistency (the person is often seen pushing her way on to buses), and low distinctiveness (she pushes her way in other places, like theater lines). We are likely to conclude that acts are due to the situation instead of the person's disposition if the opposite three conditions apply (other people are pushing to get on the bus too; she seldom does so at other times; she never does so in other places).

Events take on very different meanings if we attribute them to external instead of internal factors. If someone judged a person's pushing to be evidence of the trait of pushiness, she might think poorly of the person in general; if she realized that the person was in a hurry, she would probably judge the behavior less severely.

Imagine that two young women are

at a table in a singles bar, talking about a man standing near the bar.

"If he had blond hair, he could be Robert Redford's twin. He's gorgeous," says the first.

"I bet he's a lawyer or a doctor," says the other, "to carry himself like that. His suit must be expensive."

"I wonder what he's doing here? He's sure to be married," says the other.

Seeing the man start to walk in their direction, the women stop talking but watch him out of the corner of their eye.

He goes over to the table next to them, where a couple have just left, and picks up their check and the money they've left. All at once they realize: he's the waiter. ■

Person perception

We all continually form impressions of people we see, making assumptions about them that may or may not be true. *Person perception* is the process whereby we size up people and categorize their qualities, characteristics, and inner states. Physical appearance is one of the most obvious bases for forming impressions. The women in the singles bar perceived the handsome man as being wealthy and of high status simply because he was good-looking.

The more physically attractive a person, the more favorable an impression he or she will make. Physical appearance exerts a powerful influence on how people respond to a person. In one study, people were shown photos of three faces of either the same or the opposite sex; the photos had previously been rated as high, average, or low in looks. The people then rated the faces in the photos on personality traits such as sincerity, competitiveness, and kindness and estimated the person's chances of future marital happiness, job success, competence as a parent, and overall happiness. The more physically attractive the face, the more positive the ratings it received (Dion, Berschied, and Walster, 1972). The experimenters concluded that an attractiveness stereotype exists and that the assumption is that "what is beautiful is good"—that is, not only are good-looking people thought to be more personable, but their lives are expected to be happier and more successful.

The self-fulfilling prophecy

The expectations a person brings to a situation can affect its outcome. When we have formed an impression of a person, our impression will shape how we treat him or her. This is one form of a *self-fulfilling prophecy*, whereby a person acts on the basis of an expectation and in so doing makes it come true (Merton, 1948; Jones, 1977).

A classic demonstration of the self-fulfilling prophecy as it operates in school showed that if a teacher thinks a student will do well, the student will in fact do better (Rosenthal and Jacobson, 1968). In a California primary school, children were given a standard IQ test. The teachers were told it measured "intellectual blooming." The testers reported to the teacher that 20 percent of the children were potential "bloomers"; in fact, the label was given to children picked at random. When the children were tested a year later, the so-called "bloomers" actually showed a significant gain in IQ. Presumably the teachers' expectations of "blooming" had led them to treat these children in such a way that they actually did bloom. This kind of increase in ability brought about by positive expectations is called the *Pygmalion effect*.

A stereotype such as attractiveness can become a self-fulfilling prophecy. For example, if you expect people to be stimulating and exciting because you find them physically attractive, they may be more apt to behave that way, responding to your expectation. In one study, men and women spoke to each other on the phone, with some men (unknown to the women) led to believe they were talking to a physically attractive woman, others to an unattractive woman (Snyder, Tanke, and Berschied, 1977). Judges later concluded from listening to tapes of the phone calls that the women whose phone partners thought they were attractive showed more socially desirable qualities such as poise, sociability, and confidence than the women whose partners thought them unattractive. Additionally, the men who thought they were talking to an attractive woman were judged to have more social qualities like being warm, interesting, sexually permissive, and humorous. Liking someone, or knowing you are liked, can lead you to behave more likably.

Our preconceptions can be self-fulfilling prophecies. For example, in one study subjects were evaluated as high on a bogus personality trait, which they were told was either desirable or undesirable (Baumeister, Cooper, and Skib, 1979). They then tried to solve an anagram, after being told that people high on the bogus trait usually did poorly on such tasks. As predicted, those subjects who had been told the trait was desirable did worse on the task than those who were told the trait was undesirable—who may therefore have been motivated to disprove that they had the trait.

Judging status

A woman who steps out of a chauffeured limousine will draw more stares than she would if she pulled up in an old van. Each person you meet gives you a set of cues such as accent, clothes, jewelry, and bearing that influence your impression of that person's status—and how you judge a person's status can have a great deal to do with how you treat her or him. For example, when researchers stopped at a red light in an old beat-up car and did not move when the light turned green, drivers behind them were quick to honk. When they did the same thing in a luxury car, drivers behind them were much more patient (Doob and Gross, 1968). Status cues can even influence judgment about a person's height: in one study, students estimated a stranger's height as shorter when they thought he was a fellow student than when they were told he was a professor (Wilson, 1968).

Imagine that you like Joe and Fran. You hate Gail and Mike. You may know what attracts you to the first two and repels you about the other two. You're about to meet Kathy. What determines whether or not you'll like her? And what will decide whether she likes you? ∎

INTERPERSONAL ATTRACTION

While no one factor can predict one person's liking for another with total certainty, many factors can be strong influences. Your liking for Kathy—and hers for you—could very likely be shaped one way or the other by how familiar you become, how similar you are, whether each of you sees the other as offering something you need, whether each of you thinks you're liked by the other, and how physically attractive or important each of you perceives the other to be.

Proximity and familiarity

Suppose you notice someone who sits near you at the library. If you see each other week after week, you're likely to smile or say hello in recognition. From this sort of nodding acquaintance, friendships can grow. Frequent exposure, even to strangers, makes people seem like friends. In one study, the more strangers met, even without talking, the more they reported liking each other (Freedman, Carlsmith, and Sears, 1970); in another, the more a picture of a person was seen, the more people said they liked that person (Zajonc, 1968); and in a third, people who simply sat across the table from each other more often—without any interaction whatsoever—liked each other more than total strangers (Saegert, Swap, and Zajonc, 1973). Thus *familiarity*—the frequency of exposure—can foster attraction. So can simple proximity, or nearness. Indeed, apartment dwellers are more apt to be friends with a person who

lives within twenty feet than with one who lives within forty feet (Festinger, Schacter, and Back, 1950), probably because even twenty feet less distance makes it more convenient to get to know another person.

Similarity

Proximity and familiarity alone are not enough to guarantee liking; these factors can sometimes generate the opposite effect. In a dorm, for example, roommates paired on the basis of similar interests became good friends, while those paired because of dissimilarities did not (Newcomb, 1961); even total strangers seem more attractive if we are told they share our views (Byrne, 1969). In the college cafeteria, athletes may sit at one table, psychology majors at another, and chess players at another. Many kinds of similarity—attitudes, values, intelligence, education, social class, or ethnic group—can foster attraction.

Favors

The woman who lends you her notes for a class you missed seems more likable than she did before. In turn, if you want to be liked by her, you

Familiarity breeds friendliness more often than it leads to contempt.
(© Richard Kalvar/Magnum Photos)

might try to do her a favor. But people are often suspicious of favors. For example, subjects in an experiment involving their first impression of another person became suspicious when that person—actually an experimental confederate—treated them to a soda. They later refused to help the confederate on another task; on the other hand, subjects who had not been given any soda did volunteer to help (Brehm and Cole, 1966). The reason for their refusal was probably reactance, the negativity often evoked by attempts at ingratiation.

Indirect favors arouse little suspicion and can cause us to like people. This was demonstrated in a study with college students who had been treated either cruelly or kindly by a research assistant. Later, they overheard the assistant's supervisor berating him for a totally unrelated reason. The cruelly treated subjects tended to like the supervisor more after the incident than did subjects who had been treated kindly (Aronson and Cope, 1968). In short, indirect favors can increase your attractiveness, while obvious ones may diminish it.

An even more effective way of increasing your attractiveness may be to have someone do you a favor. Perhaps the explanation is that the helper must justify the behavior in some way. Thus, one might think, "I don't know why I went through all that trouble for Harry. It must be because he's such a nice fellow." Or one might think, "It must be because I'm such a nice fellow." Cognitive dissonance theory would support this explanation.

Reciprocity

We tend to like people who we know like us. *Reciprocity* means that feelings of being liked—or disliked—are returned in kind. Being liked gives a boost to our self-confidence, especially when we feel insecure, lonely, or anxious. One researcher (Walster, 1965) asked university women to complete a personality test and then to sit in a waiting room until the results were distributed. While she was waiting, each student had the same experience. A good-looking male confederate entered the room and began talking with a receptionist. It became evident that he, too, was participating in an experiment, one being conducted by another in-

LOVING

■ Can you think of someone you like? Someone you love?

Liking is not the same as loving. While there is no universally accepted definition of love, there are some major differences between liking and loving (Berschied and Walster, 1978). Liking is more grounded in reality, while loving often involves fantasies about the other person. Liking people means having positive feelings toward them, while in a love relationship there can be both positive and negative feelings. Liking tends to increase with the length of the relationship, while love—or at least the romantic sort—fades.

The natural history of a relationship, from the initial attraction through either longterm commitment or breaking up, is inevitably a mix of both joys and troubles. (© Lily Solmssen 1979/Photo Researchers, Inc.)

There are, of course, many kinds of love and many styles of loving. Each stage of life has its own (Bloom, 1967). The love a young child feels for its parents is different from the love that married people feel for each other; the romantic feelings of a teenage couple differ from the love of a grandparent for a grandchild.

The kind of love that people fall into is romantic. Romantic love is a state of intense absorption in another person, accompanied by feelings of physical arousal (Walster and Walster, 1978). One theory of romantic love holds that it depends on a high level of physical arousal that the person is able to label ''love'' (Schachter, 1954). As long as a person holds in mind the idea that ''this is love,'' anything her partner does to increase arousal will inflame her passion.

There is some evidence that many sorts of physiological arousal can lead to romantic passion, given the right circumstances (Dutton and Aran, 1974). Male volunteers were asked to cross a 230-foot-high wobbly bridge; another group crossed a strong bridge only ten feet over a stream. The men in both groups were met by a young woman who asked them to make up a story in response to a TAT picture. She then gave the young man her phone number and name in case he wanted more information about the experiment. The ''fear-aroused'' group who crossed the wobbly bridge used more sexual imagery in their TAT story and more of them later called the woman experimenter—presumably indicating a sexual attraction. Apparently fear became transmuted into sexual arousal.

Trust is crucial to a loving relationship. Trust begins with self-disclosure, the revealing of one's intimate feelings. The level of intimacy two people can reach will depend to a great extent on the level of self-disclosure they achieve (Altman and Taylor, 1973). While openness increases intimacy, there seems to be an optimal degree of self-disclosure. People who reveal too little of themselves are seen as cold, but those who go too far too fast in telling about themselves are seen as maladjusted (Chaikin and Derlega, 1974). Lasting intimacy comes slowly, but it is the groundwork for a loving relationship. ■

vestigator who had not yet arrived. He sat down with the subject and started telling her about himself. After about fifteen minutes of discussion, he said he wanted to see her again and asked her for a dinner date.

Just then, the experimenter arrived, took the subject to an adjoining room, and gave her the results of her personality test. These reports were rigged to raise or lower self-esteem. Half the subjects were told that they were mature, original, sensitive people. The others heard themselves described as immature, inflexible people with weak personalities. Subjects were then asked to rate a variety of people on a like-dislike scale (for example, a teacher or friend). Finally, the investigator said, "And since we have one space left, why don't you rate that fellow from the other experiment whom you were waiting with?" Subjects whose self-esteem had been lowered showed greater liking for the young man than did subjects in the high self-esteem condition. This shows that we like those who like us, especially when we feel insecure ourselves.

Complementarity: when opposites attract

While people usually like those who are similar to themselves, in some cases a person may have needs that can only be met by someone with opposite characteristics. Someone who is highly dependent and so likes to be taken care of would be attracted to someone who is nurturant and enjoys caring for others. A person who tends to be dominant might be attracted to someone submissive. In fact, people who don't share our attitudes can seem especially attractive; if they like us, we might think, they must truly appreciate our other appealing attributes (Jones, Bell, and Aronson, 1971).

SUMMARY

Attitudes. Attitudes—predispositions to react in a specific way—have cognitive, emotional, and behavioral aspects.

We get our attitudes largely from people around us. Attempts at influencing someone's attitudes can result in reactance, the adoption of the opposite point of view.

According to balance theory, when a person has two attitudes that conflict with each other, he will tend to change one of the attitudes; likewise, when two people disagree, they tend to seek agreement. This illustrates the need for cognitive consistency. The state of tension that exists when someone holds conflicting attitudes is called cognitive dissonance.

Dissonance can be reduced in several ways. Selective exposure confirms decisions already made. Discrediting an argument or its source lessens discomfort from dissonance.

Dissonance theory posits that the harder a goal is worked for, the more attractive it will seem. It also predicts that people will be more likely to perform a task the greater the reward offered them, but that a large reward will make them unlikely to change their attitude about the task.

Attitude Change and Behavior. Sometimes our attitudes influence our actions; sometimes our actions shape our attitudes. The fit between attitude and actions can best be assessed by examining the range of a person's attitudes, rather than a single opinion.

Festinger's theory of cognitive dissonance is one explanation for why people change their attitudes after they have acted a certain way. Bem proposed an alternative explanation: that people's attitudes are shaped by self-perception—what they observe and learn from their own behavior.

Persuading someone else to change his attitude can be done most effectively by establishing the prestige of the persuader, giving both sides of the argument and taking a disinterested stance, letting the other person draw his own conclusions from the argument, and having the persuader be someone well liked.

Fear can sometimes be an effective attitude and

behavior changer, especially in the area of bad health habits, if the threats are not overdone. Pleasant feelings can also enhance persuasion.

People who are easily persuaded tend to have low self-esteem; those with high self-esteem stick to their own opinions more strongly.

Inoculation theory proposes that attacks against a person's opinions make him resistant to appeals to change them.

Prejudice. Stereotyping is generally the basis of prejudice. Avoiding contact with the thing or person stereotyped allows the stereotypes and the prejudice to persist.

Stereotyping can also be useful in categorizing information and simplifying our view of the world.

Scapegoating often occurs when a group that is the target of prejudice is easily identified, accessible, unable to retaliate, and has been the scapegoat before.

Prejudice can be combatted by exposing a person to a member of the group against whom he is prejudiced or by having hostile groups cooperate in an experience of shared coping. Experiencing prejudice against oneself may also lessen the tendency to be prejudiced toward others.

Attribution. Attribution theory holds that our perceptions of and responses to another person's behavior are largely determined by the motives we attribute to her or him.

We commonly overestimate the influence of innate traits and minimize situational factors when attributing motives to people. The process of attribution includes examining consensus, consistency, and distinctiveness.

Physical appearance is a powerful influence on person perception. The qualities we attribute to a person can act as a self-fulfilling prophecy, causing a person to act as we expected. The assumptions we make about a person's status can also have a great deal to do with how we treat the person.

Interpersonal Attraction. Attraction can be shaped by familiarity and proximity, by similarity, by favors exchanged, by feeling liked, and by complementary characteristics.

There are major differences between liking and romantic love. Liking is grounded in reality; loving involves fantasies. Liking involves positive feelings; loving, both positive and negative feelings. Liking tends to increase; romantic love tends to fade.

Romantic love is a state of intense absorption in another person, accompanied by feelings of physical arousal. Trust and self-disclosure are crucial to a loving relationship.

GLOSSARY

Attitude An enduring disposition that makes a person ready to respond in a predictable manner to any sort of object; consists of cognitive, emotional, and behavioral aspects.

Attribution The process of inferring people's characteristics from what they do.

Attribution theory Holds that our perceptions of and responses to another person's behavior are largely determined by the motives we attribute to her or him.

Balance theory Proposes that people tend to change their discrepant attitudes to bring them into agreement.

Cognitive consistency The state in which one's beliefs are consistent with one another.

Cognitive dissonance The state of tension that exists when a person holds beliefs, ideas, attitudes, or opinions that are inconsistent with each other.

Inoculation theory Holds that attacks against a person's opinions make the person resistant to appeals to change them.

Person perception The process whereby we size up people and categorize their qualities, characteristics, and inner states.

Prejudice Hostility toward a member or members of a specific group based on generalizations.

Pygmalion effect An increase in ability brought about by positive expectations.

Reactance A response to an attempt to influence a person's opinion in which the person takes an opposing stance.

Reciprocity Feelings of being liked or disliked are returned in kind.

Scapegoating Displacing anger or frustration by blaming an innocent party.

Selective exposure Seeking out information that supports your own beliefs in order to reduce cognitive dissonance.

Selective perception Accepting information that fits one's stereotypes and screening out information that does not.

Self-disclosure The revelation of one's intimate feelings.

Self-fulfilling prophecy An expectation on which a person acts, thereby making it a reality.

Self-perception The way one sees oneself.

Shared coping Working together to meet a common challenge.

Stereotype The view whereby all people in a group are seen as characterized by the same qualities, regardless of their actual differences.

19

SOCIAL INFLUENCE

CONFORMITY AND OBEDIENCE

Factors in conformity ■ Conformity versus obedience ■ Personality and conformity ■ Types of conformity

COMPETITION OR COOPERATION?

ALTRUISM AND APATHY

Ambiguity ■ Diffusion of responsibility ■ The rush factor ■ Increasing altruism ■ Equity: doing what's fair

GROUPS

Leadership ■ Group efficiency ■ Facilitation

ENVIRONMENTAL PSYCHOLOGY

City life ■ Noise ■ Control ■ Crowding ■ Architectural design

THE SOCIAL PSYCHOLOGY OF PSYCHOLOGY

Bias ■ The experimental setting ■ Ethics

COMMON MYTHS

MANY PEOPLE BELIEVE ...	ACTUALLY ...
Social pressure could never force a person to harm another.	Under the right conditions, people can be pressured to do things—such as harm someone else—that they would not do on their own.
Women conform more than men.	Men and women conform to about the same extent.
People would rather cooperate than compete.	In many situations in which they can do either, people choose to compete rather than cooperate—for example, for shared resources.
A person working alone is always more effective than a group.	There are many tasks for which a group is more effective than an individual.
Being in a hurry wouldn't keep people from stopping to help someone who needed aid.	Being in a rush can keep people from stopping to help, even when the need is obvious.

If I am not for myself, who will be for
me? If I am not for others, what am I?
And if not now, when?

HILLEL

We all belong to many different kinds of groups, each of which exerts pressures on us to behave in certain ways. Human behavior is shaped to a great extent by the nature of groups (Homans, 1950). We act differently with friends at a bar, at church, in a crowd at a football game, and with our parents. Such social influences constantly affect our behavior, and a full understanding of the person is impossible without considering these social factors.

CONFORMITY AND OBEDIENCE

One powerful set of social forces upon the individual are the influences toward conformity. *Conformity* means bringing one's behavior and attitudes into agreement with those of a group as a result of social pressures. Although the word itself often raises negative thoughts in people's minds, conformity serves many useful purposes. It maintains law and order in society; our laws reflect what people consider to be socially acceptable, and group pressures to follow those norms keep peo-

ple in conformity with them even when law enforcement itself might not. Drivers keep to one side of the road, people wait in line at movie theaters. Conformity enforces the norms that make society work.

Conformity is useful in other ways. It can, for example, get you through an awkward or unfamiliar situation in which you are not sure of what to do. If you've never eaten in a fancy restaurant before, for example, you might watch the people at the next table out of the corner of your eye to see what they do. But conformity to group norms can also lead people to break rules, as when members of a teenage gang or organized crime cooperate to break the law. And conformity can also lead a person to violate his or her own sense of right and wrong.

Imagine that in response to the advertisement on the following page you come to a psychology laboratory to participate in a study of memory and learning. There you are introduced to another volunteer, a mild-mannered, likable man in his midforties. The experimenter, who is

---

Public Announcement

WE WILL PAY YOU $4.00 FOR ONE HOUR OF YOUR TIME

Persons Needed for a Study of Memory

*We will pay five hundred New Haven men to help us complete a scientific study of memory and learning. The study is being done at Yale University.

*Each person who participates will be paid $4.00 (plus 50c carfare) for approximately 1 hour's time. We need you for only one hour: there are no further obligations. You may choose the time you would like to come (evenings, weekdays, or weekends).

**No special training, education, or experience is needed. We want:*

Factory workers	Businessmen	Construction workers
City employees	Clerks	Salespeople
Laborers	Professional people	White-collar workers
Barbers	Telephone workers	Others

All persons must be between the ages of 20 and 50. High school and college students cannot be used.

*If you meet these qualifications, fill out the coupon below and mail it now to Professor Stanley Milgram, Department of Psychology, Yale University, New Haven. You will be notified later of the specific time and place of the study. We reserve the right to decline any application.

*You will be paid $4.00 (plus 50c carfare) as soon as you arrive at the laboratory.

- -

dressed in a gray technician's coat, explains that the two of you will participate in a study of punishment and learning.

You are chosen to be the "teacher," the second volunteer will be the "learner." He is led to an adjacent room where he is seated in a chair with his arms strapped down, and an electrode is attached to his wrist. He is instructed to learn a list of word pairs.

You are seated in the main experimental room before a shock generator that has a line of thirty switches ranging from 15 to 450 volts. The verbal designations for these switches range from SLIGHT SHOCK through VERY STRONG SHOCK to DANGER—SEVERE SHOCK. You are to administer a learning test to the man in the next room. Each time the learner gives a wrong answer on the word pairs, you are to give him an electric shock. The experimenter tells you to start at the lowest shock level (15 volts) and to increase the level each time the learner makes a mistake.

You proceed with the test. At 75 volts, the learner grunts. At 120 volts he complains; at 150 he demands to be released from the experiment. His protests continue as the shocks escalate, growing increasingly vehement and emotional. At 285 volts his response can only be described as "an agonized scream."

With 165 volts left to you, you turn to the experimenter for advice. "You have no other choice," he replies. "You *must* go on" (adapted from Milgram, 1974). ■

This actually happened, in a famous study by Stanley Milgram (1963). Before undertaking the experiment, Milgram asked psychiatrists, middle-class adults, college students, and faculty members what results they would expect. Virtually all predicted the subjects would categorically refuse to obey the experimenter, that people "like themselves" would stop shocking any learner who complained of distress and discomfort.

Yet Milgram found that over 60 percent of the subjects (all of whom were unaware that the "learner" was acting and received no shocks at all [see Figure 19.1]) administered shocks up to the maximum levels (labeled DANGER—SEVERE SHOCK on the apparatus)—even though the learner was groaning and screaming in pain. The experimenter had no means of forcing the "teachers" to participate, except by saying the learner was not in danger and with statements such as "It is absolutely essential that you continue." Some obedient subjects did hesitate and question the investigator about ending the procedure, and many showed obvious strain. But still they obeyed his demands.

The Milgram study is one of the more controversial in social psychology because both its findings and its design involved an elaborate series of hoaxes, in which the experimenters purposely misled their subjects (e.g., that the victim was an unwitting volunteer like themselves, that he was actually in pain). Further, most of us find its results alarming. It makes the rise of Nazism in Germany seem less remote, as it does the mass murder-suicide by 900 cult members at Jonestown, Guyana in 1978.

Since childhood we have been taught that it is morally wrong to hurt another human being against his will, especially if he has done nothing that would even remotely merit physical punishment. Yet in the Milgram study people who presumably accepted this moral standard obediently administered what they thought were painful shocks to innocent people. Each of us, on reading about the study, probably feels that we would not have given the shocks had we been subjects in the

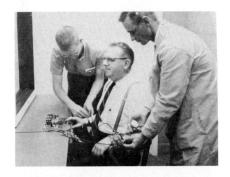

Figure 19.1 Would you shock this man?

The Milgram study of obedience used as the "victim" (actually a confederate) a like-able, mild-mannered, accountant. (From OBEDIENCE TO AUTHORITY by Stanley Milgram © 1974)

Milgram study (Safer, 1980)—yet can we be sure? What occurs in the interplay between people that could make such a thing possible?

Imagine that a small group of people are judging the length of several vertical lines, giving their estimate one by one. On the first trial, everyone agrees; on the second, the group is again unanimous. But on the third trial, a person near the end is a lone dissenter. As he gives his answer he seems amazed to find he is in disagreement with everyone else.

On the next trial and the one after that and the one after that, he remains the lone dissenter. He begins to hesitate, to speak in a low voice, to smile occasionally in embarrassment. He cannot understand why everyone else should disagree on such a simple task.

What he doesn't know is that everyone else is a confederate of the experimenter, and they have all been instructed to respond incorrectly. ■

This happened in a classic study of social pressure by Solomon Asch (1955; 1965). Although the confederates didn't fake every trial—that might arouse suspicion—their frequent unanimous but wrong judgments created a quandary for the dissenter: should he trust his senses or conform to the opinion of his peers?

Asch found that about three out of four persons tested conformed to the rigged group opinion at least once, even though they could see that the group decision was wrong. Some people conformed every time, some only on some trials, and others never conformed. But even those who remained staunchly independent later admitted to having been quite anxious.

Situations such as Asch simulated, where pressures to conform are subtle but pervasive, are quite common. Such subtle pressures lead people

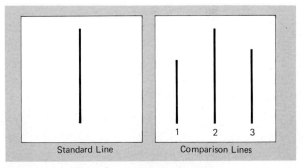

Figure 19.2 Stimuli used in Asch experiments

The subjects in the experimental groups were given the following instructions: This is a task which involves the discrimination of lengths of lines. You see the pair of white cards in front. On the left is a single line; on the right are three lines differing in length; they are numbered 1, 2, and 3 in order. One of the three lines at the right is equal to the standard line at the left—you will decide in each case which is the equal line. You will state your judgment in terms of the corresponding number. There will be twelve such comparisons. As the number of lines is few and the group is small, I shall call upon each of you in turn to announce your judgment, which I shall record here on a prepared form. Please be as accurate as possible.

in the same school, dorm, or club to dress alike, wear their hair in similar fashion, and change styles at about the same time.

The Asch study is similar to Milgram's in that no one threatened to punish a subject if he did not agree, nor did anyone offer a tangible reward for agreeing. But much that we do is done simply to get the approval of others; in these experiments, subjects seemed to conform in order to avoid disapproval from the experimenter (in the Milgram study) or the confederates (in the Asch study).

Factors in conformity

One way to understand conformity is in terms of *social comparison theory,* which holds that people have a need to evaluate themselves and, in the absence of objective measures, do so by comparing themselves to others (Festinger, 1954). People want to know how well they are doing and whether they are acting appropriately or not. If there are no clear guidelines, a person has to guess what response is appropriate. The teachers in Milgram's study had only the experimenter's assur-

ances that they should continue, and so relied on their instructions for guidance on how they should act; the subjects in Asch's study had to weigh the incorrect judgments by the confederates against their own perceptions. In both cases, social comparison may have led people to conform despite their personal reservations.

Among the factors that contribute to conformity is unanimity among group members. When everyone else in the group agrees, the lone dissenter feels more pressure to conform than he would if even one other person dissented as well. When Asch added one other truthful person to the group, subjects answered incorrectly only one-fourth as often as they did when up against a unanimous majority.

Group size can also influence conformity. When Asch varied the size of the groups in his study, he found people had no trouble answering correctly when there was only one other person to contradict their judgment. But with two against one, conformity was greater, and with three against one, greater still.

Yet numbers alone do not explain conformity;

"Well, heck! If all you smart cookies agree, who am I to dissent?"

Drawing by Handelsman; © 1972 *The New Yorker Magazine, Inc.*

many other factors can contribute. For example, the stronger a person's attraction to a group, the more likely he or she is to conform to its norms (Kelley and Volkart, 1952). Guilt, too, increases compliance; when subjects in an experiment were led to believe they had harmed a confederate, they became much more compliant (Carlsmith and Gross, 1969).

Conformity versus obedience

Milgram points out that his study differs from Asch's in one important respect: whereas Asch's subjects conformed to group pressure, Milgram's obeyed the experimenter. This marks the difference between conformity and obedience: when we conform, what we do is determined by people of equal status; when we obey, we feel that a person or group has the authority to dictate our actions. There is also a difference in explicitness. When we conform, the requirement that we do so is often implicit; no one tells us exactly what to do, but we get the message. When we obey, the command is explicit. Milgram notes that a prerequisite for obedience is that the person obeyed has to be perceived as a *legitimate authority*, one who has the right, credentials, and position to make demands. The subjects in his study saw the experimenter in just this way; if they had not, they most likely would not have obeyed to the extent they did. Some engaged in self-justification—as cognitive dissonance theory might predict—blaming their "victim" for being stupid for volunteering in the first place.

One psychological consequence of yielding to an authority is that it allows people to deny responsibility. Milgram notes that in order to reduce tension, some subjects sought reassurance that they were not responsible for giving the shocks. For example, after reaching 375 volts, one "teacher," who was under great strain, had this exchange with the experimenter:

Teacher (swiveling around in his chair): Something's happened to that man in there. You better check in on him, sir. He won't answer or nothing.

Experimenter: Continue. Go on, please.

Teacher: You accept all responsibility?

Experimenter: The responsibility is mine. Correct. Please go on.

Teacher (returns to his list, starts running through words as rapidly as he can read them, works through to 450 volts): That's that. (Milgram, 1974)

Personality and conformity

What is it that makes some people independent even under great pressures to conform—like those who refused to go along with giving a shock in the Milgram study or persisted in giving their own answers in the Asch experiment? In general, particularly in difficult situations, it is the intelligent, self-assured person who most often refuses to conform to a questionable majority judgment. The person in a group who is anxious and unsure of acceptance in the group is more careful to follow the lead of others (Jackson and Saltzstein, 1958).

People who conform tend to share certain traits. In one study, conformers were more often rated by the researchers as less intellectually competent and scored low on a scale of ego strength and higher on a scale of authoritarianism (Crutchfield, 1955). Conformers also have a higher need for affiliation (McGhee and Teevan, 1967), blame themselves more (Costanzo, 1970), and have less self-esteem (Stang, 1972). Conformers describe their parents in uncritical, idealized terms—an attitude in keeping with their greater obedience to authority (Block, 1955). A person's conformity, though, may vary widely from situation to situation; conformity does not seem to be a strong stable trait (McGuire, 1968). Some people may be more conforming than others, but their conformity seems to depend on an interaction between their personality and a given situation. Someone who was very obedient at home might be rebellious at school; a law-abiding citizen might be an agitator for unions at work.

While an old stereotype—and even some older research—held that women are more likely to conform, this is not the case (Sistrunk and McDavid, 1971). When questions are of special interest to women—for example child rearing or equal rights—they conform less than men. But when the questions matter more to men—for example, the Superbowl—then women conform more than men in giving their opinions. In short, women hold stronger and more divergent views on topics of interest to them, while men tend to conform more in giving their views on these topics.

Types of conformity

It is helpful to distinguish between the various possible consequences of pressure to conform (Kelman, 1958; 1961). *Compliance* occurs when a person agrees with the majority simply to get a reward (e.g., social acceptance) or avoid a punishment for nonconformity (e.g., group rejection). This kind of conformity attempts to attain a goal—for example, a hostage signs a statement favoring his captors in order to get better treatment. *Identification* is conforming in order to maintain or affirm a relationship. When a high school student purposely gets poorer grades than she could because her friends think it's "cool," she is doing so to affirm her group identification.

Internalization occurs when a person accepts another's influence because it fits her own attitude. The person conforms not so much because of the social pressure to do so, but rather because she truly feels so inclined. If someone asked you to sign a petition to protect whales, and you actually believed whales should be protected, then

your signing would be due to internalization, not pressures to conform.

COMPETITION OR COOPERATION?

Imagine that your friend Terry is a premed who wants nothing more in the world than to get into medical school. She's taking organic chemistry this term, and knows that her grade is critically important for admissions.

A group of students has formed a study group to prepare for the final exam together. They're eager for her to join, since she got the highest score in the class on the midterm.

After thinking it over, Terry declines the invitation. "Look," she explains to you, "I've got a good chance of doing well on the final, probably better than anyone else in the study group. If I help them and they all do better on the final, then it will raise the class average and lower the value of my own score. I'd rather take my chances on my own." ■

We often have a choice between cooperating and competing. In a simulation of such situations, volunteers were asked to play at truck driving (Deutsch and Krauss, 1960). They were given dif-

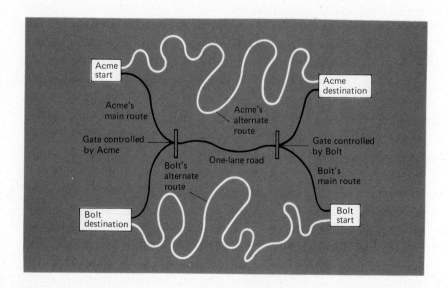

Figure 19.3 The trucking game
In the trucking game, one player is the "Acme" trucking company, the other the "Bolt." Each player can choose one of two paths: a short route, where both players may meet head-on, or a longer one where there will be no conflict.

SOLVING THE COMMONS DILEMMA

■ Does it matter in an energy shortage if you turn your heat up or your air conditioning down a few degrees? Probably not, you may say to yourself. But we all know that if enough people so excuse their excessive use of energy, the available supply will shrink.

Energy is one modern case of the "tragedy of the commons." The "commons" can be any jointly owned resource used by many people, including anything from the air we breathe to the coffee pool in an office. As long as each person uses the common resource in moderation, the system works well. But when too many people use the resources too quickly, a problem develops: the immediate needs of the individual conflict with the long-term needs of the community.

Gas shortages illustrate this dilemma. In a shortage, drivers hoard gasoline, buying as much as possible so that they won't run out. This results in lines at the pumps, with some drivers not having any gas at all—and worsens the shortage.

There are actually two conflicts here: individual versus group needs, and short-term versus long-term benefits. When resources are low, some kind of regulation must be agreed upon and enforced to keep the commons system working. How to do this effectively, though, remains a dilemma.

One problem is the "free rider," someone who uses the commons without restraint to satisfy his own needs, while others limit their consumption to preserve the resource. In a gas shortage, a free rider would buy as much gas as he could as often as he could, while others would keep themselves to a limit in order for there to be enough gas for all.

Edney (1979) staged an experiment to see how problems like free riders might be managed. He set up a "commons" of points in which three people could take as many points as they wanted. A scoreboard showed them how many points were left after each of them had his turn. After everyone had taken two turns, the points left in the pool would double. If the subjects took only a few points, the doubling would be substantial and the pool would grow quickly, resulting in long-term benefits. If the subjects took too many points for themselves, the overall supply would diminish.

More than three out of four trials ended with the pool of points collapsing. Even subjects who were told to take only one or two points at a time ended up exploiting the resources. Communication was the key to a successful commons. The only time the system seemed to work was when the participants were allowed to talk to each other before and during the exercise.

Regulation of resources also helps. In Maine, for example, lobstermen set up group territories in which daily fishing was strictly regulated. Compared to lobstermen using free waters, these territorial groups kept their supply of lobsters higher, had bigger catches, and earned about $6,000 a year more.

Timing offers another means to conserve. For example, oyster beds are a commons off the Atlantic coast. Sailboats take so long to reach the beds for harvesting that the oysters have time to regenerate. Motorboats, however, get there too fast, leaving no time for regeneration. If the oyster harvesters can agree to use sailboats rather than motorboats, or limit the size of catches or number of times they go out, the commons can be preserved.

Whether the commons is the air we breathe, whales, or gasoline, the problem is balancing use with renewal rate—and that is, in fact, a social problem. Whatever solution is found, it must resolve the conflict between the needs of the individual and the needs of the group without imposing costs on future generations. ■

ferent starting and destination points on a game board and told to get to the end of their route as fast as they could. Although each player had a different destination, the fastest route for both overlapped at one point on a one-lane road. If both entered this one-lane stretch at the same time, one would have to wait for the other to pass, just as happens at an old-fashioned one-lane bridge when cars start to cross from both ends at once. There was an alternative route, but it was much longer and meant certain lost time. Given the choice, what would you do?

Both players typically try to use the direct route. But instead of cooperating, they meet head-on and then stubbornly refuse to back up. Most choose to compete even though it is self-defeating. And whether players compete or cooperate, they tend to assume other players feel as they do; this means that someone who feels the urge to compete is likely to justify competition by attributing the same urge to others—often falsely (Messe and Sivacek, 1979).

Not all people choose to compete in situations where they have the choice of cooperating. In a similar game, children from an Israeli communal *kibbutz* were more cooperative than children from cities (Shapira and Marsden, 1969). In Canada, Indian children were more cooperative than non-Indian children (A. G. Miller and Thomas, 1972). Middle-class American children, on the other hand, compete even when cooperation is a more reason-

able strategy. The difference seems to be in socialization. Kibbutz children are taught to depend on each other and cooperate; Indian children in some tribes are trained to cooperate to such a degree that they would not start a race, knowing the winner would be ridiculed for caring so much about winning (Erikson, 1963). Middle-class Americans, on the other hand, teach their children the value of competition and winning, making it less likely they will learn the virtues of cooperation.

The tendency to choose competition rather than cooperation has been called "the tragedy of the commons" (Hardin, 1968). In the early days of this country and throughout Europe, a commons was an open pasture where anyone could bring herds of sheep or cattle to graze. As the population grew, however, the commons became overgrazed, and once-lush pastures turned barren. The tragedy is that the commons could have been kept lush if each herder had voluntarily restricted the size of the herd brought to graze. But since it immediately benefited each to bring as many cattle or sheep as possible to graze, and since the penalty for overgrazing lay years in the future, none chose to restrict grazing. In such situations, short-term gains are far more powerful as rewards than long-term costs are as deterrents. People think it doesn't pay to cooperate, and so they compete.

One way to resolve the "tragedy of the commons" is through mutually accepted coercion—making it more difficult or costly to exploit the

commons (Hardin, 1968). This is the strategy, for example, adopted by those who advocate solving a gas shortage by rationing gas or increasing its cost to the consumer. Improving communication may also increase cooperation (Dawes, McTavish, and Shaklee, 1977). For one, communication increases familiarity and concern. It also allows people to share information that might lead them to cooperate. Finally, it lets each person understand that the intentions of everyone else are to be trusted.

ALTRUISM AND APATHY

Imagine that you're visiting a friend in New York City. It's a hot, muggy August afternoon, and somehow you've managed to be on the subway at the peak of rush hour. People are packed together like sardines, yet no one pays any attention to anyone else.

As you squeeze out of the subway at your station, you notice a portly man in a sweat-soaked white shirt gasping for breath. Suddenly he falls to the ground.

People rush on to their train, ignoring him. Nobody seems to notice him. You stand there frozen in your tracks, not knowing what to do. Agonizing moments pass.

Just then several people run over to the man and begin to help him. As you stand watching, still stunned, the question hits you: why didn't I help? ■

People who live in large cities are often thought of as aloof and unwilling to get involved. Any city-dweller knows of cases similar to the scene in the subway station. The drunk who falls into the gutter, the old woman whose purse is stolen by muggers—no passerby helps either victim. Several years ago, newspapers carried the story of a young woman named Kitty Genovese, who was attacked and killed on a New York street in the early hours of the morning. Her screams and cries for help awakened at least thirty-eight neighbors, who watched in horror out their windows for over a half-hour, until her death. Not one came to her aid or even called the police. In Cincinnati in 1979, eleven people were crushed to death by a crowd

scrambling for seats at a rock concert. A student who tried to save three victims with mouth-to-mouth resuscitation failed; he said "people just didn't seem to care" as they rushed by the accident scene on the way to their seats.

What determines when people will help out and when they will not?

When people help someone in danger, they sometimes put themselves at risk while doing so (Schwartz, 1977). Rushing into a burning building, struggling with a drowning person, and fighting off attackers are all risky situations. Often helping out is less dramatic: donating to a charity, volunteering your time for a good cause, lending a hand to push a car stuck in snow. *Altruism* is the term for an act performed to help someone else when there is no expectation of reward. If you have an ulterior motive—say, the hope of getting paid or receiving a favor in return—your act is not altruistic. It is, though, *prosocial*, a broader category that includes any acts that are meant to help others. The motives behind prosocial acts, though, can include the expectation of reward, while altruistic ones do not. *Apathy*, on the other hand, refers to a bystander's failure to intervene on behalf of someone needing help. A good deal of research has attempted to sort out the factors that determine when people will be altruistic, when apathetic.

Ambiguity

Can you always be sure when and how to help in an emergency? Often you cannot. Latané and Darley point out that a person's decision is based on (1) noticing that something is happening; (2) interpreting the event as an emergency; (3) taking responsibility for helping; (4) deciding what help is appropriate; and (5) deciding how to help. Any or all of these points of decision can be unclear, and so keep someone from helping.

For example, in one study, waiting subjects heard the sounds of a woman in the next room falling off a chair and then screaming for about two minutes. When the subjects waited alone, 70 percent came to help her. Of those who waited in pairs, however, only 40 percent helped; when one of the two was a passive confederate who ignored the screams, only 7 percent helped. The experi-

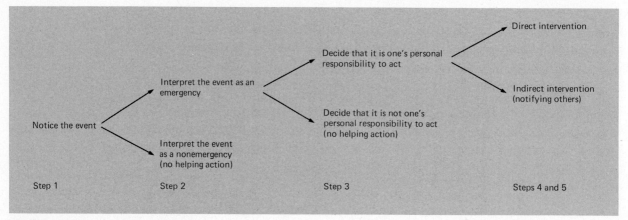

Figure 19.4 The decision to help
Before bystanders can decide to intervene, they must (1) notice what is happening; (2) interpret it as an emergency; (3) decide that action is up to them; (4) and (5) figure out what
to do and how to do it.

menters conjectured that the ambiguity of the situation made the subjects uncertain about whether
or not there was a real emergency, and so they
looked to the other person for cues to guide them
(Latané and Rodin, 1969). If that person seemed
unsure or indifferent, then both might be less likely to help. In a less ambiguous situation, when the
victim actually cried for help, many more people
helped. Thus being in a group seems to lead to bystander apathy when the need for help is ambiguous (Clark and Word, 1974).

Deciding whether a situation is a real emergency—where the threat of harm increases with
time—is another source of ambiguity (Shotland
and Huston, 1979). If someone is bleeding profuse-
ly after a car accident, the emergency is clear. But
if a man and woman are arguing on a street, a
common interpretation is that it is a lover's quar-
rel and an outsider has no business interfering
(Shotland and Straw, 1976). If the situation is ambiguous, offering help when none is called for
raises the risk of embarrassing yourself, a factor
heightened by the presence of others.

Diffusion of responsibility

Ambiguity alone doesn't explain people's failure
to help someone in distress. Kitty Genovese called
for help. Her neighbors were all aware that others
were watching, but no one knew if anyone had

called the police or done anything else to help. No
one had.

To discover why no one acted, researchers created an experimental simulation of the situation
(Darley and Latané, 1968). Subjects were put by
themselves in cubicles where each could hear and
take part in a discussion of personal problems
with one, two, or five others. This setup, each one
was told, was designed to protect everyone's anonymity in discussing personal topics. Actually
what they heard were tapes.

When the future victim first spoke, he revealed,
with much hesitancy, that he was prone to seizures. The other voices then took their turns, and
the naive subject spoke last. When it was again
the victim's turn to speak, he began calmly but
grew incoherent, saying, "I ... er ... I think I
need ... er ... er ... er ... give me a little help
here ... I'm gonna die ... er ... er ... seizure
(chokes, then quiet)." The investigators found that
all the subjects in the two-person groups (the naive subject and the voice of the supposed victim)
eventually sought help, but only 62 percent of the
subjects in the six-person group (the subject, the
victim, and four other supposed subjects) ever
took action.

Subjects who did not report the emergency
were indeed concerned about the victim. They later asked, "Is he being taken care of?" or "He's all
right, isn't he?" But at the time of the emergency
they simply assumed that even if they did not re-

What are the factors that sometimes lead bystanders to help a person in need, while at other times they are indifferent? (Arthur Tress)

spond immediately, someone else would. The presence or absence of other people can determine whether someone will help (Latané and Darley, 1976); a review of several studies where people could have helped out in a seeming emergency showed that bystanders are more likely to help when they are alone.

To minimize the likelihood of seeming foolish, people often wait to see how others will react. The problem with this, of course, is that everyone may be waiting in this way. If there is no clear evidence of an emergency, then the group's nonchalance will tend to keep anyone from intervening. Having others present allows *diffusion of responsibility*, where each person assumes that someone else will help, and so feels less responsible. In a large city, when many people are present at an emergency, these factors may explain why people fail to help out.

Given the mix of decisions and ambiguities inherent in an emergency, a bystander seems most likely to help when the emergency is clear, the bystander feels the ability and responsibility to act, the effectiveness of helping is clear, and the potential risks to the helper do not outweigh the benefits of helping (Enzle and Harvey, 1979; Schwartz, 1977).

Imagine that you're running to catch a bus, which is just about to pull away. In your haste, you pass an elderly woman who has slipped and is trying to stand up.

Just as you reach the bus door, it slams shut and the bus pulls away. You stand there fuming for a moment, then calm down. You see the woman is trying to collect groceries that fell out of a bag. You go over and help her.

As you pick up the last of a dozen scattered oranges, she gives you a big smile and says, "Thank you, you're very kind."

You feel warm inside. ■

The rush factor

There are probably situations when even the most altruistic among us might not help out—such as rushing to catch a bus before it pulls away. Take, for example, a study done with students at Princeton Theological Seminary (Darley and Batson, 1973; Batson, *et al.*, 1978). Forty seminary students volunteered to give a speech; some were to speak on jobs that seminary students might be suitable for, others on the parable of the Good Samaritan, a Bible story about a man who helped a traveler in trouble. The students were sent alone at fifteen-minute intervals to another building to give their talk. One third were told they had plenty of time to get there, one third they had just enough time, and one third that they were late.

On the way over, the students passed a man groaning, slumped over in a doorway. Sixty percent of the seminary students did *not* stop to help the man, including those on their way to talk about the Good Samaritan. The factor that made a difference was being in a rush: 63 percent of those in no hurry stopped, 45 percent of those just on time, and only 10 percent of those who were late. In a later repeat of the study, when the stu-

ANONYMOUS

■ There is something uninhibiting in being anonymous: a face in a crowd, author of an unsigned letter, an unidentified caller on the phone. People who are anonymous seem to do things they would hesitate to do if their identity were known. The hooded Ku Klux Klan has used this principle to encourage its members to commit acts of aggression and hatred.

The relationship between anonymity and aggression has been well established in research. For example, in a laboratory study, when women were made to feel anonymous by wearing lab coats and hoods, they delivered shocks lasting twice as long as those administered by a group of women whose identity was emphasized by wearing name tags (Zimbardo, 1969).

Anonymity not only increases aggression; it can also increase other antisocial behavior. For example, children trick-or-treating on Halloween were given the chance to steal candy and money. At different homes in Seattle, a table was set up inside the door with a bowl full of small candy bars and one full of pennies and nickels. A grownup would answer the door, tell the trick-or-treaters to take one candy bar, and then go somewhere else in the house. Some children were asked their names, others were not. The anonymous children were more likely to steal candy bars or money than were those who had identified themselves (Fraser, 1974). Anonymity encouraged stealing. Conversely, people would be expected to be more prosocial when their identity was known. One reason small towns may have lower crime rates than large cities is that anonymity is easier in a city.

But anonymity may not necessarily make people

---

dents were heading to a less demanding task, 70 percent of those who were late stopped to help. The less demanding task meant they had less conflict, and so they stopped to help more readily (Batson, *et al.*, 1978).

Increasing altruism

Of all the background factors that affect personality, the only one that predicts who would help in a crisis is the size of the community in which the bystander was raised (Latané and Darley, 1970). Small towners are more likely to help, even in large cities. However, people can be made to be more likely to help by giving them the sense that they are especially responsible for what is happening. When subjects were asked to watch a suitcase or radio while the owner was away, they were much more likely to try to stop a theft of it than were people not asked to look after it (Moriarty, 1975).

Feeling good also seems to increase the likelihood of helping someone in need (Isen, 1970). For example, in one study shoppers who used a phone booth either found a dime in it or did not. After leaving the booth they saw a woman drop a folder of papers. Of twenty-five men and women who had not found a dime, only one helped the woman; of sixteen who did find a dime, all but two helped the woman (Isen and Levin, 1972). Being in a positive mood, then, makes people more prosocial. Conversely, being in a bad mood makes people less likely to help—at least in some situations (Isen, Horn, and Rosenhand, 1973).

This is most true with children; as adults we have learned that one way to make ourselves feel better is by helping someone else (Cialdini and Kenrick, 1976). A grumpy child, though, is in no mood to help someone else. Children seem to learn

more antisocial; under the right conditions, it may make them more prosocial. When subjects were left together in a darkened room, their behavior became more intimate and friendly (Gergen, Gergen, and Baron, 1973). The difference seems to be in the situational cues: when situational clues elicit aggression, anonymity seems to increase the probability of antisocial acts; when they elicit intimacy, then anonymity increases the probability of prosocial acts.

This relationship between anonymity and situational cues was shown clearly in a study by Johnson and Downing (1979). They had college women administer shocks to a young man who was supposed to be engaged in a learning task. He actually was a confederate of the experimenters; he was intentionally unlikable and a poor learner. The women could adjust the severity of the shocks after each trial.

The women were given one of two uniforms to wear during the study: a nurse's outfit or a Ku Klux Klan-type robe. Some of the women in both kinds of outfits believed that other subjects had pictures of them with their names written in while the others thought their identity was unknown to other subjects.

The results: women in the KKK robes—an antisocial cue—increased the shocks given, while those in nurses' uniforms—a prosocial cue—were more likely to decrease shock levels. In addition, the women who believed themselves anonymous also gave stronger shocks, while those who thought their identities were known gave less strong shocks. In short, anonymity in and of itself will increase antisocial behavior—but antisocial cues will, too. And the two together make for even more antisocial action. ■

to be altruistic as they grow and mature (Kenrick, Baumann, and Cialdini, 1979). Preschoolers are likely to regard the idea of sharing, for example, as a punishment; as any parent knows, toddlers have to be taught to share. But beginning in the primary grades, children learn that sharing and helping out in other ways brings social rewards such as approval. Finally, people can be taught to increase their empathy; the increased understanding of others' plights makes people more altruistic. Charitable, helpful acts can become secondary reinforcers; at this stage helping someone else becomes a way to cheer yourself up (Clark, 1980).

Equity: doing what's fair

People's sense of justice appears to determine the extent to which they will help another person. *Equity* is the term for the idea that every person should get what he or she deserves (Adams, 1965; Homans, 1961). If people make an equal effort toward a common goal, they should share equally in the rewards; if one person gets more than his or her share, then there is inequity. People tend to try to establish equity. This concept underlies social welfare programs and charities in general, and reflects the norm of social responsibility.

Equity distributes shares according to effort; *parity*, in contrast, is sharing equally regardless of individual efforts. When children divide candy equally, they are acting on parity. If, though, they divided a reward for a team effort on the basis of how much each member had contributed to the victory, that would be equity. Kindergarteners who teamed up to win a reward divided it up equally; slightly older children used equity to split their reward, giving more to kids who had done more to win it (Lerner, 1974).

One motive for equity is not altruism, but self-concern: people want to be sure that they themselves will be treated justly. Equity seems to apply most often when the resources being distributed are limited: when there is more than enough for everyone, it is irrelevant (Romer, 1979).

GROUPS

Imagine that you're visiting your cousin, who's taking care of his five children while his wife is away for a week.

"I think I'm going nuts," he tells you. "All I've done for the last four days is make meals, wash dishes, run errands, drive car pools, and stop fights between the kids. I haven't read a paper since she left, and I feel like I've deserted the office."

You're about to give him some sympathetic response, when he adds, "But you know, I don't really mind. I feel more a part of what's happening at home, and I haven't talked to the kids this much in years." ■

Everyone belongs to groups of many kinds, from small groups like families, friends, or a study group to larger groups like a student body, political party, or nation. When people are together in a group, they naturally differentiate themselves within it. Members adopt different roles, divide tasks, and develop often unspoken rules or patterns for interaction. Your cousin, for example, found himself taking on the tasks and roles normally relegated to his wife within the family group. As a group forms, it evolves a unique pattern of *group dynamics*, the processes that rule how people in the group will make decisions, align themselves within it, and conduct activities.

The common denominators of groups are that all in them see themselves as members, depend on one another to attain the group's goals, and generally share goals, interests, or beliefs. There are many kinds of groups. *Primary groups* involve face-to-face contact, like a family or team; *secondary groups* involve little or no personal interaction among members, like subscribers to a

magazine or members of an auto club. Some are informal, with little defined structure, like a group of teenagers that hangs out on a street corner; others are formal, with organized rules and a structure, like the ROTC.

Leadership

You can often tell who the leader of a group is just by listening while members discuss something: the leader is the one who talks the most. No matter who is the official leader of a group (e.g., the president of the club or the chair of a meeting), people will perceive the person in the group who talks the most as having leadership abilities (Sorrentino and Boutillier, 1975). Oddly enough, a person who talks a lot in a group can be seen as a leader even if that person is disliked.

Who will be seen as leader by people in a group can be changed simply by changing the amount of time people within the group spend talking. In one study, college students were put in four-member discussion groups. During the first session, as often happens, one person did most of the talking; that person became the acknowledged leader. The people who spoke least in the groups were rated low on leadership qualities. In a second meeting, though, the amount each person talked was regulated by signals. The talkative student was kept more quiet by flashing a red light when he spoke, while the quiet student was always given a green signal to keep talking. As the quiet student became more talkative, his leadership ratings increased (Bavelas, *et al.*, 1965).

But talk alone does not keep one a leader: *what* is said matters, too. Another attribute of perceived leaders is their ability to state feelings and goals the group shares, but which have not been voiced before (Bales, 1970). Personality, too, can mark a person as a leader. For example, people of high status, intelligence, and self-confidence are more likely to become group leaders.

There are no "born leaders": different situations require different leaders. The *contingency theory* of leadership holds that the situation determines what kind of leader will be best at a given juncture (Fiedler, 1969). For example, if a group is trying to raise money, an experienced fund raiser

GROUPTHINK

■ Groups do not always make the best decisions; people in groups can get carried away by the atmosphere of a shared enthusiasm and become oblivious to the stark facts. Using the decision by John F. Kennedy and his advisers to invade Cuba's Bay of Pigs in 1961, Irving Janis (1972) analyzed how the group process can go wrong. He labelled the process "groupthink," a type of thinking whereby people in close-knit groups become so preoccupied with maintaining agreement among themselves that they impair their ability to think critically. They no longer weigh pros and cons, seek information openly, consider alternatives, or raise moral issues. Instead they try to maintain consensus, no matter what. Their perceptions of issues become simplistic, ignoring complexity and nuance (Tetlock, 1979).

Janis names several characteristics of groupthink:

☐ Invulnerability, the illusion that the group cannot fail.

☐ Rationalization, collective justification of the group's actions that allows it to discount any opposing views or evidence.

☐ Moral superiority, the belief that the group's motives are beyond reproach, so that it can ignore the moral consequences of its acts.

☐ Stereotypes, fixed views of the opposition as weak or stupid, with the inability to evaluate "the bad guys" fairly.

☐ Pressure to conform, so that any dissension or questioning is discouraged.

☐ Self-censorship, each person carefully expressing only those thoughts that support the group's views, and

☐ "Mindguards," people in the group who take on the role of suppressing information that does not fit the group view.

An illusion of unanimity arises from all the processes just named: dissent is stifled and no objections are voiced, so the impression prevails that everyone agrees. Among the conditions that encourage groupthink are a highly close-knit group, insulated from more balanced sources of information, with a leader who endorses their policy.

The decisions made through groupthink are usually disastrous, mainly because they are based on biased and distorted information. Janis proposes several ways groupthink can be avoided. All of them aim to help members remain independent critics rather than enthusiastic endorsers. The leader, for example, can encourage the airing of doubts and criticism. Outside evaluations of group efforts should be routinely encouraged, thus preventing insulation; the views of outside experts should be sought. One member should periodically play the role of devil's advocate, criticizing the group's decision. While these are only untested suggestions, after the Bay of Pigs fiasco President John F. Kennedy did use several of these techniques with his own advisers. The apparent result: the same men who planned the Bay of Pigs in 1961 were far more effective in handling the Cuban missile crisis of 1962. ■

---

would be a natural task leader; if the group is trying to draw new members, a socially skilled person would be the better leader. These varying roles demand different leadership skills; two different people might fill them better than could a single person trying to serve both functions (Bales, 1958).

Imagine that you're sitting in your American history class when the professor announces there's a midterm next week. She's willing to let the class decide whether to have an essay or an objective exam.

The class erupts in a noisy discussion, everyone taking sides. Some people can't remember dates, and clamor for an essay. Others hate essays; they push for an objective test. One student suggests an oral exam.

Forty minutes later the class is over, with no decision. The professor says she'll wait until next Monday, and let the class vote then. You walk out wishing she had just made up her own mind—now you don't know whether to memorize dates or study for an essay.

Group efficiency

In many situations, a group effort is less efficient than a person working alone, although this is not always the case: if a task requires several different kinds of expertise, there is greater likelihood that pooling the skills found among members of a group will provide what is needed (Davis, 1969).

But as you saw with your class, group members can also distract or oppose one another so that no one does his or her best. For example, in tasks requiring both careful coordination and organization, a person working alone is likely to do better than a group (Kelley and Thibaut, 1969). How productive a group is on a task depends on several factors: (1) the nature of the task—groups tend to be more effective on simple or repetitive tasks than a person working alone; (2) cohesiveness—a group that works together in a cohesive way is more efficient than one that is splintered into factions; (3) the presence or absence of an information network—groups that communicate through a centralized control center are most efficient in completing tasks; (4) size—although large groups can be more productive in many situations, they also have more possibilities for interpersonal friction; (5) composition—total group efficiency depends on how productive each person in it is; (6) members' acceptance of group goals—people in a group will work toward group goals more vigorously if they coincide with their personal goals (Middlebrook, 1979).

Facilitation

One of the effects a group can have on an individual is *social facilitation*, where a person performs better in the presence of others than when alone. As long ago as 1920, Floyd Allport showed that people tested in small groups on tasks ranging from crossing out vowels in a newspaper column to writing a refutation of an argument did better than those tested alone. Later tests have shown the same to be true (e.g., Zajonc and Sales, 1966), although in some cases the presence of a group can have quite the opposite effect, making a person do more poorly.

One explanation of the differing effects groups can have on a person's performance suggests that other people increase a person's level of arousal (Zajonc, 1965). If the person would have tended to answer correctly regardless of the group presence, then increased arousal will enhance his or her performance; if the person would have tended to answer incorrectly, the effect of increased arousal will be to impair performance. In general, groups tend to help when the task is simple, but interfere with complex tasks.

ENVIRONMENTAL PSYCHOLOGY

Imagine that you're driving on one of the highways outside New York City when you get a flat. You pull to the side and start to change your tire.

As you're removing the tire, another car stops just behind yours. A man gets out, lifts the hood of your car, and nonchalantly starts to remove your battery.

"Hey, what do you think you're doing?" you yell.

"Take it easy," he says, "you can have the tires. All I want is the battery." ■

City life

This actually happened, according to Philip Zimbardo (1972). Such acts of vandalism have become a notorious part of life in big cities. Almost daily, schools, churches, buses, and subways are spray-painted, burned, or otherwise defaced. People in cities seem to ignore others whom they would notice or help in small towns.

One explanation of the problems unique to city life is sensory overload, a person's inability to process all the information coming from the environment (Milgram, 1970). Cities are immensely stimulating: people rush by and signs, lights, and ads demand attention; street noises assail the senses. Consider the sheer density of people in a city: one estimate says a Manhattan executive can encounter 220,000 people within ten minutes of her office, while in suburban Nassau County the figure is only 10,000. City life is a continuous series of encounters. One way to handle the sensory overload of a city street is to ignore most of it. People use selective attention in cities, noticing only what they consider of high priority and ignoring the rest.

Another way to lessen overloads is through more selective norms: in a small town, people typically greet each other if they pass on the street; in large cities, people greet only those they happen to know. City dwellers, then, develop a norm of noninvolvement, where the rule of courtesy is not to intrude, rather than to acknowledge another person.

There is a positive side to city life, too. The intensity of stimuli and density of people make it a much more exciting environment than a small town. There are many more choices, sights, people, events. Perhaps because of the ways city dwellers have found to adapt to sensory overload, there does not seem to be any great psychological cost to city life. For example, contrary to popular belief, people in cities do not have higher rates of mental disturbance than those who live in small towns or the country (Srole, 1972). Rates of psychosis and neurosis are about the same in the city and elsewhere; even though there may be more stress in the cities, people there seem able to handle it. In a survey of happiness, people who lived in cities were found to be just as happy as those in small towns, the suburbs, and the country (Shaver and Freedman, 1976).

Noise

Cities are extremely noisy, and while noise can be a great bother, it is not as serious a problem in cities as one might think. The main reason is that people adapt to noise relatively quickly, and so its

The intense, aggravating noises of the urban environment—such as this noisy subway train—are a major source of stress in cities. Noise can be a form of pollution. (© Jim Anderson 1980/Woodfin Camp & Assoc.)

disruptive effects do not last long (Broadbent, 1971; Glass and Singer, 1972). There are some exceptions to this: when a person is engaged in a task that demands careful monitoring, loud noises are extremely disruptive (Finkelman and Glass, 1970). When you're studying for a final, for example, a neighbor playing loud music can be very annoying. Because cities have many more sources of noise and noise levels are louder in general, such disruption of tasks that demand concentration is more likely to occur (Cohen, Evans, Krantz, and Stokols, 1980).

The noise of a city may lead people to be more aggressive. Loud noises are physiologically arousing. When a person already aroused by noise gets angry, he may feel even *more* angry than usual to the degree that he misattributes the noise-induced arousal to his rising anger (Geen, 1978). For example, if someone is stopped for a traffic light next to a loud construction site, he may be aroused by the noise. Should someone bump his car from behind, the anger he feels would be compounded by the arousal he already felt from the noise.

Imagine that you're studying for a final, and the noise of your neighbor's stereo keeps distracting you. You try to ignore it, but it's driving you nuts.

You thump on the wall to get her to turn down the volume. Nothing happens.

You start pounding on the wall. You hear a shout from her side, but no change in the volume. You keep pounding.

Finally she turns down the stereo and shouts through the wall, "What do you want? I can't hear you with the stereo on!" ■

Control

Whatever the nature of the task one is involved in, the less control one has over noise, the more irritating it is (Glass and Singer, 1972; Geen, 1978). If you're studying and your neighbor's stereo is too loud, it is even more bothersome if she ignores your pleas to lower the volume. A sense of being able to control your environment seems important

to your ability to adapt to it. In one study, for example, children who lived in a densely populated low-income housing project didn't attempt to exert control over as simple a task as choosing candy, but rather let the experimenter do it for them, while children from less densely populated residences were more likely to choose their own. The high-density children also did less well on learning a new task after having been discouraged by tackling an unsolvable problem. In short, the children from high-density homes seemed to have learned an attitude of helplessness, and so gave up more easily when confronted with a challenge (Rodin, 1976).

Crowding

The psychological state of discomfort associated with wanting more space than is available is *crowding*. *Density* is a physical measure of the amount of space available to each organism in an environment. Although high density is often called "crowding," the two are not the same. The subjective nature of crowding is important: one person's impression of sufficient space may seem crowded to another. Comfort may also depend on the situation (Morasch, Groner, and Keating, 1979). Six good friends stuffed into a compact car may feel less "crowded" than would six strangers in the same car on the same ride. Cultures vary greatly in this way—an Arab may feel quite comfortable talking to a person with less than a foot separating their faces, while an American would feel encroached upon at that distance (Hall, 1966).

In a classic study of the effects of crowding, rats were kept in a caged area, given all the food and water they needed, and allowed to multiply (Calhoun, 1962). The rat population grew quickly, then dropped sharply. During the period of peak density, the rats fought often, invaded each other's nests, built poor nests, and did not care well for their young—all unusual behaviors under less crowded conditions. The drop in population was largely due to infant mortality: baby rats failed to survive to adulthood. They could not nurse well, were trampled underfoot, and were sometimes even eaten. (See Figure 19.5.)

Crowding broke down the rats' usual social hab-

When people sit down in public places they typically position themselves so as to maximize their personal space—or not to intrude on someone else's. (© Jan Lukas 1976/Photo Researchers, Inc.)

Figure 19.5 The tragedy of Universe 25
In 1968, Dr. John B. Calhoun ran an experiment known as Universe 25 to test the effects of over-crowding on a population of mice. Although unlimited supplies of food were available to the mice, five years after the project began, all the mice were dead, seemingly as a direct result of overpopulation. The relevance of Calhoun's experiment to the problems of human overpopulation is not clear, given our capacity to adapt to changes and stress in our environment. (Courtesy of the National Institute for Mental Health)

its—but would the same thing happen to humans? In general, crowding among humans seems to enhance some problems, but it does not destroy the social fabric. Humans seem highly adaptable to such situations (Dubos, 1970). There is, for example, a slight rise in crime rates associated with density in cities (Freedman, Heshka, and Levy, 1973). But a survey in Hong Kong of some of the most densely populated neighborhoods in the world found no increase in pathology or crime with crowding (Mitchell, 1971).

Crowding is aversive when it interferes with a person's attempts to achieve a goal (McCallum, *et al.*, 1979). If, for example, you're rushing to get to a store before it closes, but a dense lunch-hour crowd on the sidewalk makes you late, the crowd is aversive. If, however, you're simply strolling along enjoying watching people, the crowd is a pleasure. Indeed, the simple expectation of a crowd in a room where subjects were concentrating on a puzzle was enough to hamper performance, even though the crowd never materialized.

In short, density in and of itself is not as important as how a person perceives it.

Architectural design

One of the distinctive features of a cityscape is its forest of high-rise buildings. Our physical surroundings can influence our state of mind. High-rise apartment houses, for example, have come under attack as harmful to the development of normal friendships and a sense of community. Could the psychological atmosphere of the city be due in part to the effects of its arrangements of physical space? Perhaps. Many people who live in high rises seem to suffer no ill effects (Michaelson, 1977), but in some circumstances, high-rise dwellers fare more poorly than those in lower buildings. For example, there were marked differences found between residents of high and low buildings in a housing project in the Bronx (Swae-

Figure 19.6 The risks of living in high rises
As buildings in public housing get higher, so do the number of felonies committed in them. Felonies are reported per thousand families, based on reported crimes. *(The New York Times*, Oct. 26, 1972)

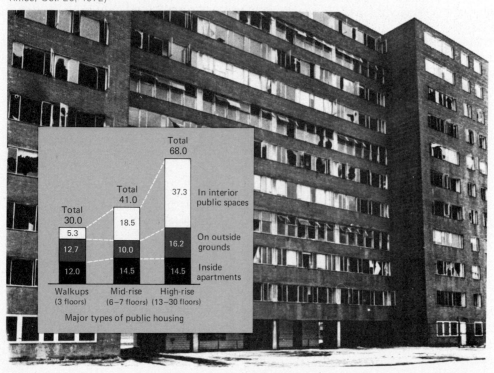

gert, 1978). High-rise dwellers had fewer friendships with fellow residents, even on the same floor. They felt that any area outside their own apartment was not in their control and was unsafe—even the hallway. They may have been right: in another study, residents of low and high apartments were asked if they would help if someone were attacked in their own building. Low risers almost always said they would, while high risers said they would not.

Height isn't the only factor in how buildings affect the people who live in them. "Defensible space," or the area that people can keep watch on, makes people feel safer (Newman, 1973). Poorly lit corridors, halls with turns, or stairways can be places of danger; crimes are more common in such areas because people don't have the protection of their neighbors' watchful eyes. If buildings are low, however, and occupants feel the area near their own apartment is part of their territory, then strangers within that zone are easily noticed and can be challenged. The lesson for architects and urban planners is clear: less massive apartment houses that are designed to give people a sense of their own territory result in happier tenants.

The same kind of question has been raised for college dorms to decide whether it is better to have the traditional dorm design of rooms with doors on a long corridor and shared bathrooms and social areas or the newer type, where suites of bedrooms surround a common living room and private bathroom. One study found that the students in suites were friendlier and more sociable (Baum and Valins, 1977)—although the students who chose to live in suites may have been that way to begin with.

THE SOCIAL PSYCHOLOGY OF PSYCHOLOGY

Imagine that you've volunteered to be a subject in a study of learning. The experimenter seems a bit rude to you, but you don't make much of it—she probably had a bad day.

As you leave the psychology lab and wait for an elevator, a woman approaches you with a small can marked "Red Cross Donations" and asks if you'd care to donate.

It seems fishy—no one ever comes up to this floor of the psychology building to get donations. Then it hits you: she must be connected with the experiment you just finished.

"Are you part of that study down the hall?" you ask.

You can tell by her embarrassed look that you're right. ∎

Have you ever been a subject in a psychology experiment? Probably as many as three-fourths of all the psychological studies ever done with human subjects have used college students. Among the issues that concern psychologists about psychological research is whether a science based in large part on studies of college students accurately reflects human nature.

Apart from these questions of the validity of psychological research, there are pressing ethical concerns. Is an experimenter abusing the rights of subjects when he or she manipulates their behavior by using deceptive instructions for experimental purposes? And how can we be sure the psychologist will be an unbiased observer?

Bias

One of the distortions that can confound the results of an experiment is *subject bias,* where subjects respond the way they suspect the experimenter desires. Subjects—especially college students—may volunteer for a study in order to please the experimenter or even to get a higher grade in a course. During the experiment itself, they may try to guess the hypothesis and respond in a way they think will support it.

Subject bias presents a serious problem to the experimenter. Subjects naturally acquiesce to the demands of the experimenter, as was seen dramatically when they gave electric shocks in Milgram's study. But even mothers who were being observed at home by an experimenter repeatedly asked the observer for instructions or even permission to handle their own baby (Beckwith and Cohen, 1974); they did so even after being told that

the purpose of the study was to see how they acted naturally in their own homes. A person taking part in an experiment can be expected to play the role of a "good subject," which means trying to help validate the experimental hypothesis (Orne, 1962). This is one of the main rationales for using deception; it prevents subjects from "helping out" the experimenter by trying to validate his or her hypothesis.

Experimenter bias is a distortion of results due to the expectations and desires of the researcher, whether conscious or unintentional. In general, the experimenter's views, personality, motives, and aims can significantly affect the results obtained from subjects.

For example, when observers asked to record the movements of worms were told to expect a high rate of turns, they reported twice as many turns and three times as many other movements as did observers who were told the worms would not move much (Cordaro and Ibsen, 1963). The ac-

tual amount of movement to be seen by both kinds of observers was, presumably, the same; the observers' expectations accounted for the different results. The distortion in findings due to such unintentional experimenter influence is referred to as the *Rosenthal effect*, after Robert Rosenthal (1966), the psychologist who pointed it out.

The experimental setting

Psychological research often takes place in special settings, such as laboratories at universities. It may be that people do not act the same outside such settings as they do within them, and so experimental results arrived at there may not reflect the "real world." Some researchers question the "ecological validity" of laboratories and other contrived conditions—the degree they represent real settings—arguing that the artificial situation in which research takes place may not produce results that are accurate (Orne, 1970).

An alternative has been to abandon psychology labs for natural settings. One advantage of *field research*, experimental studies with people in natural settings, is that it minimizes the influence of relatively unreal laboratory situations. For example, a natural setting minimizes subjects' suspicions, so their responses are more spontaneous and less biased. The disadvantages of field studies are that the situation is hard to control, it is difficult to select subjects at random, accurate measures are hard to get, and subjects may not all experience the same situation. Conversely, the disadvantages of the field setting are the very strengths of the laboratory.

Ethics

Whenever research involves using humans as subjects, some fundamental ethical concerns arise, especially when there is to be manipulation such as misrepresentation of what is happening (Patulo, 1980). Foremost among these concerns is whether there will be any harm to the person's self-esteem, psychological state, or physical well-being. The Milgram study is a particularly striking example of why psychologists have this concern, as was

STANLEY MILGRAM (1933-)

(Courtesy, Dr. Stanley Milgram)

■ One of the best known—and most controversial—experiments ever done in psychology is Stanley Milgram's study of obedience to authority, in which subjects continued to give electric shocks to another subject even though they believed he was in serious pain. This study is typical of Milgram's creative research on social issues.

Milgram, who received his Ph.D. in social psychology from Harvard in 1960, currently teaches at the City University of New York. As a graduate student he worked for Solomon Asch, who had performed the experiment in which group pressure swayed how long people reported a line to be. Challenged by the criticism of Asch's study that it was trivial in significance, Milgram looked for a way to make the study more obviously meaningful. His solution: to see how far pressure could make one person act against another.

Born and bred in New York City, Milgram has a penchant for research that deals with real-life issues and problems. Apart from his study of obedi-ence, Milgram has examined how people are linked through chains of acquaintance to just about anybody else; why people do or do not help a child or someone else in distress; the mental maps people make of their cities; and, more recently, the social meaning of photography.

In his research on when people would help a child, Milgram had a nine-year-old approach strangers on the street and ask them to help him call his home. His study of people's mental maps found that the upper and lower classes of the same city find very different landmarks meaningful; psychologically they inhabit different cities. In still another study, Milgram had his students approach people sitting on a subway car and ask to have their seat without offering any reason for the request; most people readily complied. Each of these studies reflects Milgram's fascination with studying everyday experience, with what he calls "the pulse and emotionality of social life" (Tavris, 1974). "To understand why people behave as they do," says Milgram, "you have to be aware of the feelings aroused in everyday social situations."

Milgram was aware of the broader social implications of the obedience study from its inception. Obedience in its extreme forms is the seed of fascism; when obedience is wed to the idea that one group is inferior and another superior, repression is the next step.

The study evoked a storm of protests about its ethics. Milgram felt the storm was due, in part, to the alarming nature of his results. If he had found instead that people refused to buckle under to authority and had stopped shocking the confederate, Milgram proposes, people would not have been nearly so upset by the study.

In an interview Milgram noted, "Sometimes psychology becomes so academic and removed from the ordinary nature of things that it has to be balanced by turning attention to them." His work exemplifies how psychology can shed light on the "ordinary nature" of human behavior. ■

Watson's conditioning a fear response in little Albert. Milgram lied when he told participants the study was a learning experiment; it was designed to study something very different. Moreover, subjects were led to believe that the confederates pretending to suffer from the electrical shocks they were administering were acting authentically. Milgram's critics maintain that besides deceiving his subjects, he subjected them to great emotional stress.

Milgram was certainly aware of these problems, but he also knew that these deceptions were necessary to test his hypothesis, as is often the case in much psychological research. If the subjects were warned in advance that the study was of obedience and not learning, they most likely would have behaved very differently. If they knew the confederates were faking, then the results would have been meaningless. In response to his critics, Milgram has explained how he "debriefed" his subjects afterward, informing them of the true nature of what had just happened. He also found, through follow-up questionnaires, that none of the subjects reported feeling any ill effect from having taken part in the experiment.

While the ethics of Milgram's study are debatable, certain ethical standards for research are generally agreed on. First, the researcher must weigh the scientific advantages of his or her study against the possible discomfort of subjects. The design must minimize deception. If there is a rea-

sonable possibility of bad aftereffects, the researcher should inform subjects of this before they consent to take part. Only if subjects give informed consent should the experiment be conducted (American Psychological Association, 1973). During the experiment, the welfare of the subject must override any other concerns. Afterward the subject should be debriefed, with the researcher explaining the purpose of the study, and if any deception was used, what it was and why it was necessary. Most important, the debriefing should relieve any anxiety or confusion that the subject may feel.

Psychologists don't agree on the need for a research code. A study of how people viewed the Milgram experiment revealed that what distressed the general public was not the ethical questions in the procedure, but rather what the study revealed about human nature (Bickman and Zarantonelloe, 1978). Steiner (1972) makes the point that a college exam is more stressful than most psychological experiments. One school of thought holds that until we are sure of how deception, coercion, and uninformed consent might harm subjects, these practices should not be allowed (Gergen, 1974). On the other hand, the overall benefits to society of research that uses these tactics might far outweigh their possible adverse effects (Johnson, 1974); if so, they should be allowed until proven hazardous. The controversy continues.

SUMMARY

Conformity and obedience. Despite its negative connotations, conformity serves some useful purposes. It enforces societal norms and can be helpful in an awkward or unfamiliar social situation. But conformity can also lead people to violate social rules, the law, or their own ethics.

Why do people conform? Social comparison theory holds that people need to evaluate themselves, and if there are no objective measures to use, they will compare themselves to others.

Among the factors that contribute to a person's conformity are group unanimity, group size, the

strength of the person's attraction to the group, and feelings of guilt.

Conformity differs from obedience: conformity is brought about by people of status equal to ours and by implicit, unspoken demands. Obedience is evoked by a person or group with perceived legitimate authority to dictate our actions, and by explicit commands. The presence or absence of the authority figure influences the extent of obedience. One consequence of obedience is that it allows a person to deny responsibility.

In general, intelligent, self-assured people are

more likely to refuse to conform to a questionable majority judgment. Conformers have been found to be low in intellectual competence, ego strength, and self-esteem and to have a high need for affiliation and a tendency to blame themselves.

There are several types of conformity. Compliance occurs when a person agrees with the majority simply to get a reward or avoid a punishment. Conforming in order to maintain or affirm a relationship is called identification. Internalization is the acceptance of another's influence because it fits with one's own attitude.

Competition or cooperation? People very often have the choice of cooperating or competing. In our society and many others, there is a tendency to try to maximize one's gains while treating all other parties as threatening competitors. A person's degree of competitiveness depends to a large extent on socialization.

Many of the world's current dilemmas follow the pattern of "the tragedy of the commons," in which resources that could be preserved for the future are being destroyed because of a shortsighted lack of cooperation. One way to resolve the problem is through mutually accepted coercion—making it more difficult or costly to exploit the resources in question. Improving communication also may increase cooperation.

Altruism and apathy. Altruism is the term for an act performed to help someone else with no expectation of reward. Prosocial is the term for any act meant to help others, including acts with ulterior motives. A bystander's refusal to intervene on behalf of someone in trouble is evidence of apathy.

Why are people sometimes apathetic in an emergency? If the need for help is ambiguous, people's willingness to assist is dramatically lowered.

The presence or absence of other people can determine whether someone will help. Others' presence may make a potential helper fear looking foolish if the trouble turns out to be a false alarm. Diffusion of responsibility, with each individual thinking another will act, lessens the likelihood of anyone helping. People in a rush are also less likely to help, especially if they are on their way to an important event.

A person's altruism can be increased by giving him a sense that he is responsible for what is happening. Feeling good also seems to increase the likelihood that someone will act altruistically; helping someone else can also be a way to improve one's own mood.

People's sense of justice seems to determine the extent to which they will help. Equity is the term for the idea that every person should get what she or he deserves. Parity, in contrast, is sharing equally regardless of individual efforts. One motive for equity is self-concern—not altruism.

Groups. When people are together in a group, they adopt specific roles for themselves. Group dynamics govern the ways members of a group make decisions, align themselves within it, and conduct activities.

The common denominators of a group are that all people in it see themselves as members, depend on one another to attain the group's goals, and generally share goals, interests, and beliefs. Primary groups involve face-to-face contact; secondary groups, little or no personal interaction. Some groups are formal, others informal. The person who talks the most in a group is usually perceived as a leader. The ability to voice the feelings of the group is another mark of a perceived leader, along with intelligence and self-confidence. The contingency theory of leadership holds that the situation determines what kind of leader will be best at a given time.

Group efficiency. A group effort is often less efficient than a person working alone. But if several different kinds of expertise are needed, a group may be more effective than an individual.

Several factors determine how productive a group will be on a task: the nature of the task, group cohesiveness, the presence or absence of an information network, group size, group composition, and individuals' acceptance of group goals. Belonging to a group can have an effect of social facilitation on an individual, stimulating improved performance.

Environmental psychology. One of the problems unique to a city environment is sensory overload. People learn to cope with this by using selective attention and developing a norm of non-involvement.

People adapt to constant noise fairly quickly and are not disrupted by it unless they are trying to concentrate. But if their anger is aroused, noise can increase its felt intensity.

A sense of being able to control one's environment is important to the ability to adapt to it. In general, crowding appears to enhance some problems, but it does not destroy the social fabric. People seem to be highly adaptable in this regard.

Physical surroundings can have a strong influence on one's state of mind. People feel less safe and less friendly in high rises. Lower buildings and those that provide more defensible space make people feel more comfortable.

The social psychology of psychology. A great majority of psychological studies have used college students as subjects. Among the issues that concern psychologists is whether the results of such studies are an accurate reflection of the true nature of all human beings. There are ethical concerns as well—for example, is it right to deceive experimental subjects?

Distortions such as subject bias can confound the results of an experiment. Experimenter bias, whether conscious or unconscious, is another problem.

Some critics raise the question of whether people's behavior in a laboratory might not be the same as it is in the real world. Field research avoids this difficulty, but it too has disadvantages: the situation is hard to control, selecting subjects at random is not easy, and subjects may not all experience the same situation.

There are ethical standards for research that are generally agreed upon—for example, the scientific advantages of the study must be weighed against the possible discomfort of subjects. Deception must be minimized. Subjects should be informed of possible bad aftereffects, their welfare should override any other concerns during the experiment, and they should be debriefed afterward.

GLOSSARY

Altruism An act performed to help someone else with no expectation of reward.

Apathy The failure to intervene when help is needed.

Compliance A type of conformity that occurs when a person agrees with the majority simply to get a reward or avoid a punishment.

Conformity The result of a person's bringing his behavior and attitudes into agreement with a group as a result of implicit social pressures.

Contingency theory Holds that the situation determines what kind of leader will be best at a given time.

Crowding The state of discomfort associated with wanting more space than is available.

Density An objective measure of the space available to each organism in an environment.

Diffusion of responsibility Each person assumes that someone else will help, and so feels less responsible.

Equity The idea that each person should get what he or she deserves.

Experimenter bias A distortion of results due to the expectations and desires of the researcher, whether conscious or unconscious.

Field research Experimental studies with people in natural settings.

Group dynamics The processes that evolve within a group that govern how group members will work and interact.

Identification Conformity in order to maintain or affirm a relationship.

Internalization A type of conformity that occurs when a person accepts another's influence because it fits his or her own attitude.

Legitimate authority A person or group that has the right, credentials, and position to make demands.

Obedience Compliance with explicit commands.

Parity Sharing equally, regardless of individual efforts.

Primary groups Relationships with face-to-face contact, for example, a family or team.

Prosocial A term that describes any act meant to help others.

Rosenthal effect A distortion in findings due to unintentional experimenter influences.

Secondary group Relationships with little or no personal interaction among members, for example, subscribers to a magazine or members of an auto club.

Social comparison theory Holds that people have a need to evaluate themselves and, in the absence of objective measures, do so by comparing themselves to others.

Social facilitation The heightening of a person's performance in a group.

Subject bias A distortion of results caused by subjects responding the way they expect the experimenter wants them to.

THE SEXES

HOW THE SEXES DIFFER

Is biology destiny? ■ Socializing the sexes ■ Beliefs and stereotypes

THE COSTS OF SEX ROLES

The power of stereotypes (or "She's only a woman") ■ The price of manhood ■ Androgyny: the middle way ■ Sexism ■ Does sexism have a future?

Biology is Destiny.

SIGMUND FREUD

Freud's dictum represents his opinion of the psychological impact of the differences between men's and women's genitals: he was persuaded that the difference between having a penis and having a vagina was significant in shaping personality. Because a woman's vagina makes her the recipient of penetration by the penis during intercourse, Freud theorized, women are innately passive and receptive, preoccupied with inner feelings rather than activities in the outer world. Men, on the other hand, are aggressive and concerned with manipulating the world around them.

Today Freud's emphasis on anatomy is seen as oversimplified. Anatomy plays a small role in shaping personality. Differences between the sexes are the product of both biology and learning—although there is still uncertainty about just how important each of these factors is (Frieze, *et al.*, 1978).

HOW THE SEXES DIFFER

We all know that men are different from women. But in what ways, and to what degree? In examining the psychological differences that have been found between the sexes, remember that these differences are not total. The sexes overlap on every trait. Sex differences are a matter of degree, or averages: for example, the greater aggression of little boys does not mean that little girls don't play rough or slug it out—just that boys are more prone to do so. And the differences *within* the sexes are far greater than those *between* them: there is a greater range of aggressiveness between the most and least aggressive boy than between the average girl and the average boy.

A distillation and careful review of the research on psychological differences between the sexes found the following to be well established (Block, 1979; Eron, 1980):

☐ *Aggression* One of the strongest sex differences is that men are more aggressive than women, from early childhood on. Boys fight more, are more competitive, and even prefer TV shows with aggressive content more than girls.

☐ *Activity level* Men are more active than women, at least in infancy and childhood. Boys explore more than girls, and men perceive themselves as more adventurous than women.

☐ *Impulsivity* Men are more impulsive than women, finding it harder to delay gratification and harder to resist temptation, and they react more to frustration. Even the driving habits of men reflect more impatience and impulsivity than those of women.

□ *Susceptibility to anxiety and influence* Women are more fearful, show more anxiety, and have less confidence than men. For example, between the ages of eighteen and twenty-six, women decreased in their sense of adequacy, while men during the same period increased in theirs. This may explain why women in groups are more influenced by peer pressures than men (Eagly, 1978).

□ *Achievement* While men and women are about equally persistent in achievement situations, their motives seem to differ. Achievement in men is stimulated by ego-involving challenges, while these same factors may impair the performance of women. Women may feel a conflict when achievement threatens interpersonal acceptance, and this worsens performance—they take the attitude "I'd rather be liked than win."

□ *Potency of self-concept* Men are not only more confident in problem solving, but they also have greater feelings of self-efficacy, the confidence that one can meet a challenge. Men see themselves as being more powerful, ambitious, and in control of external events than women.

□ *Social relationships* Women are more skilled at social relationships than men. Women are more empathic, have more intense relationships, and even keep a closer proximity to others than men. Women are also more dependent—in the sense of seeking help from others—and more nurturant than men.

Is biology destiny?

Could there be something in the biological makeup of men and women that would account for all these sex differences? We know that biology and environment interact to shape a person's behavior, but it is hard to say just how malleable the sexes are in what they do and to what degree their behavior is part of an invariable genetic blueprint.

No one denies that there are fundamental biological differences between the sexes—only that anatomy outweighs upbringing in accounting for all the differences between men and women. In fact, a person's psychological identity can differ totally from his or her biological sex, as is the case with transsexuals, who feel they are in a body of the wrong sex (Money and Ehrhardt, 1972). Such people may seek sex change operations so that their bodies will match their feeling of being male or female—although such operations may not improve the psychological adjustment of transsexuals.

Apart from the anatomical differences between men and women, one of the most profound biological influences on their behavior are the sex-related hormones. Men have proportionately more of the hormones called androgens, while women have more estrogens. These hormones may account for some of the differences in behavior between men and women. For example, boys are generally more aggressive than girls at all ages and in nearly all cultures (Maccoby and Jacklin, 1974). In rats, the male hormones seem to produce aggressive behavior, while the female hormones produce more passivity (Beach, 1965). When a group of girls were born with a high level of male hormones as a result of drugs their mothers took during pregnancy, they proved to prefer more aggressive, rough-and-tumble play, just like boys their age (Money and Ehrhardt, 1972).

In addition to boys' greater aggressiveness, other well-established sex differences are cognitive: girls have greater verbal ability than boys, and boys excel in visual-spatial and mathematical skills (Maccoby and Jacklin, 1974). Recent research has pegged these differences not to how boys and girls are treated, but rather to the ways their brains are organized (Wittig and Petersen, 1979). One theory is that men's and women's brains absorb differing ratios of sex hormones, which produces cognitive differences (McGuinness and Pribram, 1979).

While hormones may explain some differences, they probably won't account for the whole range of sex differences. There is no clear evidence to explain what biological factors might underlie the broad range of behavioral differences between men and women, nor to determine the extent that these differences can be altered by experience. Take, for example, the finding that male babies are more active than females, and that female infants are more vocal and use language earlier (Bardwick, 1971). Is this because boys are built differently from girls—or because mothers treat baby boys and baby girls differently, touching boys more and talking more to girls (Moss, 1967)? There is no clear answer.

While it is true that men and women in different cultures show many consistent sex differences, this does not prove that those differences transcend culture and so must be rooted in biological makeup. A survey of the ways in which boys and girls were brought up in 110 cultures found that while boys were encouraged to be self-reliant, girls were not. Instead the girls were raised to be nurturant. Thus the fact that men show more independence than women on the average all over the world and that women show more nurturance seems due to consistent patterns of socialization of the sexes, not necessarily any biological, innate difference. The evidence strongly suggests that experience accounts for such sex differences, not biology: when in one African tribe a shortage of girls meant boys were assigned to care for younger children, the boys became less aggressive and less dominant (Barry, Bacon, and Child, 1957).

Socializing the sexes

Parents treat their sons and daughters differently. The messages from parent to child about how to be a boy or girl begin very early. They include such everyday matters as what clothes a child wears, what sorts of games he or she is allowed, what sorts of chores each does. A little girl helps her mother iron; a little boy helps his father work on the car.

Children label themselves as boys and girls by around age two, and actively learn for themselves how to be a boy or girl (Kohler, 1966). Once they identify their own sex, they develop a gender identity, a sense of being a boy or girl, and what that means. They categorize objects, like toys, as for boys (tool chest) or girls (dolls). Then they value the importance of the toys to them according to their appropriateness for their gender: little girls choose dolls over tools; boys, the opposite. They also imitate grownups of their own sex, and develop a closer emotional attachment to the same-sex parent at around age four or five. A little boy likes to learn how to do things from his father, while a little girl prefers to do so with her mother.

There are a large number of ways parents shape boys' behavior into a masculine mold and girls' into a feminine one (Block, 1979). Parents encourage sons to control their emotions and be more independent, although they also punish their sons more than their daughters. Fathers also expect their sons to be competitive and achievement-oriented, although mothers do not. Daughters, on the other hand, are emotionally closer to parents, and more trust is put in them. Parents discourage roughhousing in girls, expecting them to be "ladylike," and girls are more strictly supervised (Block, 1979).

Not only do mothers and fathers treat boys and girls differently, but this differentiation increases with the child's age (Block, 1979). A toddler is given much more freedom to experiment with a wide range of sex-typed behavior than a teenager—a mother might let a little boy, for example, dress up in his mother's clothes; she would not let a teenager do the same.

Mothers are more attentive to signals from male infants than from females (Murphy and Moriarty, 1976), and from infancy through childhood both parents react more to what boys say than to what girls say (Parke and Sawin, 1976; Margolin and Patterson, 1975). Parents provide more physical activity for sons than daughters; they give boys toys that allow for inventive possibilities, while those they give girls encourage imitation (Block, 1979). Parents also give more freedom to sons, keeping a tighter rein on daughters: daughters are allowed fewer outings from home, mothers encourage their daughters to follow them around the house, and parents supervise daughters' activities more. Girls also get assigned more homebound chores like cleaning and baby-sitting.

Much of the difference in upbringing between boys and girls comes from their fathers (Block, 1979). When fathers were observed teaching their children, they set higher standards for achievement for sons than for daughters; with daughters they put more emphasis on the interpersonal aspects of teaching, joking and kidding with them.

With their sons, fathers act in a task-oriented

way that emphasizes mastery, while with daughters, they are more expressive and less intellectually rigorous (Rodin, 1976). What daughters learn from relationships with their fathers may well be that their path to success is through relationships rather than achievements (Lamb, Owen, and Chase-Lansdale, in press).

Mothers, too, reinforce these messages. Mothers of girls offer help in problem solving more than mothers of boys—even when no help is needed (Gunnar-Gnetchen, 1977), and they are more positive in responding to requests for help from daughters than from sons. Mothers also give more comfort to girls who get hurt playing than to boys (Lewis, 1972). Both fathers and mothers interrupt what their daughters are saying more than they do with their sons, conveying the message that the daughters' thoughts are less important (Grief, 1979).

Schools do their part in teaching boys and girls how to be men and women. The power structure shows them that men are dominant: principals tend to be men; teachers, women. Men typically teach science and math; women teach literature and art (Wirtenburg and Nakamura, 1976). Boys and girls are also directed toward interests in keeping with traditional images of the sexes—science and mathematics for boys, literature and languages for girls. Until recently, in junior high only boys took shop courses, and only girls took home economics. The net effect is to teach that boys and girls should master different abilities (Maccoby and Jacklin, 1974).

Block (1974) sees ready connections between how parents and teachers treat children and the differences found between the sexes. Socialization that encourages boys to be more exploratory than girls may account for many of the differences between the sexes in activity, anxiety, and achievement. The more controlled environments and circumscribed activities provided for daughters may contribute to their lesser confidence and impulsivity as well as to their greater investment in social relationships.

Beliefs and stereotypes

Another force that shapes how men and women behave is less tangible than upbringing, but potent nevertheless—the attitudes people hold about what it means to be male or female. When people are asked to describe the "average man" and the "average woman," the man is depicted as competent and independent, the woman as warm and expressive (Broverman, *et al.*, 1972). Such stereotypes about the sexes start very early. In one study, kindergarten children played with a four-month-old infant, who was dressed as a boy—in a blue playsuit—or girl—in a red dress (Smith and Barclay, 1979). When they saw the infant as a boy, they later described it as big, a good eater, not beautiful, noisy, strong, cheerful, and tough. When the same baby was dressed as a girl, they said she was little, a poor eater, beautiful, quiet, weak, fussy, and gentle.

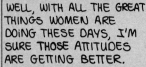

These stereotypes are not just a product of male chauvinism: women seem to hold them as strongly as men. Stereotypes such as these can become self-fulfilling prophecies. If a little girl believes girls are quiet and weak, she may act that way, just as a boy who thinks it unmanly to cry will learn to hide his tears.

THE COSTS OF SEX ROLES

The power of stereotypes (or "She's only a woman")

One of the social costs of these stereotypes is that it is harder for a woman to prove herself to be capable. For example, college students asked to judge the quality of professional articles were given two versions, identical in every way except that one was by "John McKay," the other by "Joan Mc-Kay." Both men and women rated John's version superior to Joan's (P. Goldberg, 1968; Bem and Bem, 1970). But when the same experiment was done with a wider variety of topics, college students showed a male bias only when the topics were "masculine" ones such as law. For example, when the topic was dietetics, women were seen to have the edge (H. Mischel, 1974).

When a woman *does* excel, she is more likely to be seen as successful because of luck rather than skill (Deaux and Emswiller, 1974). Indeed, men and women apply the same twist in explaining their own successes: when, for example, college

students solved a series of anagrams, the men explained their success (or failure) as their own responsibility, while the women saw it as due to good (or bad) luck (Deaux and Farris, 1974). Women and men, then, are popularly viewed as differing in abilities, and women accept this bias in viewing their own lives.

One source of women's lower evaluations of their own abilities can be traced to teachers. An analysis of evaluations given fifth-grade boys and girls by their teachers found that girls were given much more negative feedback on intellectual performance, while boys received more negative remarks about nonintellectual activities. Moreover, teachers attributed boys' failures more often than girls' to a lack of motivation, rather than intellectual inability (Dweck, *et al.*, 1975). The net result is that girls feel more helpless than boys about their ability to perform well (Dweck and Bush, 1976). In short, girls more than boys are trained to feel incompetent in the face of failure.

Because women tend to downgrade their abilities from girlhood on, they may avoid "masculine" jobs. Expecting to perform badly, they may choose jobs where there are fewer challenges—being a secretary rather than a manager, nurse rather than doctor. Such women are caught in a vicious cycle of undervaluing their successes and overestimating their failures (Frieze, *et al.*, in press). An added barrier is that family and friends—who may consider success "unfeminine"—may be threatened by a woman who succeeds (Hoffman, 1972).

The price of manhood

The costs of the male sex role are not so great socially as they are psychologically and physically: men die sooner and have fewer close friendships. In 1900, life expectancy for men was 46.3 years, for women 48.3 years. In 1975 it had risen to 68.7 years for men, 76.5 years for women. While both sexes had gained about twenty years, the difference between men and women jumped from two years to almost eight years. One reason: the unhealthy nature of the male role.

Men, remember, are more competitive, aggressive, and impulsive. This pattern is characteristic of Type A behavior, the hurried, frantic pace of life that makes people more likely to have heart attacks (Friedman and Rosenman, 1974). And, indeed, between the ages of thirty-five and seventy-five men are twice as likely to have a fatal heart attack as women. Men, perhaps because of pressures to be "macho" as well as their greater aggressiveness, are also far more likely than women to die a violent death, whether from accidents, homicide, or suicide.

The psychological costs of manliness are many. One is the price of success: men can become slaves to their jobs. Many successful men are "workaholics," putting in fifty-five-hour weeks and more to get ahead. The result is a restricted personal life, with the successful man obsessed with work and too tired to play (Kaye, 1974).

Little boys are taught that it's not manly to cry; grown men often don't seem to know how. The stifling of emotions results in men finding it more difficult to express their feelings, especially those of tenderness or vulnerability (Pleck and Sawyer, 1974). Men are also less self-disclosing about themselves in general than women (Jourard, 1971). Stereotypes of the male role demand that a man seem tough, achieving, and unsentimental, and so men learn to conceal those sides of themselves that are vulnerable, fearful, and emotional. The net result is that men more than women avoid intimacy and maintain a facade of unemotional stoicism, keeping their problems bottled up inside. Eron (1980) proposes that exposing boys to the same training girls have traditionally received would reduce the level of aggression in society: encouraging the development of socially positive, tender, cooperative, and sensitive qualities.

Androgyny: the middle way

Sex roles can be oppressive, for both men and women. But although men and women are biologically different, the concepts of masculinity and femininity are psychological ones, separate from biological identity per se. In terms of the traits that are typical of masculinity and femininity, there is not a clear-cut dichotomy: all men possess "feminine" traits to a degree, and all women, "masculine" ones. We can be both assertive and yielding, at times, and nurturant and achieving. *Androgyny* is the term for a self-concept that allows a person to engage in both "masculine" and "feminine" behavior, thus giving a person a greater range of choices.

Sandra Bem (1974) had men and women rate themselves on how well each of sixty masculine, feminine, and neutral personality traits described them. Masculine items included acting as a leader, being assertive, making decisions easily, and being independent. Feminine items included being affectionate, gentle, shy, and understanding. On the basis of their responses they were judged either masculine, feminine, or androgynous—a mix of both.

A masculine man can do "male" things well, such as be assertive and independent, but does poorly in responding to a baby or a person in need. Similarly, "feminine" women are good at womanly activities like playing with a baby or helping someone in need, but they have trouble being assertive or independent. Androgynous men and women, though, can be either masculine or feminine as the situation requires. If someone makes an unreasonable request, they can give a "masculine" assertive response; if someone is troubled, they can be "feminine" in helping.

Some believe that operating within the traditional masculine or feminine roles means limiting oneself to being half a person, while being androgynous allows a fuller repertoire of possibilities. Androgyny makes people feel that they have the potential to meet a wider range of situations with an apt response—whether it requires sharing a range of emotions or being assertive. Perhaps it is because androgynous people feel themselves capable of more responses that they have a high level of self-esteem (Orlofsky, 1977). Indeed, androgynous men and women get along better with members of the opposite sex than masculine men and feminine women (Ickes and Barnes, 1978).

It stands to reason that the most adaptive response to life situations is made by people who have the widest range of alternatives available to them. For example, in a business setting, the adaptive person can be businesslike; as a lover the person needs an entirely different set of responses; as a parent, still another. To the degree that being masculine or feminine excludes a range of behaviors from a person's possibilities, these sex roles are maladaptive.

Androgyny does not seem to be a fixed trait, but varies with situations. For example, 120 men and women were measured for androgyny; thirty each were either single but living with a lover, married but childless, married and expecting a first child, or married and the parent of an infant (Abrahams, Feldman, and Nash, 1978). Their scores on an androgyny scale showed that their life situation made a large difference. For women, androgyny was highest while living with a man before marriage, then fell after marriage; their femininity scores, meanwhile, increased steadily from marriage on. For men, androgyny was highest just after marriage. The strongest effect was

for pregnancy and parenthood: having a child made women more feminine and men more masculine. Presumably both men and women find raising children most natural in traditional sex roles. One implication of this is that parents will be more likely to pass on to their children traditional models for sex roles, rather than androgynous ones.

Sexism

The bias against women by virtue of their sex alone is *sexism*. As Bem and Bem (1970) point out, sexism is pervasive in American culture: a person's family, peers, teachers, the mass media, and even religions tend to be sexist. Sexism has been so widespread for so long that it has become a "nonconscious ideology," a set of beliefs that people accept without even realizing they do—simply because no alternative view is ever offered.

The power of sexism in American society is perhaps nowhere clearer than in the job market. Those jobs that women typically hold pay much less than those that men typically hold, and—despite laws to the contrary—women still get less pay than men in the identical job. Although only 3 percent of women in a national survey of high school seniors selected "housewife" as their first career choice, that is the job most women hold. As Bem and Bem note: "Talent, education, ability, interests, motivations—all are irrelevant. In our society, being female uniquely qualifies an individual for domestic work" (1970).

Does sexism have a future?

Strong social currents are moving against sexism. The women's movement has made people more aware of what was once an unconscious ideology, federal laws have outlawed job discrimination on the basis of sex, large corporations have been ordered by courts to pay women back wages they were unfairly denied, and more and more women are entering the job market. Attitudes, too, seem to be changing. In 1974 a study found that the higher the proportion of women in a profession, the lower its prestige (Touhey, 1974). This bias seems to have vanished. A determined attempt in 1979 to see if the same sexist effect held for a wider range of social classes, regions, and jobs failed to find the same bias among any group tested (Suchner, 1979).

Certainly among many young people the image of an ideal man or woman is hardly what it was twenty years ago. Social changes are bound to shape new sex roles. The largest impact on sex roles may be economic: as more women work, two-career marriages will become increasingly com-

mon. Men will be called on to help more with housework and children, and will need to rely on "feminine" traits like nurturance. Daughters will more often grow up with other models of a woman than the stay-at-home housewife, and children will have more equal amounts of contact with both parents. As women succeed in higher-prestige jobs, they are sure to display more competence, independence, and assertiveness—typically "masculine" traits. If these trends continue, the sexes will become increasingly similar (Hoffman, 1977).

Even so, there are undoubtedly limits to the elasticity of sex roles. Many women, for example, report that the satisfactions they get from raising children are worth any sacrifice this might mean for career goals (Frieze, et al., 1978). Over the coming years, there may be a blurring of the dichotomy between "feminine" and "masculine" traits, since both men and women may find it more necessary to call on a wider range of abilities—for example, women to be more assertive, men to be more emotional. But just how far this change can or will go and how many people in our culture it will affect, only time can tell.

BIBLIOGRAPHY

A

ABBS, J. H., and SUSSMAN, H. M. Neurophysiological feature detectors and speech perception. Discussion of theoretical implications. *Journal of Speech and Hearing Research*, 1971, *14*, 23–36.

ABEL, G. C., BARLOW, D. H., BLANCHARD, E. B., and MAVISSAKALIAN, M. Measurement of sexual arousal in male homosexuals: Effects of instructions and stimulus modality. *Archives of Sexual Behavior*, 1975, *4*, 623–629.

ABRAHAMS, B., FELDMAN, S. S., and NASH, S. C. Sex role concept and sex role attitudes: enduring personality characteristics of adaptations to changing life situations. *Developmental Psychology*, 1978, *14*, 393–400.

ABRAHAMSON, P. R., and MOSHER, D. L. Development of a measure of negative attitudes toward masturbation. *Journal of Consulting and Clinical Psychology*, 1975, *43*, 485–490.

ADAMS, H. Inequity in social exchange. In L. Berkowitz, ed., *Advances in Experimental Social Psychology*. Vol. 2. New York: Academic Press, 1965.

ADELSON, J. Adolescence and the generation gap. *Psychology Today*, February 1979, pp. 33–37.

ADLER, A. *The Individual Psychology of Alfred Adler: A Systematic Presentation in Selections from His Writings*. Edited by H. L. Ansbacher and R. R. Ansbacher. New York: Basic Books, 1956.

ADORNO, T. W., FRENKEL-BRUNSWIK, E., LEVINSON, D. J., and SANFORD, R. N. *The Authoritarian Personality*. New York: Harper, 1950.

AINSWORTH, M. D. S. Infant-mother attachment. *American Psychologist*, 1979, *34*, 932–937.

AINSWORTH, M. D. S., and BELL, S. M. Attachment, exploration, and separation: Illustrated by the behavior of one-year-olds in a strange situation. *Child Development*, 1970, *41*, 149–168.

ALGEIER, E. R. *The influence of sex roles on heterosexual attitudes and behavior*. Ph.D. dissertation, Purdue University, 1976.

ALLPORT, G. W. *Personality: A Psychological Interpretation*. New York: Holt, Rinehart and Winston, 1937.

ALLPORT, G. W. *ABC's of Scapegoating*. Chicago: Central Y.M.C.A. College, 1944.

ALLPORT, G. *The Nature of Prejudice*. Carlisle, Mass.: Addison-Wesley, 1954.

ALLPORT, G. W., and ODBERT, A. S. Trait names: A psycholexical study. *Psychological Monographs*, 1936, *47*, 1–171.

ALTMAN, I., and TAYLOR, D. *Social Penetration: The Development of Interpersonal Relations*. New York: Holt, Rinehart and Winston, 1973.

AMERICAN PSYCHIATRIC ASSOCIATION. *Diagnostic and Statistical Manual of Mental Disorders*. 3rd ed. Washington, D.C.: American Psychiatric Association, 1980.

AMERICAN PSYCHOLOGICAL ASSOCIATION. *Casebook on Ethical Standards of Psychologists*. Washington, D.C.: American Psychological Association, 1967.

AMERICAN PSYCHOLOGICAL ASSOCIATION. Ethical principles in the conduct of research with human participants. *American Psychologist*, 1973, *28*, 79–80.

AMMON, P. R. The perception of grammatical relations in sentences: A methodological exploration. *Journal of Verbal Learning and Verbal Behavior*, 1968, *7*, 869–875.

ANAND, B. D., CHINNA, G. S., and SINGH, B. Some aspects of EEG studies in Yogis. *EEG Clinical Neurophysiology*, 1961, *13*, 452–456.

ANASTASI, A. *Psychological Testing*. 4th ed. New York: Macmillan, 1976.

ANDERSON, B. F. *The Psychology Experiment: An Introduction to the Scientific Method*, Belmont, Calif.: Wadsworth, 1966.

ANDERSON, B. Thirst—and brain control of water balance. *American Scientist*, 1971, *59*, 408–415.

ANDERSON, J. R., and ROSS, B. H. Evidence against a semantic-episodic distinction. *Journal of Experimental Psychology: Human Learning and Memory*, 1980, *6*, 441–466.

ANDERSON, R. C., and AUSUBEL, D. P. *Readings in the History of Cognition*. New York: Holt, Rinehart and Winston, 1965.

ANDOLFI, M., and ZWERLING, I., eds. *Dimensions of Family Therapy*. New York: Guilford Press, 1980.

ANDREASSI, J. L. *Psychophysiology*. New York: Oxford University Press, 1980.

ANGLIN, J. *Word, Object, and Conceptual Development*. New York: Norton, 1976.

ANISFELD, M., and KLENBORT, I. On the functions of structural paraphrase: The view from the passive voice. *Psychological Bulletin*, 1973, *79*, 117–126.

ANTINUCCI, F., and MILLER, R. How children talk about what happened. *Journal of Child Language*, 1976, *3*, 167–189.

ARGYLE, M. *Social Interaction*. Chicago: Aldine-Atherton, 1969.

ARIETI, S., and BEMPORAD, J. *Mild and Severe Depression*. New York: Basic Books, 1979.

ARKES, H. R., and GARSKE, J. P. *Psychological Theories of Motivation*. Monterey, Calif.: Brooks/Cole, 1977.

ARKIN, A. M. Sleeptalking. In A. M. Arkin, J. S. Antrobus, and S. J. Ellman, *The Mind in Sleep*. New York: Lawrence Erlbaum, 1978.

ARNHEIM, R. *Visual thinking*. Berkeley: University of California Press, 1969.

ARNOLD, C. R. Role of discriminative stimuli in the formation of functional response classes. *Journal of Experimental Child Psychology*, 1970, *9*, 470–488.

ARNOLD, M. B. *Emotions and personality*. New York: Columbia University Press, 1960.

ARONSON, E., and COPE, V. My enemy's enemy is my friend. *Journal of Personality and Social Psychology*, 1968, *8*, 8–12.

ARONSON, E., AND MILLS, J. The effect of severity of initiation on liking for a group. *Journal of Abnormal and Social Psychology*, 1959, *59*, 177–181.

ARONSON, E., TURNER, J., and CARLSMITH, M. Communicator credibility and communicator discrepancy as determinants of opinion change. *Journal of Abnormal and Social Psychology*, 1963, *67*, 31–36.

ASCH, S. E. Opinions and social pressure. *Scientific American*, 1955, *193*, 31–35.

ATHANASIA, R. Pornography: A review of research. In B. B. Wolman and J. Money, eds., *Handbook of Human Sexuality*. New York: Plenum, 1980.

ATKINSON, J. W., ed. *Motives in Fantasy, Action, and Society*. Princeton, N.J.: Van Nostrand, 1958.

ATKINSON, J. W., and Raynor, J. O. *Personality, Motivation and Achievement*. New York: Halstead Press, 1978.

ATTHOWE, J. M., and KRASNER, L. Preliminary report on the application of contingent reinforcement procedures (Token Economy) on a "chronic" psychiatric ward. *Journal of Abnormal Psychology*, 1968, *73*, 37–43.

AUERBACH, S. M., and KILMANN, P. R. Crisis intervention: A review of outcome research. *Psychological Bulletin*, 1978, *84*, 1189–1217.

AUSUBEL, D. P. *Theory and Problems of Adolescent Development*. New York: Grune and Stratton, 1954.

AUSUBEL, D. P. Personality disorder is a disease. *American Psychologist*, 1961, *16*, 69–74.

AVERILL, J. R., and OPTON, E. M. Psychophysiological assessment; rationale and problems. In P. McReynolds, ed., *Advances in Psychological Assessment*. Palo Alto, Calif.: Science and Behavior Books, 1968.

AYLLON, T., and AZRIN, N. *The Token Economy: A Motivational System for Therapy and Rehabilitation*. New York: Appleton-Century-Crofts, 1968.

B

BACHRACH, A. J. *Psychological Research. An Introduction*. New York: Random House, 1972.

BALDESSARINI, R. J. Chemotherapy. In A. M. Nicholi, ed., *The Harvard Guide to Modern Psychiatry*. Cambridge, Mass.: Harvard University Press, 1978.

BALES, R. F. Task roles and social roles in problem solving groups. In E. E. Maccoby, T. M. Newcomb, and E. L. Hartley, eds., *Readings in Social Psychology*. 3rd ed. New York: Holt, Rinehart and Winston, 1958.

BALES, R. F. *Personality and Interpersonal Behavior*. New York: Holt, Rinehart and Winston, 1970.

BALL, S., and BOGATZ, G.A. *The First Year of Sesame Street: An Evaluation*. Princeton, N.J.: Educational Testing Service, 1970.

BALTES, P. B., REESE, H. W., and LIPSITT, L. P. Life-span developmental psychology. *Annual Review of Psychology*, 1980, *31*, 65–110.

BANDURA, A. *Principles of Behavior Modification.* New York: Holt, Rinehart and Winston, 1969.

BANDURA, A. *Social Learning Theory.* Englewood Cliffs, N.J.: Prentice-Hall, 1977a.

BANDURA, A. Self-efficacy: Toward a unifying theory of behavioral change. *Psychological Review,* 1977b, *84,* 191–215.

BANDURA, A., BLANCHARD, E. B., and RITTER, B. The relative efficacy of desensitization and modeling approaches for inducing behavioral, affective, and attitudinal changes. *Journal of Personality and Social psychology,* 1969, *13,* 173–199.

BANDURA, A., ROSS, D., and ROSS, S. A. Transmission of aggression through imitation of aggressive models. *Journal of Abnormal and Social Psychology,* 1962, *63,* 575–582.

BANDURA, A., and WALTERS, R. H. *Social Learning and Personality Development.* New York: Holt, Rinehart and Winston, 1963.

BANE, M. J. Marital disruption and the lives of children. *Journal of Social Issues,* 1976, *32,* 103–117.

BANQUET, J. P. EEG and meditation. *EEG Clinical Neurophysiology,* 1973, *33,* 453–454.

BARASH, D. P. *Sociobiology and Behavior.* New York: Elsevier, 1977.

BARBER, T. X. Suggested ("hypnotic") behavior: The trance paradigm versus an alternative paradigm. In E. Fromm and R. Shor, eds., *Hypnosis: Research Developments and Perspectives.* Chicago: Aldine, 1972.

BARBER, T. X. *Pitfalls in Human Research.* Oxford, England: Pergamon Press, 1976.

BARCHAS, J. D., AKIL, H., ELLIOTT, G. R., HOLMAN, R. B., and WATSON, S. J. Behavioral neurochemistry: Neuroregulators and behavioral states. *Science,* May 26, 1978, 964–973.

BARCLAY, A. M. Urinary acid phosphatase secretion in sexually aroused males. *Journal of Experimental Research in Personality,* 1970, *4,* 233–238.

BARD, P. A. Emotion I: The neuro-humoral basis of emotional reactions. In C. Murchison, ed., *Handbook of General Experimental Psychology.* Worcester, Mass.: Clark University Press, 1934.

BARDWICK, J. M. *Psychology of Women.* New York: Harper & Row, 1971.

BARKER, R. G., DEMBO, T., and LEWIN, K. Frustration and regression: An experiment with young children. *University of Iowa Studies in Child Welfare,* 1941, *18,* 1–314.

BARLOW, D. H., ABEL, G. G., BLANCHARD, E. B., BRISTOW, A. R., and YOUNG, L. D. A heterosocial skills behavior checklist for males. *Behavior Therapy,* in press.

BARNES, G. M. The development of adolescent drinking behavior. *Adolescence,* 1977, *12,* 571–591.

BARNES, M., and BERKE, J. *Mary Barnes: Two Accounts of a Journey Through Madness.* New York: Ballantine, 1971.

BARON, R. A., and BYRNE, D. *Social Psychology: Under-standing Human Interaction.* 2nd ed. Boston: Allyn & Bacon, 1977.

BARON, R. A., BYRNE, D., and GRIFFIT, W. *Social Psychology: Understanding Human Interaction.* Boston: Allyn & Bacon, 1974.

BARRON, F. Diffusion, integration and enduring attention in the creative process. In R. W. White, ed., *The Study of Lives.* New York: Atherton, 1963.

BARRON, F., and LEARY, T. F. Changes in psychoneurotic patients with and without psychotherapy. *Journal of Consulting Psychology,* 1955, *19,* 239–245.

BARRY, H., BACON, M. K., and CHILD, I. L. A cross-cultural survey of some sex differences in socialization. *Journal of Abnormal and Social Psychology,* 1957, *55,* 327–332.

BARTLETT, F. C. *Remembering.* London: Cambridge University Press, 1932.

BARTLEY, H. S. *Perception in Everyday Life.* New York: Harper & Row, 1972.

BATES, E. *Language and Context: The Acquisition of Pragmatics.* New York: Academic Press, 1976.

BATESON, G. *Steps to an Ecology of Mind.* New York: Chandler, 1972.

BATSON, C. D., COCHRAN, P. J., BIEDERMAN, M. G., BLOSSER, J. L., RYAN, M. J., and VOGT, B. Failure to help when in a hurry: Callousness or conflict? *Personality and Social Psychology Bulletin,* 1978, *4,* 97–101.

BAUM, A., and VALINS, S. *Architecture and Social Behavior: Psychological Studies of Social Density.* Hillsdale, N.J.: Lawrence Erlbaum, 1977.

BAUMEISTER, R. F., COOPER, J., and SKIB, B. A. Inferior performance as a selective response to expectancy: Taking a dive to make a point. *Journal of Personality and Social Psychology,* 1979, *37,* 424–432.

BAUMGARTNER, L. The public health significance of low birth weight in the U.S.A., with special reference to varying practices in providing special care to infants of low birth weight. *Bulletin of the World Health Organization,* 1962, *26,* 175.

BAUMRIND, D. Child care practices anteceding three patterns of preschool behavior, *Genetic Psychology Monographs,* 1967, *75,* 43–88.

BAUMRIND, D. Current patterns of parental authority. *Developmental Psychology Monographs, 4,* 1971, 1–103.

BAVELAS, A., et al. Experiments on the alteration of group structure. *Journal of Experimental Social Psychology,* 1965, *1,* 55–70.

BAYLEY, N. *Manual for the Bayley Scales of Infant Development.* New York: Psychological Corporation, 1969.

BAZAR, D. Catching up with the chimp controversy. *APA Monitor,* January 1980, pp. 4–5, 47.

BEACH, F. A., ed. Instinctive behavior: Reproductive activities. In S. S. Stevens, ed., *Handbook of Experimental Psychology.* New York: Wiley, 1951.

BEACH, F. A., ed. *Sex and Behavior.* New York: Wiley, 1965.

BEAUCHAMP, G. K., MALLER, O., and ROGERS, J. G. Flavor

preferences in cats. *Journal of Comparative and Physiological Psychology* 1977, *91*, 1118–1127.

BECK, A. T. *Depression: Causes and Treatment.* Philadelphia: University of Pennsylvania Press, 1972.

BECK, A. T. *Cognitive Therapy and the Emotional Disorders.* New York: International Universities Press, 1976.

BECK, A. T., and KOVACS, M. A new fast therapy for depression. *Psychology Today, January 1977, pp. 94–101.*

BECK, A. T., WARD, C. H., MENDELSON, M., MOCK, J. E., and ERBAUGH, J. K. Reliability of psychiatric diagnosis: A study of consistency of clinical judgments and ratings. *American Journal of Psychiatry*, 1962, *119*, 351–357.

BECK, A. T., and YOUNG, J. E. College blues. *Psychology Today*, September 1978, pp. 80–92.

BECKWITH, L., and COHEN, S. Acquiescence of mothers as research subjects. *American Journal of Orthopsychiatry*, 1974, *44*, 180–191.

BEDROSIAN, R. C., and BECK, A. T. Cognitive aspects of suicidal behavior. *Suicide and Life Threatening Behavior*, 1979, *2*, 87–96.

BELL, A. P., and WEINBERG, M. S. *Homosexualities: A study of diversity among men and women.* New York: Simon and Schuster, 1978.

BELL, R. Q. Stimulus control of parent or caretaker behavior by offspring. *Developmental Psychology*, 1971, 463–72.

BELLUGI, U. Learning the language. *Psychology Today*, December 1970, pp. 32–35.

BELLUGI, U., and KLIMA, E. S. The structural properties of American Sign Language. In L. S. Liben, ed., *Deaf Children: Developmental Perspectives.* New York: Academic Press, 1978.

BELLUGI, U., and KLIMA, E. S. *The Signs of Language.* Cambridge, Mass.: Harvard University Press, 1979.

BELSON, W. *Television Violence and the Adolescent.* London: Teakfield, 1978.

BEM, D. J. *Beliefs, Attitudes, and Human Affairs.* Belmont, Calif.: Brooks/Cole, 1970.

BEM, D. J. Self-perception theory. In L. Berkowitz, ed., *Advances in Experimental Social Psychology.* Vol. 6. New York: Academic Press, 1972.

BEM, D. J., and ALLEN, A. On predicting some of the people some of the time. *Psychological Review*, 1974, *81*, 506–520.

BEM, S. L. The measurement of psychological androgyny. *Journal of consulting and Clinical Psychology*, 1974, *42*, 155–162.

BEM, S. L., and BEM, D. J. Case study of a nonconscious ideology: Training the woman to know her place. In D. Bem, ed., *Beliefs, Attitudes and Human Affairs.* Belmont, Calif.: Brooks/Cole, 1970.

BENEDEK, E. P., and BENEDEK, R. S. Joint custody: solution or illusion? *American Journal of Psychiatry*, 1979, *136*, 1540–1544.

BERGIN, A. E. Negative effects revisited—a reply. *Professional Psychology*, 1980, *11*, 93–100.

BERKOWITZ, L. The contagion of violence. In W. J.

Arnold and M. M. Page, eds., *Nebraska Symposium on Motivation.* Lincoln: University of Nebraska Press, 1970.

BERKOWITZ, L., and LePAGE, A. Weapons as aggression-eliciting stimuli. *Journal of Personality and Social Psychology*, 1969, *13*, 200–206.

BERLIN, B., and KAY, P. *Basic Color Terms, Their Universality and Evolution.* Berkeley: University of California Press, 1969.

BERNARD, J. Infidelity: Some moral and social issues. In R. W. Libby and R. N. Whithurst, eds., *Marriage and Alternatives.* Chicago: Scott, Foresman, 1977.

BERNE, E. *Games People Play.* New York: Grove, 1964.

BERNE, E. *Principles of Group Treatment.* New York: Oxford University Press, 1966.

BERNHEIM, K. F., and LEVINE, R. J. *Schizophrenia: Symptoms, Causes, Treatments.* New York: Norton, 1979.

BERNSTEIN, I. L. Learned taste aversions in children receiving chemotherapy. *Science*, June 16, 1978, pp. 1302–1330.

BERSCHIED, E., and WALSTER, E. H. *Interpersonal Attraction.* Reading, Mass.: Addison-Wesley, 1978.

BEVER, T. G., GARRETT, M. F., and HURTING, R. The interaction of perceptual processes and ambiguous sentences. *Memory and Cognition.* 1973, *1*, 277–286.

BICKMANN, L., and ZARANTELLO, M. The effects of deception and level of obedience on subjects' ratings of the Milgram study. *Personality and Social Psychology Bulletin*, 1978, *4*, 81–85.

BILLER, H. B. Parental deprivation, cognitive functioning, and the feminized classroom. In A. Davids, ed., *Child Personality and Psychopathology: Current Topics.* New York: Wiley-Interscience, 1974.

BILLER, H. B., and DAVIDS, A. Parent-child relations, personality development, and psychopathology. In A. Davids, ed., *Issues in Abnormal Child Psychology.* Monterey, Calif.: Brooks/Cole, 1973.

BILLINGS, A. Conflict resolution in distressed and nondistressed married couples. *Journal of Consulting and Clinical Psychology*, 1979, *47*, 368–376.

BIRD, B. A. Effects of a systematic drill system on computational ability of primary children. *Dissertation Abstracts International*, 1978, *39*, 1317.

BIRK, L. Behavior therapy and behavioral psychotherapy. In A. M. Nocholi, Jr., ed., *The Harvard Guide to Modern Psychiatry.* Cambridge, Mass.: Harvard University Press, 1978.

BIRNBAUM, I. M., JOHNSON, J. K., HARTELY, J. T., and TAYLOR, T. H. Alcohol and elaborative schemas for sentences. *Journal of Experimental Psychology: Human Learning and Memory*, 1980, *6*, 293–300.

BIRNBAUM, I. M., and PARKER, E. S., eds. *Alcohol and Human Memory.* Hillsdale, N.J.: Lawrence Erlbaum, 1977.

BIRNS, B. Individual differences in human neonates' responses to stimulation. *Child Development*, 1965, *36*, 249–256.

BLAKEMORE, C. *Mechanics of the Mind.* London: Cambridge University Press, 1977.

BLANEY, P. H. Contemporary theories of depression: Critique and comparison. *Journal of Abnormal Psychology,* 1977, *86,* 203–223.

BLOCK, J. Personality characteristics associated with father's attitudes toward child-rearing. *Child Development,* 1955, *26,* 41–48.

BLOCK, J. H. *Socialization influences on personality development in males and females.* Paper presented at the annual meeting of the American Psychological Association, 1979.

BLOOD, R. O., and WOLFE, D.M. Husbands and wives. In R. Bell, ed., *Studies in Marriage and the Family.* New York: Crowell, 1968.

BLOOM, L. M., and LAHEY, M. *Language Development and Language Disorder.* New York: Wiley, 1977.

BOLLES, R. N. *What Color Is Your Parachute?* Berkeley, Calif.: Ten Speed Press, 1979.

BORNSTEIN, M., ed. *The Comparative Method in Psychology.* New York: Erlbaum, 1979.

BOWER, G. H. "Analysis of a Mnemonic Device," *American Scientist,* 1970, *58,* 496–501.

BOWER, G. H. How to . . . uh . . . remember! *Psychology Today,* October 1973, pp. 63–70.

BOWER, G. H. Memory freaks I have known. *Psychology Today,* October 1973, pp. 64–65.

BOWER, G. H. Experiments on story understanding and recall. *Quarterly Journal of Experimental Psychology,* 1976, *28,* 511–534.

BOWER, G. H., and CLARK, M. C. Narrative stories as mediators for serial learning. *Psychonomic Science,* 1969, *14,* 181–182.

BOWER, T. G. R. Repetitive processes in child development. *Scientific American,* 1976, *235,* 38–47.

BOWERS, K. S. *Hypnosis for the Seriously Curious.* Monterey, Calif.: Brooks/Cole, 1976.

BOWLBY, J. Maternal health care and mental health. *Bulletin of World Health Organization,* 1951, *3,* 355–384.

BOWLBY, J. Separation anxiety. *International Journal of Psychoanalysis,* 1960, *41,* 89–113.

BOWLBY, J. *Attachment.* New York: Basic Books, 1969.

BOWLBY, J. *Separation and Loss.* New York: Basic Books, 1973.

BRADLEY, C., and MEDDIS, R. Arousal threshold in dreaming sleep. *Physiological Psychology,* 1974, *2,* 109–110.

BRAMWELL, S. T., MASUDA, M., and WAGNER, N. N. Psychosocial factors in athletic injuries: Development and application of the Social and Athletic Readjustment Scale (SARRS). *Journal of Human Stress,* 1975, *1,* 6–20.

BRANSFORD, J. D., and McCARRELL, N. S. A sketch of a cognitive approach to comprehension: Some thoughts about understanding what it means to comprehend. In W. B. Weimer and D. S. Palermo, eds., *Cognition and the Symbolic Processes.* Hillsdale, N.J.: Lawrence Erlbaum, 1974.

BRECHER, E. M. *The Sex Researchers.* Boston: Little, Brown, 1969.

BREHM, J. W. *A Theory of Psychological Reactance.* New York: Academic Press, 1966.

BREHM, J. W., and COLE, A. H. Effect of a favor which reduces freedom. *Journal of Personality and Social Psychology,* 1966, *3,* 420–426.

BRENNER, C. Affects and psychic conflict. *Psychoanalytic Quarterly,* 1975, *44,* 5–28.

BRIDGER, W. H. Sensory habituation and discrimination in the human neonate. *American Journal of Psychiatry,* 1961, *117,* 991–996.

BROADBENT, D. E. Effects of noise in behavior. In C. M. Harris, ed., *Handbook of Noise Control.* New York: McGraw-Hill, 1957.

BROADBENT, D. E. *Perception and Communication.* London: Pergamon Press, 1958.

BRONFENBRENNER, U. *The Ecology of Human Development: Experiments by Nature and Design.* Cambridge, Mass.: Harvard University Press, 1979.

BROVERMAN, I. K., VOGEL, S. R., BROVERMAN, D. M., CLARKSON, F. E., and ROSENKRANTZ, P. S. Sex-role stereotypes: A current appraisal. *Journal of Social Issues,* 1972, *28,* 59–78.

BROWN, B. Keynote address. Mental health for the 1970s conference, MIT. Cambridge, Mass., June 1973.

BROWN, J. States in newborn infants. *Merrill-Palmer Quarterly,* 1967, *10,* 313–327.

BROWN, R. Development of the first language in the human species. *American Psychologist,* February 1973, pp. 97–106.

BROWN, R. *A First Language: The Early Stages.* Cambridge, Mass.: Harvard University Press, 1973.

BROWN, R. Introduction. In C. Snow and C. Ferguson, eds., *Talking to Children: Language Acquisition.* New York: Academic Press, 1977.

BROWN, R., and HANLON, C. Derivational complexity and order of acquisition in child speech. In J. R. Hayes, ed., *Cognition and the Development of Language.* New York: Wiley, 1970.

BROWN, R., and McNEILL, D. The "tip of the tongue" phenomenon. *Journal of Verbal Learning and Verbal Behavior,* 1966, *5,* 325–337.

BROWNELL, K., and BARLOW, D. H. The behavioral treatment of sexual deviation. In A. Goldstein and E. Foa, eds., *Handbook of Behavioral Interventions: A Clinical Guide.* New York: Wiley, 1980.

BRUNER, J. S. *Toward A Theory of Instruction.* New York: Norton, 1966.

BRUNER, J. S. *Toward A Memory of Instruction.* New York: Norton, 1966.

BUCHSBAUM, M. S. The sensoristat in the brain. *Psychology Today,* May 1978, pp. 96–104.

BUCK, C., and STAVRAKY, K. The relationship between age at marriage among child-bearing women. *Human Biology,* 1967, *39,* 93–102.

BUDZYNSKI, T. H., STOYVA, J. M., ADLER, C. S., and MUL-

LANEY, D. J. EMG biofeedback and tension headache: A controlled outcome study. *Psychosomatic Medicine*, 1973, *35*, 484–496.

BUGELSKI, B. R., KIDD, E., and SEGMAN, J. Image as a mediator in one-trial paired-associate learning. *Journal of Experimental Psychology*, 1968, *76*, 69–73.

BUMBERRY, W., OLIVER, J. M., and McCLURE, J. M. Validation of the Beck Depression Inventory in a university population using psychiatric estimate as the criterion. *Journal of Consulting and Clinical Psychology*, 1978, *46*, 150–155.

BUTLER, R. A. Curiosity in monkeys. *Scientific American*, 1954, *190*, 70–75.

BUTLER, R. H., and LEWIS, M. I. *Aging and Mental Health: Positive Psychosocial Approaches.* St. Louis: Mosby, 1973.

BYRNE, D. Attitudes and attraction. In L. Berkowitz, ed., *Advances in Experimental Social Psychology.* Vol. 4. New York: Academic Press, 1969.

BYRNE, D., and BLAYLOCK, B. Similarity and assumed similarity of attitudes between husbands and wives. *Journal of Abnormal and Social Psychology*, 1963, *67*, 636–640.

BYRNE, D., and LAMBERTH, J. The effect of erotic stimuli on sex arousal, evaluative responses, and subsequent behavior. In *Technical Report of the Commission on Obscenity and Pornography*, Vol. 8. Washington, D.C.: U.S. Government Printing Office, 1971.

C

CAIN, W. S. The odiferous environment and the application of olfactory research. In E. C. Carterette and M. P. Friedman, eds., *Handbook of Perception.* Vol. 6A, *Tasting and Smelling.* New York: Academic Press, 1978.

CALHOUN, J. B. Population density and social psychology. *Scientific American*, 1962, *206*, 139–148.

CAMPBELL, A., CONVERSE, P. E., and ROGERS, W. L. *The Quality of American Life.* New York: Russell Sage Foundation, 1975.

CAMPOS, J. L., LANGER, A., and KROWITZ, A. Cardiac responses on the visual cliff in prelocomotor human infants. *Science*, 1970, *170*, 196–197.

CANDLAND, D. K, ed. *Emotion.* Monterey, Calif.: Brooks/Cole, 1977.

CANDLAND, D. K., FELL, J. P., KEEN, E., LESHNER, A. I., PLUTCHIK, R., and TAUPY, R. M. In D. K. Candland, ed., *Emotion.* Monterey, Calif.: Brooks/Cole, 1977.

CANNON, W. B. The James-Lange theory of emotions: A critical examination and an alternative theory, *American Journal of Psychology*, 1927, *39*; 106–124.

CAPKO, M. K., and LEWIS, M. H. Authoritarianism and "All in The Family." *Journal of Psychology*, 1975, *90*, 245–248.

CAPLAN, G., MACHT, L. B., and WOLF, A. B. *Manual for Mental Health Professionals Participating in the Job Corps Program.* Washington, D.C.: Office of Economic Opportunity, 1969.

CAPUTO, D. V., and MANDEL, W. Consequences of low birth weight. *Developmental Psychology*, 1970, *3*, 363–383.

CAREY, J. O. The effects of a mnemonic on retention of verbal information from meaningful prose. *Dissertation Abstracts International*, 1977, *37*, 4222.

CARLSMITH, J. M., and GROSS, A. E. Some effects of guilt on compliance. *Journal of Personality and Social Psychology*, 1969, *11*, 232–239.

CARMICHAEL, L. The onset and early development of behavior. In L. Carmichael, ed., *Manual of Child Psychology.* New York: Wiley, 1954.

CARPENTER, P. A., and JUST, M. A. Integrative processes in comprehension. In D. La Berge and S. J. Samuels, eds., *Basic Processes in Reading: Perception and Comprehension.* Hillsdale, N.J.: Lawrence Erlbaum, 1977.

CASLER, L. Perceptual deprivation in institutional settings. In G. Newton and S. Levine, eds., *Early Experience and Behavior.* New York: Springer, 1967.

CAUTELA, J. Covert negative reinforcement. *Journal of Behavior Therapy and Experimental Psychiatry*, 1970, *1*, 273.

CHAIKIN, A. L. and DERLEGA, V. J. Liking for the norm-breaker in self-disclosure. *Journal of Personality*, 1974, *42*, 112–129.

CHAIKEN, S. Communicator physical attractiveness and persuasion. *Journal of Personality and Social Psychology*, 1979, *37*, 1387–1397.

CHASE, W. G., and CLARK, H. H. Mental operations in the comparison of sentences and pictures. In L. W. Gregg, ed., *Cognition in learning and memory.* New York: Wiley, 1972.

Chemical communication in mating. Interview with Dr. E. A. Boyse, Sloan-Kettering Institute, New York City. *Research Resources Reporter*, January 1979, pp. 6–8.

CHERRY, E. C. Some experiments on the recognition of speech, with one and two ears. *Journal of the Acoustical Society of America*, 1953, *25*, 975–979.

CHOMSKY, N. *Aspects of the Theory of Syntax.* Cambridge, Mass.: MIT Press, 1965.

CHOMSKY, N. *The Sound Pattern of English.* New York: Harper & Row, 1968.

CHRISTIE, R., and JAHODA, M., eds. *Studies in the Scope and Method of "The Authoritarian Personality."* New York: Free Press, 1954.

CIALDINI, R., and KENRICK, D. Altruism and hedonism: A social developmental perspective on the relationship of negative mood state and helping. *Journal of Personality and Social Psychology*, 1976, *34*, 907–914.

CHURCHMAN, C. W. Perception and deception. *Science*, 1966, *153*, 1088–1090.

CLARK. E. V. How young children describe events in time. In G. B. Flores d'Areals and W. J. M. Levelt, eds., *Advances in Psycholinguistics*. Amsterdam: North-Holland Publishing, 1970a. pp. 275–284.

CLARK, E. V. Locationals: A study of "existential," "locative," and "possessive" sentences. Working Papers in Language Universals (Stanford University), 1970b, *3*, L1–L36(b).

CLARK, E. V. On the acquisition of the meaning of before and after. *Journal of Verbal Learning and Verbal Behavior*, 1971, *10*, 266–275.

CLARK, E. V. Non-linguistic strategies and the acquisition of word meanings. *Cognition*, 1973a, *2*, 161–182.

CLARK, E. V. How children describe time and order. In C. A. Ferguson and D. I. Slobin, eds., *Studies of Child Language Development*. New York: Holt, Rinehart and Winston, 1973b.

CLARK, E. V. Some aspects of the conceptual basis for first language acquisiton. In R. L. Schiefelbusch and L. L. Lloyd., eds., *Language perspectives–Acquisition, Retardation and Intervention*. Baltimore: University Park Press, 1974.

CLARK, H. H., Inferences in comprehension. In D. LaBerge and S. J. Samuels, eds., *Basic Processes in Reading: Perception and Comprehension*. Hillsdale, N.J.: Lawrence Erlbaum, 1977.

CLARK, H. H., and CHASE, W. G. On the process of comparing sentences against pictures. *Cognitive Psychology*, 1972, *3*, 472–517.

CLARK, H. H., and CLARK, E. V. *Psychology and Language: An Introduction to Psycholinguistics*. New York: Harcourt Brace Jovanovich, 1977.

CLARK, H. H., CARPENTER, P. A., and JUST, M. A. On the meeting of semantics and perception. In W. G. Chase, ed., *Visual Information Processing*. New York: Academic Press, 1973.

CLARK, H. H., and HAVILAND, S. E. Comprehension and the given-new contract. In R. O. Freedle, ed., *Discourse Production and Comprehension*. Norwood, N.J.: Ablex, 1977.

CLARK, H. H., and LUCY, P. Understanding what is meant from what is said: A study in conversationally conveyed requests. *Journal of Verbal Learning and Behavior*, 1975, *14*, 56–72.

CLARK, K. B. Empathy: A neglected topic in psychological research. *American Psychologist*, 1980, *35*, 187–190.

CLARK, R. D., and WORD, L. E. Where is the apathetic bystander? Situational characteristics of the emergency. *Journal of Personality and Social Psychology*, 1974, *29*, 279–287.

CLARK, W. C., and BROWN, J. C. How the psychiatric patient's subjective criterion affects his sensory threshold. *Psychological Bulletin*, 1966, *65*, 358–366.

CLARKE-STEWART, K. A. And Daddy makes three. *Child Development*, 1978, *49*, 466–478.

CLEMENS, L. G. Effect of stimulus female variation on sexual performance of the male deermouse, *peromyscus manifulatus*. *Proceedings of the American Psychological Association*, seventy-fifth annual convention, 1967, 119–120.

CLEMES, S. Repression and hypnotic amnesia. *Journal of Abnormal and Social Psychology*, 1964, *69*, 62–69.

COFER, C. M. *Motivation and Emotion*. Glenville, Ill.: Scott, Foresman, 1972.

COGGINS, W. J., SWENSON, E. W., DAWSON, W. C., FERNANDEZ-SALA, A., HERNANDEZ-BOLANAS, J., and JIMINEZ-ANTILLON, C. R. Health status of chronic heavy cannabis users. In R. L. Dornbush, A. M. Freedman, and M. Fink, eds., Chronic Cannabis use, *Annals of the New York Academy of Sciences*, 1979, *282*.

COHEN, J., EVANS, G., KRANTZ, D. S., and STOKOLS, D. Physiological, motivational, and cognitive effects of aircraft noise on children. Moving from the laboratory to the field. *American Psychologist*, 1980, *35*, 231–243.

COHEN, L. G., DELOACHE, J. S., and STRAUSS, M. S. Infant visual perception. In J. Osofsky, ed., *Handbook of Infancy*. New York: Wiley, 1978.

COLE, C. L. Cohabitation in social context. In R. W. Libby and R. N. Whithurst, eds., *Marriage and Alternatives*. New York: Scott, Foresman, 1977.

COLEMAN, J. The fears of adolescents. In J. Adelson, ed., *Handbook of Adolescent Psychology*. New York: Wiley-Interscience, 1980.

COLLIGAN, D. The helpless feeling: the dangers of stress. *New York Magazine*, July 14, 1975.

COMFORT, A. *The Joy of Sex*. New York: Crown, 1972.

COMSTOCK, G., CHAFFEE, S., KATZMAN, N., McCOMBS, M., and ROBERTS, D. *Television and Human Behavior*. New York: Columbia University Press, 1978.

CONDON, W. S. Linguistic-kinesic research and dance therapy. *Proceedings of the American Dance Therapy Association*, third annual conference, 1968.

CONDRY, J. C., Jr., SIMON, M. L., and BRONFENBRENNER, U. *Characteristics of peer- and adult-oriented children*. Unpublished manuscript, Department of Child Development, Cornell University, 1968.

CONGER, J. J. *Adolescence and Youth*. New York: Harper & Row, 1973.

CONRAD, R. Speech and reading. In J. F. Kavanaugh and I. G. Mattingly, eds., *Language by Ear and Eye: The Relationship Between Speech and Reading*. Cambridge, Mass.: MIT Press, 1972.

COOK, S. W. Motives in a conceptual analysis of attitude-related behavior. In W. J. Arnold and D. Levine, eds., *Nebraska Symposium on Motivation*. Lincoln: University of Nebraska Press, 1969.

COOPER, J. R., BLOOM, F. E., and ROTH, R. H. *The Biochemical Basis of Neuropharmacology*. 2nd ed. London: Oxford University Press, 1974.

CORDARO, L., and ISON, J. R. Psychology of the scientist: X. Observer bias in classical conditioning of the planarian. *Psychological Reports*, 1963, *13*, 787–789.

COREN, S., and GIRGAS, J. Illusions and constancies. In W. Epstein, ed., *Stability and Constancy in Visual*

Perception: Mechanisms and Processes. New York: Wiley, 1977.

COREN, S., PORAC, C., and WARD, L. M. *Sensation and Perception.* New York: Academic Press, 1979.

COSTANZO, P. R. Conformity development as a function of self-blame. *Journal of Personality and Social Psychology,* 1970, *14,* 366–374.

COURTS, F. Muscular tension and memorization. *Journal of Experimental Psychology,* 1939, *25,* 235–256.

COUSINS, N. *Anatomy of an Illness.* New York: Norton, 1980.

COYNE, J. C., and WIDIGER, T. A. Toward a participatory model of psychotherapy. *Professional Psychology,* 1978, *9,* 700–710.

CRANNELL, C. W., and KØHLER, W. *Journal of the History of the Behavioral Sciences,* 1970, *6,* 267–268.

CRIDER, A. *Schizophrenia: A Biopsychological Perspective.* Hillsdale, N.J.: Lawrence Erlbaum, 1979.

CROCKETT, H.J. The achievement motive and differential occupational mobility in the United States. *American Sociological Review,* 1962, *27,* 191–194.

CRONBACH, L. J. *Essentials of Psychological Testing.* 3rd ed. New York: Harper & Row, 1970.

CROOK, C. K. Taste perception in the newborn infant. *Infant Behavior and Development,* 1978, *1,* 52–69.

CROOK, C. K., and LIPSITT, L. P. Neonatal nutritive sucking: Effects of taste stimulation upon sucking rhythms and heart rate. *Child Development,* 1976, *47,* 518–522.

CRUTCHFIELD, R. S. Conformity and character. *American Psychologist,* 1955, *10,* 191–198.

CSIKZENTMIHALYI, M. *Beyond Boredom and Anxiety.* San Francisco: Jossey-Bass, 1977.

CSIKZENTMIHALYI, M., GRAEF, R., and LARSON, R. *Age differences in the quality of subjective experience.* Paper presented at meeting of the American Psychological Association, New York City, September 1979.

CUMMING, E., and HENRY, W. *Growing Old: The Process of Disengagement.* New York: Basic Books, 1961.

D

DARLEY, C. F., TINKLENBERG, J. R., ROTH, W. T., and ATKINSON, R. C. The nature of storage deficits and state-dependent retrieval under marijuana. *Psychopharmacologia,* 1974, *37,* 139–149.

DARLEY, J. M., and BATSON, D. ". . . From Jerusalem to Jericho." A study of situational and dispositional variables in helping behavior. *Journal of Personality and Social Psychology,* 1973, *27,* 100–108.

DARLEY, J. M., and LATANÉ, B. Bystander intervention in emergencies: Diffusion of responsibility. *Journal of Personality and Social Psychology,* 1968, *8,* 377–383.

DAVIDS, A., and DeVAULT, S. Maternal anxiety during pregnancy and childbirth abnormalities. *Psychosomatic Medicine,* 1961, *23,* 444 (abstract).

DAVIDS, A., and HOLDEN, R. Consistency of maternal attitudes and personality from pregnancy to eight months following childbirth. *Developmental Psychology,* 1970, *2,* 364–366.

DAVIDS, A., and PILDNER, H. Comparison of direct and projective methods of personality assessment under different conditions of motivation. *Psychological Monographs* Vol. 72, No. 11, 1958.

DAVIDSON, J. M., and DAVIDSON, R. J., eds. *Psychobiology of Consciousness.* New York: Plenum, 1980.

DAVIDSON, R. Specificity and patterning in biobehavioral systems. *American Psychologist,* May 1978, pp. 430–435.

DAVIDSON, R., and GOLEMAN, D. The role of attention in meditation and hypnosis: A psychobiological perspective on transformations of consciousness. *International Journal of Clinical and Experimental Hypnosis,* 1977, *25,* 291–308.

DAVIDSON, R. J., HOROWITZ, M. D., SCHWARTZ, G. E., and GOODMAN, D. M. Lateral differences in the latency between finger tapping and the heart beat. *Psychophysiology,* 1980, *17,* 22-27.

DAVIDSON, R. J., and SCHWARTZ, G. E. The influence of musical training on patterns of EEG asymmetry during musical and nonmusical self-generation tasks. *Psychophysiology,* 1977, *14,* 58–63.

DAVIS, F. *Inside Intuition: What We Know About Nonverbal Communication.* New York: McGraw-Hill, 1973.

DAVIS, J. *Group Performance.* Reading, Mass.: Addison-Wesley, 1969.

DAWES, R. M., McTAVISH, J., and SHAKLEE, H. Behavior, communication, and assumptions about other people's behavior in a common dilemma situation. *Journal of Personality and Social Psychology,* 1977, *35,* 1–11.

DEAUX, K. and EMSWILLER, T. Explanations of successful performance on sex-linked tasks: What's skill for the male is luck for the female. *Journal of Personality and Social Psychology,* 1974, *29,* 80–85.

DEAUX, K., and FARRIS, E. *Attributing causes for one's performance: the effects of sex norms and outcome.* Unpublished manuscript, Purdue University, 1974.

DE BEAUVOIR, S. *The Coming of Age.* New York: Warner, 1972.

DECHARMES, R. *Personal Causation: The Internal Affective Determinants of Behavior.* New York: Academic Press, 1968.

DELGADO, J. M. R., ROBERTS, W. W., and MILLER, N. E. Learning motivated by electrical stimulation of the brain. *American Journal of Physiology,* 1954, *179,* 587–593.

DELLAS, M., and GAIER, E. L. Identification of creativity: The individual. *Psychological Bulletin,* 1970, *73,* 55–73.

DELUCIA, L. A. Effects of rocking on infant behavior. Un-pubished manuscript cited in L. P. Lipsitt, Infant learn-ing: the blooming, buzzing confusion revisited. In M. E. Meyer, ed., *Second Western Symposium on Learning: Early Learning.* Bellingham, Western Washington State College, 1971.

DEMBER, W. N. Birth order and need affiliation. *Journal of Abnormal and Social Psychology.* 1964, *68*, No. 5, 555–557.

DEMBER, W. N., EARL, R. W. and PARADISE, N. Response by rats to differential stimulus complexity. *Journal of Comparative and Physiological Psychology*, 1957, *50*, 514–518.

DEMENT, W. C. The Effect of dream deprivation. *Science,* 1960, *131*, 1705–1707.

DEMENT, W. C. *Some Must Watch While Some Must Sleep.* San Francisco: San Francisco Book Company, 1978.

DEMENT, W. C., and WOLPERT, E. A. The relation of eye movements, body mobility, and external stimuli to dream content. *Journal of Experimental Psychology,* 1958, *55*, 543–553.

DENNIS, W. Creative productivity between the ages of 20 and 80. *Journal of Gerontology,* 1966, *21*, 1–8.

DESOR, J. A., and MALLER, O. Preferences for sweet and salty in 9–15 year-olds and adult humans. *Science,* 1975, *190*, 686–687.

DEUTSCH, M., and KRAUSS, R. M. The effect of threat on interpersonal bargaining. *Journal of Abnormal and Social Psychology,* 1960, *61*, 181–189.

DE VILLIERS, J. G., and DE VILLIERS, P. A. *Language Acquisition.* Cambridge, Mass.: Harvard University Press, 1978.

DEWART, M. H. *A psychological investigation of sentence comprehension by children.* Ph.D. dissertation, University of London, 1975.

DEWSBERRY, D. A. *Comparative Animal Behavior.* New York: McGraw-Hill, 1977.

DIAMOND, M. C. Aging and cell loss: Calling for an honest count. *Psychology Today,* September 1978, *12*, 126.

DIAMOND, M. C., et al. Effects of aging and environment on the pyriform cortex, the occipital cortex, and the hip-pocampus. *Behavioral Biology,* 1977, *20*, 325–336.

DION, K., BERSCHEID, E., and WALSTER, E. What is beauti-ful is good. *Journal of Personality and Social Psy-chology,* 1972, *24*, 285–290.

DOERING, C. H., et al. Plasma testosterone levels and psy-chological measures in men over a two-month period. In R. C. Friedman, R. M. Richart, R. L. Vandewiele, and L. W. Stern, eds. *Sex differences in Human Behavior.* New York: Wiley, 1974.

DOLINSKY, R. *Human Learning.* 2nd ed. Dubuque, Iowa: Brown, 1973.

DOLLARD, J., et al. *Frustration and Aggression.* New Haven, Conn.: Yale University Press, 1939.

DOLLARD, J., and MILLER, N. E. *Personality and Psycho-therapy.* New York: McGraw-Hill, 1950.

DONALDSON, M., and BALFOUR, G. Less is more: A study of language comprehension in children. *British Jour-nal of Psychology,* 1968, *59*, 461–472.

DOOB, A. N., and GROSS, A. E. Status of frustrator as an inhibitor of horn-honking responses. *Journal of Social Psychology,* 1968, *76*, 213–218.

DORFMAN, D. D. The Cyril Burt question: new findings. *Science,* 1978, *203*, 117.

DORFMAN, D. D. Burt's tables–a reply. *Science,* 1979, *204*, 246.

DORNBUSH, R. L., FREEDMAN, A. J., and FINK, M., eds., Chronic cannabis use. *Annals of the New York Academy of Sciences,* vol. 282, 1976.

DOUVAN, E., and ADELSON, J. *The Adolescent Experience.* New York: Wiley, 1966.

DUBOS, R. Life is an endless give-and-take with earth and all her creatures. *Smithsonian,* 1970, *1*, 8–17.

DUFFY, E. *Activation and Behavior.* New York: Wiley, 1962.

DUNHAM, P.J. *Experimental Psychology: Theory and Prac-tice.* New York: Harper & Row, 1977.

DUSTIN, D. S. *How Psychologists Do Research. The Ex-ample of Anxiety.* Englewood Cliffs, N.J.: Prentice-Hall, 1969.

DUTTON, D. G., and ARAN, A. P. Some evidence for heightened sexual attraction under conditions of high anxiety. *Journal of Personality and Social Psycho-logy,* 1974, *30*, 510–517.

DWECK, C. S., and BUSH, E. S. Sex differences in learned helplessness. *Developmental Psychology,* 1976, *12*, 147–156.

DWECK, C. S., DAVIDSON, W., and NELSON, S. *Sex differ-ences in learned helplessness: The contingencies of evaluative feedback in the classroom.* Paper presented at the Society for Research in Child Development, Denver, 1975.

DYCHTWALD, K. *Bodymind.* New York: Pantheon, 1978.

E

EAGLY, A. Sex differences in influencibility. *Psychologi-cal Bulletin,* 1978, *85*, 86–116.

EDELBERG, R. Electrodermal activity of the skin. In N. Greenfield and R. Sternback, eds., *Handbook of Psychophysiology.* New York: Holt, Rinehart and Winston, 1972.

EDNEY, J. Free riders en route to disaster. *Psychology Today,* August 1979, pp. 80–97.

EDWARDS, A. L. *The Social Desirability Variable in Per-sonality Research.* New York: Dryden, 1957.

EHRENKRANZ. J., BLISS, E., and SHEARD, M. Plasma testosterone: Correlation with aggressive behavior and social dominance in man. *Psychosomatic Medicine*, 1974, *36*, 469–475.

EIBL-EIBESFELT, I. *Ethnology*. New York: Holt, Rinehart and Winston, 1970.

EIMAS, P. D., SIQUELAND, E. R., JUSCZYK, P., and VIGORITO, J. Speech perception in infants. *Science*, 1970, *171*, 303–306.

EICHORN, D. H. Biological Correlates of Behavior. In W. H. STEVENSON, (ed.), *Child Psychology*. Chicago: University of Chicago Press, 1963.

EISEN, S. V. Actor-observer differences in information inference and causal attribution. *Journal of Personality and Social Psychology*, 1979, *37*, 261–272.

EISLER M., et al. Mild high renin hypertension: Neurogenic human hypertension? *New England Journal of Medicine*, 1977, *296*, 405–411.

EKMAN, P. *The Face of Man*. New York: Garland Press, 1980.

EKMAN, P., FRIESEN, W. V., and ELLSWORTH, P. *Emotion in the Human Face*. Oxford, Eng.: Pergamon, 1972.

ELLIS, A. *Reason and Emotion in Psychotherapy*. New York: Lyle Stuart, 1962.

ELLIS, A. Rational-emotive therapy. In R. J. CORSINI, ed., *Current Psychotherapies*. Itasca, Illinois: Peacock, 1979.

ELLIS, H. C. Motor skills in learning. In H. C. Ellis, *Fundamentals of Human Learning and Cognition*. Dubuque, Iowa: Brown, 1972.

ELLIS, H. C. *Fundamentals of Human Learning and Cognition*. Dubuque, Iowa: Brown, 1972.

ENGEL, G. Emotional stress and sudden death. *Psychology Today*, November 1977, pp. 114–118.

ENGEN, T. Why the aroma lingers on. *Psychology Today*, May 1980, p. 138.

ENGEN, T., and LIPSITT, L. P. "Decrement and recovery of responses to olfactory stimuli in the human neonate. *Journal of Comparative and Physiological Psychology*, 1965, *59*, 312–316.

ENGEN, T., LIPSETT, L. P., and KAYE, H. Olfactory responses and adaptation in the human nenonate, *Journal of Comparative and Physiological Psychology*, 1963, *56*, 73–77.

ENGEN, T., and ROSS, B. M. Long-term memory of odors with and without verbal descriptions. *Journal of Experimental Psychology*, 1973, *100*, 221–227.

ENGLANDER-GOLDEN, P., WILLIS, K. A., and DIENSTABIER, R. A. Stability of perceived tension as a function of the menstrual cycle. *Journal of Human Stress*, 1977, *4*, 14–21.

ENZLE, M. E., and HARVEY, M. D. Recipient mood states and helping behavior. *Journal of Experimental and Social Psychology*, 1979, *15*, 170-182.

EPSTEIN, A. S., and RADIN, N. Motivational components related to father behavior and cognitive functioning in preschoolers. *Child Development*, 1976, *46*, 831–839.

EPSTEIN, S. The stability of behavior, II: Implications for psychological research. *American Psychologist*, 1980, *35*, 790–806.

ERIKSON, E. H. *Identity: Youth and Crisis*. New York: Norton, 1968.

ERIKSON, E. H., ed. *Youth: Change and Challenge*. New York: Basic Books, 1963.

ERON, L. D. Prescription for reduction of aggression. *American Psychologist*, 1980, *35*, 244–252.

ETAUGH, C. Effects of nonmaternal care on children: Research evidence and popular views. *American Psychologist*, 1980, *35*, 309–319.

EVARTS, E. V. Brain mechanisms of movement. *Scientific American*, 1979, *241*, 164–178.

EYSENCK, B. I. *Psychology Is About People*. London: Allan Lane, 1972.

F

FAGOT, B. I. Sex difference in toddler's behavior and reaction. *Developmental Psychology*, 1974, *10*, 554–558.

FANCHER, R. E. *Pioneers of Psychology*, New York: Norton, 1979.

FANTINO, E., and LOGAN, F. A. *The Experimental Analysis of Behavior: A Biological Perspective*. San Francisco: Freeman, 1979.

FANTZ, R. L. The origin of form perception. *Scientific American*, 1961, 450–463.

FARBEROW, N. L., and SCHNEIDMAN, E. S. *The cry for Help*. New York: McGraw-Hill, 1965.

FARINA, A., MURRAY, P.J., and GROH, T. Sex and worker acceptance of a former mental patient. *Journal of Consulting and Clinical Psychology*, 1978, *5*, 887–891.

FARKAS, G., Cohort, age, and period effects upon the employment of white females: Evidence for 1957–1968. *Demography*, 1977, *14*, 33–42.

FARKAS, G. M. An ontological analysis of behavior therapy. *American Psychologist*, 1980, *35*, 364-374.

FAZIO, R. H., ZANNA, M. P., and COOPER, J. Direct experience and attitude-behavior consistency: An information processing analysis. *Personality and Social Psychology Bulletin*, 1978, *4*, 48–51.

FEATHER, N. T. Positive and negative reactions to male and female success and failure in relation to the perceived status and sex-typed appropriateness of occupations. *Journal of Personality and Social Psychology*, 1975, *31*, 536–548.

FEATHER, N. T. Family resemblances in conservatism: Are daughters more similar to parents than sons are? *Journal of Personality*, 1978, *46*, 260–278.

FEATHER, N. T., and SIMON, J. G. Stereotypes about male and female success and failure at sex-linked occupations. *Journal of Personality*, 1976, *44*, 16–37.

FESHBACK, N. D., DILLMAN, A. S., and JORDAN, T. S. Children and television advertising: Some research and some perspectives. *Journal of Clinical Child Psychology*, 1979, *8*, 26–30.

FESTINGER, L. A theory of social comparison processes. *Human Relations*, 1954, *7*, 117–140.

FESTINGER, L. *A Theory of Cognitive Dissonance.* Evanston, Ill.: Row, Peterson, 1957.

FESTINGER, L., and CARLSMITH, J. M. Cognitive consequences of forced compliance. *Journal of Abnormal and Social Psychology*, 1959, *58*, 203–211.

FESTINGER, L., SCHACHTER, S., and BACK, K. *Social Pressures in Informal Groups: A Study of Human Factors in Housing.* New York: Harper & Row, 1950.

FIEDLER, F. E. Style or circumstance: the leadership enigma. *Psychology Today*, March 1969, pp. 38–43.

FIELD, T. M. Visual and cardiac responses to animate and inanimate faces by young term and preterm infants. *Child Development*, 1979, *50*, 188–194.

FINKELMAN, J. M., and GLASS, D. C. Reappraisal of the relationship between noise and human performance by means of a subsidiary task measure. *Journal of Applied Psychology*, 1970, *54*, 211–213.

FISHER, L. E. Relationships and sexuality in contexts and cultures: The anthropology of eros. In B. B. Wolman and J. Money, eds., *Handbook of Human Sexuality.* New York: Plenum, 1980.

FISHER, W. A., and BYRNE, D. Individual differences in affective, evaluative, and behavioral responses to an erotic film. *Journal of Applied Social Psychology*, 1978, *8*, 355–365.

FLAVELL, J. H. *Cognitive Development.* Englewood Cliffs, N. J.: Prentice-Hall, 1977.

FLEMING, T. C. A note on psychosurgery. In A. M. Nicholi, ed., *The Harvard Guide to Modern Psychiatry.* Cambridge, Mass.: Harvard University Press, 1978.

FORD, C. S., and F. A. BEACH. *Patterns of Sexual Behavior.* New York: Harper & Row, 1951.

FORER, B. R. The fallacy of personal validation: A classroom demonstration of gullibility. *Journal of Abnormal Social Psychology*, 1949, *44*, 118–123.

FOSS, D. J. Some effects of ambiguity upon sentence comprehension. *Journal of Verbal Learning and Verbal Behavior*, 1970, *9*, 699–706.

FOSTER, J. W., and ARCHER, S. J. Birth order and intelligence: An immunological interpretaton. *Perceptual and Motor Skills*, 1979, *48*, 79–83.

FOULKE, E. Listening comprehension as a function of word rate. *Journal of Communication*, 1968, *18*, 198–296.

FOULKE, E., and STICHT, T. Review of research on the intelligibility of accelerated speech. *Psychological Bulletin*, 1969, *72*, 50–62.

FOX, L. Effecting the use of efficient study habits. *Journal of Mathematics*, 1962, *1*, 75–86.

FOXX, R. M., and AZRIN, N. H. Rapid method of toilet training children. *Proceedings of the American Psychological Association, eighty-first annual convention*, 1973.

FRAIBERG, S. *Every Child's Birthright.* New York: Basic Books, 1978.

FRAMO, J. L. Marriage and marital therapy: Issues and initial interview. In M. Andolfi and I. Zerling, eds., *Dimensions of Family Therapy.* New York: Guilford Press, 1980.

FRANK, J. *Persuasion and Healing.* Baltimore: Johns Hopkins Press, 1973.

FRANKENHAEUSER, M. Coping with job stress: A psychobiological approach. *Report of the Psychology Department*, University of Stockholm, No. 532, November 1978.

FRASER, A., and WILCOX, W. The escalator illusion: A genetic component? *Nature*, 1980, *281*, 565–566.

FRASER, S. C. *Deindividuation: effects of anonymity on aggression in children.* Unpublished report, University of Southern California, 1974.

FRAUKENHAEUSER, M., MYRSTEN, A–L., and POST, B. Psychophysiological reactions to cigarette smoking, *Scandinavian Journal of Psychology*, 1970, *11*, 237–245.

FREEDMAN, J. L., CARLSMITH J. M., and SEARS, D. O. *Social Psychology.* Englewood Cliffs, N.J.: Prentice-Hall, 1970.

FREEDMAN, J. L., HERSHKA, S., and LEVY, A. Population density and pathology: Is there a relationship? *Journal of Experimental Social Psychology*, 1975, *11*, 539–552.

FRENCH, D. G. Effects of the interaction of motivation and feedback on performance. In J. W. Atkinson, ed., *Motives in Fantasy, Action, and Society.* New York: Van Nostrand, 1958.

FREUD, A. *The Ego and the Mechanisms of Defense.* New York: International Universities Press, 1937.

FREUD, S. *The Interpretation of Dreams.* New York: Macmillan, 1939.

FREUD, S. Analysis of a phobia in a five-year-old boy. In J. Strachey, ed., *Standard Edition of the Complete Psychological Works*, Vol. 10. London: Hogarth Press, 1956a.

FREUD, S. Studies in hysteria (1893–1895). In J. Strachey, ed., *Standard Edition of (His) Complete Psychological Works*, Vol. 11. London: Hogarth Press, 1955b.

FRIEDMAN M., and ROSENMAN, R. H. *Type A Behavior and Your Heart.* New York: Knopf, 1974.

FRIEDRICH, L., and STEIN, A. Prosocial television and young children: the effects of verbal learning and role playing on learning and behavior. *Child Development*, 1975, *46*, 27–38.

FRIEZE, I. Being male or female. In P. N. Middlebrook, *Social Psychology and Modern Life.* 2nd ed. New York: Knopf, 1980.

FRIEZE, I., PARSONS, J., JOHNSON, P., RUBLE, D., and ZELLMAN, G. *Women and Sex Roles: A Psychological Perspective.* New York: Norton, 1978.

FRISBY, J. P. *Seeing: Illusion, Brain and Mind.* New York: Oxford University Press, 1980.

FROMKIN, V., and RODMAN, R. *An Introduction to Language.* New York: Holt, Rhinehart and Winston, 1974.

FURTH, H. G. The influence of language on the development of concept formation in deaf children. *Journal of Abnormal and Social Psychology,* 1961, *63,* 386–389.

FURUKAWA, J. M. Cognitive processing capacity and learning mode effects in prose learning. *Journal of Education Psychology,* 1979, *69,* No. 6, 736–743.

G

GAGNON, J. H., and DAVISON, G. C. *The enhancement of sexual responsiveness in behavior therapy.* Paper presented at the annual meeting of the American Psychological Association, New Orleans, August 30, 1974.

GALIN, D. The two modes of consciousness and the two halves of the brain. In P. R. Lee, et al., *Symposium on Consciousness.* New York: Viking, 1976.

GALTON, F. *Hereditary Genius.* London: Macmillan, 1869.

GANTT, W. H., and PAVLOV, L. P.: A biographical sketch. In I. P. Pavlov, *Lectures on Conditioned Reflexes,* Volume I. New York: International Publishers, 1928 (W. H. Gantt, translator).

GARB, J. L., and STUNKARD, A. J. *American Journal of Psychiatry,* 1974, *131,* 1204.

GARCIA, J., and BRETT, L. P. Conditional responses to food odor and taste in rats and wild predators. In M. R. Kare and O. Maller, eds., *The Chemical Senses and Nutrition.* New York: Academic Press, 1977.

GARDNER, R. A., and GARDNER, B. T. Teaching sign languages to a chimpanzee. *Science,* 1969, *165,* 664–672.

GARFIELD, C. A., ed. *Psychosocial Care of the Dying Patient.* New York: McGraw-Hill, 1978.

GARMEZY, N. DSM-III never mind the psychgologists: Is it good for the children? *Clinical Psychologist,* 1978, *31,* issues 3 and 4, 1.

GARTELL, N., and MOSBACHER, D. *Sex differences in the naming of genitalia.* Unpublished manuscript, Harvard Medical School, 1979.

GAYLIN, W. *Feelings: Our Vital Signs.* New York: Harper & Row, 1979.

GAZZANIGA, M. S. The split brain in man. *Scientific American,* 1967, *217,* 24–29.

GAZZANIGA, M. S. *The Bisected Brain.* New York: Appleton-Century-Crofts, 1970.

GAZZANIGA, M. S. One brain—two minds? *Scientific American,* 1972, *60,* 311–317.

GEEN, R. G. Effects of attack and uncontrollable noise on aggression. *Journal of Research in Personality,* 1978, *12,* 15–29.

GEER, J. H. Direct measurement of genital responding. *American Psychologist,* 1975, *30,* 415–418.

GEER, J. H., and FUHR, R. Cognitive factors in sexual arousal: The role of distraction. *Journal of Consulting and Clinical Psychology,* 1976, *44,* 238–243.

GEER, J. H., MOROKOFF, P., and GREENWOOD, P. Sexual arousal in women: The development of a measurement device for vaginal blood volume. *Archives of Sexual Behavior,* 1974, *3,* 559–564.

GEER, J. H., and QUARTARARO, J. D. Vaginal blood volume responses during masturbation and resultant orgasm. *Archives of Sexual Behavior,* 1976, *5,* 403–413.

GERBNER, G. Violence in television drama: Trends and symbolic functions. In G. A. Comstock and E. A. Rubinstein, eds., *Television and Social Behavior.* Washington, D.C.: U.S. Government Printing Office, 1972.

GERGEN, K. J. The codification of research ethics: Views of a doubting Thomas. *American Psychologist,* 1973, *28,* 907–912.

GERGEN, K. J., GERGEN, N. M., and BARTON, W. H. Deviance in the dark. *Psychology Today,* October 1973, pp. 129–130.

GERSCHWIND, N. *The Development of the Brain and the Evolution of Language.* Washington, D.C.: Georgetown University, Institute of Language and Linguistics, 1964.

GESELL, A. The ontogenesis of infant behavior. In L. Carmichael, ed., *Manual of Child Psychology.* 2nd ed. New York: Wiley, 1954.

GIBBONS, P. A., and KOPELMAN, R. E. Maternal employment as a determinant of fear of success in females. *Psychological Reports,* 1977, *40,* 1200–1202.

GIBSON, J. J. *The Senses Considered As Perceptual Systems.* Boston: Houghton Mifflin, 1966.

GLASS, D. C. *Behavior Patterns, Stress, and Coronary Disease.* Hillsdale, N.J.: Lawrence Erlbaum, 1977.

GLASS, D. C., and SINGER, J. E. *Urban Stress.* New York: Academic Press, 1972.

GLICK, J. Cognitive development in cross-cultural perspective. In F. D. Horowitz, ed., *Review of Child Development Research.* Vol. 4. Chicago: University of Chicago Press, 1975.

GOETHALS, G. R., COOPER, J., and NAFICY, A. Role of foreseen, foreseeable, and unforeseeable consequences in the arousal of cognitive dissonance. *Journal of Personality and Social Psychology,* 1979, *37,* 1179–1185.

GOFFMAN, E. *Stigma: Notes on the Management of Spoiled Identity.* Englewood Cliffs, N.J.: Prentice-Hall, 1963.

GOLD, D., and ANDRES, D. Developmental comparisons between 10-year-old children with employed and nonemployed mothers. *Child Development,* 1978, *49,* 75.

GOLDBERG, P. Are women prejudiced against women? *Transaction,* 1968, *5,* 28–39.

GOLDFARB, W. Effects of psychological deprivaton in infancy and subsequent stimulation. *American Journal of Psychiatry*, 1945, *102*, 18–33.

GOLDIAMOND, I. Self-control procedures in personal behavior problems. *Psychological Reports*, 1965, *17*, 18–46.

GOLDIAMOND, I. A diary of self-modification. *Psychology Today*, November 1973, pp. 95–102.

GOLDSTEIN, M. J., KANT, H. S., and HARTMAN, J. J. *Pornography and sexual deviance*. Berkeley: University of California Press, 197 .

GOLEMAN, D. *The Varieties of the Meditative Experience*. New York: Dutton, 1977.

GOLEMAN, D. Who's mentally ill? *Psychology Today*, January 1978, pp. 34–41.

GOLEMAN, D. 1,528 little geniuses and how they grew. *Psychology Today*, February 1980, pp. 28–44.

GOLEMAN, D., and BUSH, S. The liberation of sexual fantasy. *Psychology Today*, October 1977, pp. 48–53, 104–107.

GOLEMAN, D., and ENGEL, J. A feeling of falling. *Psychology Today*, November 1976, pp. 107–108.

GOLEMAN, D. J., and SCHWARTZ, G. E. Meditation as an intervention in stress reactivity. *Journal of Consulting and Clinical Psychology*, 1976, *44*, 456–466.

GOODMAN, 1976. Cited in Herzog, Bachman, and Johnston, 1979. Paid work, child care, and housework: A national survey of high school seniors' preferences for sharing responsibilities between husband and wife. Unpublished report, University of Michigan, February 1979.

GOTLIB, I. H., and ASARNOW, R. F. Interpersonal and impersonal problem-solving skills in mildly and clinically depressed university students. *Journal of Consulting and Clinical Psychology*, 1979, *47*, 86–95.

GOTTLIEB, G. *Neural and Behavioral Specificity*. New York: Academic Press, 1976.

GOULD, S. J. Jensen's last stand. *The New York Review of Books*, May 1, 1980, pp. 38–44.

GREEN, D. M., and SWETS, J. A. *Signal Detection Theory and Psychophysics*. New York: Wiley, 1966.

GREENBERG, B. S., ATKIN, C. K., EDISON, N. G., and KORZENNY, F. *Pro-social and Anti-social Behaviors on Commercial Television in 1975–76*. Washington, D.C.: U.S. Office of Child Development, 1977.

GRIEF, E. F. A comparison of individual and group parent-child interaction training. *Dissertation Abstracts International*, 1978, *39*, 1436.

GRINDER, R. E. *Adolescence*, New York: Wiley, 1973.

GRINSPOON, L. *Marijuana Reconsidered*. Boston: Harvard University Press, 1977.

GRINSPOON, L., and BAKALAR, J. B. *Cocaine: A Drug and Its Social Evolution*. New York: Basic Books, 1977.

GROF, S. *Principles of LSD Psychotherapy*. New York: Hunter House, 1979.

GUERIN, P. J., ed., *Family therapy*. New York: Gardner Press, 1976.

GUNNAR-VON GNETCHEN, M. R. Changing a frightening toy into a pleasant toy by allowing the infant to control its actions. *Developmental Psychology*, 1978, *14*, 157–162.

GUSTAVSON, C. R., and GARCIA J. Aversive conditioning: Pulling a gag on the wild coyote. *Psychology Today*, August 1974, pp. 68–72.

H

HABER, R. N. Eidetic images. *Scientific American*, 1969, *220*, 36–44.

HAGBERG, B. Defects of immediate memory related to the cerebral blood flow distribution. *Brain and Language*, 1978, *5*, 366–377.

HAITH, M. M., BERGMAN, T., and MOORE, M. J. Eye contact and face scanning in early infancy. Unpublished manuscript, University of Denver, 1977. Cited in Heatherington, E. M., and Parke, R. D. *Child Psychology: A Contemporary Viewpoint*, 1979.

HALEY, J. *Leaving Home*. New York: McGraw-Hill, 1980.

HALL, C. S., and LINDZEY, G. *Theories of Personality*. 3rd ed. New York: Wiley, 1978.

HALL, C. *The Meaning of Dreams*. New York: McGraw-Hill, 1971.

HALL, D. T., and LAWLER, E. E. Job pressures and research performance. In I. L. Janis, ed., *Current Trends in Psychology*. Los Altos, Calif.: E. William Kaufmann, 1977.

HALL, E. T. *The Hidden Dimension*. New York: Doubleday, 1966.

HALL, G. S. *Founders of Modern Psychology*. New York: D. Appleton, 1924.

HALPERIN, K. M., and SNYDER, C. R. Effects of enhanced psychological test feedback on treatment outcome: Therapeutic implications of the Barnum effect. *Journal of Consulting and Clinical Psychology*, 1979, *47*, 140–146.

HAPKIEWICZ, W. G. Children's reactions to cartoon violence. *Journal of Clinical Child Psychology*, 1979, *8*, 30–34.

HARDIN, G. *Population, Evolution, and Birth Control: A Collage of Controversial Ideas*. 2nd ed. San Francisco: Freeman, 1969.

HARDIN, G., and BADEN, J. *Managing the Commons*. San Francisco: Freeman, 1977.

HARE, R. D. *Psychopathy: Therapy and Research.* New York: Wiley, 1970.

HARITON, E. B., and SINGER, J. L. Women's fantasies during sexual intercourse: Normative and theoretical implications. *Journal of Consulting and Clinical Psychology*, 1974, *42*, 313–322.

HARLOW, H. F., and HARLOW, M. K. Learning to love. *Scientific American*, 1966, *54*, 244–272.

HARLOW, H. F., and KUENEE, M. Learning to think. *Scientific American*, 1949, *181*, 36–39.

HARRELL, J. P. Psychological factors and hypertension. A status report. *Psychological Bulletin*, 1980, *87*, 482–501.

HARRIS, B. Whatever happened to Little Albert? *American Psychologist*, 1979, *34*, 151–160.

HARRIS, T. A. *I'm Ok—You're Ok.* New York: Harper & Row, 1969.

HART, C., and HOLMES, T. H. *College life change score.* Unpublished report, University of Washington, n.d.

HARTMANN, E. L. *The Functions of Sleep.* New Haven, Conn.: Yale University Press, 1973.

HASSETT, J. *A Primer of Psychophysiology.* San Francisco: Freeman, 1978.

HASSETT, J. Sex and smell. *Psychology Today*, March 1978, pp. 40–45.

HAVIGHURST, R. J., NEUGARTEN, B. L., and TOBIN, S. S. Disengagement and patterns of aging. In B. L. Neugarten, ed., *Middle Age and Aging.* Chicago: University of Chicago Press, 1975.

HAYDEN, B., and SILVERSTEIN, R. The effects of tachistoscopic Oedipal stimulation on competitive dart-throwing. *Journal of Abnormal Psychology*, in press.

HEATHERINGTON, E. M. Divorce: A child's perspective. *American Psychologist*, 1979a, *34*, 851–858.

HEATHERINGTON, E. M. *Children and divorce.* Paper presented at the annual meeting of the American Psychological Association, New York City, 1979b.

HEATHERINGTON, E. M., COX, M., and COX, R. The development of children in mother-headed families. In H. Hoffman and D. Reiss, eds., *The American Family: Dying or Developing?* New York: Plenum, 1978.

HEATHERINGTON, E. M., and PARKE, R. D. *Child Psychology: A Contemporary Viewpoint.* 2nd ed. New York: McGraw-Hill, 1979.

HEBB, D. O. *A Textbook of Psychology.* Philadelphia: Saunders, 1966.

HEIDBREDER, E. *Seven Psychologies.* New York: Appleton-Century-Crofts, 1961.

HEIDER, F. *The Psychology of Interpersonal Relations.* New York: Wiley, 1958.

HEIMAN, J. R. The physiology of erotica: Women's sexual arousal. *Psychology Today*, April 1975, pp. 90–94.

HELD, R., and HEIN, A. Movement-produced stimulation in the development of visually guided behavior. *Journal of Comparative and Physiological Psychology*, 1963, *56*, 872–876.

HEMSLEY, D. R. A two-state model of attention in schizo-phrenic research. *British Journal of Social and Clinical Psychology*. 1975, *14*, 81–89.

HENDRICK, C. Effects of salience of stimulus in consistency on impression formation. *Journal of Personality and Social Psychology*, 1972, *22*, 219–222.

HENLE, M. One man against the Nazis—Wolfgang Køhler. *American Psychologist*, 1978, *33*, 939–944.

HERINK, R., ed., *The Psychotherapy Handbook.* New York: New American Library, 1980.

HERON, W. The pathology of boredom, *Scientific American*, 1957, *196*, 52–56.

HERRNSTEIN, R. I.Q. *Atlantic Monthly*, September 1971, pp. 43–64.

HERZOG, A. R., BACHMAN, J. G., and JOHNSTON, L. D. Paid work, child care, and housework: A national survey of high school seniors' preferences for sharing responsibilities between husband and wife. Unpublished report, University of Michigan, February 1979.

HESS, E. H. Imprinting. *Early Experience and the Developmental Psychology of Attachment.* New York: Van Nostrand, 1973.

HESS, R. D., and CAMARA, K. A., 1979a. In Heatherington, 1979b.

HESS, R. D., and CAMARA, K. A. Post-divorce family relations as mediating factors in the consequences of divorce for children. *Journal of Social Issues*, 1979b, *35*, 79–96.

HIGGINS, E. T., RHODEWALT, F., and ZANNA, M. P. Dissonance motivation: Its nature, persistence, and reinstatement. *Journal of Experimental and Social Psychology*, 1979, *15*, 16–34.

HILGARD, E. *Hypnotic Susceptibility.* New York: Harcourt Brace Jovanovich, 1965.

HILGARD, E. *Divided Consciousness: Mutiple Controls on Human Thought and Action.* New York: Wiley, 1977.

HILGARD, J. *Personality and Hypnosis: A Study of Imaginative Involvement.* Chicago: University of Chicago Press, 1970.

HILL, C. T., RUBIN, Z., and PEPLAU, L. A. Breakups before marriage: The end of 103 affairs. *Journal of Social Issues*, 1976, *32*, 147–168.

HOCK, E. Working and nonworking mothers with infants: Perceptions of their careers, their infants' needs, and satisfaction with mothering. *Developmental Psychology*, 1978, *4*, 37–43.

HOFFMAN, H. S., and DEPARLO, P. Behavioral control by an imprinting stimulus. *American Scientist*, 1977, *65*, 58–66.

HOFFMAN, L. W. Early childhood experiences and women's achievement motives. *Journal of Social Issues*, 1972, *28*, 129–155.

HOFFMAN, L. W. Changes in family roles, socialization, and sex differences. *American Psychologist*, 1977, *32*, 644–657.

HOFFMAN, L. W. Fear of success in 1965 and 1974: A follow-up study. *Journal of Consulting and Clinical Psychology*, 1977, *45*, 310–321.

HOLMES, T. H. Life situations, emotions, and disease. *Psychosomatics*, 1978, *19*, 747–754.

HOLMES, T. H., and MASUDA, M. Life changes and illness susceptibility. In B. S. Dohrenwend and B. P. Dohrenwend, eds., *Stressful Life Events: Their Nature and Effects*. New York: Wiley, 1974.

HOLMES, T. H., and RAHE, R. H. The social readjustment rating scale. *Journal of Psychosomatic Research*, 1967, *11*, 213–218.

HOMANS, G. *Social Behavior: Its Elementary Forms*. New York: Harcourt Brace, 1961.

HONZIK, M. P. Values and limitations of infant tests: an overview. In M. Lewis, ed., *Origins of Intelligence*. New York: Plenum, 1976.

HOOK, E. B. Behavioral implications of the human XYY genotype. *Science*, 1973, *179*, 139–150.

HORNER, M. S. *Sex differences in achievement motivation and performance in competitive and noncompetitive situations*. Ph.D. dissertation, University of Michigan, 1968.

HORNEY, K. *Neurotic Personality of Our Time*. New York: Norton, 1937.

HORROCKS, J. E., and BUKER, M. E. A study of the friendship fluctuations of preadolescents. *Journal of Genetic Psychology*, 1951, *78*, 131–144.

HOVLAND, C. I., and JANIS, I. L.,eds. *Personality and Persuasibility*. New Haven, Conn.: Yale University Press, 1959.

HOVLAND, C. I., LUMSDAINE, A., and SHEFFIELD, F. *Experiments on Mass Communication*. Princeton, N.J.: Princeton University Press, 1949.

HOVLAND, C. I., and WEISS, W. The influence of source credibility on communication effectiveness. *Public Opinion Quarterly*, 1951, *15*, 635–650.

HUBEL, D. H., and WIESEL, T. N. Receptive fields of cells in striate cortex of visually inexperienced kittens, *Journal of Neurophysiology*, 1963, *26*, 994–1002.

HUBEL, D. H., and WIESEL, T. N. Brain mechanisms of vision. *Scientific American*, 1979, *241*, 150–162.

HUDSON, L. *Human Beings*. New York: Doubleday, 1975.

HUNT, M. *Sexual Behavior in the 1970s*. Chicago: Playboy, 1974.

HUTT, C. Effects of stimulus novelty on manipulatory exploration in an infant. *Journal of Child Psychology and Psychiatry and Allied Disciplines*, 1967, *8*, 241–247.

HUTTENLOCHER, J. The origins of language comprehension. In R. L. Solso, ed., *Theories in Cognitive Psychology*. Potomac, Md.: Lawrence Erlbaum, 1974.

HUTTENLOCHER, J., EISENBERG, K., and STRAUSS, S. Comprehension: Relation between perceived actor and logical subject. *Journal of Verbal Learning and Verbal Behavior*, 1968, *7*, 300–304.

HUTTENLOCHER, J., and WEINER, S. L. Comprehension of instructions in varying contexts. *Cognitive Psychology*, 1971, *2*, 369–385.

I

ICKES, W., and BARNES, R. The role of sex and self-monitoring in unstructured dyadic situations. *Journal of Personality and Social Psychology*, 1977, *35*, 315–330.

IMMELMANN, K. Sexual and other long-term aspects of imprinting in birds and other species. In D. S. Hehrman, R. A. Hinde, and E. Shaw, eds., *Advances in the Study of Behavior*. Vol. 4. New York: Academic Press, 1972.

INGRAM, D. Surface contrast in children's speech. *Journal of Child Language*, 1975, *2*, 287–292.

Institute for Social Research Newsletter. New survey shows whites resist integration. Summer 1979, pp. 4–5.

ISEN, A. M. Success, failure, attraction and reaction to others: The warm glow of success. *Journal of Personality and Social Psychology*, 1970, *15*, 294–301.

ISEN, A. M., HORN, N., and ROSENHAND, D. L. Effects of success and failure on children's generosity. *Journal of Personality and Social Psychology*, 1973, *27*, 239–247.

ISEN, A. M., and LEVIN, P. F. Effect of feeling good on helping: Cookies and kindness. *Journal of Personality and Social Psychology*, 1972, *21*, 384–388.

IVERSEN, L. L. The chemistry of the brain. *Scientific American*, 1979, *241*, 134–148.

IZZETT, R. Authoritarianism and attitudes toward the Vietnam War as reflected in behavioral and self-report measures. *Journal of Personality and Social Psychology*, 1971, *17*, 145–148.

J

JACKLIN, C. N., and MACCOBY, E. E. Social behavior at thirty-three months in same-sex and mixed sex dyads. *Child Development*, 1978, *49*, 557–569.

JACKSON, J. M., and SALTZSTEIN, H. D. The effect of person-group relationships on conformity processes. *Journal of Abnormal and Social Psychology*, 1958, *57*, 17–24.

JAFFE, P. G., THOMPSON, J. K., and PAQUIN, M. J. Immediate family crisis intervention as preventative mental health: The family consultant service. *Professional Psychology*, November 1978, pp. 551–560.

JANDA, L. H., O'GRADY, K. E., and CAPPS, C. F. Fear of success in males and females in sex-linked occupations. *Sex Roles*, 1978, *4*, 43–50.

JANIS, I. L. Effects of fear arousal on attitude change: Recent developments in theory and experimental research. In L. Berkowitz, ed., *Advances in Experimental Social Psychology*. Vol. 3. New York: Academic Press, 1967.

JANIS, I. L. *Victims of Group Think: A Psychological Study of Foreign-Policy Decisions and Fiascoes*. Boston: Houghton Mifflin, 1972.

JANIS, I. L., KAYE, D., and KIRSCHNER, P. Facilitating effects of "eating-while-reading" on responsiveness to persuasive communication. *Journal of Personality and Social Psychology*, 1965, *1*, 181–186.

JEFFREY, R. W., BENDER, M., and WING, R. R. Weight loss and behavior change 1 year after behavioral treatment for obesity. *Journal of Consulting and Clinical Psychology*, 1978, *46*, 368–369.

JENCKS, C., et al. *Inequality: A Reassessment of the Effect of Family and Schooling in America*. New York: Basic Books, 1972.

JENCKS, C., et al. *Who Gets Ahead?— The Determinants of Success in America*. New York: Basic Books, 1979.

JENKINS, J. G., and DALLENBACH, K. M. Obliviscence during sleep and waking. *American Journal of Psychology*, 1924, *35*, 605–612.

JENNINGS, M. K., and NIEMI, R. G. The transmission of political values from parent to child. *American Political Science Review*, 1968, *62*, 169–184.

JENSEN, A. R. The differences are real. *Psychology Today*, December 1973, pp. 79–86.

JENSEN, A. R. The current status of the IQ controversy. *Australian Psychologist*, 1978, *13*, 7–27.

JENSEN, A. R. *Bias in Mental Testing*. New York: Free Press, 1980.

JOHN, E. R. How the brain works. *Psychology Today*, May 1976, pp. 48–51.

JOHN, E. R. Multipotentiality: A statistical theory of brain function. In J. M. Davidson and R. J. Davidson, eds., *Psychobiology of Consciousness*. New York: Plenum, 1980.

JOHNSON, A. J. Comment on Gergen. *American Psychologist*, 1974, *29*, 470.

JOHNSON, R. D., and DOWNING, L. L. Deindividuation and valence of cues: Effects on prosocial and antisocial behavior. *Journal of Personality and Social Psychology*, 1979, *37*, 1532–1538.

JOHNSTON, L., and BACHMAN, J. Monitoring the future: A continuing study of the life styles and values of youth. Ann Arbor, Mich.: Institute for Social Research, 1975.

JOHNSTON, L. D., BACHMAN, J. G., and O'MALLEY, P. M. *Drug use among American high school students*. U.S. Department of Health, Education, and Welfare, National Institute on Drug Abuse, 1977.

JONES, E. E. *Ingratiation: A Social Psychological Analysis*. New York: Appleton-Century-Crofts, 1964.

JONES, E. E., BELL, L., and ARONSON, E. The reciprocation of attraction from similar and dissimilar others: A study in person perception and evaluation. In C. G. McClintock, ed., *Experimental Social Psychology*. New York: Holt, Rinehart and Winston, 1971.

JONES, E. E., KANOUSE, D. E., KELLEY, H. H., NISBETT, R. E., VALINS, S., and WEINER, B. *Attribution: Perceiving the Causes of Behavior*. New York: General Learning Press, 1972.

JONES, K. L., SMITH, D. W., ULLELAND, C. N., and STREISSGUTH, A. P. Patterns of malformation in offspring of chronic alcoholic mothers. *Lancet*, 1973, *1*, 1267.

JONES, M. C. Psychological correlates of somatic development. *Child Development*, 1965, *36*, 899–911.

JONES, M. C. The later careers of boys who were early- or late-maturing. *Child Development*, 1957, *28*, 87–111.

JONES, R. A. *Self-fulfilling prophecies*. Hillsdale, N.J.: Lawrence Erlbaum, 1977.

JOURARD, S. *The Transparent Self*. New York: Van Nostrand, 1964.

JOURARD, S. *Self-Disclosure: An Experimental Analysis of the Transparent Self*. New York: Wiley, 1971.

JUNG, C. G. *Collected Works of C. G. Jung*. rev. ed. Princeton, N.J.: Princeton University Press, 1970.

JUST, M. A., and CARPENTER, P. A. Comparative studies of comprehension: An investigation of Chinese, Norwegian, and English. *Memory and Cognition*, 1975, *3*, 465–473.

JUST, M. A., and CARPENTER, P. A., eds. *Cognitive Processes in Comprehension*. Hillsdale, N.J.: Lawrence Erlbaum, 1977.

K

KAATS, G. R., and DAVIS, K. E. The dynamics of sexual behavior of college students. *Journal of Marriage and the Family*, 1970, *32*, 390–399.

KAGAN, J. Personality development. In P. London and D. Rosenhan, eds., *Foundations of Abnormal Psychology*. New York: Holt, Rinehart and Winston, 1968

KAGAN, J. *Change and Continuity in Infancy*. New York: Wiley, 1971.

KAGAN, J., KEARSLEY, R. B., and ZELAZO, P. R. *Infancy: Its Place in Human Development*. Cambridge, Mass.: Harvard University Press, 1978.

KAGAN, J., and KLEIN, R. Cross-cultural perspectives on early development. *American Psychologist*, 1973, *28*, 947–961.

KAHLE, L. R., and BERMAN, J. J. Attitudes cause behaviors: A cross-lagged panel analysis. *Journal of Personality and Social Psychology*, 1979, *37*, 315–326.

KAHN, E., FISHER, C., and EDWARDS, A. Night terrors and anxiety dreams. In A. M. Arkin, J. S. Antrobus, and S. J. Ellman, eds. *The Minds in Sleep*. New York: Lawrence Erlbaum, 1978.

KAMIN, L. J. *The Science and Politics of I.Q.* Potomac, Md.: Lawrence Erlbaum, 1974.

KASAMATSU, A., and HIRAI, T. An EEG study on the Zen meditation (Zazen). *Folio Psychiatry & Neurology Japan*, 1966, *20*, 315–336.

KATCHADOURIAN, H. A., and LUNDE, D. T. *Fundamentals of Human Sexuality*. New York: Holt, Rinehart and Winston, 1975.

KATZ, R. J., and LIEBLER, L. GABA involvement in memory consolidation: Evidence from posttrial amino-oxyacetic acid. *Psychopharmacology*, 1978, *56*, 191–193.

KAUFMAN, L., and ROCK, I. The moon illusion. *Scientific American*, 1962, *207*, 120–130.

KAUFMANN, H. *Introduction to the Study of Human Behavior*. Philadelphia: Saunders, 1968.

KAYE, H. *Male Survival: Masculinity Without Myth*. New York: Grosset & Dunlap, 1974.

KEESEY, R. E., and POWLEY, T. L. Hypothalamic regulation of body weight. *American Scientist*, 1975, *63*, 558–565.

KELLEY, H. H. *Causal Schemata and the Attribution Process*. Morristown, N.J.: General Learning Press, 1972.

KELLEY, H. H. The processes of causal attribution. *American Psychologist*, 1973, *28*, 107–128.

KELLEY, H. H., and THIBAUT, J. Group problem solving. In G. Lindzey and E. Aronson, eds., *The Handbook of Social Psychology*. Vol. 4. Reading, Mass.: Addison-Wesley, 1969.

KELLEY, H. H., and VOLKART, E. H. The resistance to change of group-anchored attitudes. *American Sociological Review*, 1952, *17*, 453–456.

KELMAN, H. C. Compliance, identification, and internalization: Three processes of attitude change. *Journal of Conflict Resolution*, 1958, *2*, 51–60

KELMAN, H. C. Processes of opinion change. *Public Opinion Quarterly*, 1961, *25*, 57–78.

KENNEDY, E. Are we short-changing the mentally ill? *New York Times*, October 28, 1978, p. 27.

KENNEDY, W. A. *Child Psychology*. Englewood Cliffs, N.J.: Prentice-Hall, 1971.

KENRICK, D. T., BAUMANN, A., and CIALDINI, R. B. A step in the socialization of altruism on hedonism: Effects of negative mood on children's generosity under public and private conditions. *Journal of Personality and Social Psychology*, 1979, *37*, 737–744.

KENRICK, D. T., and CIALDINI, R. B. Romantic attraction: Misattribution versus reinforcement explanations.

Journal of Personality and Social Psychology, 1977, *35*, 381–391.

KESSEN, W., HAITH, M. M., and SALAPATEK, P. H. Human infancy: A bibliography and guide. In P. H. Mussen, ed., *Carmichael's Manual of Child Psychology*. Vol. 1. 3rd ed. New York: Wiley, 1970.

KESSEN, W., and LEUTZENDORFF, A. M. The effect of non-nutritive sucking on movement in the human newborn. *Journal of Comparative and Physiological Psychology*, 1963, *56*, 69–72.

KETY, S. S., et al. A sustained effect of electroconvulsive shock on the turnover of norepinephrine in the central nervous system of the rat. *Publication of the Proceedings of the National Academy of Science*, 1967, *58*, 1249–1254.

KIMBLE, G. A. *How to Use (and Misuse) Statistics*. Englewood Cliffs, N.J.: Prentice-Hall, 1978.

KIMMEL, D. *Adulthood and Aging*. New York: Wiley, 1974

KINSBOURNE, M. Biological determinants of functional bisymmetry and asymmetry. In M. Kinsbourne, ed., *Asymmetrical Function of the Brain*. Cambridge: Cambridge University Press, 1978.

KINSBOURNE, M. *An organizing principle for distinguishing between the function of the two cerebral hemispheres*. Paper presented at the Society for Research in Child Development, Work Group on the Development of Emotions and Cerebral Asymmetry, Tarrytown, N.Y., October 1980.

KINSEY, A. C., POMEROY, W. B., and MARTIN, C. E. *Sexual Behavior in the Human Male*. Philadelphia: Saunders, 1948.

KINSEY, A. C., POMEROY, W. B., and MARTIN, C. E. *Sexual Behavior in the Human Female*. Philadelphia: Saunders, 1953.

KLAUS, M. H., and KENNELL, J. H. *Maternal-infant bonding*. St. Louis: Mosby, 1976.

KLEINMAN, R. A. The development of voluntary cardiovascular control. *Dissertation Abstracts International*, 1971, *31*, 5666.

KLING, J. W., and RIGGS, L. A., eds. *Woodworth and Schlosberg's Experimental Psychology*. 2 vols. 3rd ed. New York: Holt, Rinehart and Winston, 1972.

KLUCKHOHN, H. C., and MURRAY, H. A., eds. *Personality in Nature, Society, and Culture*. New York: Knopf, 1948.

KNOTT, J. R., PLATT, E. P., ASHBY, M. C., and GOTTLIEB, J. S. A familial evaluation of the electroencephalogram of parents with primary behavior disorder and psychopathic personalities. *EEG and Clinical Neurophysiology*, 1963, *9*, 263–370.

KOHLBERG, L. The development of children's orientation toward a moral order, I. Sequence in the development of moral thought. *Vita Humana*, 1963, *6*, 11–33.

KOHLBERG, L. Development of moral character and moral ideology. In M. L. Hoffman and L. W. Hoffman, eds., *Review of Child Development Research*. Vol. 1. New York: Russell Sage Foundation, 1964.

KOHLBERG, L. A cognitive-developmental analysis of children's sex-role concepts and attitudes. In E. E. Maccoby ed., *The Development of Sex Differences*. Palo Alto, Calif.: Stanford University Press, 1966.

KÖHLER, I. Experiments with goggles. *Scientific American*, 1962, *206*, 62–72.

KÖHLER, W. *Gestalt Psychology*. New York: Liveright, 1929.

KOLB, B., and WHISHAL, I. Q. *Fundamentals of Human Neuropsychology*. San Francisco: Freeman, 1980.

KOPFSTEIN, J. M., and NEALE, J. M. A multivariate study of attention dysfunction in schizophrenia. *Journal of Abnormal Psychology*, 1972, *80*, 294–299.

KORCHIN, S. *Modern Clinical Psychology*. New York: Basic Books, 1976.

KOSS, M. P. Length of psychotherapy for clients seen in private practice. *Journal of Consulting and Clinical Psychology*, 1979, *47*, 210–212.

KOVAC, L. Critical analysis of chemical theories of memory. *Studia psychologica*, 1977, *19*, 191–200.

KREUZ, L. E., and ROSE, A. M. Assessment of aggressive behavior and plasma testosterone in a young criminal population. *Psychosomatic Medicine*, 1972, *34*, 321–332.

KRINGLEN, E. *Heredity and Environment in the Functional Psychosis: An Epidermiological-Clinical Twin Study*. Oslo: Universitforlaget, 1967.

KRONSTADT, D., OBERKLAID, F., FERB, F. T., and SWARTZ, J. P. Infant behavior and maternal adaptations in the first six months of life. *American Journal of Orthopsychiatry*, 1979, *49*, 454–464.

KRUMBOLTZ, J. D., and THORESEN, C. E., eds. *Behavioral Counseling*. New York: Holt, Rinehart and Winston, 1969.

KUBLER-ROSS, E. *On Death and Dying*. New York: Macmillan, 1970.

KÜNNAPAS, T. M. Multidimensional similarity of letters. *Reports from the Psychological Laboratories of the University of Stockholm*, No. 266 (1968).

KUSUMO, K. S., and VAUGHN, M. Effects of lithium salts on memory. *British Journal of Psychiatry*, 1977, *131*, 453–457.

L

LACHMAN, R., LACHMAN, J. L., and BUTTERFIELD, E. C. *Cognitive psychology and information processing*. New York: Halstead Press, 1979.

LAMB, M. E. Twelve-month-olds and their parents: Interaction in a laboratory playroom. *Developmental Psychology*, 1976, *12*, 237–244.

LAMB, M. E. Father-infant and mother-infant interaction in the first year of life. *Child Development*, 1977, *48*, 167–181.

LAMB, M. E. Paternal influences and the father's role: A personal perspective. *American Psychologist*, 1979, *34*, 938–943.

LAMB, M. E. Influence of the child on marital quality and family interaction during the prenatal, perinatal and infancy periods. In R. M. Lerner and G. D. Spanier, eds., *Contribution of the Child to Marital Quality and Family Interaction Through the Life-span*. New York: Academic Press, in press.

LAMB, M. E., OWEN, M. T., and CHASE-LANSDALE, L. The father-daughter relationship: Past, present, and future. In C. B. Kopp and M. Kirkpatrick, eds., *Becoming Female*. New York: Plenum, 1979.

LANCE, J. W. *Headache*. New York: Scribner's, 1975.

LANGACKER, R. W. *Language and Its Structure*. New York: Harcourt, Brace and World, 1968.

LANGER, E. J., and ABELSON, R. P. A patient by any other name...: Clinical group differences in labelling bias. *Journal of Consulting and Clinical Psychology*, 1974, *42*, 4–9.

LARNED, J. Do you take Valium? *Ms.*, November 1975, pp. 26–28.

LARSON, L. E. *The relative influence of parent-adolescent affect in predicting the salience hierarchy among youth*. Paper presented at the annual meeting of the National Council on Family Relations, Chicago, October 1970.

LATANÉ, B., and DARLEY, J. M. *The Unresponsive Bystander: Why Doesn't He Help?* New York: Appleton-Century-Crofts, 1970.

LATANÉ, B., and DARLEY, J. M. Help in a crisis: Bystander response to an emergency. In J. W. Thibault, J. T. Spence, and R. C. Carson, eds., *Contemporary Topics in Social Psychology*. Morristown, N.J.: General Learning Press, 1976.

LATANÉ, B., and RODIN, J. A lady in distress: Inhibiting effects of friends and strangers on bystander intervention. *Journal of Experimental Social Psychology*, 1969, *5*, 189–202.

LAWLESS, H. L., and ENGEN, T. Associations to odors: Interference, mnemonics, and verbal labeling. *Journal of Experimental Psychology: Human Learning and Memory*, 1977, *3*, 52–59.

LAZARUS, A. A. Multimodal behavior therapy: Treating the basic id. *Journal of Nervous and Mental Disease*, 1973, *156*, 404–411.

LAZARUS, R. S. *Psychological Stress and the Coping Process*. New York: McGraw-Hill, 1966.

LAZARUS, R. S. *The power of positive thinking*. Conference paper presented at Haifa University, June 10, 1979.

LAZARUS, R. S. Positive denial: The case of not facing reality. *Psychology Today*, November 1979.

LAZARUS, R. S., KANNER, A. D., and FOLKMAN, S. Emotions: A cognitive-phenomenological analysis. In R. Plutchik and H. Kellerman, eds., *Emotions: Theory, Research, and Experience.* Vol. 1. New York: Academic Press, 1980.

LEAR, M. W. Save the spouses, rather than the marriage. *New York Times Magazine,* August 13, 1972.

LEAVITT, H. J., and SCHLOSBERG, H. The retention of verbal and motor skills. *Journal of Experimental Psychology,* 1944, *34,* 404–417.

LENNEBERG, E. H. *Biological Foundations of Language.* New York: Wiley, 1967.

LEON, G. R., GILLUM, B., GILLUM, R., and GOUZE, M. Personality stability and change over a 30-year period—middle age to old age. *Journal of Consulting and Clinical Psychology,* 1979, *47,* 517–524.

LEPPER, M. P., GREENE, D., and NISBETT, R. E. Undermining children's intrinsic interest with extrinsic reward. *Journal of Personality and Social Psychology,* 1973, *28,* 129–137.

LERNER, M. L. Social psychology of justice and interpersonal attraction. In T. L. Huston, ed., *Foundations of Interpersonal Attraction.* New York: Academic Press, 1974.

LESHNER, A. I. Hormones and emotions. In D. K. Candland, ed., *Emotion.* Monterey, Calif.: Brooks/Cole, 1977.

LESTER, D., BECK, A. T., and MITCHELL, B. Extrapolation from attempted suicides to completed suicides: A test. *Journal of Abnormal Psychology,* 1979, *88,* 78–80.

LEVENTHAL, H., WATTS, J. C., and PAGANO, F. Effects of fear and instructions on how to cope with danger. *Journal of Personality and Social Psychology,* 1967, *6,* 313–321.

LEVINGER, G., and SENN, D. J. Disclosure of feelings in marriage. *Merrill-Palmer Quarterly,* 1967, *13,* 237–249.

LEVINSON, D. J. *The Seasons of a Man's Life.* New York: Knopf, 1978.

LEVITSKY, A., and PERLS, F. S. The rules and games of gestalt therapy. In J. Fagan and I. L. Shepherd, eds. *Gestalt Therapy Now.* Palo Alto, Calif.: Science and Behavior Books, 1970.

LEVY, J. Cerebral lateralization and spatial ability. *Behavior Genetics,* 1976, *6,* 171–188.

LEWIN, K. *A Dynamic Theory of Personality.* New York: Holt, Rinehart and Winston, 1935.

LEWINSOHN, P. H. A behavioral approach to depression. In R. J. Freidman and M. M. Katz, eds., *The Psychology of Depression: Contemporary Theory and Research.* Washington, D.C.: Winston-Wiley, 1974.

LEWINSOHN, P. H., and GRAF, M. Pleasant activities and depression. *Journal of Consulting and Clinical Psychology,* 1972, *41,* 215–228.

LEWIS, D. J., and DUNCAN, C. P. Expectation and resistance to extinction of a lever-pulling response as a function of percentage of reinforcement and number of acquisition trials. *Journal of Experimental Psychology,* 1958, *55,* 121–218.

LEWIS, M. Culture and gender roles: There's no unisex in the nursery. *Psychology Today,* May 1972, pp. 54–57.

LEWIS, M. S., GOTTSMAN, D., and GUTSTEIN, S. The course and direction of crisis. *Journal of Consulting and Clinical Psychology,* 1979, *47,* 128–134.

LEZAK, M. D. *Neuropsychological Assessment.* New York: Oxford University Press, 1976.

LIBBY, R. W. In R. W. Libby and R. N. Whithurst, eds., *Marriage and Alternatives.* New York: Scott, Foresman, 1977.

LIEBERT, R. M. and SPIEGLER, M. D. *Personality Strategies and Issues.* 3rd ed. Homewood, Ill.: Dorsey Press, 1978.

LIEBERT, R. M., and BARON, R. Some immediate effects of televised violence on children's behavior. *Developmental Psychology,* 1972, *6,* 469–475.

LIEBERT, R. M., and POULOS, R. W. Television and personality development: The socializing effects of an entertainment medium. In A. Davids, ed., *Child Personality and Psychopathology: Current Topics.* New York: Wiley, 1975.

LINDNER, W. A. *Statistics for Students in the Behavioral Sciences.* Benjamin/Cummings, 1979.

LINDSAY, P. H., and NORMAN, D. A. *Human Information Processing.* 2nd ed. New York: Academic Press, 1977.

LINDSLEY, D. B. Emotion. In S. S. Stevens, ed., *Handbook of Experimental Psychology.* New York: Wiley, 1951.

LIPSITT, L. P. The study of sensory and learning processes in the newborn. *Symposium on Neonatal Neurology, Clinics in Perinatology,* 1977, *4,* 163–186.

LIPSITT, L. P. Critical conditions in infancy: A psychological perspective. *American Psychologist,* 1979, *34,* 973–980.

LIPSITT, L. P. Conditioning the range to live. *Psychology Today,* February 1980, p. 124.

LIPSITT, L. P., ENGEN, T., and KAYE, H. Developmental changes in the olfactory threshold of the neonate. *Child Development,* 1963, *34,* 371–376.

LIPSITT, L. P., and KAYE, H. Conditioned sucking in the human newborn. *Psychonomic Science,* 1964, *1,* 29–30.

LIPSITT, L. P., and LEVY, N. Pain threshold in the human neonate. *Child Development,* 1959, *30,* 547–554.

LISHMAN, W. A. The speed of recall of pleasant and unpleasant experiences. *Psychological Medicine,* 1974, *4,* 169–177.

LLOYD, G. G., and LISHMAN, W. A. Effect of depression on the speed of recall of pleasant and unpleasant experiences. *Psychological Medicine,* 1975, *5,* 173–180.

LOFTUS, E. F. Alcohol, marijuana, and memory. *Psychology Today,* March 1980, pp. 42–56, 92.

LOFTUS, E. F., and LOFTUS, G. R. On the permanence of stored information in the human brain. *American Psychologist,* 1980, *35,* 409–420.

LOFTUS, E. F., and ZANNI, R. Eyewitness testimony: The influence of the wording of a question. *Bulletin of the Psychonomic Society,* 1975, *5,* 86–88.

LOFTUS, G. R., and LOFTUS, E. F. *Human Memory the Processing of Information.* New York: Halstead Press, 1976.

LONDON, P. The psychotherapy boom: From the long couch for the sick to the red button for the bored. *Psychology Today*, June 1974, pp. 63–68.

LORENZ, K. Der Kumpan in der umvelt des vogels. *Journal of Ornithology*, 1935, *83*, 137–213.

LORENZ, K. *On Aggression*. New York: Harcourt Brace Jovanovich, 1970.

LOVAAS, O. I., FREITAG, G., GOLD, V. J., and KASSORLA, I. C. Recordings apparatus for observation of behaviors of children in free play settings. *Journal of Experimental Child Psychology*, 1965, *2*, 108–120.

LOWELL, E. L. The effect of need for achievement on learning and speed of performance. *Journal of Psychology*, 1952, *33*, 31–40.

LUBENCHEVCO, L. O. *The High Risk Infant*. Philadelphia: Saunders, 1976.

LUCE, G. G. *Your Second Life*. New York: Delacorte Press, 1979.

LURIA, A. R. *Higher Cortical Functions in Man*. New York: Basic Books, 1966.

LURIA, A. R. *The Working Brain: An Introduction to Neuropsychology*. New York: Basic Books, 1973.

LUNCH, J. J., PASKEWITZ, D., and ORNE, M. Intersession stability of human alpha rhythm densities. *EEG and Clinical neurophysiology*, 1974, *36*, 538–540.

LYNN, D. B. *The Father: His Role in Child Development*. Monterey, Calif.: Brooks/Cole, 1974.

LYONS, J. *Noam Chomsky*. New York: Viking, 1970.

M

MCBURNEY, D. H. *The persistence of parapsychology*. Paper presented at the American Psychological Association, Montreal, September 1980.

MCBURNEY, D. H., and COLLINGS, V. B. *Introduction to Sensation/Perception*. Englewood Cliffs, N.J.: Prentice-Hall, 1977.

MCCALL, R. B. *Fundamental Statistics for Psychology*. New York: Harcourt Brace Jovanovich, 1975.

MCCALLUM, R., RUSBULT, C. E., HONG, G. K., WALDEN, T. A., and SCHOPLER, J. Effects of resource availability and importance of behavior on the experience of crowding. *Journal of Personality and Social Psychology*, 1979, *37*, 1304–1313.

MCCARTHY, D. P. The effects of tenant population size on low-income public housing residents. *Dissertation Abstracts International*, 1978, *39*, 154–155.

MCCARTHY, D. P., and SAEGERT, S. Residential density, social overload, and social withdrawal. *Human Ecology*, 1978, *6*, 253–272.

MCCARY, J. L. *Human Sexuality*. New York: Van Nostrand Reinhold, 1973.

MCCLELLAND, D. C. *The Achieving Society*. Princeton, N.J.: Van Nostrand, 1961.

MCCLELLAND, D. C. *Assessing Human Motivation*. New York: General Learning Press, 1971.

MCCLELLAND, D. C. Testing for competence rather than for intelligence. *American Psychologist*, 1973, *28*, 1–14.

MCCLELLAND, D. C. *Power: The Inner Experience*. New York: Wiley, 1975.

MCCLELLAND, D. C. Managing motivation to expand human freedom. *American Psychologist*, 1978, 201–210.

MCCLELLAND, D. C. Inhibited power motivation and high blood pressure in men. *Journal of Abnormal Psychology*, 1979, *88*, 182–190.

MCCLELLAND, D. C., and BOYATZIS, R. E. Opportunities for counselors from the competency assessment movement. *Personnel and Guidance Journal*, January 1980, pp. 368–372.

MCCLELLAND, D. C., and STEELE, R. *Motivation Workshop*. New York: General Learning Press, 1972.

MCCLELLAND, D. C., and WATSON, R. I., Jr. Power motivation and risk-taking behavior. *Journal of Personality*, 1973, *41*, 121–139.

MCCLINTOCK, M. K. Menstrual synchrony and suppression. *Nature*, 1971, *229*, 244.

MACCOBY, E. E., 1979. In Heatherington, 1979b.

MACCOBY, E. E., DOERING, C. H., JACKLIN, C. N., and KRAEMER, H. Concentration of sex hormones in umbilical cord blood: Their relation to sex and birth order of infants. *Child Development*, 1979, *50*, 632–642.

MACCOBY, E. E., and JACKLIN, C. N. Stress, activity and proximity seeking: Sex differences in the year-old child. *Child Development*, 1973, *44*, 196–200.

MACCOBY, E. E., and JACKLIN, C. N. *The Psychology of Sex Differences*. Palo Alto, Calif.: Stanford University Press, 1974.

MCCORD, W., MCCORD, J., and HOWARD, A., "Familial Correlates of Aggression in Nondelinquent Male Children." *Journal of Abnormal and Social Psychology*, 1961, *63*, 493–503.

MCDOUGALL, W. *An Introduction to Social Psychology*. New York: Barnes & Noble, 1929.

MACFARLANE, J. A. Olfaction in the development of social preferences in the human neonate. In M. A. Hofer, ed., *Parent-Infant Interaction*. Amsterdam: Elsevier, 1975.

MCGHEE, P. E., and TEEVAN, R. C. Conformity behavior and need for affiliation. *Journal of Social Psychology*, 1967, *72*, 117–121.

MCGLOTHLIN, W. H., and WEST, L. J. The marijuana problem: An overview. *American Journal of Psychiatry*, 1968, *125*, 370–378.

MCGUINNESS, D., and PRIBRAM, K. The origins of sensory bias in the development of gender differences in perception and cognition. In M. Bortner, ed., *Cognitive Growth and Development—Essays in Honor of Herbert G. Birch*. New York: Brunner/Mazel, 1978.

MCGUIRE, W. J. Personality and susceptibility to social influence. In E. E. Borgatta and W. W. Lambert, eds., *Handbook of Personality Theory and Research*. Chicago: Rand-McNally, 1968.

MCGUIRE, W. J. The nature of attitudes and attitude change. In G. Lindzey and E. Aronson, eds., *Handbook of Social Psychology*. Vol. 3. 2nd ed. Reading, Mass.: Addison-Wesley, 1969.

MCGUIRE, W. J., and PAPAGEORGIS, D. The relative efficacy of various types of prior belief-defense in producing immunity against persuasion. *Journal of Abnormal and Social Psychology*, 1961, *62*, 327–337.

MACHT, L. B. Community psychiatry. In A. M. Nicholi, ed., *The Harvard Guide to Modern Psychiatry*. Cambridge, Mass.: Harvard University Press, 1978.

MCINISH, J. R., and COFFMAN, B. *Evaluating the Introductory Psychology Course*. Reading, Mass.: Addison-Wesley, 1970.

MCKEACHIE, W. J., POLLIE, D., and SPEISMAN, J. Relieving anxiety in classroom examination. *Journal of Abnormal and Social Psychology*, 1953, *50*, 93–98.

MACKINNON, D. W. The nature and nurture of creative talent. *American Psychologist*, 1962, *17*, 484–495.

MACKWORTH, J. F. *Vigilance and Habituation*. Baltimore: Penguin, 1970.

MACLEAN, P. The paranoid streak in man. In A. Koestler and J. R. Smythies, eds., *Beyond Reductionism*. Princeton, N.J.: Princeton University Press, 1968.

MADDUX, J. E., and ROGERS, R. W. Effects of source expertness, physical attractiveness, and supporting arguments on persuasion. *Journal of Personality and Social Psychology*, 1980, *39*, 235–244.

MAHER, B. A. *Principles of Psychopathology: An Experimental Approach*. New York: McGraw-Hill, 1966.

MAHER, B. A. The language of schizophrenia: A review and interpretation. *British Journal of Psychiatry*, 1972, *120*, 3–17.

MAIR, R. G., CAPRA, C., MCENTEE, W. J., and ENGEN, T. Odor discrimination and memory in Korsakoff Psychosis. *Journal of Experimental Psychology: Human Perception and Performance*, 1980, *6*, 445–458.

MANDEL, A. J. Toward a psychobiology of transcendence. In J. M. Davidson and R. J. Davidson, eds., *Psychobiology of Consciousness*. New York: Plenum, 1980.

MANDLER, G. Verbal learning. In P. Mussen, et al., eds., *New Directions in Psychology*. Vol. 3. New York: Holt, Rinehart and Winston, 1968.

MARGOLIN, G., and PATTERSON, G. R. Differential consequences provided by mothers and fathers for their sons and daughters. *Developmental Psychology*, 1975, *11*, 537–538.

MARGULES, D. L. Obesity and the hibernation response. *Psychology Today*, October 1979, p. 136.

MARK, V. H., and ERVIN, F. R. *Violence and the Brain*. New York: Harper & Row, 1970.

MARKS, L. *The Unity of the Senses*. New York: Academic Press, 1978.

MARLER, P., DOOLING, R., and ZOLOTH, S. Comparative perspectives on ethology and behavioral development. In M. Bornstein, ed., *The Comparative Method in Psychology*. New York: Lawrence Erlbaum, 1979.

MARTIN, B. *Abnormal Psychology. Clinical and Scientific Perspectives*. New York: Holt, Rinehart and Winston, 1977.

MARTIN, J., and WESTIE, F. The tolerant personality. *American Sociological Review*, 1959, *24*, 521–528.

MARTINSON, F. M. Sexual knowledge, values, and behavior patterns of adolescents. *Child Welfare*, 1968, *47*, 405–410, 426.

MARTINSON, F. M. Childhood sexuality. In B. B. Wolman and J. Money, eds., *Handbook of Human Sexuality*. New York: Plenum, 1980.

MASLACH, C. Burned-out. *Human Behavior*, 1976, *5*, 16–22.

MASLACH, C. The client role in staff burnout. *Journal of Social Issues*, 1978, *34*, 4.

MASLACH, C., and JACKSON, S. E. Burned-out cops and their families. *Psychology Today*, May 1979, pp. 59–62.

MASLOW, A. H., *Motivation and Personality*. New York: Harper & Row, 1954.

MASLOW, A. H. *Toward a Psychology of Being*. Princeton, N.J.: Van Nostrand, 1968.

MASTERS, W. H., and JOHNSON, V. E. *Human Sexual Response*. Boston: Little, Brown, 1966.

MASTERS, W. H., and JOHNSON, V. E. *Homosexuality in Perspective*. Boston: Little, Brown, 1979.

MATARAZZO, J. D. *Wechsler's Measurement and Appraisal of Adult Intelligence*. 5th ed. Baltimore: Williams and Wilkins, 1972.

MATARAZZO, J. D. Behavioral health and behavioral medicine: Frontiers for a new health psychology. *American Psychologist*, 1980, *35*, 807–817.

MATARAZZO, J. D. The history of psychotherapy. In G. Kimbee and K. Schlesinger, eds., *History of Psychology*, New York: Wiley, in press.

MAY, R. R. Mood shifts and the menstrual cycle. *Journal of Psychosomatic Research*, 1976, *20*, 125–130.

MAYS, D. T., and FRANKS, C. M. Getting worse—psychotherapy or no treatment: The jury should still be out. *Professional Psychology*, 1980, *11*, 78–92.

MELTZER, H., and STAGNER, R. The social psychology of aging in industry. *Professional Psychology*, 1980, *11*, 436–444.

MELTZOFF, A. N., and MOORE, M. K. Imitation of facial and manual gestures by human neonates. *Science*, 1977, *198*, 75–77.

MELZACK, R. The perception of pain. *Scientific American*, 1961, 41–49.

MELZACK, R. *The Puzzle of Pain*. New York: Basic Books, 1973.

MELZACK, R. The promise of biofeedback: Don't hold the party yet. *Psychology Today*, July 1975, pp. 18–22, 80–81.

MENNINGER, E. Proud to be a bleeding heart. Conversation with Daniel Goleman. *Psychology Today*, June, 1978, pp. 80–91.

MERTON, R. *Social Theory and Social Structure*. Glencoe, Ill.: Free Press, 1948.

MESSÉ, L. A., and SIVACEK, J. M. Prediction of others' responses in a mixed-motive game: Self-justification or false consensus? *Journal of Personality and Social Psychology*, 1979, *4*, 602–607.

MESSER, S. B., and WINOKUR, M. Some limits to the integration of psychoanalytic and behavior therapy. *American Psychologist*, 1980, *35*, 818–827.

MICHAELSON, W. *Environmental Choice, Human Behavior, and Residential Satisfaction*. New York: Oxford University Press, 1977.

MIDDLEBROOK, P. N. *Social Psychology and Modern Life*. New York: Knopf, 1974.

MIKA, K. *Adjustment to separation among formerly cohabitating men and women*. Ph.D. dissertation, University of Colorado, 1979.

MILGRAM, S. Behavioral study of obedience. *Journal of Abnormal and Social Psychology*, 1963, *67*, 371–378.

MILGRAM, S. The experience of living in cities: A psychological analysis. In F. F. Korten, S. W. Cook, and J. I. Lacey, eds., *Psychology and the Problems of Society*. Washington, D.C.: American Psychological Association, 1970.

MILGRAM, S. *Obedience to Authority*. New York: Harper & Row, 1974.

MILLER, A., and BYRNE, D. *Observational effects of erotica on sexual behavior preferences*. Paper presented at the annual meeting of the American Psychological Association, 1979.

MILLER, A. G., and THOMAS, R. Cooperation and competition among Blackfoot Indian and urban Canadian children. *Child Development*, 1972, *43*, 1104–1110.

MILLER, A., BYRNE, D., and FISHER, J. D. *Preliminary scaling of 40 erotic slides for sexual arousal and disgust*. Unpublished manuscript, Purdue University, 1976.

MILLER, G. A. "The magical number seven. Plus or minus two. *Psychological Review*, 1956, *63*, 81–97.

MILLER, L., et al. Marijuana and memory impairment: The effect of retrieval cues on free recall. *Pharmacology, Biochemistry and Behavior*, 1976, *5*, 639–643.

MILLER, M. L. *Life satisfaction and adaptation of the elderly*. Paper presented at the annual meeting of the American Physiological Association, Montreal, September 1980.

MILLER, N., and CAMPBELL, D. T. Recency and primacy in persuasion as a function of the timing of speeches and measurements. *Journal of Abnormal and Social Psychology*, 1959, *59*, 1–9.

MILLER, N. E. Fear as an acquired drive. *Journal of Experimental Psychology*, 1948, *38*, 89–101.

MILLER, N. E. Learning of visceral and glandular response. *Science*, 1969, *163*, 444–445.

MILLER, N. E. *From the brain to behavior*. Invited lecture at Twelfth Inter-American Congress of Psychology, Montevideo, Uruguay, March 20 to April 6, 1969.

MILLER, N. E. Biofeedback: Evaluation of a new technic. *New England Journal of Medicine*, 1974, *290*, 684–685.

MILLER, N. E., and DWORKIN, B. Visceral learning: Recent difficulties with curarized rats and significant problems for human research. In P. A. Obrist, et al., eds., *Cardiovascular Psychophysiology*. Chicago: Aldine, 1972.

MISCHEL, H. N. Sex bias in the evaluation of professional achievement. *Journal of Educational Psychology*, 1974, *66*, 157–166.

MISCHEL, W. *Personality and Assessment*. New York: Wiley, 1968.

MISCHEL, W. Toward a cognitive-social learning reconceptualization of personality. *Psychological Review*, 1973, *80*, 252–283.

MISCHEL, W. On the interface of cognition and personality: Beyond the person-situation debate. *American Psychologist*, 1979, *34*, 740–754.

MITCHELL, R. E. Some social implications of high density housing. *American Sociological Review*, 1971, *38*, 18–29.

MONAT, A., and LAZARUS, R. S. *Stress and Coping: An Anthology*. New York: Columbia University Press, 1977.

MONEY, J., and EHRHARDT, A. A. *Man and Woman: Boy and Girl*. Baltimore: Johns Hopkins Press, 1972.

MONEY, J., and WIEDEKING, C. Gender identity role: Normal differentiation and its transpositions. In B. B. Wolman and J. Money, eds., *Handbook of Human Sexuality*. New York: Plenum, 1980.

MONTEMAYOR, R., and EISEN, M. The development of self-conceptions from childhood to adolescence. *Developmental Psychology*, 1977, *13*, 314–319.

MOODY, R. A. *Life after Life*. Harrisburg, Pa.: Stackpole, 1976.

MORASCH, B., GRONER, N., and KEATING, J. P. Type of activity and failure as mediators of perceived crowding. *Personality and Social Psychology Bulletin*, 1979, *5*, 223–227.

MORIARTY, T. Crime, commitment, and the responsive bystander: Two field experiments. *Journal of Personality and Social Psychology*, 1975, *31*, 370–376.

MORIN, S. F. Educational programs as a means of changing attitudes towards gay people. *Homosexual counseling Journal*, 1975, *1*, No. 4, 160–165.

MORRIS, N. M., and UDRY, J. R. Pheromonal influences on human sexual behavior, an experimental search. *Journal of Biosocial Science*, 1978, *12*, 34–42.

MOSHER, D. L., and O'GRADY, K. E. Sex guilt, trait anxiety, and females' subjective sexual arousal to erotica. *Motivation and Emotion*, 1979, *3*, 235–249.

MOSS, M. A. Sex, age, and state as determinants of mother-infant interactions. *Merrill-Palmer Quarterly*, 1967, *13*, 19–36.

MURCH, G. M. *Visual and Auditory Perception*. New York:

Bobbs-Merrill, 1973.

MURDOCK, B. B. The retention of individual items. *Journal of Experimental Psychology*, 1961, *62*, 618–625.

MURPHY, G. *The Challenge of Psychological Research.* New York: Harper, 1961.

MURPHY, G., and MURPHY, L. B., eds. *Asian Psychology.* New York: Basic Books, 1968.

MURPHY, L. B., and MORIARTY, A. E. *Vulnerability, Coping and Growth from Infancy to Adolescence.* New Haven, Conn.: Yale University Press, 1976.

MURRAY, H. A. The effect of fear upon estimates of the maliciousness of other personalities. *Journal of Social Psychology*, 1933, *4*, 310–329.

MURRAY, H. A., and OSS ASSESSMENT STAFF. *Assessment of Men: Selection of Personnel for the Office of Strategic Services.* New York: Holt, Rinehart and Winston, 1948.

MUSSEN, P. H., CONGER, J. J., and KAGAN, J. *Child Development and Personality.* 5th ed. New York: Harper & Row, 1979.

MYERS, D. G. Social comparison processes in choice dilemma responding. *Journal of Psychology*, 1974, *86*, 287–292.

NEUGARTEN, B. L., and WEINSTEIN, K. K. The changing American grandparent. In B. L. Neugarten, ed., *Middle Age and Aging.* Chicago: University of Chicago Press, 1975.

NEWCOMB, T. M. *The Acquaintance Process.* New York: Holt, Rinehart and Winston, 1961.

NEWMAN, E. B. Forgetting of meaningful material during sleep and waking. *American Journal of Psychology*, 1938, *50*, 65–71.

NEWMAN, O. *Defensible Space.* New York: Macmillan, 1973.

NISBETT, R. E. Eating behavior and obesity in men and animals. In F. Reichsman, ed., *Hunger and Satiety in Health and Disease.* White Plains, N.Y.: Phiebig, 1972.

NOMIKOS, M. S., OPTON, E. M., AVERILL, J. R., and LAZARUS, R. S. Surprise and suspense in the production of stress reaction. *Journal of Personality and Social Psychology*, 1968, *8*, 204–208.

NOBACK, C. R., and DEMAREST, R. J. *The Nervous System: Introduction and Review.* New York: McGraw-Hill, 1972.

NORMAN, D. A. *Memory and Attention: Human Information Processing.* New York: Wiley, 1969.

NOTZ, W. W. Work motivation and the negative effects of extrinsic rewards. *American Psychologist*, 1975, *30*, 884–891.

N

NAKAZIMA, S., and SAHEKI, O. A study of an English teaching method in Japan based on a comparative study of Japanese and English. *Japanese Journal of Educational Psychology*, 1968, *16*, 127–141.

NATIONAL INSTITUTE ON DRUG ABUSE. *Marijuana and Health.* Washington, D.C.: Department of Health, Education and Welfare, 1980.

NAUTA, WALLE, J. H., and FEIRTAG, M. The organization of the brain. *Scientific American*, 1979, *241*, 88–110

NEISSER, U. *Cognition and Reality.* San Francisco: Freeman, 1976.

NEISSER, U. The Multiplicity of thought. *British Journal of Psychology*, 1963, *45*, 1–14.

NELSON, K. Structure and strategy in learning to talk. *Monographs for the Society for Research in Child Development*, No. 149, 173.

NEUGARTEN, B. L. Dynamics of transition of middle age to old age: Adaptation and the life cycle. *Journal of Geriatric Psychology*, 1970, *4*, 71–87.

NEUGARTEN, B. L., et al. *Personality in Middle and Late Life.* New York: Atherton, 1964.

O

ODEN, M. H. The fulfillment of promise: 40-year follow-up of the Terman gifted group. *Genetic Psychology Monographs*, 1968, *77*, 3–93.

OGILVIE, B. C. Stimulus addition: The sweet psychic jolt of danger. *Psychology Today*, October 1974, pp. 88–94.

O'GRADY, K. E., and JANDA, L. H. Psychometric correlates of the Mosher Forced-choice Guilt Inventory. *Journal of Consulting and Clinical Psychology*, 1978, *46*, 1581–1582.

OLDS, J. Pleasure centres in the brain. *Scientific American*, 1956, *195*, 105–116.

OLDS, J., and MILNER, P. M. Positive reinforcement produced by electrical stimulation of septal area and other regions of rat brain. *Journal of Comparative and Physiological Psychology*, 1954, *47*, 419–427.

OLSON, D. Marital and family therapy: Integrative review and critique. *Journal of Marriage and the Family*, 1970, *32*, 501–538.

OLSON, J. M., and ZANNA, M. P. A new look at selective exposure. *Journal of Experimental Social Psychology*, 1979, *15*, 1–15.

OLTMANNS, T. F. Selective attention in schizophrenic and manic psychoses: The effect of distraction on information processing. *Journal of Abnormal Psychology*, 1978, *87*, 212–225.

ORLANSKY, H. Infant care and personality. *Psychological Bulletin*, 1949, *46*, 1–48.

ORLOFSKY, J. Sex-role orientation, identity formation, and self-esteem in college men and women. *Sex Roles*, 1977, *3*, 561–575.

ORNE, M. The nature of hypnosis: Artifact and essence. *Journal of Abnormal and Social Psychology*, 1959, *58*, 277–299.

ORNE, M. T. On the social psychology of the psychological experiment: With particular reference to demand characteristics and their implications. *American Psychologist*, 1962, *17*, 776–783.

ORNE, M. T. Demand characteristics and the concept of quasi-controls. In R. Rosenthal and R. C. Rosnow, eds., *Artifact in Behavioral Research*. New York: Academic Press, 1969.

OSIS, K., and HARALDSSON, E. *At the Hour of Death*. New York: Avon, 1977.

OTIS, L. S. If well-integrated but anxious, try TM. *Psychology Today*, April 1974, pp. 45–46.

OWEN, D. R. The 47, XYY male: A review. *Psychological Review*, 1972, *78*, 209–233.

P

PALERMO, D. S. More about less: A study of language comprehension. *Journal of Verbal Learning and Verbal Behavior*, 1973, *12*, 211–221.

PARKE, R. D., and SAWIN, D. B. The father's role in infancy: A reevaluation. *Family Coordinator*, 1976, *25*, 365–371.

PARKER, E. S., BIRNBAUM, I. M., and NOBEL, E. P. Alcohol and memory: Storage and state dependency. *Journal of Verbal Learning and Verbal Behavior*, 1976, *15*, 691–702.

PARLEE, M. B. Stereotypic beliefs about menstruation: A methodological note on the Moos Menstrual Distress Questionnaire and some new data. *Psychosocomatic Medicine*, 1974, *36*, 229–240.

PARLEE, M. B. First-borns have higher hormone levels. *Psychology Today*, April 1979, p. 102.

PASAMANICK, B., and KNOBLOCH, H. Retrospective studies on the epidemiology of reproductive causality: Old and new. *Merrill-Palmer Quarterly*, 1966, *12*, 7–26.

PATULLO, E. P. Social science and research. *Hastings Review*, April 1980.

PEASE, D., WOLINS, L., and STOCKDALE, D. F. Relationship and prediction of infant tests. *Journal of Genetic Psychology*, 1973, *122*, 31–35.

PELLETIER, K. R. *Mind as Healer, Mind as Slayer*. New York: Delacorte, 1977.

PENFIELD, W. Functional localization in temporal and deep Sylvian areas. In *The Brain and Human Behavior*. Baltimore: Williams & Wilkins, 1958.

PENFIELD, W., and RASMUSSEN, T. *The Cerebral Cortex of Man*. New York: Macmillan, 1957.

PEPLAU, L. A. Impact of fear of success and sex-role attitudes on women's competitive achievement. *Journal of Personality and Social Psychology*, 1976, *34*, 561–568.

PEPLAU, L. A. Power in dating relationships. In J. Freeman, ed., *Women: A Feminist Perspective*. Palo Alto, Calif.: Mayfield, 1978.

PEPLAU, L. A., and PERLMAN, D. Blueprint for a social psychological theory of loneliness. In M. Cook and G. Wilson, eds., *Love and Attraction*. New York: Pergamon, 1979.

PEPLAU, L. A., RUBIN, Z., and HILL, C. T. The sexual balance of power. *Psychology Today*, November 1976, pp. 142–151.

PETERSON, L. R., and PETERSON, M. J. Short-term retention of individual items. *Journal of Experimental Psychology*, 1959, *58*, 193-198.

PETRIE, A. *Individuality in Pain and Suffering*. Chicago: University of Chicago Press, 1979.

PIAGET, J. *The Moral Judgment of the Child*. London: Routledge & Kegan Paul, 1932.

PIAGET, J. *The Grasp of Consciousness: Action and Concept in the Young Child*. Cambridge, Mass.: Harvard University Press, 1976.

PLECK, J. H. *Men's new roles in the family: Housework and child care*. Unpublished manuscript, University of Massachusetts, 1976a.

PLECK, J. H., 1976b. Cited in Herzog, Bachman, and Johnston, 1979. Paid work, child care, and housework: A national survey of high school seniors' preferences for sharing responsibilities between husband and wife. Unpublished report, University of Michigan, February, 1979.

PLECK, J. H., and SAWYER, J., eds. *Men and Masculinity*. Englewood Cliffs, N.J.: Prentice-Hall, 1974.

PERLS, F. *Gestalt Therapy Verbatim*. Lafayette, Calif.: Real People Press, 1969.

PETTIGREW, T. Race relations. In R. Merton and R. Nisbet, eds., *Contemporary Social Problems*. New York: Harcourt Brace Jovanovich, 1971.

PETTY, R. E., and CACIOPPO, J. T. Issue involvement can increase or decrease persuasion by enhancing message-relevant cognitive responses. *Journal of Personality and Social Psychology*, 1979, *37*, 1915–1926.

PLACE, E. J. S., and GILMORE, G. C. Perceptual organization in schizophrenia. *Journal of Abnormal Psychology*, 1980, *89*, 409–418.

PLUTCHIK, R. *Emotions: A Psychobioevolutionary Synthesis*. New York: Harper & Row, 1980.

POCS, O., and GODOW, A. G. The shock of recognizing parents as sexual beings. In D. Burne and L. A. Byrne, eds., *Exploring Human Sexuality*. New York: Crowell, 1977.

POKORNY, A. D. Myths about suicide. In H. L. P. Resnick, ed., *Suicidal Behaviors: Diagnosis and Management*. Boston: Little, Brown, 1968.

POLEY, W., LEA, G., and VIBE, G. *Alcoholism: A Treatment Manual*. New York: Gardner, 1979.

PORTER, B., and O'LEARY, D. K. Marital discord and child behavior problems. *Journal of Abnormal Child Psychology*, 1980, *8*, 287–295.

POSTMAN, L., and EBBINGHAUS, H. *American Psychologist*, 1968, *23*, 149–157.

PRIBRAM, K. H., and GILL, M. M. *Freud's 'Project' Reassessed*. New York: Basic Books, 1976.

PROCHASKA, J. O. *Systems of Psychotherapy: A Transtheoretical Analysis*. New York: Dorsey, 1979.

PROVIDENCE JOURNAL, September 25, 1979.

R

RADIN, M.E., and WITTMAIER, B.C. Effects of state and trait anxiety on retention and clustering. Paper presented at American Psychological Association, New York, September, 1979.

RAGOZIN, A. S. Attachment behavior of day-care children: Naturalistic and laboratory observations. *Child Development*, 1980, *51*, 409–415.

RAKOFF, V., ed. *Psychiatric Diagnosis*. New York: Brunner/Mazel, 1977.

REED, G. *The Psychology of Anomalous Experience*. Boston: Houghton-Mifflin, 1974.

REICHARD, S., LIVSON, F., and PETERSON, P. G. Adjustment to retirement. In *Aging and Personality*. New York: Wiley, 1962.

REISS, I. L. How and why America's sex standards are changing. In *The Social Context of Premarital Sexual Permissiveness*. New York: Holt, Rinehart and Winston, 1967.

RIESEN, A. H. Arrested Vision. *Scientific American*, 1950, *183*, 16–19.

RIMLAND, B. Savant capabilities of autistic children and their cognitive implications. In G. Serban, ed., *Cognitive Defects in the Development of Mental Illness*. New York: Brunner/Mazel, 1978.

RIMM, D. C., and MASTERS, J. C. *Behavior Therapy*. 2nd ed. New York: Academic Press, 1979.

ROBERTS, M. C., and HORNER M. M. A comprehensive intervention for failure-to-thrive. *Journal of Clinical Child Psychology*, 1979, 10–14.

RODIN, J. Perceived choice, and response to controllable and uncontrollable outcomes. *Journal of Experimental and Social Psychology*, 1976, *12*, 564–578.

RODIN, J. The effects of stimulus-bound behavior on biological self-regulation. In G. Schwartz and D. Shapiro, eds., *Consciousness and Self-regulation*. Vol. 2. New York: Plenum, 1977.

RODIN, J., and SLOCHOWER, J. Externality in the non-obese: The effects of environmental responsiveness on weight. *Journal of Personality and Social Psychology*, 1976, *33*, 338–344.

RODIN, J., SLOCHOWER, J., and FLEMING, B. Effects of degree of obesity, age of onset, and weight loss on responsiveness to sensory and external stimuli. *Journal of Comparative and Physiological Psychology*, 1977, *91*, 586–597.

ROGERS, C. R. *On Becoming a Person*. Boston: Houghton Mifflin, 1961.

ROGERS, C. R. *Carl Rogers on Personal Power*. New York: Delacorte, 1977.

ROKEACH, M., and KLIEJUNAS, P. Behavior is a function of attitude-toward-object and attitude-toward-situation. *Journal of Personality and Social Psychology*, 1972, *22*, 194–201.

ROMER, D. Further limitations in the equity approach theory: A reply to Samuel. *Personality and Social Psychology Bulletin*, 1979, *5*, 249–252.

ROSCH, E. On the internal structure of perceptual and semantic categories. In T. E. Morre, ed., *Cognitive Development and the Acquisition of Language*. New York: Academic Press, 1973.

ROSE, S. *The Conscious Brain*. New York: Random House, 1976.

ROSENBAUM, C. P. *The Meaning of Madness*. New York: Science House, 1970.

ROSENHAN, D. L. On being sane in insane places. *Science*, 1973, *179*, 250–257.

ROSENTHAL, D., and KETY, S. S., eds. *The Transmission of Schizophrenia*. Elmsford, N. Y.: Pergamon, 1968.

ROSENTHAL, R. *Experimenter Effects in Behavior Research*. New York: Appleton-Century-Crofts, 1966.

ROSENTHAL, R., and JACOBSON, L. *Pygmalion in the Classroom*. New York: Holt, Rinehart and Winston, 1968.

ROSENZWEIG, M. R. Auditory localization. *Scientific American*, 1961, 132–142. Oct.

ROSENZWEIG, M. R. Effects of heredity and environment on brain chemistry, brain anatomy, and learning ability in the rat. In M. Monosovitz, G. Lindzey, and D. D. Thiessen, eds., *Behavioral Genetics.* New York: Appleton-Century-Crofts, 1969.

ROSKIES, E., and LAZARUS, R. S. Coping theory and the teaching of coping skills. In P. Davidson, ed., *Behavioral Medicine: Changing Health Life Styles.* New York: Brunner/Mazel, 1979.

ROSS, H. L., and SAWHILL, I. V. *Time of Transition: The Growth of Families Headed by Women.* Washington, D.C.: Urban Institute, 1975.

ROSS, J., and LAWRENCE, K. A. Some observations on memory artifice. *Psychonomic Science,* 1968, *13,* 107-108.

ROTTER, J. B., and STEIN, D. K. Public attitudes toward the trustworthiness and altruism of twenty selected occupations. *Journal of Applied Psychology,* 1971, *1,* 334-343.

ROZIN, P., and SCHILLER, D. The nature and acquisition of preference for chili pepper by humans. *Motivation and Emotion,* 1980, *4,* 77-101.

RUBENSTEIN, C. M., and SHAVER, P. *Loneliness: Longing for Love and Community.* New York: Delacorte, 1980.

RUBIN, Z., HILL, C. T., PEPLAU, L. A., and DUNKEL-SCHETTER, C. Self-disclosure in dating couples: sex roles and the ethic of openness. *Journal of Marriage and the Family,* 1980, *42,* 305-317.

RUBLE, D. N., FELDMAN, N. S., and BOGGIANO, A. K. Social comparison between young children in achievement situations. *Developmental Psychology,* 1976, *12,* 192-197.

RUSSELL, P. *The Brain Book,* New York: Hawthorne, 1980.

RUSSELL, P. L., and BRANDSMA, J. M. A theoretical and empirical investigation of the rational-emotive and classical conditioning theories. *Journal of Consulting and Clinical Psychology,* 1974, *42,* 389-397.

RUTTER, M. Protective factors in children's responses to stress and disadvantage. In M. W. Kent and J. E. Rolf, eds., *Primary Prevention of Psychopathology.* Vol 3. Hanover, N.H.: University Press of New England, 1978.

RUTTER, M. Maternal deprivation 1972-1978: New findings, new concepts, new approaches. *Child Development,* 1979, *50,* 283-305.

S

SADACCA, R., RICCIUTI, H. N., and SWANSON, E. O. *Content Analysis of Achievement Motivation Protocols: A Study of Scorer Agreement.* Princeton, N.J.: Educational Testing Service, 1956.

SAEGERT, S., SWAMP, W., and ZAJONC, R.B. Exposure, context, and interpersonal attraction. *Journal of Personality and Social Psychology,* 1973, *25,* 234-242.

SAFER, M.A. Attributing evil to the subject not the situation: Student reaction to Milgram's film on obedience. *Personality and Social Psychology Bulletin,* 1980, *6,* 205-209.

SALAPATEK, P., and KESSEN, W. Visual scanning of triangles by the human newborn. *Journal of Comparative and Physiological Psychology,* 1968, *66,* 247-248.

SALZMAN, C. Electroconvulsive therapy. In A. M. Nicholi, ed., *The Harvard Guide to Modern Psychiatry.* Cambridge, Mass.: Harvard University Press, 1978.

SAMELSON, F. J. B. Watson's Little Albert, Cyril Burt's twins and the need for a critical science. *American Psychologist,* 1980, *35,* 619-625.

SAMPSON, E. A., and HANCOCK, F. T. An examination of the relationship between ordinal position, personality, and conformity. *Journal of Personality and Social Psychology,* 1967, *5,* 398-407.

SANDER, F. A. *Beyond the adversarial process.* Paper presented at the annual convention, American Psychological Association, Montreal, September, 1980.

SANDERS, J., and ROBINSON, W. Sexual terms used by men and women. *Journal of Communication,* 1979, *2,* 24-38.

SANFORD, N. Collective destructiveness: Sources and remedies. In G. Usdin ed., *Perspectives on Violence.* New York: Brunner/Mazel, 1972.

SAPIR, E. *Selected Writings of Edward Sapir in Language, Culture, and Personality.* Berkeley: University of California Press, 1949.

SARASON, I. G. *Abnormal Psychology.* 2nd ed. Englewood Cliffs, N.J.: Prentice-Hall, 1976.

SATIR, V. *Conjoint Family Therapy.* Palo Alto, Calif.: Science and Behavior Books, 1967.

SCARF, M. The more sorrowful sex. *Psychology Today,* April 1979, pp. 47–52.

SCARR, S., and WEINBERG, R. IQ test performance of black children adopted by white families. *American Psychologist,* 1976, *31,* 726-739.

SCHACHTER, S. Birth order, eminence and higher education. *American Sociological Review,* 1963, *28,* 757-786.

SCHACHTER, S. *Emotion, Obesity and Crime.* New York: Academic Press, 1971.

SCHACHTER, S. Some extraordinary facts about obese humans and rats. *American psychologist,* 1971, *26,* 129-144.

SCHACHTER, S., and GROSS, L. P. Manipulated time and eating behavior. *Journal of Personality and Social Psychology,* 1968, *10,* 98-106.

SCHACHTER, S., and SINGER, S. E. Cognitive, social and physiological determinants of emotional states. *Psychological Review,* 1962, *69,* 379-399.

SCHAEFER, E. S., and BAYLEY, N. Maternal behavior, child behavior, and their correlations from infancy through adolescence. *Monographs of the Society for Research in Child Development,* 1963, *28,* No. 3.

SPIELBERGER, C. D. "The effects of anx
learning and academic achievement.
C. D., ed., *Anxiety and Behavior*. New
Press, 1966.

SPIELBERGER, C. D., and SARASON, I. G.
Anxiety. Vol. 4. New York: Wiley, 19

SPITZ, R. A. Hospitalism: An inquiry int
psychiatric conditions in early childho
lytic Study of the Child, 1945, *1*, 53–

SPRAFKIN, J. N., LIEBERT, R. M., and POUL
of a prosocial televised example on ch
Journal of Experimental Child Psych

SROLE, L. Urbanization and mental hea
mulations. *American Scientist*, 1972,

STAMPFL, T. G., and LEVIS, D. J. Essent
therapy: A learning-theory-based psy
havior theory. *Journal of Abnormal P
72*, 496–503.

STANG, D. J. Conformity, ability, and sel
sentative Research in Social Psych
97–103.

STEINER, I. D., and JOHNSON, H. Auth
"tolerance of trait inconsistency." *Jo
mal and Social Psychology*, 1963, *67*

STEINER, I. *Group Process and Product*
Academic Press, 1972.

STENGEL, E. Psychogenic loss of memo
Whitty and O. L. Zangwill, eds., *A*
Butterworth, 1966.

STEPHAN, W. G. School desegregation:
predictions made in Brown vs. Boa
Psychological Bulletin, 1978, *85*, 217

STERN, L. Prematurity as a factor in chil
Practice, May 1973, 117–123.

STERN, P. C. *Evaluating Social Science*
York: Oxford University Press, 1979

STEVENS, C. F. The neuron. *Scientific
241*, 54–65.

STEVENS, J. C., and MARKS, L. E. Cross-m
functions generated by magnitude es
tion and Psychophysics, 1980, *27*, 37

STEVENS, S. S. *Psychophysics*. New Yo

STOLZ, H. R., and STOLZ, L. M. *Somatic
Adolescent Boys*. New York: Macmil

STONE, L. J., and CHURCH, J. *Childhood*
3rd ed. New York: Random House,

STONE, L. J., and CHURCH, J. *Childhood*
4th ed. New York: Random House,

STRUPP, H. Some observations on the
free psychotherapy and the empty
ments on a case study. *Journal of A
logy*, 1974, *83*, 199–201.

STUART, R. B. Behavioral contracting w
of delinquents. *Journal of Behavior
perimental Psychiatry*, 1971, *2*, 1–11

STUNKARD, A. J. Eating patterns and ob
Quarterly, 1959, *33*, 284–295.

SCHAFFER, H. R. *The Growth of Sociability*. Baltimore: Penguin, 1971.

SCHAFFER, H. R., and CALLENDER, W. M. Psychologic effects of hospitalization in infancy. *Pediatrics*, 1959, *24*, 528–539.

SCHAFFER, H. R., and EMERSON, P. E. The development of social attachments in infancy. *Monographs of the Society for Research in Child Development*, 1964, *29*, No. 94.

SCHAFFER, R. *Mothering*. Cambridge, Mass.: Harvard University Press, 1977.

SCHEFLEN, A. E. Family communication and social connectedness in the development of schizophrenia. In M. Andolfi and I. Zwerling, eds., *Dimensions of Family Therapy*. New York: Guilford Press, 1980.

SCHELL, R. E., and HALL, E. *Developmental Psychology Today*. New York: Random House, 1979.

SCHILL, T., and CHAPIN, J. Sex guilt and males' preference for reading erotic magazines. *Journal of Consulting and Clinical Psychology*, 1972, *39*, 516.

SCHLESINGER, I. M., and NAMIR, L. *Sign Language of the Deaf*. New York: Academic Press, 1978.

SCHMIDT, G., and SIGUSCH, V. Sex differences in responses to psycho-sexual stimulation by films and slides. *Journal of Sex Research*, 1970, *6*, 268–283.

SCHNEIDER, A. M. and TARSHIS, B. *An Introduction to Physiological Psychology*. 2nd ed. New York: Random House, 1980.

SCHOFIELD, W. *Psychotherapy: The Purchase of Friendship*. Englewood Cliffs, N.J.: Prentice-Hall, 1964.

SCHONBERG, W. B., COSTANZA, D. J., and CARPENTER, R. S. Menstrual cycle: Phases and reaction to frustration. *Psychological Record*, 1976, *26*, 312–325.

SCHREIBER, F. R. *Sybil*. New York: Regnery, 1973.

SCHULTES, R. E. *Hallucinogenic Plants*. New York: Golden Press, 1976.

SCHULTZ, D. *A History of Modern Psychology*, New York: Academic Press, 1975.

SCHUMAN, M. The psychophysiological model of meditation and altered states of consciousness. In J. M. Davidson and R. J. Davisdon, eds., *Psychobiology of Consciousness*. New York: Plenum, 1980.

SCHUTZ, F. Zur sexuellen Prägbarkeit und sensiblen Phase von Gänsen und der Bedeutung der Farbe des Prägungsobjecks. *Zoologisher Anzeiger Supplement*, 1969, *33*, 301–306.

SCHWARTZ, G. E., DAVIDSON, R. J., and GOLEMAN, D. Patterning of cognitive and somatic processes in the self-regulation of anxiety: Effects of meditation versus exercise. *Psychosomatic Medicine*, 1978.

SCHWARTZ, S. H. Normative influences on altruism. In L. Berkowitz, ed., *Advances in Experimental Social Psychology*. Vol. 10. New York: Academic Press, 1977.

SEARS, P. H., and BARBEE, A. H., 1977. Cited in Herzog, Bachman, and Johnston, 1979.

SEARS, P. H., and BARBEE, A. H. Career and life satisfaction among Terman's gifted women. In *The Gifted and the Creative: Fifty-year Perspective*. Baltimore: Johns Hopkins Press, 1978.

SEARS, R. R. Sources of life satisfaction of the Terman gifted men. *American Psychologist*, 1977, *32*, 119–128.

SEARS, R., and SEARS, P. Still learning from Terman's children. *Psychology Today*, September 1980, *9*, 44–53.

SEAY, B., ALEXANDER, B. K., and HARLOW, H. F. Maternal behavior of socially deprived rhesus monkeys. *Journal of Abnormal and Social Psychology*, 1964, *69*, 345–354.

SEGAL, M. H., CAMPBELL, D. T., and HERSKOVITS, M. J. *The Influence of Culture on Visual Perception*. Indianapolis: Bobbs-Merrill, 1966.

SEIGEL, R. K. Hallucinations. *Scientific American*, 1977, *237*, 4.

SELIGMAN, M. E. P., *Helplessness*. San Francisco: Freeman, 1975.

SELIGMAN, M. E. P., and HAGER, J. L. *Biological Boundaries of Learning*. New York: Appleton-Century-Crofts, 1972.

SELIGMAN, M. E., and MAIER, S. F. Failure to escape from traumatic shock. *Journal of Experimental Psychology*, 1967, *74*, 1–9.

SELYE, H. *The Stress of Life*. Rev. ed. New York: McGraw-Hill, 1976.

SELYE, H. *The Stress of Life*. New York: McGraw-Hill, 1978.

SHAH, F., and SELNICK, M. Sexuality in adolescence. In B. B. Wolman and J. Money, eds., *Handbook of Human Sexuality*. New York: Plenum, 1980.

SHAKOW, D. H., Ebbinghaus. *American Journal of Psychology*, 1930, *42*, 505–518.

SHANTEAU, J., and NAGY, G. F. Probability of acceptance in dating choice. *Journal of Personality and Social Psychology*, 1979, *37*, 522–533.

SHAPIRA, A., and MARSDEN, M. C. Cooperative and competitive behavior of kibbutz and urban children in Israel. *Child Development*, 1969, *40*, 609–617.

SHAPIRO, A. K. Placebo effects in medicine, psychotherapy and psychoanalysis. In A. E. Bergin and S. L. Garfield, eds., *Handbook of Psychotherapy and Behavior Change*. New York: Wiley, 1971.

SHAPIRO, D. *Meditation: Self-regulation and Altered States of Consciousness*. New York: Aldine, 1980.

SCHATZ, M. *The comprehension of indirect directives: Can two-year-olds shut the door?* Paper presented at the summer meeting of the Linguistic Society of America, Amherst, Mass., July 1974.

SHAVER, P., and FREEDMAN, J. Your pursuit of happiness. *Psychology Today*, August 1976, pp. 26–34.

SHAVER, P., and RUBENSTEIN, C. M. *Living alone, loneliness, and health*. Paper presented at the meeting of the American Psychological Association, New York City, September 4, 1979.

SHEARD, M. H. Testosterone and aggression. In M. Sandler, ed., *Psychopharmacology of Aggression*. New York: Raven, 1979.

SHELDON, W. H. *The Varieties of Human Physique*. New York: Harper & Row, 1940.

SHELDON, W. H. *The Varieties of* : York: Harper & Row, 1942.

SHEPARD, R. N. Recognition memor; ces, and pictures. *Journal of V. Verbal Behavior*, 1967, *6*, 156–16;

SHEPARD R. N. Form, formation, ar internal representations. In R. Sol *Processing and Cognition: The* Hillsdale, N.J.: Lawrence Erlbau

SHEPARD, R. N., and METZLER, J. Men dimensional objects. *Science*, 1971

SHEVRIN, H., and DICKMAN, S. The scious: A necessary assumption theory? *American Psychologist*, 1

SHNEIDLING, M. M., and PEDERSON, L teacher and student on children's and verbal performance. *Journal 76*, 79–84.

SHNEIDMAN, E. S. *Voices of Death*. N Row, 1980.

SHNEIDMAN, E. S. *Deaths of Man*. N gle, 1973.

SHOPE, D. F. *Interpersonal Sexuality* ders, 1975.

SHOTLUND, R. L., and HUSTON, T. L. are they and do they influence vene? *Journal of Personality and* 1979, *37*, 1822–1834.

SHOTLAND, R. L., and STRAW, M. K. B an assault: When a man attacks *Personality and Social Psycholog*

SHUTTE, J. G. *Everything You Alwa about Elementary Statistics (But* Englewood Cliffs, N.J.: Prentice-

SILVERMAN, L. H., ROSS, D. L., ADLEF A. Simple research paradigm for minal psychodynamic activation: E uli on dart-throwing accuracy in co *of Abnormal Psychology*, 1978, *8*

SIMON, H. A. *Models of Thought*. Nev University Press, 1979.

SINGER, D. G., and REVENSON, T. New York: International Univers

SINGER, J. L. *The Inner World of* York: Harper & Row, 1975.

SIQUELAND, E. R. Reinforcement pa in human newborns. *Journal of Psychology*, 1968, *6*, 431–442.

SIQUELAND, E. R., and DELUCIA, C. ment of nonnutritive sucking in ence*, 1969, *165*, 1144–1146.

SISTRUNK, F., and MCDAVID, J. W. Se: ing behavior. *Journal of Person chology*, 1971, *17*, 200–207.

SKEELS, H. M. Adult status of child early life experiences. *Monograp Research in Child Development,*

TERRACE, H. S. *Nim: A Chimpanzee Who Learned Sign Language*. New York: Knopf, 1979.

TESSMAN, M. *Children of Parting Parents*. New York: Aronson, 1978.

TETLOCK, P. E. Identifying victims of groupthink from public statements of decision-makers. *Journal of Personality and Social Psychology*, 1979, *37*, 1314–1324.

THOMAS, A., CHESS, S., and BIRCH, H. G. The origin of personality. *Scientific American*, August 1970, 102–109.

THOMPSON, G. G., and HORROCKS, J. E. A study of the friendship fluctuations of urban boys and girls. *Journal of Genetic Psychology*, 1947, *70*, 53–63.

THOMPSON, J. S., and THOMPSON, M. W. *Genetics in Medicine*. Philadelphia: Saunders, 1966.

THOMPSON, R. F. *Foundatins of Physiological Psychology*. New York: Harper & Row, 1967.

TIZARD, B., and REES, J. The effects of early institutional rearing on the behavioral problems and affectional relationships of four-year-old children. *Journal of Child Psychology and Psychiatry*, 1975, *16*, 61–73.

TORRANCE, E. P. *Torrance Tests of Creative Thinking, Verbal Forms A and B*. Princeton, N.J.: Personnel Press, 1966.

TOUHEY, J. C. Effects of additional men on prestige and desirability of occupations typically performed by women. *Journal of Applied Social Psychology*, 1974, *4*, 330–335.

TOWER, R. B., SINGER, D. G., SINGER, J. L., and BIGGS, A. Differential effects of television programming on preschoolers' cognition, imagination, and social play. *American Journal of Orthopsychiatry*, 1979, *49*, 265–281.

TREISMAN, A. M. Verbal cues, language and meaning in selective attention. *American Journal of Psychology*, 1964, *77*, 206–219.

TRESSEMER, D. Fear of success: Popular, but unproven. *Psychology Today*, March 1974, pp. 82–85.

TRIPPI, J., MICHAEL, R., COLAO, A., and ALVAREZ, A. Housing discrimination toward mentally retarded persons. *Exceptional Children*, 1978, *44*, 430–433.

TRUAX, C. B., and CARKHUFF, R. R. *Toward Effective Counseling and Psychotherapy*. Chicago: Aldine, 1967.

TULVING, E. Episodic and semantic memory. In E. Tulving and W. Donaldson, eds., *Organization of Memory*. New York: Academic Press, 1972.

TULVING, E., and PEARLSONE, Z. Availability versus accessibility of information in memory for words. *Journal of Verbal Leàrning and Verbal Behavior*, 1966, *5*, 381–391.

U

UNDERWOOD, B. J. Forgetting. *Scientific American*, March 1964, 91–99.

UNDERWOOD, B. J., and SCHULTZ, R. Sources of interference associated with differences in learning and retention. Studies of Distributed Practice: XX. *Journal of Experimental Psychology*, 1961, *61*, 228.

UNGAR, G., HO, I. K., GALVAN, L., and DESIDERIO, D. M. Isolation, identification and synthesis of specific behavior-inducing brain peptide. *Nature*, 1972, *238*, 196–197.

UNITED PRESS INTERNATIONAL. Nevada has top suicide rate. April 23, 1980.

V

VALENSTEIN, E. S. *The Psychosurgery Debate*. San Francisco: Freeman, 1980.

VALENSTEIN, E., COX, J., and KØKOLEWSKI, V. Reexamination of the role of the hypothalamus in motivation. *Psychological Review*, 1970, *77*, 16–31.

VAUGHN, E. Misconceptions about psychology among introductory psychology students. *Teaching of Psychology*, 1977, *4*, no. 3, pp. 138–141.

VEATCH, R. M. *Death, Dying, and the Biological Revolution*. New Haven, Conn.: Yale University Press, 1976.

VON BÉKÉSY, G. The ear. *Scientific American*, 1957, 66–78.

VONNEGUT, M. *The Eden Express*. New York: Praeger, 1975.

VYGOTSKY, L. S. K. *Thought and Language*. Cambridge, Mass.: MIT Press, 1962.

W

WAGNER, T. L. The effect of frustration on cognitive processes. *Dissertation Abstracts International*, 1976, *37*, 3433.

WALBERG, H. J., and RASHER, S. P. The ways schooling makes a difference. *Phi Delta Kappa*, 1977, *58*, 703–707.

WALK, R. D., and GIBSON, E. J. A comparative and analytical study of visual depth perception. *Psychological Monographs*, 1961, No. 75.

WALKER, C. E. Treatment of children's disorders by relaxation training: The poor man's biofeedback. *Journal of Clinical Child Psychology*, 1979, *8*, 22–25.

WALL, P. D., and MELZACK, R. Pain mechanisms: A new theory. *Science*, 1965, *150*, 971–979.

WALLACE, D. H., and WEHMER, G. Evaluation of visual erotica by sexual liberals and conservatives. *Journal of Sex Research*, 1972, *8*, 147–153.

WALLACE, K. and BENSON, H. The physiology of meditation. *Scientific American*, 1972, *226*, 84–90.

WALLACH, M. A., and KOGAN, N. *Models of Thinking in Young Children: A Sudy of the Creativity-Intelligence Distribution.* New York: Holt, Rinehart and Winston, 1965.

WALLERSTEIN, J. S. *Children and parents 18 months after parental separation: Factors related to different outcomes.* Paper presented at NIMH conference on divorce, Washington, D.C., February 1978.

WALLERSTEIN, J. S., and KELLY, J. B. *Surviving the Breakup: How Children Cope with Divorce.* New York: Basic Books, 1980.

WALLS, G. I. The problem of visual direction. Part II: Experimental attacks and their results. *American Journal of Optometry and Archives of the American Academy of Optometry*, 1951, *28*, 173–212.

WALSTER, E. The effect of self-esteem on romantic liking. *Journal of Experimental Social Psychology*, 1965, *1*, 184–197.

WALSTER, E., ARONSON, E., ABRAHAMS, D., and ROTTMANN, L. Importance of physical attractiveness in dating behavior. *Journal of Personality and Social Psychology*, 1966, *5*, 508–516.

WALSTER, E., and FESTINGER, L. The effectiveness of "overheard" persuasive communications. *Journal of Abnormal and Social Psychology*, 1962, *65*, 395–402.

WALSTER, E., and WALSTER, W. G. *A New Look at Love.* Reading, Mass.: Addison-Wesley, 1978.

WARREN, R. M., and WARREN, R. P. Auditory illusions and confusion. *Scientific American*, 1970, *232*, 169–174.

WATKINS, J. G., and WATKINS, H. H. Ego states and hidden observers. *Journal of Altered States of Consciousness*, 1979, *5*, 3–23.

WATSON, J. B. *Behaviorism.* New York: Norton, 1924.

WATSON, R. I. *The Great Psychologists from Aristotle to Freud.* 2nd ed. Philadelphia: Lippincott, 1968.

WATTS, W. A., and HOLT, L. E. Persistence of opinion change induced under conditions of forewarning and distraction. *Journal of Personality and Social Psychology*, 1979, *37*, 778–789.

WEAVER, W. The mathematics of information. In *Scientific American*, New York: Simon and Schuster, 1955, pp. 97–110.

WEBB, E. J., CAMPBELL, D. T., SCHWARTZ, R. D., and SECHREST, L. *Unobstrusive measures: Nonreactive research in the social sciences.* Chicago: Rand McNally, 1966.

WEBB, W. B. *Sleep: The gentle tyrant.* Englewood Cliffs, N.J.: Prentice-Hall, 1975.

WEIL, A. T. The letdown. *Psychology Today*, 1974, pp. 74–77.

WEIL, A. T., ZINBERG, N., and NELSEN, J. M. Clinical and psychological effects of marijuana in man. *Science*, 1968, *162*, 1234–1242.

WEINBERG, M. A., and WILLIAMS, C. J. *Male homosexuals: Their problems and adaptations.* New York: Oxford University Press, 1974.

WEINER, M., and WRIGHT, F. Effects of undergoing arbitrary discrimination upon subsequent attitudes toward a minority group. *Journal of Applied Social Psychology*, 1973, *3*, 94–102.

WENDER, P. H. *Minimal Brain Dysfunction in Children.* New York: Wiley-Interscience, 1971.

WERTHEIMER, M. Hebb and Senden on the role of learning in perception. *American Journal of Psychology*, 1951, *64*, 133–137.

WESTFALL, T. C., FLEMING, R. M., FUDGOR, M. F., and CLARK, W. G. Effect of nicotine and related substances upon amine levels in the brain. *Annuals of the New York Academy of Science*, 1967, *142*, 83–110.

WESTONE, H. S., and FRIEDLANDER, B. Z. The effect of word order on young children's responses to simple questions and commands. *Child Development*, 1973, *44*, 734–740.

WHITE, B. L. Child development research: An edifice without a foundation. *Merrill-Palmer Quarterly*, 1969, *59*, 49–79.

WHORF, B. L. *Language, Thought and Reality.* Cambridge, Mass.: MIT Press, 1956.

WICKLUND, R. A., AND BREHM, J. W. *Perspectives on Cognitive Dissonance.* Hillsdale, N.J.: Lawrence Erlbaum, 1976.

WICKER, A. W. Attitudes versus action: The relationship of verbal and overt behavioral responses to attitude objects. *Journal of Social Issues*, 1969, *251*, 41–78.

WICKER, A. W. An examination of the "other variables" explanation of attitude-behavior inconsistency. *Journal of Personality and Social Psychology*, 1971, *19*, 18–30.

WILKINS, L., and RICHTER, C. P. The great craving for salt by a child with a cortico-adrenal insufficiency. *Journal of the American Medical Association*, 1940, *114*, 866–868.

WILLIAMS, J. H. Sexuality in marriage. In B. B. Wolman and J. Money, eds., *Handbook of Human Sexuality*. New York: Plenum, 1980.

WILSON, E. O. *Sociobiology: The New Synthesis*. Cambridge, Mass.: Harvard University Press, 1975.

WILSON, P. R. Peceptual distortion of height as a function of ascribed academic status. *Journal of Social Psychology*, 1968, *74*, 97–102.

WINER, D. Anger and dissociation: A case study of multiple personality. *Journal of Abnormal Psychology*, 1978, *87*, 368–372.

WINICK, M., and ROSSO, P. the effect of severe early malnutrition on cellular growth of the human brain. *Pediatric Research*, 1969, *3*, 181–184.

WINOCUR, G., and OLDS, J. Effects of context manipulation on memory and reversal learning in rats with hippocampal lesions. *Journal of Comparative and Physiological Psychology*, 1978, *92*, 312–321.

WINTER, D. G. *The Power Motive*. Boston: Free Press, 1973.

WINTER, R. *The Smell Book: Scent, Sex, and Society*. New York: Lippincott, 1976.

WINTERBOTTOM, M. R. *The relation of childhood training in independence to achievement motivation*. Ph.D. dissertation, University of Michigan, 1953.

WIRTENBURG, T., and NAKAMURA, C. Education: Barrier or boom to changing occupational roles of women. *Journal of Social Issues*, 1976, *32*, 165–179.

WISPÉ, L. G. and THOMPSON, J. N., JR. The war between the words: Biological versus social evolution and some related issues. *American Psychologist*, 1976, *31*, 341–347.

WITTING, M. A., and PETERSEN, A. C., eds. *Sex Related Differences in Cognitive Functioning: Developmental Biases*. New York: Academic Press, 1979.

WOLF, M., RISLEY, T. R., and MEES, H. L. Application of operant conditioning procedures to the behavior problems of an autistic child. In *Behavior Research and Therapy*. Vol. 1. Elmsford, N.Y.: Pergamon Press, 1964.

WOLMAN, B. B., ed. *Historical Roots of Contemporary Psychology*, New York: Harper & Row, 1968.

WOLMAN, B. B., ed. *The Therapist's Handbook*. New York: Van Nostrand-Reinhold, 1976.

WOLMAN, B. B., ed. *Handbook of Parapsychology*. New York: Van Nostrand-Reinhold, 1977.

WOLMAN, B. B., and MONEY, J., eds. *Handbook of Human Sexuality*. New York: Plenum, 1980.

WOLPE, J. *Psychotherapy by Reciprocal Inhibition*. Palo Alto, Calif.: Stanford University Press, 1958.

WOODS, N. B. The unsupervised child of the working mother. *Developmental Psychology*, 1972, *6*, 14–15.

WOOLFOLK, R. L., CARR-KAFFASHAN, L., MCNULTY, T. F., and LEHRER, P. M. Meditation training as a teatment for insomnia. *Behavior Therapy*, 1976, *7*, 359–365.

WOODWORTH, R. S., and SCHLOSBERG, H. *Experimental Psychology*. Rev. ed. New York: Holt, Rinehart and Winston, 1954.

WRIGHT, R. L. D. *Understanding Statistics*. New York: Harcourt Brace Jovanovich, 1976.

Y

YALOM, I. D. *The Theory and Practice of Group Psychotherapy*. New York: Basic Books, 1970.

YANKELOVICH, D. *Generations Apart: A Study of the Generation Gap*. New York: Harper & Row, 1973.

YANKELOVICH, D. How students control their drug crisis. *Psychology Today*, October 1975, pp. 39–44.

YERGIN, D. The Chomskyan revolution. *New York Times Magazine*, December 3, 1972.

YERKES, R. M., and DODSON, J. D. The relation of strength of stimulus to rapidity habit-formation. *Journal of Comparative Neurology and Psychology*, 1908, *18*, 459–482.

YESSEN, S. R., and SANTROCK, J. W., *Child Development: An Introduction*. Dubuque, Iowa: Brown, 1978.

YOCHELSON, S., and SAMENOW, S. E. *The Criminal Personality*. New York: Jason Aronson, 1977.

YOUNG, P. T. *Emotion in Man and Animal*. 2nd rev. ed. Huntington, N.Y.: Krieger, 1973.

Z

ZAJONC, R. B. Social facilitation. *Science*, 1965, *149*, 269–274.

ZAJONC, R. B. Attitudinal effects of mere exposure. *Journal of Personality and Social Psychology*, 1968, *9*, 1–27.

ZAJONC, R. B. Family configuration and intelligence. *Science*, 1976, *192*, 227–236.

ZAJONC, R. B. Feeling and thinking: Preferences need no inferences. *American Psychologist*, 1980, *135*, 151-175.

ZAJONC, R. B., and BARGH, J. Birth order, family size, and decline of SAT scores. *American Psychologist*, 1980, *35*, 662-668.

ZAJONC, R. B., MARKUS, H., and MARKUS, G. B. The birth order puzzle. *Journal of Personality and Social Psychology*, 1979, *37*, 1325-1341.

ZAJONC, R. B., and SALES, S. Social facilitation of dominant and subordinate responses. *Journal of Experimental Social Psychology*, 1966, *2*, 160–168.

ZANNA, M. P., and AZIZA, C. On the interaction of repression-sensitization and attention in resolving cognitive dissonance. *Journal of Personality*, 1976, *44*, 577–593.

ZELAZO, P. R., ZELAZO, N. A., and KOLB, S. "Walking" in the newborn. *Science*, 1972, *176*, 314–315.

ZIMBARDO, P. G. The human choice: Individuation, reason, and order versus deindividuation, impulse, and chaos. In W. J. Arnold and D. Levine, eds., *Nebraska Symposium on Motivation*. Lincoln: University of Nebraska Press, 1969.

ZIMBARDO, P. G. Vandalism: An act in search of a cause. *Bell Telephone Magazine*. July–August 1972, pp. 12–17.

ZIMBARDO, P. G. *Shyness*. Reading, Mass.: Addison-Wesley, 1977.

ZUCKERMAN, M. Sensation-seeking. In H. London and E. Exner, eds., *Dimensions of Personality*. New York: Wiley, 1978a.

ZUCKERMAN, M. The search for high sensation. *Psychology Today*, February 1978b, pp. 30–46, 96–99.

ZUCKERMAN, M., BUCHSBAUM, M. S., and MURPHY, D. L. Sensation seeking and its biological correlates. *Psychological Bulletin*, 1980, *88*, 187–214.

CREDITS AND ACKNOWLEDGEMENTS

CHAPTER 1

P. 12, Figure 1.2: © 1977 by the American Psychological Association. Reprinted by permission.

AP/ONE

P. 17, drawing by Levine, © 1980 The New Yorker Magazine, Inc.

P. 19, Figure A.1: © 1980/1972 by The New York Times Company. Reprinted by permission.

P. 20, Figure A.2: From *Stanford Binet Intelligence Scale*, by L. M. Terman, and M. A. Merril. Houghton

Mifflin, 1960, p. 18. Reprinted by permission of the Riverside Publishing Company.

CHAPTER 2

P. 33, epigraph from "Woodstock" by Joni Mitchell, © 1969 Siquomb Publishing Corporation. Used by permission. All rights reserved.

P. 38, drawing by Fagan, © 1980 United Feature Syndicate, Inc.

P. 40, Figure 2.4: Skinner, Cumulative Record, © 1961 page vii. Reprinted by permission of Prentice-Hall, Inc., Englewood Cliffs, New Jersey.

P. 43, drawing by Unger, Copyright © 1980, Universal Press Syndicate. All rights reserved.

P. 43, Figure 2.6: From "A Methodological Study of Extinction Following Aperiodic and Continuous Reinforcement," by W. O. Jenkins and H. McFann. *The Journal of Comparative and Physiological Psychology*, 1950, *43*, 155–67.

P. 48, drawing by Dougherty, © *Saturday Review*, 1978.

P. 49, drawing by Gahan Wilson, © Gahan Wilson.

CHAPTER 3

P. 55, epigraph from *Zen Flesh, Zen Bones*, compiled by Paul Reps. Reprinted by permission of the publisher, the Charles E. Tuttle Co., Inc. of Tokyo, Japan.

P. 56, Figure 3.1: From *An Introduction to Language*, by Victoria Fromkin and Robert Rodman. Copyright © 1974 by Holt, Rinehart and Winston, Inc. Reprinted by permission of Holt, Rinehart and Winston.

P. 57, Figure 3.2: From "The Implication of Short-Term Memory for a General Theory of Memory," in *The Journal of Verbal Learning and Verbal Behavior*, 1963, *2*, 1–21.

P. 64, drawing by Unger, ©1980 Universal Press Syndicate. All rights reserved.

P. 67, Figure 3.6: From "Narrative Stories as Mediators for Social Learning," by G. H. Bower and M. C. Clark. In *Psychosomatic Science*, 1969, *14*, 181–182. Reprinted by permission.

P. 71, Figure 3.7(a): From *University of California Publications in Psychology*, Vol. 8, no. 3 (a monograph), 1957 (November) by Postman and L. Rau. Reprinted by permission of the University of California Press.

P. 71, Figure 3.7(b): From "Alcohol, Marijuana, and Memory," by Elizabeth F. Loftus, in *Psychology Today*, 1980, p. 46. Copyright © 1980, Ziff-Davis Publishing Company.

P. 71, Figure 3.7(c): From "Alcohol, Marijuana and Memory," by Elizabeth F. Loftus, in *Psychology Today*, 1980, pg. 54. Copyright © 1980, Ziff-Davis Publishing Company.

CHAPTER 4

P. 78, Table 4.2: From *Aspects of Language*, by D. Bollinger, Harcourt Brace Jovanovich, Inc., 1968, p. 18.

Pp. 79, 81, Figures 4.1, 4.2: From *An Introduction to Language* by Victoria Fromkin and Robert Rodman, 1974, pp. 177, 313. Copyright © 1974 by Holt, Rinehart and Winston. Reprinted by permission of Holt, Rinehart and Winston.

P. 83, Table 4.3: Adapted from "Two-Way Communication," by B. T. Gardner and R. A. Gardner, in *Behavior of Nonhuman Primates*, Vol. 4, edited by A. M. Schrier and F. Stollnitz, 1971, Copyright © Academic Press.

P. 85, Table 4.4: From "Three Processes in the Child's Acquisition of Syntax," by R. Brown and U. Bellugi, *Harvard Educational Review*, *34*, Spring 1964, 133–151, Copyright 1965 by the President and Fellows of Harvard College.

P. 89, drawing by Johnston, Copyright © 1980 Universal Press Syndicate. All rights reserved.

P. 89, Table 4.6: From *An Introduction to Language* by V. Fromkin and R. Rodman, 1974, p. 318. Copyright © 1974 by Holt, Rinehart and Winston. Reprinted by permission of Holt, Rinehart and Winston.

P. 91, Table 4.7: From *Word, Object and Conceptual Development*, by J. M. Anglin, 1977, p. 190. Reprinted by permission of W. W. Norton & Co., Inc.

P. 93, Figure 4.3: Adapted from *The Signs of Language*, by U. Bellugi and E. S. Klima. Harvard University Press, 1979, p. 17. Copyright © 1979 by the President and Fellows of Harvard College. Reprinted by permission.

AP/TWO

Pp. 101, 102, 104, drawings by Batiuk, FUNKY WINKERBEAN by Tom Batiuk, © 1980 Field Enterprises, Inc. Courtesy of Field Newspaper Syndicate.

CHAPTER 5

P. 112, Figure 5.1: From *Physiological Psychology*, by A. Schneider and B. Tarshis, 2nd Edition, p. 66, Copyright © 1980 by Random House, Inc.

P. 113, Figure 5.2: From *Physiological Psychology*, by A. Schneider and B. Tarshis, 2nd Edition, p. 65. Copyright © 1980 by Random House, Inc.

P. 114, Figure 5.3: From *Physiological Psychology*, by A. Schneider and B. Tarshis, 2nd Edition, p. 115. Copyright © 1980 by Random House, Inc.

P. 115, Figure 5.4: From *Physiological Psychology*, by A. Schneider and B. Tarshis, 2nd Edition, pp. 120, 121. Copyright © 1980 by Random House, Inc.

P. 116, Table 5:1: Adapted from *Biological Aspects of Mental Disorder*, by S. Snyder, 1980, Oxford University Press.

P. 117, Figure 5.5: From *Physiological Psychology*, by A. Schneider and B. Tarshis, 2nd Edition, p. 64. Copyright © 1980 by Random House, Inc.

Pp. 120, 121, Figures 5.6, 5.7: Reprinted with the permission of Macmillan Publishing Company, Inc. From *The Cerebral Cortex of Man* by W. Penfield and T. Rasmussen. Copyright © 1950 by Macmillan Publishing Company, Inc., renewed 1978 by Theodore Rasmussen.

P. 122, Figure 5.8: From *Physiological Psychology*, by A. Schneider and B. Tarshis, 2nd Edition, p. 469. Copyright © 1980 by Random House, Inc.

P. 123, Figure 5.9: From *Physiological Psychology*, by A. Schneider and B. Tarshis, 2nd Edition, p. 99. Copyright © 1980 by Random House, Inc.

P. 127, Figure 5.10: From *Life: An Introduction to Biology*, by G. G. Simpson, C. S. Pittendrigh, and L. H. Tiffany, Copyright © 1957 by Harcourt Brace Jovanovich, Inc. Reproduced by permission of the publisher. Originally adapted from A. S. Romer, *The Vertebrate Body*, W. B. Saunders, 1962.

CHAPTER 6

P. 142, Figure 6.3: Adapted from *Sensation and Perception*, by S. Coren, C. Porac, and L. M. Ward (New York: Academic Press, 1979).

P. 143, Table 6.2: Reprinted from *Human Information Processing*, by P. H. Lindsay and D. A. Norman (New York: Academic Press, 1972).

Color display: Reprinted from *An Introduction to Color* by R. M. Evans (New York: John Wiley, 1946).

P. 152, Figure 6.10: From *Sensation and Perception* by S. Coren, C. Porac, and L. M. Ward (New York: Academic Press, 1979).

P. 152, DENNIS THE MENACE® Courtesy of Hank Ketcham and ©1980 by Field Enterprises, Inc.

P. 153, Figure 6.11: From *The Skin Senses* by D. R. Kenshalo (Springfield: Charles Thomas, 1968). Courtesy of Charles C. Thomas, Publisher.

CHAPTER 7

P. 159, Figure 7.1: From "Impossible Objects: A Special Type of Illusion," by L. S. Penrose and R. Penrose. *The British Journal of Psychology*, 1958, *49*, p. 31.

P. 164, "The Escalator Illusion," Courtesy of A. Fraser, F. A. A., University of Cincinnati.

P. 167, "The Impossible Triangle," devised by L. S. Penrose and R. Penrose. The University College London.

P. 167, Figure 7.4: From "The Perception of Disoriented Figures" by I. Rock. Copyright © 1974 by Scientific American, Inc., All rights reserved.

P. 170, drawing by Brilliant, © Ashleigh Brilliant, 1979. POT SHOTS® No. 1515.

P. 171, Figure 7.7: Reprinted from *Intonation, Perception, and Language*, by P. Lieberman. By permission of the MIT Press, Cambridge, Massachusetts. Copyright © 1967 by the Massachusetts Institute of Technology.

P. 172, drawing by Thanes, © 1978, NEA, Inc.

P. 173, "Dartmouth vs. Princeton" from "They Saw A Game: A Case Study" by A. H. Hastorf and H. Cantril. *Journal of Abnormal and Social Psychology*, 1954, *49*, 129–134. Copyright © 1954 by the American Psychological Association. Reprinted by permission.

P. 175, Figure 7.8: Adapted from *Human Information Processing*, by P. H. Lindsay and D. A. Norman, New York: Academic Press, 1972.

CHAPTER 8

P. 187, Figure 8.1: From *Physiological Psychology*, by A. Schneider and B. Tarshis, 2nd Edition, p. 318, Copyright © 1980 by Random House, Inc.

P. 193, drawing by S. Harris, from *Human Behavior*, March 1977.

P. 197, Figure 8.2: The Department of Data. The Division of Motor Vehicles, New Jersey.

AP/THREE

P. 208, drawing by Sansom, © 1979 NEA, Inc.

CHAPTER 9

P. 216, drawing by Thanes, © 1980 by NEA, Inc.

P. 218, drawing by Johnston, Copyright © 1980 Universal Press Syndicate. All rights reserved.

P. 219, drawing by Guisewite, Copyright © 1979 Universal Press Syndicate. All rights reserved.

P. 222, Figure 9.2: From *Physiological Psychology*, by A. Schneider and B. Tarshis, 2nd Edition, p. 272, Copyright © 1980 by Random House, Inc.

P. 223, drawing by Guisewite, Copyright © 1980 Universal Press Syndicate. All rights reserved.

P. 224, Box adapted from "Weight Lost by Keeping Eating Record," *The Los Angeles Times*, reprinted in Providence *Sunday Journal* (June 30, 1974).

P. 226, Figure 9.3: From "Pleasure Centers in the Brain," by J. Olds, Copyright © 1956 by Scientific American, Inc. All rights reserved.

P. 231, drawing by Schulz, © 1979, United Feature Syndicate, Inc.

CHAPTER 10

P. 241, epigraph from "Like a Rolling Stone," by Bob Dylan, © 1965 Warner Bros. Inc. All rights reserved. Used by permission.

P. 242, Figure 10.1: From *Emotion: A Psychoevolutionary Synthesis*, by Robert Plutchik, p. 164. Copyright © 1980 by Robert Plutchik. Reprinted by permission of Harper & Row Publishers, Inc.

P. 246, Figure 10.2: From *Physiological Psychology* by A. Schneider and B. Tarshis, 2nd Edition, p. 371. Copyright © 1980 by Random House, Inc.

P. 248, drawing by D. Fradon, © 1980 The New Yorker Magazine, Inc.

P. 249, drawing by William Hamilton, © 1979 The New Yorker Magazine, Inc.

P. 254, Figure 10.4: Adapted from *Physiology of Reproduction* by William D. Odell and Dean L. Moyer (St. Louis: C. V. Mosby, 1971).

P. 258, Figure 10.5: From "Imitation of Facial and Manual Gestures by Human Neonates," by A. N. Meltzoff and M. K. Moorgin, *Science*, 1977, *198*, 75–78.

P. 263, Figure 10.7: Copyright © 1976 by Glenn Wilson and David Nias. Reprinted by permission of Times Books, a division of Quadrangle/The New York Times Book Co., Inc. From *The Mystery of Love*.

P. 264, drawing by Guisewite, Copyright © 1979, Universal Press Syndicate. All rights reserved.

CHAPTER 11

P. 273, Figure 11.3: From *Human Sexual Response* by Masters and Johnson, 1966. Reprinted by permission of the publisher, Little, Brown and Co.

P. 277, Figure 11.5: From *Human Sexualities* by John H. Gagnon. Copyright © 1977 by Scott, Foresman and Company. Reprinted by permission.

P. 282, Figure 11.6: From *Sexual Behavior in the Human Male*, p. 502, and from *Sexual Behavior in the Human Female*, p. 149, both by Alfred Kinsey.

CHAPTER 12

P. 305, quote: From "Arcs," *Parabola* iv, 64–65, 1979. Copyright © Society for the Study of Myth and Tradition.

P. 309, Table 12.1: "Incidence of Mongolism and Diagnosis in the Newborn" by C. O. Carter and D. MaCarthy. *British Journal of Social Medicine*: 1951, 5, 83–90.

P. 310, Figure 12.1: From The White House Conference on Children, 1970, p. 48.

P. 312, Table 12.2: From "Reflexes in the Newborn" by Hertherington and R. Parke, in *Child Psychology: A Contemporary View*, McGraw-Hill, 1975.

P. 316, Table 12.3: From "The Origin of Personality," by Alexander Thomas, Stella Chess and Herbert B. Birch. Copyright © August 1970 by Scientific American, Inc. All rights reserved.

P. 319, Figure 12.2: From *The First Two Years* by Mary M. Shirley. University of Minnesota Press, Minneapolis. Copyright © 1933, by the University of Minnesota.

P. 320, Figure 12.3: From "The Perception of Disoriented Figures" by Irvin Rock. Copyright © January 1974 by Scientific American, Inc. All rights reserved.

P. 321, Figure 12.4: Photo by William Vandivert. Copyright © 1960 by Scientific American, Inc. All rights reserved.

P. 321, Figure 12.5: From "Plasticity in Sensory-Motor Systems," by Richard Held. Copyright © November 1965 by Scientific American, Inc. All rights reserved.

P. 325, Table 12.6: From Kohlberg, *Moral Education*, Copyright © Harvard University Press. Reprinted by permission.

P. 328, drawing by Browne, © King Features Syndicate, Inc., 1979. World rights reserved.

P. 329, drawing ALBERT HERBERT HAWKINS by Frank Dickens, © 1980 Field Enterprises, Inc. Courtesy of Field Newspaper Syndicate.

P. 331, drawing by Browne, © King Features Syndicate, Inc., 1977. World rights reserved.

CHAPTER 13

P. 340, epigraph from *As You Like It*, Act II, scene vii, by William Shakespeare.

P. 340, Figure 13.1: From Levinson, *The Seasons of a Man's Life*, p. 57. Copyright © 1978, Alfred A. Knopf, Inc.

P. 341, Table 13.1: Adapted from *Childhood and Society*, by Erik H. Erikson, with the permission of the publisher, W. W. Norton & Company, Inc. Copyright © 1950, 1963 by W. W. Norton and Company Inc.

P. 342, Figure 13.2: From "Standards from Birth to Maturity for Height, Weight, Height Velocity, and Weight

Velocity: British Children," by J. M. Tanner et al. In *The British Medical Journal*, 1965, Part 1, 1966, Part II 41: 467.

P. 343, Figure 13.3: From *Growth at Adolescence* 2nd Edition, by J. M. Tanner, in Oxford: Blackwell; Philadelphia: Davis, 1962. By permission.

P. 345, drawing by E. Opie, © 1978 The New Yorker Magazine, Inc.

P. 347, drawing by Fagan, © 1980 United Features Syndicate, Inc.

P. 349, Figure 13.4: From "How Happy is Your Marriage" by Carol Tavris and Toby Jayaratne from *Redbook Magazine*, June 1976.

P. 349, Figure 13.5: From the United States Department of Health, Education and Welfare.

P. 354, Table 13.3: From Schulz, *The Psychology of Death, Dying and Bereavement*, © 1978 Addison-Wesley Publishing Company, Inc. Chapter 5, pp. 97 and 98, "How Long Will You Live." Reprinted with permission.

P. 355, Figure 13.6: United States Bureau of the Census.

CHAPTER 15

P. 394, drawing by Barsotti, © 1979 The New Yorker Magazine, Inc.

P. 397, Figure 15.1: From "Dumber by the Dozen" by R. B. Zajonc, *Psychology Today Magazine* January 1975, *8*, 37–43. Copyright © 1974. Ziff-Davis Publishing Company.

P. 403, drawing by Myers, reprinted by permission of the Chicago Tribune-New York News Syndicate, Inc.

P. 406, Figure 15.3: From *The Rorschach Technique: An Introductory Manual*, by B. Klopfer and H. H. Davidson, p. 432. Copyright © 1975 by Harcourt Brace Jovanovich, Inc. Reprinted by permission.

P. 407, Figure 15.4: From *Thematic Apperception Test* by Henry A. Murray. Copyright © 1943 Harvard University Press. Reprinted by permission.

P. 408, Figure 15.5: Kinetic Family Drawings (K-F-D), edited by R. C. Burns and S. H. Kaufman, New York, Brunner/Mazel, Inc.

P. 409, drawing by Sansom, © 1979 NEA, Inc.

CHAPTER 14

P. 370, epigraph from "Personality" by Lloyd Price and Harold Logan. © 1959 by Lloyd and Logan Music. All rights reserved. Reproduced by permission.

P. 372: drawing by Dana Fradon, © 1979 The New Yorker Magazine, Inc.

CHAPTER 16

P. 418, Table 16.1: From *Abnormal Psychology*, 3rd edition by R. Bootzin, p. 7. Copyright © 1980 by Random House, Inc.

P. 426, drawing by Sansom, © 1979 NEA, Inc.

P. 429, drawing by Fagan, © 1979 United Feature Syndicate.

P. 430, Figure 16.1: From the United States Department of Health, Education and Welfare.

P. 432, drawing by Chon Day, © 1977, as appeared in *Psychology Today*, February 1977.

P. 435, Table 16.3: Reprinted with the permission of the American Psychiatric Association.

CHAPTER 17

P. 444, drawing by Guisewite, Copyright © 1980 Universal Press Syndicate. All rights reserved.

P. 449, drawing by Wilson, Copyright © 1979 Universal Press Syndicate. All rights reserved.

P. 451, drawing by Fagan, © 1979 United Feature Syndicate, Inc.

P. 454, Figure 17.1: Reprinted with permission from *Journal of Behavior Therapy and Experimental Psychiatry*, Vol. 2, R. B. Stuart, "Behavioral Contracting Within the Families of Delinquents," Copyright © 1971, Pergamon Press, Ltd.

AP/SIX

P. 468, box table: From *The Psychology of Death, Dying, and Bereavement*, by R. Schulz. © 1978, Addison-Wesley Publishing Company, Inc., pp. 97 and 98, "How Long Will You Live." Reprinted with permission.

CHAPTER 18

P. 480, Figure 18.1: From *Social Psychology and Modern Life*, by Patricia Niles Middlebrook. Copyright © 1973 by Alfred A. Knopf, Inc. Reprinted by permission of Alfred A. Knopf, Inc.

P. 482, Figure 18.2: From "Cognitive Consequences of Forced Compliance" by L. Festinger and J. Carlsmith. Copyright © 1959 by the American Psychological Association. Reprinted by permission.

P. 485, drawing by Ed Arno, © 1979 The New Yorker Magazine, Inc.

P. 491, drawing by Browne, © King Features Syndicate, Inc., 1979. World rights reserved.

P. 495, drawing by Guisewite, Copyright © 1979, Universal Press Syndicate. All rights reserved.

CHAPTER 19

P. 503, Figure 19.2: From *Social Psychology* by Solomon E. Asch, p. 452. © 1952 Prentice-Hall, Inc., Englewood Cliffs, New Jersey. Reprinted by permission.

P. 504, drawing by Handelsman, © 1972 The New Yorker Magazine, Inc.

P. 506, Figure 19.3: From *Social Psychology and Modern Life*, by Patricia Niles Middlebrook. Copyright © 1973 by Alfred A. Knopf, Inc. Reprinted by permission of Alfred A. Knopf, Inc.

P. 508, drawing by Schulz. © 1980 United Feature Syndicate, Inc.

P. 520, Figure 19.6: © 10/26/72 by the New York Times Company. Reprinted by permission.

P. 522, drawing by Trudeau, Copyright, 1980, G. B. Trudeau. Reprinted with permission of Universal Press Syndicate. All rights reserved.

AP/SEVEN

P. 532, drawing by Guisewite, Copyright © 1979, Universal Press Syndicate. All rights reserved.

P. 533, drawing by Guisewite, Copyright © 1979, Universal Press Syndicate. All rights reserved.

P. 535, drawing by Johnston, Copyright © 1980, Universal Press Syndicate. All rights reserved.

SUBJECT INDEX

NAME INDEX

DANIEL GOLEMAN, the new coauthor for this edition, is a Senior Editor of *Psychology Today*. He received his Ph.D. from Harvard University, where he specialized in the areas of clinical, personality, and developmental psychology. He has published over 50 articles during his career, which have appeared in such journals as *Journal of Clinical and Consulting Psychology*; *Journal of Abnormal Psychology*; *Psychosomatic Medicine*; as well as *Psychology Today*, where he is a regular contributor. He has coauthored *What Psychology Knows that Everyone Should*, and coedited *Consciousness*, and *The Therapist's Craft*. Dr. Goleman won the American Psychological Foundation 1980 Media Award for magazine articles with his February 1980 *Psychology Today* article, "1,528 Little Geniuses and How They Grew."

TRYGG ENGEN is an experimental psychologist whose field of specialization is sensory psychology—especially the psychology of odor. His research has concerned the development of taste aversions and preferences in children, human factors in injury control, as well as psychophysics of the chemical senses. He received his Ph.D. from the University of Nebraska, and received an honorary Doctor of Science degree from Central Michigan University. He received a Fullbright Scholarship for research and teaching at the University of Stockholm, Sweden. Dr. Engen is now Professor of Psychology at Brown University, where he has taught introductory psychology for twenty-five years. Dr. Engen is the author of the psychophysics chapters in the third edition of Woodworth and Schlosberg's *Experimental Psychology*; and the author of a book entitled *The Perception of Odors*. He has had more than 60 articles published in professional journals.

ANTHONY DAVIDS is a clinical psychologist whose fields of specialization are child development, personality, and abnormal psychology. He received his Ph.D. from Harvard University, and is presently a professor of Psychology at Brown University. He has served as a Special Research Fellow at The Institute for Personality Assessment and Research at The University of California, Berkeley, and was a Visiting Scholar at the Boys Town Research Center at Stanford University. He has been a member of the Psychology Department at Brown University since 1955. He is the author of three books: *Abnormal Children and Youth: Therapy and Research*, *Issues in Abnormal Child Psychology*, and *Children in Conflict: A Casebook*. He has edited a series of three volumes on Child Personality and Psychopathology. Dr. Davids has published more than 75 articles in professional journals. He has served as Advisory Editor for *Contemporary Psychology*, and is now a Consulting Editor for the *Journal of Consulting and Clinical Psychology*.